MIMESIS, EXPRESSION, CONSTRUCTION

"Jameson on Adorno? It's like reading Benjamin on Brecht, or Sartre on Baudelaire. A great Oedipal drama."

T.J. CLARK, AUTHOR OF *THE PAINTING OF MODERN LIFE: PARIS IN THE ART OF MANET AND HIS FOLLOWERS*

"Dialectics, understood performatively, means experiencing the drama of exploration and discovery, while remaining alert to the contradictions and obstacles to closure that inevitably arise on the journey. In rescuing Jameson's 2003 lectures on Adorno's *Aesthetic Theory* from oblivion and presenting them to us in all their messy vitality, Octavian Esanu allows contemporary readers to experience vicariously the struggles of one master dialectician to explicate and criticize the efforts of another."

MARTIN JAY, AUTHOR OF *IMMANENT CRITIQUES: THE FRANKFURT SCHOOL UNDER PRESSURE*

"Octavian Esanu's idea to edit the transcript of Fredric Jameson's seminar on Adorno's *Aesthetic Theory* at Duke University in 2003 is a mind-blowing acheivement... What we get here is not the insight into some secret core of Jameson's thought lost in later gentrified published versions but, on the contrary, a flow of improvisations and mental experimentations where the detours through secondary topics are often more precious than the main line of argumentation. When Jameson was delivering his seminar, he wasn't aware that his words are recorded by some students, so we see him stumbling, looking for the right word, getting interrupted and even corrected by students... in short, what we are getting is a live thought, a thought in its painful process of gestation. Again and again, we see how *la verite surgit de la meprise*, how a genuinely new insight emerges only through unexpected deadlocks."

SLAVOJ ŽIŽEK, AUTHOR OF *TOO LATE TO AWAKEN*

MIMESIS, EXPRESSION, CONSTRUCTION

FREDRIC JAMESON'S SEMINAR ON *AESTHETIC THEORY*

TRANSCRIBED AND EDITED
BY OCTAVIAN ESANU

Published by Repeater Books
An imprint of Watkins Media Ltd
Unit 11 Shepperton House
89-93 Shepperton Road
London
N1 3DF
United Kingdom
www.repeaterbooks.com

A Repeater Books paperback original 2024
1
Distributed in the United States by Random House, Inc., New York.

ISBN: 9781915672162
Ebook ISBN: 9781915672179

Printed and bound in the United Kingdom by TJ Books Limited

CONTENTS

INTRODUCTION
BY OCTAVIAN ESANU

1

Mimesis, Expression, Construction offers to readers the transcripts of Fredric Jameson's seminar lectures on Theodor W. Adorno's *Aesthetic Theory.* I recorded the seminar while taking part in it, at Duke University in the winter/spring of 2003. Since that time, I have been intermittently transcribing the audio files over the years while thinking of a form in which they could be made publishable. This book comprises twenty-one lectures presented in a form reminiscent of both a high modernist play and contemporary closed captioning. Each lecture/act begins with a stage set, and contains footnotes with references and sources mentioned by Jameson or by student presenters in the seminar, along with other information on the aesthetics of modernism. In addition, some of the lectures incorporate a few longer endnotes with fragments from a body of research (conducted during and after this seminar), which explores the three main impulses of Adornian aesthetics, also highlighted in the title of this book, namely: Mimesis, Expression, and Construction. This introduction discusses the form and content of the book, elucidates the context in which the project originated, and generally prepares the way for the original mimetic act to be expressed and constructed into a historico-dramatic play of Jameson's seminar on Adorno and other aspects of modernist aesthetics.

2

The history of aesthetics knows many examples of disciples reproducing the oral discourses of their teachers. The art of retelling, dictating, transcribing, or using a recording device to turn scholarly speech into writing has its own history and aesthetics: from Plato putting into Socrates's mouth various dialogues regarding the nature of the beautiful (*kalon*) in oral Ancient Greece, to Heinrich Gustav Hotho's note-taking during Hegel's 1820s Berlin lectures on aesthetics, to Theodor W. Adorno's seminars on aesthetics delivered in Frankfurt in the late 1950s, which were in this century transcribed from audio tapes, edited, and published as *Aesthetics (1958/59)*.[1] Even Adorno's posthumous *Aesthetic Theory* — the main character of this book — was initially dictated.[2] In all of these human and machine operations, one comes across not only the problematic of speech and writing in relation to meaning and truth, which has been at the center of poststructuralist thought (as, for example, the Derridean duality between the "natural" voice and writing as "supplement" and instrument of power), but also some of the most fundamental issues of aesthetics. The latter includes mimetic impulse and imitation, semblance and fictional play, expression, construction, composition — all crucial to Adorno's theory of aesthetics. We will never know exactly whose definition of beauty is presented in the Platonic dialogues — given the debated nature of the Socratic conversations — and scholars have questioned the accuracy of Hotho's handwritten transcripts of Hegel's lectures on the philosophy of art (for example, the much-disputed Hegelian definition of beauty or art as the "sensual appearance of the idea").[3] In the late twentieth century, however, oral discourses and university lectures delivered by distinguished philosophers and theorists were edited or published based on transcripts made from audio tape recordings. For example, Adorno's late-1950s lectures on aesthetics were transcribed from what may have originally been analog tapes preserved at the Institute for Social Research. And, if we are to trust the accuracy of the transcripts (occasionally marked by gaps "[...]" footnoted as "The gap in the text resulted from a change of tape"), *Aesthetics (1958/59)* is a word-by-word reproduction of Adorno's lecturing voice in one of the auditoriums of the University of Frankfurt. In these seminar transcripts, one discerns a different Adorno from that of *Aesthetic Theory*. This Adorno seems more approachable and more friendly perhaps, which might be explained by the proximity of his voice — the so-called "intimate kernel of subjectivity," as Mladen Dolar defined it.[4] Adorno's seminar transcripts give us a chance to compare his speech in *Aesthetics (1958/59)* to his writing in *Aesthetic Theory*. While the former is a verbatim record of his impromptu speech — an act of subjective expression (extracted from the audio tapes by the mimetic impulse) — the latter (albeit with some parts originally dictated) was mostly composed, edited, or constructed over the years by Adorno and later by his wife and editor for the purpose of being read. These two late books of Adorno, both with the word "aesthetic" in their titles, give two different images of this thinker: that of a teacher using a more "natural" and conversational syntax, versus that of an abstract thinker, or even an artist invested in the "law of form," a negative dialectician whose writing — to put it in Fredric Jameson's words — is a "towering wall of water of a text that carries us forward across bewildering shifts and changes in its topics and raw material."[5]

A similar dialectic of phonic and graphic substance, of expression and construction, of subjectivity and objectivity, of the didactive and dialectical, but also of theory and art, form, and content, lies at the heart of this project. In the seminar, Jameson discusses the impact of the invention of the typewriter on the prose of Henry James and of Friedrich Nietzsche (see Lecture Four). It is common knowledge in literary history that Henry James's so-called "late style" emerged as he began to dictate to a secretary who typed his words on a typewriter. The new medium radically altered his prose, producing a more convoluted and ambiguous style. Something similar has happened here, with regard to the personal voice recorder that I used to record the seminar. This device was invented in order to provide a more "personal," intimate, and precise knowledge of the subject or/and the object, but has paradoxically reminded us of the fundamentally fragmentary nature of human speech, divided by "empty" spaces (i.e., incomplete utterances, prolongations, stuttering, hesitations, repetitions, or false starts). This fragmentation is part of the subject-object split and the associated crisis of representation that has been one of the main themes of modernist aesthetics.

It is first of all the nature of the "raw material" — twenty-one digital files containing many disturbances, gaps, interferences, silence, and noises — that called for a distinct form of organization, encouraging a less expected and even an artistic approach to the main characters of this play (i.e., Jameson, Adorno, *Aesthetic Theory*, the fragment, mimesis, expression, construction). Often, in the secondary literature, one comes across an image of an Adorno who "thought of himself as an artist,"[6] or who was "both an artist and a scientist, a composer and a writer, a philosopher and a sociologist."[7] Such views have persisted despite the fact that Adorno regarded science (including philosophy or theory) and art in oppositional terms. For Adorno, the term "artistic," when brought into close proximity with "theory," is fraught with difficulties and unsolvable problems. On one hand, art cannot be reduced to its concept, for artistic practice is ultimately extralogical,[8] and on the other, a theory of aesthetics cannot be fetishized or made to look like a work of art because it would lose its rigor or betray the concept. Art and theory are some of the key antinomies of *Aesthetic Theory*, and the dilemma is expressed in the form of its presentation: Adorno adopts a paratactical form of writing,[9] and a sentence structure that has been described as "empty in the middle" (see Lecture Thirteen). This very distinct way of writing is not a result of his connecting art and theory — or trying to be an artist — but rather is a way of expressing their unapproachability. His style of writing *Aesthetic Theory* is the negative result pointing to the impossibility of bridging art and theory, rather than a positive sign of their possible reconciliation. The impossibility of this task is expressed in Adorno's idea of using Friedrich Schlegel's observation that "what is called the philosophy of art usually lacks one of two things: either the philosophy or the art" as the motto of *Aesthetic Theory*.[10]

Adorno did not think very much about the written form of his seminar transcripts on aesthetics, which became *Aesthetics (1958/59)*. The current project shares some of Adorno's concerns and perspectives, although it is the product of different circumstances. Unlike Adorno's *Aesthetics (1958/59)* — which is a written record of Adorno speaking directly into a microphone (installed in front of him by a technician, as I imagine it), later edited by Adorno himself and reused in part for *Aesthetic Theory*[11] — Jameson did not "work on" the present transcripts. These recordings of Jameson's seminars were made by a member of his audience, if not in secret, then more or less discreetly using a cheap "personal" recorder in the pre-smartphone era. This should explain why some parts of the transcripts appear incohesive and fragmentary, where sometimes, for example, the lecturer's voice is drowned by the audience's clatter, along with other random sounds picked up by the disoriented microphone (coughs, sneezes, sniffling, footsteps, page-flipping, accidental chattering, Amtrak trains passing by, jackets and backpack zippers zipping up and zipping down, police sirens, and so on). During the transcription of these lectures, these "empty" spaces, noises, and "distractions" (to invoke a familiar Benjaminian aesthetic concept) raised questions regarding their role and place in a project dedicated to the art and aesthetics of modernism.

From the beginning, this project aimed to offer the reader several things: a historical record of Jameson's seminar as I attended it in the early 2000s; a practical application of some key aesthetic concepts (mimesis, expression, and construction) to the form and content of Jameson's transcripts; and a presentation of Jameson's pedagogical or lecturing "style." The latter has also posed multiple technical challenges, which the book has tried to address by adopting, or rather surrendering to, the current dramatic form. The difficulties of transcribing the seminar owed not only to the uneven quality of the audio recordings, or the restless, crowded audience, but also to Jameson's voice. His classroom speech changes intonation depending on the character of the utterance: raising his voice to state a political belief — i.e., to historicize! — or lowering it to the point of fading into a mumble, as if in order to lessen the importance of certain descriptive moments (for example, anecdotal or biographical information about the interrelations between the members and affiliates of the Frankfurt School was often spoken in a low *sotto voce*, as if it were shameful gossip). It is all of these variations that the book has attempted to retain: the "empty" gaps, the audience noises, disturbances, and voice fluctuations, but also thought caught in the act of being thought through, the toil of dialectical thinking that is not ashamed of its accidents or errors, along with the effort to address the fragmentary nature of speech, knowledge, and representation — the central characters in the drama of the aesthetics of modernism.

The book also comes as an opportunity to compare Jameson's lecturing voice to his writing. The latter has won him many accolades, as a complex dialectical writer and eloquent thinker of Marxist cultural criticism and of art, aesthetics, and society. The book also aims to offer a sense of the working conditions in the workshop of his literary criticism, as well as throw some light on his relation to Adorno. In critical theory, Jameson has often been discussed in connection to Adorno not only due to his pioneering studies of Marxist aesthetics and dialectical thinking (from his early 1970s *Marxism and Form* to the early 1990s reassessments of Adorno for the context of postmodernism in *Late Marxism*[12]), but also because of a sense of semblance or even lineage between these two critics. And even though Jameson has also been called "the American Lukács" — the latter being Adorno's main theoretical opponent in the field of Marxist aesthetics — his connection to Adorno is equally important. Adorno (along with Sartre and Lukács, or Barthes) was among Jameson's greatest influences during his formative years,[13] and was one of the four figures (along with Sartre, Brecht, and Lewis) to whom Jameson has dedicated full-length books (at the time of the seminar).[14] Jameson shared with Adorno a commitment to totalizing thought. He often defended the latter's "difficult" or "obscure" writing, as both critics heavily emphasized the role of theory in resisting the reification and commodification of language in the totally administered world. Like Adorno in his own time, Jameson has understood critical writing in terms of delivering "dialectical shocks" to a reality in urgent need of defamiliarization. There is also their common dedication to the "law of form," or to the pleasure — and for their opponents, the pain — of crafting and constructing textual worlds. The affinity between the two critics is certainly more complex, as it also involves negotiating a position within a camp of twentieth-century Marxist aesthetics divided into sectors and zones of "Soviet" and "Western Marxism," or into parties of so-called "committed," materio-historic, and/or politicized aesthetic experience and artistic practice (after Lukács, Sartre, and Brecht) and those whom Robert Kaufman once designated as the "red Kantians"[15] — that is, Marxist thinkers who have not been completely dismissive of "bourgeois" preoccupations with form or "formalism." Kaufman describes this category by altering Jameson's most famous dictum: *Always aestheticize!* It is such preoccupations with form, and "reservations about the overhasty or antagonistic positing of opposition between the materio-historical and the aesthetic," that have earned Jameson a place within this tradition of late-twentieth-century "red Kantianism."[16]

But the continuity within this "tradition" should also be viewed dialectically, in a way perhaps akin to Adorno and Horkheimer's *Dialectic of Enlightenment*, wherein a newer phase of cultural criticism both preserves and cancels the previous one. The continuity from Adorno to Jameson's version of "red Kantianism" is reflected not only in their close attention to form and to the construction of the work of art. In Adorno's modernist vision, artworks are monads (both forces or fields of tension and things) interacting with society through their "windowless facades"; art is both autonomous and a *fait social;* "authentic art," which is the only art that Adorno recognizes (or to reverse it, the only art that he accepts is "authentic art"), offers in its form symbolic resolutions to social contradictions; and finally, art is an act of negation, which takes the side of the suppressed and exploited natural and/or social world. For Adorno, there is only "high" or "authentic art," which only a select few cultured individuals can grasp, and everything else is the culture industry, jazz, barbarism, and Hollywood. In his dialectical leap, Jameson moves beyond, taking the elitist version of high modernism as a point of departure in order to articulate his aesthetics of postmodernism. The latter, by contrast, presents us with new features that are to be extracted from the mode of cultural production under late capitalism, which Adorno only saw in its early stage. The postmodern work of art is the product of a new world in crisis of a unified agency, like the "ruling class"; it is part of a world that has been shattered by the multiplication and randomization of the economic and political power of multinational corporations. And therefore, the aesthetics of postmodernism is an aesthetics of populism and of difference, following the fragmentation of political, economic, and cultural agency and power. It is an aesthetics of deathlessness, of simulacrum, of the weakening of historicity and the waning of affect, an aesthetic of the surface, of consumer fetishism, kitsch, schlock, pastiche, bravura, and disassociated affinities. These are some of the predominant "themes" in postmodern aesthetics that Jameson worked on building on the aesthetics of high modernism, including Adorno's ideas. He worked on these subjects in his 1970s and 1990s books, and later on during his teaching career in the 2000s when I attended his seminars. The reflection on the transformation of high modernist aesthetics into postmodernism has become an enormous field of literature.

This book would also like to contribute to this field, albeit by other means. During one of our last meetings in the spring of 2015, I showed Jameson the transcripts of his lectures and informed him of my plans to give this "raw material" a publishable form. He looked through the transcripts, then said something to the effect that he had not realized until then how inarticulate he may have sounded in some parts of his lecturing. What he saw on the pages of these early transcripts was indeed very different from his masterfully written prose. The transcripts presented me with multiple challenges as I struggled to keep my editorial interventions to the minimum. But while working on the chapters, it also occurred to me at some point that perhaps the incoherence that Jameson perceived may also have something to do with the problems raised in his seminar on aesthetics, and that perhaps I was betraying the *mimetic* impulse — the primordial drive which *Aesthetic Theory* and especially the *Dialectic of Enlightenment* places, along with expression and construction, at the origin and center of art, knowledge, progress, and aesthetic experience.

Thus "mimesis," "expression," and "construction" came to constitute the mode of aesthetic production, or the main tools, for this project. Remaining faithful to the innate predisposition of the raw material, and to those aesthetic drives that shape each substance into its immanent form, the project unfolds from the initial effort to *imitate* Jameson into that of *expressing* and ultimately (re)*constructing* a significant academic event and document of modernist aesthetics.

3

Mimesis, Expression, Construction introduces Jameson's seminar transcripts on Adorno's *Aesthetic Theory* in a format reminiscent of a play, or rather a combination of theatrical script (inspired in particular by Samuel Beckett's play *Krapp's Last Tape*) and closed-captioning. In its presentation, the project rests on the belief that these three aesthetic impulses play a central role in Adorno's aesthetic theory and in artistic experience.[17] The triad not only allows us to grasp art in both historical and structural terms — that is, along the diachronic and synchronic axes (Jameson's preferred temporal dimensions of cultural analysis) — but it also recognizes some of the primary urges that inform or predispose art-making. On the first day of the seminar, Jameson pointed to the dialectics between "expression" and "construction," describing it in terms of a ceaseless tension between the subjective and the objective poles in art, and citing the famous first sentence of *Aesthetic Theory*: "It is self-evident that nothing concerning art is self-evident anymore, not its inner life, not its relation to the world, not even its right to exist."[18] This sentence sets the main theme of *Aesthetic Theory*, locating art and aesthetic experience between the dialectical poles of "expression" (denoted by the phrase "its inner life") and "construction" (inscribed in "its relation to the world").

But there is still the problematic notion of "mimesis." On numerous occasions in the seminar, Jameson expresses his ambivalence towards the notion of "mimesis," as discussed in *Aesthetic Theory* and the *Dialectic of Enlightenment*. This ambiguity was associated with what he perceived to be Adorno's anthropological preoccupations with notions of the "origins" of art. As coiner of the dictum "Always historicize!," Jameson felt perhaps that Adorno's mimesis reached too far into the dark *pre*-historical days of primeval magic and ritual. But Adorno was not alone in his susceptibility to such theories about the distant or mythical origins of art. They had been popular in his day: from the anthropological accounts of James George Frazer and Roger Caillois to Aby Warburg's iconology of mimesis, and even the historical-materialist interpretation of mimesis as "imitative" or "naturalistic" during the period of Stone-Age "primitive communism," as in Arnold Hauser's first volume of social art history.[19] In the seminar, Jameson attempts over and over to explain mimesis in light of other impulses, as, for example, in Lectures Nine and Ten where he makes construction and expression into two "possibilities" of mimesis. In one of our most recent communications, Jameson advised a closer look at Robin Collingwood's discussion of mimesis, expression, and construction in *The Principles of Art* (1938), in which such terms as "representation" and "imitation" stand in for mimesis, and in which the three come together to form compounds like "emotional representation," a form of "expressive mimesis," or "imaginative construction," which expresses a given emotion.[20] Yet despite these attempts to interconnect the drives, Collingwood's theory of aesthetics is a continuation of Croce's investment in the aesthetics of expression.

For the remaining part of this introduction, I will discuss each of the impulses separately. This may be perceived as not fully in the spirit of the seminar, but I discuss them in connection to the development and the making of this book. The book takes Jameson's seminar transcripts as an opportunity to weave between these aesthetic drives not in or only in theory but also in practice, such that it is not always easy to distinguish where mimesis ends, and where expression or construction begin.

4

Mimesis is the most recognizable of the three drives, as it is enacted in the verbatim graphic imitation of Jameson's seminar audio recordings. In Adornian anthropology, mimesis lies at the origins of art. It is art's original sin, so to speak, having migrated or rather been banished into art from the primordial phase of archaic ritual and magic. As art advances historically towards its modern autonomy — passing through magic, myth, metaphysics, contemporary scientism, and/or the culture industry — the mimetic impulse is pushed deeper and deeper, repressed into the subconsciousness of artistic experience and practice. Mimetic behavior originates in early humans' identification with the forces of the environment and is part of their instinct for self-preservation. Mimesis is pre-conceptual and intuitive, constituting the main form of early human knowledge and power. In the historical stage defined by magic, humans identify with demons, animals, and birds, with their natural surroundings or those forces of nature that they also seek to control. The urge for domination turned mimesis into one of the main drives in the general unfolding of reason and the suppression of nature. The culmination of the archaic mimetic impulse is the project of enlightenment, and the process of the de-mythologization, disenchantment, and finally the de-mimeticization of the world. Magic and myth become science, and through a dialectical reversal or distortion, this progressive demystification and disenchantment turns scientific instrumental rationality into the new myth of the modern age. For this very reason, early romantic art and modernist philosophy protest the disenchantment of the world seeking to bring back pre-conceptual and mimetic forms of knowledge (as in Husserl's phenomenology or Bergsonian intuition).

The mimetic impulse also stands at the origin of this project, as it does in the Adornian theory of art. From magic and myth to modern science, the drive to imitate is fueled by the quest for knowledge and for reconciliation with the object. For many graduate and undergraduate students on the East Campus of Duke University, Jameson's seminar served as a rite of initiation into modernist aesthetic theory. In the concrete case of this project, the mimetic impulse has the sense of magic mimicry or ritual imitation, where mimetic behavior is a response to an encounter with the fearful forces of nature, just as for many young scholars of culture, *Aesthetic Theory* comprised the "enigma"[21] of modernist aesthetics. Just as one "mimics" a beloved music piece by learning to play it, or a poem by learning it by heart, the simulation, or verbatim mimicry of Jameson's lectures and their transcription into written form, have the goal of reconciliation with the object of study: *Aesthetic Theory*. Imitation is particularly helpful to those lacking a background in philosophy or philosophical aesthetics, or a Western liberal education for that matter, offering the choice to move ahead by the path of the ignorant schoolmaster. The power of writing in this mimetic imitation *supplements* the deficiencies of the voice, its lack of extension in space.[22] For Adorno, mimesis is an immanent part of *artistic* experience, and bears no relation — or even stands in firm opposition — to mimesis understood as realism, be it the Platonic mimesis of appearances, Lukácsian social realism and/or naturalism, or a Leninist version of art as a reflection of reality. Instead, Adornian mimesis is an imitation of the inner truth of the spirit, or to put it in Hegelian terms: it is the imitation of the *idea* of natural beauty. As tested in this project (through my attempts to provide an accurate factual record of Jameson's lectures), a "truthful" mimesis is an impossibility, which of course we knew all along. Being the oldest and the most archaic of the aesthetic drives, mimesis is part of the subconsciousness of every socially symbolic act.

If mimesis is the residue of antiquated forms of knowledge, the drive seeking to subdue archaic forces of nature, then *expression* is the enduring voice of nature, or what is left of it. Adorno's interpreters have often debated the relation of expression to mimesis and construction, setting them sometimes in oppositional and other times in non-oppositional terms.[23] In this project, expression is understood as a historical residuum of mimesis, or as a repressed and inverted mimesis. In simplified terms, and based on this interpretation, expression is the modern version of mimesis, or what is left of mimesis after the complete domination of nature by the "enlightened" mind. When there is nothing left to mimic, or simulate and adapt to, following the rationalized mastery over the natural world, the alienated modern subject can only imitate its own inner emptiness. Expression is the dominant aesthetic drive of the modern subject who has lost touch with the natural world. Expression is mimesis of the modern subject's reified spirit, of its broken internal nature. For Adorno, expression is also the voice of suffering, which is the "cry" of the tragic consequences of the dialectics of enlightenment, and of culture and the human spirit after Auschwitz. It is the crisis of experience,[24] "of life that does not live" (Ferdinand Kiimberger's phrase, which Adorno often repeats), and of the idea that something worse than death — namely the gas chamber — is possible. For our generation today, it may also be the "cry" of climate collapse and the disappearance of animal and plant species and of life on Earth as it has been known. With the advance of enlightened reason, modern art can only express the cry of subjugated nature, mimicking the subject's depleted internal world. Modern art is the powerlessness of the human subject when faced with this reality, and ultimately the subject's desperate attempt to escape it by expressing itself, which fatally leads to even more fragmentation and singularization. In this book, the expressive impulse is perhaps the attempt to externalize an internal personal experience, and although expression is not as manifest here as imitation or mimesis, it is doing its work behind the scenes. It may be that here, artistic expression takes the side of repressed nature by giving voice to what is often suppressed during the transformation of speech into writing: the silencing of gaps, of murmurings and distractions, of the spoken incoherencies and other mumblings that the reader will find here. In its relation to pain, expression gives voice to what is often bracketed by reason, by technology, and in this case by the supplement of writing. Expression gives voice through objectification of the non-objective, of what is mute and cannot speak. It is the voice of the disappearing world.

Finally, *construction* is the aesthetic drive sometimes described as a corrective to expression. It continues to serve as an instrument for those who have not lost hope in progress and enlightenment. Construction is the impulse responsible for the organization of raw material — the drive associated with the latest phase of modernity, technique, and technology. It is the impulse that wants to confer objectivity on the structure of the artwork. Once art has lost its various historical forms — following the advance of nominalism and the crisis of the universals that once conferred objectivity externally (i.e., through the imposition of cultural forms, norms, languages, and stylistic conventions) — the modern artist is compelled to organize fragments of the world into artistic form without recourse to external rules or codes. Construction is the most advanced principle of modern artistic production. Although it is sometimes regarded as the dialectical opposite of mimesis, construction shares a purpose with the latter, namely full control over nature. However, if, for Adorno, mimesis is the archaic pre-conceptual and pre-spiritual impulse that art has carried out since the beginning of humankind — the drive that today is deeply buried in art's unconsciousness — construction is the manifest principle of modernity, modernism, and modernization, "fueling" the dialectics of progress. In modern art, mimesis and construction are caught in a dialectical to and fro, where the former is childish infantile play, and the latter is the work of "enlightened" or matured reason. Overall, construction is the organization of the shattered world as a consequence of the fragmentation of bourgeois subjectivity, of the individual monad.

In this project, construction is the form-giving principle. Here, the rule of aesthetic construction can be sought in the overall organization of mimetically extracted lectures. It is no accident that the principle of construction sends us first to architecture and to practices of heritage or historical reconstruction. In the seminar, we read fragments from Peter Weiss's *Aesthetics of Resistance*, on an edition of which Jameson was busy at the time, bringing early drafts into the classroom.[25] Weiss's discussion of the Pergamon Altar can serve as an illustration of the role of construction as an aesthetic-historic process. Splinters of the Pergamon frieze were brought to Berlin from Asia Minor and were then reconstructed by restorers and museum workers to bring back to life the story of the battle between the Giants and the Olympians. Certainly, in high modernist artistic practices, the principle of aesthetic construction is encompassed in the techniques of cinematic montage, cubist collage, twelve-tone music, surrealist association, and later in contemporary practices of assemblage or today in network aesthetics. It is a principle of modern rational organization and management and of territorialization or production of space, which Jameson once defined as a primary feature of postmodernist aesthetics. In the concrete case of this project, it is overall the intention to organize the raw material by constructing and construing some of the distinctive traits of high modernism as seen through the prism of Adornian aesthetics elaborated by Jameson in the Duke seminar.

The transcripts that follow contain not only interpretive material on *Aesthetic Theory,* but also analysis of other books that Jameson discusses in the seminar, namely Thomas Mann's *Doctor Faustus,* Kant's *Critique of Judgment*, Peter Weiss's *Aesthetics of Resistance*, along with shorter writings and works by Schoenberg, Freud, Beethoven, Nietzsche, Beckett, and other representatives of modern and modernist music, literature, or theory. These are some of the prisms through which Jameson regards Adorno's theory of aesthetics. Altogether, they provide the most paradigmatic examples of theory and practice in the aesthetics of high modernism, which may also have repercussions and implications for our own age. The form in which the seminar transcripts are presented in this volume occupies the position of "postmodernism" (or depending on one's favored periodization, "contemporaneity") — the cultural paradigm of late global capitalism for which mimesis, expression, and construction remain valid categories for engaging with artistic experience and production.

CHARACTERS

FREDRIC JAMESON

In 2003, the sixty-nine-year-old distinguished Marxist literary critic, the Knut Schmidt-Nielsen Professor of Comparative Literature and Romance Studies (French), and the director of the Center for Critical Theory at Duke University.

AUDIENCE

Undergraduate and graduate students, and occasionally junior faculty from various departments at Duke University.

LECTURE ONE

JANUARY 9, 2003

SEMINAR INTRODUCTION

CURTAIN RISES

Moving chairs, squeaking door, coughs, other sounds filling the noise environment of a large classroom in the Literature Department at Duke University. Undergraduates, graduate students, and junior faculty from various humanities departments have gathered for the first seminar on Adorno's Aesthetic Theory. *Most of the students are enrolled for credit, but there are also many who are simply auditing. Jameson's seminars usually run over capacity, which often creates tensions with the administration. Out of concern for safety, the university has proposed to either move the seminar to a larger, newer, and brighter-lit auditorium on East Campus, which Jameson resolutely refuses, or limit enrollment and thus restrict access to those students or faculty who are auditing. The issue of crowded classrooms and auditing (which is lost revenue for increasingly corporatized academia) has been one of his many contentions with the administration. Those arriving late often have no places to sit. Therefore, during Jameson's seminars, one can frequently see students wondering along the corridors of the Literature Department desperately looking for or carrying chairs.*

Jameson enters the classroom carrying a few books and a large college notebook. The latter contains his notes for the course, which usually consist of one or two words, or phrases written in large letters across the otherwise empty pages. Jameson wears a fitted plaid flannel shirt, regular trousers with a chain to a watch in his pocket, and black sneakers. In the chest pocket of his flannel shirt, he always carries a red pen.

[*Microphone turns on.*]

JAMESON: Mm-hmm... [*Long pause. Speaks without bothering about the noise.*] Mm-hmm. This is the first draft, and he wrote it in sentences... [*Sounds of chairs scraping against the floor. Footsteps. Backpacks and jackets' zippers unzipping. The audience gradually turns to silence.*]

Hmm... [*Pause.*] I'm sure if he had completed it, he would have done other things, but it is more or less what, hmm... [*Hesitates.*][1]

[*Long pause.*]

It is certainly very satisfactory in itself, Aesthetic Theory, and it came out I suppose the year after his death... [*Tries to remember*] in 1971 maybe? No, in 1970; I think he died in 1969.[2] At the end, hmm... [*Hesitates.*] Mm-hmm... [*Pause.*] At the end, there are some appendices, and that is called "Paralipomena," which are other thoughts he had on various things, a hundred pages of those, they're very interesting and worth reading, but I want you to separate those off; then there is an earlier piece called "Theories on the Origin of Art," and finally a "Draft Introduction." Making abstraction of those final three parts,[3] you will please number all of these sections in such a way that they come out to twelve chapters... [*Door creaks open. Footsteps. Sounds of chairs scratching against the floor. Audience members move closer to the front to make space for those arriving late*] which critics say Adorno didn't do it himself.[4] I believe that the German was originally published without any breaks, but with running heads that I think Adorno, you can look the story up, and I think that Adorno, hmm... [*Hesitates*] made up the running heads, that is to say what's on the top of these chapters.[5] And I believe that the editor Tiedemann has gone through and made more substantial breaks, which in later editions involve, hmm... [*Examines his notes*] involve the kind of index that you have here,[6] the kind of chapters, or table of contents that you have with indications of what's in these series of pages but without numbers. And indeed, now the German and the English both have an index of names and of topics, which is very useful. [*Firmly*.] Use the index of names — don't use the index of topics for reasons I'll tell you in a moment.

[*Long pause*.]

There was an older translation of this book that wasn't very meritorious. Mm-hmm. This man... [*Quietly*: I forget who he was, thought that after all these are very complicated sentences, let's break them down into simpler sentences.[7]] I assure you that, hmm... [*Hesitates*] it's a very strange thing to read because you look at this and you follow some kind of ideas going on and then you look at the German and you can, maybe by what Adorno calls "second reflection," you can see, oh yes, those are sort of the same things, but it's a wholly different text from Adorno's. So, this translator made a... [*Pause*.] He made the wrong decision, or maybe it was the publisher who insisted on making the text more readable by simplifying the English translation, I don't know. And finally, Hullot-Kentor did this translation... [*Words indistinct*] this new English version of Aesthetic Theory. And I think it is quite excellent, as it gives you the spirit of Adorno's writing.

[*Long pause*.]

It is supposed to be difficult.

Mm-hmm... [*Pause*.]

Well, there are certainly lots of references here to everything possible, some of which he will explain to you, some of which... [*Sighs*] he doesn't, and I will have to, and maybe I will know some of them myself. But the main thing is that there is certain kind of style going on here, a certain stylistic procedure, which is one of — I don't want to call it "paradox" even — and if I call it "dialectical" that would be maybe also not the right way to describe it. Mm-hmm... [*Pause*.] But it's quite unique, and I also think that Aesthetic Theory is not a discursive work, but a

[*Stressing*] literary product. I hope that there will be enough of this in English, for those of you who don't read German, to take some pleasure in reading this text. It's certainly not something you can read fifty pages at a time, and once you'll get into the spirit of this, and you see the interesting operations going on, you realize that it is like aesthetics itself lying halfway between the cognitive and the artistic.

[*Long pause.*]

This will be our... [*Door creaks open. Footsteps*] our principal text here, or one of the only three texts that we're gonna look at. However, because aesthetics really starts with Kant, and I think, hmm... [*Hesitates*] if one wants to get some idea of what we're doing here and what these initial references are all about, we must also talk about Kant. Therefore, I also ordered the latest edition of Kant's Critique of Judgment. Now, the Critique of Judgment is on two things: it's on forms of beauty and natural forms, or the teleology of nature. That's very important, and when we look at Kant, we'll take a look at that too. But we will only focus on the first half of the Critique of Judgment, and here are the pages which you'll get from... [*Talks to himself while leafing through the Table of Contents of Kant's last* Critique.] Mm-hmm... [*Pause.*] The first section is on beauty and the second section is on the sublime.[8] These are both parts of what in the division here is called... [*Sighs*] Part One, which is the "Critique of Aesthetic Judgment,"[9] that's the first half of the book. Book One of Part One is the "Analytic of the Beautiful" and Book Two is the "Analytic of the Sublime," and those are the parts that we need to, hmm... [*Hesitates*] that we need to take on. And I would suggest that what we are going to do today is look at the very opening of Aesthetic Theory, and at the moment when this passes to, questions of, hmm... [*Reflects.*] Here, in what I call the first chapter of Aesthetic Theory, when this chapter passes over into questions of effect,[10] suddenly we are confronted with two thinkers. One of them is... [*Sound of chalk on the blackboard*] K-A-N-T, and the effect of the beautiful, or, how can I say it, the pleasure without interest, and purposiveness with no purpose, or Zweck, hmm... [*Hesitates*] Zweckmäßigkeit ohne Zweck, and the other thinker is... [*Chalk on the blackboard*] F-R-E-U-D. It would be appropriate to get this part out of the way today, to look at the first few pages in detail, then we'll go into Kant and Freud. If someone wants to give us an introduction to Freud's "Der Dichter" essay, which is sometimes called "Daydreaming and Creative Writing," come talk to me after the class.[11] And then we'll go back to Adorno.

[*Long pause.*]

Obviously, we will not be holding to this schedule as such, because, hmm... [*Hesitates*] some things take more time than the others. So, this is very approximate, and our main plan of action is simply going through all of the Aesthetic Theory in its order, chapter by chapter. [*Decisively.*] However, because this can be tiresome, and I don't know, maybe at a certain point we may get exasperated with Adorno and his book... [*Quietly*: and after you've learned some of the mistakes and some of his tricks by now] then we will take a break. At that point then we will, hmm... [*Hesitates*] do something else, namely read Thomas Mann's novel Doctor Faustus. [*Addresses the audience.*] How many people have read Doctor Faustus?

[*Long pause. A few students raise hands.*]

JAMESON: Oh, that's not too many. How many read some Thomas Mann?

[*Silence.*]

JAMESON: Death in Venice I suppose, or The Magic Mountain? [*Pause.*] Mm-hmm. This is really Mann's greatest book, I think... [*Quietly*: I mean a lot of people think so, and he wrote it, hmm... (*Pause*).] It's a book about a musician who makes a pact with the devil... [*Cough in the audience*] and whose musical work then evolves into the twelve-tone system. Schoenberg, who was also living in LA at the time when Mann wrote the novel, was very unhappy. Doctor Faustus was written during the war, published in the last days of the war, in May probably, and it came out almost simultaneously in German and English. First it was published in German in Switzerland, and soon it appeared also here in English to become an American bestseller at that time... [*Achoo. Sneeze in the audience.*][12] Mm-hmm... [*Pause.*] Schoenberg was furious... [*Quietly*: he wrote a very angry letter to Mann in which he accused Mann of misrepresenting his ideas and using him to create a character.[13]] I'm not going to go into biography today, or into the history of the Frankfurt School. There are two books you can look at, one is Martin Jay's famous book, hmm... [*Tries to remember*] Dialectical Imagination, or something like that I think it's called,[14] which is the history of the Frankfurt School up to their return to Germany in 1953. This book essentially tells the story of the Frankfurt School from the point of view of Adorno's collaborator and the head of the school Max H-... [*Chalk strokes on the blackboard*] H-O-R-K-H-E-I-M-E-R, with whom Adorno wrote Dialectic of Enlightenment. We'll come back to it at some point. That's one version.

[*Long pause.*]

Much more recently in the last ten years there is a much more detailed history of the Frankfurt School, including the German period. Horkheimer presided over the school up to the 1960s, hmm... [*Pause.*] It was of course very dramatic like everything else in the 1960s, hmm... [*Pause*] up to Adorno's death. This is the so-called "first" Frankfurt School because then Habermas is supposed to be the "second" Frankfurt School, which is not altogether so. At any rate, this book I think... [*Tries to remember*] is by Rolf, and I cannot think now of his last name...

STUDENT: Wiggershaus.

JAMESON: Yes, Rolf Wiggershaus and he gives you the whole story of the Frankfurt School but now from Habermas's point of view.[15] Mm-hmm... [*Pause.*] Horkheimer fired Habermas and here you will see quite a different view from the one you get from Jay. It is very well done. Wiggershaus uses a lot of letters and documents that were unknown at the time and has also the biographies of all the major figures that are put in smaller type, inserted in the text, and also some of the more minor figures, like Leo Löwenthal, for example, who had his teaching career at Berkeley, or Erich Fromm, and people like that who have been associated with the School, and obviously Horkheimer... [*Quietly*: who is made a central figure in... (*Achoo. Sneeze in the audience.*)]

[*Long pause.*]

Anyway, we'll come back to all of that. What I wanted to say is that Adorno, hmm... [*Hesitates*] started really... [*Quietly:* I don't know what kind of degree he first had, but he finally got a philosophy degree.] I believe his first work was on Husserl and today there are some interesting essays and more and more of his work is being translated today.[16] But his real interest was music. He went to Vienna. He didn't study with Schoenberg, but he studied with Alban Berg, who was Schoenberg's student... [*Quietly*: and they both had a complicated relation.] There are now compositions of Adorno on CDs that you can listen to, and I have those, and I will play some for you — they are pretty much in the style of Berg. He composed his music in the 1920s and 1930s... [*Quietly*: people said he knew a lot about music and about the twelve-tone system, but in practice he was very slow at composing.] So, music becomes a major reference throughout his aesthetics, and a lot of his writings on music have now also been translated.

[*Long pause.*]

How many people read German? Let's see, raise your hands...

[*Silence.*]

Well, that's a pity because it would be nice to look at his work in German. But the... [*Pause.*] But whether all his books are still in print, or translated, I don't know. The important book on Schoenberg is called <u>The Philosophy of Modern Music</u>... [*Quietly*: <u>Philosophie der neuen Musik</u>] and there are also little books he wrote on Mahler, on Berg, hmm, a sort of memoir of Berg.[17] [*Pause.*] There is now an entire collection coming from Verso, a collection of his musical books, and what is that one called... [*To himself*: I was looking at it this morning, well I can't remember it now but is very new... (*Pause*).] And finally, there is also the posthumous work on Beethoven that he was working on.[18]

You will see that Adorno is never philosophically continuous, as you can observe this in Aesthetic Theory, which proceeds by blocs of themes. There are paragraph breaks that correspond to various themes, and then you go on to another theme, and in a way the same thing is being said in all of those themes… [*Choo-choo. Amtrak train whistle in the distance.*] So, clearly there is a change of topic, and a sort of a shifting of gears. The fact that the Beethoven essay was unfinished is maybe not necessarily the worst thing and there are a lot of other essays… [*Choo-choo. Loud Amtrak train whistle.*] There are a lot of musical references in here. I don't know to what degree we need to look into those. There are fewer references to the visual arts in Adorno and that we will have to make up for ourselves by trying to see how his aesthetics works across various arts. And in literature… [*Pause.*] Suhrkamp used to publish these little volumes, a little smaller than this [*Holds up* Aesthetic Theory], and there were four or five of these little volumes called Noten zur Literatur. Mm-hmm, and those have all been translated now, as… [*Chalk on the black-board*] N-O-T-E-S T-O L-I-T-E-R-A-T-U-R-E.[19] But these texts are not just on literature, there are also musical essays, there is an essay on essay… [*Quietly*: "Essay as Form," which I hope we will talk about in this seminar] and other ones on Beckett, on surrealism, and so forth. And there are a number of literary references there, which I don't… [*Pause*] you can decide later on for yourself whether you think that this perspective on the arts allows for criticism. Proust was very important to him but is he a good critic of Proust, I'm not sure about that… [*Quietly*: you can look at his Proust essay and decide for yourself.] There is a wonderful little essay "On Dickens' The Old Curiosity Shop" and there are other titles as well. The German classics were important. He had a running kind of relationship with Benjamin, and they exchanged many letters which have been now published.[20] [*Clears throat.*] Adorno read to Benjamin chapters of his work on Wagner, which I believe has also been translated as In Search of Wagner… [*Quietly*: Versuch über Wagner.][21] Maybe that would be also a place to look at Wagner's work, where he illustrates the problem of value plus ideology, and if anybody knows anything about Wagner, they know about the role that's played in it by a certain kind of nationalism, a certain kind of anti-Semitism, and all the rest of it. This is certainly one of the problems that comes up in Aesthetic Theory at a certain point, and we will look at that when time comes. But there is the other book on Wagner, which Adorno had connections with...[22] [*Mumbles indistinctly.*] But overall music was very important for Adorno, and we will have a few sessions dedicated exclusively to music theory. Music also runs through Mann's novel, which we will discuss.

[*Long Pause.*]

Now, I bring that up because Adorno was Thomas Mann's musical adviser in Doctor Faustus. Mann knew music very well, he played the piano, there are some famous stories... [*Quietly*: Bruno Walter was playing something from the Tristan and Isolde, and at some point, Mann pointed out that he left out the low B-flat in a certain passage.] This is a period in which music was practiced in the households of the German grand bourgeoisie, and it was very important to Mann, who has written some very important essays on Freud and on Wagner.[23] But Doctor Faustus, hmm... [*Hesitates*] you'll see that it's more than just the twelve-tone system which Adorno advised Mann on music philosophy. Indeed, some of the compositions mentioned in the book have some Adornesque, or Alban Bergesque... [*Raps his knuckles against the desk*] resonances. Also, by some happy coincidence they just published the correspondence between Thomas Mann and Adorno,[24] so we have more material on that front... [*Mumbles indistinctly.*] Anyway, but that's... [*Pause.*] I think you'll find in Doctor Faustus a somewhat more clear discussion of music, or more immediately entertaining than Aesthetic Theory, and so the novel shall furnish us with a useful break.

[*Long pause.*]

Mm-hmm... [*Looks over the syllabus. Reaches for the red pen.*]

You will note several days without class, and this is January 23rd, January 28th, February 6th, besides the break, hmm… [*Pause.*] You will also note a series of topics that I would like some oral presentations on. These presentations can be brief, fifteen-minute exposés on certain topics, so I'm not the only one talking here.

[*Long pause.*]

You also need to add two further topics which are on the list there… [*Breathes on the lenses and begins to polish them with his handkerchief.*] It is a way of introducing some practical considerations, some of the artists, works of art here, or themes because Aesthetic Theory itself is fairly abstract, as we shall see. And those two themes here are, first of all, Herbert Marcuse's early essay called "On the Affirmative Character of Culture."[25] This is an [*Whispering*] absolutely fundamental essay for the whole view of the Frankfurt School on culture and art. Mm-hmm. Adorno… [*Pause.*] In the first few pages of Aesthetic Theory, you will find Adorno recapitulating some of Marcuse's ideas on the inescapable affirmative essence of art. And there you have to know, and so I pointed out to you in the very beginning… [*Tries to remember.*] Mm-hmm, oh yeah, this essay is in Marcuse's collection of essays called Negations, and I would very much appreciate if somebody would like to give us a kind of précis of that article. I must also tell you right away… [*Pause.*] I must give you a lexical idiosyncrasy because it's important to know from the very beginning of this seminar some of these specific uses of words in the vocabulary of Frankfurt School, which you might otherwise be tempted to misunderstand.

[*Long pause.*]

[*Softly.*] It is that "affirmative" here means bad.

[*Long pause.*]

There are several words that are connected here, and these are "emphatic," "affirmative" and finally "positive" or "positivistic." Now you can see why much of Adorno, the whole dialectical side of Adorno, is an attack on positivism. This is the idea that only things that, hmm… [*Hesitates.*] The only thing that we can think about is what exists empirically, or what we can see and touch, and all the rest — according to positivism — is somehow subjective and odd or in the realm of the fantastic… [*Quietly:* or superstition.] The way the Frankfurt School understood and denounced it was basically to say that positivism insisted on being the empirical model of the natural sciences and the proper way to knowledge, and that the only path to truth and knowledge lies through these verifiable sciences. In the 1960s, the Frankfurt School had a whole debate with some of the representatives of the so-called positivist sociology.[26] Positivism is not exactly materialism, as we shall see, but it's for Adorno the dominant thought in this society. Increasingly, we only believe in what we see, what we can touch and what's there, and we will also talk about another related aspect in Adorno's aesthetic critique, and that is "nominalism," which has to do with the crisis of "universals" and the repudiation of the general or universal forms.[27] So, it is against this background of positivism and nominalism, which have become the laws of this modern… [*Cough in the audience*] society of late capitalism, that "affirmative" comes to mean something, which is related to but somewhat different. It means a… [*Pause.*] A… [*Softly.*] It means… [*Pause*] a ce… [*Stammering*] a celebration of what-is.

[*Long pause.*]

It's not just believing in [*Stressing*] what-is — in what Heidegger would call the "ontic," but… [Quietly: I guess it would be the ontological, which is in Heidegger not beings, the world of things, but Being with a capital "B"] — but somehow [*Whispering*] affirming it. An affirmative culture is one which somehow celebrates the existence of things as they are. You can say that Adorno is Hegelian in this sense, and that for him what-is is not primary… [*Quietly:* …Hegel has this formula that Adorno also likes to use from time to time, namely that, reality is not equal to its concept.] That is to say that this world of existing things is an imperfect world. There are concepts of everything in the world, but those concepts correspond to something only partially and incompletely or in unsatisfactory way. So, reality is not what it "ought to" be in some Kantian ethical sense, but what — for Hegel now — is implicit in the concept, in the realm of concepts rather than in the positivistic world of what exist now. When Hegel says "the real is the rational and the rational is the real" — I've told some of you this story in another class... [*Mumbles indistinctly.*] When Heine was a student... [*Quietly:* the poor Heine, he was very unhappy] he is supposed to have come, according to the story, to some of Hegel's lectures. Mm-hmm, I'm not sure if that's historically possible but anyway, let's say it happened. Heine is the first ironist in the German tradition; the first real critic of the emerging German modern realities; he is the Baudelaire of German poetry in some sense. So, Heine was supposed to go up to Hegel afterwards and say [*Impersonates Heine*] "Meister, this thing of yours 'the real is the rational and the rational is the real' isn't that sort of a reactionary slogan?" And then Hegel supposedly had said... [*Impersonates Hegel*] "I can see that you are a very intelligent young man, so to you only I will reveal the secret meaning of this saying; it is that the real *[Stressing]* must become rational and the rational must become real."[28] And obviously, if you can put it this way, suddenly everything changes. Anyway, this is the framework in which words like "affirmative" — mm-hmm, besides "positivism" — emphatically takes on a negative meaning. Whenever you see that in the language of the Frankfurt School, you understand that a praise is not being given to these subjects.

[*Examines his notes. Page flipping.*]

The other work, besides Marcuse's affirmative culture essay that I want you to look at... [*Pause.*] I'm not gonna, hmm... [*Hesitates*] unless we have to... [*Pause.*] I'm not going to put together a reader this time as we used to do in the past and this is because... [*Quietly*: I think a lot of these texts are now available on the Internet probably.] I don't know about Marcuse, but certainly Freud's essay you can probably find yourself online. The other thing that belongs on to this list of topics, and it isn't here, is the one writer whom, hmm... [*Hesitates*] one literary figure to whom Adorno feels to be the closest, and that is Samuel Beckett.

[*Long pause.*]

Adorno wrote a very famous essay about Beckett's Endgame, which is called, hmm... [*Tries to remember*] "An Attempt to Understand or to Interpret Endgame," or something like that.

STUDENT: "Trying to Understand Endgame..."[29]

JAMESON: Yes, right, "Understanding Endgame." Adorno thought that Beckett was that one figure, who like himself, was able to make utterances about a primitive situation, that is to say a situation of irredeemable negation. [*Pause.*] If you say anything about this situation, you are affirming it, and thereby implicitly celebrating the existence of this hopeless situation. There is another possibility for dealing with it, and that's the famous... [*Cough in the audience*] you fall silent, and you say nothing... [*Quietly*: this is not exactly the Wittgensteinian motto of what we cannot talk about must remain silent,[30] but it is a (*Stressing*) refusal to speak.] Then there is also a third possibility, which will be called with some of Adorno's philosophical work "negative dialectics" — the non-affirmative form of philosophizing, hmm... [*Hesitates*] in which you are able to speak about something even though it is literarily unspeakable. And I think "unspeakable" is the word that one must use for this whole process. [*Softly.*] How to understand this point of view? I think there are several ways of understanding it, and I'll give you two. One is that these people all emerged in the 1920s, in a revolutionary period. Mm-hmm. They all flee Nazism in the United States, but then they discover that the United States is a caricatural form of society. [*Gloomily.*] When you read a book like Dialectic of Enlightenment that he wrote with Hork... [*Cough-cough. Jameson*]... Horkheimer, or even his autobiographical writings, which is called Minima Moralia,[31] you will see... [*Quietly*: and this is part of the great tradition of many Europeans traveling to the US, like Tocqueville, Martineau, Dickens[32]] that they found the United States an abomination. They hated everything about it: the way people behave, its crudeness, its barbarous materialism, the consumerist modernity, and the culture industry. [*Exhales* *deeply.*] They discover that United States is not the future of the modern society. On the other hand, they also distrust the Soviet system, and this started already in the 1930s with the purge trials in the USSR. Then later, owing to the uniqueness of the German situation which had two Germanies, a... [*Achoo. Sneeze in the audience*] Soviet, or communist Germany, and a capitalist one, they became increasingly anti-communist. In a sense, there was nothing for them in this modern society, so they went back to Frankfurt and re-established their center. Horkheimer became rector, that is president of the University of Frankfurt, the most modern of all German universities after that point. [*Footsteps.*] Mm-hmm... [*Pause.*] And this is very interesting, because after all this is Hitler's territory. I mean you can say that Rhineland wasn't as bad as Bavaria, but everybody knows to what degree denazification was not really applied in West Germany... [*Quietly*: and was scarcely applied to old Nazis and reactionaries, and these reactionaries the ones who were able to escape without great public dishonor — unlike Carl Schmitt and Heidegger, who were, if not put on trial, at least removed from the system.] Mm-hmm. The universities in Germany were still full of conservatives, if not Nazis then at least quite old-fashioned right-wingers. So, there cannot be an affirmation of West Germany either... [*Quietly*: and although there are close ties with France and Britain, these are also not the model, they would find... (*Mumbles indistinctly*).] We must look at his impossibility to speak from this perspective, namely the bleakness that they have encountered after experiencing different social models. And one other perspective is the one found in the famous remark by Adorno that "no poetry is possible after Auschwitz." It is from [*Stressing*] this perspective of complete desolation that Adorno interprets Endgame. It is Auschwitz, and this is when Clov climbs up and looks up the window and sees the desert — what he sees is the concentration camp.

[*Long pause.*]

Adorno was half-Jewish. His mother, I believe, was Mediterranean — it's a Thomas Mann kind of combination that shows in various places in Doctor Faustus, as well. His name was actually... [*Chalk on the blackboard*] W-I-E-S-E-N-G-R-U-N-D. He had a very Jewish sounding name, and after a certain point in his thirties, I guess, he drops that name and starts using his mother's name "Adorno."[33] He re-transposes Wiese, placing the "W" in the middle and you'll see that this is very good, as it means "meadow" in German. [*Softly.*] There is a funny part in Doctor Faustus, which is like the thing in Proust, where he thanks... [*Quietly:* Mann inscribes his thanks to Adorno, and there is passage in Beethoven which is interpreted in terms of this theme which goes (*Intoning*) Wie-sen-grund — mead-ow-land.][34] [*Chuckles.*] That's Mann's "thank you" to Adorno... [*Quietly*: but he didn't like it.] So, this notion of "no literature is possible after Auschwitz," "no speech" in a sense, that's another way of defining this impossibility of art. And I think it has very much to do with the guilt of the survivors, which will persist in the Jewish communities of this generation — the idea that the European Jews... [*Addresses the audience.*] Did I talk about this? The idea is that you could have been in Auschwitz yourself. You could have died, and nothing justifies you going on living. It was sheer accident that you were able — by whose choice, God's or accident or something — that you were able to live on and all these other people were killed. So, I think this is the product of another deep psychological trauma, if you like, that plays its way into the alleged pessimism of this work, and his aesthetic theory. But it is not pessimistic, and you will see what other kind of forms this takes.

[*Long pause.*]

So that's more or less our program. I haven't put any Hegel in here but I'm going to give you a few pages from his Aesthetics. The whole introduction is only about a hundred pages, and you get all of his aesthetics. There is in fact a Penguin edition of the introduction to what sometimes is called "Philosophy of Fine Arts," and sometimes is called "Aesthetics," and so forth, which is an excellent summary.[35] [*Looks over the syllabus.*] And you have possibilities for other topics here, so please think about it and let me know if you would like to present. We can use the one on Freud's daydreaming very soon, if anyone knows this text, it's a short essay, really easy to fill us in on it. As for the rest of it, we'll see as we go on.

[*Long pause.*]

Mm-hmm... [*Pause.*] Now, how many undergraduates are actually enrolled in this course anyway?

[*A few students raise their hands.*]

JAMESON: You're enrolled?

STUDENT: Yes.

JAMESON: You?

STUDENT: Yes.

JAMESON: Okay. We will need to talk... [*Cough in the audience*] you'll do the same kind of work as the others, but essentially the way I imagined this is writing a single long paper, on whatever variety of possible themes, and if you're doing an oral presentation then that could get rid of that or be regarded as first draft or something of that sort. I also will need to talk to all our first-year literature students... [*Pause.*] Who are those? Okay, there is about... [*Counts in the course list*] one, two, three — just four of you. [*Softly.*] Hmm, one, two, three, four. Well, we've got to figure out something too for reasons that I will explain to you, and that doesn't necessarily need to be today.

[*Long pause.*]

Are there questions about the practical side of this course?

[*Silence.*]

Okay well, now as much as possible, I would like to go back to these first few pages of Aesthetic Theory and do a kind of tiresome virtual line-by-line reading of some of the most important sentences, to give you a little idea of how a text like this works. And in fact, I think ideally the whole course... [*Quietly*: if it's a real seminar] should be, simply a line-by-line, page-by-page reading and interpretation. But, when you have a three-hundred-fifty-page book, to do that in a single course is impossible... [*Pause.*] In Europe sometimes, they had... [*Quietly*: oh, I remember in the 1950s it was very funny.] They were reading, I don't remember what was on the syllabus... [*Tries to remember*: was it Camus's L'étranger?] It was a large three-hundred-page book, or something like that, and they went line-by-line, text-by-text in that seminar which must have lasted three or four years... [*Chuckles.*][36] I feel that we can, hmm... [*Chuckles continue*] we can pursue this course, perhaps not quite to that degree, but it's very important to identify topics, as well as some of the positions that are being taken. Now, I'm not asking you... [*Agitated.*] Sometimes, I ask you to make a sort of journal of your readings, and just keep notes on your computer, which you regularly turn in, and which are in effect noticing things of interest, turns of phrases that you find interesting, cross-references that appear important to you, and so forth. I asked you to make a note of anything that catches your attention, but I think we won't do it this time. What I was thinking... [*Cough-cough. Jameson*] is that you could on the other hand... [*Quietly*: that's why I said earlier that you should not bother with the book's index of themes] but try and make a kind of conceptual index for yourselves and send it to me. As you're doing your reading of Aesthetic Theory, and as you noticing a theme appearing, invent a category, and a page number for that topic, and make a note on the appearance of the topic that could go a little bit beyond a word and page number. You can say, for example, here he discusses aesthetic autonomy in terms of this and that, hmm... [*Hesitates*], then here he attacks Kant, here he is engaging with Benjamin... [*Pause*] and so on and so forth. That way you would not be doing this index in a chronological way but rather in terms of themes that you are mapping out, as you're going through the book. I think you may find that this method can give you an interesting way to engage with Adorno... [*Audience murmuring.*] If the progression of the argument is the melody, so to speak, these themes are the harmonics of these melodies. That is, here we get a discussion of art's autonomy in relation to this particular topic, whereas later on it will be the other way around. But anyway, play with this idea and see what you can do, using that as a way of exploring the text, because otherwise the editors have very well picked out for you what's going on in these various chapters. You have already a sort of very vague and general index, or in this case a ready-made table of contents, and a sequence of... [*Exhales deeply*] "On the Relation of Art and Society," "Critique of the Psychoanalytic Theory of Art," and so on. These is a very general list of topics, but I think it may be more interesting to do it the other way around and compile a more detailed constellation of concepts.

[*Clears throat.*]

Now, one of the most striking things, which is part of the aesthetics of this book, is the first sentence. One other very famous first sentence in Adorno is the one in <u>Negative Dialectics</u> and that's... [*Student raises hand.*]

JAMESON: Yes.

STUDENT: This conceptual index can be handed...

JAMESON: Come again. Can be...?

STUDENT: Can be handed over instead of being sent by email?

JAMESON: [*Surprised.*] Oh, people don't use computers anymore, yes, of course, sure, sure, yes, print it and hand it to me.

[*Long pause.*]

Mm-hmm. The most famous of these introductory sentences that sort of blasts off his mode of philosophizing, if you can call it that, is the one in <u>Negative Dialectics</u>, which is also poorly translated but not as badly as this one. There you have the famous sentence: "Philosophy lives on... because the moment to realize it was missed..." [*Quietly*: I'm translating from memory here.][37] In other words, in the nineteenth century with Hegel, and presumably Marx as well, there is a moment when philosophy might have been realized in the real world — and that is the revolutionary moment. But the moment was missed, and therefore, what used to be called "philosophy" is still living on as an independent discipline. It did not change the world and with the world but has been absorbed into a world, which itself has become rational, and turned into a specialized separate discipline of rationality. You can make of this first sentence any number of philosophies. But this one is not as dramatic but there is a lot here that announces the future of his theory... [*Reads from* Aesthetic Theory.] "It is self-evident that nothing concerning art is self-evident anymore, not its inner life, not its relation to the world, not even its right to exist."[38] [*Pause.*] Mm-hmm, I think this means that aesthetics, as a kind of philosophy, is a questionable and self-contradictory field. If art is in question as he states in "its right to exist"... [*Choo-choo. Amtrak train whistle in the distance*] then a philosophy of art is doubly questionable, right? How can you philosophize about something whose very existence is problematic, what kind of philosophy would that be? And indeed, I think the question that aesthetics as a philosophy raises is precisely that: What is the coherence of this reflection on... [*Pause*] what is the reflection on? You could say, well it's supposed to be about art. Yeah, but is this a criticism of art, is it, hmm... [*Hesitates*] is it some kind of category of thought, which is art, and if so then what kind of category is that? All of that I think is implied here. Okay, next comes "it's inner life..." [*Pause.*] Here Adorno means to raise the question of subjective versus objective in art, which was particularly strongly argued in the early years of the twentieth century, in the 1920s and so forth. Is art to become an exploration of subjectivity, is it the inner subjective impulse of art that needs to be expressed somehow, with those subjectivities interiorized — or is art to be an [*Stressing*] objective thing? The German word for this, and there are several German words to look at is... [*Chalk on the blackboard*] S-A-C-H-L-I-C-K-E-I-T...

STUDENT: [*Quietly.*] Spelling is wrong...

JAMESON: Sache is "thing." The Neue Sachlichkeit was a kind of art that was to be wholly objective; they wished to get rid of all interiority and subjectivity. [*Looks at the blackboard.*] Mm-hmm. Did I spell it right?

STUDENT: Missing the second "H"... [*Inaudible.*]

JAMESON: Huh? Oh, I see... [*Chalk on the blackboard*] S-A-C-H-L-I-C-H-K-E-I-T. That's okay now. The subjective and objective in art are the two seemingly and radically incompatible matters. Does art exist in order to develop new forms of subjectivity, to reflect new forms of interiority... [*Quietly*: that's something that one sometimes associates with music, and one of the great breakthrough pieces which, I have to play it one day for you, is Erwartung which is... *Mumbles indistinctly*).]

JAMESON: How many of you listen to any classical music at all?

STUDENTS: Ha, ha, ha. [*Audience laughing*.]

JAMESON: Because I find that it is one of the hardest things to really listen to the classics today. Anyway, Schoenberg's Erwartung is this vocal short one-act monodrama using atonality... [*Quietly*: it is not that short actually] a vocal piece, which conveys all the great fantasies of the neurotic. These fantasies are obviously of a woman, because hysteria, neurosis and so on, that used to be predominantly considered a condition for the middle-class modern women. This would be one of the high points of what you would think as a purely subjective art of inwardness. The dominant category of this kind of art, and here I'm anticipating an aesthetic concept that will be overtly discussed later on, if not now... [*Pause*.] Let's see if you know it. [*Addresses the audience*.] How would we call this kind of art? I mean, you've got something inside, and you are going to make art out of it, and as I say it's also clear that music will play some central role in that, even though you could also imagine it in paintings, books, literature, and other examples of art showing anxieties, fear, things that are invisible. What is this kind of art called? [*Pause*.] What would be the dominant category that that art would function under such conditions?

[*Long silence*.]

STUDENT ONE: [*Quietly*.] Expression?

JAMESON: Yes. [*Firmly*.] Expression.

So, we have a fundamental category of aesthetics, which is that of [*Stressing*] expression. It is an aesthetics of inwardness, of subjectivity, an aesthetics that thinks of itself in terms of conveying or expressing some inner nature. And you can imagine that Adorno will demolish this idea that expression is possible. But then the reaction would be, okay, we don't want that, we don't want inwardness, we don't want subjectivity, we don't want expression. We want objectivity and things... [*Quietly*: you may want to think about Mondrian, for example, and people seeing the colors of Broadway Boogie-Woogie, or something like that — hmm, we wanna make things, we don't want to express anything, we are not interested in subjectivity.] Or we make collages, hmm... [*Hesitates*] do people know John Herzfeld, and the political collages he made in the late 1920s? Or you take Picasso, for instance, all of these works by Picasso and Braque, the collages of cubism. They seemingly have less to do with subjectivity, and instead they want to put things from the world together, like scraps of paper, pieces of wood glued to the canvas and mixed with paint, and so on. Alright. If there is a category called "expression," on one hand, and it stands for all the inner and subjective in art, what's the category for the objective in art?

[*Long silence.*]

STUDENT TWO: Realism...?

JAMESON: Not, exactly, not exactly, and that's gonna be a problem. And I'm not sure whether this is a very good term... [*Mumbles indistinctly*] to Adorno. [*Exhales deeply*] But we'll come to these issues of representation some other time.

STUDENT THREE: Well, I'm trying to remember, Mondrian is neo-plasticism...

JAMESON: Yeah, yeah, yeah...

STUDENT THREE: ... so maybe for him art and the value of art itself is to be found in...

JAMESON: Right, right, right, yeah, well Mondrian may or may not be a very good example. It is not about Mondrian, or a style of art. I want a more general, abstract category which would govern the world of the people who are on the objective side of this strange but quite fundamental opposition in art?

[*Long pause.*]

JAMESON: They don't want to deal with their inner world, they don't want to express anything, so what are they gonna do with things?

STUDENT FOUR: Co- co- [*Stammers*] concept? Conceptualism?

JAMESON: No, not concept, not conceptualism, it is not conceptual art...

STUDENT THREE: How about...

JAMESON: Ah?

STUDENT THREE: I mean art as an object that is... [*Words indistinct.*]

JAMESON: Yea, yea, yea, what do you do with that? How do you get to that stage of the object?

STUDENT THREE: I don't know.

JAMESON: [*Softly.*] Construction. Constructivism.

AUDIENCE: [*Murmuring in unison.*]

JAMESON: [*Chalk on the blackboard.*] C-O-N-S-T-R-U-C-T-I-V-I-S-M.

AUDIENCE: [*Murmuring to each other*] Construction... constructivism.

JAMESON: To construct! It is an art that [*Whispering*] wants to construct something. So, in this first sentence we already have one of the dominant themes of this book, which is the opposition between expression and construction. It is an opposition that one finds in aesthetics, in artistic production, and as you can imagine, both of which are contradictory. And you could assume, and I think he does assume that all great art is gonna be a combination between construction and expression. That is to say... [*Quietly:* a construction which expresses, or an expression which constructs.] But this is after the fact, and we have to find the work first, and then show how these categories operate... [*Pause.*] We can't deduce a manifesto from this. Certainly, you can have manifestos of expressionism, and you can have manifestos of constructivism, right... [*Quietly:* Soviet constructivism and so on] but an aesthetics which can put the two together — that can't be assumed. So, this tension between expression and construction will be the basic dialectical opposition of this book, and we have them encoded in the first sentence. "Not its inner life"... [*Pause.*] "Not its relation to the world." Mm-hmm, and here we get Marcuse's "affirmative culture..." [*Cough in the audience.*] Art is apparently some kind of reproduction of the world, but which is not the world. Art is imaginary. It doesn't have to be a picture of it, but everything has to be taken from the world. If you take, hmm... [*Hesitates*] take something that's even better than Mondrian. If you take Malevich. You all know what the Black Square is? [*Pause.*] It's a painting which is all black, and it was made as the ultimate answer in Malevich's explorations of painting, which was... [*Tries to remember.*] I don't recall what his style of art was called... [*Raps his knuckles on the desk*] ... Supre... something.

STUDENT: Suprematism.

JAMESON: Right, suprematism. Okay, now The Black Square. [*Pause.*] It's an object. The black is in the world somewhere, right... [*Chair-back creaks.*] It is like that blackness has been borrowed from the world and put somewhere else. Now, we know where it is — I think I saw it somewhere in the world — so we know maybe that there is a piece of canvas painted all over black by Malevich, and we can testify that we got it from somebody important, a rich collector who told us that it was Malevich who did that, and that it's very expensive now [*Chuckles.*] But if you say that the painting is in Stedelijk Museum, or Munich or some other place, hmm... [*Hesitates*] well, it is not anywhere. It's only the object, the canvas and frame that's in the museum, but the [*Stressing*] work of art itself cannot be contained in any physical place. The material can, but the image, or the idea that art puts into our heads, that is nowhere — it is immaterial. Alright, so that is what art is: it's made of pieces of the world, but at the same time it lives outside the world somehow. If you look at it, if you take this painting and if you take some machinery and start to analyze the kind of paint that was used, or you look at the canvas and how it was preserved, or you look at the wood and how the frame was made — you are looking at all of this as an [*Stressing*] object, but then you're looking at it from the point of view of the scientist, or the curator or something. You are not looking at it as a work of art, and as a work of art, it is not there. [*Pause.*] So, art in that sense is always somehow duplicating the real world; it is a zone of reality that is not in the world but somehow floats above it... [*Achoo. Sneeze in the audience*] and in some way or another has a relationship to it. What are the two obvious relationships that art can have to the real world?

[*Long pause.*]

STUDENT: Representation?

JAMESON: [*Hesitates.*] Hmm... yeah, yeah and mimesis. We will get to that later. That's a very complicated thing, but that wasn't the kind of relationship I was thinking. What can art say about the real world?

[*Walks around classroom.*]

I think it can say at least two things... [*Quietly*: that the world is wonderful, or the real world is a bummer.] Art can be a subversion, a [*Stressing*] critique or a negation of the real world — a favored Frankfurt School word — or, it can be an affirmation of the real world, and there is no way of choosing between these two. What Marcuse is trying to say in his essay about affirmative culture is that you may start off with the one and you will end up in the other: you start off wanting to make a critique but then it ends to be an affirmation. [*Exhales deeply.*] Let me illustrate this in terms of war novels because there are some very nice examples. Let's say you wish to denounce war, so you write a novel like, what was that novel called... [*Raps his knuckles on the desk*] hmm, oh yes: All Quiet on the Western Front.[39] This is the famous novel showing how terrible war is, and how inhuman it is, and what it does to people, and so on and so forth. Yes, but as one critic said... [*Quietly:* this one was not anybody from the Frankfurt School, this was an American critic that pointed out to this paradox] you know, that many people who are reading this book would think: war is truly abominable, who would like such an experience, the novel is very powerful in denouncing the cruel reality of war. But then as this critic said, there are people in this world who find peacetime boring and unsatisfying, and who may actually find this novel rather exciting as a way of life or representation of war. For them — and this is certainly the case in European history and probably in our own in various places — so for them, this work is not a denunciation or a critique of the world, but it is an [*Stressing*] affirmation of it. That is, it points out to an experience in which excitement still exists, in which a heightened sense of life is possible in the midst of death, and so on and so forth, and therefore what set out to be an anti-war novel becomes a kind of advertisement for a certain kind of military existence. You could also look at it the other way around... [*Pause.*] Mm-hmm, this is an example from Sartre: he once said that the artist is always negative and critical, even when he tries not to be so. You have, for example, the great periods like the golden age in France, the court of Louis the Fourteenth, where art was to serve the splendor of the monarch. So, you have the whole history of portraiture, I guess from the end of the Middle Ages on, which is about the glorification of the court, of the monarch, of the great figures. They painted these sumptuous paintings and portraits of court life. But as Sartre says, you know, the problem is that no matter how close the representation is, hmm... [*Hesitates*] it is always a little bit different, and the subject who was being painted always feels that this is not the way he or she really looks. [*Softly.*] The artist has somehow betrayed the subject in the slight difference between the way I want to see myself and the way this artist is seeing me... [*Quietly*: and this is then a critique of me.] So, the most affirmative kind of art, it also tends to have its moment of criticism. At any rate, this dialectic back-and-forth between the positive, the affirmative and the critical is part of this question of what the relationship of art to the world is. What happens when art becomes part of the world, when it becomes private property and is used to endorse the system, thus betraying that moment when art was still mainly an imaginary alternative or negation of the status quo, when it did not exist in the world as a collectable object or a commodity. All of that is also implicit in the second phrase: "not its relation to the world." And I should also say that this part has to do with autonomy. If art is part of the world, then it is not autonomous... [*Pause.*] Then you have to say, eh, what is the biography of the artist and what does this correspond to? Or maybe the pieces of art are in the world — the traditions — look, he just imitated so-and-so, and the musical combinations here are really just derived from previous compositional innovations, and so on and so forth, and at that point the whole thing is stuck back into this context. If it's purely autonomous though, then it's not connected to anything, but isn't that purely utopian? Even utopias are connected to the real world. So, the question of autonomy becomes central at once in aesthetics as a discipline, and as I said these questions go back to Kant... [*Quietly:* Kant is the first great early inventor of the aesthetics, and nothing after Kant goes that far in thinking about these questions the way he does.] And so, the notion of aesthetic autonomy, or the autonomy of the aesthetic experience is central here. Don't you have to be yourself... [*Pause.*] If this art object is outside in the world... [*Reflects*] it has some marks and paint on the canvas, and then you go and look at it, hmm... [*Hesitates*] well, is that inside your life or outside it? Is something happening there, as you're looking at this which is not really part of your biography? For example, it's very difficult to put those things into a narrative... [*Exhales deeply*] it's very hard for aesthetic experience to become part of a novel, let alone the creation of a work of art within the novel. We will look at that in the case of Thomas Mann obviously.

[*Long pause.*]

Now... [*Page flipping. Looks at his notes.*] But then one has to go further and say that this art-piece that you're putting together... [*Quietly*: and I don't think that you are putting it together only purely objectively, you are still looking at it using your eyes, or thinking and imagining it] because even though these are pieces of paint, you are synthesizing them into something which is physically not there. It's appearance, and a little bit like a show, but far superior to a show — there is a whole set of relations there, which is no longer physical. [*Pause.*] But you're doing that. Now, are you still doing that in the real world? And are you yourself not also outside of it? Mm-hmm, Sartre called this process "derealization." It is not a word that Adorno uses but it could be useful here... [*Chalk strokes on the blackboard*] D-E-R-E-A-L-I-Z-A-T-I-O-N.[40] And I think, derealization means in very simple terms that if you're gonna deal with a work of art, if you're gonna read a book, look at a picture, listen to a piece of music, you have to abstract yourself from your surroundings. Mentally, you are detached from your reality, and you are somewhere else, where the novel or the painting is. Now, is this always true of music because music is not part of space, or how about dance music? But then there are works of art which expand and include all of that. So, the question is not only about the autonomy of the work of art but about the autonomy of so-called "aesthetic experience." That's all, hmm... [*Hesitates*], that's all part of this book, and I think that one of the points of Aesthetic Theory — which does not call itself an aesthetic by the way, but it could call itself [*Whispering*] a critique of aesthetic, we'll see later on what that is — is to take those things apart and find out how many contradictions... [*Cough in the audience*] there are in this thing called "aesthetics," which is, hmm... [*Hesitates*] which is as imposable and contradictory as it is inevitable and necessary, if you see what I mean. That is sort of a fundamental Adornian, hmm... [*Hesitates*] — a fundamental Adornian paradox.

[*Long pause.*]

"Not even its right to exist." Okay, now this is modernism. Adorno's aesthetics is an aesthetics of modernism. Remember that music... [*Reflects.*] What he is really thinking about here is music; it is modern music which comes into being in the eighteenth century, according to Adorno's system. There is a lot of music before, and there is a lot of music and sonorous techniques in other cultures, but music in the sense that he is thinking about is only two or three hundred and fifty years old. We will come to a point... [*Exhales deeply*] ah, it is later on one of these pages where he says [*Impersonates Adorno*] "Look, maybe there was only a certain moment when there could be great music, and maybe that moment is over."[41] [*Pause.*] Mm-hmm. Maybe Phil Glass, and all of that stuff now is not music anymore... [*Quietly*: hmm, I heard Tim Clark say a similar thing, when he was talking about his new book, which is relevant to us and we should look at it, and his new book is called Farewell to an Idea.[42]] What is the "Idea"? [*Pause.*] It sounds like socialism but it's really modernism. I think what Tim is saying... [*Impersonates Clark*] "Look, when I entered this field" — he is one of the great modern art historians — "I came to realize that I wasn't interested in all possible marks. I was only interested in this weird thing, this unnatural thing, which is stretching a canvas on some pieces of wood and putting some marks on it. I wasn't interested in happenings; I'm not interested in installations, I'm not interested in any of this stuff that is going on now, so it is as though I had committed myself to a form of production which was temporarily limited, which came into being and died." Mm-hmm... [*Sighs*] and I think Adorno is saying something similar here only about music.

[*Long pause.*]

Now, you can look at this in several ways. You can look at this as the end of modernism... [*Pause.*] Adorno was certainly very interested in new kinds of music... [*Quietly*: I'll play something for you next time] but it is as though modernism as art — and that's the way it is essentially taught in the university today — was the limit of his horizon. Or you can talk about it also in terms of Hegel's famous formula of the "end of art." [*Sound of pen dropped on the floor.*] And there it's a little bit different. Hegel's idea was that art... [*Addresses the audience.*] What time is the class supposed to end?

STUDENT: Twelve thirty...

JAMESON: Oh, okay we are almost at the end of… [*Quietly:* we will get to these other pages next time, obviously we cannot continue today.] Hegel's idea was that art was part of the Spirit, and part of the sequences as forms of consciousness and activity in human history. It begins with religion, then religion becomes art, in the moment of the classical Greeks, and then art and what remained of religion becomes philosophy. [*Footsteps. Walks towards the blackboard.*] So, when we make a transition from the historical moment of art to the moment of philosophy, and for Hegel that has taken place around the time of the German Reformation, and probably Kant, then art no longer has the function of the… [*Chalk on the blackboard*] A-B-S-O-L-U-T-E. The earlier forms: it is first religion, which deals with the Absolute, then art and so on, and now it is philosophy. At that point then, art no longer has its vocation in the Absolute, and therefore it comes to an end as art. [*Page flipping.*] Now, my friend Peter Bürger… [*Quietly*: who's written on this in his famous avant-garde essay[43]] says [*Impersonates Bürger*] "You see, if you really look at the Aesthetics carefully you can see that Hegel didn't mean that people will stop painting, only that art would sink to a decorative level." Yes, people still paint, they make still-lifes or decorate their houses, and so forth, but overall art is today present on some peripheral level, some kind of subconsciousness as if it does not have any longer a… [*Mumbles indistinctly*] to impact our everyday life, and human history. And the Absolute would be then that… [*Exhales.*] Mm-hmm. Well for some, it is the human community itself and no longer in the distorted forms of religion, or of some religion of art. That would have been the realization of philosophy, which Adorno points out earlier with his other famous sentence, was missed. [*Pause.*] So, in my view, what happens is that art doesn't end but becomes modernism, which supremely has the vocation of the Absolute… [*Sighs.*] And that comes to an end with modernism. Ah, but, hmm… [*Hesitates.*] But, hmm… [*Words indistinct*] into postmodernism. So, this is certainly one of the basic themes of this book. Is art mortal?

[*Long pause.*]

One view is that art is profoundly historical. Under what circumstances can it cease to exist? Does it die? And if so, is there anything else to replace it? Anyway, in this first sentence we have a whole set of such questions, and we can go on and follow these pages through next time. Now, for Kant I can give you that stuff next time. So, next try and read as much of this first section of <u>Aesthetic Theory</u> as you can, concentrating on the themes and subjects and the index that I was... [*Words indistinct*] and maybe... [*Chairs screeching across the floor.*]

Feet shuffling. Audience stands up. Objects drop on the floor. Door squeaks. Backpacks and jackets zipping up. Students return chairs to other classrooms. Some in the audience form a line to discuss their assignments with Jameson. General noise. Screeching microphone noise.

[*Microphone turns off.*]

CURTAIN

LECTURE TWO

JANUARY 14, 2003

ART, SOCIETY, AESTHETICS (CHAPTER) — AUTONOMY — HEGEL'S AESTHETICS — SUBLIME

CURTAIN RISES

Moving chairs, squeaking door, coughs, other sounds filling the noise environment of a large classroom in the Literature Department at Duke University. Students are getting settled. Some are taking off their jackets, making themselves comfortable. Others are milling around chatting. Students tend to sit in groups formed by acquaintance, department, or degree sought. The undergraduate students in the seminar stick together in small clusters, feeling intimidated by "critical theory" or by the confidence projected by the graduate students. Some students are still chewing, or sipping their coffee, and a few continue with their breakfast even during the seminar. This is apparently a common practice in North American universities and is part of the "culture shock" for many foreign students or visiting faculty.

Jameson enters the classroom carrying a few books, his scattered notes, and the red pen in the chest pocket of his flannel shirt. On the way to the front of the class he stops to chat with a few students on practical matters.

[*Microphone turns on.*]

JAMESON: Mm-hmm, I wanted to draw your attention to this book… [*General noise. Footsteps. Chairs scratching the wooden floor.*] This is a somewhat more systematic way to deal with the idea of… [*More footsteps. Students whispering.*] I don't know if it incorporates all of Adorno's themes, but I think it can give you a certain idea about some of the basic themes, which we will discuss in more detail later on. Then we will go on to, hmm… [*Hesitates*] to Kant, at least the first part of the text… [*Door creaks open and closes again. Zippers unzipping.*]

[*Long pause.*]

I've been talking a lot about autonomy, and you understand that this business of autonomy has to do with the notion of the [*Stressing*] critical, which is fundamental for the Frankfurt School, and under which you can arrange a number of synonyms, like the "negative," or "negative dialectics" famously, and this is what is it called because, hmm… [*Addresses audience.*] Because why?

[*Long pause.*]

How does this fit into Adorno's scheme of things, the "negative," or the "critical"? Anyone?

[*Silence.*]

Look. The term "critical theory" is the euphemism they adopted from Marxism in the late 1920s and 1930s, and that remained. When you adopt these euphemisms sometimes… [*Chairs scraping the floor*] they take on a life of their own. But why would it be so important for Adorno to call this, hmm… [*Hesitates*] to talk about the negative?

[*Long pause. More footsteps. Door creaks open.*]

You see this oscillates back and forth and it is something that we would now identify with… [*Quietly*: but they were doing it a lot earlier] with deconstruction. It is a sort of deconstructive stance aimed at destabilizing an ideological position. I mean, the whole argument on autonomy is, I think, a sort of a textbook kind of… [*Clears throat*] deconstruction, in that it seeks to locate some fundamental contradiction or antinomy at the heart of the notion of autonomy. [*Softly.*] Art is autonomous, and yet it can't be autonomous. And autonomy means, or should mean, separation from what-is, and therefore a critique of what-is, but at the same time, and this is inevitable, it is part of and an affirmation of what-is. What I'm looking for is this business of how to elude... [*Cough in the audience*] affirmation, or affirmativeness. [*Firmly*.] And affirmativeness is bad. As with deconstruction, you can't say anything, you can just undermine everything, right? You can show that any attempt to say something is doomed to internal contradictions that... [*Door creaks open. Footsteps*.] I would say that very often in Adorno that's the case, but unlike — what at least looks like a sort of Derridean style, or stance — it seems to me that Adorno always says you have to do both in some sense: both to keep up the critique and the inevitable affirmation... [*Quietly*: whereas in Derrida you never know what are you supposed to do once you realize that these are meaningful antinomies, meaningless sort of unresolvable forms of meaning, speech, contradictions.]

[*Long pause*.]

Now, hmm... [*Hesitates*.] In Adorno, you have to assume that art's very separation from life, from social life, from being, from the world, is in and of itself critical and negative because art is not life, art is not being, and so forth. But on the other hand, you must also say that, for some strange reason, art can also very easily slip into the affirmation of what-is, into the celebration of what-is, into being taken for or confused with life and being... [*Cough in the audience*.] This parallelism of the world of art and of the real world does not guarantee that the separation is gonna be negative, or critical, and therefore art can always slip into the ideological affirmation of the world. This is, in some sense, imposable to decide in advance. And this fundamental ambiguity raises the question of, hmm... [*Hesitates*] of the autonomy of art.

[*Long pause*.]

This raises the question of the negativity of art, which Adorno would answer in a historical way. I think that what he would say is: there were moments in history when art could have been more negative than it is now. This is because... [*Cough in the audience*] late capitalism... [*Quietly*: in its various manifestations that he denounces as "positivism," "scientism," "nominalism"] is driving out negation and critical reflection. [*Pause.*] Negation is the ability to take a distance from what-is, which increasingly becomes more difficult, given that the whole logic of our society is based on an ideology which insists that only what-is exists, or is possible, and that there is no place for anything outside of what already exists. [*After prolonged reflection.*] Well, little by little that's gonna mean that you can't imagine a future that's different from this one, and finally that there is no real place for negativity, for imagination, fantasy, and so forth. Therefore, one of the great... [*Cough in the audience*] laments of the Frankfurt School — as the postwar went on into the 1960s, and so forth — is that this society of late capitalism is removing all the possible spaces from which any negation of it could be achieved. This means that the question about the criticality of art, its negativity, its subversion... [*Quietly*: and we have a lot of words for it: undermining, dissidence, rebellion, condemnation, critique... (*Pause*) what are the other words that you know, what are artists supposed to do in the face of the status quo] is that one cannot make an ahistorical statement about the nature of art. Adorno insists that one always has to be in the moment of history... [*Audience move their chairs to make space for new students.*] And therefore, he assumes that negativity is central to art [*Pause.*] It seems to me that his position as a modernist is that negativity was far more possible in the heyday of modernism, in the early years of modernism, in the 1910s, or from the 1890s to the First World War, than it is after World War Two — a period when negativity is gradually disappearing. [*Footsteps.*] Now, it seems to me that that is a very interesting proposition, and even in the postmodern — whatever one thinks about this question of modernism — this problem occurs. There is a very real crisis today of what functions as being subversive of the current system. Mm-hmm... [*Pause.*] One should say maybe two things about that. First of all, politically, Adorno has made the point that in the early years of the century, on the whole, political radicalism and aesthetic radicalism went together. There is really not any great distinction between art and politics. You think of the great formalists, if you wanna call them that. [*Exhales deeply.*] Malevich, and many other artists of that time and place, I mean they are revolutionaries, and until Stalin, until socialist realism, ex... [*Clears throat*] experimentation or radicality in the arts and in politics go hand in hand up until the late 1920s. This later position by which the communists turn against radical modernism, that doesn't occur in these early years. Now, looking at the other end of this, I think you would have to say that this crisis of subversiveness has also something to do with... [*Reflects.*] Maybe one would have to explain this in a different way... [*Pause.*] Maybe one would have to add something to Adorno's notion of creeping positivism, of creeping nominalism, as well... [*Quietly*: have I talked about nominalism?]

[*Long pause.*]

You see how this could be also described, for he very frequently talks about modernity in terms of an intensifying nominalism, that is to say an increasing, hmm... [*Hesitates*] an increasing inability of language to carry universals, or abstractions. [*Softly.*] Nominalism is a doctrine that rejects the existence of concepts and entities, such as universals, classes, properties, insisting that only particular things, or "nominals," exist, and that the universals are only labels attached to things, and as labels they do not, hmm... [*Hesitates*] exist. And if you think of these universals or abstractions not as we do today, in postmodernism as a matter of conformity or difference, but in terms of the future, and of some future social change and so on, then you see that nominalism also is a process whereby we are reduced to the particulars themselves... [*Cough in the audience.*] We're reduced to the positive affirmation of the existing thing, of the status quo. Now, today one would have... [*Quietly*: this is a German invention... (*Pause*) he is pretty much a pamphleteer still, although he would like to be seen as a kind of a German Baudrillard, I think, but he is not exactly that.] His name is Peter... [*Mumbles. Chalk strokes on the blackboard*] S-L-O-T-E-R-D-I-J-K, and his big book in the old days was called Critique of Cynical Reason.[1] And I think it would be very important to add to this diagnosis of positivism, nominalism, affirmatism, and whatever else Adorno has to say about late capitalism — this one, which in effect says that nothing is subversive anymore because everybody knows the whole thing; there aren't any taboos, nothing shocks us anymore, and everybody knows very well what's bad with this system. [*Pause.*] And therefore, you can't... [*Gloomily.*] Everybody has criticized the system already, there is no further critique to be made of it, and so an art that wishes to be subversive can't do anything because it will just say what everybody already knows. Art has lost... [*Achoo! Sneeze in the audience*] its critical edge. So "cynical reason" would be another way of speaking about the disappearance of negativity. The negative has been absorbed into the positive, into what-is, and we all know now that capitalism is bad... [*Softly*] but also that capitalism has the power to absorb any form of critique, and even exploit it to its own advantage, and therefore nothing that we've pointed out about this can serve as a critique of capital because everybody knows that, and because capital can absorb it and turn into profit.

[*Long pause.*]

But, hmm... [*Shuffling papers. Mumbles to himself while looking at a list of enrolled students.*] I hope that some of you are here, hmm... [*Hesitates.*] Yeah. At least a few of you, let me see... [*Counts the students*]: one, two, three... [*Addresses student.*] You're enlisted?

STUDENT: Yes, I enlisted.

JAMESON: Four...?

STUDENTS: [*In unison.*] I'm also enlisted. Me too.

JAMESON: What? Ah, okay.

[*Pages flipping.*]

So that's another way in which negativity is reproduced, but I think that we think about it in a rather different way than the

Frankfurt School. And finally, the Frankfurt School's lamentations about this tend to seem querulous and old-fashioned and have a modernist undertone... [*Quietly*: what a pity that is, you don't get to criticize anything anymore, you cannot make an efficient critique, and so on and so forth.] Mm-hmm... [*Pause.*] So, these are some of the changes that one notices when one moves from modernity to postmodernity, and this is also one of the central problems of his aesthetics. It is that for these people... [*Gloomily*] after Stalin and Hitler, there really isn't any political subversion possible. There is a big discussion about the student movement in Frankfurt. Mm-hmm. Adorno... [*Tries to remember*] I think Horkheimer was retired at that point. It's certain that at least Horkheimer was becoming much more conservative when he went back to Germany. In his case, you can say the opposite of what Brecht said about West Germany, and he said [*Impersonates Brecht*] "There cannot now be a theater over there in the West, and since Ulbricht is giving me a theater in East Germany I could stay here."[2] But in the case of the Frankfurt School, after all, the regime, the restoration so to speak, the conservative reinstitution... [*Cough in the audience*] gave them not a theater but a whole center; it made Horkheimer rector of the university, which was a very prestigious position in Europe at the time. This inclined them to a certain conformity with the authorities in such a way that, for example, some of the radical stuff they wrote earlier in the 1930s Horkheimer kept locked up in the basement. [*Chuckles.*] But the students then acquired those writings and reprinted them illegally in the 1960s as part of their own radical literature, much against the wishes of Horkheimer. Now, in the case of Adorno, we're told that he [*Stressing*] <u>did speak</u> to the students in private, but he also famously — and this is something that had tarnished his reputation — in one of these student occupations he called in the police... [*More chuckles.*] You do with this what you want but I would like to say that Adorno was more sympathetic to the radical students than the other side... [*Quietly*: although Habermas was very close to the student movement until a certain point.][3]

Mm-hmm. But on the other hand, you don't really see any political sympathies with the radical political movements in Adorno later on, and maybe there never was any, hmm… [*Hesitates*] and certainly he was not somebody who was fully committed or involved politically. [*Firmly.*] But this principle of negation remained. Here he doesn't make any compromises with the critique of capitalism, and in fact it seems to me that the aesthetic is the only place in which, he thinks, that one can supremely make that critique, hmm… [*Exhales deeply*] unlike political philosophy, or metaphysics, or whatever. It's in the aesthetics, it is the aesthetics and the problems of aesthetics that serves as place where social contradictions can be registered for Adorno, and the whole <u>Aesthetic Theory</u> is based on that, it seems to me, although there are moments in which … [*Mumbles indistinctly*: eh, I don't know, it becomes rather…(*Words indistinct*).]

[*Long pause.*]

Now, the point about the historicity of art is that the problems of art are historical indexes of the problems of society.

[*Long Pause.*]

The other language that they use about society was <u>Vergesellschaftung</u>, hmm… [*Quietly:* this is how they were translating this term, as "socialization," "social integration," of "subsumption" I would say, and this is a vaguer translation.] That is to say, the system itself increasingly subsumes more and more of the social life and of the individual parts of social life. Therefore, what existed in, let's say, earlier modernity, in the earlier nineteenth century, as the private spaces outside of society, is increasingly subsumed under it. And when they talk about socialization they mean two kinds of things in that respect, and that is, hmm… [*Hesitates.*] I would talk about it in this way: the colonization of nature, and the colonization of the unconscious. These are facets of the subsumption of things that were once outside of the social realm, and the absorption of all those things into the modern social system. With nature, I think it's pretty obvious, hmm… [*Hesitates*] I do not mean here the metaphysical category "nature," but let's simply say pre-industrial agricultural production and the peasantry, and so on. As the peasantry is turned into a workforce that has a wage and a salary — that is to say, as agriculture becomes agribusiness — little by little that nature ceased to exist. And I think you could see that almost everything you see in the way of plant life, and so on, are artificial and now it's that genetic stuff. [*Pause.*] It's obvious that there is a humanization of nature going on... [*Cough in the audience*] which is, if you put it that way, sounds very exciting but if you look from another point of view it is quite terrifying... [*Quietly*: these artificially-made genetically-engineered plants that are spreading and taking over everything, these are whole processes whereby they do infect the more traditional forms of plants and vegetation and so on... (*Mumbles indistinctly*). There is a very interesting article I read the other day about how genetically modified... (*Words indistinct*).] So, it is in that sense that nature is disappearing. Everything is becoming humanized, everything is becoming part of the human praxis, that is to say social practice, and that would be okay if it wasn't for the complete commercialization and commodification of every... [*Zipper unzipping*] aspect of life that's going on. In terms of the unconscious, well here we're talking about advertising, and the spread of mass culture, and the way in which these spaces presumably outside of social control are being absorbed into commodified fantasy; all of these things that need to be desired themselves are being absorbed into this machinery of commodification. So, I think that's really in the spirit of Adorno's pessimism to look at things that way.

[*Long silence.*]

Now, this does raise — and I need to say this at this point to prepare you — a question about the curious return to the problem of natural beauty, to which he devotes a whole chapter in Aesthetic Theory. We will see that in Kant, hmm... [*Hesitates*] natural beauty occupies an important place, but it isn't something that people really seem to ask very much nowadays. Natural beauty is certainly part of all the older aesthetics. Why does Adorno go back to it then? What is the distinction between natural beauty — and nature in that sense — and the aesthetic? You will see this in some of the very first chapters here when we'll deal with this, but we also need to get some idea eventually of where this fits into his system. Because in a sense there is a myth of the destruction of nature, which is at work here. This famous book the Dialectic of Enlightenment that he wrote... [*Quietly*: it was really written by three people because it's Adorno, Horkheimer and Adorno's wife who took all these notes down and wrote them up, so this is really a, hmm... (*Hesitates*) a collaboration.[4]] This book gives us a picture... [*Pause.*] I think probably the most... [*Quietly*: hmm, I shouldn't say that] but it was a very influential critique of enlightenment understood to be the reign of science and progress. [*Pause.*] Mm-hmm. And this is because... [*Clears throat*] the process of enlightenment, as they saw it in this book, it's a constant wiping out of nature itself — a constant cancelation of each preceding stage, and an attempt to eliminate the natural portions of that in the name of a new kind of progress which for them is ultimately... [*Quietly*: they wrote it in... (*Pause*) I think these things were being written in 1943 or 1944, and I don't know if they knew about the gas chambers, I don't know, but I mean in a sense Auschwitz is the final stage of enlightenment in some sense, where everything is programmed and timed, human labor is becoming absorbed into this, and technologies for mass killing and death are being developed, and so on and so forth.] It's a very bleak picture of enlightenment, which goes along with this picture of universal pessimism, of universal commodification, the extinction of the negative that I was just talking about earlier. And nature, in some sense, fits into that.

[*Long pause.*]

Now, our main question would be — and that fits into this as well — essentially, it's the idea of the [*Stressing*] domination of nature. I think we can make a case that, hmm... [*Hesitates*] if you want to say that Adorno and Horkheimer were not Marxists, you would have to insist that their primary thematic is one of domination and power, and that's a Nietzschean rather a

Marxist line... [*Quietly*: later we will dedicate some time to discuss their relationship to Nietzsche.] But I think that's not altogether true. I mean, we'll see in here that their critique is social, and it has to do with historical materialism. But the theme of domination, I think it's very important — but also very ambiguous — and we'll see it here again in the opening pages, where he talks about art as being itself a form of domination; that is, art is a way of taking outside reality and somehow controlling it but maybe in a different way or sense from what industry or power does. [*Sighs.*] But the notion of "domination of nature" I think fits them into — what you can really call — sort of "nascent feminism" in Adorno and Horkheimer, and also a nascent ecological strain, and maybe even animal rights strain. These are all forms of domination; they are closely related to the notion of a society of domination. So, subsumption or socialization for them is domination... [*Pause*] and I guess that may be the right way to put it. Mm-hmm. They want to think of subsumption — which one could normally think of in an economic way, as a mode of colonizing the smallest pores and cells of reality — but colonizing, or subsuming: those are all modes of domination. But of course, if you insist on that as the fundamental theme then you turn it into... [*Reflects.*] I don't know, not exactly into Foucault but something closer to that... [*Cough in the audience.*] And I think this is not wished to be that, hmm... [*Hesitates.*] Maybe it's a little more like Derrida, for it is something that it's not wished to be pinned down to a theme. I'll give you another theme in a moment that has been widely used for Adorno and which I think is very misleading. So, you can't thematize Adorno by saying "well, Adorno's social philosophy is essentially against domination..." but the minute you say that, it then becomes ideology. You have limited Adorno to a certain horizon... [*Pause.*] Can you see how subtle this is and how difficult it is to negotiate all of these thematics? I mean, they are all in some sense parallel, but we're jumping from one theme to another because the minute a single issue is... [*Quietly*: Paul de Man liked this word]: <u>thematized</u>...[5] [*Softly.*] You pick out an issue and you say: "Okay, the most important thread here in Adorno is domination." The moment you start to thematize it along these lines... [*Quietly*: you have lapsed into a kind of affirmative philosophy that we talked about last time.] [*Pause*.] If you say "it's a philosophy that denounces domination," then you've turned it into an ideology. And so, we have to constantly go back and forth, and the minute we register a theme... [*Quietly*: be it domination, suppression, beauty, expression and so on] then that must be swiftly undermined by another theme. We have to constantly move on to another theme in order to put all that into a different perspective and in order to avoid having it arrested or reified into an ideological position. There is a constant movement here in the thematics of his philosophy that is meant to keep it from turning into an affirmative philosophy — into a philosophy that takes a position, or gives you manifestos... [*Quietly*: like, this is what's the matter with this society, and if we fix this then everything is gonna be okay.] It does not wish to be locked into that because that's exactly the very mode of this society.

[*Long pause*.]

And as I say, I think there are some similarities to the way in which Derrida avoids... [*Pause*] he attempts to avoid thematization, hmm... [*Cough in the audience*.] But if you think of écriture, of writing or something like that, you see that it has been very possible to thematize Derrida and to turn him into some philosophy of nature, or some philosophy of whatever. I think it's a little bit more difficult here because Adorno always stays on an abstract plane jumping from one theme to another, and the moment you feel like you have something on him, he quickly switches to another idea and theme... [*Mumbles indistinctly*.]

STUDENT: I just want to know how successful you think was Adorno in staying away from ideology?

JAMESON: Well, I think this is about what you can do with Adorno. Most of the books on Adorno, they have to tell you that he was really about this, or about that, because they have to interpret him, and to interpret means to thematize. And the minute they do that, I think, they really are somehow untrue to the spirit of his work, hmm... [*Hesitates.*] This does not mean that they are necessarily wrong about certain individual points, but that they betray Adorno somehow.

[*Long pause.*]

Okay, now... [*Pause.*] So, history is fundamental in this notion of... [*Contemplates.*] You see, the other thing I wanted to talk about... [*Quietly*: hmm, maybe I said it the other day.] If you look at page 139, you have a discussion of philosophy that I think is very suggestive. [*Page flipping. Reads from* Aesthetic Theory.] "That the logic of artworks is a derivative of discursive logic and not identical with it, is evident in that art's logic — and here art converges with dialectical thought — suspends its own rigor and is ultimately able to make this suspension its idea; this is the aim of the many forms of disruption..."[6] hmm, and so on and so forth. And here is more:

> The autonomous law of form of artworks protests against logicality even though logicality itself defines form as a principle. If art had absolutely nothing to do with logicality and causality, it would forfeit any relation to its other and would be an a priori empty activity; if art took them literally, it would succumb to the spell; only by its double character, which provokes permanent conflict, does art succeed at escaping the spell by even the slightest degree.[7]

[*Long pause.*]

So, one-dimensionalities are threatening the work of art from all sides. Now, I think that by "logicality" he means all of the philosophical discourse. [*Pause.*] I think this means that systematic philosophy is impossible... [*Quietly*: you could also say that, historically, Hegel was the last systematic philosopher... (*Words indistinct*).] And the whole point of Nietzsche is that this kind of philosophical systematicity, which reveals itself in Hegel's Logic, or metaphysics itself as a model of the whole world that this effort is somehow — by modern times itself, or in modern times — is doomed to... [*Chair-back creaks*] failure. But the opposite view in which one should simply let philosophy go... [*Quietly*: the famous case of Rorty's Mirror of Nature who's done this in a gesture in which he says, that since philosophy is constructed the history of philosophy doesn't exist. Kant just put that together and later philosophers built a discipline, and all of this is simply a construction of something that didn't have a proper history, and so I'm not gonna be a philosopher because there is no philosophy. I will just be a commentator on various issues of life.] Mm-hmm. That means that then you abandon that logicality, those contradictory categories. Meanwhile, aesthetics as a philosophy is also... [*Cough in the audience*] contradictory, but somehow the autonomy of aesthetics allows us to see the contradictions of these philosophical categories better than philosophy itself... [*Quietly*: but which we don't do anymore.] So, in a funny kind of way, hmm... [*Pause*] the failure of aesthetics allows us to see why philosophy is imposable. In a sense, all of the problems of philosophy come into this effort which is doomed to create a systematic aesthetics. Or they are all dramatized by, hmm... [*Pause*] by, hmm... [*Hesitates*.] Or that the problems of philosophy become visible in this attempt to create an aesthetics.

[*Long pause*.]

Aesthetic Theory is Adorno's first systematic book. His book on philosophy, Negative Dialectics, is extremely episodic. Mm-hmm. There are various probes, hmm... [*Hesitates*] and how could it be otherwise, when... [*Quietly*: I think he would agree that the history of philosophy is a construction and then in that case you're reduced to just writing about individual moments: the "moment" of Heidegger, the "moment" of Kant, the "moment" of Hegel, and so on and so forth.] And then the whole history of philosophy breaks down, and one cannot have a systematic history. And I think you will see when you read a few other kinds of works that there is definitely an episodic and anti-systematic quality to Adorno's thought, hmm... [*Hesitates*.] You are constantly moving forward from paragraph to paragraph, then you jump, you cannot connect all these things and yet they are connected in some way... [*Cough in the audience.*] But somehow in Aesthetic Theory, this lack of connection becomes the object of study... [*Pause*] and all of these problems that render philosophy impossible are now what renders the work of art possible. And in this crisis of aesthetics, you can see the crisis not only in metaphysics, in logic in political philosophy, and so on and so forth. So, it seems to me that's one reason why this is important, it's not that aesthetics is the most important issue of the day, it's not that in this society there is only aesthetics nowadays — although sometimes it sounds like that — it is that aesthetics is this [*Stressing*] peculiar laboratory experiment — the only one in which one can see why all the other experiments don't work. It is as if aesthetics holds the secrets to all these other disciplines.

[*Long pause.*]

Okay, but now historicity. Well... [*Pause.*] He attributes to Nietzsche... [*Shuffling paper. Talks to himself*: Where is that page? Mm-hmm. It's here... (*Pause*).] He attributes to Nietzsche that even this, ah here inside page 3: "Nietzsche's late insight, honed in opposition to traditional philosophy, that even what has become can be true, is axiomatic for a reoriented aesthetic."[8] I spoke to you the other day about the moment of truth, or the "truth content." That's what this means. It means that, whereas hmm... [*After prolonged reflection.*] Or maybe that's related to what I said a moment ago about that other... [*Chair-back creaks*] kind of expression of the historical moment... [*Quietly*: I don't know: late feudalism, the Greeks, or the Romans, or whatever] that those epochs are further timed, and we are different from that, they are in a sense outmoded in what is known and useful for us. But in art this outmoded situation that has no correspondence to modern experience still has its truth content. In one sense, I suppose this means that, for certain moments of the past, these epochs are still alive in an aesthetic way... [*Quietly*: you can look at a medieval painting and have an immediate contact with it even though the great techniques of painting have been altered.] But I think it also means something deeper, it means that there is a truth of the historical situation that comes through these paintings and that's still there; and that is, if you like, maybe it is the most privileged contact with the past. [*Softly.*] But this contact is not fully possible, this is a [*Stressing*] negative contact... [*Quietly*: what you have contact with is the contradictions of the past and what gives the work its power are precisely those contradictions.] And the place you find that contact — and here we have this systematic argument again — is not in the content of the artwork, or its subject matter. Remember, this is modernism, this is not realism, this isn't a representation of past societies, or of the contradictions that all the societies have. The contact is in the form... [*Cough in the audience*] or rather what he calls "technique." And this is the [*Stressing*] constructivism of Adorno.

[*Long pause.*]

[*To himself*: where's that sentence... (*Page flipping*). Mm-hmm. Ah here... (*Begins reading*).] "The aesthetic force of production," page 5, "is the same as that of productive labor and has the same teleology; and what may be called aesthetic relations of production — all that in which the productive force is embedded and in which it is active — are sedimentations or imprintings of social relations of production."[9] [*Pause.*] This is an aesthetics based on productivity. It is based on what the form at that moment is doing to its content and the content is several-fold: it is content in a sense of the social experience, right? You can't probably... [*Quietly*: there is this famous thing in Hegel where he says... (*Pause*) or in Marx, where he says] look, the Greeks, they didn't have the telegram and the railroad, and so on and so forth, you can't find in the Greeks the kinds of experience of alienation that we know from the Industrial era. Well, that was the social experience that was available in that period, right? Then you could say, it's part of the same experience but we often distinguish it — the emotions involved are also historical. There are certain kinds of emotions that you don't yet feel in Greece, let's say, and on the contrary, there are emotions that they felt, and we can't feel anymore. So, there is an absolute historicality of emotional content. Then there is that content, which is the raw material of the work, a certain kind of subject matter... [*Cough in the audience*] a certain configuration of colors, a certain stage of the aesthetic process which means that you are limited, and in order to do something new you have to see and go beyond the productive processes that exist in your own time [*Pause*.] All of those things and the raw material are part of the productive process. The state of the art, the, hmm... [*Hesitates*] the state of social relations, subjectivity itself as a historical matter and its various configurations, and finally no doubt the biography of the artist, what art is and what this artist wants to do — all of these things are the raw material [*Stresses*] on which the work of art builds and which it produces in another form. This is also the way industry, or social productivity produces new things and new objects out of raw materials in nature, and machinery, and things, and hats, right? In order to produce that industrially you have to have certain raw materials at hand, certain kind of machines, and you have to have certain kinds of people who can run those things. I mean it's an old, old apprenticeship and the working class, to come to be able to participate in certain kind of factory work, they have to be part of the time, and so forth. All of that are the raw materials of the process of production. But what this means in fact in criticism is that this will always be a politics of form... [*Pause*] rather than a politics of representation. It's not because a given novel represents production, it's because in its form itself this is [*Stressing*] production. And these are very strong statements about the politics of art and they're very modernist, I mean — politics, the political comes through formal innovation.

[*Long pause. Paper rustling.*]

Hmm, "Art's double character as both autonomous and fait social..." — as a social fact, as well as an autonomous thing in its own right — this "is incessantly reproduced on the level of its autonomy."[10] This is a little bit different, this relationship of art to the outside world than the ordinary notions of autonomy that we are all familiar with. This is not like saying...

[*Thud! Heavy object falls on the floor*] that the autonomy of art simply means art is not sacred anymore, or it freed itself from the church. Mm-hmm... [*Pause.*] Hmm... [*Hesitates.*] It doesn't exactly have to do with that kind of separation of art as a distinct activity or realm, although that's part of it, too. But here it has to do with the way in which the two productive processes — the rate of production and the quality of production of a given society, and that of the work of art — mirror each other in some way. In what way, that may not be altogether clear in Adorno, but he hasn't worked it out, he doesn't want us to inspect the one and then make deductions about the other, and it's pretty obvious that there isn't exactly a one-to-one straight parallel between these processes. [*Reflects.*] I mean, if you look at the art of futurism, for example, you see that the artists who had the keenest sense of what the machine was, and the way in which a new art has to capture the energies of the machine, these were artists in the relatively, hmm... [*Hesitates*] not backward, but less developed European country. It is Italy where the industrial complex is centered essentially in the north and where industrial production is nowhere near as advanced as it is in England or France, but by that very token they understand in a sense something about the novelty of industrial production, and the machine that British art... [*Cough in the audience*] isn't aware of, and this is because, in Britain, the machine became part of the lifeforce very early on. So, it's not a one-to-one process. One can't say that it is the most advanced industrial countries who will produce the most advanced forms of art. In fact, if you assume that England is the most advanced industrial country... [*Quietly*: hmm, I don't know if you want to do that] but there is hardly any modernism in England until very late and it's relatively weak. You know this book of Terry Eagleton called Exiles and Émigrés where he shows that there is no English modernism... [*Quietly*: it's all done by foreigners, outsiders, women, by Poles and Americans.][11] So, hmm... [*Pause.*] So, this is not a correlational reflection, but it has to do with directing our attention to these properties, which are those of advanced aesthetic production. And this is why, hmm... [*Hesitates*] I think we get these very formulations on page 6: "The unsolved antagonisms of reality return in artworks as immanent problems of form."[12] So, formal contradictions in the work of art, which in a funny kind of way you can say are resolved because we can see them as contradictions, in real life you can see a contradiction, but seeing it doesn't resolve it, right? But in the work of art, the very fact that a contradiction is somehow articulated... [*Quietly*: it has been represented and therefore it means that it has been resolved in some sense.] The work of art is the place in which, hmm... [*Pause*] ...slight, hmm... [*Hesitates.*] Mm-hmm. Let me think of an example... [*Pause.*] I'm sure there are experimental situations, like something where you're working on some materials in a laboratory in order to predict some behaviors or analyze how something will behave in real life, right? You are looking at some forms in order to understand what's going on in these elements or materials in a larger-scale situation. Well, something like this also takes place here. Art is not an X-ray, the work of art is not allowing you to look closer at things in society, but it is giving you clues and hints in a completely distant area that seem to have no relationship with those contradictions of life that you encounter in your daily life. And once again, this takes place on the formal level of the work of art.

[*Long pause.*]

But this has to be turned around as well because it has to do with aesthetic reception. Mm-hmm. [*Pause.*] So, we have this sentence at the bottom of the page: "Art perceived strictly aesthetically is art aesthetically misperceived."[13] That's translated rather weakly, but what he means is that if you hear Beethoven and this is, I'm quoting Adorno here so... [*Words indistinct.*] If you hear Beethoven in a purely musical sense, and you're aware of the state of compositional techniques immediately before these innovations of Beethoven and you perceive them purely as musical innovations, as expansions of the sonata form, and so forth, and if you perceive these on purely formal basis —

you're still not hearing it because what you should be hearing through those innovations is the French Revolution. [*Pause.*] Now, is that something extra aesthetic? [*Footsteps.*] Well, I think what he's saying is that the [*Stressing*] absolute of these works is the social and historical absolute and they are not representations of the moment of history, and yet the moment of history has to be heard in them or you're not hearing it right. So, if you're perce... [*Hesitates*] if you're receiving works of art in a purely aesthetic way you are not even perceiving them aesthetically. They have to be understood also in terms of this other dimension, which is I think a very characteristic rebuke of his own formalism. I quoted pieces of these that sounded very formalistic, but on the other hand, it has to be in the view of the fact that the doubleness, the duality of the work of art has to mean that we do both. [*Pause.*]

[*Long pause.*]

Adorno comes back to the raw material... [*Page flipping*] hmm, on page 7, and I think this is an important section to think about. It's... [*Pause.*] It's in... [*Quietly*: hmm, a lot of people have said it, and Adorno talks about this too] that one of the great vehicles for the negativity, and criticality of the work of art in the late nineteenth century is adultery, that is to say, it is the situation of women. [*Pause.*] Hmm, here we have Madame Bovary references, but in Minima Moralia, which is, as I said, his book of fragments and kind of his autobiography... [*Page flipping*] he also talks about Ibsen, and I think this is very interesting [*Reads from* Minima Moralia.] "No sooner is a name like Ibsen's mentioned, then he and his themes are condemned as old-fashioned and outdated."[14] All this stuff about syphilis, or about women's liberation, I mean we know all that, so this was what... [*Words indistinct.*] "Sixty years ago, the same voices were raised..." [*Quietly*: sixty years ago, meaning in Ibsen's time, of course] "...were raised in indignation against the modernistic decadence and immoral extravagance of the Doll's House and Ghosts. Ibsen, the truculent bourgeois, vented his spleen on the society from whose very principle his implacability and his ideals were derived."[15] Hmm... [*Hesitates.*] "But perhaps this is the way of all outdatedness." It's the whole thing, maybe I'll read this all for you:

> It is to be explained not only by mere temporal distance, but by the verdict of history. Its expression in things [outdatedness] is the shame that overcomes the descendant in face of an earlier possibility that he has neglected to bring to fruition. What was accomplished can be forgotten, and preserved in the present. Only what failed is outdated, the broken promise of a new beginning. It is not without reason that Ibsen's women are called 'modern.' Hatred of modernity and of outdatedness are identical.[16]

So, in a sense, as with "philosophy which is living on because its promises were unrealized"[17]... [*Quietly:* the Adornian sentence that we discussed last time] what the modern sees as being outdated in Ibsen's representations is precisely this failure to solve this moment of social contradiction. "The fanatic linguistic perfection of Madame Bovary is probably a symptom of precisely this contrary element; the unity of both, of reportage and linguistic perfectionism, accounts for the book's unfaded actuality."[18] [*To himself*: Hmm, sorry, this is not it... where is it? Ah, here.] "At the height of its form, in the nineteenth century, the realistic novel had something of what the theory of so-called socialist realism rationally plotted for its debasement: reportage, the anticipation of what social science would later ascertain."[19] At any rate, these are... [*Pause.*] This is the way in which negativity gets inscribed in these works in a, hmm... [*Hesitates*] in a kind of strange sort of stasis where, in a sense, the contradiction is present on the level of the form, and we can say that these are not yet completely modern plays; they have these elements of representation and of didacticism, and that modernity or modernism will attempt to get rid. But for Adorno, noticing these seeming flaws is the key to what's still alive to the "truth content," if you like, of those representations. Now, hmm... [*Very quietly:* and this is a critique of Hegel, and we'll come back to it later on.]

[*Long pause.*]

But I wanted to mention another feature of this discussion. "Hegel's content aesthetics [Inhaltsästhetik] recognized that element of otherness immanent to art..." Mm-hmm. "Hegel's idealist dialectic, which conceives form as content..." this is for Adorno an advance "...regresses to a crude, preaesthetic level; it confuses the representational or discursive treatment of thematic material with the otherness that is constitutive of art."[20] [*Pause.*] Hegel confused, or conflated, I would rather say, truth content and actual social content. So, Hegel gives us an example which has to be somehow modified. This theme of the otherness of the work is another, let's say, generalization that people have used about Adorno's work, but I want to warn you against it. It is often said that Adorno is the philosopher of non-identity, right? Adorno is constantly stressing the [*Stressing*] non-identical. [*Pause.*] Well, I think that... [*Quietly*: and you'll find this in Martin Jay, and so forth, and obviously in some sense that's not wrong but I think it really... (*Words indistinct*).] This is the way the French understood Adorno when he was finally translated in the post-structuralist period, [*Whispering*] as a philosopher of difference. Well, yes and no. Identity is, for Adorno, what the system does. The subsumption under the system that I spoke about is the increasing power of identity, of the logic of identity, which is also positivism and so on. But I also think that, with the emphasis on otherness, you don't want to turn Adorno into Levinas. It seems to me that's only at certain points or the crucial theme to which one would want to describe this process. And non-identity, I think essentially, is here connected to the notion of "truth content" and that is another situation for... [*Cough in the audience*] you have to recognize [*Stressing*] that radical difference in this "truth content" but not preserving non-identity as the fundamental theme. You could also, as I said a moment ago... [*Softly*] bottom of page 7: "This unites the aesthetic element of form with noncoercion."[21] You can also talk about power. And I think that is an underrepresented theme but it's also not a fundamental one. Mm-hmm... [*Pause*] and, hmm... [*Page flipping*] and, so on and so forth.

[*Long pause.*]

I think, I'm gonna break off, hmm... [*Hesitates*] this discussion of Adorno at this point, and I wanted to give you a little idea of Hegel before we go on to... [*Door slams shut*] which has to do with the... [*Mumbles to himself*: what are the pages?] Mm-hmm. It has to do with... [*Pause*] this historical system of Hegel, which is the progression from symbolic art to classical art and to romantic art. In symbolic art, the Idea is not yet completely articulated in the raw material. The raw material dominates the Idea, and there the example Hegel gives is the pyramids. The pyramids are this massive matter which overwhelms their idea and speaks for itself in some name, and in a sense it's very interesting that [*Stressing*] <u>that</u> will be the moment that Hegel identifies as that of the sublime... [*Quietly*: which, I think, is not at all necessarily the case with other readings of the sublime when we come to Kant.]

[*Page flipping. Starts reading from Hegel's* <u>Aesthetics</u>]:

> The first form of art is therefore rather a <u>mere search</u> for portrayal than a capacity for true presentation; the Idea has not found the form even in itself and therefore remains struggling and striving after it. We may call this form, in general terms, the <u>symbolic</u> form of art. In it the abstract Idea has its shape outside itself in the natural sensuous material from which the process of shaping starts... [*Reads Note 1.*] An unknown block of stone may symbolize the Divine, but it does not represent it. [So, hmm... *Hesitates*] the abstractness of this relation brings home to consciousness even so the foreignness of the Idea to natural phenomena. [So now...*Continues reading*] ...it seeks itself in them in their unrest and extravagance, but yet does not find them adequate to itself. So now the Idea exaggerates natural shapes and the phenomena of reality itself into indefiniteness and extravagance; it staggers round in them, it bubbles and ferments in them, does violence to

> them, distorts and stretches them unnaturally, and tries to elevate their phenomenal appearance to the Idea.[22]

... and so on and so forth. [*Pause*.] Now, Hegel is talking about the pre-modern but from a safely Western context, and this can certainly be taken as the Eurocentrism of Hegel. [*Quietly:* There are those horrendous pages in the Philosophy of History where he talks about other parts of the world.] But what's interesting I think is that one could then really recover this kind of testimony for contemporary analysis, and now I'm sort of quoting it from memory: "the imperfection of the form is the key to the imperfection of the Idea."[23] And I think that something like that is what's going on in Adorno, but if you make it a little more sophisticated — and it is — then you have to transfer that from some mere perception of "otherness" in history and culture to modern art.

[*Long Pause*.]

At any rate, the second notion will clearly be the one in which the Idea and the form come together... [*Quietly*: and that's the human body — that's ancient Greece.] Mm-hmm. That's the classical Form. So, hmm... [*Page flipping*.] "...in classical art the peculiarity of the content consists in its being itself the concrete Idea, and as such the concretely spiritual, for it is the spiritual alone which is the truly inner [self.]" This has to do with anthropomorphism, and so forth and where "...the spirituality, which is the content, must be of such a kind that it can express itself completely in the natural human form, without towering beyond and above this expression in sensuous and bodily terms."[24] Then you have to talk about the limits of art in ancient Greece, about the limits of this type of classical humanism. You can see that what's going on here in terms of history is the idea that Christianity brings some special new kind of internalization, and certain new forms that the Greeks did not know. So, the Greeks are on one hand this perfect moment in human history, and yet there is a limitation in Greek art, which would be... [*Quietly:* you could also talk in terms of the limitations of their city state, or their polis.] With Christianity all of a sudden, we reach the moment... [*Cough in the audience*] when the mind-body balanced relation achieved in the classical age is in doubt, and this has to do with many things, but one central cause is Romanticism and irony. If in Hegel's symbolic moment of art the body is enormous, and the mind is still trying to find its form, in the classical moment, mind and body, spirit and material, reach some equal state or ground — they come together. With Christianity, and what he will call romantic art... [*Quietly*: which in Hegel's language that does not necessarily correspond to historical Romanticism but is something that emerges already in the Middle Ages] there is another kind of disproportion where the content is too large for the form. The Idea can't any longer express its subject matter and becomes reflexive and so on and so forth. What's... [*Raps his knuckles on the desk.*] What's confusing about all this, or paradoxical, is that Hegel hated the romantics... [*Quietly*: I mean, you have the famous remark of Goethe, who attempted problematically to revive the classical; we would call it the neo-classical.] For Goethe, and many other people of that time, Classicism is the healthy, and Romanticism is the sick... [*Quietly*: mm-hmm, and people like Kleist and Hölderlin, these people were indeed very sick, but they were also busy doing things that may not be... (*Mumbles indistinctly*).] So, on the one hand, Hegel... [*Pause.*] And for Hegel as a thinker the prime representative of everything that's abominable in the modern age was Romanticism... [*Chair-back creaks.*] He hated the romantics for their individualistic and irrational feelings that witnessed a tremendous revival in his days. Those were the people whom he considered the real enemies of philosophy, and of everything else. And yet the whole period, this whole enormous... [*Cough in the audience*] modern period that predates modernity back to the Romans, or to the Christians and at least from the Middle Ages, gets back to us as the romantic one. Well, what does that mean? [*Pause.*] I think it suggests the reason why, for Hegel, art has to be overcome by a new form of spirit, which is philosophy. Only philosophy is adequate to this predominance of the mind, only philosophy can articulate this heightened sense of reflexivity and all of that. The work of art can't do that anymore. So, the romantic moment in art, this advanced moment, it has in itself the seeds of its own transcendence of art in general by philosophy — the transcendence of that mode of achievement of the Absolute made by this new form which is modern philosophy.

[*Long pause.*]

At any rate, you see, that for Hegel art is a means of expressing the spirit. It is a means through which the spirit achieves a form of self-understanding, and it is a form of reconciliation of the subjective and objective... [*Pounds his fist on the desk.*] In any case, this is also what Adorno wants to convey here, that this is, hmm... [*Reflects.*] Art is something objective, that is, it is an objective historical process, it reveals things about history, and about matter, and historical periods and all those things. It is not a matter of aesthetic appreciation at all — art is profoundly historical, and this is Hegel's revolution over and against Kant. [*Pause.*] And I think it's also very crucial for Adorno to insist on the aesthetic as being an area of the objective. This is a place... [*Quietly*: this is what I am trying to say in some other kind of ways.] This is a place in which the, hmm... [*Hesitates*] the... [*Pause*] ...in which, hmm... [*Hesitates.*] It is a place in which art has also to do with fantasy, no doubt, but these fantasies are all objective... [*Achoo! Sneeze in the audience.*] Everywhere you move in this theory you don't find anything that is purely subjective. The subjective is already objectified. What I said the other day about emotions as raw materials, that's one example of that. Art is not the place of subjectivities but of objectivized subjectivities, which have already been objectivized by the fact that they are historical. So, history and objectivity become related.

[*Long Pause.*]

Okay, hmm, any thoughts about that... [*Tapping his thumb on the desk*] before we get on to Kant?

[*Long pause.*]

Questions, or observations? Comments?

[*Long pause.*]

Okay. I think what's going on in Kant is... [*Quietly*: well, a lot of things are going on in Kant, of course, and we can't address them all in this seminar.] You could say that Kant is a very interesting language experiment or a thought experiment, if you like. But I would say what's... [*Cough in the audience*] going on here is something of this nature. Kant feels already, I think, that the nature of aesthetics, the vocation of aesthetics, is the analysis of beauty. Beauty is his word for this... [*Reflects*] hmm, his term for the object which aesthetics deals with. "Beauty" is the word for aesthetic autonomy, or the specificity of aesthetic experience and all of these terms are contained in this object of study. Kant goes through this phenomenon, which is that of the beautiful, and analyzes it to his satisfaction, creating a whole system of the beautiful and how to deal with it. [*Softly.*] And it's a very impressive system to look at, but after having done that, he has realized, in the first eighty pages or so, the real task of aesthetics, and of aesthetic philosophy. When he gets to the end of it, it's as though he says to himself... [*Impersonates Kant*] "Well, this is very satisfying, and this is what art is, or the essence of it is, but on the other hand there is something else that hasn't got enough attention at all." And this "something else," this sort of supplement, if you wish to call it this way, is [*Whispering*] <u>the sublime</u>. In our analysis of beauty, we forgot about the sublime, but it had to be forgotten, because it isn't part of beauty, it's something else, but it's still part of the aesthetic. So, what we have with the sublime is this immense addendum to the aesthetics that Kant thought he had completed. The task of aesthetic philosophy is complete, but then all of a sudden it produces a supplement, and it condemns itself as insufficient... [*Quietly*: if you like paradoxes] by virtue of its very sufficiency. The Kantian nature of the aesthetic judgment is so perfect that it leaves the most important thing out, and the most important thing turns out to be not the beautiful but the sublime.

[*Long silence.*]

Now, this whole idea of the sublime has been around for

some time; you can find it with the Romans,[25] but in modern times... [*Quietly*: that is in the eighteenth century] it comes yet from another text from the fringes of England — in this case Ireland rather than Scotland — and that's Edmund Burke's Reflections on the Sublime and the Beautiful,[26] which is something you should all one day read. Burke's Reflections is much more down-to-earth than Kant's Critique: it's not philosophizing, it's mostly description. And it essentially comes down to this [*Pause*.] Mm-hmm. The beautiful is sensual pleasure and the sublime is fear, and these are the two great oppositions. Burke is a very interesting and complicated figure who is more controversial than Swift, I think. Burke was very conservative; although he was also for the American colonies, he also condemned the colonization of India, but on the other hand, he also condemned the French Revolution. His political pamphlet called something about the French Revolution is the most famous counter-revolutionary tract he had written, containing all of the most famous arguments against revolutions that have ever been tracked down.[27] And indeed, if you look at what Burke calls the "sublime," this is all related to terror and fear, and you will find the sublime in his descriptions of the French Revolution. The violent excesses during the Reign of Terror with these masses of people, wandering around and committing the most horrible massacres, and the bloody horrible things, the slaughter of the aristocrats, and finally the execution of Louis the Sixteenth, and even worse of Marie Antoinette. There is a great couple of passages about the Queen, and for Burke the Queen's execution is a particularly appalling example of the violence and bloodshed which then [*Whispering*] becomes the sublime. But you also see that the sublime is this tremendous, fearful, excess of cruelty that's also happening in the human mind.

[*Long pause*.]

Burke is an extremely complicated and interesting and contradictory figure, but this is also, if you like, a starting point for Kant. I mean this is why the sublime has to begin here... [*Pause*.] And you'll notice that the way Burke deals with beauty as sensual pleasure, you will not find this in Kant. Nonetheless, hmm... [*Cough in the audience*] even after that clarification of the central notion of art, there remain these other things... [*Softly*] and these other things, of course, they have been the motor of the moderns. And I'm tempted to say... [*Quietly*: I mean I have said that in one of Adorno's very famous sentences] that philosophy lives on because the moment to realize it was missed. So, the way in which philosophy lives on — that's taken in a Hegelian way in relationship with the Absolute, which is either art in Hegel's sense or later on philosophy... [*Pause*] — hmm, philosophy was not able to achieve that relationship with the Absolute by realizing the promise of freedom and other demands of the great revolutions, and therefore it lives on as a discipline. The same could be also said about art, namely that the Absolute then had to retreat into art, but this time not into the beautiful... [*Cough in the audience*] but into the sublime. [*Pause.*] And it seems to me that the sublime is always this relationship, this vocation of art to become a kind of religion or something of that sort, and that's what Kant called the "sublime." And then what we call "modernism" is really the hijacking of art, and of beauty, in general by the sublime... [*Pause.*] And when this process stops, then I think modernism is also over. And it's no accident that nowadays all these... [*Quietly*: everybody is talking about the return of the beautiful. Well, to be sure, postmodernism wishes to be beautiful; it doesn't want to be extravagantly metaphysical anymore but wants to be a matter of pleasure.] This is, you can read any of the arts and this would be the rhetoric that's used and that's used in aesthetics. When you read the current reactionary Minister of Culture of France, what's his name, I keep repressing his name... [*Quietly: ...*what's his name... (*Looks around*) hmm, anyone?] He was the... [*Taps his fingers on the desk*: hmm, who was a philosopher and an aesthetician, who wrote a book about aesthetics.[28]] When you read his aesthetics, oh yeah, Luc Ferry, hmm... [*Pause.*] When you read his aesthetics, you see that all things are going back to pleasure or going back to classical modernism as though modern art was a form of pleasure, which I think is very wrong or misreading. For critics on the left, Baudelaire means the sublime, but for reactionaries in the French establishment, it is not the sublime, but on the contrary — that was the beautiful. For them, we have to get rid of these strenuous ambitions of art to touch the Absolute, to have political ideals or social implications. You will see this relation in everybody that we are going to read; you'll see it in Adorno, in Thomas Mann, hmm... [*Hesitates.*] But this is the conservative aesthetic credo of our days: we have to give rid of the relation between art and Absolute and go back to art as detached pleasure and beauty. Hmm, because... [*Student raises hand.*] Yes.

STUDENT: Hmm, I wonder when do you think it was that people started these discussions about the difference between beauty and sublime?

[*Long pause.*]

JAMESON: Well, they go on for a long time but in this modern sense... [*Pause*] I think it's happening in the eighteenth century, when suddenly there are a lot of questions and discussions about art, and when art gets... [*Pause.*] Oh, oh... [*Agitated.*] Wait, wait a minute. The first place where you can see this split appear, it is in the moment when the historicality of art is raised, and this is in the famous debate which was called the "Querelle des anciens et des modernes." The debate begins in the time of... [*Quietly:* I think Racine is still alive; and it's the fairytale writer Perrault who institutes... (*Words indistinct*) and then, with Boileau and Perrault, there are a number of exchanges on the notion of the genius, and the sublime is also debated.] The basic question of the Quarrel is who is greater, the ancients or the moderns? Sophocles or Racine? [*Pause.*] And in these first debates — in 1680, or something like that — these questions get raised... [*Cough in the audience*] and all of a sudden you have "modernists" and "classicists" standing against each other. Hans Robert Jauss has written a study on this extensively,[29] and he points out that what happens is something very amazing. This debate goes on for twenty or thirty years and includes the beginnings of the revival of all kinds of classical texts. And in the end, the debate is finally resolved... [*Clears throat*] because all of a sudden both sides decide that Greek art isn't greater than modern art, nor is modern art greater than Greek art, [*Whispering*] they are just different. [*Chuckles.*] And the minute you say it, then history appears.

[*Long pause.*]

At any rate, this kind of debate about values start to take place in history, and that's also when a certain kind of differentiation in aesthetics also begins. And I think that the whole revival of classical antiquity also evolves from the French classical debates, which also begin to appear in England with people like John Dryden and William Temple and Jonathan Swift on the other side. [*Softly.*] I'm not sure who the first commentators on all of those things are but that's been around for a long time.

[*Long pause.*]

Other... [*Raps his knuckles on the desk*] questions?

[*Silence.*]

Okay, we'll move back to Kant. Now I want to point out to pages 53, 64, 84 and 90. What is beauty? The four aspects of beauty? It is devoid of interest. It is universal... [*Quietly:* this is very strange.] Mm-hmm... [*Pause.*] It is purposiveness without purpose... [*Quietly*: is that the same as the interest thing?] We'll see. And finally, art is without a concept, it's not cognitive and yet, hmm... [*Hesitates*] what does it do? Well, it seems that it puts various faculties of the mind to work together in some kind of harmony. And that would be the pleasure of beauty or of art, which is, however... [*Quietly*: let's remember this is not a pleasure in the senses.] Okay, next time on Tuesday also try to... [*Chairs scratching the floor.*] We still have three, four, five, six openings. I think that some of you are still able to make a presentation and they should come forward... [*Words indistinct.*] I'm gonna give this list of enlistment to Joan... [*Footsteps. Chairs scratching against the floor*] and those of you who are not yet enrolled... [*Door creaks open. Zippers zipping up*] go talk to Joan...

Feet shuffling. Audience stands up. Objects drop on the floor. Door squeaks. Members of the audience talk among themselves. Students return chairs to other classrooms. Some students form a line to discuss their assignments. General noise. Screeching microphone noise.

[*Microphone turns off.*]

CURTAIN

LECTURE THREE

JANUARY 16, 2003

ART, SOCIETY, AESTHETICS (CHAPTER) — KANTIAN BEAUTY AND THE SUBLIME

CURTAIN RISES

Moving chairs, squeaking door, coughs, other sounds filling the noise environment of a large classroom in the Literature Department at Duke University. Jameson's teaching assistants are going around distributing some papers to the arriving audience. Students are joking about more readings for the course. This is material additional to what has already been announced in the beginning of the seminar. In his previous seminars, Jameson used to compile a reader. At the beginning of the semester, each participant received a heavy document compendium containing articles, book chapters or even whole books, and copied pages, all with a table of contents. For this seminar on aesthetics, however, there was no usual "Jameson Reader," as most of the assigned texts were books: Adorno's Aesthetic Theory, *Mann's* Doctor Faustus, *Beckett's* Endgame, *Kant's* Critique of Judgement, *Freud's "Creative Writing and Daydreaming," and so on. One additional reason for renouncing the heavy reader is the rise of the Internet, and the fact that many secondary or shorter texts can be now found online, at the click of a mouse.*

Jameson enters the classroom carrying his college notebook and the red pen in the chest pocket of his flannel shirt.

He stops to chat quickly with a student who sent him a chapter of his thesis. He always offers generous feedback to papers and has had long after-class conversations with students coming from different departments to discuss their research projects.

JAMESON: *Come see me after class, let's think more about this...*

STUDENT: *Okay, will do. Thank you.*

[*Microphone turns on.*]

JAMESON: [*Audience hubbub. Microphone distortions*] ... and which was therefore an illustration of many of his theories. [*Hubbub fading to silence.*] On Thursday, I will not be here, but I want you to come and watch Beckett's Endgame, a play that was very important for Adorno. He wrote about it in a very famous essay that is called "Trying to Understand..." [*Quietly*: Versuch, das Endspiel zu verstehen, which literally means "An Attempt to understand Endgame," and later in the semester we will talk about another meaning of the word Versuch.] You can find it in, hmm... [*Hesitates*] in Notes to Literature...[1] [*Quietly*: which I believe... (*Mumbles indistinctly*) we must have it in the university library?] [*Addresses student assistant.*] Did Joan give you a copy of that book? It's supposed to be in print, in the compiled... [*Page flipping.*] And we should also have it in our department library, unless somebody's pinched it... [*Chuckles.*] Mm-hmm. And if we need it, ask and we can make a copy of this essay. There is a lot of other essays in Notes to Literature that I think you'll find very interesting. It's not just about literature, it's also about music... [*Pause.*] In fact, most of it's [*Stressing*] not literature but music and all other kinds of stuff.

[*Long pause.*]

Anyway, the Beckett essay, it's the most systematic reading of a literary piece in Adorno, and I think it's very emblematic for him of what art does today... [*Quietly*: that is, in his "today," in the post-World War Two period of the 1950s and 1960s.] Mm-hmm. Because it raises all the problems of the impossibility of representation... [*Door creaks open. Footsteps*] and all the problems of silence as opposed to expression, and of all the problems of suffering and how one can possibly put that into words when by definition it is wordless. Now, what happens in Beckett is that this tends towards a certain minimalism... [*Pause.*] I think it is worth... [*Quietly*: I don't know whether Adorno says this or not, I don't remember it... (*Pause*) but I'm thinking about this for a moment as we will be moving towards discussing Kant later on in the hour... (*Mumbles indistinctly*).]

[*Long pause.*]

How many of you know what the second Viennese school of composers are?

[*Silence.*]

STUDENT: Schoenberg, Berg, Webe... [*Words indistinct.*]

JAMESON: Schoenberg, Berg, Webern... [*Chalk on the blackboard*] S-C-H-O-E-N-B-E-R-G. In the demise of the tonal system, Schoenberg invented a new kind of system — the twelve-tone system in which a different kind of musical law is maintained. Namely, you can't repeat a note, hmm... [*Hesitates*] unless... [*Pause.*] There are twelve tones in the scale, right? That is to say, they are twelve if you include the white/black keys on the piano, they're twelve keys... [*Cough in the audience.*] So, you can't repeat any one of those until you gone through the entire scale. Now, this seems very strange, I mean... [*Reflects.*] What happens is that, with these twelve tones, each composition will be dominated by a row that is a kind of melody, if you wanna call it that way, which is a certain order of these tones. But it has to keep repeating. It can repeat horizontally or vertically, in a form of a chord or in all kinds of other places and so forth. [*Music Ph.D. Student raises hand.*]

STUDENT: I think that this thing about repeating is sort of a secondary consideration, and it is much more about this idea of the [*Stressing*] <u>mechanical</u> order of the...

JAMESON: Yes, the order of the things... [*Pause.*] The point about repeating... [*Agitated.*] No, of course you can have a way of a single note at a given point, but the point about repeating, or the ban on repetition of a single note is because Schoenberg was afraid that, given our habits, music would lapse back into tonality. You can think of his work as setting up rules that would assure that new music doesn't become tonal again. And it is true, some believe that tonality is part of our human nature... [*Quietly*: I read an article recently in the Times which was referring back to all kinds of... (*Mumbles indistinctly*).] There was a very strong twelve-tone movement in the immediate post-World War One period — I would say up to the 1960s, which I would call the period of "late modernism." Then, with the break between the likes of Philip Glass and Steve Reich, who introduce this new kind of postmodern pleasant semi-lyricism, and which have also some relationship to non-Western music, twelve-tone music seems to have receded or was restricted to the circles of specialists... [*Quietly*: of music critics and academics.] And of course, many of the twelve-tone people thought that all this new kind of postmodernist music was just kitsch, and the other side thought that the twelve-tone people were repulsive and authoritarian. Mm-hmm. But at its triumph, at its height, twelve-tone music was sort of the music of the future. [*Exhales deeply*.] I mean even Stravinsky — who was the major representative of a different kind of avant-garde musical tradition — ended up writing twelve-tone music. So, that part of it is very interesting. Anyway, as I was saying, I read a Times article which was saying... [*Quietly*: this must have been a couple of months ago] somebody in the featured article in the Sunday Times[2] did a long diatribe not only against the twelve-tone music but the author was also saying somehow that what Schoenberg didn't understand was that tonality is part of the human nature, and therefore twelve-tone music was unnatural. Schoenberg's attempt to replace the tonal system with something else was somehow unreasonable. [*Pause*.] But I think that this is rather unlikely, since the tonal system as we know it comes into being in the eighteenth century. Bach is famously the completer of musical tonality, and now the question is, where was tonality in the rest of human history?

[*Pause.*] If tonality is supposedly in the human nature, then where is it in non-Western music? Anyway, Schoenberg, hmm... [*Reflects.*] The point about the repetition of notes is that Schoenberg was afraid, hmm... [*Hesitates*] that if you laid any emphasis on a single note, it would organize itself again into a tonal center, and thus it would bring back the habits of tonality.

[*Long pause.*]

Mm-hmm... [*Pause.*] And therefore, in his efforts to make music radically [*Stressing*] de-centered, there's gotta be a sort of constant movement of these notes so that they don't get reified around a single tone and its various vibrations. It seems to me that's more or less the main rationale of the musical method that Schoenberg invented. Anyway, so you can say that Schoenberg invented a system of some kind. But then, with Berg and Webern, we have the two antithetical results of this movement. Webern, if you play any Webern... [*Quietly*: I'll play you some of his stuff one day, because... (*Loud cough near the microphone*) as I am about to say, these are pieces that last about a minute or so, and they are very much, hmm... (*Hesitates*) interspersed with silences, and so it might be interesting to hear it, and you may like it.] And as I said, these pieces of Webern, if they last five minutes it's a miracle, I mean but mostly they don't. Now, Berg, on the other hand, is this artist who incorporates into his music everything. When you get to the final works of Leverkühn in Doctor Faustus with a jazz orchestra, and all kinds of other stuff going on, that's more like Berg. [*Pause.*] And whereas you would pretend to think of Adorno, given what he says about Beckett, I tend to think of him being more of a Webern person... [*Quietly*: although he was a student of Berg himself, and there is a way in which he somehow forgets his own doctrines and he appreciated (*Stressing*) the impurity of Berg's music.] And in the case of Berg, I think you could say that Berg is like Joyce in literature... [*To himself*: it would be enough to think of Joyce and the Finnegans Wake] where, what they tried to do is incorporate everything. Joyce throws everything into this novel and somehow makes up a multiple system that includes all... [*Qui-*

etly: places, languages, the world, puns, sounds], whereas in the minimalist artist like Webern, there is an attempt to get rid of everything... [*Cough in the audience*] to eliminate everything but the virtual silence. The other name that's mentioned in literature in connection to this is Paul Celan, and I think one can at least play with the idea that... [*Quietly*: that is much more closely... (*Words indistinct*) as is Adorno's interpretation of Beckett.]

[*Long pause*.]

The reason I am telling you all of this is because I think that, in a way, there are two antithetical movements in modernism. You can call one [*Stressing*] <u>maximalism,</u> if you want to call it that way, and this is when you try to include everything in the artwork; and the other one is [*Stressing*] <u>minimalism</u>, and this is when you leave out as much as possible, or you strip away all but the essential. These are the two contradictory and yet dialectically identical movements in high modernism [*Pause*.] And why do we think that would be the case?

[*Long silence. Chair scrapes against the floor*.]

Well, it's not a ques... [*Pause*.] Ah, it's not a... [*Pause*.] I think it's because, hmm... [*Hesitates*.] Look, if modernism has something to do with Hegel's Absolute — or, maybe as we will try and see today — with the Kantian sublime, then clearly it wants to go to excesses. And if we're talking about art, then there are only two directions for excess, and this is: everything or nothing. [*Pause*.] So, everything is the "Book of the World," and that is Joyce, Proust, maybe Musil, and people like that who have tried to represent that kind of [*Stressing*] <u>immense</u> excess. The artist wants to incorporate the whole universe, and everything must become part of the artwork. And, on the other hand, the absolute minimalism involves, hmm... [*Hesitates*] nothingness, silence, blank poems, empty canvases... [*Quietly*: who's the painter who, hmm... (*Hesitates*) who, hmm... (*Tries to remember*) that, hmm....] What's his name? There is also a critic who talks about him in his theory of modernism. What's his name... [*Taps his fingers on the desk*.] Who is the most important theorist of modernism in American postwar painting... [*Tries to *remember*.] Mm-hmm... [*Raps his knuckles on the desk*] hmm, he started over as a literary...

STUDENT: Gr... Greenberg?

JAMESON: Uh-huh. Who?

STUDENT: Clement Greenberg?

JAMESON: Greenberg, exactly. [*After prolonged reflection*.] And who is the painter that Greenberg came to endorse after Pollock, and that he thought that he could replace Pollock as the bad boy of American abstract expressionism... [*Pause*.] There has been just recently his major show... [*Quietly*: hmm, there is nothing but one little strip of color on bare canvas.] Maybe you can also say that about Malevich, and that the Black Square is some form of absolute minimalism but somehow, I'm tempted to think that the Black Square does include everything, I mean, everything is supposed to be drowned into that total emptiness, especially the White Square, right? Whereas in this case... [*Quietly*: that name I won't remember now, but maybe somebody will... (*Reflectively*).] He had a big retrospective recently in one of the major museums, and he does this very interesting work that could be seen as the ultimate minimalism in modern painting.[3] And you see this opposition between maximalism and minimalism taking place in all of the arts... [*Quietly*: I mean, one could also add to this dance, theater, and poetry... (*Mumbles indistinctly*).] So, now Beckett's play is important for us, and I would like you to see this production, which as I understand Beckett himself directed. Endgame is a better play than Waiting for Godot, which Beckett himself came to hate because... [*Softly*.] I think because, hmm... [*Hesitates*] Waiting for Godot looks like it still means something as people tend to ask: Who is Godot? Is Godot God? What are they waiting for, and so forth... [*Quietly*: these are questions that drove Beckett crazy later on in life... (*Chuckles*) because people were imagining a project with these interesting questions which Beckett kept dismissing, asking why people should complicate simple things.] And therefore, I think you could say that there is this sort of a... [*Achoo. Sneeze in the audience*] modernist symbolism in that work, which is not the case with Endgame. But this would be my, hmm... [*Hesitates*] hypothesis, and I invite you to make one for yourself. You can do it like Webern, try and write these little text impressions after you watch this play. Anyway, Endgame, it's pure... [*Door slams in the distance*] play, and so you'll come to see it here in this classroom on Thursday. Then I will be curious to learn what you think when I'm back. What else did I want to announce... [*Mumbles indistinctly*.]

[*Long pause*.]

Now, let's get back to Kant because I would like to do some more work with the Critique of Judgment today. [*Chalk on the blackboard. Starts drawing the Kantian table of categories on the blackboard. Whispers each category*.]

Q-U-A-N-T-I-T-Y
Particular
Universal
Singular

Q-U-A-L-I-T-Y
Affirmative
Negative
Infinite

R-E-L-A-T-I-O-N
Categorical
Hypothetical
Disjunctive

M-O-D-A-L-I-T-Y
Problematic
Assertoric
Apodictic

[*Looks at the blackboard*.] This is not in Kant's last Critique, but it's part of the first one, hmm... [*Hesitates*] the Critique of Pure Reason, although in Kant all of these critiques are related.

[*Long pause*.]

Now, those of you who really believed me when I said that you could use the four sets of categories corresponding to the four rules in order to make a judgment of taste, or to determine a work of art, must have had an interesting time trying to fit them together. I think any self-respecting Kantian scholar would spend two to three hundred pages trying to do just that but… [*Examines his notes.*] It's only certain categories in Kant I think where this is obvious… [*Pause.*] I mean, for example, when he talks about universality, and how a judgment of taste is well grounded only when it is valid for everyone. Well, that fits under Quantity, and when he insists that a judgment of taste involves a sort of disinterested pleasure, that would relate to Quality. But some other categories are a little bit harder to link together, and I don't think you have to worry except to know that in Kant you've always got subsystems that are at work. We have four of these conditions for the judgment of taste and they always lead somewhere else, to his previous work and the table of categories in the Critique of Pure Reason.[4] [*Pause.*] But this is not so visible in his discussions of the sublime, and that would be an interesting clue for us. The four-fold categories run through the Analytic of the Beautiful, and I think it's a process of matching a little bit its own notion of the faculties. You can also look at it another way and say that, for Kant, any truthful statement about the world has to answer these four questions… [*Knocking the chalk against the blackboard*], or run its way through the four categories, because each category is radically different: Modality is different from Relation and from Quality, and so on and so forth. But in Kant, any scientific, hmm… [*Hesitates*] any judgment on the world has to satisfy all four categories or will [*Stressing*] necessarily be expressed through these four categories in order for the possibility of knowledge and experience to be valid. Mm-hmm… [*Pause.*] What's the relationship to each other in social or historical terms? Well, you don't get an answer to that until you come to Hegel, where Hegel really tries to break up this four-fold Kantian division and put them together in some way, showing their inner relations with each other… [*Quietly*: because after all, someone invented this, human beings invented these schemas, so it must be subsumed under its own kind of logic, but that's a different matter.]

[*Long pause.*]

Mm-hmm. So, I think we've got those, and then the other thing that I wanted to mention in relation to Hegel, but we didn't have enough time the other day... [*Pause.*] For those of you who know Hegel... [*Chair scrapes across the floor*] Hegel would call this...

[*Starts drawing a two-column chart on the blackboard.*]

V-E-R-S-T-A-N-D Understanding	V-E-R-N-U-N-F-T Reason

Now, if you... [*Pause.*] If those of you — we did some Hegel... [*Quietly*: I don't know when, was it in the last semester or earlier?] you know that for Hegel this [*Strikes the word* Verstand *on the blackboard*] is bad, and this [*Strikes* Vernunft] is good.

[*Long pause.*]

For Hegel, Verstand is this lower faculty of seeing everything in terms of space and objects, of bringing sensible data into static concepts, whereas Vernunft is the dialectic. [*Pause.*] Now, when you're reading Kant, please understand that this relation in Kant is exactly the reverse. In Kant, this... [*Points to* Verstand] is the healthy mind, which can make scientific thinking possible, and which organizes this innerworldly unity of consciousness, that is our judgments about events, objects, experience and so forth. His Critique of Pure Reason urges us — as far as knowledge is concerned — to confine ourselves to the powers of Understanding. For Kant, Reason, hmm... [*Hesitates*] the minute we've got into Reason or Vernunft, we know that we've gone beyond experience; we are beyond those boundaries, and we are in a world where nothing is amenable to experience and senses anymore, and that beyond-world involves the soul, God, totality of the universe, creation, and freedom. And those have to be under principles. They are not anywhere in the sensible world, they are not objects, they can never be really known in any sense — they are just [*Stressing*] posited. And all of these objects and things can come because we assimilate them, and we are sort of confusing appearances with things-in-themselves, hmm... [*Hesitates*] and he calls it [*Stressing*] amphiboly, the "amphiboly of pure reason." That is when you think that concepts, which are simply ideal, don't have any... [*Achoo. Sneeze in the audience*] they are only applicable to our objects of possible experience and cannot be used beyond experience... [*Mumbles indistinctly.*] So, in Kant, Understanding and Reason must be kept radically separated,[5] and you will see this is going on also in his aesthetics, in the Critique of Judgment, because he doesn't get rid of them. And you know this is a great dualism, and this dualism is bound to somehow keep coming back and... [*Words indistinct.*] Now, even without jumping ahead, I think you might suspect that in the realm of the aesthetic, this one... [*Taps on the Verstand/Understanding* part of the column] which measures the relationship to the inner world of sensory data and is responsible for organizing a coherent representation of the world, and so forth, is gonna be on the side of beauty, and this one... [*Taps on Vernunft/Reason* side of the column] which ultimately enables our thinking of abstract concepts that lie beyond the sensible... [*Quietly*: God, freedom, and so forth] this one is going to eventually end in the sublime. (*See full chart below*). But I don't... [*Pause.*] This is not crystal clear in Kant. It is only clear that this dualism plays itself out in this other place, whether it is actually... [*Pause.*] This is more of an implication than it is an actual part of the argument. Because once he gets to the sublime, you see, this all gets very tricky and it's very hard to figure out even what he thinks, and indeed what he thinks is profoundly ambiguous... [*Quietly*: ah, as is with this little story, I told you last time, the sublime is a supplément, as Derrida would say; it's the excess of a thing; it's the overload of the thing and it can't fully be integrated into the scheme of things.] But as precisely an overload, as something, which is unreasonable, paradoxically it would fall under Reason rather than under Understanding, which is the realm of the finitude...

[*Quietly*: and Reason is realm of the infinite, and what lies beyond experience... (*Voice fades into mumbling*).]

[*Long pause*.]

Okay, now I think we've been over these four features of the beautiful, but we can go over them quickly again because some of them are very strange. Mm-hmm... [*Reads from the* Critique of Judgment] "...it is devoid of interest," page 52.[6] Okay, that's... [*Reflects*.] "A liking or disliking devoid of all interest."[7] Well, interest, hmm... [*Pause*.] As I've already said it, in Kant interest has to do with desire, it has to do with utility, practicality, usefulness, and all of those things. And therefore, interest means of course, hmm... [*Hesitates*] that so-and-so is an "interested party" and, as an interested party, someone may have a stake in something. Someone [*Whispering*] is getting something out of it, and all of this and the torturous use of the word "pleasure" — which he can't really avoid using but that he would like not to be using about the characteristics of beauty — this is all directed towards trying to secure for beauty a place which has no practical interest. Now, that will be a major thing in the evolution of aesthetics, because if you're in a place where there is interest — in the sense of getting some practical advantage out of the object... [*Quietly*: gaining, profiting, fulfilling a desire, and so forth] — if you can find a place like that then you found a place that lies outside society, outside the laws of the modern business society. [*Pause*.] Then you found a place, if not completely outside of the world, then a kind of utopian space in which the laws of the business society and of profit and desire, and of all those things, no longer apply. This is a space of what in some sort of later tradition will be called "freedom." And little by little the later aesthetics will defend beauty or art as the place of an essential freedom from the economic ideas, governing systems or the passions that are ruling the world, including ethics, because the moral good itself is... [*Quietly*: hmm, it's also really (*Stressing*) interest in some sense.] So, this realm of beauty must then be established somehow outside of the practical world, outside of the daily reality of the bourgeois society. Well, we'll see what else is outside of it.

[*Long pause.*]

So, as I said the other day, if there is pleasure involved, physical pleasure, then there is interest too. Take your glass of fresh orange juice... [*Points to student's drink*] here, it will not be considered beautiful because you enjoy it too much [*Chuckles*] and this is gonna be, I think, a problem for aesthetics. As I also said last time, when we get to the evolution of art... [*Cough in the audience*] in the twentieth century, this would then become more problematic as it will involve new forms of materialisms. Because the passion for oil paint is a material passion; it has a physical interest... [*Quietly:* there is a famous story in the autobiography of... (*Words indistinct*).] Wait, it's not the biography, it's a questionnaire they asked Gertrude Stein and that's in the Little Review journal. They asked her, "What is your attitude towards modern art?" And Gertrude Stein said, "I liked to look at it, at least at the picture part the other parts interest me much less."[8] Well okay, the "other part," that's the story, that's the content. But to look at it, you're looking at paint, at oil paint essentially. And oil paint offers a unique kind of sensory or sensual experience. It represents the return of the body, and what are the pictorial means in which this return manifests? This is then... [*Chalk on the blackboard. Adds to the column*] L-I-N-E and C-O-L-O-R. Okay, now color represents a return of the body. I would say this is the domination of poetry by the sound of language, by the materiality of language later on in the nineteenth century, certainly from Baudelaire, Mallarmé, and then in English... [*Quietly*: they always say that the English equivalent of Baudelaire would be Tennyson but it doesn't really get that... (*Words indistinct*) strangeness, materiality and all these weird words and sentences.] And then, little by little, modern poetry will become [*Stressing*] material... [*Quietly*: in the sense that it is the sonorous and material and even visual shape of the words that one is consuming.] And the same for musical color, which you can really take that... [*Quietly*: Beethoven is not, doesn't use instrumental coloration the way Wagner does... (*Pause*) you get the beginnings of Berlioz and Schumann, and so forth, but Wagner is the central place for color.] Then, after that, all of music is really this... [*Zipper unzipping*] of coloration in the orchestra and the addition of various new instruments and richer orchestral palette.

[*Long pause*.]

Mm-hmm. So, all of that is very [*Whispering*] un-Kantian, and it becomes very worrisome for any true Kantian, because whatever the parties there is something that you have to call physical stimulus, which would involve pleasure and interest, and that shouldn't be there. Now, can we say... [*Pause*.] But then there is also Freud's question... [*Quietly*: and we have Adorno counterposing Kant and Freud's theories of art in this first section of Aesthetic Theory.] Can we... [*Reflects*.] Couldn't we use the word "sublimation" and wish-fulfilment for this, and say, but look [*Impersonates Freud*] "Yes, sure those might be material images, but this is a sublimation of some real material pleasures"? I mean, you don't... [*Quietly*: remember Hegel's remark about the animal] he says that the animals also desire, of course they do, but they don't think about it. When they desire something, they walk up to it and eat it up. Well, so one might like to... [*Quietly*: eat up the canvas, for example (*Chuckles*).] This might be... [*Pause*.] You might approach some notion of almost physical appropriation, but you don't get there so you could say that all of that desire to eat up comes through the other senses, through the eyes and ears essentially... [*Quietly*: I don't know what sense language comes through, ears in this case.] So, the desire for the beautiful and art is a form of sublimation of the physical, and although we cannot say that it's completely spiritual, it is a lot closer to spirit than all these other basic bodily pleasures. Because if you look back at Burke, I mean, Burke's great opposition is sexuality and fear, I mean pleasure and pain. That entire tradition of aesthetics for these people was based on the relation between pleasure/beauty and pain/ugliness. In Burke, there is a completely unashamed connection of beauty with sex, hmm... [*Hesitates*] and it does seem to me that's... [*Cough in the audience*] what is being critiqued here. Kant is trying, he is working very hard to get away from it and find some new formula, which will somehow repress and eliminate the bodily pleasures. And clearly the theory of sublimation is not present in Kant, but we always have this constant worry about the physical, about the so-called "interest."

[*Long pause.*]

Now, on the other hand... [*Pause.*] Mm-hmm. These works of art are disinterested in some sense because we don't do anything with them. If we look at them to appraise them or to invest in them in order to get a tax write-off, well that's [*Stressing*] <u>interest</u>. But normally... [*Reflects.*] Or even, you know, if you're looking at them to write your thesis or a monograph to promote your career... [*Quietly*: hmm, that's probably interest too, or write a piece of criticism about it so that the museum could use it to bring more audiences.] I mean, the critique of interest is a very useful critical tool, I think, because it allows us to track one's motives and keep this place, which as I said earlier, must lie outside the business society. It allows us to keep this place of freedom clean. So, for Kant, this is a very interesting and important obsession, and we must see that it's also a very controversial proposition that is not so easy to defend... [*Quietly*: especially when we get to modernism where... (*Mumbles indistinctly*).]

[*Long pause.*]

Okay, now beau... [*Clears throat.*] "<u>Beautiful</u> is what, without a concept..." — we'll come back to that later on — "is liked universally."[9] This is the strangest part of this book. The aesthetic judgment is supposed to be universal. But what does this mean? I mean, he explains right away because clearly, he knows like everybody else that people don't have the same taste, and so you like something and somebody else, other people, don't like it. Mm-hmm. So how can these judgments be universal? [*Pause.*] I think what's meant — this will later on become the famous antinomy of taste precisely because we [*Stressing*] <u>want</u>

our judgments to be universal, and on the other hand "there is no...", what's the famous phrase that "there is no disputing about taste"... [*Quietly*: or whatever it is.][10] So, the antinomy of taste is: it's universal but it isn't universal. Mm-hmm, and I think what's meant here... [*Quietly*: and we'll see how he solves this later on because that's the closest thing to an antinomy that we get with this as opposed to... (*Words indistinct*).] I think that what he means is that taste only claims to be universal. It's not that empirically we know that everybody is gonna like the same thing we do, but that our liking must include the demand that it be universal... [*Door creaks open. Footsteps.*] That is to say, if we, hmm... [*Hesitates.*] You know, there are things that we like all by ourselves, right? So, let's say we have some weird tastes, you know. You might like to combine salt with, I don't know, something sweet... [*Quietly*: I'm trying to think of something. I like to have sweet Chinese things with... (*Words indistinct. Chuckles*).] Or, you know some people like salty watermelons or peanut butter and pickle, and so on and so forth, so maybe that is not so peculiar, but think of some [*Stressing*] really peculiar things, something that is peculiar to you, something that you don't want other people to know you're doing at night in the kitchen... [*Chuckles.*] That isn't a problem when you're eating it by yourself, on your own, not with everybody else. You happen to like that and you're doing it in secret, and that's not a big deal. But you can't feel that way about a film, a painting, or a book, or something like that, because you have to believe that you're liking something in it and that everyone else should also like it, and that people who don't like that, then something is very wrong with them. [*Pause.*] I mean, I think it can't be an aesthetic judgment unless you have that basic requirement. You know that you will never succeed in convincing everyone to like something that you like, I mean... [*Pause.*] Or by the time something becomes universal... [*Quietly*: Shakespeare, for example, it took what, four centuries for his literary recognition to grow and it would be completely... (*Mumbles indistinctly*).] Somehow you want to feel that you discovered something, and that here is something that people don't know about yet, but which will someday grow and become truly [*Stressing*] universal. Everyone will like it one day. But as I say, what it is it's... [*Student raises hand.*] Yeah...

STUDENT: It seems like Kant wants to say that if there isn't something universal about taste, then there are absolutely no bases whatsoever forever in telling anyone what to say about it.

JAMESON: Yeah, that's the other...

STUDENT: That's seems to be...

JAMESON: Yes. That's the other version of this. Yeah, yeah... [*Excited.*] Or, that you can't even have an idea of taste if it isn't universal, if there isn't something that everybody could agree to like. I would say that's what is coming out of these eighteenth-century traditions about taste. There is a famous essay of Hume on taste,[11] where he deals with the question of subjectivity of taste raising the same issue of objectivity. This is a... [*Pause.*] But in the eighteenth century, this notion of goût and taste, and so forth, or Geschmack, this is part of the whole repertoire of neo-classical themes as it develops out of France in the late seventeenth century, and it immediately gives rise to precisely such discussions. Normally, there are some of the neoclassicists who are saying... [*Impersonates a neoclassicist*] "Well, if you don't like something, then you are barbarian, you have no taste," right? [*Chuckles.*] But Kant is the one who tries to maintain this universal form, and at the same time really thinks it out in his last Critique. And I would say for us... [*Searches for words.*] Mm-hmm. For us, this is probably the way to think about it existentially, and if you're making this aesthetic judgment on a purely individually basis, particular basis without any appeal to the taste of other people... [*Quietly*: this is a concept that involves other people; it is about otherness, that's what universality is, and if you are able to experience the work without any appeal to otherness, then probably you're a schizophrenic, or something like that, and what you like is clearly not taste or art.] Mm-hmm. And even though a lot of people would say this, I mean, "Well, I don't care what everybody else thinks, I like this regardless of what others think," that is not claim to high spiritual value, or art as we understand it. So, Kant is closer to the truth, and this is what the universal means, it means precisely [*Stressing*] that.

[*Long pause.*]

Mm-hmm, hmm... [*Page flipping.*] Okay, now page 84. Mm-hmm. Purposiveness. Ah, "...it is purposiveness... without the presentation of a purpose."[12] This is probably the most famous thing in the whole third Critique. And what does it mean? Well, you have to understand that the second half of the Critique will deal with nature, and the whole point about nature is that it seems to be purposeful. That is to say, nature has a design, it's not random, it is organized and self-organizing, it has an inherent teleology... [*Cough in the audience.*] And yet nobody is there doing it... [*Quietly*: I mean, Kant has it somewhere of course that God is somewhere, but God is... (*Mumbles indistinctly*) the ideal reason for something.] So, all we can know about nature is that it seems purposeful... [*Pause.*] It seems to be functional, that is, the natural world is organized in a functional way and our relationship to nature is precisely that. You can't have a non-functional relation to nature, so this becomes a study of teleology in the second half of the third Critique, and the connection to the aesthetic part is precisely that — that the work of art is organized, even when it appears random, and seemingly absolutely contingent and given over to chance... [*Quietly*: the frame of the work turns the painting back into something purposeful.] So, if you think about action painting and Jackson Pollock... [*Pause.*] Mm-hmm. The whole aesthetic of action painting is gonna be one of purpose, but a purpose that has no purpose, it is doing and not doing anything; it is, and it is not, in the world; it's a kind of functionality that is not functional, and so on and so forth. Here we touch the edge of language in a sense; this is a language we're speaking like all... [*Words indistinct.*] Purposefulness without a purpose, that's really pushing the envelope... [*Door creaks open*] of language to its extreme. How could we understand something? I mean, what would that be? Maybe something in science fiction where... [*Quietly*: you see some strange object that seems to have a function, but no one knows what's their function is because it's not an earthly or known function... (*Mumbles indistinctly*).]

STUDENT: But it seems to me that all of these Kantian formulae are very paradoxical, or they have a sort of...

JAMESON: Yeah, yeah...

STUDENT: [*Agitated. Continues*] ...take "liking without interest" ...

JAMESON: Yeah...

STUDENT: [*Continues*] ...or again "purposiveness without purpose" ...

JAMESON: Yes, yes, yes...

STUDENT: .... and [*Stressing*] "subjective universality." Kant introduces this differentiation, subjective universality, and isn't that already a contradiction in the first place?

JAMESON: Mm-hmm.

STUDENT: ... or an antinomy based on contradictory conclusions... [*Cough in the audience.*]

JAMESON: Yeah, yeah. [*Determined.*] No, I think that's... [*Pause.*] That's what's interesting about this, that these formulas are pushed to a limit in which, all of a sudden, they verge on the incomprehensible because of the final thing here, which is simply... [*Page flipping.*] Ah here: "...without a concept." Mm-hmm. [*Reads from the* Critique of Judgement] "Beautiful is what without a concept is cognized as the object of a necessary liking."[13] [*Pause.*] We have the keywords here: "without a concept" and the "necessary." "Without a concept," this means that art or beauty is not [*Whispering*] an object of knowledge. You can know things about it, but the thing as a whole is not knowable... [*Pause.*] And remember that, in Kant, knowledge is related to... [*Quietly*: what's the technical word for this?] It involves the a priori categories, and of course they are a priori because they are not derived from the laboratory, from experience, and all of Kant's philosophy is based on the idea that there is a combination somewhere between the unique event or experience and some a priori principles... [*Quietly:* take, for instance, the whole relation to time and space.] Well, in aesthetics, seemingly there can't be an a priori. In other words... [*Quietly*: and I think I also said this the other day] you can't say, okay because I read this treatise on classical beauty, I've been told that the most beautiful picture would be something that's about fifteen inches by ten inches, and it's got some stuff balancing here and here, and it uses such colors... [*Quietly*: here is a list of them] and then light must come from above, and that the most beautiful depicted object is a landscape or a still life painted from nature, and blah, blah, blah and so on. And then you go in front of a work of art, and you start checking with your list, and at the end you pronounce: "oh, thus, it must be beautiful," right? [*Chuckles*.] Well, that's really not the way we operate. Everything we say about a beautiful object is a posteriori... [*Quietly*: it's not a priori.] But... [*Pause*.] But it is [*Stressing*] as though it is based on the logic of the concept. And indeed, we can find out very shortly... [*Quietly*: how do you explain this weird thing, why would anybody...? (*Pause.*) What are these things and what is this kind of experience that we call "aesthetic experience"?] Why does this give us a certain pleasure, but a pleasure without pleasure? Well, because, and this is again an obsession of Kant with parts of the mind and powers or faculties, and him insisting that it has also something to do with these faculties achieving a state of harmony, a harmony between the imagination and the cognitive faculty.

[*Long pause*.]

Page 92... [*Page flipping*] "Only a lawfulness without a law, and a subjective harmony of the imagination with the understanding without an objective harmony..."[14] [*Door creaks open. Footsteps*.] The understanding is busy trying to cognize these things... [*Quietly*: objects of nature or art] and put them together. The imagination, on the other hand, is free-drawing all sorts of alternative realities, visualizations, and aspirations... [*Words indistinct*]. So here suddenly we have an exercising of the cognitive faculty, which is filled with a wholly different set of things that is normally more appropriate for a scientific laboratory [*Pause.*] In the scientific laboratory, we have all of these empirical experiments and sensations, and we're trying to think... [*Cough in the audience*] about them and understand them and turn them into laws. Understanding provides the rules to organize our experience. The imagination, on the other hand, synthesizes and forms mental representations and sensory information into these... [*Pause*] into these, hmm... [*Hesitates*] forms. There isn't a concept or rule involved. Well, the ultimate effect of the aesthetic then, in Kant, or what he calls [*Stressing*] the beautiful, is the result of clicking together of these two faculties — so one could say a harmony of [*Stressing*] freedom and knowledge. In ordinary knowledge, we are not free, and that is why we do our experiments. We don't take up the world as it is but base our actions on observations and experiences. You could say this in a different way. There has been a lot of aesthetics which talks about how any aesthetic object is the, hmm... [*Hesitates*] symbol, or if you like, the allegory of human creativity. We're condemned to a certain number of constraints in the real world... [*Quietly:* all kind of constraints, I mean food, clothing, shelter, and other necessities.] But in the world of the aesthetic, the human being has made these necessities irrelevant, and imagination is that faculty of freedom because... [*Quietly:* you could imagine whatever you want.] If you want to go back to Vico and say that people can understand only what they made, and therefore... [*Quietly*: this is still in the 1700s, no, 1800s.] Ah, God made nature so we can't understand that, but... [*Quietly:* and this is what is so revolutionary about Vico] is that human beings made history, and that is something that we can understand. We can understand human history but not nature.[15] Well, from this other point of view, one could say that the work of art is also something that has been completely made, so all of the constraints of the body and the world, and so forth, go away and this becomes a kind of state in which freedom seems to be recognized in, say, a painting, a piece of music, a book. Or as Adorno says, "production," because freedom is then production. Freedom is and can be completely produced by human beings, but the world or nature cannot. The world of nature is alien to us but not the work of art. So, this is a kind of utopian situation in which, in and as though the human beings completely made this world, and therefore are thus fully responsible for it.

[*Long pause*.]

Now, that's what this means. But I also think that in Kant there is a more basic meaning with this idea of the harmonious interaction of these various mental faculties. As I said to you before, all of this is very strange. [*Reflects*.] How would you know... [*Pause*.] It's like saying: all music is a combination of numbers and vibrations, as if the key to music is the right combination of your economic or mathematical faculties... [*Quietly*: when you start counting and doing numbers] and then you get these very funny sensations or pleasant physical vibrations that we call music, right? And it's like... [*Pause*.] Hmm... [*Hesitates*.] Who, who... [*Stammering*.] Ah, who... [*Pause*.] Who even knows about these faculties? [*Pause*.] I mean, who has ever experienced them? Or who can prove their existence? They all sort of have been deduced and made up by Kant, who says that there is a faculty of desire, and a faculty of understanding, and a faculty of reason, that's all very Platonic but who says we're cut up and separated like that? Mm-hmm. It is again, and this is Kant's genius, in that he sets up a kind of representational experiment where he says well, we're all divided up in these various powers, or faculties, and that sometimes these faculties overlap and play together, and when this takes place, then interesting stuff starts to happen. And in this case, the interesting stuff is this combination of the imagination and understanding, or cognition, and the minute we get them combined... [*Pause*] ah, that something very special happens, and that very special thing is aesthetics... [*Quietly:* the judgment of taste, the appreciation of the beautiful, or art.]

[*Long pause*.]

[*Stressing.*] Now, there will be yet another justification and it also sounds like pleasure to me. I mean, this harmony of the faculties, you know, they still sound very much like, hmm... [*Hesitates*] as though we're getting something out of it. [*Firmly.*] There will be a later justification of this... [*Takes a sip of water*] and it has to do with the idea of the good. I will jump ahead here — this is at the end of the later section, but we'll probably come back to it later on — and there he's saying... [*Impersonates Kant*] "Okay, I'll tell you this: it's as though these aesthetic experiences were preparations for the exercise of the good..." [*Pause.*] Mm-hmm. Beauty is somehow symbolic of virtue. And then he says... [*Impersonates Kant*] "Oh it would be nice, and everything would be much clearer, if the good and the beautiful were related." Then we could understand it, as this is part of what we're doing in this world: God wants us to behave, we can't deduce that out of our limited understanding, so God has implanted this aesthetic faculty in us to sort of [*Stressing*] civilize us and make us harmonious and make us more susceptible to acting properly and to having all the virtues. But... [*Pause.*] But Kant says, after all, that we can't say that because then we're exercising reason, and this also involves some form of interest. [*Pause.*] So, although it would be nice to think that; it would be nice to think so, we can't really accept it. If... if... [*Stammers*] ...if life had a meaning, maybe the aesthetic would be part of it... [*Words indistinct.*] It's a very candid suggestion, but there is always a further question, right? If beauty or art doesn't prepare us for the exercise of virtue or of the good, then what is art for? How do you justify it? [*Softly.*] Is this just some weird accident that happens to me because, after all, I got this faculty of imagination that's the key to all, and then sometimes these faculties set off some connections and combinations? Well, yeah, could be that, could be that. But that could be also historical? [*Reflecting.*] I mean, it isn't until certain moment of the development of science, and a certain liberation of the imagination, that one gets not art in general... [*Quietly*: that is religious art, or magic] but autonomous secular or modern art. Well, I mean it is around the time of Kant that autonomous art and its institutions, the discipline of aesthetics, is coming into being... [*Quietly*: or maybe a little earlier or later...(*Pause*).] So, art comes to become a practice, which is self-justified, and then at that moment we need the justification that might be this conscious one of the harmonies between the two faculties as they are developing. And then this is historical. Then there would be a moment in which precisely that harmony becomes possible to look at it in historical terms, and this comes to... [*Quietly*: and then this comes to justify this modern understanding that we must have a thing called "autonomous art"... (*Raps his knuckles on the desk*).]

[*Long pause*.]

Okay, now let's go to the sublime... [*Page flipping*.] Kant doesn't seem to think, hmm... [*Hesitates*.] You will have to read this carefully in order to figure it out, but I don't think that he believes that there could be a form of sublime art. [*Pause*.] I think that if you read this, the sublime is some kind of experience that has to be explained, and it has something to do with the feeling of awe when faced with something that is beyond ordinary human experience, the overwhelming... [*Cough in the audience*.] It's got something to do with nature, but what we are wondering today is: can anybody sit down and make sublime art? I think it's always... [*Pause*.] When he talks about this, it's a combination of beauty and the sublime. It's something that beauty is the central focus of the work of art. A work of art is supposed to be that, but then in certain things a movement of the sublime begins to push the bounds of beauty, and we get one of these combinations. But none of the examples of the sublime are works of art, as far as I can see... [*Student assistant hands the list of students enrolled in the course*.]

STUDENT ASSISTANT: This is the list you've asked for...

JAMESON: Ah... [*Looks at the list. Talks to himself*.] Yeah. Okay. Thank you. But for the most part, hmm... [*Hesitates*.] But for the most part, the category of the sublime is not about paintings, or literary works, or whatever, and so here too this new thing that has to be taken up, this new topic, this new category of the sublime... [*Quietly:* this has to be somehow closely examined.] Okay, so I think that... [*Pause.*] Mm-hmm. As I said, here, hmm... [*Looks at the columns on the blackboard.*] Art will be more or less judged within the domain of beauty, and reason will be in the domain of the sublime. But it is also, speaking in terms of the Kantian categories, that beauty will be quality and the sublime will be quantity. Ah, and as you know from this, the two areas in which the sublime manifests itself are either size or power and any of the multiple combinations of them. Size, quantity and so forth is the mathematical sublime. Power is the dynamic sublime. These are the forms that this strange manifestation can take. Mm-hmm "...since judgments about the sublime," page 100, "are made by the aesthetic reflective power of judgment, the analytic must allow us to present the liking for the sublime, just as that for the beautiful as follows: in terms of quantity, as universally valid; in terms of quality, as devoid of interest; in terms of relation, as a subjective purposiveness; and in terms of modality, as a necessary subjective purposiveness."[16] We've gone through all of that stuff and yet that's not what we can look for, a specific differentiation of the sublime. So, we have to look now into other directions. And despite this division, and if we look at it from another way, we can see that there's some kind of overlap or overwash here with these other three Critiques because... [*Reflects.*] Mm-hmm. "...While... the beautiful presupposes and sustains the mind in restful contemplation, the feeling of the sublime carries with it a mental agitation..." "...and so the imagination will refer this agitation either to the cognitive power or to the power of desire."[17] That is to say, either to science or to ethics. So, we're spilling out of this empty place of the aesthetic, over where it's washing back and forth into these other impure places... [*Quietly*: it seems to me, or at least it looks as if the aesthetics must have some form of connection with those other realms.] The cognitive power would be the mathematical sublime, the power of desire dynamic attunement of the mind, and...

[*Pause.*] The point is that, at least in the dynamic area, or maybe in both probably, what's presupposed is [*Stresses*] fear. Sublime, he says, has to do with negative pleasures.[18] [*Reflecting.*] There is a fear involved in the contemplation of these natural objects. The mathematical sublime shows an enormous quantity next to which I'm nothing but an ant, or something like that, and the dynamic sublime shows something that threatens people. Ah, maybe there is more fear on that side, I'm not sure, but very much close to Burke's idea that when we get to the sublime we talk about pain and the management of sublimation of pain.

[*Long Pause.*]

Now... [*Pause.*] Now the temples. I mentioned St. Peter's Basilica, okay you've got... [*Pause.*] Obviously, everybody knows the famous themes that have been used with regard to the sublime... [*Quietly:* this certainly has to do with the interest of Romanticism, and the famous examples of the Alps, and the mountains... (*Cough in the audience*), or the open sea. What are the other great motifs of the sublime?][19] These are the main themes, which somehow come to be occasions for the matters of representing the sublime. The St. Peter's Basilica in Rome was interesting as an episode in itself... [*Page flipping.*] "Perhaps the same observation can explain the bewilderment or kind of perplexity that is said to seize the spectator who for the first time enters St. Peter's Basilica in Rome. For he has the feeling that his imagination is inadequate for exhibiting the idea of a whole, [a feeling] in which imagination reaches its maximum..."[20] and so on. These are the great colonnades of St. Peter's that stretch to infinity... [*Quietly*: and these may also have to do with Hegel... (*Mumbles indistinctly*) and the "bad" form of infinity, the infinite regress, and the failure to reach a final conclusion.] These colonnades are physical forms, or man-made forms of representing infinity, which is another motif of the sublime. But then we also arrive at questions that are very interesting for modernism, and they require a language which is somewhat different from Kant's because these are clearly problems of representation. [*Footsteps. Walks across the classroom.*] Ah... ah... this other... [*Pause.*] These three examples used to represent the sublime, and there will be one more which is the ban on graven images. All of these examples involve a relationship to an object, which transcends our powers to understand or to perceive it. [*Chair-back creaks.*] In some way, the object itself stands in the way of perceiving it — it is something so immense that we can't possibly absorb it. The bed of the sea, the stormy sea, the tops of the mountain — these are sort of hints as to something that we can't really take in because we are just too small and too powerless, and our perceptive apparatus cannot really absorb them, and yet it's a moment in which you also suddenly realize that there is something else immense... [*Achoo. Sneeze in the audience*] beyond them that we precisely can't grasp. And then we get to a very odd idea, which is a little bit like Hegel's critique of Kant. [*Pause.*] As you all know, Hegel's famous critique of Kant has to do with the limit. Kant wanted us to fix a limit and stop there, but then as Hegel said, if there is a limit, it is a limit on both sides, and the minute you set the limit you are sort of seeing it from the other side too, which means that you've already gone beyond it. For Kant, the limit is, for example, his famous thing-in-itself. But if you decided to name it, if you characterize it in all of these ways, then how can it be "in-itself"? It's as though we are somehow intuitively transcending the "thing," it's already there without being able to be there on its own. Well, okay, so much for that argument against Kant... [*Quietly*: I think Slavoj has some more attacks on this somewhere in his books.]

[*Long pause.*]

But what's also interesting for us and for modernism is that Kant's own prospect of the sublime seems already to anticipate a limit. Because he says, look, this thing that you're feeling in the sublime is not in the world. [*Pause.*] It is not in those objects precisely because, insofar as you can see those objects, they're not bigger than you are, right? I mean your percept about other states means... [*Reflects*.] What they're doing is they're promising to overwhelm you and to contain things that are beyond your sense of perception. And what's beyond your sense of perception is not something that you find in the object, and therefore this is subjective. This is something the sublime reaches in itself; the sublime is a subjective reaction on certain occasions to these worldly circumstances. So, Kant says, the sublime is something that has to do with [*Whispering*] the limits of the mind, so long as we understand that we are unable to comprehend things. But on the other hand, he seems to tell us that the sublime is also a way of acknowledging those limits, so we sort of go over them and, in a way, our pleasure is that we have mastered something that's more enormous than we are. Our various experience of the sublime suggests that somehow this affect that we're drawing from the thing is a way of absorbing it; it's a way of appropriating it. So, there is a funny mixture here... [*Quietly*: which I think, as I say, I think that this is very... (*Words indistinct*).] I'm not sure if it sounds unclear or incoherent, but the incoherencies are also in Kant's reactions to this situation. I think that if you put it all together it's a fairly coherent statement of every paradoxical kind of thing about which he is not sure what he wants to do. [*Pause*.] For example, what is "negative pleasure" — we're not supposed to have any pleasures. Is that still pleasure or is it something else? Or, if it is unpleasure, then we have nothing on it, we don't even react, we don't see it. So, there is a lot in here that hints towards something from which he also wants to draw back. But he points to it in such an articulated way that we can know his own ambiguities. This is not "fuzzy thinking" or anything, it seems to me; it's "mixed feelings," which is a little bit different. If the mixed feelings are clear enough and articulated enough, it can also be described beyond it. So here, when we are looking at one of the motifs of the sublime, it means that we're overwhelmed by it, but on the other hand, the fact that we can make an experience out of being overwhelmed means that we also surrender to it, and you've got both of those feelings going on at once. In the case of the sublime, it is that you are experiencing it ... [*Quietly*: but it's also true that we have to feel safe, I mean, when you see the raging sea, or glaciered mountains, or something like that, you have to be in a safe place in order to experience it rather than be thrown into... (*Words indistinct*). It would be great to experiment one day and study the physical conditions of experiencing the sublime, but unfortunately, we don't have very much time for this kind of aesthetic experiments (*Chuckles*).] But the sublime really has to do with this... [*Page flipping*.] If the human "... mind is nonetheless to be able even to think the given infinite without contradiction, it must have within itself a power that is supersensible..."[21] [*Quietly*: ...that's another thing we could add to our chart.] Here is the... [*Chalk on the blackboard. Talks to himself*] S-E-N-S-E P-E-R-C-E-P-T-I-O-N under Understanding, and on this other side of Reason we write the... [*Chalk on the blackboard*] S-U-P-E-R-S-E-N-S-I-B-L-E. So, hmm... [*Hesitates*.] So, in the sublime we are coming in close contact with the faculty of Reason as Vernunft; we engage with these strange powers that are no good, that are contradictory, unlimited, something that we could delegate to science... [*Words indistinct*] and yet which are somehow now also here with us, in the human mind. [*Page flipping*.] The mind "must have within itself a power that is super..." [*Quietly*: yeah, it is (*Stressing*) supersensible.] "It must have within itself a power that is supersensible, whose idea of a noumenon cannot be intuited but can yet be regarded as the substrate underlying what is mere appearance, namely, our intuition of the world."[22] So this is a concrete exercise not of understanding, which as we have said has to do with real experience and empirical knowledge and what we call Verstand, but of reason. And yet reason cannot be exercised in some sort of way... [*Quietly*: reason is not a reliable faculty but pleasure, still in some sense, comes out of it, and that's on page 111 where there's this paradox involved.]

[*Long pause*.]

After that, hmm... [*Page flipping*.] After that, he goes on to discuss various features of the sublime. One has to do with...

[*Door creaks open.*] Well, in a way you should look at the people who don't feel the sublime. These are like that boy who didn't feel any fear, or these are the people who Adorno, and other critics of his generation, called the "philistines" — a problematic term today, as you all know. But in those days it was used to refer to people who are sort of stunned and unresponsive to beauty, or to great ideas because the sublime is also the main source of ideas. And ideas are different from concepts. This is the realm of... [*Adds more words to the chart. Chalk on the blackboard*] I-D-E-A-S, and this is the realm of... [*Chalk on the blackboard*] C-O-N-C-E-P-T-S. Then, let's see here, page 124: "In order for the mind to be attuned to the feeling of the sublime, it must be receptive to ideas."[23] So, we say that someone has no feeling if he remained unmoved to the presence of something that we judge as sublime. These are people who are... [*Pause.*] They don't get any kind of content out of this, it doesn't teach them a specific... [*Quietly*: if we are blinded by the sublime, it is like being unmusical... (*Pause*).] There is this famous remark by Max Weber, the great German sociologist, who once said, "I'm religiously unmusical." Well, according to Kant, if people are unattuned to the sublime, then something is the matter with them, and they won't reach some fuller sense of morality or have access to all the kind things presupposed by Reason. This is still the eighteenth century, remember. Hmm, so... [*Pause.*] So, these are ways in which one could think of the uses or the meaning of the sublime in Kant. There is also this sociology business, which it's quite interesting I think, on page 121 and 122. [*Page flipping.*] "Even in a fully, hmm..." [*Hesitates.*] "Even in a fully civilized society there remains this superior esteem for the warrior..." [*Pause.*] He's writing this in Prussia of the eighteenth century, during the emergence of a modern commercial society, and the advent of the ideas of the Enlightenment all across Europe... [*Quietly*: and there is also the figure of the warrior who goes into these big battles, like Napoleon, and some other heroes] "...except that we demand more of [the warrior]: that he also demonstrate all the virtues of peace-gentleness, sympathy, and even appropriate care for his own person — precisely because they reveal to us that his mind cannot be subdued by danger. Hence, no matter how much people may dispute, when they compare the statesman with the general, as to which one deserves the superior respect, an aesthetic judgment decides in favor of the general."[24] The general has the sublime, he has danger, fear, and courage. That's a very curious sociology of the sublime if you like. Mm-hmm. But as I say, I think finally, here on page 129 you have again a great celebration of the limit:

> The imagination thereby acquires an expansion and a might that surpasses the one it sacrifices: but the basis of this might is concealed from it; instead the imagination feels the sacrifice or deprivation and at the same time the cause to which it is being subjugated. Thus any spectator who beholds massive mountains climbing skyward, deep gorges with raging streams in them, wastelands lying in deep shadow and inviting melancholy meditation and so on is indeed seized by amazement bordering on terror, by horror and sacred thrill...[25]

...and so on and so forth. And these are then also objects that seem purposeful without a purpose... [*Quietly*: that is, they seem to have a teleology like beautiful objects, and the fear is also part of that because this is all in some sense material.] I'm gonna show you, hmm... [*Hesitates*.] Well, we don't have time today, but I'll show you a few examples of the eighteenth-century sublime because we tend to think of the eighteenth century in terms of Rococo and excessive decoration and so on and so forth, but he uses specific forms of the sublime from his time, and if we see them, then I'm sure it would help us get a better understanding of what he means. Mm-hmm... [*Looks at the chart he drew on the blackboard*.]

V-E-R-S-T-A-N-D	V-E-R-N-U-N-F-T
Understanding	Reason
Beauty	Sublime
Beethoven	Wagner
Line	Color
Modernism	Absolute (Sublime)
Concept	Ideas
Sense perception (of the world)	Supersensual (or supersensible)

In the next section he goes on to deal with what he calls the "Deduction of Pure Aesthetic Judgment," that is what is involved in [*Stressing*] the actual judgment of taste, and I think that he recapitulates something that we already know, but here he tries to come to terms with the whole notion of taste. And to do so, he introduces two rather special ideas. One is the notion of "common sense," hmm... [*Hesitates*] — the sensus communis. This will be then this internal universal sense of communicability of feeling that is supposed to be shared somehow by everybody else. The claim to universality is important because otherwise we're living in a state of... [*Reflecting*] not even in the dark ages but... [*Quietly:* what is often called... (*Raps his knuckles on the desk*)] oh yeah, in the "state of nature." This is the state of absolute savagery; it is the pre-political state where everybody is engaged in a perpetual struggle for survival, where everyone thinks something different, and where everybody's got something different going on. So, there is something here that has to be theorized as the sensus communis and this also has something to do with politics and democracy and all the rest of that. The other idea that we're going to see here, and we will only quickly mention, is the notion of "genius." This is of course the moment in which this pre-romantic part of Kant surfaces. I don't think genius here is meant... [*Quietly*: because you see, with the romantics the genius becomes this resisting part of nature in human beings.] Romantic genius is untheorizable and yet, since it's there, it has to be named — it is this whole new productive power of innovation with a heightened sensitivity and imagination that sees the world in a different way. But this comes later after Kant. Kant's genius has something to do with taste but it's always a certain kind of distance because geniuses are not necessarily tasteful... [*Mumbles indistinctly*.] Now... [*Pause*.] When you think that genius will become very shortly the source of the sublime in art, then you're already over into the Romantic period that is this whole new... [*Shuffling papers near the microphone*] productive notion. It seems to me that genius is not yet this explosive natural force that will become very soon, but Kant's theory puts it on the table and then, from now on, it can be developed by all kind of other people, and all kind of other voices, and therefore it is historically that the notion becomes very important here... [*Chair scrapes the floor. Door creaks open. Footsteps*.]

[*Long pause*.]

I want you also to note the notion of [*Stressing*] enthusiasm, which is as a sort of inner sublime. And, as Lyotard makes it clear... [*Quietly*: Lyotard's whole book is probably taken down to a quarter or something[26]] but his book is a lengthy commentary just on the pages of the sublime. [*Pause*.] It's very thorough, it's very useful, and I encourage everyone to take a closer look at it. Lyotard underscores the importance of enthusiasm — and this is the moment of the French Revolution, and maybe Kant's reaction to revolutionary Europe. This is the emergence of the political... [*Pause*.] As Lyotard points out, Kant couldn't get around by writing a "Critique of Political Reason," but this is the moment in which... [*Words indistinct*] and he already found it in Burke in a sense because the French Revolution, also for Burke, is the pain and horror of the sublime. [*Exhales deeply*.] But enthusiasm refers to these events, which are world-historical: the getting rid of the monarchy and the building of a radically new political order.

[*Long pause.*]

Then there is another division… [*Quietly*: Division II, and the so-called Dialectic of Aesthetic Judgment. I mean, we are jumping around the Third Critique, which we are not supposed to do, and this is not how things are usually done with respect to Kant, but I only want to point certain things out to you… (*Mumbles indistinctly*).] Now as for the antinomy of taste… [*Pause.*] Mm-hmm. The antinomy has to do with the paradoxical nature of the aesthetic judgment, where we have first the individual taste, or "everyone has his own taste," and this attempt to seek some form of validity for everyone. Taste wants to be universal but there is no disputing of individual taste, which is then solved for you, see on page 211 called "Solution of the Antinomy of Taste," and here Kant says that we have these antinomies because of some misuse of the concept, hmm… [*Hesitates.*] It's enough to think that all contradictions disappear by saying: "A judgment of taste is based on a concept (the concept of a general basis of nature's subjective purposiveness for our power of judgment), but this concept does not allow us to cognize and prove anything concerning the object because it is intrinsically indeterminable…"[27] So again, a kind of conceptuality without a concept, right? The form of the conceptuality is universal, but since art is radically singular, we can't make the connection. And so, everybody is picking on a different singular and arguing about that and the argument must take place and it can never be solved. But it's not an antinomy; it's not a contradiction between the two things. Anyway, such is the argument… [*Pause.*]

[*Footsteps.*]

Okay… [*Chairs scraping the floor*] let's break up at this point, and I'll see you then in a week, on Thursday. And please make sure you… [*Words indistinct.*]

Feet shuffling. Audience stands up. Objects drop on the floor. Door squeaks. Students return chairs to other classrooms. Zippers zipping up. Some students form a line to discuss their papers with Jameson. General noise. Screeching microphone noise.

[*Microphone turns off.*]

CURTAIN

LECTURE FOUR

JANUARY 30, 2003

ART, SOCIETY, AESTHETICS (CHAPTER) — FREUD, "CREATIVE WRITERS AND DAYDREAMING"

CURTAIN RISES

Moving chairs, squeaking door, coughs, other sounds filling the noise environment of a large classroom in the Literature Department at Duke University. Students are arriving. Some are discussing the play they watched last week. When Jameson travels, he assigns a movie, play, concert, or other work of art or culture in accordance with the topic of the seminar. The screenings usually take place in the same classroom, where the Teaching Assistant turns on the TV and VCR for the audience. A few students are talking about last week's screening of Samuel Beckett's Endgame, *a 2000 production directed by Conor McPherson.*

Jameson enters the classroom carrying a few books, his scattered notes, and the red pen in the chest pocket of his flannel shirt.

[*Microphone turns on.*]

JAMESON: ... and so forth [*Pause.*] That will be at three o'clock, up in the north gallery, and there will be a reception afterwards... [*Zippers unzipping. Footsteps.*]

[*Long pause.*]

Mm-hmm. How did you like the movie, or the play I should say, the other day?

[*Silence. More footsteps.*]

JAMESON: I haven't seen this production, so I cannot say anyth... [*Chair scraping the floor.*] Have you seen, or do you have Adorno's...? [*Pause.*]

JAMESON: [*Addresses his Student Assistant.*] Do you have a copy of the Notes?[1]

STUDENT ASSISTANT: No, but there is a copy in the university library...

JAMESON: Not the printout but the actual book?

STUDENT ASSISTANT: Yes.

JAMESON: Do you have it with you?

STUDENT ASSISTANT: Ah no, I don't have it with me.

JAMESON: Hmm, okay then... [*Another student hands over a copy of* Notes to Literature.] Mm-hmm. Okay good, alright. [*Nods.*] I just want to pass this book around, so people know what's in this first part. [*Hands* Notes to Literature *to be passed around the class.*] Now, there are four or five volumes of these notes. He delivered them as radio, hmm... [*Hesitates*] as radio addresses which they used to do in the more cultured countries of Europe, and West Germany. Mm-hmm... [*Pause.*] It seems odd... [*Addresses a student who is looking at* Notes to Literature.] Just look at the table of contents to get an idea of all of the things he wrote about, and keep in mind that there is another volume, which hopefully we will have one of these days. One of those texts is of course the "Endgame" essay that you have just watched. I think probably the difficulty of the language is less apparent verbally, orally, and this maybe has to do with... [*Pause.*] For example, you know that the typewriter was invented in 1860s, or so I guess... [*Quietly*: and they say that Mark Twain apparently was the first writer to have used a typewriter] but the actual functioning typewriter, I think it came into the use in the 1880s. Mm-hmm. We're told by Heidegger, I think, that Nietzsche was the first philosopher to use a typewriter... [*Quietly*: now, picture Nietzsche with a typewriter (*Audience* *laughing*).] Henry James... [*Laughter continues.*] Henry James at that time, or a little later I guess, started to dictate... [*Chair scrapes the floor*] to a secretary, or a scribe or something, and at that point you have the emergence of his "late style," because as he dictated his writing got more complicated, and his sentences more convoluted, and they have been characterized by an increased ambiguity and complexity. [*Softly.*] You would think that it would be the other way around, and that the oral would be simpler than writing, but that's not necessarily true.

[*Longue pause.*]

Anyway, as I said, these essays in Notes to Literature are all short, probably one-hour radio talks, which are very interesting because they give us an idea about Adorno's reactions to various things. This one on Endgame I think is particularly significant for all kind of reasons, and we'll look at it... [*Quietly*: maybe on Tuesday... (*Page flipping. Looks at his notes*). Yes, it will fit into our program around that point.] Now, as I told you before, I will again be away this next Thursday, a week from today, and I'll show you something else. I think, hmm... [*Hesitates.*] I think that you should see... [*Pause.*] There is a name that is very significant here in the German context, you don't know much about him. Mm-hmm. His name is Frank... [*Chalk on the blackboard*] W-E-D-E-K-I-N-D, who was like Brecht. He would play songs and sing in public on his guitar, but he was mainly noted as being one of the great rebels against taboo and particularly sexual taboo. His plays were probably the most radical thing in the German theater of the naturalist period, before you get into all of the 1920s stuff, and the most famous of those plays are... [*Quietly*: a set of two, I don't know what you call that.] One is on a, hmm... [*Hesitates*] a sort of demonic woman figure called "Lulu." In German, the two plays are called... [*Cough in the audience*] I don't remember: Pandora's Box and Spring Awakening, or something like that.[2] [*Pause.*] Now, Pabst made one of the last silent films reducing these two plays by Wedekind to a single film.[3] It's a very famous film based on the Wedekind's play... [*Quietly*: I don't know if this is telling you very much, but it ends with

Jack the Ripper.] The film stars one of the most intriguing and legendary actresses in film... [*Cough in the audience*] at that time [*Deep coughing persists.*] What is her name... [*Raps his knuckles on the desk.*] I'm trying to remember, oh... [*Pause.*] Uh-huh, God, what was her name? She was very famous...

STUDENT: [*Softly.*] Louise Brooks?

JAMESON: Louise Brooks, yes. [*Looks around.*]

So, I think I will show you that movie next time and I hope that we have a decent copy because it will give you a little idea of some of these theatrical references in Adorno. And then if we have another occasion, we will also watch Alban Berg's last opera, hmm... [*Hesitates*] which was allegedly incomplete, but I think it's been sort of completed since.[4] It's an opera which — if Wedekind's play ends with Jack the Ripper — the opera ends with a chord of all twelve notes... [*Quietly*: which is the equivalent of the Malevich's Black Square, if you like.] Anyway, I think it would be interesting to look at that too.

[*Long pause.*]

Now, what I wanted to do... [*Pause.*] We're gonna talk a little bit about Freud today, and I also have a few extra things that I wanted to do with Kant. Then I want us to move on to what I call chapter two, that is the chapter called "Situation," which I think is probably, hmm... [*Hesitates*] in some way this is the most important chapter in Aesthetic Theory, or at least the [*Stressing*] central one in the early part of this book. The so-called "beauty chapters,"[5] I think they are less interesting, for various reasons... [*Quietly*: we'll touch on them later on.] But the "Situation" chapter could almost be printed on its own because I think that we are getting here many of Adorno's most important positions. So hopefully, if we don't have time today, we'll have time in the next few days to go over it.

[*Door creaks open.*]

Okay, now, hmm... [*Looks at his notes.*] Alright, now what I wanted to do, just to wrap up our Kant discussion from last time... [*Quietly*: you can never really be done with Kant but anyway.] I wanted to bring back again these two ideas of genius and of, hmm... [*Hesitates*] enthusiasm. What the remark on genius does is not establish a hierarchy, although that happens later on with this notion of genius, which undergoes all kinds of different variations, but with Kant it is meant to integrate the aesthetic into nature. The genius does not become a characteristic of the artist, but somehow a characteristics of the nature of the artist, and this is once again a way for Kant of solving some problems, or of making some problems — false problems — and also a time in the overall framework that we are not gonna have an occasion to look at, namely — natural teleology, the teleology of nature... [*Quietly*: as I said a moment ago, the matter of nature will come back in Adorno's chapters on beauty.] On the matter of enthusiasm, if you look at Lyotard's commentary... [*Pause.*] It's very interesting, this is a man whose formation... [*Quietly*: I presume some of you read something of Lyotard.] You should look at the so-called <u>différend</u>, and I wouldn't translate that either, just leave it as <u>différend,</u> I guess. This is a really interesting and important book,[6] which sets out the notion of what I would call "incommensurability." Under certain circumstances, the juridical <u>différend</u> refers to differences, or conflicts between parties, that cannot be resolved. They are incommensurable and they can only resolve in antagonisms and mutual destruction. It's a book that contains a lot of arguments about language and language games and so on that are quite interesting, a section on Gertrude Stein, which is quite astonishing for a French reference... [*Quietly*: he visited this country often and taught at many universities, San Diego, Irvine.[7]] There is also a running commentary on Kant, so if you don't have the stamina for the big commentary on the sublime, which is very, hmm... [*Hesitates*] let's say very serious and it's a really line-by-line matter, you might look at the four — I believe there are four, little inserts about Kant — those are distinguished from the body of the book... [*Quietly*: I think they are... (*Words indistinct*) internal digressions or something like that. He works a lot with these paragraphs by Kant, a number of paragraphs and then these various inserts.] At any rate, Lyotard was somebody who was I think by temperament a profoundly political character... [*Quietly*: hmm, he was in the Communist Party; he did his military service, you could do your military service in social work in France in those days; he was a teacher in Algeria, which at that time was still a French protectorate.] He was quite horrified by this situation... [*Softly*.] This was at the time of the first Vietnam War. The Communist Party was very bad on all of this as it continued to be during the Algerian revolution, and he broke with them; I don't know what they wanted to call him, a... [*Cough in the audience*] "Trotskyist" or something. He was part of the Socialisme ou Barbarie group and like all these people who are on the left but then essentially anti-Stalinist... [*Quietly*: not all of them but many of them, he finally ended up abandoning politics.] So, for him the question of enthusiasm is a very crucial one, as you can see. Kant had [*Stressing*] enthusiasm for the French Revolution. I mean, it's clear throughout Kant's work that for him the French Revolution was one of the great events in human history. For the next generation of Germans, they saw — Kant witnessed this but did not attack it — they saw the terror of it, and therefore... [*Quietly*: that is 1793-94 as opposed to early 1790s] hmm, and they tried to wriggle out of it. In other ways, Schiller's aesthetic education[8] is a kind of attempt to frame a notion of revolution which is not revolutionary or not based on terror, hmm, which passes through education and culture, and so forth and which is... [*Softly*] somehow very common for Germany. What Lyotard does with this... [*Quietly*: but Kant kept playing to a certain degree with the French Revolution.] I do think that Lyotard's reading is very ingenious and, hmm... [*Hesitates*] and very interesting, and maybe it's true, I don't know. So Lyotard says, look, if you read this closely, enthusiasm, it's no longer a religious term but it is revolutionary — for it is enthusiasm for other people's revolution.[9] [*Pause*.] It is a [*Stressing*] spectatorial enthusiasm. The people in the middle of the revolution are busy slaughtering away and executing people and so on, but from the outside, or "for us" as opposed to "for them," the revolution is a manifestation of human freedom. So, this is a very interesting notion that there is a politics of otherness involved here and that one should analyze some of these works in those terms. At any rate, I think this is a, hmm... [*Hesitates*] a very curious notion... [*Chair scrapes the floor.*] Mm-hmm... [*To himself*: no, that's something else.]

[*Long pause.*]

Okay, now I promised myself to say something about the eighteenth-century conception of the sublime. [*Pause.*] That is of course the French Revolution and that's what it meant for Burke. For Burke, the French Revolution was the manifestation of the sublime in the abruption of these mass-murdering events... [*Quietly*: abuses, killings in the streets, and so on and so forth.] In Burke's Reflections on the French Revolution,[10] you have these vivid descriptions of the royal family and of the angry mob, of the ferocious men and women of Paris screaming and yelling that seemed to be part of the hell... [*Words indistinct.*] But I think that one should also look for other examples. The ones that I wanted to illustrate for you are some of the great, hmm... [*Hesitates*] some of the great sculptural pieces in the Per... [*Pause*] in the Berlin Museum Island, which used to be in East Berlin, the Pergamon Altar, and that is the frieze which shows the struggle between the Giants and the Gods — that is to say, between the powers of the earth and the Olympians. These are only fragments, but that is enough for you to see that they are incredibly violent and ferocious. The fact that this is not an eighteenth-century work doesn't really matter because, as I said, Neoclassicism has a relationship to these ancient works [*Pause.*] There were some other things... [*Hesitates.*] The Metropolitan used to have some really magnificent heads, which were supposed to be Etruscan, but at some point they were discovered to be forgeries... [*Quietly*: so, they removed them, which was a pity because they were nonetheless an acknowledgment of the forgery, which is a little bit of recognition of the work.] Instead, I thought I would give you some examples from the work, which George Steiner[11] has once said, this is the greatest narrative form in the English language, [*Softly*] namely Pope's translation of Homer. [*Turns towards the blackboard.*] This is a volume that's illustrated by Flaxman's drawings,[12] and it should give you a little idea of the... [*Quietly:* I'll send this book around afterwards.] As calm and peaceful as Flaxman's drawings look... [*Cough in the audience*] you should understand that what's behind it is the ferocity of the Iliad. Goethe said that reading Iliad was like looking into hell. Hmm... [*Hesitates.*] If you remember the Iliad, it's not unlike — to use a contemporary reference — what goes on in the Gangs of New York.[13] I mean, this is really physical butchering of an incredibly bloody type, where these people are hacked to pieces, and half of the poem is this simply enormous repertoire... [*Absorbed*] hmm, inventory of all the physical horrors that are carried out in this form of virtually hand-to-hand warfare. [*Stomping feet.*] Now, hmm... [*Clears throat.*] So that already I think makes the connection between an eighteenth-century aesthetic and the sublime as something fearful and terrifying. But I thought I would illustrate this with Pope because that's a combination that we are not used to anymore of the very measure of kind of classicism... [*Quietly*: the equivalent to French would be Racine, really, I suppose, but as far as I know there is no real... (*Pause*). Even though Racine is earlier than Pope, so I don't think there is really an equivalent of this.]

[*Longue Pause.*]

So, I wanted to read you a few lines from Book Three of the Iliad, but in order to do that, hmm... [*Hesitates.*] I'll tell you just a little bit about this book, which is quite astonishing in itself, the first... [*Quietly*: well, I suppose it gets going in every book but I mean this is a very special one in which Achilles, as you recall, is sulking under his tent and not participating any longer in the battle.] So, the Greeks decide, they approach perilously, their boats on shore, to attack the Trojan army without him. Now... [*Page flipping.*] Well, let me first read you the opening which describes the two armies:[14]

Thus by their leader's care each martial band
Moves into ranks, and stretches o'er the land.
With shouts the Trojans rushing from afar,
Proclaim their motions, and provoke the war:

So when inclement winters vex the plain
With piercing frosts, or thick descending rain,
To warmer seas, the Cranes embodied fly,
With noise, and order, through the mid-way sky;
To pigmy nations wounds and death they bring,
And all the war descends upon the wing.
But silent, breathing rage, resolv'd and skill'd
By mutual aids to fix a doubtful field,
Swift march the Greeks: the rapid dust around
Darkening arises from the labor's ground.
Thus from his flaggy wings when Notus sheds
A night of vapors round the mountain-heads,
Swift-gliding mists the dusky fields invade,
To thieves more grateful than the midnight shade;
While scarce the swains their feeding flocks survey,
Lost and confus'd amidst the thicken'd day:
So wrapt in gathering dust, the Grecian train
A moving cloud, swept on, and hid the plain.[15]

So, you see how, in this opposition, you have the aerial numbers of the Trojans... [*Softly*] you know that in legend and myth there is a war between the Cranes and the Pigmies, hence that reference. So, this are not only the flight of birds, but birds who are dangerous and can bring death and reduce the sizes of their human adversaries. Well, the Greeks, on the other hand, are associated with the soil, this mist and tremendous dust that comes out of lakes, that's a different kind of force. I think from the very beginning... [*Pause.*] Well, let's see, hmm... [*Hesitates.*] Anyway, let's see what Chapman... [*Continues reading from Chapman's translation of* The Iliad]:

When every least commander's will best soldiers had obey'd,
And both the hosts were rang'd for fight, the Trojans would have
  fray'd
The Greeks with noises, crying out, in coming rudely on
At all parts, like the cranes that fill with harsh confusion

Of brutish clangés all the air, and in ridiculous war
(Eschewing the unsuffer'd storms shot from the winter's star)
Visit the ocean, and confer the pigmy soldiers death.
The Greeks charg'd silent, and, like men, bestow'd their thrifty breath
In strength of far-resounding blows, still entertaining care
Of either's rescue, when their strength did their engagements dare.
And as upon a hill's steep top, the south wind pours a cloud,
To shepherds thankless, but by thieves that love the night, allow'd,
A darkness letting down, that blinds a stone's cast off men's eyes,
Such darkness from the Greeks' swift feet (made all of dust) did rise.[16]

[*Long pause.*]

Hmm... [*Pause.*] And that's Chapman. How would we do it? Okay. Now... [*Reads from Richard Lattimore's translation of* The Iliad]:

Now when the men of both sides were set in order by their leaders,
the Trojans came on with clamor and shouting, like wildfowl,
as when the clamor or cranes goes high to the heavens
when the cranes escape the winter time and the rains unceasing
and clamorously wing their way to the streaming Ocean,
bringing to the Pygmaian men bloodshed and destruction: at daybreak they bring on the baleful battle against them. But the Acaian men went silently, breathing valor, stubbornly minded each in his heart to stand by the others.
As on the peaks of a mountain the south wind scatters the thick mist,
no friend to the shepherd, but better than night for the robber,
and a man can see before him only so far as a stone cast,
so beneath their feet the dust drove up in a stormcloud
of men marching, who made their way through the plain in great speed.
(Book III 1-7).[17]

Now, I think it's not yet clear... [*Pause*] in neither of these versions yet, how the oppositions have played out so far.[18] But you hear birds, the sky birds, cries and so forth — a multiplicity. The Greeks, as Homer points out, are:

> But silent, breathing rage, resolv'd and skill'ed,
> By mutual aids to fix a doubtful field,[19]

The Greeks have a different sort of relationship to all of this. If the Trojans are this multiplicity, the Greeks are a kind of unity — the unity of the dust clouds and so on. [*Walks towards the blackboard.*] Now, what's gonna happen is that, as these armies come together, hmm... [*Hesitates*] the hero or the villain steps out. This is Paris who takes off with Helen, who is in some legendary fashion the most beautiful, and also very elegant and eloquent as well, but feminine in some special way. And he dares the Greek army with these lances... [*Quietly*: I imagine it a little bit like the bullfighter in, hmm... [*Hesitates*] what are called those things? Like daring the bull, you know.] At that point, Menelaus leaps out, I won't read you all of this but... [*Page flipping.*] Menelaus is a... [*Starts reading*] "two pointed spears..." this is Paris:

> ...the panther's speckled hide
> Flowed o'er his armour with an easy pride,
> His bended bow across his shoulders flung,
> His sword beside him negligently hung;
> Two pointed spears he shook with gallant grace,
> And dared the bravest of the Grecian race.
> And thus, with glorious air and proud disdain,
> He boldly stalked, the foremost on the plain,
> Him Menelaus... [*Whispers*: now this is the husband]
> Him Menelaus loved of Mars, espies,
> With heart elated, and with joyful eyes:
> So joyous a lion, the branching deer,
> Or mountain goat, his bulky prize, appear;

Eager he seizes and devours the slain,
Pressed by bold youths and baying dogs in vain.[20]

Hmm, and this is obviously a very frightening operation, right? Well, while Paris disappears, goes and hides, hmm... [*Hesitates*] Hector, his cousin, rebukes him, he comes out again, and this is to be a hand-to-hand fight... [*Pause.*] Menelaus, the Spartan king, knocks him down, I believe, and at that point his protectors... [*Quietly*: because they go out... (*Words indistinct*)] Aphrodite wraps him in a cloud and whisks him away to Helen's bedchamber. And so, as this battle continues, there is no longer individual duels but collective slaughters that I evoked and which happen as... [*Words indistinct.*]

[*Long pause.*]

So, what's going on in here, I think, is very precisely suited for our purpose of beauty, and the sublime.

[*Long pause.*]

Hmm... [*Hesitates.*] You have... [*Pause.*] And this reflects, I think, a... [*Quietly*: I don't think you should necessarily think of this in terms of racism, but this is certainly having to do with the Other.] All relations with other collectivities are in some sense racist, or they involve some kind of distorted vision or caricature. Because you see, there isn't any such thing as collectivity, so you have to make it up, and it has to be an image of some kind and that image becomes something like a scornful image, or it involves turning it into an enemy. It's one of the two, or it can be both. And obviously, The Iliad is the Greeks' version of the story. So, for them, the Trojans are Orientals, and the Orientals, back in later times, the Persians of course are different: they are fond of external trappings; they like to wear their leopard skin on the shoulders as it is here, they like rich apparel, curved bows, and swords... [*Achoo. Sneeze in the audience.*] And this is the sense in which I'm using the word "effeminate" in the classical sense, as you find it in Foucault, that is, they represent pleasure and ostentation and luxury and all of those things. The Greeks, in the meantime, represent, hmm... [*Hesitates*] modesty, self-control, and abstinence, which are the well-known stereotypes... [*Quietly*: as we know them form the whole conflict between West and East.] Well, so you see how this dualism of beauty and sublime is at work here in what we may call the clash of cultures or civilizations. This is very much, hmm... [*Hesitates*] not the West in our current sense but a masculine culture versus a feminine culture, and obviously, as in any dualism, the gender associations come first, and they always have to inevitably be a strong component in this opposition. So, with Paris we may associate the concept of physical beauty, sexuality or love and whatever... [*Pause*] whereas Menelaus is the sublime, he is fear, bloodshed, and so forth.

[*Long pause.*]

At any rate, it seems to me that it's only through these dualisms that the Greek tragedies have been perceived by the neoclassicists later on. None of the Greeks tragedies are ... [*Searches for words*] are just calm and serene works of beauty, but they all have some violence at their heart, or beauty combined with violence. Violence is always [*Stressing*] <u>underlying</u> classical beauty. This, it seems to me, is working its way through the eighteenth century, from this first opposition, and as I said, from the 1680s when the first Quarrel between the Ancients and the Moderns takes place over the, hmm... [*Hesitates*] which was this dispute over the nature of classicism, all the way up to Kant's final formulations. And as far as Pope is concerned, he was also caught in the English side of this Quarrel, as a strong proponent of the aesthetics of the Ancients... [*Words indistinct*] "An Essay on Criticism," which was his famous contribution to the debate between the Ancients and the Moderns.[21] I'll pass this book around. I've marked some of these places, but take a closer look at Flaxman's illustrations, which will give you an idea of how classicism works. As I said, this is a classicism of the line, and with Romanticism, which becomes part of the Quarrel, new aesthetic sensibilities start to appear and that is when in place of the line we have materiality and color.[22]

[*Students are passing around Homer's* <u>Iliad</u> *and* <u>Odyssey</u>, *illustrated by John Flaxman.*]

So, this is a very odd and new kind of relationship to the body. In Burke, as you know, beauty is what we associate with the pleasures of life, with happiness and friendship, and with those qualities that cause love. And the sublime in Burke is something totally different — it is astonishment and horror; it is terror and something that could go all the way to extreme religious experience. But with Kant the sublime is the product of the mind confronting its own limits; in Kant, the sublime is something more than the spiritual because it refers to something that overwhelms and transcends reason. And then the question is: what is the sublime good for...? [*Quietly*: Because, as you recall with Kant, we always have to ask the question of purpose, insisting that beauty or art is this... (*Words indistinct*) purposefulness without purpose.] Well, he says, the sublime is a way of relating to ideas, it's a relationship to ideas with a capital "I." Kant somehow suggests that there may be non-metaphysical people who are not stirred by great concepts found beyond their immediate senses. Anybody can react to beauty. This is a universal reaction... [*Quietly*: and what he doesn't say, I think, is that beauty can also slip very easily into these forms of physicality or physical pleasure, which Kant wishes to preserve true beauty from.] But with the sublime, only people who have a sense of freedom, only those who think of their soul, only those concerned by transcendental ideas, hmm... [*Hesitates*] those who are sensitive to them, or vice versa — it is only those people who have this sense of the sublime; only they can feel these... [*Cough in the audience*] higher forms of relationship as something greater than individual objects. Only those people can be sensitive to these ideas with a capital "I." And... [*Quietly*: I can't say that in the Platonic sense, but in the metaphysical sense, I think that this is also a very interesting reflection on Kant's part... (*Mumbles indistinctly*).]

[*Long pause.*]

Okay, so, maybe now we can move to... [*Chair scratches the floor.*] Mm-hmm. Are there any thoughts on all of this?

[*Long pause.*]

The Iliad of Homer Engraved from the Compositions of John Flaxman, R.A., Sculptor, book, John Flaxman, William Blake, Tommaso Piroli, James Parker (MET, 1970.565.63). Public Domain. Wikimedia commons.

Kant's thoughts come back from time to time, and in a way this initial gesture of cutting beauty or art off from any practical purpose is a crucial foundation for aesthetics as an autonomous discipline. It doesn't matter that later on — on the basis of that initial autonomy — people would claim that art is not really autonomous. But somehow this is the first drawing of a line around this area in some sense. And so, in that sense, Kant is inaugural and foundational: his Critique separates this, hmm... [*Hesitates*] discipline, or experience, or whatever you like to call it, from others. Then later on, you might want to connect it back up to the others, but you won't do that because it's missing this initial separation... [*Mumbles indistinctly.*]

STUDENT: [*Words indistinct. Far away from the microphone a student is asking a question about Lessing.*]

JAMESON: Yeah, I don't know. I'm not sure if there is an immediate discussion here about Lessing... [*Words indistinct.*] Let me research it and we will talk about it again. Are there other questions? [*Page flipping. Talks to himself while looking at his notes.*]

[*Long Silence.*]

As you saw in this first so-called "chapter" of Aesthetic Theory, Adorno engages with two major theories of art, and that is Kant, which we discussed last time, and also Freud. He plays them against each other in some dialectical way, suggesting that they are opposed, yet somehow... [*Chair-back creaks.*] So now I would like us to have a discussion about Freud. [*Pause.*] How many of you have had a chance to read Freud's short piece called "Writers and Daydreamers," or "Creative Writers and Phantasy," or something like that?

[*Long Silence.*]

JAMESON: Nobody. Mm-hmm. Okay. Well, look, this is an article he first published in a newspaper; it is not too long, so you can read it, but let's have our first presentation in this seminar. [*Addresses student.*] Do you want to step up here in front of the class? [*Chair scrapes hard against the floor. Footsteps.*]

Student Presentation: Freud, "Creative Writers and Daydreaming"[23]

STUDENT ONE: Mm-hmm. Okay. [*Page flipping. Starts reading.*] By Freud's own admission, this short 1908 essay on the relation between creative writers and daydreaming tells you much more about daydreaming than creative writing. Creative production is primarily understood as a special case of phantasy creation common to all adults, as what precisely accounts for the specific qualities of the special case... [*Chair scratches the floor.*] Freud is looking clearly to some suggestive preliminary remarks, and we can supplement them with other moments in Freud's writing. [*Pause.*] But we will ultimately leave unformed the properly psychoanalytic — as distinct from the psychological — understanding of the creation and reception of aesthetic productions.

[*Long pause.*]

Freud begins by saying that, if we wish to understand how a poet achieves his art, we will never get a satisfactory answer from the poet, but we must look to analogies for creative activities in ourselves, the laymen. [*Page flipping.*] Imaginative activity begins with a child at play. As anyone familiar with Freud will know, this analogy between a child at play and the artist in no way suggests that the artist's work is in any way childish — that is, frivolous or light. On the contrary, the child takes play very seriously. As Freud says... [*Quietly*: I quote] "the opposite of play is not serious occupation but — reality."[24] [*Pause.*] The child at play rearranges the things in his world and orders them in a new way that pleases him better. The child uses the visible, tangible elements of reality and restructures them towards the fulfillment of his long wish, which is that of being an adult. The adult phantasy or daydreaming is seen as a substitution for, and continuation of, childhood play. [*Pause.*] What distinguishes it from the childhood play is that it is no longer a... [*Cough in the audience*] reality. The adult's play as a child was conducted with a seriousness and intensity that the would-be seriousness of his everyday life does not match up to; this... [*Words indistinct*] is the genesis for the necessary but socially unacceptable creation of day-dreams. The adult must give up real objects and create what Freud calls "castles in the air."[25] The adult then can see if his day-dreams are childish because it can no longer play at being an adult. [*Page flipping.*] Freud says that it is likely, from time to time, everyone has phantasies, but he also says that half of the people never make phantasies because phantasies presume being unsatisfied. Since phantasies are generally concealed because they are necessarily shameful, we are aware of the main truth of the neurotic, whose raison d'être is the need to confess them. Presumably, when the neurotic confesses, the normal or healthy individual keeps the occasional phantasies to himself, whereas the creative artist sublimates them, or he gets the best out of them. Freud raises phantasies into two primary categories: ambitious or egotistic phantasies and erotic phantasies. He claims that the former are primarily male and the latter female, but then he goes on to claim that these two features tend to be denied more often than not. Another quality of phantasy stressed by Freud is its distinctive temporality... [*Door creaks open. Footsteps*] ...to that that arouses desire is linked back to infancy when the wish was fulfilled and towards the future representing the fulfillment of the wish. [*Quietly*: and this is Freud.] "So past, present, and future are threaded, as it were, on the string of the wish that runs through them all."[26] He suggests that the motivation of the work of the creative writer holds the same pattern. [*Pause.*] Freud then briefly links phantasies to dreams and claims that the difference is that the former are more transparent and don't require the level of dreamwork needed to disguise their mechanisms. He doesn't state this explicitly, but it seems that, since phantasies are more naïve and less connected to the more painful, repressed unconscious elements of the psyche, they are more ego-oriented than dreams. This fact will have significance when we see the type of creative work Freud choses to demonstrate the analogy between the day-dream and the [*Words indistinct*]... at work, that is the popular novel.

[*Long pause.*]

According to Freud, popular novels all have a hero who is the center of attention for whom the author chose to win our sympathy by every possible means and whom he places under the protection of a special providence. This inv.... [*Pause.*] Hmm... [*Hesitates.*] This invulnerability of the protagonist betrays his majesty the Ego, hero of all daydreams and novels. Freud's analogy is a variation on this theme in novels as, for example, when the Ego is no longer the hero, but is split up into component Egos, or is relegated to the role of spectator. Freud then briefly mentions adaptive writers who, instead of inventing their own stories, reimagined shared social histories. Freud claims that we all are now attached to groups, the structure of phantasy remains here, and suggests that myths are distorted vestiges of the wish-phantasies of whole nations. [*Page flipping.*] I think that, in this parallel between the creative work and phantasy, what is left to be understood is the question of form. Freud is very aware that the analogy between the day-dream and the work of the imagination can only go so far and that there are fundamental differences. [*Quietly*: and this is Freud.] "We have not touched on the other problem at all, i.e. what are the means which writers use to achieve those emotional reactions in us that are roused by their productions."[27] [*Pause.*] Freud finds out that the transcript of a neurotic's phantasy — well, it might in many ways have a similar narrative logic to the popular novel — is missing something crucial found in the latter. That something is pleasure. [*Quietly*: and this is Freud.] "... the day-dreamer hid his phantasies carefully from other people because he had reasons to be ashamed of them..." and "... even if he were to communicate them to us, he would give us no pleasure..."[28] [*Pause.*] In fact, we are naturally repulsed by other people's day-dreams. So, the art of the imaginative writer becomes the attempt to overcome... [*Thud. Backpack falls on the floor*] this repulsion. He does this by two methods. The first method is the writer softens the egotistical character by changes and disguises, and the second is that he rides us by a purely formal — that is, aesthetic — pleasure in the presentation of his phantasies. This is the most interesting yet all too brief moment in Freud's essay. [*Pause.*] The crude... [*Words indistinct*] ... which to the author appears in a way of a dreamwork through displacement, through the unacceptable, and that is formalized through a process of condensation to become pleasurable. But the tricky part is that this formal or aesthetic pleasure is only a small amount of the pleasure that the creative work yields. Instead, it is still the wish-fulfillment aspect, the experience of our daydreams preci... [*Clears throat*] precisely what is repulsive to us in its raw immediate form that is the source of deeper pleasures. Yet again, this deeper pleasure is only possible by the bribe of aesthetic rendering which he calls "fore-pleasure."

[*Long pause.*]

The most immediate question that seems left open is what is the relation between fore-pleasure and the phantasy. Presumably, they are both necessary for the creative production, and yet they function across purposes. Freud's primary example is the popular novel precisely because it demonstrates necessarily the egotistic or erotic wish-fulfillment that Freud sees as the necessary elements of the artwork. Nonetheless, we might consider the way popular novels are often considered by the educated middle classes, for example, as shamely... [*Self-correcting*] as shameful for precisely this reason, as the fore-pleasure is minimal in relation to the relatively transparent wish. Therefore, we may wonder how much fore-pleasure we need as access to the psychic pleasure of wish fulfillment. Too much would presumably lose sight of the egotistic pleasure, which is the basis of our pleasure of the creative work; yet too little would fail to disguise the shameful wish and inspire revulsion for a milder case for them. Is it merely an economic question of the appropriate balance?

[*Long pause.*]

The question of fore-pleasure gets more thorough but still speculative treatment in "Jokes and their Relation to the Unconscious." The term emerges in the context of Freud's explanation of what he calls "tendentious jokes," often racist, sexist, obscene or cruel. And this is Freud [*Page flipping. Reads from Freud's* Jokes and their Relation to the Unconscious.] "A possibility of generating pleasure supervenes in a situation in which another possibility of pleasure is obstructed so that, as far as the latter alone is concerned, no pleasure would arise. The result is a generation of pleasure far greater than that offered by the supervening possibility. This has acted, as it were, as an incentive bonus with the assistance of the offer of a small amount of pleasure, a much greater one, which would otherwise have been hard to achieve, has been gained."[29] Freud continues, hmm... [*Hesitates*] "I have good reason to suspect that this principle corresponds with an arrangement that holds good in many widely separated departments of mental life."[30]

[*Long pause.*]

Here we have a clear texture of the fore-pleasure principle, as the aid or incentive bonus that is used to bribe reason, critical judgment, and suppression to release the true pleasures found in the relinquishing of an ambition. [*Pause.*] Fore-pleasure gets its most sustained treatment in "Three Essays on Sexuality."[31] Here it is contrasted with "end-pleasure." Fore-pleasure is associated with the excitement of the erotogenic zones and the creation of sexual tension, whereas end-pleasure as sexual discharge is associated with the release of tension... [*Zipper unzipping.*] It is fore-pleasure that is here related to the infantile sexuality. This is seen as a danger of fore-pleasure, which can develop into perversion if the fore-pleasure is too great in comparison with the tension that needs to be released. There seems to be something of a reversal here. In all cases, fore-pleasure functions as a kind of bribe for the eventual release of tension. On the other hand, the positions are reversed when it comes to deeper psychical pleasures and social acceptability. When fore-pleasure is associated with aesthetic pleasure or humor, it is the more socially acceptable aspect of the pleasure received from the artwork or joke that allows us to have access to diverse psychical and potentially more shameful infantile pleasures.

[*Pause.*] But in "Three Essays on Sexuality," the end-pleasure is seen as the necessary mature completion of the sexual process, whereas the fore-pleasure is associated with infantile desires. Whereas perverse sexuality, we are told, focuses on fore-pleasure in the form of, for example, "the fetish," presumably the perverse experience in part would focus less on the aesthetic aspect, the bribe of fore-pleasure, and more on the aspects that are not assimilated and made acceptable by the aesthetic function of work. Hence, for example, the more perverse pleasure derived from reading someone's diary found in the street or perhaps from some reality television. [*Pause.*] This reversal is due to a lack of explanation of how fore-pleasure with a sexual end is translated into the non-explicitly sexual pleasure of creative production or experience of jokes or poetry. The term for this translation is "sublimation," a term which is notably absent from both "Creative Writers and Daydreaming" and "Jokes and their Relation to the Unconscious." In "Introductory Lectures on Psychoanalysis,"[32] Freud suggests that the artist's constitution probably includes a strong capacity for sublimation, and a certain degree of lacks in the repression, which will be decisive for the conflict. According to Jean Laplanche and Jean-Bertrand Pontalis, the lack of a coherent theory of sublimation remains one of the lacunae of the psychoanalytic thought.[33] For Cornelius Castoriadis, sublimation is precisely the area where Freud thought to go beyond psychic eminence and find a way of theorizing the psyche's relation to objects and temporality that have no meaning on that plane. According to Castoriadis, what Freud's thought was trying to grasp when he wrote on sublimation was the process by which the psyche opens itself up to the social and historical world.[34]

[*Page flipping.*]

According to Freud, the sexual instinct places extraordinarily large amounts of force at the disposal of civilized activity, and it does this in virtue of the especially marked characteristics of being able to displace aim without diminishing its intensity. This capacity... [*Clears throat.*] This capacity to exchange its originally sexual aim for another one, which is no longer sexual, or which is psychically related to the first aim, opens the capacity for sublimation. Or, in another context, Freud says, "we call this process 'sublimation,' in accordance with the general estimate that places social aims higher than sexual ones, which are at bottom self-interested."[35] Sublimation is consistent with the principle of fore-pleasure in "Three Essays on Sexuality," and it attempts to be associated with component instincts or partial drives that are not sufficiently integrated and therefore associated with perversion. [*Quietly:* and this is Freud.] "The forces that can be employed for cultural activities are thus to a great extent obtained through the suppression of what are known as the perverse elements of sexual excitation."[36] In this way, we can see aesthetic fore-pleasure as the sublimated manifestation of excessive attachment to sexual fore-pleasure. [*Cough in the audience.*] Yet, if we agree with Adorno, the question of the artwork might be an area that reveals the inadequacy of the theories of sublimation. As he states in Minima Moralia, "in renouncing the goal of instinct, [artists] remain faithful to it, and unmask the socially desirable activity naively glorified by Freud as sublimation — which probably does not exist."[37] For Adorno, psychoanalysis has an advantage over the anthropological theory of art, in that it does not rely on aesthetic notions of human nature but has an advantage of an idealess theory of art, in that it doesn't imagine that art is Absolute Spirit. Bu... [*Pause.*] But he claims that, by making art wish-fulfillment, and asserting its intrinsic relation to interest or pleasure, Freud's theory of art is too instrumental. In Freud, the artwork, like the phantasy, is always tied to some form of psychic dissatisfaction; sublimation becomes an instrumental psychic mechanism to overcome that dissatisfaction or to put it to work. What's more, we can then measure the success of the artwork based on its activity of overcoming that dissatisfaction, which, in Freud's weakest moment on the subject, seems directly tied to the highly conventional social success desired by the suffering male individual. As Freud states in the "Introductory Lectures on Psychoanalysis": the artist "...achieves through his phantasy what he had originally achieved only in his phantasy: honor, power and the love of women."[38] As Adorno will suggest, legitimate works of art today are without exception socially undesired. For Adorno, Kant provides a counterpoint to Freud by attempting to wrest art from interest, but Kant made the separation of art from the empirical static. Adorno suggests that, in Freud, we find a more dynamic relation, but what is so objectionable about the theory of sublimation in Freud is that Freud makes the negativity of experience nearly a means for affirmation. As Adorno says, artworks should, in themselves, imply relation between interest and its renunciation.

[*Deep breath. Long pause.*]

If we agree with Adorno that Freudian sublimation is inadequate to understanding the artwork, do we need to junk the concept entirely? If it is not adequate to the artwork, could it still be adequate to the popular novel? We might ask instead whether or not sublimation is only a particular and ultimately limited way for the psyche to go beyond itself. That is, if sublimation with fore-pleasure is about an economic way of managing the potentially perverse component drives to affirm the ego and has its example in any given work of popular genre fiction. Might we need a different psychoanalytic term to explain the writing of Endgame or the Flowers of Evil? Or, on the other hand, is the problem nearly with the terms "affirmative" and "ideological character" and could we use Adorno's Aesthetic Theory as an attempt to ground a more dialectical and historical contingent theory of negative sublimation?

[*Long pause.*]

STUDENT ONE: I'm done.

[*Audience applauding.*]

JAMESON: This is very good. [*Chair scrapes the floor.*] Hmm... [*Hesitates.*] Questions? [*Addresses Student One.*] Why don't you wait a bit longer here to see if there are questions or comments.

STUDENT ONE: [*Quietly*: I suppose I can.]

JAMESON: Or objections? Mm-hmm... [*Quietly*: have I told you the story of a colleague of mine who gave a political talk and somebody in the rear said, "I'm sorry I had to miss the talk, but I have the following objections..." (*Laughter. Words indistinct*). You know what people's positions are... (*Laughter continues*).]

[*Long silence.*]

Okay. [*Firmly.*] Well look, I mean I think this is, hmm... [*Hesitates.*] I'm not sure that Adorno solves this, but it all turns out to be about desire, and one could almost call it the "antinomy of desire" that enters the discussion of the work of art. [*Pause.*] Kant and Freud are, [*Looks at Student One*] as you said, the two opposing figures of this antinomy, and it cannot be solved. And I think that, finally, almost everything in Adorno's version of the aesthetic involves in some sense an antinomy that can't be solved; and if you pose aesthetic as an antinomy and insist that the truth lies on both sides — is that dialectical? [*Pause.*] I mean, hmm... [*Hesitates.*] But that's another question... [*Quietly*: we'll have to leave that aside for a moment.] So, when Kant says... [*Exhales deeply.*] For Kant, aesthetics becomes paradoxically a "desire without desire," a sort of "castrated hedonism" as Adorno calls it one place. And in both he has the notion of the "universal," that is, this is something that has to be addressed by all people, and therefore the work of art in Kant makes this universal claim, or rather you in your reaction to it make a universal claim for it. It should be, hmm... [*Hesitates.*] Everyone should acknowledge this object as beautiful, even though you know that this is not gonna happen, it's not possible and so forth, but I think it contains this universal appeal.

[*Long pause.*]

In Freud, those marvelous passages that you've read are exactly that — we are repulsed by other people's wish-fulfillments. [*Pause.*] But the work of art wants naturally to be as universal as possible, so the wish-fulfillments have to be... [*Quietly:* disguised and hidden away.] The "bonus of pleasure" is another expression that he uses for aesthetic pleasure, I believe... [*Quietly*: but maybe that's... (*Mumbles indistinctly*).] And I thought that your discussion of the fore-pleasure, and the aesthetic side of this where you have the [*Stressing*] disguising part in the creative process... [*Quietly*: oh, it's not me who has these weird phantasies but various characters, each one has a different phantasy, you see... (*Words indistinct*). This is not a personal matter with me, these are not my private thoughts but of these characters that I invented... (*Chuckles*).] But the bonus of pleasure, the fore-pleasure, is apparently a more formal one. Well, for example, there is also this funny word used in the dreams, which has since had all kinds of other affects and uses, and which is translated as "over-determination." Over-determination in the analysis of "The Interpretation of Dreams" is this process of connecting everything with everything else, as the dream is [*Stressing*] over-determined by multiple fears, unconscious desires, repressed memories. Hmm, so... [*Hesitates*.] So, the result in dream analysis is that you can really free-associate from any moment of the dream, you can take anything and eventually it will lead you back to the unconscious wish... [*Quietly*: this is obviously the case of the dreamwork... (*Mumbles indistinctly*).] But it's because, in what he calls — in another translation "over-determination" is called "secondary elaboration" — you have the primary crystallization of the dream, and then the unconscious or something goes to work on that and starts to make connections like crazy. [*Pause*.] And that's what Freud thinks of as the work of art. So, there you've got another one of these oppositions, right? I mean, you have another dualism in which we have the very crude personal egotistical wish-fulfillment and the more purely [*Stressing*] formal aesthetic or cultural process. And I think that you are quite right to talk about mass culture and all that popular stuff, because all those bestsellers and romances and those correspondences are obviously exclusively about wish-fulfillments in the most obvious kind of way... [*Clears throat*.]

[*Long pause*.]

Mm-hmm, but with sublimation, hmm... [*Hesitates*.] I also think that Lacan has a lot of problems with the notion of sublimation, because it is the moment of moving from body to mind, so to speak. I mean, it's also Freud's explanation of the professions. In the eighteenth century, with the Enlightenment — and you want to think of this also when you think about Kant and the notion of "genius," because now the great slogan is: la carrière ouverte aux talents.[39] [*Pause.*] In the eighteenth century, suddenly, hmm... [*Hesitates*] not only the middle classes approach political power, but suddenly the professions come into being... [*Cough in the audience*] and the métiers are secularized. So, you don't have to be a blacksmith like your father, you can go on to become... [*Softly*] a minister of state, or something else... [*Quietly*: like Napoleon, I mean, at twenty-five you can become a general and conquer of all of Europe.] Now. So, hmm... [*Hesitates.*] So, the secularization of professions means that, unlike in the feudal system, where being a noble wasn't regarded as a profession at all... [*Quietly*: except they also got their trainings on how to ride, how to be a noble, with private tutors at home where they were taught literature, history, religion, languages, in order to prepare them for their special social status... (*Mumbles indistinctly*).] Now, suddenly, there is a moment of freedom... [*Metal screeching. Tries to open the window*] where somehow you gotta figure out what's your relationship to all these various social activities, and then we are also told that we are all endowed with some special talents and aptitudes and are to be attracted to one or the other of these occupations. Well, in Freud, that's sublimation. [*Pause.*] Because, hmm... [*Hesitates.*] For example, science — they have the passion to know everything... [*Quietly*: which he argues has its origins in infantile looking, in wishing to stare at the woman's body, or the female parts, of voyeurism, or there is the crazy story of the boy who cut up animals and became a surgeon.] So, the voyeurism and the cruelty of the infant, which is part of the infantile sexuality, has now been transfigured into unveiling of the secrets of nature... [*Quietly*: which is a voyeurism on a superior and more serious level of science (*Chuckles*).] Well, you can see then how Castoriadis, as Nico has described in his presentation, is quite right in stating that this is Freud's attempt to throw a bridge to collective and social reality, but it's not clear... [*Quietly*: hmm, I think it's likely to go right to the famous Freudian idea, in that sense that you have to renounce the immediacy of pleasure or sense-pleasure, and I think you are quite right to underscore ambition. Freud was tremendously ambitious, and he understood that this relationship of the renunciation of pleasure and body and work and the passions of the mind are somehow connected.] But then, we are back in Kant, aren't we? Because the renunciation of the body, that's disinterested pleasure, hmm... [*Hesitates*] for as long as we exist, there is always interest of a physical kind. So, there is a great difficulty in trying to integrate desire or integrating pleasure in any theory of the aesthetic, and that's very odd because most of us think that this is what it is all about somehow. Mm-hmm... [*Hesitates*.] So, so this impossibility to account for desire is sort of built into this opposition of Freud and Kant.

[*Long pause*.]

Now... [*Raps his knuckles on the desk*] there is also a... [*Pause*.] There is another thing that arrives later on that I don't think is directly related to Freud, or it is older than all of this, older than the psychoanalytic... [*Cough in the audience*] explanation I would say, and that's what you could call, on the one hand, "imaginary satisfaction," or "imaginary gratification," and on the other hand, the "resolution of a contradiction," and there is a way in which these two are the same. Mm-hmm. In... [*Pounds the desk*.] Here is someone worth looking at in a lot of ways, and whose name is... [*Chalk on the blackboard*] E-R-I-K-S-O-N... [*Quietly*: I think this wasn't his real name but a pseudonym.] Erik Erikson is rather primary, and maybe not always as interesting as other forms of psychoanalysis, but he was best known for the psychosocial theories and the so-called eight psychosocial stages of an individual's personality.[40] In his books, and I'm thinking especially of <u>Young Man Luther</u>, he offers a kind of basic explanation of the relationship of Protestantism and history and society, and one other book called <u>Childhood and</u>

Society includes some case studies: Hitler, Gorky... [*Quietly*: is someone else there?][41] What Erikson said was that, at the heart of these people's personalities, there is always... [*Quietly*: and this is of course at the heart of most depressed people, including Freud himself or Dostoevsky] there is of course the Oedipus complex. I mean, here is the decisive wound that they have to traverse. But you know, that's somehow a very different thing than talking about wish fulfillments. Obviously, if you can resolve the Oedipus complex somehow, that would satisfy your wish, hmm... [*Hesitates*] and not bother you anymore, right? I mean, maybe these two things... [*Quietly*: wish fulfillment and Oedipus complex] maybe these are older versions of something similar, because if you put it in terms of a conflict, or even contradiction, then it would look very different. So, The Brothers Karamazov is classically the resolution of this Oedipus complex... [*Quietly*: that's where the whole point turns around the ignoble father, the humiliating father, and so on and so forth.] Now, what Erikson says is, look, certain of these things, and of course he attaches Luther's crisis here... [*Quietly*: you know that in Luther's case, mm-hmm, (*Hesitates*)... he was crossing a field and there was a great bolt of lightning that struck a tree, and as a result of this, a revelation of the sublime no doubt followed, leading to this powerful conversion which resulted in one of the basic experiences of the Protestants in this period, as opposed to the whole Catholic institution; and this Protestant experience is fueled by personal anxiety, guilt, terror and so on and so forth.] Well, Erikson says what you have here are resolutions of contradictions that are built into the historical family structure at any given period, and therefore someone — whether it's Hitler, Luther, or whoever — someone who resolves this contradiction of family structure in some very dramatic or original way, will suddenly have the power of attraction for a lot of other people, because this will then serve as a kind of daydreaming resolution of their own personal contradictions. In Sartre, there is the... [*Clears throat*] the fact of the work of art, which itself is included in this kind of resolution, but for him these things are always misunderstandings — that is, these are moments in which the whole activity is mesmerized by a personality or by a work; they are always, in some sense, collective mirages and misunderstandings because — and then one can go back here to Lacan or whatever — because the desire, the contradiction [*Stressing*] can't be resolved, and the desire [*Stressing*] can't be fulfilled. So, evidently, there is here some sort of cultural mirage, some notion that the work of art offers the satisfaction of this deeper malaise or conflict... [*Quietly:* and that's a structural one rather than personal.]

[*Long pause.*]

But this is another form of what Lévi-Strauss developed in his cultural criticism, where there is a fair amount of dialectical thinking on how structures of thought and behavior affect human societies... [*Door creaks open.*] It's odd not to find it so much in Adorno, and I think that's because, as we'll see later on, he wants to move aesthetics towards the objective, towards the work itself and away from the subjective, away from the human experience. As we'll see later on, Adorno wants to insist on the [*Stressing*] objectivity of the subjective. In other words, what we've been calling "subjective" is always historical and objective. But with Freud, or at least the way we interpret Freudianism for art criticism, and also with later generations of people like Erikson, this tends to be simply about going back to the life story... [*Quietly*: what happened to this writer as a child, what was the family structure and the missing father or the mother who died giving birth, and how all of this registers in the work of art.] But I don't imagine that many people are too attentive to that, even though, on the other hand, that battle led by Freud has been won in mainstream criticism, but also in most of academic criticism. [*Pause.*] We live in a period when we have again these great biographies, some of them four or five hundred pages long, which don't feel the necessity for that taboo on the biographical detail anymore. I would say that we almost have to protest or repress biographical criticism in the same way that they did it in the early twentieth century,[42] but we're not likely to do it... [*Chair-back creaks.*] The titles of these biographies are often like The Life and Loves of So-and-So... [*Quietly*: let's say of Goethe or Rilke or whoever... (*Chuckles*) and you'd go to find detailed anecdotal evidence about their personal lives... (*Words indistinct*) lovers and so on, and all these things correspond to various periods of criticism... (*Mumbles indistinctly*).] I don't think anybody is tempted by that kind of criticism anymore, and therefore you can look at the life as a text along with all the others. I mean, it is similarly embedded, and although things could be said in parallel, and you could look at them as all parts of a single corpus if you like. And I think this narrativization of the life story or explanation of all works of art in terms of personal stories, of mom and dad, and of the traumas of the bourgeois family, this really has been one of the basic fears that people had with this orthodox Freudianism and its impact on art and criticism. But on the other hand, I also think that Freud is much more subtle about this, and there is a good deal more to be said.

[*Long pause.*]

Mm-hmm, now, in Adorno what you get at the end of this chapter... [*Quietly*: the section called "The Art Theories of Kant and Freud"] is the mistake that, hmm... [*Hesitates*] or at least this is how I read that. The mistake is this. Both of these people, Kant and Freud, who lived a hundred years apart from each other, they assumed that desire can be satisfied. [*Pause.*] And so, Kant wishes [*Stressing*] not to get desire involved in the judgment of taste because we don't want satisfaction, because we don't want the work of art to be stirred up by everyday practical interests. In Freud, on the other hand, the satisfaction becomes sublimated into an imaginary and symbolic form, and so on and so forth. But what if — and here Adorno and Lacan have some very distant echoes of each other — what if desire can never be satisfied? [*Pounds his fist on the desk.*] It is implicit in Freudianism, this whole notion of the maturation process, this idea that the human animal is seething with these instinctive and sexual aggressive drives, and that the drive is directed towards a specific object or aim that will satisfy the desire, which it does so from the early childhood. But then there are other interpretations of the drive, when obviously the drives have no, hmm... [*Hesitates*] as if they are not... [*Pause*] they don't have a figure; they're not expressed in anything and therefore they're simply... [*Pause.*] I guess this is what the Lacanians call the "drive" rather than desire... [*Quietly*: because, in Lacan, the drive is a force that is not directed towards an object or thing, it's just there doing the repetitive and circular movements and it kind of folds over into instincts in the natural world, and therefore it has no relationship to an object anymore, so you can't satisfy it in that sense.] Okay, but then Adorno does something very interesting, I think, which puts him closer... [*Shuffling papers*] to Lacan. He brings a reference to Stendhal, hmm... [*Quietly*: Stendhal, who hated France anyway... (*Chuckles*), and who participated in the Napoleonic wars, witnessed the burning of Moscow, and later ended up in Italy as a counsel. He wrote non-fiction, travel books, and even a book on Italian painting...[43] (*Mumbles indistinctly*).] So, Stendhal had a very interesting expression for the mixture of the pleasures of painting and other forms of desire. This is still the time when Renaissance figuration still dominates in art, and he talks about [*Softly*] la promesse du bonheur — a promise of happiness, where bonheur is stronger in French and means real satisfaction.

[*Long pause.*]

Mm-hmm. The [*Stressing*] promise of happiness. Well, that's a little different from happiness, right? You can have the promise of happiness without ever getting happiness. The promise of the satisfaction of desire without it ever being satisfied. So, with that, all of a sudden, we have Adorno's whole theory of utopia. He had a very different idea of how you deal with pleasure in the work of art — the work of art cannot bring pleasure... [*Quietly*: number one, it's like Freud's broken pots, you know the famous story about the person who borrows the pot and then he is taken to court because it's broken, and so forth. And the lawyer gets up and he says, well, we're putting up three arguments here upon the defendant: first of all, he never borrowed the vase... (*Self-corrects*) ...the pot. (*Chuckles*). Second, when he borrowed it, it already had a hole in it. And three, he returned it intact, thus proving himself innocent on all three counts.[44]] Well, it's a little bit like that in Adorno, there isn't any satisfaction in desire because one, desires can't be satisfied, and two, because the imaginary work or the artwork are not made in order to satisfy desires, but have a totally different function that we will be talking about later.

[*Long pause.*]

Mm-hmm. So, what happens next? [*Pause.*] Then, suddenly, there is a way of understanding how and this is how this chapter one ends in Aesthetic Theory, and this is obviously symbolically very important for the aesthetic, for music, and indeed for Doctor Faustus... [*Quietly:* as we will see.] Satisfied desire can be rendered in the form of dissonance, and of longing. The promise of happiness is also a longing for happiness. So not only does it not in fact physically have to be satisfied, but you can also experience it in a form of the pain of longing and of not knowing the satisfaction... [*Footsteps.*] And as I think we've said the other day, in music, when you get the turn towards Wagner and then towards later modern music, you have this precisely in the utopia of, hmm... [*Hesitates*] of dissonance. [*Starts reading.*] "The source of the immense importance of all dissonance for new art since Baudelaire and Tristan..." which is 1865, or something like this... [*Words indistinct*] "... — veritably an invariant of the modern — is that the immanent play of forces in the artwork converges with external reality: Its power over the subject intensifies in parallel with the increasing autonomy of the work."[45] The renunciation of the practical or the satisfaction of interest by the artwork allows it to become this closed laboratory in which all of these social longings, utopian social aspirations, are far more intensely felt. Well, that will be a, hmm... [*Hesitates*] a contribution to the later notion of utopia that runs through this whole book, but at least it's a rather unexpected displacement, if you like, of the whole notion of pleasure and desire from Kant and Freud into another social position altogether, or at least into what Adorno thought was another position. Again, whether that's dialectical, I think you'll have to wait and see... [*Quietly*: hmm, and of course we can talk further about the notion of the dialectical that corresponds to it, and it might be Hegel's or it might be Marx or... (*Mumbles indistinctly*).]

[*Long pause*.]

Alright, so next time we will talk about this whole next large chapter called "Situation," that's part two, and which runs from page 16 to 45, I believe, in your edition and you... [*Addresses a student*] you will tell us something about Hofmannsthal's "Letter to Lord Chandos" as we agreed... [*Words indistinct*.]

Audience stands up. Objects drop on the floor. Zippers zipping up. Door squeaks. Students return chairs to other classrooms. General noise. Screeching microphone noise.

[*Microphone turns off*.]

CURTAIN

LECTURE FIVE

FEBRUARY 4, 2003

SITUATION (CHAPTER) — MIMESIS — HOFMANNSTHAL, "THE LORD CHANDOS LETTER" — NOMINALISM

CURTAIN RISES

Moving chairs, squeaking door, coughs, other sounds filling the noise environment of a large classroom in the Literature Department at Duke University. A few students are discussing Jameson's influence in post-Mao China. In 1985, he taught a full semester at Peking University. His seminars exposed a generation of Chinese intellectuals to the idioms and modes of American academic Marxism, opening the way to what became known as lilun *(theory), and the launching of its key institutions, such as the Institute of Comparative Literature and Culture at Peking University. Following his teaching in China, it became common to have many Chinese students in the Literature Department. This seminar on* Aesthetic Theory *also had one Chinese student, who was now talking to his American colleagues about Jameson's influence at home. He mentions Jameson's books that have been translated into Chinese, and the fact that his influence in China extends beyond the walls of academia, as his ideas about modernity and postmodernism are widely known and discussed.*[1]

Jameson enters the classroom carrying a few books, his scattered notes, and the red pen in the chest pocket of his flannel shirt.

[*Microphone turns on.*]

JAMESON: ... based on Wedekind's two plays about Lulu called Pandora's Box, and I would like to start this a little earlier.[2] [*Footsteps across the classroom.*] It seems like everybody can get here by 10am on Thursday? [*Looks at the class.*] Uh? [*Pause.*] This is, hmm... [*Hesitates.*] How many people will miss some of it if we start earlier?

[*Long pause. A few students raise their hands.*]

Oh, I think that's okay then. How about we meet quarter to ten? [*Audience murmuring.*]

STUDENT: I have another class...

JAMESON: [*Talks to the student.*] You're still in class?

STUDENT: Yeah...

JAMESON: Ah, okay, everybody else can be here? Let's try to start the film at a quarter to... [*Chairs scrapes the floor*] and... [*Foot shuffles.*] We will start and let's try to make it in time so we.

STUDENT: How long is the film?

JAMESON: The film is one hour and fifty minutes, so we will be out of here, I think, before Michael Hardt's class, which is at 12:45.

STUDENT: Twelve... [*Words indistinct.*]

JAMESON: Uh?

STUDENT: Twelve forty.

JAMESON: Ah, twelve forty, so twenty to one.

STUDENT: Yes.

JAMESON: Ah well, this is not the right time, but it doesn't matter. They know that we're gonna be here and so we can... [*Zippers unzipping*] hopefully stay till the end of it. I hope it's a good copy because some... [*Cough in the audience*] of them are always, hmm... [*Hesitates*] eh, they are subject to scratches and other mishaps. I don't think this DVD is too old or too bad. But Pandora's Box will be helpful because the film will give you frequent allusions to Wedekind here. These plays date from... [*Softly*.] I think they are from the 1890s or so, and are sort of, not really the first wave of German modern theater... [*Quietly*: the first is Büchner, and people like that... (*Words indistinct*) von Kleist, Tieck, but there isn't anyone like him... (*Mumbles indistinctly*).] This is a kind of first wave of something that looks like naturalism, but is maybe closer to modernism in the German context. And these are definitely those two writers precisely... [*Quietly*: Büchner, I'd say, which is from the 1830s, is a very strange and very modern portrayal of all sorts of contradictions, conflicts, of the individual and society, of freedom and determinism, of faith and atheism, and... (*Words indistinct*) and the other one is Wedekind, whose work comes later in the century and who also deals with controversial issues of sexuality, youth, mental struggles, authority and freedom.[3]]

[*Long pause. Footsteps.*]

Okay, so much for that. Now, people have been complaining to me about the index I asked you to do. Is that working out for you, or does it tend to be a drag? [*Pause.*] Hmm, give me some testimony on this.

STUDENT: It slows down the reading considerably.

JAMESON: That's what people say, yeh, yeh. How many people have done any... [*Cough in the audience*] extensive work on this index of Aesthetic Theory? [*Looks around.*] Oh, not very many. Mm-hmm. Well, those of you who have, just turn in what you have, and we'll sort of cancel it. Maybe at the very end, what you can do is a kind of [*Stressing*] retrospective look at these themes. [*Pause.*] It'd give me a kind of a sense of what you think the major themes are and how they're connected through pages or something like that. But I, hmm... [*Hesitates*] but I agree with you that it's not easy... [*Pause.*] To do it as you go along without knowing what the rest of it is... [*Gloomily.*] I mean, normally, when you do something sensible with an index, it's because you have all the references already and then you can look back and put them together. But to do as you're going along is probably not a good idea... [*Zipper zipping up near the microphone*] so we will cancel that part of the assignment. But as I say, people who've done some work on it, please... [*Quietly*: how this whole thing can be even indexed] but if you have it, just print it out and give it to me, of course, if it's not just some scribble on the margins, or something.

[*Addresses a student*:] You have it on your computer?

STUDENT: Ah, no... no... I will work... [*Embarrassed.*]

JAMESON: Ah, no. You don't have to. It's not... [*Pause.*] I'm just saying if you've done it in some computerized form that you can print out, hmm... [*Hesitates*] if you haven't done it already.

[*Long pause.*]

Mm, hmm, it's unfortunate that, hmm... [*Hesitates*] or maybe it's not unfortunate. I was thinking that the German speakers or readers can benefit from an extraordinary register of themes and ideas in the German edition of this... [*Holds up the German edition of* Ästhetische Theorie.] But Hullot-Kentor decided not to include that, as far as I can see, and I think that, in a way, this is a good idea. I think that it's very convenient to have these indexes, one of which I use today, and I'll show you, but on the other hand, it also prevents you from doing a lot of important work with the content, so maybe it's not so good after all.

[*Long pause.*]

Mm-hmm... [*Looks at his notes.*] I was also hoping today to make a quick commentary on Lessing... [*Quietly*: we had a question about Lessing last time, and I presume when it comes to aesthetics and modernism, we would have to talk about his essay on Laocoön.[4]] One of the main points in the Laocoön book was a distinction of temporality... . [*Quietly*: oh, we are now calling it "synchronic" and "diachronic," I guess] but that is to say it is about arts that provide instantaneous visual gratification, which we have in painting, and the temporal or narrative line... [*Door creaks open. Footsteps.*] The story of Laocoön is in, I don't know what book of the... [*Chalk on the blackboard*] A-E-N-E-I-D...

STUDENT: Second.

JAMESON: Is it in the second? Okay, it is in Book Two of the Aeneid,[5] where Virgil gives us this great depiction of Laocoön... [*Quietly*: the Trojan priest who tries to warn his fellow Trojans about the wooden horse left by the Greeks in the city, and then the gods send the serpents who strangle his two sons, leaving Laocoön to suffer.] And of course, the Roman, hmm... [*Hesitates*] sculpture of Laocoön, which is I think a reproduction of a Greek sculpture,[6] shows these figures caught and being suffocated by the snake. And so, there is a comparison in this treatise of how aesthetic affects are made, based on the discussion and description of differences between the visual arts and literature. [*Determined*.] I think in our... [*Pause*.] In some way, Lessing opting for the story of Laocoön to talk about the limitations of each art brings us back to the Kantian themes that we were talking about before. I would certainly want to do something with this idea of the relationship between classicism... [*Quietly*: or let's say the management of a kind of monstrous and terrifying event via a certain kind of classicism or neo-classicism.] It seems to me that something like that is what we're finding in Kant's own moment. But from our perspective, which will emerge at certain points in Adorno and which I think it's more interesting and which you'll find very strongly in Doctor Faustus: it will be the opposition of harmony and counterpoint. [*Pause*.] That's what is going on here. [*After prolonged reflection*.] Counterpoint is this movement of melodic lines in time, and harmony is this sort of static cross-section combination of sounds, a "satisfied unity" as someone described it, based on rules and you'll find the music theorist in Doctor Faustus... [*Quietly*: behind whom stands Adorno, of course] saying that counterpoint is designed as melodic harmony, and every chord or harmony is really just a moment of counterpoint that should be re-dissolved into the various lines that presumably make it up. And this is obviously the complete reversal of the structuralist position, for which synchrony is predominant and diachrony is just a series of these synchronies displacing each other... [*Quietly*: but we can take that up when we get to that part.]

[*Long pause*.]

Mm-hmm, the other thing that I wanted to do today... [*Quietly*: before we get to the matter of the Lord Chandos Letter] is a set of themes that Adorno mentions, and I think you need to know about that. I don't want to wait with that because some of them are characteristic leitmotifs or obsessions or whatever is the technical terminology and some of them have to be explained. [*Pause*.] And I would just go down a list of these things because I think you should know... [*Cough in the audience*] you should know what they are. Mm-hmm... [*Pause*.] Non-identity, we talked about that already. I think that's frankly, this is, hmm... [*Hesitates*] a post-structuralist idea and I don't think the importance that Martin Jay gives it is really that important or... [*Words indistinct*.] There is stuff about "otherness," there is stuff about "difference," but these are not themes of the type that we talked about. But if we see it as we go by, we will stop and talk about it some more.

[*Long Pause*.]

The <u>Dialectic of Enlightenment</u> I've already discussed with you, but let me do it in terms of this other dominant theme, which is... [*Decisively*] "mimesis." I think that this concept in Adorno is never explained philosophically but only presupposed. Did he get it from Benjamin? What does it mean? I don't know, but this idea of mimesis plays a very central role in his theories about art. In Adorno, mimesis is this primordial activity, and hmm... [*Quietly*: it's both good and bad in some respects.] Mimesis, it's almost a mythical activity and there is a layer of this activity which does refer back to some sort of primitive society; it is some sort of [*Stressing*] <u>anthropological</u> thesis from which modernity and contemporary culture, hmm... [*Hesitates*] needs to be distinguished. But I think, in this case, mimesis, it's even pre-animistic, that is, it's not yet even religious or cultic or whatever. [*Softly*.] What does mimesis suggest? Does it suggest that there is some impulse or drive in human nature to make pictures of things? I think it's very hard to figure this out and it comes in at various points, as though Adorno had already written a treatise on this, which he never did. I don't believe myself that Benjamin's early essays on this — "speech as mimesis," and so forth, those are Benjamin's essays form the 1930s[7] — I don't think that they shed any light, and frankly I don't think these two essays by Benjamin are talking about the same thing, though Adorno sometimes says they are. [*Pause.*] So, it's very hard to know what to do with this notion of mimesis. I suggest that we begin thinking about it in terms of contemporary philosophical discussions, in that part that I'm going to refer to here... [*Page flipping.*] At the very end of the "Draft Introduction," pages 358-359, he says this about art: "The principle of method here is that light should be cast on all art from the vantage point of the most recent artworks, rather than the reverse, following the custom of historicism and philology, which, bourgeois at heart, prefers that nothing ever change."[8] This means that, hmm... [*Cough in the audience.*] This means that the most contemporary developments in the arts, or let's say... [*Sighs*] that in trying to grasp the history of modern music we must start from Schoenberg, who sheds light on Wagner, Bach, and so forth, rather than the other way around. And I think one could also do this with philosophy, in the sense that the contemporary form of what Adorno talks about as mimesis is the theme of representation. [*Pause.*] That essentially comes from Heidegger, hmm... [*Hesitates*] and it's sort of at one with all kinds of post-structuralist theories. These ideas are essentially based on the problematic nature of representing anything, and it ends up in a situation in which we come to the conclusion that no representation is possible — that representation must always be a failure in one way or another. It also has to do with the subject-object split that is for Heidegger the beginning of modernity... [*Quietly*: in the bad sense.] It is the split between subject and object and it's out of this split that representation necessarily comes. [*Pause.*] Because then, at that point, the subject has to breach the gap and move from the thing-in-itself out there, from reality, to some picture of reality, which it then absorbs, domesticates, and uses for its cultural production. Mm-hmm. Mimesis is then... [*Hesitates.*] So, for Heidegger, this is a fall out of some more satisfactory mode of being, let's say, and it determines the weak spot of all modern culture from which Heidegger wishes of course to find an escape... [*Quietly*: hmm, the solutions of the post-structuralists, I think, are not precedent in that sense but we still turn on that matter of naïve representation as being a sign of this subject-object split and the po... or re-posing the problem of representation as a mode of philosophical or maybe cultural critique.]

[*Long pause.*]

Mimesis obviously is... [*Sighs.*] If he starts from the idea — not of representation but of mimesis — lots of things change, because the mimetic doesn't necessarily suggest that it is going to be true to reality. I mean, it doesn't necessarily imply any kind of belief in the success of representation... [*Raps his knuckles on the desk.*] On the other hand, it also could imply... [*Quietly*: this is the stuff he gets from Frazer and The Golden Bough, the kind of magic belief, that when the bison on the floor of the cave is allegedly designed to somehow capture the spirit of the bison for the hunters, to serve hunting rituals and to capture the outside world.[9]] That would also not necessarily suggest a full representation, but it would certainly imply some kind of relationship with the world. Mm-hmm... [*Pause.*] At any rate, I think that's the way to think of mimesis and we'll come back to it as it comes up.[10]

[*Long pause.*]

Now, in the Dialectic of Enlightenment we have some such mythic narrative, if you like, which begins in the earliest stages of human culture, and it moves gradually on to the later stages, and the place you can find this is... [*Pause.*] This is laid out for us in the very beginning of the Dialectic of Enlightenment, in the first chapter.[11] The idea is that science emerges out of some primal instinct for basic survival and of conquering nature. As with Hegel, you've got two kinds of reason. You have

Verstand, which is "understanding..." [*Chair scratching across the floor*] and this is, let's say, a reified forms of reason, or what the Frankfurt School will end up calling... [*Quietly*: at least in English] and I think it's better than the translation of "understanding" in the Hegelian terms... [*Chalk on the blackboard*] I-N-S-T-R-U-M-E-N-T-A-L R-E-A-S-O-N. And that's... [*Pause.*] It is [*Stressing*] instrumental rationality because it is reason that wishes to achieve something, it is an efficient means to achieve a specific goal, and you can see that there is an anti-scientific bias here, because that's a type of understanding which seeks to appropriate and dominate the world; a form of thinking whose scientific analysis of things is a way of conquering the world and doing something with it, right? And this form of reason is opposed to... [*Quietly*: in Hegel, again, there is another term, Vernunft, which is often translated as "reason"], and which would be something like... [*Chalk on the blackboard*] D-I-A-L-E-C-T-I-C-A-L R-E-A-S-O-N, and maybe it would have something to do with what we are interested in here in this seminar, with a form of value-thinking, which is essentially based on the nature of society and certain utopian ambition of these societies to become [*Stressing*] non-exploitative. This instrumental reason, which is denounced throughout the work of the Frankfurt School — especially by Horkheimer — is very definitely a form of power and a form of exploitation. This would be their version... [*Cough in the audience*] the Frankfurt School's version of a kind of a historical fall into some sort or other of subject-object relationship.

[*Long pause.*]

Now, the point they wanna make in the Dialectic of Enlightenment is a kind of a complicated and cumulative one. That is to say... [*Softly.*] Power over nature. Yeah, because when humanity is powerless, this is a positive achievement. But the history of reason has been so far progressing in the opposite direction... [*Quietly:* the domestication of fire, all the knowledge, which gave us control over phenomena, the acquisition of the rudiments of some form... (*Pause*) of various forms of what today would be science.] These are all forms of control and, to that degree, one can hardly denounce them on some ethical ground. But the point about instrumental reason, or what they're now calling Enlightenment, is that it — like revolutions — it devours its own children. [*Pause.*] Each successor stage of enlightened reason denounces the previous one or dismisses it by calling it "superstition." And this is obvious. Take alchemy. Mm-hmm... [*Pause.*] Alchemy is this pre-, hmm... [*Hesitates*] it's the superstitious pre-stage of modern chemistry, right? But presumably, there is a moment with alchemy — maybe we need to go back to some pre-alchemist times or something like that, when alchemy was the dominant form of annexing and understanding the world... [*Quietly*: the way chemistry is today.] The later stage always ends up being a form of rationality, which, by virtue of the progress of history and of science, has to be mastered, and which it does by denouncing the very stage that preceded or constituted it. It cancels the previous stage, calling or denouncing it as a "superstition." Now, their point about this history... [*Pause.*] So, you've got a history of Enlightenment from... [*Clears throat*] from the caves, because magic, as they point out, is an early form of Enlightenment; magic as in the cave paintings of the bison, and all the rest of it, are the earliest ways in which people tried to master nature. And you have to imagine that the... [*Achoo. Sneeze in the audience*] combinations and the ratio of nature to human praxis is almost completely reversed... [*Quietly:* increasingly, humans manage to bring under their control this immense, terrifying thing.] As instrumental reason increases, it becomes a negative force. Mm-hmm... [*Hesitates.*] And I must say, the good things that are in nature — that could be natural beauty, it could be various parts of the psyche, Kant's genius, for example, is part of... [*Cough near the microphone*] nature in some sense, art itself is presumably part of nature — all of those things also get canceled in this movement of progress, of science, of instrumental reason and Enlightenment.

[*Long pause.*]

The end products of this historical process — and these are some other terms you need to know — are, for example, hmm... [*Hesitates*] what he calls "administration," verwaltete Welt... [*Stressing*] the administered world. This is a world in which bureaucracy and humanization has spread so thoroughly into the very pores of social life that everything is an object of these forms of domination by instrumental reason. So, this is a progressive process, which gets worse and worse. There is less and less nature. There is more and more domination, which takes place now at micrological levels... [*Pause*] and we can go on with that to various places. Well, what are the places? Mm-hmm, [*Hesitates.*] Hmm, Verwaltung, or verwaltete Welt, or another very odd word that I think they got it from Max Weber, Vergesellschaftung, which means... [*Chalk strokes on the blackboard*] S-O-C-I-E-T-A-L-I-Z-A-T-I-O-N. This, I think, would be my translation of it. [*Pause.*] Mm-hmm, and that is not a good thing. That's another form of the way in which the social order and social power gradually subsumes... [*Quietly*: that's a nice word for this] subsumes more and more of what was either nature or tradition before. So, in effect, the division of labor, the Taylorism, it's a form of this subsumption. You have... [*Zipper unzipping*] relatively natural or traditional work processes, even with an industry. In the early days, the workers knew what the entire form of the labor process was in their industry, and they had a clear idea of where they stood within those processes. When you get to Taylorization, which is the breaking down of the production process to smaller tasks, and out of which comes the assembly line at Ford... [*Quietly*: but of course, Lenin was also very enthusiastic about it] you get the dissolution of those unified labor processes. It's a story that's told in... [*Pause.*] The great book on this subject is Harry Braverman's The Degradation of Work, I think it's called or something like that...[12] [*Mumbles indistinctly.*] Mm-hmm. You break up the labor process into smaller specialized jobs and tasks. Everybody does a little bit of everything. Labor is scientifically managed — the production process is standardized and specialized. Obviously, this is all implicit with Adam Smith, but anyway, in the factory, hmm... [*Absorbed*.] It's the comical situation in Modern Times movie, if you like.[13] At that point, the various participants in this process, who were doing one little bit, no longer see the unity of the entire work process. And this gets a bonus for Taylor, as he says this very explicitly... [*Quietly*: it is very important that the workers no longer have control over the labor process.] It is therefore important that the knowledge of the whole, and of these old working traditions, be destroyed, hmm... [*Hesitates*.] It's important that the worker be [*Whispers*] powerless, and only know one little operation or task... [*Quietly*: you remember that, in Chaplin's Modern Times, Tramp is screwing on these bolts at the conveyer belt, and he cannot keep up.] Okay. But then who knows the entire labor process? [*Softly*.] Well, it is the new class of managers. If the workers know, if they still had knowledge of the labor processes, they're gonna argue with the managers, they're gonna tell the managers that they are not gonna do it. [*Firmly*.] And then, there will be trouble and rebellion and strikes and so on. There must be absolute obedience, so the worker is no longer to know anything besides their small tasks, and the manager is now the one who only knows and sees the full picture. Well, that's an example, I think, of the... admin... [*Pause*] of the administered world, an example of the way in which now this new world is subsumed under power, control, knowledge, and so on and so forth. Hmm, this is not exactly Foucauldian power-knowledge... [*Door creaks open*] but that could be itself subsumed under as part of it.

[*Long pause*.]

Now, in some ideological sense, what else is related to this? [*Pause*.] Well, they use a number of other terms that I have already mentioned, and we will talk more about... [*Cough in the audience*.] One such word is "positivism," and that is part of a larger dispute... [*Quietly*: they had a big debate that took place in Tübingen] and it revolved around what the Frankfurt School considered a sort of monopoly of science and technical progress on knowledge, and any other aspect of modern life. In their language, "positivism" encompasses a range of critiques brought against modern science, including its reliance on empiricism and sense-certainty, the technical utility, and instrumentality or technical power over nature and society. Part of this process also includes the assault on totality, and the totality of the labor processes mentioned above... [*Quietly*: or an assault on the producers of historical life in its totality, reducing this life to individual existence, or individuelle Existenz, I guess we would say... (*Mumbles indistinctly*).] The individual objects which exist, which were condemned to a world of ontic things, as Heidegger would say, or ontic phenomena in which there is no negative. [*Pause*.] And for Adorno, positivism is this attitude that imposes a prescriptive framework... [*Quietly*: you make an empirical observation, an experiment, you turn it into law or fact and impose it on all future experience, which in some way means you are putting a stop to the new.] This is what, for Adorno, positivism is as a philosophy. Its main tool is instrumental reason, which is increasing its hold over things, and there is a, hmm... [*Hesitates*] a kind of phenomenological experience that either results from this, or on which this whole process is based... [*Quietly*: that would be interesting to talk about.]

[*Long pause*.]

Another term that you will also find frequently mentioned in Aesthetic Theory and his other writings is what Adorno — going back to the Middle Ages — calls "nominalism" ... [*Quietly*: and we'll have a look at that in a moment.] This is a very crucial concept for Adorno, the notion of "nominalism." And talking about these two concepts, you see, with positivism we could denounce it because it has to do with a certain method of acquiring knowledge and power, which has no doubt to do with people who, hmm... [*Searches for words*] with people who are part of the system, with the apologists for power and domination, who want to maintain the status quo and have their ideological task performed. You could say that they produce a positive theory in order to maintain their form of life, their mode of being, and they attack dialectical philosophy, which tries to reassert these twin notions of the negative and of totality. [*Pause.*] Positivism, as an ideology, wishes us to entrust ourselves to science and modern technology, to live in a world of individually existing objects without a sense of totality, without any wish for negativity, critique, or social change. But nominalism, on the other hand, is a historical process, hmm... [*Pause.*] We can attack positivism... [*Quietly*: because it imposes a certain structure on knowledge, by reducing it to discussions about methodology and the study of separate facts and verifiable phenomena, which is all part of, or is done in the interest of capitalism.] You will also find that positivism is not limited only to this philosophical school called "Positivism," or "Logical Positivism," but is to be found everywhere in every field and in different versions. [*Exhales deeply.*] But you can't exactly attack nominalism because that's what history has made of this world for us. The positivists are ideologists, but on the other hand, they reflect the structure of a world which has been positivized, so to speak, and this is part of the human effort to impose control on nature, or is related to the instinct of self-preservation, as we will see later with Adorno, hmm... [*Hesitates*] and so the world was reduced to a collection of these exisistents, where the sense of totality is weaker and weaker, and more and more feeble. But nominalism, on the other hand, is historical, and it corresponds to a new form of experiencing the world... [*Quietly*: a world which rejects the existence of universal concepts, of abstract entities, and this tendency to treat objects and concepts as isolated.] And in this case, there you've gotta do something else about it... [*Quietly*: and we'll see maybe... (*Mumbles indistinctly*) what else, hmm... (*Talks to himself*) what else comes of that.]

[*Long pause.*]

Mm-hmm. Another word that will come into play here is... [*Quietly*: sometimes I think this one of the ugliest words that Adorno invented (*Chuckling*).] It is what he calls... [*Chalk on the blackboard*] E-N-T-K-U-N-S-T-U-N-G, which means de-... [*Pause.*] Ent in German is like de- in English, and Entnazifizierung, for example, is "denazification"... [*Quietly*: that is, getting rid of Nazis.] But Entkunstung here means "de-arting"... [*Cough in the audience*.] Hullot-Kentor translated this as "deaestheticization," and I don't think that's the right way to do it, but the other way... [*Quietly*: "deartification" is certainly extremely ugly.] Adorno connects that to... [*Pause*.] But you'll see it in this first chapter, and we have seen it already,[14] that it pops up in various places without much explanation, and it means this other unique form of positivism, which now takes place in art and which he also calls the "culture industry," which is discussed in another chapter of the Dialectic of Enlightenment. And the culture industry is, hmm... [*Hesitates*] essentially a... [*Pause*.] It means, at least in this context, an industry which takes things that might have had elements of works of art, or might have been part of art before, and turns them into cultural commodities. That is to say it... [*Stammers*] it, hmm... [*Hesitates*] it removes their aesthetic dimensions and turns them into things which are for sale [*Quietly*: like labor power] and what you sell then is not called art anymore, it's called [*Whispering*] entertainment... [*Quietly*: after all, Adorno was spending the war years in Hollywood, so he heard a lot of it.] And remember that this is a period when the great dominance of Hollywood as an industry and as a factory of dreams, and so on, hmm... [*Hesitates*] brings the reign of a certain kind of radio production... [*Quietly*: it's pre-television era] and also, because this is one of those scandalous parts of Adorno, the more public existence of a certain form of really entertainment-oriented light music, which he calls "jazz." Now, he knows something about jazz in its full form... [*Quietly*: he knows that the jazz musicians are extraordinarily virtuosos, and their technical capacities may make orchestra players pale, and so forth.] But I insist that, for him, for the most part, he passionately disliked this anyway; he was not very temperamentally equipped to understand what was really going on in some of the great forms of jazz. And I also think that he was thinking more of... [*Zipper unzipping*] white jazz dance like Paul Whiteman,[15] which was a kind of degraded jazz that really falls under all of these appropriated forms of mass entertainment… (*Words indistinct*). Because at that point… [*Quietly*: well, I'm not… (*Pause*). I don't have any great pretenses to know or listen to jazz] but it seems to me that the very great players, in 1930s or 1940s I think, a lot of them were dead, some of them have lost their teeth, they were drug addicts or in retirement homes, I mean, or some of them are… [*Softly*] like Jelly Roll[16] playing in the brothels of New Orleans. I mean, the recovery of the golden age of real jazz, it's not there, and I don't know what was going on in Los Angeles at that time… [*Quietly*: I mean great jazz was either in New Orleans or Chicago, but not in LA.] So, I don't think he had access to any real jazz. I don't think he would have really liked it if he had to listen to it, but he was a great… [*Quietly*: he was a passionate observer of music, and I think some of great forms of jazz of his time would have looked different to him.] But then, the chances, then, in that limited negative sense, is also part of this process of Entkunstung that could have been, hmm… [*Hesitates*] could have been a musical work of art that was turned into a commodity to be used at the lowest level [*Stressing*] instrumentally. Entertainment at that time is instrumental. You go there to kill a few hours, right? Whereas remember that this whole discussion of the affects of art is very paradoxical, I mean, it's not clear whether the realm of high aesthetics, like the one discussed in terms of Freud or Kant, whether one can really talk about affects here. But certainly, from either standpoint — that of Kant's relationship to pleasure and the body, or Freud's sublimation, and so on — in neither of those cases is entertainment per se an issue. It is not theorized… [*Achoo. Sneeze in the audience.*] And then, what is entertainment? I mean, this is clearly an ideological concept that has to be looked at… [*Quietly*: it is not a critical or philosophical idea.]

[*Long pause.*]

Mm-hmm… [*Hesitates.*] Now. [*Talks quietly to himself.*]

[*Pause.*]

There is a lot of other stuff that needs discussion of these objects produced by the culture industry, but they're not very interesting. He says [*Impersonates Adorno*] "Look, the whole point is that Hollywood thinks you have to have the same things every time — it's all about repetition." If you go to a film of some sort, let's say, we're talking about the 1940s and early 1950s and 1930s, hmm... [*Hesitates*] you are going to see a comedy, a western or a musical, you don't want to see something which is unclassifiable and unique. You wanna see more of the same, you wanna see another one of those, you wanna see that form repeated over and over again. It would be... [*Pause.*] It is like in those discussions in which people try to say, "Oh, the detective story after all is a great art form because things like The Brothers Karamazov is just too boring... [*Mumbles indistinctly.*] Well, if you are a detective story reader, you don't wanna read The Brothers Karamazov [*Chuckles.*] It's not what you want to do in your free time... [*Chuckles continues.*] If you're watching situation comedy on television, or cop shows or whatever, you do not wanna see something unique and interesting. Mm-hmm. You want to see this process repeated over and over again, and Adorno then says, [*Impersonates Adorno*] "Look, this is a repetition exactly of the same kind that the worker is doing in the daytime at the assembly line." And so, having gone through this whole formulaic process of physical work, as a kind of alienation... [*Quietly*: he needs full rest and recovery] and so the worker sits in a movie theater where he goes through the same process again. Only this time it is symbolic. Anyway, there is a lot of very interesting stuff in there, and I think that the last word about the culture industry has not been said. I also think that we are taking a rather different position on the culture industry today, and this is partially because mass culture itself has changed. [*Pause.*] And I think, you know... [*Quietly*: it's not just from the World War Two, and the latest television shows, which can also be surely pretty bad too] hmm, but also from Hollywood to contemporary film, from the golden age of Hollywood to contemporary film, from the golden age of anything in mass culture, which is, what, 1930s, 1940s and 1950s, to what's going on now, there have been substantial changes in mass culture itself. So, we cannot use this 1940s kind of cultural analysis to understand what's going on now. On the other hand, I think it's not altogether… [*Hesitates*] it's not altogether irrelevant or different either. Mm-hmm. But you have a long section on the culture industry here, in this first chapter, in the second chapter I meant…[17] Hmm, which… [*Cough in the audience*] in some new way goes over some of these issues he first discussed with Horkheimer. And this notion of Entkunstung is analogous to some of the points they raise in the Dialectic of Enlightenment as the process of, hmm… [*Hesitates*] of cultural reification. Mm-hmm. It is instrumental, it's an [*Stressing*] instrumentalization of these early forms of art as they are then picked up in mass culture and exploited.

[*Long pause.*]

A couple of more things. I don't want to take too much more time here. The so-called "second reflection…" [*Pause.*] Well, look at pages 348 and 358 at the very end of the "Draft Introduction." They don't exactly tell us what we need to know about this weird idea. I would say that "second reflection" must have something to do with the Dialectic of Enlightenment, but what it has to do, we'll have to figure it out on our own. We will dedicate more time in our future session to talk about "second reflection," and I'm bringing it now just for you to be aware that it exists and that's very important in Adorno.

[*Long pause.*]

Mm-hmm. What else? [*Decisively.*] Ah yeah, the term "content." There is an excellent footnote by Hullot-Kentor on page 368.[18] The footnote sets the difference between… [*Chalk on the blackboard*] I-N-H-A-L-T and G-E-H-A-L-T, and that's, I think, very important here because normally when we say in English "content," it's sort of refers to the meaning of the work, or what's the work about. Here content is broken into thematic or subject matter… [*Page flipping. Reads from note* 7] "the idea of thematic content or subject matter"… [*Quietly*: and this is Inhalt] and then content as Gehalt, which is in a sense about the substance or import of the work. And then, of course, when Adorno talks about "truth content," then we're also into something else, which is far more historical and thematic, but we will come back later to those things. [*Pause.*] You have also some Greek words here that I think you need to know. Of course, this is hmm... [*Chalk on the blackboard*] χ-ω-ρ-ὶ-ς[19] and I think this is a Platonic term which means "apart," "outside" or "separated from." [*Pause.*] So, you would have a Platonic idea, as a kind of autonomous realm, and then there would be something [*Stressing*] exterior to that idea, hmm... [*Hesitates*] or, if you like, something outside of it, and that's what χωρὶς means. Mm-hmm. It would be like the good, the true and the beautiful. Well, the good is χωρὶς to the beautiful, in some sense. Kant makes these rather doubtful attempts to connect out why the experience of the beautiful could be helpful informing an ethical personality, but very allegorical and not very satisfying. The ethics is outside of aesthetics. So, translate χωρὶς as "separation" and that would be okay for the moment.

[*Long pause.*]

And finally, a very strange word, which this translator uses on page... [*Quietly*: hmm, I'm quite annoyed by this because he hasn't translated it... (*To himself*). Where is it? (*Page flipping*).] Anyway, this is the German word called Innervierung, which we would be tempted to translate as, hmm... [*Hesitates*] "enervation." And he does that on page 19, but that's not the right word I think, and it is strange for the translator to use this already rather weird English word. Mm-hmm. Innervierung, I think... [*Pause.*] "Enervation" to me in English means that you're exhausted, or you are fatigued, right? [*Addresses the audience.*] Is this how you also understand it? [*Silence.*] Your nerves have been sort of wiped out, and so you're enervated, you're... [*Quietly:* or maybe you have too many nerves, but it also leaves you sort of powerless, and you are just sort of lying there not doing anything.] Innervierung does not mean that in German. None of the Germans I talked to really know what it means... [*Audience laughing*] they always thought it is the same as the English. [*Laughter continues.*] And I think in German it means to [*Stressing*] activate in some way, eh, to animate the elements that are within the artwork. But frankly, I've never been able to explain this myself or get any clarity, and I just warn you about this strange term, which you'll find popping up every so often, and maybe you can yourself find some way of dealing with it... [*Quietly*: this is a kind of term that can't be simply looked up in a dictionary, although I tried... (*Mumbles indistinctly*).] Mm-hmm. And other people who've used it say that this is a Frankfurt School usage, and I don't even know if it comes out of Horkheimer, but this is one of these very confusing words. It's obviously a word that Adorno likes, and it means something to him, but I'm not sure what it means any more... [*Quietly*: it is a little bit like "mimesis," which we also do not always know what it means, but the problem with this mimesis is much more... (*Door slams in the distance*) because of this cunning English closeness.]

[*Long pause.*]

[*Decisive.*] Okay, listen, that's a few of these terms that I wanted to mention to you. Mm-hmm. This second chapter that we were supposed to discuss today, called "Situation"... [*Pause.*] Ah, one more thing. You notice that in every case that I've been telling you — or Adorno is telling us — is like a historical story that sounds a little bit like this. [*Impersonates Adorno.*] "Well, before it was like this, and now it's like that." I think every sentence that Adorno wrote was secretly a narrative sentence of this kind. It doesn't have to do with nostalgia for the past, hmm... [*Hesitates*] but it certainly has something to do with what the theme of "degradation..." [*Quietly*: degraded culture, degraded society, degraded art, life, and so on.] All of these sentences, it seems to me, somewhere and somehow, they are dealing with the profound form of social change; they are dealing with history — they are not dealing with structures, or something like that, whatever they look like on the surface. There is always a historical process, a process generally of getting worse and worse, which is at stake in these sentences. So, we have a couple of ways of looking at Adorno's style. I mean, one is this attempt not to come down on either side of an antinomy but to [*Stressing*] set forth a proposition in such a way that, by the end of the sentence, you will understand why — as true as it may be — you can't really fully accept this proposition because of a deeply-seated contradiction or antinomy within it. [*Pause.*] He is setting up or writing sentences that are self-canceling somehow. Mm-hmm. And the other thing is his degrading narrative — and obviously these two tendencies are interrelated — but they are also a way for us to look at his prose, and theory.

[*Long Pause.*]

Okay, so the chapter "Situation" begins on page 16 with what he calls the "materials," and the materials represent history... [*Quietly*: because ultimately, it's history that you can detect in the state of the materials.] Mm-hmm. The famous example is that of the, hmm... [*Hesitates*] of the tonic chord, which is the chord that serves as the root or center of a melody, or the key, and has been an essential element in Western tonal music. It's the major chord, which is very powerful in the period in which tonality is being invented or [*Stressing*] constructed, but which very quickly... [*Cough in the audience*] became absolutely insipid and it started to have no effect at all. Or look at it the other way around, and that's when very simple forms of musical dissonance start to emerge in the early to mid-eighteenth century, let's say, and they are very troubling. But the more dissonance is used, the more it gets worn out and nobody's shocked anymore, nobody hears the ugliness of it, nobody understands what's at stake in this business, so it has to get worse. [*Pause.*] This is one way of looking at what happens to the materials... [*Quietly*: or what Adorno calls the "materials."] The materials are in history, and they are being transformed by history. And therefore, what you've used... [*Cough in the audience*] earlier in the work, you can't use it in the same way later on. Now, one of the most famous examples of this, one of the first signals and great documents that speaks of this condition of degradation of the materials in history and the, hmm... [*Hesitates*] and the onset of these new kind of problems, which are... [*Sighs*] central to what we call "modernism"... [*Quietly*: and perhaps also for postmodernism] is a document called "The Letter of Lord Chandos," which was written by Hugo von Hofmannsthal in 1902, I believe. [*Addresses a student*.] And you're going to tell us something today about this "Letter." Why won't you come up here in front of the class. [*Chair scrapes against the floor*.]

STUDENT ONE: Okay.

[*Footsteps*.]

Student Presentation: Hugo von Hofmannsthal, "The Lord Chandos Letter"

STUDENT ONE: Before I begin, I would like to acknowledge my tutor at Oxford, Professor Richard Shepperd... [*Door creaks open*] whose chapter "Lord Chandos and His Discontents," from his book Modernism-Dada-Postmodernism, I will quote on many occasions in this presentation. Professor Shepperd's chapter has been very helpful... [*Chair-back creaks*] grasp the significance of Hofmannsthal's "Letter of Lord Chandos" ... [*Words indistinct*.][20]

[*Long pause*.]

[*Starts reading*.] Hugo von Hofmannsthal's "The Lord Chandos Letter"... [*Quietly*: which is also known as "The Letter of Lord Chandos" and the "Chandos Letter"] is a letter allegedly written in 1603 by a fictitious English gentleman, a young aristocrat named Lord Philip Chandos. [*Pause*.] Hofmannsthal published it first in 1902 in the Berlin newspaper Der Tag (The Day) and was originally titled "Ein Brief..." [*Quietly*: "A Letter.... "] It was addressed to Francis Bacon... [*Quietly*: known also as Lord Verulam] considered one of the early modern philosophers of empirical science and a strong advocate of the scientific method. [*Softly*.] It seems significant to underline that Chandos chose to address the letter to the father of modern empiricism, which may reveal Hofmannsthal's views regarding the role of modern science in the modern perception of the world. [*Pause*.] The

"Letter" starts with an apology for not writing for two years, as Chandos informs Bacon of a crisis, or a "mental paralysis," and he is also thanking Bacon for the medical advice; next... [*Page flipping*] it provides a nostalgic account of the state of the world in which Chandos lived before the presumed crisis; and finally, the "Letter" proceeds to describe the origins of the crisis, and the author's state of mind.

[*Long pause.*]

First, Chandos narrates in nostalgic words the days before the moment of said crisis. He talks about his intellectual endeavors, asking himself how he could have been so enthusiastic and self-confident in pursuing so many of his learned projects. Before the mental paralysis, he lived in a literary world writing a pastoral at the age of nineteen, which was marked by an excess of baroque splendor. [*Pause.*] And at the age of twenty-three, he "discovered in himself an edifice of Latin prose whose abstract plan and structure gladdened his heart more than the buildings of Palladio and Sansovino,"[21] during a trip to Venice. He then asks... [*Quietly*: he is twenty-six years old now] whether these treatises, which are looking back at him, could have been written by the same person. Chandos thinks of that very productive period in his life as an architectural space dominated by the anthropocentric humanism of Renaissance, as a well-structured, well-ordered, static, and solid rational world extending in time; it was the time when it was so easy to lend order to the earthly objects, materials and forms, thanks to the eternal forces that kept flowing to him from the distant Antiquity.

[*Long pause.*]

This was the secure world that Chandos inhabited, and in this part of the "Letter," he asks himself what divine forces held it together, and what motivated him to engage and pursue so many projects; what forces gave him the confidence in that world and the language and words that he had used to describe or glorify it. First, Chandos had a very secure place in that world... [*Quietly*: I will draw now on Shepperd's interpretations.] First, he was [*Stressing*] <u>socially</u> secure, as Chandos was a member of the aristocracy, and he also contributed to the security of his own class or order by making literary images of it, like the pastorals. [*Quietly:* I quote.] "He had also been historically secure and had possessed so strong a sense of history as a linear continuum that when he wanted to write a history of the early years of the reign of Henry VIII, his mind instinctively turned to the writings of the Roman historian Sallust."[22] Then Shepperd adds that Chandos was also epistemologically secure, supporting this claim with details of Chandos's plan to put together a collection of utterances and maxims, which he collected during his extensive travels. These were to be parts of conversations, manuscripts, intellectual baubles, all combined with descriptions of festivals, or of buildings that he saw in France, Netherlands, and Italy — and this was a project that was to be titled Nosce te ipsum (Know yourself).[23] Finally, Shepperd continues... [*Clears throat*] Chandos was [*Stressing*] ontologically secure, because he lived at a time... [*Quietly*: that is, still before his crisis] when there was no sign of a split in his reality, there was no rupture between the mental and physical worlds, and when his universe was one absolute unity. [*Pause.*] Chandos talks about a fully constituted world, a world of unity between materials and language, which he described in the following allegorical terms... [*Page flipping*]: "To me there was no difference between drinking warm foaming milk which a tousled rustic at my hunting lodge had squeezed into a wooden bucket from the udder of a fine, mild-eyed cow, and drinking in sweet and frothy spiritual nourishment from an old book as I sat in the window seat of my study. The one was like the other."[24] [*Softly.*] This was a world with no separation.

[*Long pause.*]

As we proceed to the next part of Chandos' "Letter," we begin to learn about a crisis. At a certain point, the young gentlemen realized that his previous sense of security was false... [*Cough in the audience*] and his views were based on some arrogant assumptions. As his confidence in a unified world began to leave him, his soul sank into a state of inner exhaustion, which soon become permanent. He felt fragile as he sensed that he was losing his ability to think coherently or relate the material to the spiritual... [*Quietly*: and I quote from Sheppard] "Indeed, this sense of loss becomes so corrosive that Chandos starts to feel an inexplicable uneasiness [Unbehagen] about uttering the words Geist [spirit/mind], Seele [soul/spirit], and Köper [body] — three concepts that form the cornerstone of his conceptual world."[25] [*Quietly*: End quote.] He then describes his inability to form an opinion on current events, explaining this by the sense that the abstract concepts that he usually used to construct opinions began to disintegrate in his mouth like rotten mushrooms. [*Pause*.] And it wasn't only the matter of forming opinions but also of passing moral judgments... [*Quietly*: he gives this example of his four-year-old daughter whom he wanted to scold for telling a little lie] but then discovered that he was not capable of instructing her on how to tell the truth, as any attempt to do so, any idea or words that he tried to utter merged into each other as if unable to form themselves into moral rules and principles. [*Quietly*: and I quote.] He lost his former Archimedean point from which he surveyed the world with sovereign confidence. "All of which means that Chandos is beginning to realize affectively what Saussure is beginning to formulate scientifically at about the same time: that language is an arbitrary system and that there is gap between the illusory security afforded by language and the fluid complexity of reality."[26]

[*Long pause*.]

As the crisis deepens, Chandos is completely losing his grasp on language; he is incapable of sustaining even the simplest opinions, which used to be part of his most trivial conversations in his social circles. This leads to a profound sense of self-examination and self-scrutiny of his language, as well as of his relation to other people, which he describes in terms of the experience of looking at the skin on his finger through a magnifying glass, which "looked like an open field with furrows and burrows."[27] Again, Chandos emphasizes the shattered unity, where everything... [*Quietly*: his language, his relation to the world] broke into multiple fragments which could not be held by one idea. Looking for cure and escape from this sense of fragmentation and void, he turns to the orderly world of classical antiquity, to the writings of Seneca and Cicero, but soon realizes that they could not help him either. We then proceed to what is often considered the central or most important part of the Letter: the so-called "rats in the cellar" episode. Chandos describes the shattered unity of the old world, the dissolution of language and materials in terms of dying rats — an allegory that has been triggered by a recent event when he asked for a large amount of rat poison to be spread in the milk cellars at one of his diary farms. [*Quietly*: I will read you the whole paragraph and the way he describes the rats in the cellar event, using the translation from Professor Sheppard's chapter.] [*Shuffling papers*.]:

> As I was trotting along over the freshly-ploughed land, nothing more alarming was in sight that a scared covey of quail and, in the distance, the great sun sinking over the undulating fields, there suddenly loomed up before me the vision of that cellar, resounding with the death-struggle of a mob of rats. I felt everything within me: the cool, musty air of the cellar filled with the sweet and pungent reek of poison, and the yelling of the death-cries breaking against the mouldering walls; the vain convulsions of those convoluted bodies as they tear about in confusion and despair; their frenzied search for escape, and the grimace of icy rage when a couple collide with one another at a blocked-up crevice. But why seek again for words which I have foresworn! You remember, my friend, the wonderful description in Livy of the hours preceding the destruction of Alba Longa: when the crowds stray aimlessly through the streets which they are to see no more... when they bid farewell to the stones beneath their feet. I assure you, my friend, I carried this vision within me, and the vision of burning Carthage, too; but there was more, something more divine, more bestial; and it was the Present, the fullest, most exalted Present. There was a mother, surrounded by her young in their agony of death; but

> her gaze was cast neither toward the dying nor upon the merciless walls of stone, but into the void, or through the void into Infinity, accompanying this gaze with a gnashing of teeth! — A slave struck with helpless terror standing hear the petrifying Niobe must have experienced what I experienced when, within me, the soul of this animal bared its teeth to its monstrous fate.
>
> Forgive this description, but do not think that it was pity I felt. For if you did, my example would have been poorly chosen. It was far more and far less than pity: an immense sympathy, a flowing over into these creatures, or a feeling that an aura of life and death, of dream and wakefulness, had flowed for a moment into them — but whence?[28]

For the final part of the "Letter"... [*Quietly*: and of my presentation] I would like to offer a very basic outline of Shepperd's interpretation of this passage, as well as of the significance of Lord Chandos' "Letter" for our study of the aesthetics of modernism. [*Pause*.] Shepperd draws attention to the fact that the episode was triggered by the sunset, and he then resorts to several interpretative models to describe the process. His main model used in the chapter, and also alluded in the title of the chapter, is of course Freud's 1930 book, Civilization and its Discontents... [*Quietly*: Das Unbehangen in der Kultur] where Freud argued that Western civilization was caught in a fundamental contradiction between the individual and society. Freud is not the only model and Shepperd is making frequent references to other thinkers and poets as, for example, when he is proposing that the rats in the cellar episode could be seen as a vision of the Nietzschean death of God, or the Dionysian will to power, or a Marxist allegory of the total war of all against all in capitalism... [*Achoo. Sneeze in the audience*.] But overall, he places Chandos' experience between Freud's two centrals drives, Eros... [*Quietly*: the instinct representing the drive towards life] and the death drive, Thanatos, in arguing that the rat episode was not in his memory but part of Chandos' inner experience and the work of his unconscious.[29]

[*Sighs.*]

Ultimately, what happens with Chandos during the period of his crisis is significative of the experience of the modern world, and of modernism. [*Pause.*] His post-crisis experience changes insofar as he doesn't perceive the world as a stable object of contemplation, where Nature seems in abundance, static and eternal in its form... [*Quietly*: like something experienced in classical antiquity or medieval theology] but following the dying rats in the cellar episode, he perceives of the natural world as being less stable, more dynamic, horrifying, violent, incompressible, and subject to chance.[30] If, before the crisis, his attention was mainly concentrated on universal forms and cultured images, on eternal forces and laws, now he develops an empathy for the particular, for the insignificant creatures of life... [*Quietly*: he talks about dogs, rats, insects, about moss-covered stones, and other mute, inanimate beings that raise in him feelings of love and joyful eyes.] Chandos likes to compare himself to Crassus, the Roman stateman, orator, military commander, and politician who had a pet eel... [*Quietly*: and by other accounts, it was a lamprey, apparently, they are not the same fish] and which was the reason Crassus was often ridiculed by other senators. But Chandos found Crassus's sympathy for a lower creature, for this ugly fish, and the whole absurdity of the situation, central to his new state of mind and view of the world.

[*Long pause.*]

Ultimately, Shepperd argues that "Chandos has arrived at the threshold of a new way of relating to the world, he announces to Bacon that he will never write another book."[31] He leaves behind a static world of Renaissance humanism encapsulated in reified universalized forms in order to embrace a new world of particulars in constant flux of dynamic change. Chandos relates to this new world through a gesture, which has been central to modernism, a gesture that revolves around two extreme aesthetic positions, which we discussed in one of our past lectures, and this is the choice of complete fullness... [*Quietly*: the book of the world] or complete emptiness and minimalism. [*Pause.*]

He chooses the latter. His refusal to write is not a surrender, like the gesture of Arthur Rimbaud, who at the age of twenty-one gave up writing poems when he got disillusioned with the literary world... [*Quietly*: as Shepperd interprets this] which is a nihilistic surrender to the drive of Thanatos, but out of "a sense of humility and respect for [the] mysterious creative power" of Eros.[32]

[*Long pause.*]

Shepperd then offers some of the major implications of Hofmannsthal's "Lord Chandos Letter" for our understanding of modernism... [*Quietly*: and I quote.] "He flirts with nihilism; he knows moments of ecstasy and (quasi-) mystical insight; his way of writing about the epiphanies and the inability of language to grasp them reminds us of Symbolist aestheticism; his withdrawal from public life prefigures Rilke's and Yeats's withdrawals from modernity; his enjoyment of simple objects connected with rustic life has something of the modernists who tried to reinstate a 'more modest humanism' shorn of its illusions together with the experimental, eccentric openness to life; and his positive appreciation of folly and the absurd point forward to Dada and Leopold Bloom."[33]

[*Long pause.*]

Chandos concludes the "Letter" with an apology for the lengthy description of his state of crisis. He restates his determination to stop writing, asserting that he will write no more books in English or Latin in the next or all the coming years. He explains his position by the realization that he does not know a single word of the new language that he had discovered, and this is "a language in which mute things speak to me and in which I will perhaps have something to say for myself someday when I am dead and standing before an unknown judge."[34] And I will conclude this presentation with my favorite closing sentence from Professor Sheppard's chapter that interprets the Lord Chandos' gesture in terms of learning to deal with death, with Thanatos, and... [*Quietly*: here is my favorite part] "if he is to find his proper place within Creation, he has to dethrone reason from its earlier position of imperial sovereignty and allow it to find a much less exalted place within the democratic federation of faculties that constitutes the human personality."[35]

STUDENT ONE: Thank you.

[*Audience applauding.*]

JAMESON: Okay, let me... [*Footsteps.*] Let me also say a word or two about this Letter. This is a very short document, hmm... [*Addresses Teaching Assistant*: we should make some extra copies for people who want to read it.] It is something that anybody interested in modernism needs to know, as I think it's a [*Stressing*] <u>fundamental</u> document of modernism. It's not an idea, it is the record of an experience, and this experience can be analyzed in a whole variety of ways, and you... [*Addresses Student One*] brought some of those very well. [*Pause.*] The multiple interpretations of "The Lord Chandos Letter" are not, I think, all clear and decidable, but they vary in their analysis. The most obvious way to think about it — and you mentioned some of them, like the centrality of the sun, the sunset and so on and so forth — is the breakup of the cosmos or of the old view of the world... [*Quietly*: it is the new order that comes much earlier with Galileo challenging the Earth-centered universe.] The hierarchically organized world of the cosmos has been settled down and broken into pieces by the rise of modern science, and, hmm... [*Hesitates*] and this then instills some crisis of meaning. And even later, the view of the cosmos built on a Newtonian architecture challenged the older Ptolemaic model of the universe, which was widely accepted in the Middle Ages, and this is the very familiar notion we all have, and I think we would have to also ask ourselves why it happens again in the late nineteenth and early twentieth century, right... [*Quietly*: because we are now around the time of the Einsteinian theory.] So, that can be one way of looking at the Letter, through the reorganization of the universe, the dissolution of the old worldview. That's often been said about modernism... [*Quietly*: that it is a world that was turned into fragments, into isolated individuals, people with angst, psychological dread, anxiety and so forth.] And I don't mean to say that that view would not be true, but it seems to me that there are other ways of looking at it and they are all in this text. [*Pause.*] Then you could talk about it in terms of psychopathologies, as with Deleuzian schizophrenia, and I think this is one of the great documents of what's lost by the schizophrenic. There is no particular causality there; I mean, one can really see why this should be happening except as a kind of strange accidental, hmm... [*Hesitates*] convulsion of things or some purely personal and private experience. [*Pause.*] Mm-hmm. But I also think that it's in terms of language that this Letter is supposed to reach us. Hofmannsthal is not saying that the world doesn't mean anything anymore; he's saying that language and words don't function anymore... [*Quietly*: and that's obviously a very different thing.] And this is then what Adorno, in this chapter, calls nominalism. [*Pause.*] "The Lord Chandos' Letter" is a test case of an exemplar of nominalistic experience, but you can look for such experience in other more familiar places. [*Addresses the audience.*] Who knows William Carlos Williams's famous line: "So much depends on a red wheel barrow..." How does the rest of it go? [*Looks around.*] Anyone? These are... [*Pause.*]

AUDIENCE: [*Murmuring.*]

JAMESON: Hmm?

STUDENT: "...glazed with rain water beside the white chickens..."

JAMESON: Right. [*Excited.*] "So much depends on a red wheel barrow glazed with rain water beside the white chickens."[36] Alright. This is the nominalism of images, which is more or less contemporary with Hofmannsthal's Letter. Mm-hmm. And that somehow does not... [*Quietly:* they are not fragments anymore; I don't think what is evoked at the end of the Letter in somewhat positive sense are really fragments in the strict sense of this word... (*Mumbles indistinctly*).] They are things, they're even little unities, they may be micrological unities — they are unities which don't fit into anything anymore. When you say "fragment," it suggests a broken piece of something, but that's not what is going on here, I think. [*Softly*.] There wasn't anything for this to be pieced off, hmm, that something has disappeared. Now, in terms of classical nominalism, obviously that something, of which these so-called "fragments" were once a part, are what in logical philosophy are called "universals." Hence, his remarks about abstract values, opinions, moral judgments, and truth and things like that... [*Cough in the audience*] these universals can also be classifying devices, abstractions, and so on. Now all of these universals are gone, and you only have the contact with the thing. [*Pause*.] There is no universal under which this particular can be subsumed. Nowadays, in current language, these are called singularities, and the point with singularities is that they are particulars without generalities. Right? [*Softly*.] You've got these things: universals, particulars, singularities.[37] Nominalism is the crisis of the universal, hmm... [*Hesitates*] because it turns the particularity, which would be an example of this universal, into a [*Stressing*] singularity, which is an example of nothing, but which is a kind of event... [*Quietly*: and this would be if we put it in a very contemporary language... (*Mumbles indistinctly*) which is the language of nominalism.] Here Adorno is sort of insisting on singularity, he is holding on to the singularity, which could be a positive thing to say... [*Cough in the audience*] and even ethically, because at least you've got a genuine experience there, a genuine event, a reality that you hold on to. Nonetheless, this is in some sense symptomatic of a whole decay of language, and of the universal, and of thinking.

[*Long pause*.]

Mm-hmm. So, there are all those... [*Pause*.] There are all those different levels on which this narrative of decay is taking place. Hofmannsthal himself was, hmm... [*Hesitates*] I don't know if you can call him a fin-de-siècle poet, or maybe a post-fin-de-siècle poet? But on this first page of chapter two of Aesthetic Theory... [*Quietly*: and we'll come back to this next time] Adorno enumerates a number of people who belong to the general fin-de-siècle period, which would be called symbolisme in

French, Jugendstil in German, and so forth.[38] This is a moment in which... [*Pause.*] And the names here are... [*To himself*: who are they, hmm] Stefan George is one of them. [*Determined.*] There is a new biography of Stefan George, a very important poet and figure in German literary history, which we don't know very much about. In the latest New Left Review, there is a very enlightening review of this new book, Secret Germany, which gives you a little biography of George...[39] [*Quietly*: but you can find this also in some other place.] Mm-hmm, Oscar Wilde... [*Pause.*] In French, I think it wouldn't be Mallarmé so much, but maybe Verlaine, and some other people. It is about beauty and decadence in some sense. And it's not only Wilde, it's William Morris, so there is also a political component in this. I believe that the social and political content of the decadence, or the fin-de-siècle, is the idea that, in this nascent industrial society, the evocation of beauty and the idea of beauty can be subversive. And the... [*Pause.*] The dandyism of Wilde is as subversive as the politics of Marx or Ruskin, as far as that's concern, because it is out of Ruskin that a lot of this comes. And this is a pan-European development.

[*Long pause.*]

Alright. Hofmannsthal inherits this; he is the next generation of this fin-de-siècle Vienna; he practices it for a while, and then suddenly there is the crisis. [*Pause.*] And the crisis means... [*Quietly*: so, I'm assuming that it is corresponding to something personal, or at least to the imagination of something possibly personal.] What the crisis corresponds to, in fact, is the emergence of modernism. This is a... [*Pause.*] Schoenberg in music is right around the corner, and Schoenberg is also a central part of this process. Brecht once said that Schoenberg's music was too sweet, which is rather an odd idea, but he was thinking of early Schoenberg, which is this post-Wagnerian.... [*Door slams shut*] longing hysteria and very beautiful sorts of things. If you know the famous early piece by Schoenberg, which is called "Transfigured Night" or Verklärte Nacht...[40] [*Quietly*: which was one of the great tonal pieces with these lush harmonies and romantic… (*Words indistinct*) one of his, the early days of (*Mumbles indistinctly*).] And again, it's based on some psychoanalytic notion of hysteria, as that quintessential form of longing and desire and so on and so forth. But Schoenberg moves from that into something that are not at all like that, or that one can still feel some sweetness inside of his later work. Mm-hmm. In the early years of the century, you can't write in the traditional way anymore. It's clear that Jugendstil, based on natural forms, and that symbolisme or the fin-de-siècle, or even the decadence, that these are not any longer possible or alive and that a more substantial break has to be made with those artistic forms. [*Pause.*] Mm-hmm. And that break will be a break with the natural objects of beauty, and will go on over and out of harmony, out of the natural forms of Jugendstil into something which is easiest to talk about in terms of… [*Slams his palm on the desk*] dissonance. With the impressionists in painting being an example of that? We are now, I think, making the connection with Cézanne, and even beyond Cézanne with the cubists maybe in two continuous ways. Yeah, maybe but there is also a symbolist painting you know, which is Puvis de Chavannes[41] and people like that… [*Door slams.*] But maybe one could say that, even in their case, what we call here elements of nominalism are developed to a point where the cubism then finally results, and it has nothing to do with that sort of aesthetic of impressionism anymore. Well, what is that to say is that Chandos can't… [*Pause.*] Hmm, literary history, poetry, modernism have gone into directions that he can no longer follow. [*Cough in the audience.*] So, he can't write modernist poetry anymore for whatever reason. And this is in that sense a farewell to [*Stressing*] that form of literature… [*Pause*] or let's say farewell to literature, insofar as literature or art has gone on beyond what it can do. [*Cough in the audience.*] And I think this is a very familiar notion, right, that somehow you reach a line and that you can't pass over, either in terms of appreciating it or in terms of producing it. But remember that one of the most… [*Reflects*] hmm, already one of the most emblematic gestures in something that will become modernism is Rimbaud's silence. [*Pause.*] And this is the more reason Rimbaud... [*Quietly*: I don't think you can find, or you can have it in A Season in Hell.[42]] And I don't know if Rimbaud is really an account of the type of silence that you find in here, but this falling silent is certainly another version of that. And so, you can say okay, but the silence is a form of art itself, as in Beckett, or you can talk about the historical break, or indeed and I think [*Addresses Student One*] you were tempted to do this — you can seize on somebody's later perceptions and see in those the form of something new. [*Pause.*] Certainly, the individual perception, when he talks about his sympathy for these objects and insignificant things, and as I said, Chandos is associated with Imagism and that suggests a rather different aesthetics than that of Victorian excess and sentimentality by advocating a more direct, concrete form focused on the visual image... [*Quietly*: one could even talk about Heidegger and Being] that is to say, it's the way in which a single object, a singularity, connects not to abstract ideas but to being itself in some Heideggerian sense. He also talks about vitalism, and I think this is probably the more appropriate reference where there is a sense of life itself that started under all of these things, hence the ploughed field, and the notion of death, and the rats. And so, all of these things are manifestations of the vital. [*Decisively.*] Vitalism is one of the dominant post-Nietzschean currents in European art and culture around this period, from D.H. Lawrence, for example... [*Quietly*: who else? I mean, it's also a bit naturalist. I mean, you have this sense of the unity of an enormous sort of vitalistic force rather than any architecture of the universe.] So, one could interpret the Letter in that way too, and indeed, I think it's, hmm... [*Mumbles indistinctly.*]

[*Long pause.*]

One of the undecidable features of this Letter is whether this is a happy ending or not, right? [*Pause.*] You will no longer write verse; you will no longer use language. But has he not [*Stressing*] used it though? And it is not that you have to still use language in order to say that you can't speak, which is itself already like overstepping the Kantian limit, or boundary as Hegel might say. I mean, as you draw the line, you're already beyond it, and in some sense, and so Chandos is already beyond this limit, which is his own experience.

[*Long pause.*]

Mm-hmm, so it could be all of these things, I think. Mm-hmm. But it is a document of all of these manifestations, and I also think... [*Achoo. Sneeze in the audience*] it is quite amazing how this Letter was written in a period of relative European harmony. Therefore, it could be said that it anticipates all the coming tragedies and genocides on the continent in some historical way... [*Quietly*: it's really a kind of experience of death and of genocide to which nothing can compare, except maybe in the colonial territories, but then Austria did not quite have colonies, even though... (*Mumbles indistinctly*) the Austro-Hungarian Empire had its own experience with violence committed against the Serbian population and some other things.] But I'm not sure that it is... [*Pause.*] That's yet another interpretation of these processes, in the sense of death or mortality. Hofmannsthal went on to write some very remarkable plays, in which he used the Viennese dialect, and they are quite dazzling in their style. There are also these various other sketches; he never wrote a full novel, I believe, but he does get back to modernism, but now it's through something that Adorno... [*Quietly*: and Adorno and Benjamin were close to him, he was a patron of Benjamin.] In his journal... [*Raps his knuckles on the desk*] what was the journal called? Anyone? Hmm, it was the first one to print Benjamin's major essay on "Goethe's Elective Affinities," so there is some correspondence there.[43] I think Adorno must have had... [*Quietly*: he died fairly young, Hofmannsthal.] So, there are all kind of other connections, but what I wanted to say is, hmm... [*Hesitates*] what happens is that Hofmannsthal ends up writing the librettos for Richard Strauss, and he is the author of Elektra, Der Rosenkavalier, and all of those. And Strauss is also one of these figures who some people think that, with Elektra, Strauss touches the [*Stressing*] outside point of his modernism, and then retreats again, but that's another question. But certainly, via music, Hofmannsthal does break into the world of modernism again, but in some new way. Mm-hmm... [*Pause.*] So, I think this really is a very basic outlook to Adorno's ideas about modernism and nominalism.

[*Long pause.*]

Okay, listen, we went beyond our time, and I get to... [*Pause.*] I get to stop here. Let's see then... [*Chair-backs creaks*] what we do with this film you will watch next time... [*Chairs scratching the floor. Zippers zipping up.*] At quarter to eleven, and we will then go on... [*Noise.*]

Audience stands up. Objects drop on the floor. Door squeaks. Feet shuffling. Students return chairs to other classrooms. Some form a line to discuss their papers with Jameson. General noise. Screeching microphone noise.

[*Microphone turns off.*]

CURTAIN

LECTURE SIX

FEBRUARY 11, 2003

SITUATION (CHAPTER) — ANTINOMIES OF MODERNISM — ART AS PRODUCTION — INNOVATION

CURTAIN RISES

Moving chairs, squeaking door, coughs, other sounds filling the noise environment of a large classroom in the Literature Department at Duke University. A few graduate students discuss Jameson's teaching style, and how it differs from what they experience in other seminars on campus. For the most part, they consist of him lecturing in front of a relatively passive audience, and the only engagement from the audience is the spontaneous questions or comments, and the presentations made by his graduate students. His teaching methods differ from other pedagogies. Occasionally one hears complaints that his seminars are "old-fashioned," "monological," "non-democratic" (or are a form of "communist propaganda"), or that they "discourage dialogue and hybridity," or are generally detrimental to the education of future leaders. Indeed, Jameson's teaching style has not kept pace with corporatized academia, where the professor is increasingly a service provider and the student a consumer who is entitled to an opinion on every subject. One student says, taking off her coat, that she prefers this old-fashioned lecturing, or — as she puts it —

this thinking-in-progress, to the "interactive" seminars where classroom participation is reduced to exchanges of unformed opinions.

Jameson enters the classroom carrying a few books, his scattered notes, and the red pen in the chest pocket of his flannel shirt.

[*Microphone turns on.*]

JAMESON: [*General audience hubbub. Floor creaking.*] Mm-hmm. Please pass the German text, if anyone wants a copy... [*Zipper unzipping.*] Hmm... [*Hesitates.*] I would like today to... [*Footsteps. Chairs scratching against the floor.*]

[*Audience hubbub fading away.*]

Oh, a couple of other announcements. Here is an interesting Japanese film I've never heard of... [*Audience laughing.*] Tomorrow at 8pm and it's called Welcome Back, Mr. McDonald.[1] [*Laughter continues.*] Then... [*Quietly*: I'm sure there are some other things going on, so if anyone has other announcements to make, please go ahead.] I did want also to say a few words about our bigger event... [*Raps his knuckles on the desk.*] Please keep in mind that our Slovenian friends are arriving on Sunday, and next week there will be three lectures which will take place at noon in... [*Cough in the audience*] you know where that is? It's in that room up there in the Union Building. What is that place called, I don't know, hmm... [*Quietly*: which is never used, except by us, so it's a good place to hang out.] Slavoj will be first on Monday the 17th with a talk called "Against Deleuze"... [*Chair scraping the floor*] then Alenka Zupančič on Wednesday at 12 o'clock will give a paper called "Lacan with Nietzsche." She is the author of this very important book on Lacan's ethics, which... [*Cough in the audience*] shows how that works out in Lacan's "Seminar Seven." She explores the relation between ethics and psychoanalysis and there is also a relationship to Kant's moral philosophy.[2] But her talk this time will be about Nietzsche. And then we will also host Mladen Dolar on Friday... [*Quietly*: also, at noon] and his talk is called "Voice as a Political Category." This is a very interesting theme that he has been working on for a long time. Mm-hmm. He thinks that singing opera... [*Quietly*: he's written a book on opera, and he's also written a book on Mozart, which is only in German, as far as I know right now.[3]] So, Mladen thinks that voice is a central element of subjectivity and that singing is there to obliterate the voice... [*Door creaks open. Footsteps.*] There will be thoughts like this. He did something... [*Tries to remember*] he did an older work on voice four or so years ago, and it is in the copies of Sic,[4] and maybe I should copy that too for you. Then he also worked on Descartes,[5] linking cogito to desire and the unconscious, and then there is also another one on voice. I'll bring them all and then we will make copies.

[*Long pause.*]

Now, the actual seminar that the Slovenians will give will be the next two weeks after that. There will be one session every day for the duration of two weeks. Every day, from one to three in that same room in the Union Building, they will all be doing something which I don't exactly know... [*Quietly*: I mean, they will give you a reading list, which I believe is from Slavoj's Lenin book.] This is a collection of texts which people don't really know, except for the "State and Revolution"... [*Quietly*: the stuff that Lenin wrote between the February revolution and the October revolution — very interesting stuff, with huge essays by Slavoj.[6]] You also have this joint book that Dolar and Slavoj wrote about the opera — The Second Death of Opera, or something like that and the latest book on ethics.[7] But I think that their seminar will range in all kind of other directions. This seminar can be taken [*Stressing*] for credit, but you will need to sign up for it. There is a number down in Caroline's office... [*Quietly*: for those of you who are from other departments, you can also sign up and that's down... (*Mumbles indistinctly*) in the basement.] You all will get credit for it... [*Pause.*] I think we're gonna do it this way — anybody who comes for the entire ten sessions will get credit. I will take attendance and we'll just turn in advance... [*Achoo. Sneeze in the audience*] the grades. So, the seminar can be on your transcript, and it merely requires you going, and hopefully even maybe doing some readings that they will give you... [*Quietly*: I don't know, have I quoted Slavoj's favorite reply to a student?] "Yes, you can write a paper. If you don't write a paper, you get an A — everybody gets an A. If you write a paper, I can't promise anything." [*Audience laughing*.] So, anyway, that's the... [*Laughter continues*.] So that's the story on that. I don't know how exactly their seminar is supposed to take place, who is going to say what. Maybe the three of them will talk all at once, I don't know... [*Laughter*] that's for them to know and for us to find out.

[*Long pause. Laughter continues*.]

Okay, next thing... [*Addresses a student*.] Do you think you could pass this paper around so people can sign for the seminar? Just pass it around and make everyone interested in the seminar, put a mark against their names... [*Audience passing around the enrolment sheet for the Slovenian seminar*.]

STUDENT: What mark shall I use?

JAMESON: Why don't you just... [*Pause*.] What's the other nice sign for this sort of things?

STUDENT: Can I use a checking mark? Or a vertical line?

JAMESON: Oh, that's what I use for "delete," but anyway. Make sure you don't mean delete... [*Chuckles*.] Just put a cross or something next to your name...

JAMESON: Alright. Then, I would also like to know how many people have signed up so far to produce short exposés in this seminar. Just raise your hand... [*Quietly*: one, two, three, ah, and there was another one... (*Cough in the audience*).] Ah, Erin, is she here?

STUDENT: Yes, I'm here.

JAMESON: Are you still going to do your presentation on Beckett?

STUDENT: Yes, I can do it.

JAMESON: Okay. Alright. Let me see all of you, the exposé people, after class, and I hope more of you will get into the swing of this and do something... [*Quietly*: because it's a welcome change from hearing only my voice in this classroom all the time.]

[*Long pause.*]

The other thing is... [*Chair legs scrapes against the floor*] how do we want to go ahead with this? Of course, we are falling behind... [*Clears throat*] but that's in the nature of things. Today I will try to get through very rapidly this second chapter of Aesthetic Theory... [*Quietly:* "Situation" chapter] and after that, I want us to go very swiftly to the chapters on beauty, and those are the next three chapters: chapters three, four and five, which is to say, in English, they range from page 45 to 100... [*Cough in the audience.*] Mm-hmm. All of this is very interesting and important, but somehow, I feel that the themes of those three chapters on beauty are somehow less immediate than some of the other ones, namely the first and the second chapters... [*Quietly*: but we won't have any time left if we slow down and try to do everything.] In any case, the way Adorno writes, you can't really go line by line with him... [*Pause.*] We'll see how we will do it today, but you really just have to grab some of his essential themes. [*Pause.*] Aesthetic Theory is really a little bit like a suite of themes and variations, in some sense... [*Quietly*: maybe in some twelve-tone music sense.] You have a certain number of themes that go and come back all the time, because a lot of these matters, he will mention, then they come back in a secondary way or they get fully addressed later on, and part of the mapping of this book will be to figure that out, to see what the repetitions and proportions are. For example, we get a little bit on the culture industry on the first page of the second chapter,[8] and I think we already started on that the other day, and then later on in the book we'll get another twenty pages on the culture industry... [*Quietly*: in the case of the culture industry, I think we don't, but I use it as an example of how one of his themes may work throughout this book.] So... [*Exhales deeply.*] There is a repetition, but repetition in the sense of being a variation, not in any obsessive-compulsive sense. But still, we have to see what makes this thing up, what is Aesthetic Theory composed or how it is [*Stressing*] constructed.

[*Long pause.*]

Now, are we just... [*Exhales deeply.*] Are we just banging our heads against the wall to assume that there really is a unity in these chapters? [*Pause.*] But I think that we still have to try and find one, even if we fail. I think you should also notice the way the paragraphs are set up, because there is certainly a kind of unity in these paragraphs, which is very difficult to identify because the editors have made a... [*Quietly*: they pulled all the paragraphs to the right inside and you can only tell it by looking at the unfinished lines on the left, I mean on the right... (*Mumbles indistinctly*).] But nonetheless, these paragraphs do seem to be arranged... [*Sighs.*] There is a kind of thematic or philosophical breathing here, where he starts a theme; he works it out for a while and then runs out of breath and that's the end of the paragraph. Then we have a new theme. I also think that there is no philosophical [*Stressing*] argument in Adorno, as that is normally been understood. Somebody asked the other day about "proof," like what proof can he offer that everything is going downhill? I think there is no proof with the matter that we are dealing with here... [*Pause.*] In his world, works of art are not about proof, but they are [*Stressing*] symptoms of everything, including of what's going down the hill or you can call it crisis.

[*Addresses student signing the enrollment sheet.*] This column here, you can use this one. Just put a checking mark or something.

[*Long pause.*]

Mm-hmm. And actually, I also think that the philosophical texts, the various texts are also symptoms... [*Chair scrapes the floor*] because in them, as in a work of art, a formal contradiction will come out. In the philosophical or other texts, the ideological contradictions will emerge, and here we read statements about these superstructural symptoms. So maybe I'm wrong, maybe there is a kind of proof in that sense, but it's certainly not the kind of proof where you'd say... [*Quietly*: "Oh, all is lost, culture is going downhill, look at the quality of these TV programs, if you analyze this or that movie, or this or that novel", and so on and so forth.] It's not that kind of crisis, although as I already suggested, there is a kind of narrative of decline here — there is a historical narrative if you wish... [*Quietly*: a kind of philosophy of history I guess you could call it, in either a good or bad sense.] In each of these narratives, there is always something developing I think, and that would be one way of putting it... [*Quietly*: and on so many occasions, we can see that over and over again, and we feel that every time we read and re-read these sentences, there is a direction they point in if you wish.] So, we can't really... [*Pause*.] We can't really discuss this book sentence by sentence, but we can at least go over... [*Cough in the audience*] some of its major themes and follow them up by paying attention to how they come back as we're moving along.

[*Long pause*.]

Okay, now before we start on that, we may need to make some readjustment. What I forgot to say was that, according to our schedule, we should be up to chapter seven or something and then move on to Doctor Faustus next week. I think that's probably not a good idea. [*Pause*.] Mm-hmm, how many of you have started reading Mann...? [*Pause*.] How is Doctor Faustus coming...? [*Looks at the audience*.] How many of you have started reading it?

[*Long silence*.]

Okay. [*Cheerfully*.] How many of you will have read it eventually? Uh-huh?

STUDENTS: [*Chuckles*.]

JAMESON: Well, I suggest we put Doctor Faustus off for a few more weeks. Would you like to do it after the break? [*Audience murmuring*.] Maybe that's the best way to go about it because that would be a change of pace and it would give you time over the break to read it, and then in the meantime we can do a few more of these Aesthetic Theory chapters by then. [*Quietly*: Alright, so we will readjust this then.]

[*Long pause*.]

[*Enthusiastically*.] Oh. Did you see the movie the other day? [*Softly*.] How was that, how did you like it? Did you manage to see it?

[*Silence*.]

STUDENTS: [*Audience murmuring. Nodding*.]

JAMESON: What were your reactions? [*Pause*.] Had anybody seen it before, Pandora's Box by Georg Pabst and starring Louise Brooks? [*Pause*.] It's sort of classic Weimar, or the underside of Weimar, although... [*Mumbles indistinctly*.] And the kind of transgression that goes on in this period looks as if everything is breaking down... [*Quietly*: or whatever you want to describe these times.] Mm-hmm. But it's much more of a social and sexual transgression obviously... [*Raps his knuckles on the desk*] more of a transgression than in the Victorian era... [*Quietly*: which we should maybe call it the Wilhelminian Era, after the last Kaiser.] But on the other hand, Pandora Box's themes of sexuality, decadence, and moral decay in Weimar-era Germany often gets tied to a kind of very traditional gender relations... [*Quietly*: as if wanting to say, we're not necessarily equal because, after all, women incite male desire, as this is often put together in a very odd way (*Mumbles indistinctly*).] I mean, the collective murder is obviously a punishment for all of this. And the film is rather paradigmatic of the whole Weimer period, where these themes of violence run through the whole cultural production of Wedekind's plays, which was very important for Brecht and for many other German expressionists. [*Gloomily*.] Well, you don't seem very enthusiastic about that film. [*Chuckles*.] Mm-hmm. I have been trying to see if there is anything else, like DVDs or video tapes and other movies on this Weimar period in German history... [*Mumbles indistinctly*.]

STUDENT: There is a DVD of Woyzeck in the library.

JAMESON: There is?

STUDENT: [*Imperceptible*.]

JAMESON: Of Woyzeck?

STUDENT: [*Imperceptible*.]

JAMESON: I see, I see. But this is of Woyzeck according to… [*Words indistinct*]?[9]

STUDENT: Yes.

JAMESON: Ah, but that's… [*Slams his palm on the desk.*] We'll see about that and maybe we can set that up at some other time when we don't have to rush through Aesthetic Theory. Hmm, anyway.

[*Long pause.*]

Okay, so let's begin again with this second chapter called "Situation," which at least gives you an idea of how Adorno sees that the work of art is in some sense determined by the situation, but also it's a free choice or a free reaction to the situation. Now, I start with that — although I could come to it later on — because the other thing that will happen in this chapter is a series of, hmm… [*Hesitates*] antinomies. It is as if he wants to ask about the work of art: is the work the product of freedom or of determinism? [*Pause.*] And in fact, it's the product of both: the work of art is freedom, which is determined by a situation… [*Cough in the audience.*] And therefore, we ask ourselves what do we do with these ideas? It is simply that there is a bad side of the situation in the work of art and a good side of it? The bad side is determination and historical anchoring, and the good side of art is that it is the product of free will. But it is not only the fact that the artwork is historically anchored in a situation… [*Quietly*: because that could be simple materialism, or social history… (*Cough in the audience*) or whatever] but that the situation is bad, because the artwork is a reaction to a situation of stifling, naming, disintegration, whatever you want to call it. Mm-hmm. So that would be the bad part, but the act of freedom of expressing the situation, that is certainly the good part. But I don't know if this solves the philosophical problem… [*Cough in the audience.*] Is this dialectical to say that freedom and determination in a situation, which is art, are the same? [*Pause.*] Probably, but that way of putting it doesn't do us any good either. So, I think that this leaves us with these antinomies, which we will see a lot of them running through here... [*Quietly*: there are two or three or more of them.] This is then a crucial example of the way in which the chapter is not only laying out a set of uses of aesthetics, but it's also producing some philosophical test cases. And I tried to tell you the other day — and I think I didn't do a very good job of it — that it does seem to me that, hmm... [*Hesitates*.] For example, later on he says that negative and... [*Shuffling paper*] that's meaningless in philosophy, but in aesthetics it might have a meaning. Well, it's as if almost everything is meaningless in philosophy, that is to say in real life. All of those traditional philosophical themes, which in real life fail to do whatever they are supposed to do, if you look at them in this closed world of aesthetics, suddenly they take on a justification... [*Cough in the audience*.] And therefore, once again, art is a kind of sealed laboratory experiment in which all of philosophy or life comes in and adds some kind of genuine content, partly because this is only an imaginary content, right? So, I believe this is one of the paradoxes that is going on here. Now... [*Pause*.] And we'll try to find a number of such antinomies like this one, and maybe even make a table of these antinomies, because it seems to me that whatever else is going on in Adorno, hmm... [*Hesitates*] this one is sort of central, this location of things within these oppositions... [*Pause*.] I don't think we could yet call it "contradictions," but at least they are antonymic in the sense that they have a positive and negative pole, and we don't have a way of expressing that difference somehow.

[*Long pause*.]

We start with the materials,[10] which lead us at once to commodities and thus to the culture industry and Entkunstung — the fact of taking a work of art and sort of stripping it of everything that's art and turning it into a commodity that way. Alright, that's one way of talking, and a very interesting way of talking about the commodity, instead of the cultural problems. [*Pause*.] And it is clear that everything has succumbed to that. So, when you have... [*Quietly:* my favorite is, I haven't heard this on TV anymore] "buy this record which contains the ten all-time loveliest melodies of Western classical music," or something like that. Adorno always thought that this reification of the theme plays some central part in these processes of commodification of culture precisely by means of disjoining and fragmenting the... [*Mumbles indistinctly.*] What you want out of Beethoven, Tchaikovsky, Wagner is not the symphony or opera [*Stressing*] as a whole, but you divide it, you take the most likable part, turn it into a possessed object and listen to it over and over again. And this is the crudest way in which something that had some formal unity was turned into a commodified fragment. But the most common way of talking about this is [*Stressing*] reification. Mm-hmm, and reification simply means, hmm... [*Hesitates*] res- ...[*Pause*] Verdinglichung, Ding, "thingification," or la chosification is the term that the French existentialists liked to use... [*Quietly*: which we sometimes translate this as "thingification" as well] and that seems to me, refers to turning something which is not a thing into a thing. Now, what is it not? Well, one thing the commodified fragment is not is a production process, right? [*Pause.*] The work of art is number one: a process in time; and it is a production process because there is a whole connection with production present in it. Alright, but then it's produced — there it is as an obj... [*Cough in the audience*] and it's no longer production process. Now, I think... [*Clears throat*] that behind this notion there is something that you can understand maybe in this way. [*Reflecting*] Mm-hmm... [*Pause.*] But first let me give you a quick historical example, which should explain to you where Adorno is coming from with this.

[*Long pause.*]

In the tradition of German families... [*Quietly*: and I think in East and West Germany these things are much more so than they are here in America] people actually played music. They learned to play the piano early on and it was part of their custom to have home concerts. They approached these musical works... [*Quietly*: you could buy the latest scores for the piano and run home and learn how to play them in front of the entire family] so they approached music from the standpoint of [*Stressing*] production, hmm... [*Hesitates*] as opposed to those who just heard music on the radio, or on a record or something, and is a completely contemplative experience... [*Quietly*: as if they have nothing to do anymore with the production of these things; we don't play music anymore, we just listen to it, we lost our way, and I think the proportion in the United States would be pretty small of people who actually play music.] But for the German bourgeoisie at least, the home musical culture was almost a religion... [*Mumbles indistinctly*.] So, there would be a way of approaching a piece of music through the habit of production that doesn't exist for those who simply consume it. Now, let me give you an even better example of this. Mm-hmm. It is said that... [*Pause*.] This is something that also illustrates for you the difference between West and East and that is what one sometimes hears that the Chinese can understand Bach, and we can't understand the Chinese characters. Well, I don't know if this is true of Bach, or of China, but it is certainly true of the Chinese characters... [*Quietly*: you know that the great calligraphers, who are... (*Pause*).] For example, one of the greatest of all Chinese calligraphers, his work is almost entirely lost because the Emperor had all of them buried with him in his tomb, which is of course also lost... [*Cough in the audience*] and now they only have imitations by the disciples. Now, if I take a bunch of you through the museum and show you Chinese calligraphy, I think that — like myself — you will be embarrassed and find some difficulty in understanding what the greatness of these signs is. [*Softly*.] But that's because you don't draw characters. [*Pause*.] If one is in the habit of drawing these characters at least, then you have some sense of how the process works, and everybody in China draws characters and therefore they can sense the squiggle of lines as a production process. Mm-hmm... [*Hesitates*.] They can see things that are going on there and understand the momentum of this, and complexity of it in ways that those of us for whom this is just a spread of marks cannot. [*Pause*.] Hmm, now I think that's one way of understanding reification in this sense, namely: as separation, or non-participation in the process of cultural production.

[*Long pause.*]

But here is the problem — here is the antinomy. [*Pause.*] Modern society is becoming increasingly reified, that is to say [*Whispers*] commercialized. Another definition of reification is simply what's sold for money, with time and labor which are abstract and intangible things being treated as concrete objects sold on the market. Mm-hmm, labor power is reified when it becomes a commodity, that it to say when you get a wage. Wage labor is reified labor. If you're working for a lord in a feudal era... [*Zipper unzipping*] if you are a slave or if you're living in some ideal socialist or communist society like Thomas More,[11] you don't work for a wage, and here labor is not measured in that way, although exploitation may be present of course. So, the commodity is also [*Stressing*] what is paid, and, in that sense, society and everything in society is increasingly monetized... [*Exhales deeply.*] Everything carries a price tag; nobody does anything for nothing; all forms of labor are somehow measured, and you might get a bargain in a special kind of situation... [*Quietly*: I don't know if you know. We don't have it here, but up there in Connecticut they have this system where you exchange labor... (*Words indistinct*). You do something and you get a certain script and then someone else will do some form of labor for you, so it's a kind of barter labor transaction process, a kind of underground utopia of mutuality and collectivity still around in certain places in the United States... (*Mumbles indistinctly*).] It's been since, I would say, since Proudhon in the nineteenth century... [*Footsteps*] and this is part of the anarchist thought about how you could create a society which is no longer commodified around wage, but in which labor is exchanged directly. On the other hand, you have to remember that Marx says in a marvelous denunciation of Proudhon... [*Quietly*: I think it's in Grundrisse in the chapter on money] where Marx says, [*Impersonates Marx*] "Okay, so you get your labor record, you get your little... [*Knock his thumb on the desk*] your little ticket certifying that you have worked a certain number of hours and that somebody else will have to work the same number of hours for you, but then you don't understand that this becomes money." There is a process that is irreversible, where little by little this seemingly non-alienated exchange, it's gonna turn back into the form of money.[12] There is no way of getting away from this. Mm-hmm... [*Hesitates*] but... [*Pause*] but one vision of non-commodification has always been this dream of getting rid of money, and the attempt has had a very long history which somehow has only produced substitutes... [*Quietly*: from shells and mollusks, to metals, copper and gold, to the exchange of labor time, of gems, and agricultural barter.... (*Mumbles indistinctly*). Getting rid of the exchange is the utopia.]

[*Long pause*.]

Okay, but now here is the thing. Everything in society is getting commodified, including the work of art. However, for Adorno, the work of art is a form of [*Stressing*] <u>resistance</u> to, hmm... [*Hesitates*] to reification. But how does art resist reification?

[*Long silence*.]

[*Softly*.] By becoming material, by becoming an object. But isn't that reification too? Is there good reification that the work of art performs in order to strike back at this reified society? Is there good and bad reification? Is it all the same? This is the first of these antinomies that you'll see here. Mm-hmm... [*Pause*] and... and... [*The microphone catches a short exchange between two students*.]

STUDENT ONE: [*Whispers*: What part of the chapter is he talking about, what page?]

STUDENT TWO: [*Whispers back*: I have no idea.]

JAMESON: And what this means... [*Students continue whispering*] is that in modernism... [*Quietly*: and this is a book about modernism, as it unfolds from Baudelaire, and from Manet, and Wagner in music, I guess] in modernism the work of art wants to become more and more material. It wants to be an object. It wishes not to be meaning but to be language.

It wishes not to be some lyric tunes of some sort but the sound of the timbre of various instruments. Mm-hmm. It wishes not to be a picture [*Stressing*] of something but to be real paint on canvas. This is the process by, whereby art reifies itself and turns itself into material in order to combat social reification.

[*Long pause.*]

Now, we can do the same thing with subjectivity. Remember that the orientation of this is towards... [*Pause.*] Mm-hmm. Hegel says, see page 23: "Hegel named this comportment freedom to the object."[13] And I don't know what is being translated there, because this is not English... [*Cough in the audience*] but Hegel's may not be German either. [*Mumbles indistinctly while searching for the sentence in the German version of* Aesthetic Theory.] Mm-hmm... [*Making whistling sounds: WHEW. WHEW. WHEW.*] Mm-hmm... [*Raps his knuckles on the desk. To himself.*] Where is it? [*Exhales deeply.*] Ah here you go: "Hegel nannte solche Verhaltensweise generell die Freiheit zum Objekt."[14] Well, okay then — it's "freedom [*Stressing*] to the object." In other words, Hegel's aesthetics, Adorno says over and over again, unlike Kant's, which is very ambiguous... [*Pause.*] You see, Kant's aesthetic seems clearly to be oriented around subjectivity, that is about the categories of the mind, and how the mind operates and so on and so forth. [*Decisively.*] But — and I think this is quite true — what Kant is trying to do is to show that subjectivity isn't objective. [*Pause.*] If you're talking about mental categories, you are talking about a rigid structure that is the mind in some sense. Hmm... [*Hesitates.*] So, Kant is very ambiguous in respect to the relation of the mind and categories or faculties to the object, whereas Hegel deliberately pushes all of this onto the object. Hegel's aesthetic will always be about [*Stressing*] what the structure of the object shows, not our reactions and feelings to it. If you wanted to include our reactions to the object, then you would have to make them objective too, and they are, as emotions are objective for, they are historical...

[*Quietly:* that would be another way of saying "objective" in a sense... (*Mumbles indistinctly*).]

[*Long pause.*]

Okay, but then, let me give you another antinomy, and it has to do with reification and with the subject? Alright, so with Hegel, we want to get rid of the subject and talk increasingly about the objective, about the historical and the material, and so forth. [*Pause.*] Yeah, but isn't getting rid of subjectivity also a bad thing? Isn't this repressing subjectivity in the name of flattening out of the subject in this new objective world of historical laws... [*Quietly*: like with the things that I was telling you last time.] Or with positivism. Isn't positivism precisely about getting rid of the subject in some sense, in its quest for objectivity, truth and method? [*Pause.*] How can that be good? So, evidently... [*Sighs.*] But on the other hand, this is inciting us to a kind of what I would rather call "depersonalization": we're getting rid of the ego, we're getting rid of personality... [*Cough in the audience*] and so on and so forth; we're getting rid of all this [*Hesitates*] hmm, fluid and elusory, impalpable features of subjectivity. But yet, we are confronted, as with reification, with something that looks the same on either end. Mm-hmm. Repressing a subject or nodding and approving the increasing depersonalization — both of those look the same, right? Well, it seems as if both are telling us "subjectivity is bad so we can get rid of it," but then one is doing it anyway, like what psychoanalysis is telling us... [*Quietly*: I mean that compulsive repression of your own desires and the stuff that comes back, or the return of the repressed and all different kinds of neurosis and so on.] And there are other ways of getting rid of subjectivity, which would be like, I don't know, in Buddhism or something, where you kill your desire for the object in order to achieve liberation or enlightenment, and so on... [*Pause.*] And this is I think actually is the trend in much of contemporary philosophy, and in art in the second half of the twentieth century, with all those influences of Eastern spiritual practices. I think that if you look at phenomenology, for example, that really evolves into something that is about getting rid of the ego or arriving at some form of more depersonalized relationship to reality. Certainly, that's true of Sartrean existentialism, hmm… [*Hesitates*] and Heidegger, a yeah, I think that being-toward-death, it's meant to be similar for there is a constant underground or overground thematic of the idea that the ego is the thing that you should get rid of… [*Quietly*: and in psychoanalysis this is obvious, maybe less so in psychology.]

[*Long pause*.]

We have then this range of antinomies, and let's see, let's count up these antinomies. Okay, we have… [*Chalk on the blackboard*.] R-E-I-F-I-C-A-T-I-O-N antinomy, then we have… S-U-B-J-E-C-T-I-V-I-T-Y antinomy. Then I also mentioned earlier on F-R-E-E-D-O-M and determinism. What else do we have here? Ah, the… [*Quietly*: we also have the critique of art, which is another key antinomy.] Adorno criticizes the culture industry, then he says… [*Quietly*: this is page 18 now] yeah, but it's not that easy. We can't just separate these cultural products out and say [*Impersonates Adorno*] "Oh, television is bad because it degrades art, but Woyzeck production by, let's say, Herzog is great art." He says the minute you start to criticize the culture industry, you are entering on a path which is finally the critique of art itself [*Pause*.] And in fact, all great art — for instance, he uses all the time one of these terms like "authentic art" or "great art" or… [*Words indistinct*] — is implicitly a critique of art. All great art wants to say that art itself is limited and we have to go beyond it, or it also wants to critique all the previous art… [*Quietly*: all great art is a critique of other art, right?] Ah, and here is another antinomy that could be formulated like this: [*Softly*] all great art is the same as the critique of art. And the critique of the culture industry is the same as the critique of art, because you can't really start denouncing culture unless you engage with it. What these people do — I've observed this in various places and you can find it among the modernists too — they say, look, art is great but this concept of culture we have to get rid of because that is very suspicious… [*Quietly*: that concerns excerpts of meaning, and you start to talk about (*Stressing*) the social and the political and then you start to talk about all these philistines, and people who hate art and... (*Zipper zipping up*) what you really do is trying to quarantine the use of the concept of culture and allow people only to speak about art.] Elitism. And Adorno does that, and he says that very explicitly. But on the other hand, this is very revealing because what this says is: once you start on that path, you cannot accept art's critique of itself. Mm-hmm... [*Hesitates*] and I think the notion is simply if you think of modernist works, they're all... [*Pause.*] You can say this is the relation of the sublime and the beautiful, I don't know. If you think of, specially the modern moderns — but I think this is true also of Baudelaire and Wagner — who are saying, [*Impersonates the modernists*] "Look, everybody is producing this regular form of art, but my art is gonna be much more than that, my art is gonna be the explanation of the world, the Book of the World, the negation of all art, or whatever you want to call it." [*Pause.*] So, that's already saying that art has its practice, but a practice that is limited. I want to produce an art that's more than art itself. So, the critique is already there inside the work of art. This is then another key antinomy... [*Chalk strokes on the blackboard*] C-R-I-T-I-Q-U-E O-F A-R-T. [*Looks at the column of antinomies on the blackboard*]

R-E-I-F-I-C-A-T-I-O-N
S-U-B-J-E-C-T-I-V-I-T-Y
F-R-E-E-D-O-M
C-R-I-T-I-Q-U-E O-F A-R-T

[*Long pause.*]

Okay, now I want you, hmm... [*Hesitates.*] I wanted you to look at the bottom of page 18... [*Page flipping. Audience murmuring.*] I want to come to another issue that I feel I need to explain in a kind of philosophical way, and that's the matter of ideology in Adorno. It's not something that Adorno uses very much... [*Quietly*: and this is my own use of this concept here...

(*Words indistinct*) you all know Deleuze's denunciation of ideology.[15]] I would say that by the time you get to the 1960s and the 1970s, there is a whole critique of the concept of "ideology" going on, which even leads to new definitions of ideology: "Oh, let's get rid of the concept of ideology altogether, let's call it 'practices'..." [*Quietly*: that was a great alternative that went on for a few years.][16] Mm-hmm. I think that it might be interesting to say that ideology is something like [*Stressing*] <u>the content</u>... [*Quietly*: mm-hmm, I don't know if this will make any sense.] Ideology is something like the content of philosophical positions that ought to remain purely formal. [*Pause*.] And why they should be purely formal, we will get to when we get to second reflection. Mm-hmm... [*Very quietly:* and indeed, maybe... (*Mumbles indistinctly*).] The problem with ideology is that it is making an endorsement... [*Quietly*: hmm, people call it also "affirmative," right, but when you say "affirmative culture," that's a bad word, for an affirmative statement about reality, any kind of reality, is endorsing it.][17] If you say life is such and such a thing, or a work of art is such and such a thing, if you go back to fundamental definitions — hmm, you are in some form of metaphysics, this is the same as ideology. [*Pause*.] If you wanna think in terms of deconstruction, that's fine, and that is to say for those of you who have some background in classical Derrida, you know that from a completely different point of view... [*Quietly*: and that is typical Derrida] that if you say anything you are subject to deconstruction, right? To say a thing, to make a statement is to, hmm... [*Hesitates*] emit a metaphysical proposition. So, if you look at the form of these classical Derrida essays, you'll see that they neither affirm nor deny it, that is to say it's a form which is set up so that Derrida himself will make no statement... [*Quietly*: but he does it sometimes, although he is not supposed to.] The aesthetic of deconstruction is to admit no positive or affirmative content. To admit no proposition. To make no statement. In other words, to have no ground or foundation, which is another way of saying all of this... [*Door creaks open*.] Any foundationalism, any essentialism — this is all the deconstructive attack on thematization... [*Quietly*: as Paul de Man liked to call it.] It is a taboo on propositions, on metaphysical positions, like: What is life? What is good? What is history? What is art? And things like that. All of those things are, I think, related, and one form of ideology, at least, is to be found there, in this remainder after you went through all of your deconstructive stuff, or through Adorno's contradictory or antinomic state, and you are still left over with [*Stressing*] something. [*Sniffing near the microphone.*] And is this something still ideological? [*Addresses the audience.*] Do you see anything like this going on in Adorno? Is there something metaphysical or ideological in Adorno that you notice?

STUDENT: Is it supposed to be something there?

JAMESON: [*Excited.*] Yes.

[*Long pause.*]

STUDENT: I guess that he is trying to practice his theory of constellations in a way in which...

JAMESON: Mm-hmm...

STUDENT: ... that becomes ideological... [*Words indistinct.*]

JAMESON:. By constellation, you mean Versöhnung, or reconciliation? [*Pause.*] It's a kind of, hmm... [*Pause.*] I don't know how we would... [*Strikes the chalk against the blackboard.*] I think, if it simply sounds like patting someone on the head, that's not it exactly, it is stronger than that. I, hmm... [*Agitated.*] I think you are onto something, but that would not be the way I would define this final reality for Adorno, and the moment in which all of this, in my opinion, becomes an ideology among others. What comes out of this ideology, of course, is a remarkably complicated theory but, and maybe everybody has this and goes back to a certain kind of individual foundation... [*Cough in the audience*] or essence of something which is necessarily once put in the language has to be deployed in some way. But what would it be? [*Addresses the same student.*] I think you are on the right track here... [*Pause.*]

[*Long silence.*]

[*Door creaks open. Footsteps.*] It's not that... [*Pause.*] The constellation also isn't to be thought of exactly as a Hegelian synthesis, that is, it's not a full reconciliation. Holding that, the other phrase that I like — and this is an important phrase that I should have mentioned the other day — which I think is in the Introduction to the Philosophy of New Music, but you'll find this phrase everywhere and this is... [*Chalk on the blackboard*] D-E-T-E-R-M-I-N-A-T-E N-E-G-A-T-I-O-N. And the "determinate negation," or holding to the determinate negation — that's sort of the [*Stresses*] absolute point of a work of art, of a thought and so forth, and it means that you can't overcome negation because it's there, it's in reality. But you can articulate it and hold to it in its historical specificity somehow. Mm-hmm. You don't swim out of it, up into some illusive kind of transcendence; you don't imagine you solved it, you don't think you can get away from it, but you [*Stressing*] hold to it in some way and not just a negation in general, which would be... [*Quietly*: some form of nihilism] maybe Benjamin's destructive character, or Karl Krauss as the ultimate satirist who just refutes and repudiates everything. It's not that. It has to be [*Whispering*] determined. It is the negation of [*Stressing*] this historical situation. So, I think what you're calling "constellation" is that, and when we come back at the end of this chapter... [*Quietly*: I really want to finish this chapter today] to negation and happiness... [*Very quietly*: that's what happiness must mean and how our understanding of how happiness works... (*Mumbles indistinctly*).] Remember I said the other day, quoting from Stendhal — a thing that they were very fond of — la promesse du bonheur... [*Pause.*] Not happiness but only the promise of happiness. That sort of thing. It's the idea of happiness but we all know that nobody has it.

[*Long pause.*]

So, what is this ideological leitmotif in Adorno? [*Pause.*] Because I think that it's this leitmotif that ages and dates in his philosophy... [*Quietly*: you can say, oh yeah, that's his ideology... (*Words indistinct*) or whenever you see ideology is like this, it's like a form of undigested content.] Well, I would say, and... [*Ad-*

dresses student] you may see how it ties into what you just said; I would say that this central motif is what he calls "suffering." This is sort of a re-connection with Auschwitz... [*Quietly*: and his famous remark whether poetry after Auschwitz is possible.] The notion that the bottom line of all human reality is physical suffering... [*Cough in the audience*] is what I think is ultimately irreducible in Adorno. It seems to me that this is the ideological kernel in Adorno; I mean, you can say "well, this is true and so forth," but that's not exactly the point that I'm making. What I say is that suffering then becomes the metaphysical foundation for his whole philosophy... [*Pause*.] Mm-hmm. Everything I think gets built on this very concept of physical suffering, of material suffering, and of something which cannot be expressed, or solved, or gotten rid of. And this theme of suffering, of course, obviously lends the coloration of this whole project, which is this sort of melancholic, nihilistic... [*Quietly*: not nihilistic, but... hmm, pessimistic overtone.] But it's not a wailing musical pessimism... [*Quietly*: this is not Spengler or Wagner, I mean; that's a kind of pessimism where the world is going to pieces and is sinking and so on and so forth, and this is something that one can take great aesthetic and personal enjoyment in.] Mm-hmm... [*Zipper unzipping*.] I don't think that's the case with Adorno and as I said earlier... [*Looks at the audience*.] Have we talked about the Holocaust and the survival guilt which the survivors often felt, a sense of responsibility for having survived while so many other people died? [*Audience murmuring*.] Yeah, I think we did talk about that. Adorno got out but he used to go back and forth between England and Nazi Germany until quite late, in the late 1930s,[18] and he did not suffer like many other people... [*Quietly*: Benjamin of course suffered in a different way, by suicide] and this theme of suffering that is at the heart of his work perhaps may also have something to do with that. So even his suffering is somehow somebody else's suffering. I mean, you could see that this very leitmotif of [*Stressing*] suffering, as the kernel of reality, can itself be opened up and unpacked and analyzed in all kinds of ways, which I think Adorno does not... [*Quietly*: he does not philosophically consider it.] Hmm, you can also look for this if you are interested in the very last chapter of Negative Dialectics... [*To himself*: the translation of which is very bad though, not as bad as the first one but still... (*Mumbles indistinctly*).] Okay, so I just want to alert you... [*Cough in the audience*] to this mode of analysis which consists in looking for ideological foundations, for something that is irreducible. Because it seems to me that when we get to suffering in Adorno, we get to it in one way that you can then trace it in most of his works, including aesthetics. [*Softly*.] But you may yourself be of a completely different, hmm... (*Hesitates*) different point of view on this matter.

[*Long pause*.]

Okay then, on to the fantastic. This is a very odd, hmm... [*Hesitates*.] This is the paragraph on page 19, starting out again, and which has to do with all kinds of things, with realism and with the place of the non-... [*Chair-back creaks*] and the non-ontic in the objectification of reality, in realistic fiction, and incidentally, when you get to this sentence [*Page flipping*]: "new art is so burdened by the weight of the empirical that its pleasure in fiction lapses."[19] [*Softly*.] This will become one of the great themes of Doctor Faustus, but today, in our world, this tendency is even more pronounced. I mean, I don't know how many people still read novels or go to movies; instead, there is this great interest in reality TV and how all the things have to be somehow real because you don't want to waste your time reading these imaginary things. This is what is meant here by the "the weight of the empirical..." [*Pause*.] And you can see how modernism could be driven already back into some classical modern period by this kind of... [*Achoo. Sneeze in the audience*] by this lost and depreciation of the fictional, and of the fantastical... [*Mumbles indistinctly*.]

[*Long pause*.]

Then coming out of this, all of a sudden, is [*Stressing*] the new. Look at bottom of that page [*Page flipping*]: "...the category of the new has been central"[20] and so on. Now, how does one get from the fantastic to the new? [*Pause.*] That would be the proper reading of this paragraph in which we can't indulge right now, but when we get to the "new," we are clearly at the center of a whole new view on modernism. Now, there are several features, hmm... [*Hesitates*] and we sort of have to pull them out and then look at them separately... [*Chalk on the blackboard*] A-B-S-T-R-A-C-T-I-O-N. For him, abstraction is the negation of the world, so when we have Malevich's Black Square and this means that everything in reality, including color... [*Quietly*: because, of course, black is not... (*Pause*). Is black considered color? Maybe it is, or I guess it may depend on the theory that you adopt.] So, everything in the world is negated by this square, but if you look at it from another side, for Malevich this square is also the source of a new energy, or a new beginning. So, you see how this works? The increasing abstraction is a way of doing something to the world, and that's one thing. And the production process [*Stressing*] creates objects that are not part of the natural objects. So, in that sense, abstraction is also a kind of production process; you're producing man-made things that are not just natural things that you are [*Stressing*] imitating. And this is why... [*Pause.*] This is if you want to emphasize this second break in the modern between Jugendstil and the true machine-type modernism, between the Jugendstil people with their flowery ornamentations and so on, and let's say futurism, which is the glorification of the machine, between symbolism fin-de-siècle late-nineteenth century and then, clearly I think from 1913... [*Quietly*: but 1913 is certainly only one of the dates, and there are other possible ways of periodization... (*Mumbles indistinctly*). So, this break will have to be before that.] That would be how we would do that... [*Pause.*] But with abstraction, we then also pass from mimesis [*Stressing*] to construction, and as I told you the other day, this is a very important opposition in Adorno. Another one would be [*Stressing*] mimesis and expression. How many opposites like that we can find, do you think? This is what we need to be making, we need to make a collection of these possible oppositions and what possible combinations they may have.

[*Long pause.*]

So, abstractness is then one thing, if we make abstractness a determinate negation — a reaction to the whole situation of art. Another one... [*Pause.*] And abstractness would be the "new" ... [*Cough in the audience*] because, like Dialectic of Enlightenment, it eats its own children, so you can say that the impressionists certainly negated the tradition of academic salon and literalism, but then Cézanne negates them even more substantially, so we can't tell whether these are represented objects anymore or pieces of paint... [*Creaking floor.*] And then the cubists come along and they negate Cézanne, I mean this is a process which is like in Dialectic of Enlightenment... [*Cough in the audience*] where each new stage of progress discredits and deserts the previous one; it is a constant outcome against what goes before, and that [*Stressing*] before led in fact to the present stage; it is, hmm... [*Hesitates*] a kind of, hmm... [*Raps his knuckles on the desk.*] It's dialectical when the older stage is negated but also contained in the new one, but the main point of this dialectics is the constant negation of these stages. [*Pause.*] Now, seemingly... [*Quietly*: and this is our problem rather than Adorno's] seemingly, once we get to concrete music, or Stockhausen and Boulez or something, once we get down to abstract expressionism and other post-World War Two forms... [*Quietly*: what else do we get to?] hmm... [*To himself:* all sorts of other things then (*Door slams in the distance*)] something comes to an end. At this point, it doesn't seem possible to negate any of those aesthetic conventions of forms anymore. It is as if the telos of modernism had exhausted itself. [*Pause.*] Suddenly, the modern comes to an end, and different kinds of strange "new," seemingly much more popular and anti-modern begin to form... [*Quietly*: what you negate at that point is the whole of the modern itself.] So, if you want to talk about the negation of the negation, then the postmodern becomes one way... [*Quietly*: the beginning with pop art, and going on into this newer kind of music, and all of this negates the whole modernist thing.] But what Adorno would have thought of that, we don't know. [*Student raises hand.*] Yes.

STUDENT: How does Greenberg or Michael Fried's positions on modernism as flatness… [*Words indistinct*] …absorption, literalness resonates or contrasts with Adorno?

JAMESON: Hmm, yeah. When you say Michael Fried, what are you talking about? Where do you see that? In his older writings? [*Tapping his thumb on the desk.*]

STUDENT: In essays and the trilogy… [*Pause.*]

JAMESON: Does he actually go out to…? [*Pause.*] I don't remember his writing very well now. Does he actually go to the modern period and then sort of traces out this process as an overall…[21]

[*Pause.*]

STUDENT: Yes, in the trilogy he talks about Courbet's realism and Manet's modernism, and then absorption, theatricality, but also his version of modernism…[22]

JAMESON: Mm-hmm [*Nods.*] Yeah, so you see that as his different version of modernism… [*Pause.*] I think Greenberg is a little easier to understand, but Fried's absorption stuff is also quite interesting too… [*Words indistinct.*] For Greenberg, art increasingly gets rid of its picture content or illustrative function as it starts dealing with the material constraints like canvas and paint, which is its essence. But then you reach the end of that, and people start painting pictures of things again, or using pictures like in postmodernism and pop art, and so on. I would say myself that there has been a shift in the very medium itself… [*Pause*] and what takes over at that point, it's not a return to figuration but a grappling with the image… [*Quietly*: which is now a whole new problem… (*Door slams shut*) it has nothing to do with matter in that Greenbergian sense of canvas and paint.] This is a different aesthetic project altogether or a different aesthetic dynamic. [*Agitated.*] But I mean, all of this, it's fair game. I mean, everybody sees that this way of painting has come to an end, I think… [*Quietly*: or let's say most of them do] but the older adherents of modernist, for those like Greenberg who saw in abstract expressionism the ultimate essence of painting, the return to figuration and image is obviously a terrible idea, right... [*Quietly*: and I'm sure other people did to.] We don't have to think [*Stressing*] <u>that</u>, but I mean there is a historical narrative to be worked out here, which is almost as big a leap as from one mode of production to another, from one aesthetic system to another. I don't think we are any longer... [*Quietly*: after 1960 or something] in a process of decay or reduction of the old system — I think that a whole new thing came in, which is a completely new society of late capitalism with a completely new set of problems.

[*Long pause*.]

Now, if you want, we could talk also about contemporary reactionaries, I mean people who... [*Quietly*: they are very influential in France but also here, who believe that all of this new art is taking us astray.] There are some excellent books along these lines by Antoine... [*Chalk strokes on the blackboard*] C-O-M-P-A-G-N-O-N. This one is in English, it's called "the five somethings of modernity, or of modernism."[23] The conservatives usually say no... [*Pause*] this new art is all too cheap and degraded and we have to go back to Baudelaire, we have to go back to [*Stresses*] <u>real</u> modern art and beauty. And then that gets tied into politics. Mm-hmm. That is becoming a political position, and of ethics and so on and so forth, and we get to the current Minister of Culture in France... [*Quietly*: what's his name, who likes to connect the beautiful with freedom and political circumstances, such as elections and so on, and all the rest of Western values?][24] Hmm... [*Hesitates*.] But I consider that only a pastiche of modernism; I don't think that's real or even possible to do that anymore... [*Quietly*: nobody can go back and bring back the poetry of Baudelaire... (*Mumbles quietly*) all of this is so senseless.] But what they mean is this [*Impersonates a conservative cultural critic*] "Oh, let's have an education organized around the modern classics. Let's instruct the young in the ideas of beautiful art." And that's what I was saying the other day, but the problem is that nobody's writing poetry this way anymore; I mean, it is not possible for an artist to go back and write in that style... [*Quietly*: for what is possible for an artist, I don't know, but for sure it's not that of going back to Baudelaire... (*Mumbles indistinctly*).] So, I think the real modernism, or what I call "late modern" ends around 1960 or so, when all of these people die... [*Quietly*: we can pick that just as a date, and I know that it's very fun to argue about dates and about periodization and when all of these breaks occur.] But can we say that this starts with the beginning of the 1960s... [*Pause*] well, yes and no... [*Cough in the audience*.] But how did we get started on all of this... [*Lightly pounds his fist against the desk*.] Hmm...

[*Long pause*.]

But [*Stammering*] the... the... the dialectic of the process, or the <u>telos</u> of this process and the periodization... [*Pause*.] Because you take whatever we see happening up to that point and then you can also push your dates back a little bit... [*Quietly*: hmm, I suppose you can try to absorb Stendhal into this process, there are certainly precursor artists like... (*Cough in the audience*) Piranesi, and so on.] Then you get to identify what's the process that begun even earlier, hmm... [*Hesitates*.] Proust likes to quote... [*Pause*.] Proust liked very much the letters of Madame de Sévigné. I don't know if any of you know about them, but these letters were quite famous in France. She wrote them in a very rapid sort of shorthand style, and they provide a glimpse into the life of a French noblewoman in the seventeenth century... [*Quietly*: all sort of gossip, the Parisian society and culture, family news (*Mumbles indistinctly*).[25]] Madame de Sévigné, she wasn't an artist, she wasn't a writer; these were letters to her daughter where she wrote things as she saw them. And Proust was quite astounded by these letters, and at some point, he says, "this is what I like to call" ... [*Quietly*: "the Dostoevsky side of the letters of Madame de Sévigné."] Well, so that's how, once you get to it in the present, then a large piece of the past also gets reabsorbed into this whole story. [*Pause*.] But the point that I'm trying to make is related to this telos or this process of negation which is going on in modernism.

[*Long pause.*]

Okay, but now all of a sudden, we gonna talk about it in slightly different terms, and I think I've insisted on this before. [*Pause.*] There are people who want to say that, hmm... [*Impersonates critics of Adorno*] "Well, Adorno is not a Marxist, or that he had some affinity with post-structuralism." And I think that you have to take this into account, but it is also his insistence on aesthetic production. [*Reads from* Aesthetic Theory] "The new is the aesthetic seal of expanded reproduction."[26] [*Stressing.*] Expanded reproduction means this process whereby machinery also has its own loss, and it is developing at a pace with the larger social context, and the process is somehow penetrating everywhere. So, you have in the beginning people making their own clothing, but then all of a sudden there is... [*Cough in the audience*] some new machinery that does the weaving and knitting, and so on, and the machine is now making what we would call "store clothes," or "ready-to-wear clothing." Well, [*Stressing*] expanded reproduction means that everybody starts making clothing this way. So, this is a technological version or image of aesthetic production, and you have to think also that this is part of Adorno's competition with Benjamin... [*Clears throat.*] Benjamin said this too, but in a rather more orthodox way, I think. And it's as though Adorno was saying that he always had some [*Stressing*] reserves about a lot of these formulations by Benjamin... [*Impersonates Adorno*] "Okay, well yes, I agree with that part in Benjamin and I accept it, but I want to say it this way." And then the production process itself becomes central. And with the production process, if you have a better machine to produce shoes, or whatever, and when this happens, it drives the older ones out because that means you can produce shoes cheaper and more quickly. Someone is busy taking five hours to produce your shoes with their old machinery whereas you can do it in two — and therefore you win, and they go out of business. [*Softly.*] And this is also the dynamic, or the dialectic of art. Once you outtrump those older sounds and you don't hear in the harmonies... [*Pause*]; this is what he calls the "aging of modern music," or the aging of all music, that is to say that the consonance that forms the resolutions don't shock us anymore; they don't do anything for us anymore. Once you outtrump those and you make your own production machine which is more modern, then nobody can produce music in the old way anymore... [*Quietly*: or at least it is not worth talking about it and is considered second rate.] And the drawing back from this old stuff is the fear to go on... [*Pause*.] I think that's why Hofmannsthal and Strauss both... [*Quietly*: I told you the other day that Hofmannsthal wrote some of Strauss's librettos] so they both come to a point where they as if said, "Look, I'm afraid I'm not really modern, and I can't go on with this anymore; I cannot follow into modernism even though I see that this is where poetry and art should go." [*Pause*.] And the same for Strauss's music, for whatever other reasons, could be social theories, personal fears and so on, but after Electra, Richard Strauss said [*Impersonates Strauss*] "That's as far as I'm gonna go with the modern"... [*Raps his knuckles on the desk*] and he retreated into writing some very interesting stuff... [*Quietly:* but which was more tuneful, and more consumable, and traditional and so on.] It's very interesting I think when you find artists like that, both of them, and there are many artists who retreated into tradition, and this is because, with this kind of artists, you can register and take a look at both sides of modernism..

[*Long pause*.]

Mm-hmm. And there are critics like that too. Those of you who work with American poetry perhaps know a figure who was quite central at Stanford, I think... [*Pause*] someone called... [*Chalk on the blackboard*] Y-V-O-R W-I-N-T-E-R-S. So, Yvor Winters, he was a modernist poet and friend of Hart Crane doing the early non-rhyming free-versing imagism — very interesting stuff. [*Pause*.] He wrote theories of free verse that I think is still the basic publication, talking about why free verses aren't free. Hmm... [*Hesitates*.] Then he comes to a crisis — I think these are always personal crises, a nervous breakdown or something like that... [*Pause*] and then he retreats into classical poetry, into rhyming poetry and so on and so forth, and he decides that modernism is [*Whispering*] evil in some way. Mm-hmm. And so the stuff he writes... [*Quietly*: and this is a very smart man] but the stuff he writes on modernism I think is some of the best things that has been written because he saw it, as somebody who both was and wasn't a modernist, and who had to stand out for himself. He saw things... [*Zipper unzipping*] about modernism that its adherents didn't. Mm-hmm. And this is in an essay called... [*Quietly*: Jesus, what is that book called, hmm, something like... (*Words indistinct*).] There is a collection of his three volumes of essays in one book, the title of which I also don't remember... [*Quietly*: I'll give you that reference later.][27] Even Lukács himself is in a way part of this process of resisting modernism. Because Lukács is certainly following and theorizes contemporary art up to a certain point and then he draws the line, and I think that he was not just simply posturing but it reflects a deeper-seated anxiety about the... [*Mumbles indistinctly.*]

[*Long pause.*]

STUDENT: When you put it this way, it makes seem that it's not just the production process which gets registered in aesthetic production, but it's also this fundamental contradiction of the production process that Marx once admitted; you know, it's precisely this drive to increase productivity which makes profits possible but it's also the same increase in productivity which drives the price down, right? So, you could then have to sell more to make more out of the pocket which continues to drive the price down, right. So, this is this fundamental contradiction in capitalism...

JAMESON: Yeah, but...

STUDENT: So, I was just wondering if this is the same sort of reaching of a limit that you are pointing out, that also takes place in aesthetic production?

JAMESON: Yeah, it's certainly the paradox of the limit here as well. I'm not sure you can, hmm... [*Reflecting*.] Well, there is certainly a way in which one can talk about a limit in the production process when all the modernist stuff becomes so well-known and it's not shocking us anymore; and in fact, I think it's also important to remember the commercial side of modernism. I mean, modern art, if you think of Doctor Barnes' collection in Philadelphia, of his... [*Quietly*: I don't know if any of you knows more about Barnes Collection; he was one of the great collectors of modern or modernist art. And people went and laughed and booed and hooed, and so he shut it down and didn't let anybody visit it except on his own terms, and somewhat later.][28] If you think of the ugliness and dissonance of modern art for the people of that period, and then if you think of the way in which fashion production today... [*Quietly*: furniture, clothes, anything] is unthinkable without the forms that modernist art invented: images and patterns, soundtracks, Muzak boxes were unthinkable without Schoenberg. I mean, if you think of the way in which all that stuff has been harnessed to serve commercial production, hmm... [*Hesitates*] there is some sort of analogy there, I think. Mm-hmm. But I was thinking of it more in terms of... [*Pause*.] It's in a later section of Aesthetic Theory... [*Quietly*: I may be accused of being... *Mumbles indistinctly*] but in that other section he says [*Impersonates Adorno*] "Look, subjectivity of the art is genius, but what's genius? Genius is not something subjective. Kant didn't mean it to be. It's only the romantics who made it into something subjective. Genius means being able to do away with your personality in such a way as to be on the cutting edge of this innovation of production."[29] But if you still have a personality and you're trying to oppose that and say something personally, or you try to [*Stressing*] express yourself and so on, well, then you got other interests and you're really not interested or invested in the process of artistic production... [*Pause*.] So that's a part of this process too, how these artists are not... [*Quietly*: because there are many painters today who still paint in the old-fashioned ways, and they'd say, "Oh, I only want to express myself."] But then, how relevant are their paintings for contemporary art today, except perhaps as objects of interior decoration? But for innovative or authentic artists, it is not that they are saying something about themselves, or they are telling us something like that; they can be doing this too, but they are also keeping up with [*Stressing*] innovation. Yes, I think that's essentially what's underscored here.

[*Long pause.*]

But this notion of production would not necessarily be the same as the critique of capitalism because capitalism uses production and innovation for a certain contradictory purpose, whereas one can imagine production presumably free of such contradictions… [*Quietly*: mm-hmm, this was presumably the case of the university before the big investments, and back then when the university was not just about big money but presumably the place where scientists were busy inventing instruments; the university was the place of innovation for its own sake; well, try and imagine this today, a university without investments… (*Mumbles quietly*).] But these contradictions in the process of production and innovation come back in the work of art; not even in the culture industry, but in the artwork itself, and art is part of the reification process because works of art… [*Cough in the audience*] can scarcely help but become commodities. And they are certainly bought and sold and then something happens resulting in a sort of confusion in art's reception.

[*Long pause. Another student raises their hand.*]

JAMESON: Yes.

STUDENT: Do you think these dynamics of innovation and production has always been part of art and culture or this is only the case in the modern age…?

JAMESON: I think, hmm… [*Hesitates.*] Well, it's whatever you think the path of modernity is, or it depends on how you define art in historical terms. I mean… [*Pause.*] Obviously, we can see that Racine has been doing something different from Corneille, and that he did in fact innovate things, and we can see the same process in early art and certainly in painting… [*Door creaks open. Footsteps*] who did something different from

Rafael, and so on. But it seems to me that once the conventions of the old regime were destroyed, and art had to become more commercial, then I think the rate of this process of innovation picks up. [*Pause.*] I think it's a little bit connected to that, hmm... [*Hesitates*] and that there are analogies to the factory system, as Adorno points out. But on the other hand, the connections are always mediated, they are never direct reproductions of things... [*Cough in the audience.*] So, the way in which the speed of capitalism is registered in a work of art is not necessarily as with the naturalists... [*Quietly*: we will portray for you a real financial crisis that follows everybody around, which to be frank can also be quite astounding... (*Words indistinct*)] but it's in the way in which the artistic form itself, or the established forms are canceled. And this is a completely mediated, hmm... [*Quietly*: it's not even a reflection but a reproduction of the same process and perhaps we don't have yet the right words to express that kind of mediation.] And in general, I think Adorno was... [*Pause.*] What Adorno uses this production idea... [*Quietly*: and maybe we'll stop at this point... (*Watch chain dangling*)] is that it is a formal process. The production process is a formal process, and when you're talking about it in such terms, then everything else becomes simply raw material. [*Pause.*] So, on another page he is gonna tell you "the meaning of the work of art, the message... [*Quietly*: "message" or... (*Pronounces in French*) message was a very popular theme in the 1920s and 1930s.] The [*Stressing*] message of the work, the meaning of the work,[30] Adorno says, that's not something separate from the work, it is part of the raw material of the work. How about the intention of the artist? [*Impersonates the artist*] "What I wanted to show you here was the decline of civilization, or the beauty of my soul and the nature of the color green," or something like that [*Chuckles.*] Mm-hmm. The intention of the artist is also part of the raw material of the work and nothing else. So, the production standpoint allows you to draw everything else inside the work of art and make it look formal. This is a formalist idea, but it's an [*Stressing*] absolute formalism and that is the lesson of this kind of experiment for other kinds of thinking. That's why you think, hmm... [*Hesitates.*] That's... [*Stammering*] that's... [*Pause.*] It's in terms of that kind of formalism that I said what I said about ideology. Because, ideology is Adorno's message, right? What's his message? [*Stressing.*] Suffering. [*Pause.*] And that's not... [*Looks for words.*] The problem, hmm... [*Hesitates.*] But then, from the standpoint of his analysis of the work of art, of his macrocosm and aesthetic theory, you can't really do that because "suffering" would be raw material too. You cannot posit suffering as the ultimate horizon because that would then be ideology, right? Is suffering the raw material, is suffering the post-war hero? And how does that relate to Europe that felt the shock of American commercialization and that's... [*Words indistinct.*] That's... [*Pause.*] That's the situation that can be drawn out of this... [*Slams his palm on the desk*] but it must be seen as part of, it's the situation, and not be understood as some kind of meaning or essence of his philosophy or aesthetics.

[*Raps his knuckles on the desk.*]

Okay... [*Chairs scraping the floor. Feet shuffling.*] Please let's try and gallop ahead through these next chapters, especially the chapter on beauty, because we will deal with it soon... [*Words indistinct.*]

Audience stands up. Objects drop on the floor. Feet shuffling. Door creaks open. Students talk among themselves. Zippers zipping up. Students return chairs to other classrooms. Some form a line to discuss their assignments with Jameson. General noise. Screeching microphone noise.

[*Microphone turns off.*]

CURTAIN

LECTURE SEVEN

FEBRUARY 13, 2003

SITUATION (CHAPTER) — IRRATIONALISMS — THE ISMS — THE NEW — UTOPIA

CURTAIN RISES

Moving chairs, squeaking door, coughs, other sounds filling the noise environment of a large classroom in the Literature Department at Duke University. Students are taking their seats — some arrive early to sit in the front row. Many students in Jameson's seminars pride themselves on maintaining a critical *perspective on society. His courses gather young "radicals" from different regions of the world: most are from the United States, but there are many students from Latin America (Chile, Colombia, Venezuela), Eastern Europe, Turkey, and China. Students who enroll in Jameson's courses establish a form of camaraderie that extends beyond the perimeter of the campus and university hours, through various graduate parties, reading groups, and discussions of shared authors. They often call each other "comrade," and when they meet, they like to talk about the latest news and books or to gossip about the stars of critical theory (e.g., have you heard about* that *theorist who just married a fashion model in Argentina, or* this *good-looking Marxist professor on campus who just appeared in a men's fashion magazine advertising a clothing brand?). Sometimes they jokingly pronounce Jameson's name in the Spanish manner, as "Hameson."*

Jameson enters the classroom carrying a few books, his scattered notes and the red pen in the chest pocket of his flannel shirt. He stops for a quick chat with one of the students waiting by the door.

[*Microphone turns on.*]

JAMESON: [*Door creaks open. Footsteps shuffle across the floor.*] Mm-hmm, are there any questions? [*Audience chattering.*] Okay.

[*Audience hubbub fades into murmur.*]

Okay, we'll just go on with it. I'm sorry not to have finished this chapter last time, hmm... [*Hesitates*] and this section here. I don't... [*Chair scratches the floor.*] I guess the proper kind of reading of this... [*Zipper unzipping*] would be to figure out the unity of these sections here, being understood that Adorno didn't finish this book, and he might have lifted parts from one place to another and made it somehow more orderly. But I would say — unless you have another idea — that when it starts out with this whole notion of the raw materials, and what happens to them and the production of raw materials and the... [*Chair scrapes against the floor*] aging of the process of artistic production and innovation — all of that would seem to be the organizing principle of this chapter. And it's very interesting that the chapter is called [*Stressing*] "Situation." That is, what comes first is not the situation of art in society, or history or something, but the most immediate situation of the artist — that is to say, the artist dealing with the raw materials, with the initial state of these materials. And as I've tried to say again and again, and I think this is right — but again, you don't have to agree with me — it seems to me that this is what's, hmm... [*Reflecting*] hmm... [*Hesitates*] hmm... [*Pause.*] This is what is meant here by situation. It is the mediation of the raw materials and what you can do with them, and what you can't do with them, or how they expect the form to be produced which constitutes the political and historical symptoms, or the historical situation. Mm-hmm.

And you don't... [*Examines his notes.*] I think this is dialectical insofar as it insists on mediation.

[*Long pause.*]

And this brings us back to Hegel. The thing you remember about Hegel... [*Quietly*: I mean, if you want to have a little snap summary of the Hegelian strategy and moves there] or one way of taking Hegel I think is that, for him, there is no [*Stressing*] immediacy in the philosophical sense. You never have direct contact in some way. We always... [*Pause.*] First of all, we're always mediated through ourselves, so it's like the Heisenberg principle. Our direct contact with all that is out there is by way of ourselves: how we've been formed, our subjectivities, our personalities, subconscious and so on and so forth, but then there are many other forms of mediation. But the point is that you never get to the thing... [*Door slams shut. Footsteps*] but by ever enlarging sorts of versions of these mediations, you can finally get to a totality in which, for German objective idealism in general, this is when the subject and the object are the same, or the subject and the system reconcile... [*Quietly*: or whatever you want to call it, I mean that's the final form of Hegel's philosophy.] But Hegel begins with the debunking of the idea... [*Zipper unzipping*] that it is possible or real to just look at the thing being right there, or of having unmediated contact with the thing. Mm-hmm, so this is in some way the beginning of phenomenology. Now, when you put it that way... [*Quietly*: hmm, deconstruction is also pretty close, right, because of the debunking of presence, it seems to me, and it is very much a Hegelian... (*Words indistinct*) and the idea that there is a reality we are in immediate contact with.] There is a reality, but we only get to it through a lot of mediated contact. Well, I would say that this would be one way of looking at Adorno's Hegelianism, namely that, insofar as history and politics are concerned, the primary form of mediation... [*Cough in the audience*] for him at least, is through the work of art, it is through aesthetics and through aesthetics as [*Stressing*] symptom... [*Quietly*: a word which he of course does not use in that sense at all.]

[*Long pause.*]

Now, I've said that this notion of "message," and the meaning of the work is not, hmm... [*Hesitates*] is really not a very reliable way of looking at art. There is a meaning to the work of art, but that is rather a different meaning which Adorno will call its "truth content," [*Pause*] and that is not meaning in the traditional sense which we find in... [*Quietly*: I think most traditional literary criticism, up to the New Criticism, which we're trying to find out exactly what it was even though they had their own structures on translating the aesthetic object into some abstract set of ideas, and then you say that those sets of ideas were the meanings, and so on and so forth.] But it seems to me the notion that a work is supposed to be something [*Stressing*] meaningful is certainly the vice of much of the twentieth-century criticism... [*Quietly*: even though there isn't much criticism before twentieth century, or I don't think that anyone calls it criticism seriously.] And since Anglo-American criticism was relatively untouched either by Freud or Marx, the so-called traditional criticism ends up being some sort of Weltanschauung or search for message and meaning or whatever. [*Pause.*] Now, we'll come back to this whole notion of "truth content," but we can leave it with that for now.

[*Long pause.*]

Now, mm-hmm. This going against certain kinds of meanings and messages is... [*Door creaks open. Footsteps.*] That is to say that the raw materials of the work, as they are produced in the work of art, do not have meaning, but their newness or their new use and articulation is crucial. [*Pause.*] And what that might mean I think is what we have to try and figure out in this section. [*Page flipping.*] Page 22: "The new is not a subjective category... it is a compulsion of the object itself, which cannot in any other way come to itself and resist heteronomy. The force of the old presses toward the new, without which the old cannot be fulfilled."[1] [*Sighs.*] And this takes us back to something else I yanked out of context towards the end of this section, namely that you must look at things... [*Reflecting.*] If you're doing good criticism, you must look at art from the standpoint of [*Stresses*] the newest form of production and not of what it thought it was doing in the past. It is to look at art from the latest state of production as it appears at that moment. So, this is an argument against... [*Raps his knuckles on the desk*] nostalgia and archaism, which are sort of two different things here. But on the other hand, once you get to the postmodern, we have to wonder how valid these ideas still are, because in a sense, what was the most modern form of artistic production for Adorno, and for the modernism? [*Softly*] Well, you could say twelve-tone music, or you could also say abstract expressionism, and you could also say... [*Quietly*: what would it be in poetry? Well, I think the way the canon has been worked out it would be Wallace Stevens, or something, and maybe Eliot or... (*Mumbles indistinctly*) certain American forms of modernism. Mm-hmm. Or Proust and Joyce or something like that.] But once you get over to the postmodern today, it's not clear anymore what's going on in that respect. Most contemporary artistic products are a lot simpler than those of high modernism, but they are also more advanced; and they are more advanced because all of that advanced modernism has been absorbed and simplified and then mixed up with mass culture. Mm-hmm. I think you might wanna make an argument that technology... [*Cough in the audience*] has itself changed and therefore, if postmodernity is an ideology or an experience of the computer age, then there is a sense in which the most advanced kind of production in the modern period... [*Quietly*: and that's iron and steel, heavy industry, and so forth] is no longer the most advanced kind of production today, and therefore art and cultural production takes on a new characteristic, which no one has yet worked out in these terms. [*Exhales deeply*.] Or you could go on... [*Quietly*: but that would be very self-defeating for us] you could go on and say: "Well, Adorno is a thinker of the modern age and therefore he has nothing to say about all of this contemporary stuff." Mm-hmm. There is a remark of Schoenberg, I think I quoted it the other day, and Adorno quotes it as well, where Schoenberg says at some point [*Impersonates Schoenberg*] "Right now the whole question of harmony is not on my agenda."[2] [*Audience murmuring.*] That means... [*Quietly*: because by harmony, I'm thinking of a certain return of the harmonic and the tuneful in postmodernist music with composers like Philip Glass and Terry Riley and people like that.] Mm-hmm. That could mean that, later on, harmony may come back on the agenda, but right now for us... [*Quietly*: that is, for Schoenberg, who died in what, forty-seven, or forty-eight or nine...]

STUDENT: Fifty-three...

JAMESON: Uh-huh?

STUDENT: Fifty-three...

JAMESON: Fifty-two, alright.[3] So right now, for us, harmony is out of the question — that's old stuff. [*Pause.*] But one day, who knows, maybe harmony could again be considered advanced, and there would be a historical dialectics there. If you are listening to nothing else but serial or twelve-tone music or something, and you listen to it all the time, then maybe all of a sudden in some far future the return of consonance will be a shock to you, and it won't be perceived as something so terrible as it was at the height of musical modernism... [*Softly.*] Stanley Aronowitz once said that if you're used of thinking in those terms, and if you're used to very rapid transitions and endings of the kind that you get on television in the American Hollywood films, then what can be very shocking is Ozu... [*Quietly*: because, in Ozu, the camera just stays there in one place and people move in and out slowly; I mean, in a sense, he offers a very different kind of cinematic rhythm.][4] So, if we're just talking about [*Stressing*] defamiliarization... [*Quietly*: that is, when the artist finds a way, a shocking way that could sort of shake you out of your habitual perception, then we are in a different situation.] But I also think that postmodernity is a little bit more than that and... [*Mumbles indistinctly.*]

[*Long pause.*]

Anyway, I think it's in the spirit of Adorno to interrogate this productivity from time to time, from all those other perspectives, and he is still working while the other composers are advancing new forms... [*Quietly*: Stockhausen, Boulez and... (*Cough in the audience*).] And whatever you think of them, they certainly went beyond Schoenberg. And so, Adorno can still believe in this advanced productivity, of which the bourgeois notion of progress is a caricature, right? [*Pause.*] Advanced productivity doesn't necessarily mean everything is getting better and better, but it means that there is a whole new logic of production... [*Achoo. Sneeze in the audience.*] Now, how does one...? [*Hesitates.*] But how one then get out of technological determinism? I think that's another great basic question. Isn't this emphasis on...? [*Absorbed.*] There was a period when a lot of people in the 1970s... [*Quietly*: Baudrillard's Mirror of Production is a famous book that accused Marxism of being a productivist philosophy because it was, hmm... (*Exhales*) neglecting other so-called modes of production.[5]] Mm-hmm. I think that's not true, but on the other hand, there are ideologies of productivism on one side, and of the technological determinism on the other, which menace this viewpoint. If you look at Benjamin, for example, there is a great deal and even more than an emphasis on technology, mechanical reproduction, and the technological age, which maybe in his days totally made historical sense, but today — in the light of ecology, in the light of all those other problems that we are facing — they seem to appear very questionable. [*Pause.*] I think especially ecology would be the classic demonstration that advanced production is not perfect in itself, given its impact and domination of nature, and so forth.

[*Long pause.*]

Well, but the moment we get to Adorno... [*Stomp, stomp. Footsteps*] he says the opposite, because you will see that the domination of nature is also a very important theme here. As Adorno puts it from time to time, I guess what we have to realize is that none of these thematic concepts by themselves — [*Softly*] "advanced productivity," and the "new," or the "domination of nature" — that none of these thematic concepts are satisfactory in themselves. I'm tempted to say they always have to be canceled out by another concept. There is a point later on where he is talking about beauty, which I'll just mention now, it's actually... [*Quietly*: where is it? where is it... (*Flips through* Aesthetic Theory) yeah, I think it's on this page.] It is on page 51 of this text, but I'm not gonna quote it, but he says, [*Impersonates Adorno*] "Look, given all of these internal contradictions, we should have just gotten rid of the idea of beauty." [*Pause.*] But then, he says, you can't get rid of this concept entirely. In order to do anything worthwhile, we have to work out of its concrete oppositions. If we just say, "Look, these oppositions cancel each other out, let's just eliminate beauty," then we are back at square one. When you eliminate a concept because you find it inappropriate, we have nothing to work with. And even though beauty may be a flawed concept, and an internally contradictory concept, we need it to bounce the other things off of it. That is to say, the critique of beauty is a productive step in our thinking. Mm-hmm. And if beauty wasn't there at all... [*Reflecting*] hmm, then we would not be able to take that step. That's also a Hegelian idea. [*Pause.*] In Hegel, for example, truth is something you can only come to through error. You can't think... [*Pause.*] You can't get a list of mistakes from your philosopher in residence in the beginning and say: "Alright, let's ignore all that and proceed immediately from the truth." It's by making the mistakes, going through them, and criticizing them, and getting out of them, it is how you're taking to the next step towards truth... [*Quietly*: and it seems to me that's very much the nature of truth... (*Mumbles indistinctly*).]

[*Long pause.*]

Okay, but nonetheless, here is our friend again, "advanced productivity." [*Reads from* Aesthetic Theory]: "If in accord with its model, the fetish character of the commodity, the new becomes [*Stressing*] a fetish, this is to be criticized in the work itself, not externally simply because it became a fetish; usually the problem is a discrepancy between new means and old ends."[6] [*Pause.*] So, even the ends themselves are presumably transformed in the process, so that the kind of problem... [*Cough in the audience*] that you would experience in modern music is different from... [*Zipper unzipping*] a nineteenth-century symphony; the kind of satisfaction you get in modern literature has to be different from the satisfaction of the naturalistic novel, of the realist novel, and so on and so forth. [*Pause.*] However, here is something a little bit different [*Page flipping*]: "Scars of damage and disruption are the modern's seal of authenticity..."[7] If you look at dissonance... [*Quietly*: dissonance means internal, sort of unpleasant and harsh combinations of sounds.] But dissonance also means the discrepancy, if you like, between the self and the world, it means longing, it means demanding satisfaction and so on and so forth, that is what dissonance means after Barthes. So, dissonance is one way that we can talk about this, and a little bit later in the next chapter we will talk about it in terms of... [*Softly*] ugliness. Right now, we're talking about it in terms of scars. Well, here I think... [*Quietly*: there is a nice, hmm... (*Hesitates*).] There is a nice line in Gertrude Stein, who had all kinds of wonderful sayings that I think explains this passage in a way better than Adorno. [*Quotes Stein from memory.*] "Every new, or really new thing," she once said, "comes into the world with a measure of ugliness," which is the scar... [*Quietly*: I don't know if she used that word "scar," but since its related to what we are talking about here, let's use it] ...which is the scar of its difficulties in coming into being as something radically new. And then she added: "Our tasks as critics in front of the..." [*Quietly*: okay, what's the most beautiful thing in the world? Let's say Raphael's Sistine Madonna] "so our tasks as critics is to recover the traces of that original ugliness."[8] Well, if you think of Raphael and what we do with Raphael, that's quite a proposition. I mean, it's very hard to recover the "scars" and the traces of the original ugliness of the Sistine Madonna, which is probably why, whatever its reputation... [*Quietly*: but maybe today nobody cares too much about Raphael; it's too perfect, it's absolutely beautiful... (*Words indistinct*) and that's why there is perhaps more interest in Michelangelo, with all those distortions and the scars or the materiality of the marble.] That is what catches our attention today.

[*Long pause.*]

Hmm, so this is now... [*Pause.*] That's another way of thinking about the new and its scars, but the scars are also the traces of suffering, as we were saying last time. And suffering is somehow wordless and mute. You can't express it, and therefore, in a way, [*Stressing*] that could be the suffering, right? That could be the very essence of suffering... [*Quietly*: the inability to express it, the inability to let the other know about the nature of your suffering.] But since you can't express it, trying to express it is gonna leave big scars, so... [*Pause.*] And I, hmm... [*Hesitates.*] And I would like to think... [*Quietly*: I don't know if he does it here] but if everything is in history, if everything is changing, if everything is getting new — maybe suffering is getting new too. There are some new kinds of suffering that didn't exist in the previous age, some new forms of suffering that we can't handle? Perhaps. And I think that the situation of this, with Auschwitz still in the picture of the post-WWII period, makes that very possible.

[*Long pause.*]

But here is something else... [*Pause.*] It comes immediately after that on page 23 [*Page flipping*]: "Antitraditional energy becomes a voracious vortex." "...art desperately negates the closed confines of the ever-same." Art is [*Stressing*] against identity, against repetition and so on and so forth. Mm-hmm. "Explosion is one of its invariants." "To this extent, the modern is myth turned against itself; the timelessness of myth becomes the catastrophic instant that destroys temporal continuity."[9] [*Raps his knuckles on the desk.*] Well, I think we have to know what's meant in Adorno and in Benjamin by the term "myth"... [*Cough in the audience.*] I think that this is a language that they used consistently, and it involves... [*Quietly*: I'm tempted to say a kind of myth of a myth, or the myth of origins and so forth, which is constantly shorthanded then.] Myth is the formless, the unformed, the irrational; myth is everything that comes before the emergence of rationality, or Vernunft. Myth is everything that stands at the dawn of the dialectic of enlightenment. So mythic forces are always, for these people, [*Stressing*] negative forces. Now, they are writing in a period in which... [*Pause.*] Mm-hmm. I don't myself think that the language of the irrational makes any sense for us anymore, and I'll explain that in a minute. But in this period, you definitively have — what are called the "irrationalisms." [*Pause.*] Mm-hmm. And I would say, how many of those are we familiar with anymore, but there's a lot of irrationalisms in the German tradition. Some of those people went right through the Nazi period, kept their professorships on into West Germany in the Bundesrepublik and are the objects of Adorno's attacks... [*Cough in the audience.*] They are not... [*Pause.*] They don't have to do with party politics but very much with the politics of the university and of the disciplines. Adorno played a very important role after 1953 in being a remarkable left and dialectical voice, criticizing these reminisces of the mythical. [*Softly.*] I won't say there were no Nazis, but I mean, they're certainly some of the great traditions of German irrationalism in all of the disciplines, particularly in sociology, political theory. And in philosophy, [*Stressing*] that form of new irrationalism in German philosophy was Heidegger, for him. As you all know, Heidegger was denied the right to teach for some years after the war... [*Quietly*: he thought he was gonna be executed. When the ally troops moved into Baden-Württemberg, he had taken refuge out in the country around Freiburg.] And when the allied troops arrived — these were French troops, I believe, that came in with the Americans... [*Mumbles indistinctly*] — Heidegger hid in the forest and was captured by a couple of French soldiers, imagining that he would be shot on the spot. But instead, when these soldiers found out who he was, they gave him a cigarette and asked for his autograph [*Chuckles.*] But, hmm... [*Hesitates*] nonetheless he was too well-known to be allowed to sneak out of this, and we know that he had his party card all through the period... [*Quietly*: and I don't mean that he wasn't critical of the party, but that's another story...

(*Mumbles indistinctly*).] And when he started to lecture again... [*Quietly*: he started lecturing again a few years after the end of the war] there was a very rapid Heideggerian revival, especially of the late Heidegger — the so-called Heidegger after the turn, or the Heidegger of Being and anxiety and death instinct and so on. Heideggerianism becomes a very powerful force in West Germany right after the immediate post-World War Two period. I don't think that Frankfurt School caught up to that because many of their things were not in print until the 1960s, and in fact, the 1960s are — via the radical student movement — the triumph of the Frankfurt School over this almost universal Heideggerianism of the immediate post-World War Two period. So, there was plenty of irrationality to attack here. And... [*Pause*.] But I think the name that you want to think of from the pre-war period... [*Quietly*: because it's best known to us, and if you deal with Freud, you understand what's the matter with this] is the name of Jung.

[*Long pause*.]

Let's say that one primary thinker of myth is Jung. The archetypes, collective unconscious, the persistence of all of these primordial things. I don't think... [*Quietly:* hmm, if you think of somebody like Northrop Frye, he used some of these Jungian concepts... (*Words indistinct*) but his was a very pale version of literary Jungianism, quite harmless I think, and very literary and not at all in the original spirit.] But Jung I think is... [*Pause*.] And Jung too had some Nazi sympathies, we know that, and he was friends with some high-ranking SS members... [*Cough in the audience*] and so he did not have to worry about anything. But Jungianism would be one way of thinking about the term and the use of the concept of "myth" as it runs through Adorno and Benjamin. It is this irrationalism of the Ur-self constituted of variety of symbols and archetypes found in fairytales and other ancient cultural traditions. [*Sighs*.] And the reason I think that this is no longer a useful term, although people still use it... [*Quietly*: Habermas's book on the modern is essentially a denunciation of irrationalisms, which he considers to still persist today, and which for him are mainly French.] Habermas once said [*Impersonates Habermas*] "You know" — and this was before he had his reconciliation with Derrida — "hmm, irrationalism which used to have its capital on this side of the Rhine seems now to have moved to Paris." He was referring to Bataille, Artaud, and perhaps even Deleuze I suppose — all those things for Habermas are manifestations of irrationalisms... [*Mumbles indistinctly.*]

STUDENT ONE: What is Habermas's book on modernity?

JAMESON: Hmm, that's his twelve lectures...

STUDENT TWO: Discourse of modernity?

JAMESON: Yes, the Philosophical Discourse of Modernity, which is his history of modern philosophy.[10] [*Clears throat.*]

And I would say for Habermas, you know, hmm... [*Hesitates*] this Frankfurt School or some of the Frankfurt School stuff, in particular Dialectic of Enlightenment, would sort of be on the irrational side because it attacks reason, right? [*Pause.*] The thing that Adorno and Horkheimer are doing with Enlightenment, with their critique of Enlightenment — the source of all Western progress, and of bourgeois progress and so on and so forth — it's pointing out the destructive and irrationalist nature of Enlightenment, equating it with... [*Quietly*: with instrumental reason] and for Habermas, I think, he does not make that distinction. [*Pause.*] Mm-hmm. And therefore, in order to salvage something out of the Frankfurt School... [*Quietly*: he sort of assimilates them with aesthetics] but I think there is not a real continuity between him and them... [*Exhales deeply.*] Habermas begins by being politically more radical than they are in the 1960s... [*Chair-back creaks*] but then, once his communicational philosophy emerges,[11] I think that he wishes to break his ties with the Frankfurt School's radicalism. And I think that he has succeeded in this. The reason that I think this is a bad slogan[12] is that reason means, in a sense, understanding things... [*Pause.*] Now, I think that if you have a society like ours in which... [*Quietly*: oh, look at all the stuff about the serial murderers.] In the old days, the great example of the serial murderer... [*Quietly*:

the thing that is closest maybe to us is in Musil's Man Without Qualities, hmm... (*Finger snapping*) and the murderer, what's his name... (*Taps two times on the desk*).] Nobody reads Musil anymore... [*Quietly*: that's quite remarkable because those sections on the mass murderer and how Musil thinks his way into his mind are quite... (*Mumbles indistinctly*).] To say "irrational" means it's not thinkable by reason, right? Whereas it seems to me that today, as horrible as all these things are, most of them are thinkable. And therefore, as reason expands its field of action, it becomes less and less meaningful to call anything "irrational," I mean, hmm... [*Hesitates*.] So, I think that's a poor... [*Pause*.] That's a poor and very old-fashionable kind of slogan, but it still certainly works here with this denunciation of myth that I do because you will see the notion of myth re-emerging. It will never be explained, but it will pop up and it means all the irrationalisms of Weimar, of the Weimarian era, of the bourgeois period from Bismarck through Weimar to the post-World War Two and the neo-Nazis... [*Quietly*: and by "neo-Nazis," I don't mean the skinheads, but those conservatives and Nazi sympathizers who survived Germany's catastrophe.]

[*Long pause*.]

Okay, so then we move on at once to [*Stressing*] experiment, which is associated with the "new" in Adorno.[13] And I suppose that's also a way in which you try to make a, hmm... [*Hesitates*] you try to open up a role for the work of art, which is not epistemological — that is the work of art still doesn't have a concept, as in Kant. [*Words indistinct*.] ...even though the dialectic of modernity — or of modernism, I should say — is analogous over and over again to the dialectic of enlightenment. The dialectic of modernism is as ambiguous as the dialectic of enlightenment: you gain something new; you gain a new form of reason over the old one, but at the same time, you're losing some of the, let's say, some more humane qualities of either the work of art or reason itself... [*Quietly*: as we saw, reason is moving towards positivism and the work of art is moving towards something absolutely dehumanized and abstract and so on.] Why? Not because it wants to be so, but because this is the only way art can survive in a context of absolute dehumanization. [*Softly*.] Well, on the other hand, as everybody knows, that makes art less and less accessible, less and less pleasurable, and so forth. Mm-hmm. To talk about experiment is to move away from that epistemological realm, where the artwork is gonna teach us something or have some kind of message or be didactic... [*Quietly*: these are absolute taboos for the modernists.] Yet the work must have this formal and technological impetus because what has to be new is somehow finally articulated... [*Quietly*: not just in the new materials] but in the form itself. Because if you have these new materials, these changes in the way in which language is used, or colors and tones in painting, then the very form of the work of which they are a part has to necessarily be modified. [*Tap. One quick tap on the desk.*]

[*Long pause.*]

Mm-hmm. And so, all of a sudden, from experiment we get to [*Stressing*] construction, as a, hmm... [*Hesitates*] as a fundamental principle in contemporary art... [*Quietly*: see on page 24.] But construction is certainly a leitmotif here, and we will see it again many times. On the other hand, construction can't become a fundamental principle, because then we would simply have one kind of monolithic theory of art or aesthetics. We're gonna have to undercut construction at some point, or at least put it in negative opposition to something else, and one of the things that that will form this opposition... [*Pause.*] What's the opposite of aesthetic construction?

[*After a long silence.*]

STUDENT: Expression?

JAMESON: Expression, right. That would be one of the other aesthetic principles that... [*Pause.*] The more the principle of construction goes on in art, the harder it becomes to see how you can [*Stressing*] express the suffering of something. But is that what we are supposed to do? You can see how then the subject and object again slip into this. [*Whispers.*] Construction is objective, even if you use parts of subjectivity. And [*Stressing*] expression — no matter how subjective it is — ends up being on the objective side because, after all, we all eventually have to express. We're getting this sort of fundamental opposition again... [*Pause.*] And as I said, Adorno really wants to come down on the side of objectivity, even though I would also say that the whole movement of the Frankfurt School was to continue to have or leave some place for the menaced subject... [*Quietly*: the subject which has not been repressed, which has not yet been functionalized and turned into an operator of dehumanized codes and standards, into a commercialized and commodified subject.] But their position is that subjectivity, or the space of subjectivity, is shrinking. I think you can put it... [*Pause.*] I have put it myself this way, I think...[14] [*Quietly*: maybe I got it from somebody else, I don't know.] But I think it's a good shorthand way that is linked to the disappearance of nature, to which we will come to in the next chapter and the disappearance of the unconscious... [*Raps his knuckles on the desk.*] Mm-hmm. Nature is gradually technologized by agrobusiness and science, so if there ever was anything original in nature, it's all gone, and you all know about these new genetic experiments... [*Quietly*: and these horrible stories of how the new sort of plants, they spread like this... (*Finger snapping*) and how peasants in Mexico have found that in areas where corporations have experimented with genetic corn, they found that this new genetic corn, hmm... (*Hesitates*) has moved on into their own fields.] The genetic corn is famously — the so-called "terminator seed" — [*Audience agitated. Murmuring*] ominous nutrition... [*Quietly:* it's a seed you can't replant, and you have to buy new ones every season.] Because, you see, all traditional agriculture was based on storage of seeds, where some you eat and the rest you're saving for planting. Now we've reached the supreme point of production of new forms of temporality... [*Quietly*: where you're gonna have to buy new seeds, except that now this changes the whole picture of traditional agriculture.] Anyway, and as far as the colonization of the unconscious is concerned, I would say that's [*Stressing*] mass culture. That is to say, the colonization of the unconscious by mass-cultural images, by commodified forms of desire and so on and so forth. So where before dreams could be a source of something not touched by the practical world of business, as with nature, now those enclaves are shrinking more and more, and for the Frankfurt School this was the shrinking space of the true subject... [*Quietly*: I hesitate to slip over into all this language, but let's say the "subject of desire" or the "authentic subject."] And this shrinking space is also the shrinking space of negativity, because negativity is associated with the subject. [*Pause.*] So, you can't say Adorno was an objectivist exactly. Mm-hmm. But on the other hand... [*Pause.*] It's... it's like... it's like the people who were against the expressionists after World War One. Expressionism was this oozy sentimental stuff, full of explosions and cravings, a kind of ideological outcry about all kinds of sad things in the theater, in poetry, in painting and so forth, especially in Germany... [*Quietly*: the devastation and trauma of the war has led to the rejection of traditional cultural forms, bringing into focus inner experience, emotion, angst, fear, individualism... (*Mumbles indistinctly*)] and expressionism was sort of associated with humanism, right? Normally, the emphasis on subjectivity slips into some kind of humanist complaints about "how terrible the world has become" and so on and so forth. But the Frankfurt School, they wanted to do these complaints in a much more rigorous way, hmm, and for them the whole language of subjectivity in that sense, it's not, hmm... [*Hesitates*] it's not just a matter of simple emotional grievance.

[*Long pause.*]

Alright now, we followed the artwork this far, and all of a sudden, on page 24, something new appears. The problem with any history of art... [*Door slams shut in the distance*] and about the work of art itself, is that there are lots of them. [*Pause.*] Adorno quotes, hmm... [*Hesitates*] he quotes this famous phrase, "the war of all against all"...[15] [*Quietly*: Hegel takes it up again in the master and slave struggle, where he says "each consciousness wishes the death of the other," and this becomes then sort of the central motif in Sartrean existentialism, that the struggle with the other, it's essentially this impossible thing to solve, in which I can't be myself when the other exists.] Now, hmm... [*Pause.*] Adorno... [*Quietly*: I don't think there is an existential remnant here in Adorno, but there is a Hegelian remnant.] And so, Adorno translates that remnant to the work of art itself. Each work of art wishes the death of all the other ones. It's a fairly obvious kind of thing, I mean, if we turn to these modernist works of art, many of them wish to be absolute, to be everything. They want to be masters. [*Pause.*] So, if you are in Wagner, somehow, it does not tolerate relativity. For works of art, relativism is a threat, because if Berlioz or Brahms or someone else can be just as good as Wagner, then... [*Quietly*: or if we can get out of them only a slightly different kind of pleasure] then the absolute claims of Wagner's work — [*Stressing*] to be everything — are then canceled. And so, the work of art has to somehow wish to be everything — it wants to be a perfect Gesamtkunstwerk, or a "Book of the World," as it emerges in modern times with Proust or Joyce... [*Quietly*: either Ulysses or Finnegans Wake.] This problem of "the war of all against all" in art is sort of that. They wanted to... [*Quietly*: or the famous Livre,[16] which had implications for most futuristic kind of performances.] And they did that as a kind of [*Whispers*] conversion, because if you're reading D.H. Lawrence, then you had to become a Lawrencian, I mean you have to convert yourself to his language and everything else that it involves. Because if it's just another novel... [*Quietly*: then all of this sinks to the level of the mundane or something like this.] But of course, and their tragedy, if you wish, is to... [*Quietly*: they were not everything but just another work of art... (*Mumbles indistinctly*)] for obviously, there is no solution to this. First of all, you can't... [*Pause.*] It's very hard to write history of these absolutist works because they are very self-contained, they are at least semi-autonomous, and what is the connection between Finnegans Wake and Ulysses...? [*Quietly*: I mean, it shouldn't be any, they are two separate books, two separate worlds.] So, what would be the historical narrative then? It would have to be either by choice or by the situation — you'd have [*Stressing*] to construct a history of the aesthetic situation — something that Adorno is asking us to do by putting it in the context of other situations, works or epochs. [*Pause.*] What's at best... [*Hesitates.*] Mm-hmm. There have been experiments with writing various... [*Words indistinct.*] There is, for example, this critic, I don't know... [*Quietly*: is he at Columbia in the history of French literature department, what's his name?] He asked people to do a history of literature by years, so someone will do — hmm, let me think of a year — 1678 as the emergence of the novel, or the first year of La Peau de Chagrin, or the first Balzac, and things like that.[17] And then, the notion of heterogeneity is therefore preserved in those discontinuities, and there have been other similar attempts. But I think if you think of that problem both in historiographic terms and in terms of the relationship to the individual works, because all of a sudden, a very different solution appears, which are these so-called [*Stressing*] Isms.[18]

[*Long pause.*]

And this is very interesting, because I think normally Adorno is hostile to these Isms. There is... [*Pause.*] In modern art, you've got to really have this immense tension between the great artworks and the art movements, or the Isms. [*Pause*] And each of them... [*Quietly*: and here again we have the case where there is an ongoing struggle to death between the master and the slave.] Mm-hmm. Thomas Mann does not want to be just a representative of a certain Ism, but he wants to be writing the greatest novel of all time; and Proust, the same... [*Quietly:* you could talk about impressionism in Proust, for example, and in Conrad] but impressionism was not exactly a manifesto movement. In the meanwhile, the manifesto movements themselves... [*Quietly*: they haven't produced anything really important.] What's the greatest work of futurism? [*Pause.*] Nude Descending a Staircase... [*Quietly*: I don't know, I don't know... (*Mumbles indistinctly*).] What's the greatest work of surrealism? [*Pause.*] Yeah, but those people who produced the great works of surrealism, Breton threw them out, he excommunicated them because they were "right-wing deviationists" only interested in aesthetics, and surrealism wanted to offer something more than an aesthetics. But he also threw the communists out, I mean. They wanted to be political, but to be more than political, they had to be surrealists. Well, so... [*Quietly*: and even Breton, there are marvelous things written by Breton, but those are not really such great works, like so many other kinds of writings produced at the same time.] Or think of music, I suppose. Take concrete music, there is no individual work that you can think of, and I think on the whole Adorno did not... [*Quietly*: you might say that the Second Viennese School and the twelve-tone music is a sort of a school, but a school of only three or four people? I don't know. They did do some... (*Mumbles indistinctly*).] Or let's say that people who stood for higher status or something always feel as Harold Bloom might say that the works of the Isms are not very good when compared to great individual works. Mm-hmm. And I think that this is an ongoing debate and could be... [*Cough in the audience*.] But in this section, all of a sudden you get a very positive thing now that Adorno's taking on it philosophically, because his point here is that: the Isms are an advanced form of the concept of art, which can't be realized in individual works. There is a gap between the new concepts of art that follow or emerge with the Isms — like, futurism, surrealism, even abstract expressionism, I suppose... [*Quietly*: each saying "art should be like this or like that"] — and the individual works. And in a way, the Isms have their own "truth content." That they should have produced a new... [*Hesitates*.] Mm-hmm. Surrealism, I think, is the parody or the archetype of all of these movements, for better or for worse, and it is a remarkable idea — the liberation of the unconscious — and it's true, it can't be reduced to any of its individual works, although it has produced lots and lots of things, from painting to poetry and all kinds of film. But then, the paradox is that main idea of surrealism is more advanced than the individual artworks. [*Pause*.] And so, in a way, there will be also a lesson for the other side of this, which is the works of art as opposed to these movements — it's that maybe... [*Quietly*: even though the work of art never realizes itself] that is to say, the most [*Stressing*] advanced concept of art is something that is irreducible to any individual work and that they are certainly part of the modern, but then maybe we want to look more closely at the works and see whether any of them are successful [*Pause.*] Either way, and if you want to use that language, then I think we have a certain failure here. And that's, I think, a much healthier position for critics than Harold Blum's glorification of the masterpieces and so forth,[19] because I think you don't do justice to these artworks by adopting a celebratory position, which I consider essentially a commodification of these works when you start calling them "masterpieces." Rather, if you see it as a monumental failure... [*Zipper unzipping*] it is then, I think, that you can truly see the full production process. Whereas if it's an achieved masterpiece, then there is nothing you can do about it... [*Quietly*: it's like a meteorite that's come down and it has no history, and you just have to admire it and list its beauties and move on.] But if it's something that could never have been realized, or if it's a prodigious thing, then you could look at it in order to see how it was put together, see what it is, see what materials were used and so on and so forth, and it seems to me that this is, hmm... [*Hesitates*] that's part of what Adorno is implying here.

[*Long pause.*]

Now, interestingly, he takes as an example of this, on page 25, Benjamin's... [*Clears throat*] baroque book[20]... [*Quietly*: because all of the German baroque tragedies, hmm... (*Mumbles indistinctly*) were these unreadable things.] They're not even... [*Pause.*] You can't even, hmm... [*Hesitates.*] They are not even in print. I mean, you would think that a country so aware of its traditions, and with such a magnificent publishing industry, it would have collections of baroque books, but the problem is they don't exist. And Benjamin says so in the... [*Door creaks open.*] I mean, first of all, you must understand that, when it comes to baroque books, there are maybe two masterpieces, but they are not German... [*Words indistinct*.] But the German baroque tragedy as a movement produces nothing. [*Page flipping. Starts reading*.] "The truth content of many artistic movements does not necessarily culminate in great artworks; Benjamin demonstrated this in his study of German baroque drama."[21] I think that's a remarkable idea, and it's sort of... [*Quietly*: it pushes to one side this eternal quarrel between the avant-garde movements, which don't exist today anymore, and these masterpieces, which maybe also don't exist today anymore.] Page 26: "...new art accents the once hidden element of being something made, something produced." Mm-hmm... [*Page flipping*] "The truth of the new... is situated in..."[22] Alright, the truth, it's something produced [*Stressing*] <u>but</u>... Now, let's make another distinction. Is it intended, hmm... [*Hesitates*.] What does it also mean to say that... [*Quietly*: you know that, in French, "mean" is <u>vouloir-dire</u>, which you probably learned from Derrida] and it means "wanted to say." Mm-hmm. What did so-and-so mean by this, or what did he wanna say? Well, he didn't wanna say anything in the end... [*Quietly*: that's the crucial point that Adorno makes... (*Words indistinct*).] Or rather, as a person, yes, probably, hmm... [*Hesitates*] probably some of these artists did mean to say something, or they did have their intentions, but once again, those intentions are not to be taken subjectively [*Stressing*] <u>but objectively</u> — they are part of the work, and when you see some didactic intentions in the work, that's part of it, that's not the meaning of the work, it's part of the raw materials of the work itself, it is objective and not what the author had in mind. [*Pause*.] And here, finally, we do arrive at this very strange thing, called "second reflection" [*Page flipping*] "The truth of the new... is situated in the [*Pronounces letter-by-letter*] I-N-T-E-N-T-I-O-N-L-E-S-S."[23] And I guess this is also a kind of a... [*Pause*.] This could be a kind of matter of taste or judgment for the work of art, because the less intentions you have in it, the more it becomes a kind of a strange event in its own right, and presumably the more it... [*Cough in the audience*] exists sort of as a thing-in-itself [*Mumbles indistinctly.*] And at that point, it has become somehow objective, and it ceased to be part of those old-fashioned literary or art criticism, you know... [*Quietly*: the life and loves of the artists and their lovers and children (*Chuckles*) and all that old stuff, which is also part of the contemporary criticism as well.] So, the matter of intention is quite an important [*Stressing*] motif running through here — it is an attack on intention. It is the difference between the meaning of the work... [*Quietly*: what the artist intended; what did he mean to say by that; what does this mean; well, maybe sometimes one should not even ask these questions, generally these things are so idiotic that you can't imagine what it mattered in the first place] as opposed to what Adorno calls "second reflection." [*Pause.*] So, what is this "second reflection" about?

[*Long pause.*]

Okay. [*Shuffling paper.*] "This sets the truth in opposition to reflection, which is the motor of the new, and raises reflection to a second order, to [*Stressing*] second reflection."[24] [*Pause.*] I suppose that, if there is anywhere a new word for dialectic in Adorno, it might be that, "second reflection." I don't think this is a very satisfactory term, I mean, this is very confusing and it raises more questions than it solves, and so forth, but I think we can figure out what he means by this... [*Quietly*: whatever we think of the appropriate means of using this kind of language.] I think it means the moment in which... [*Quietly:* it's a kind of second experiencing of the work, but not exactly a re-reading of the work.] You enlarge your horizon on this... you enlarge your point of view on this work in such a way that you see it — if you like, as an event — or as a [*Stressing*] construction, which includes all of its subjective elements. In the first reading... [*Quietly*: I think he doesn't talk very much about first reading of the... (*Cough in the audience*)] but I assume here that the first reading involves just such questions: "What does this mean?" and "What's going on here?" I mean, these are all things that go through one's mind when you experience a work of art. In the "second reflection," all of these questions get included in the object. So, the question about what this character might mean in its ambiguity and so on, becomes part of the aesthetic object itself from this new vantage point, which is "second reflection." [*Pause.*] I would say that "second reflection" essentially grasps the object as a construction, hmm, as a... [*Softly.*] I don't like to say a synthesis of objectivity and subjectivity, but something in which that difference no longer obtains because everything is raw material here, and I think it moves towards what I would call some ultimate kind of formalism — an absolute formalism in which political and historical judgments also take place, but they take place in the form of the object. [*Pause.*] They don't take place on the, hmm... [*Hesitates*] in the thoughts of the author. That Céline or Flaubert had, let's say, any democratic thoughts or personal positions is not something that gives their works its meaning. To call works "fascist"... [*Pause.*] Even to call works "fascist" ... [*Quietly*: I mean, Sartre took another position, which meant there couldn't be any fascist prose and... (*Cough in the audience*) before you had to say, "Well, but wasn't Céline a fascist?" "Yeah, sort of, but he was also a populist and what comes out of... (*Words indistinct*).] My favorite is his Death on Credit, or Mort à crédit, which is this tremendous, somewhat sentimental view of the poor, or let's say, it wasn't about the poor, it was about the... [*Mumbles indistinctly.*] And so yeah, it's anti-Semitic and Nazi or fascist... [*Quietly*: you know, Céline fled to Germany and Denmark, and was later convicted of collaboration, then pardoned and so forth.] Yes, all of that is part of Céline's, but in this works, hmm... [*Hesitates*] whether or not they are mindless diatribes, which he also wrote, they become sedimented in a very different way and become part of this construction and can therefore be appropriated in different ways. [*Pause.*] I think that the process of rising above the work and seeing it as a construction in which the intentions are the raw material — I would say that's the formalism that appears in the Adornian "second reflection." And it's a formalism which involves some kind of judgment; it involves a historical judgment because it relates to the work. It sees the work in some ways as an autonomous symptom of the historical situation, but it doesn't involve judgment of the Nuremberg variety... [*Quietly*: of the indictment and trial, which is what Lukács much more intelligently did, or the other ones which did it less intelligently... (*Words indistinct*).] Or take the Nazis' famous exhibit of degenerate art in the Haus der Kunst, where they gathered together all the expressionist paintings they could find and put them up... [*Quietly*: I think that people were delighted to see them for one last time, because you would not have this experience of truly modern art again in Nazi Germany.] But those judgments, I think, are very useful... [*Raps his knuckles on the desk*] in terms of social psychology, I mean how ideologies are formed, how does someone get to be a... [*Pause*.] Or what's the connection between populism and fascism, for example? Because these are very important questions. And what is the relationship between bourgeois ressentiment and art? And Flaubert can tell us something about that. But that's not exactly what Adorno thinks of this as "second reflection," I think. [*Pause*] But we'll come back to it and see if we can, hmm... [*Hesitates*] see if we can make of it a little more sense. [*Page flipping*.]

[*Long pause*.]

Now, in these next pages, I think things begin to, hmm... [*Hesitates*.] I think things begin to... [*Pause*.] We go back to subjectivity and talk about the ambiguity of this business of depersonalization. You wanna move away from subjectivity, but... [*Quietly*: I think I already mentioned this the other day] but moving away from subjectivity can also be thought as a repression of the subject. Mm-hmm. Depersonalization: Is that also repression, or isn't it similar to repression? This is one of these paradoxes or antinomies... [*Quietly*: like the one I pointed out to you the other day.] Hmm, commodification turns production into an object, but the artwork fights commodification by way of commodification, so it wants to become an object too, and everything in modern art moves towards the condition of [*Stressing*] being an object and then, later on, moves towards the dissolution of the object and the break-up of the object into, hmm... [*Hesitates*] into various objective pieces, but it doesn't go back to subjectivity. So, what do we do with these ambiguous formulations or views of the process? It is the ambiguity that he says, on page 29, of the Dialectic of Enlightenment, so: "As soon as artworks make a fetish of their hope of duration, they begin to suffer from their sickness unto death"[25]... [*Pause.*] They wanna last, they wanna be things, but maybe the solution is — and you will see this in the next chapters — they have to be ephemeral, like fireworks: "as the only art that aspires not to duration but only to glow for an instant and fade away."[26] [*Pause.*] Mm-hmm. And this will link in the next chapters to the notion... [*Quietly*: he uses this French word, apparition, the work of art has a fireworks-type apparition or is an event... (*Mumbles indistinctly*) then it disappears.] That is something that would resist reification.

[*Long pause.*]

But on the other hand, works of art survive all that. Now... [*Pause.*] Page 29: "If the whole of modern art can be understood as the perpetual intervention of the subject, one that is at no point disposed to allow the unreflected governance of the traditional play of forces within the artwork, the permanent interventions of the ego are matched by a tendency of the ego to abdicate out of weakness."[27] In a way, what I've been calling "depersonalization" — moving away from subjectivity — can also be thought of... [*Quietly*: and maybe that could clarify things] as a movement away from the ego. In Lacan, and most psychoanalysis, in Proust and a lot of other places, it's not the subjectivity that's bad but the ego, hmm... [*Hesitates*] the... the... the personality. "True to the age-old mechanical principle of the bourgeois spirit, this abdication takes the form of the reification of subjective achievements..."[28] [*Pause.*] So, as the abdication of the ego, as the subject gives up its freedoms in this new society, which is dominated more and more by collective institutions... [*Quietly*: like the great businesses that are all around us, or this university and so on] as it does that, it compensates by sentimentally admiring subjectivities... [*Quietly*: uh, it could be powerful personalities, charismatic political leaders and so forth, but it could also be a fusion of all kinds of the type that I mentioned for German expressionism.] That is the reification of subjective achievements, and then he goes on to denounce mass culture again. [*Pause.*] And then the section on Beckett that we'll discuss hopefully later on. And finally, we get to... [*Knocks lightly on the desk*] page 32, in which he tries something else on the notion of the "new."

[*Long pause.*]

Because you see here is also the problem with the fetishization of the new... [*Door creaks open.*] Mm-hmm. We might be able to know that... [*Exhales deeply.*] In the contemporary period, we might be able to know that... [*Quietly*: I don't know, let's say] the novel Infinite Jest is something that people haven't done before right, whatever you may think of it.[29] Mm-hmm. What else... [*Quietly*: I'm sure there are many other things like that.] But when we're talking about the importance of Baudelaire, how would we know that he is an important poet except by reading it in the book? Somebody tells us that nobody has done what Baudelaire did. Jauss[30] used to say, [*Impersonates Jauss*] "Well, I read all the poetry published in 1857 in French, all of the volumes of poetry printed in that year, and I can testify that Baudelaire is different from all of those other poets," right? I mean, there is supposedly something in Baudelaire that none of the other poets have. [*Pause*] And I think, I'm sure Jauss is right, and I believe him; I'm sure he did read all of those poems, but then that's some kind of external knowledge, and how does that affect our reading of Baudelaire? And how can that still be alive in our reading of Baudelaire? Or how could we explain the fact that Baudelaire was once new, in the strong Adornian modernist sense? Hmm... [*Hesitates*] but it's not new anymore because the later poets have gone on far beyond that? Do we have to know something else and add it to our reading situation or is there something in the work itself that, hmm... [*Hesitates*] ...that... [*Reflects*] allows us to recapture that newness which was once a form-creating tool? Well, I would say maybe two things. One is what Adorno says here, which is very interesting. [*Page flipping.*] "The new is the longing for the new, not the new itself."[31] [*Pause.*] So, that you can still find in Baudelaire, that is, this commitment to the new, to the radical, to the extreme. As he points out, you can't really have people doing something new and who are not destroying the old, or maniacs who are intent on one thing, or... [*Chair-back creaks.*] I mean, the new is this destructive... [*Words indistinct.*] Mm-hmm. There is this expression about capitalism, "creative destruction," right? The new is also about this process of creative destruction, but in a way... [*Words indistinct*] that there never is anything new. Or the new tendency is already present in the old, and so on, so it would be this longing for this value of the new that has to come through, and not just the fact of the new. "That is what everything new suffers from..." This is page 32: "What takes itself to be utopia remains the negation of what exists and is obedient to it. At the center of contemporary antinomies is that art must be and [*Stressing*] <u>wants</u> to be utopia, and the more utopia is blocked by the real functional order, the more this is true; yet at the same time art may not be utopia in order not to betray it by providing semblance and consolation."[32]

[*Long pause.*]

Mm-hmm. In other words, if you had what... [*Pause.*] He believed in a fully realized utopia, this guy, and it would be in the world and not out of the world, and you would think, well, at least the one good thing that you can say about this world is that you can have this vision of utopia. [*Pause.*] Well, in that case then, we are back in the world of the status quo; we have affirmed the status quo because the status quo did one good thing — it allowed this utopia to come into being... [*Quietly: so, utopia is not the... (Words indistinct) and everything that's utopian about this moment of the new.*] And here is the thing. [*Page flipping.*] "If the utopia of art were fulfilled, it would be art's temporal end. Hegel was the first to realize that the end of art is implicit in its concept,"[33] but in a somewhat different way... [*Mumbles indistinctly.*] "Art is no more able than theory to concretize utopia, not even negatively."[34] [*Pause.*] And then you get the possibility, which seems to have been the only one that Adorno could really imagine here, as... [*Achoo. Sneeze in the audience*] as the realization of the utopian dreams. "In the image of catastrophe, an image that is not a copy of the event but the cipher of its potential, the magical trace of art's most distant prehistory reappears under the total spell, as if art wanted to prevent the catastrophe by conjuring up its image."[35] This is how this book is a real utopia... [*Doors slams shut.*] Mm-hmm. The image of negativity, the horrors of... [*Zipper zipping up*] it's only possible through this kind of image that we can imagine, through the positive. If we imagine the positive directly... [*Quietly*: then we just... (*Pause*) that's just another one of these thematic treatments that become commodities, but in this train of thought, it becomes an image, or as he says, an "image of consolation."] And whenever he says "consolation," that's bad — it consoles you with the order of things as they are. [*Pause.*] Whereas, as he puts it in a later chapter, which we will discuss hopefully next time, hmm... [*Pause.*] Mm-hmm... truth... [*Talks to himself. Page flipping.*] Truth is... [*In German:* Denn wahr ist nur, was nicht in diese Welt paßt.][36] Hmm, "For only what does not fit into this world is true."[37] [*Pause.*] Only what negates [*Stressing*] what is, only what negates Being is true. Mm-hmm. And I think that sums up some of the Adorno and... [*Feet shuffling*] and at the same time, maybe points to the limits of happiness. And Adorno reflects very seriously on happiness as we will see, and I've already said that this notion of a promise of the something, or the longing for something is another way of getting around this; it is the longing for the new, you won't find happiness in the aesthetic and the work is — as I keep repeating through this seminar — only the promesse du bonheur: the Stendhalian promise of happiness, not, hmm... [*Hesitates*] not the thing itself.

[*Long pause.*]

Okay, we will go on with this part next time and I will try to get into these... [*Feet shuffles. Chairs scraping against the floor*] so-called "nature chapters." So, go ahead and read as much as you can from... [*Audience hubbub*.]

Audience stands up. Feet shuffling. Objects drop on the floor. Door creaks open. Students return chairs to other classrooms. Zippers zipping up. Some form a line to discuss their assignments with Jameson. General noise. Screeching microphone noise.

[*Microphone turns off*.]

CURTAIN

LECTURE EIGHT

FEBRUARY 17, 2003

SITUATION (CHAPTER) — THE UGLY, THE BEAUTIFUL, AND TECHNIQUE (CHAPTER)

CURTAIN RISES

Moving chairs, squeaking door, coughs, other sounds filling the noise environment of a large classroom in the Literature Department at Duke University. In a corner, a few students are chatting about the Slovenians who will be giving a series of talks and a seminar this and next week. Some students are asking one of their Eastern European colleagues to explain why Slovenia in particular (and not, say, Russia, Hungary, or Poland) has produced such an interesting phenomenon in contemporary critical theory. The student talks in broad terms about the history of this small Alpine republic and its unique position in Central Europe as a "strange God's kindergarten in the heart of Europe" (as one Austrian clergyman once described it)[1]*; he describes its convenient geopolitical position, bordering a few Western nations while still claiming to be part of the "East," and its relative openness during the days of Yugoslavian socialism. Its position and its openness during self-managed socialism facilitated uninterrupted cultural dialogue with the West. Many Slovenian intellectuals had been trained in the West, while others remained stuck behind the Russian curtain. After the Wall fell, they were the ones best equipped to speak in the name of the "East," as they also claimed to have* *been part of the...* [makes quotation marks with his fingers] *"terrible communist experiment." They sort of became a bridge between East and West. Then the student tells an anecdote about his visit to a Slovenian embassy (for a conference visa) and how the consular clerk proudly informed him that Slavoj Žižek was their country's best asset, and that he alone had brought Slovenia more capital than many subsidized local private industries. Students are laughing.*

Jameson enters the classroom carrying a few books, his scattered notes, and the red pen in the chest pocket of his flannel shirt.

[*Microphone turns on.*]

JAMESON: [*Chair scratching the floor. Footsteps across the floor.*] ...tomorrow at twelve in that room up there in the Union Building... [*Zipper unzipping.*] And that will be the first talk called "Against Deleuze," and then we will move... [*Quietly:* I think that Alenka's lecture will be on Thursday right after this class, which will end a little early at twelve, and then Mladen is on Friday and Slavoj again the week after that.] Mm-hmm. I had copies made of some of the articles in this Duke journal SIC ...[*Pause*] that Slavoj edits, and which has articles by Alenka and Mladen, and those are in the office next door. Just sign them out so we know who has them and try to bring them back fast so everybody else, or whoever needs them, could see them and we'll get a few more copies of the book, and the same will be true for the book... [*Quietly*: you just sign them out if you can.] But I guess... [*Addresses student assistant.*] I guess we have ordered the books, right... [*Pounds his hand on the desk.*] Did we not, hmm... [*Hesitates*] order them?

STUDENT ASSISTANT: For the seminar?

JAMESON: Yeah. Yeah. Those are all there. Oh, then you don't need to get any of those, but if you see any extra books by Slavoj lying around... [*Quietly*: I don't imagine a lot of them that we don't know of... (*Mumbles indistinctly*).] Otherwise, you could get a copy... [*Deep, spasmodic coughing in the audience.*] Mm-hmm. And as I said, if you are registered for the course and you come to all the meetings — unless you have an excused absence — then you will get it, hmm... [*Hesitates*] you'll get it on your transcript. As I said, it's very hard to fail Žižek's course. Mm-hmm. Any other question about any of that?

[*Long silence.*]

Okay, I wanna go back and today I wanna [*Stressing*] finish this chapter, "Situation." I'm simply gonna add to what we were saying that the, hmm... [*Hesitates*] that the... [*Violent coughing continue*] that the general movement of this theory is... [*Zipper unzipping*] against subjectivity. I think that the book is in principle against expression, and thus, for the opposite of expression — whatever that would be — and that's generally [*Stressing*] construction. [*Pause.*] Although, it could also be mimesis, but maybe mimesis understood as construction. These are obviously very complicated categories, or categories that shift their meaning in all kinds of relational ways so that, in one historical period, you've got mimesis being one dominant aesthetic principle, and maybe even it is a positive principle, but then later on, in the modern age, mimesis becomes negative... [*Quietly*: mimesis is only achieved by the negation of the taboo on mimesis.] But overall, I think that his aesthetic theory is not on the side of subjectivity, or of expression,[2] as some may infer. So, these are, hmm... [*Hesitates*] these are, for Adorno, the main categories in terms of which one has to think about art in any given historical period. And they are not in themselves [*Stressing*] substantive ideas; they are formal categories and I think you should always accustom yourself to imagining that they work in pairs, like mimesis-construction, or expression-mimesis and expression-construction... [*Quietly*: or they could even work in thirds, like mimesis-expression-construction, and once you get beyond the thirds, they can turn to fourths, and then to pairs again.] They are always relational. [*Sighs.*] Mm-hmm, I think that's another way of saying the same thing, because if a theme is relational, then it can't really be substantive, hmm... [*Hesitates*] unless you substantify the whole opposition itself... [*Achoo. Sneeze in the audience.*] Anyway, we'll be observing this relation and I strongly encourage you to keep an eye on them as we move along.

[*Long pause.*]

Now, with this movement against subjectivity and towards objectivity, there are really two kinds of things going on here. [*Deep coughing continues.*] One is the objectivity of subjectivity. [*Pause.*] Mm-hmm. That is, in other words, when you express something, things are going... [*Talks to student who arrived late.*] Here, come take this chair...

STUDENT: Thank you... [*Footsteps. Chair legs scrape hard against the floor. Zipper unzipping.*]

JAMESON: So, when you express something in words... [*Deep coughing*] or say it in some other form of expression, then that form of expression is always gonna be objective, somehow. [*Exhales deeply.*] Mm-hmm. So there will always be a tendency of what we call "subjectivity" in that, and one could always locate an objective form for it, and then that objective form will probably have to do something with language. [*Pause.*] It's a question of thinking of a standpoint from which it is clear that expression is no longer just subjective, but it is also objective because of its material form. However, there is another feature of this that we haven't really looked at, and that is... [*Quietly*: look at page 41-42 (*Page flipping*)] and that is what we call "subjectivity," which we also tend to confuse with individual feelings, whereas if we look at feelings historically, it becomes apparent that they are not only subjective. Take, for example, emotions. All the emotions are... [*Clears throat*] again relational, they are to be defined against each other, and you have the whole series of handbooks through time in which the local or the historical chart of emotions has been mapped out. It's sort of like with colors... [*Pause.*] In the structuralist period, they loved color charts because it was clear that there were modifications that you could deduce from the local language of how colors were seen. So, in Greece... [*Quietly*: hmm, I hope I have this right, or maybe it's not Greece, but in Japan or some parts of Asia] there is no real distinction between green and blue. Well, what does that mean? Does it mean that they have different eyes than we do, and they don't see the color spectrum in the same way? [*Pause.*] Well, if you don't have a word for it, then it isn't articulated really, and these articulations, these color schemes are generally done in terms of various kinds of complicated oppositions in any case. Mm-hmm. So, we think our perception is purely scientific, and therefore it escapes all error, but that is not necessarily true either. But the same would be then true of emotions, that you have a series of emotions which have to be historicized. Take anger. Yeah, but maybe in this society there are different kinds of anger... [*Softly*] and you have to distinguish between them. And indeed, when you have an interesting language... [*Quietly*: hmm, in French, for example] you can have what they call colère du lait and it's called a "milk anger." What would that be? [*Long silence.*] Well, have you ever had your milk... [*Quietly*: you wanna warm up some milk, right?] And you leave it on the fire a little too long and all of a sudden "Kshhhh" — it overflows very quickly, right? [*Audience laughing.*] Well, there are people who get angry like that. They are not angry at first, but then they start to think about it and all of a sudden they take to become... [*Laughing continues.*] Well, that's a different kind of anger than the kind of slow anger that burns and burns inside. So, you can see that difference in articulated language, or in language which is articulated historically, there could be a number of distinctions that drop... [*Cough in the audience*] out these complicated emotions and feelings. Mm-hmm. And it's very hard to register them because you should need lots and lots of information, and you need to write them down, but sometimes there is nobody to write them down. However, the philosophers occasionally try to think this through, and therefore we have the Nicomachean Ethics of Aristotle, which is, at least for classical Greece, is a certain kind of mapping procedure for what we call the emotions, mixed up with the virtues and all kind of things. Then we have Descartes'

Treatise of Passions, which, for the early seventeenth century, that is the moment of the replacement of the feudal age by absolute monarchy, and we get a rather different version of all of this. Then we can compare emotions also from a class point of view. [*Pause*.] Aristotle's is absolutely from a class point of view... [*Quietly*: he says, (*Impersonates Aristotle*) "Really to be happy you gotta have money, and social position, and health and so forth."] This is not for slaves... [*Very quietly*: probably not for women] but for a certain kind of gendered class. For Descartes, it is a set of feudal values that are being domesticated and absorbed into the ideology of the new absolute state. For example, for Descartes, the most admirable of all emotions or "passions," as he calls them, is [*Stressing*] admiration... [*Quietly:* and that's very strange, but very interesting.] You have a system in which there is a certain relationship to people of an immediate personal type, and which includes valorization, authority, submission. In Descartes, the objects of our admiration must possess something divine, some godly quality, which makes admiration foundational for the pursuit of knowledge, as I freely abdicate my own value with respect to this supreme thing that I admire in other persons or objects. Then when you get to the eighteenth century, of course, hmm... [*Reflecting*] a lot of new kind of emotions are coming up with the new classes and then you get things that are sort of not named. I would say, for example, you get very peculiar feelings like ennui... [*Quietly*: but what is boredom, what kind of emotion is that, or fear? When do you fear?] You have to say that perhaps people are bored throughout human history, but at least they have a name for it and boredom is not exactly ennui either. [*Pause*.] Mm-hmm... [*Violent coughing continues*] so when you put a name to it, you register it and then you say, "Oh, that's what I feel," then it enters this register or system of things. And then, towards the end of the nineteenth century, it seems to me, we have what we call the "irrational" ... [*Quietly*: that is, the things that don't have any names.] They're the drives. And then with Freud in the twentieth century, new drives and feelings get catalogued and explained and so on and so forth.

[*Long pause.*]

Mm-hmm, so... [*Pause.*] So, hmm... [*Hesitates.*] So what Adorno is saying here is that all of those emotions and feelings are collective. You think that they are individual, but after all, this is a social system through which these emotions get organized and so another way — but a fundamental way in which the subjective becomes objective — is not necessarily through reification... [*Quietly*: that would be a standard problem throughout, as we've seen in Musil] but through the fact that they are in their deepest nature, so to speak [*Stressing*] social. [*Pause.*] Mm-hmm, and once they are social, they no longer belong to an individual and they are even... [*Tries to open the window.* Let's open this window. If it gets too cold, I'll close it. Mm-hmm. It's nice and very fresh outside.] So, passions, drives, emotions then become objective again, and therefore that also puts this whole matter of expression in a different way. Now, obviously this is a view from which Adorno will have to draw back and say, [*Impersonates Adorno*] "Hold it. I didn't mean that expression, subjectivity and all those things are bad..." [*Cough in the audience.*] Because, in the earlier twentieth century, this tendency towards subjectivity will end up, hmm... [*Hesitates*] and the German word is... [*Chalk on the blackboard*] S-A-C-H-L-I-C-H-K-E-I-T or Die Neue Sachlichkeit, which emerges as a reaction against sentimentality and emotional excesses of the previous generation of expressionists. In the United States, in the West, it's stuff like... [*Pause.*] Well, you can already see this in images and language, which we have with Pound and Eliot, which wishes to be something without any subjective points of view, but I'm thinking maybe about Picasso and the collage with all these newspaper fragments. You move towards... [*Clears throat*] an objectification, which really ceases to have anything subjective in it, and which gets very sterile. And therefore, however important it is to insist on the objective, on the collectivity of art, hmm... [*Hesitates*] if you pass over a certain boundary, you're gonna end up in something [*Stressing*] purely reified, which is no longer of any interest. So, at a certain point, he is going to redress the balance, so to speak... [*Quietly*: I think the expressionists pushed their rhetoric into another direction] and then they would argue for objectivity in some form. But it's clear that he wishes to rescue art from subjectivity and push it towards objectivity. And this should be deduced from its social situation... [*Zipper zipping up*] that is to say, they are in an aesthetic context which is full of kitsch and sappy or sentimental sorts of emotions and so on, a kind of humanism of the individual which is always talking about art and existential individual feelings. It is obviously against a number of those enemies that the thesis of objectivity is important in Adorno.

[*Long pause*.]

But if everything were [*Stressing*] objective, then you would have to do this in another way, and it's equally clear that on some other level here Adorno is also arguing against so-called "commitment," against socialist realism, against, hmm... [*Hesitates*] other forms of political art like Agitprop that have a purely political content... [*Quietly*: and for him, these no longer have any kind of aesthetic value... (*Words indistinct*) at all.] I think there you have to remember that... [*Quietly*: well, we're in the period of... (*Raps his knuckles on the desk*).] Obviously, the Cold War is important, but we are in the period after the Stalinist purge trials, and after the famous meetings on socialist realism that stretch from the early days of literature congresses with Zhdanov in the USSR before the war, to the situation with socialist art in East Germany after the war. [*Pause*.] And, as much as Adorno is waging a battle against conservatives in Germany — if not Nazis, then at least the irrationalist traditions of which Germany was so rich — mm-hmm, he is also waging a battle against artistic styles that are going on in the East... [*Quietly*: and so Brecht becomes this very strange figure for him.] Any time Adorno mentions Brecht, there are some ulterior motives, either he wants to tell us that Brecht was very modernist, but without knowing it, or that Brecht is different from the standard horrible didactic political stuff that the East Germans were recommending. Mm-hmm. But I think to place this form of aesthetic objectivity properly, you always gotta understand these two, hmm... [*Hesitates*] these two sides of the discussion which are present in Germany at the time, given the division of the country into two blocs. Now, other countries would also have that, but they wouldn't be dealing with another part of their country, they would be dealing with their communist parties. In France, Sartre has to do a lot of arguing against standard communist positions; and in Italy, the communist positions come out of Gramsci and therefore that's a little bit different. So again, this position on new objectivity and commitment is a situational and historical one, as everything else. Alright, I think that's what really is at stake... [*Page flipping.*] Now, page 42:

> Whoever resists the overwhelming collective force in order to insist on the passage of art through the subject need on no account at the same time think underneath the veil of subjectivism. Aesthetic autonomy encompasses what is collectively most advanced, what has escaped the spell. By virtue of its mimetic preindividual elements, every idiosyncrasy lives from collective forces of which it is unconscious. The critical reflection of the subject, however isolated that subject, stands watch that these forces do not provoke regression.[3]

So, there is a regression possible on either side. [*Pause.*] There is a regression possible in objectivity, there is a regression possible in subjectivity, and that makes life more complicated for us because these regressions often tend to take the form of reification. Whereas there is another sense of reification or objectification in art... [*Quietly*: which, as I tried to show you the other day] is a positive part of modernism as it resists social reification. [*Page flipping.*] Mm-hmm. [*To himself:* this is also something we know, and hmm... (*Mumbles indistinctly*).]

[*Long pause.*]

Okay, that is all for this very important chapter of Aesthetic Theory called "Situation," and let's go on then to chapter three where he deals, in chapters three, four, and five, with the notion of "beauty." Mm-hmm. [*Pause.*] I think that, in the postmodern, you have many people going back; hmm... [*Hesitates*] it is in many ways a kind of return from the sublime of modernism to beauty. Postmodernist architecture... [*Quietly*: which was the first to swallow up its offspring] was certainly now to restore the value of decoration and of sensual pleasure and thus of beauty in the opposite sense. And this has worked its way up through what I would call the "still surviving late modernists" — a lot of those reactionaries from the New Criterion, who are telling us that we need an aesthetic of beauty again and not this modernist sublime.[4] I think, for example, of the distinguished Irish critic who has just published a whole book on the revival of beauty... [*Quietly*: what is it called (*Mumbles indistinctly*) which I think is very characteristic of this whole beauty revival movement.][5] But I would say this takes several forms: there is a postmodernism, which is a... [*Stressing*] pure form of the revival of beauty in the aesthetic, and then there is a late modern, or reactionary modernism, that calls for a return of the so-called "old beauty." [*Clears throat.*] But they are obviously linked by something, and this is maybe by the end of the modern and the impossibility of the sublime — by the impossibility of all these things that Adorno is always talking about.

[*Long pause.*]

However, now we need to go back to the very beginning of this and talk about the original concept of "beauty," which is certainly not that of... [*Quietly*: in Kant at least] not that of sensual pleasure but rather something else. [*Pause.*] And you have read enough of the Third Critique to know that what's being defined here is somehow a different matter than what later on becomes to be called "beauty." The question of beauty... [*Pause.*] The reason there are three chapters that are dedicated to beauty in Aesthetic Theory is the following:[6] first, we have to ask ourselves questions... [*Quietly*: or Adorno has to ask himself] questions about the very... [*Raps his knuckles on the desk*] about the very nature of this concept. And it will not be any great surprise to you to learn that Adorno deals with this by turning beauty around and saying, [*Impersonates Adorno*] "Look, if you want to talk about beauty philosophically, then we have to also talk about ugliness. And ugliness [*Stressing*] comes first. Beauty is defined against it." Mm-hmm. So, this is a general philosophical discussion... [*Quietly*: chapter three] of the historical place of the concept of beauty. I'm trying to... [*Cough in the audience*] to not oversimplify this relation between beauty and ugliness, because as you all know... [*Quietly*: with Adorno, any digression is no longer a matter of deviation... (*Mumbles indistinctly*).] Then we get to the discussion of this strangest thing, which is the notion of "natural beauty," on which Adorno wishes to insist, and which he wishes to, hmm... [*Hesitates*] he wishes not to revive it in some romantic sense of going out and staring at trees, but to show that it is a fundamental form and that, without some sense of natural beauty and of its otherness... [*Quietly*: that "Not-I" as the German philosophy may put it, as that "Not-I" which is nature] everything becomes then resubjectified. [*Addresses a standing student.*] There is a chair right over there. [*Footsteps.*] Without a sense of natural beauty, we sort of lose any sense of reality and in particular with respect to the importance of the work of art. [*Door slams shut.*] There has to be some kind of... [*Zipper unzipping*] residual notion, and this is natural beauty. And then... [*Quietly*: chapter five] we go back to the beautiful in art and ask what we are to do with that. Mm-hmm. I suppose we won't get through all three of these chapters today, but I think it's important to see the progression of his argument.

[*Long pause.*]

Now, even before we came to this, we have to have some sense of what natural beauty was earlier. [*Pause.*] I'll give you a few different versions of nature. Let's say a classical... [*Quietly*: not a classical one] but an earlier nineteenth-century one, very much in the Kantian spirit, and then I'll give you a very modern one. [*Pause.*] The figure who comes out of Kant most immediately is the playwright Friedrich Schiller, who began his life as a revolutionary and gradually became more conservative... [*Cough in the audience.*] For all of these people, it was the terror... [*Quietly*: not for Kant] but for many of the English and German admirers of the French Revolution — the "enthusiasts," as Kant might say — the year of the terror, 1793, is the self-defining line. But... [*Quietly*: this tells you something when you start to get nervous about this tremendous historical event, the greatest event in human history, as they all called it.] Friedrich Schiller will say that there are three greatest events, at least in his lifetime, or in the life of the modern time, so to speak, and these were: the French Revolution, the publication of Goethe's Wilhelm Meister and Fichte's Wissenschaftslehre, hmm... [*Hesitates*] Fichte's first book of philosophy which announces this [*Stressing*] act, whereby the "I" produces the "not-I"... [*Quietly*: the self produces the world, which is a sort of philosophical take of a genuine (*Stressing*) subjective German idealism, quite different from Hegel and also quite different from Kant.[7]] Fichte is also an intermediary here, because what Schiller came to believe... [*Pause.*] Well, there are two things that Schiller tries to do later on here: he continues to write plays... [*Quietly*: which become more and more classical in the German sense, as he connects up with Goethe, who lived next to Weimar, and they saw each other. There is also a marvelous correspondence between them up until Schiller's death.[8]] Mm-hmm. And the first thing he writes is called... [*Quietly*: in a stupid English translation, it would be called "On Naïve and Sentimental Poetry"[9]] that means on, hmm... [*Hesitates*] on spontaneous versus reflexive or self-conscious poetry. And what Schiller is trying to do in this important little essay is evidently to draw a distinction between himself and Goethe. So, Goethe is this naïve poet who somehow produces his poems the way a tree produces, hmm... [*Hesitates*] a tree produces air or oxygen. And Schiller, on the other side, is the [*Stressing*] reflexive poet, who has to think and reflect on the form and be involved in this part of the production process.

But that's less important than the section I'm gonna read you about the role of the poet. The other major work, and probably one of the most important aesthetic documents of this period, is a series of letters called On the Aesthetic Education of Man, and this... [*Holds book up for the audience*][10] is a nice edition in German facing pages with the English. It has an enormous introduction and a vast bibliography and... [*Thud! Object drops on the floor.*] The book is very important because it marks out a use of aesthetics... [*Quietly*: that may have always been there, but it was probably never said] and which is historically very significant because it says that [*Whispering*] aesthetics is a way of avoiding revolutions.

[*Long pause.*]

[*Looks through the pages of* On the Aesthetic Education of Man.] What Schiller says here is that the terror has taught us that revolutions are somehow contradictory. [*Pause.*] They are made by people... [*Quietly*: I'm getting mixed up in all of these languages, but it doesn't matter.] Revolutions are made by people who were crippled by the old regime, by the old system, by power, and who have enough anger, rage, violence, and passion to destroy the old regime, but for that very reason, they are unable to become the citizens of a wholly new era, the right kind of citizens who would have nothing to do with the old regime. I would say that, from a modern... [*Pause.*] From a contemporary standpoint, we could give this question a rather different name and call it the question of [*Stressing*] the cultural revolution... [*Chair leg scraping the floor.*] How are the personalities, these evolving personalities of the old regime, to be transformed into the new people of this new revolutionary era of freedom? Well, now you can see the role of aesthetics. [*Softly.*] It is the aesthetic education of man... [*Quietly*: and how the experience of beauty can help harmonize the sensuous faculties of people, and their sense of communities leading to a more balanced human society.] Mm-hmm. Aesthetics is the sort of black box in which the subjectivities of the old regime are to be transformed into the citizens of the new modern regime of freedom, as opposed to old tyranny and oppression... [*Quietly*: and all those things that are characteristic of the ancient regimes in the eighteenth century.] Now, there is a bonus to this... [*Cough in the audience*] because if this non-violent transformation is able to take place, if culture can transform all of these subjectivities, then we won't need revolutions at all because we will be there already. [*Chuckles.*] So, this is a very interesting proposition, right, that culture is... [*Zipper unzipping.*] Here he is thinking more in terms of... [*Quietly*: but if you want more empirical evidence, then let's say the German National Theater, which he and Goethe tried to establish in Weimar.] They tried to establish a national theater in which somehow a whole new sense of nationhood would take place in this Germany of the provinces... [*Quietly*: where there is no Germany yet, and there are just individual princedoms and lands... (*Words indistinct*) with various kinds of local personalities, but there isn't as yet a unified notion of Germany, so that would be one example of aesthetic education; and then the rest of these places would also be training in this transformation of the passions into the behavior of the senses.]

[*Long pause.*]

Now, in Kantian language, what Schiller is trying to do, he is trying to take the Third Critique and insert it in between the First and the Second Critiques, because this is what Kant was doing anyway.[11] [*Pause.*] So far, he is merely drawing the consequence... [*Achoo. Sneeze in the audience*] of Kant's scheme. We have the limits and possibilities of human knowledge, we have the feeling of duty, and then what's the connection here... [*Quietly*: that takes us up in a liminal realm of affects and so on.] Well, remember the harmony of the aesthetic is supposed to be this harmony between the idea of freedom and the categories of understanding, which gives us some kind of a new connection between the Kantian Critiques. [*Pause.*] Now, it isn't so clear how the opposition of beauty and sublime plays into this because, remember Kant says ... , [*Impersonates Kant*] "Look, if there were a function of the sublime there, we don't know anything about it, it's the transcendental realm and so on." But if you could posit some reason for being of the sublime, it would be to generate notions of freedom, to generate transcendental notions, to generate a form of ethics, to train people into what is not yet imaginable. [*Pause.*] So maybe the sublime generates freedom, beauty generates the good and so on and so forth. Nothing in Kant can support this argument. Mm-hmm, and this is somewhat against the Kantian system, and nonetheless, Kant has to point out that you could maybe connect them... [*Cough in the audience*] or maybe you can use a sentence like that. Well, Schiller marches ahead and [*Whispers*] uses a sentence like that.

[*Long pause.*]

So, aesthetics will build the bridge between matter and spirit, between the drive of the corporeal, and the values of the transcendental, which is to say, hmm... [*Hesitates*] freedom, or in Schiller this becomes the material drive and the formal drive. [*Pause.*] And form and matter are somehow reconciled in the aesthetic, and the aesthetic is the place in which these two principles learn to get along and to form a synthesis and thus — in my language — to create a new form of political subjectivity, which is not dependent on, hmm... [*Hesitates*] on... [*Pause*] on final revolution. Obviously, on the side of matter you have "people going hungry," and they have no time for the transcendental, and they'll make a revolution. On the other side, I suppose you have people who are only interested in order, and obviously they don't insist on the revolution. But the middle classes, hopefully, can combine these two poles... [*Pause.*] And the middle classes, via certain processes, would perhaps achieve... [*Quietly*: that doesn't appear in Schiller] but they would somehow achieve this harmony, which then has a political purpose. It's very interesting to note... [*Door slams in the distance*] that Le Corbusier a hundred years later would do the same thing... [*Quotes Le Corbusier from memory*] "Hmm, my architecture," he said, "is to replace the revolution..." [*Quietly*: he frames it more poetically... (*Mumbles indistinctly*).] Because his idea was that, if you could create the right kind of space, the space would do the mediation and revolution would not be necessary... [*Quietly*: and he says that in Vers une architecture, or Toward a New Architecture is the name of the book.][12]

[*Long pause.*]

So, this is a... [*Pause.*] This is really a pipedream which recurs throughout the history of the modern aesthetics: this relationship between art and revolution. I mean, if you take somebody like Malevich, hmm... [*Hesitates.*] Or even the surrealists, I mean — these are people who thought that they had a little bit of a superiority over the plain old Leninist revolutionary parties, because they were gonna add to political radicalism culture and cultural transformation, and somehow that's something that the standard communist parties didn't have, because they were too busy doing all the other things, and that therefore these crazy... [*Zipper zipping up*] artistic revolutionaries like Malevich wanted really to be the center of all political activity — they wanted to be this... [*Slams his palm on the desk*] transformatory kind of medium. And the surrealists did it in the same way. Now, of course, if you are dealing with a finished revolution, then this could look probably a little bit more plausible because... [*Cough in the audience*] all the violence has already happened, so you don't need to conquer the state — you have the state, but you still need... [*Quietly*: what I said earlier will later on be called in China the "cultural revolution."] You need to transform all these peasants, all of these subjects of an old repressive political order into the new subjects of a new kind of revolutionary situation. Mm-hmm. I think that aesthetics in the older period... [*Quietly*: obviously those matters didn't arise since in older forms of history you don't really have a revolution as such, but only gradual transformations in the social system.] But there I think probably aesthetics has something to do with sublimation, that is to say with the management of unruly bodily forces and drives. Well, those are not exactly absolutely different from each other, right, except that one would play itself out in terms of the law, of religion, and the other will play itself out in terms of... [*Words indistinct.*]

[*Long pause.*]

Mm-hmm. So, Schiller's relationship to this relation between art and revolution... [*Pause.*] I'll just read you a little section, a very [*Stressing*] famous section from his "On Naïve and Sentimental Poetry," and you will find the beginnings of this also in Rousseau, but I mean this passage really gives you an idea about the political and aesthetic content of nature and natural beauty during this period. [*Translates directly from German*]:

> This shows that this kind of pleasure in nature is not aesthetic but rather an ethical one, hmm... [*Hesitates*] for it is mediated by an idea, not immediately through observation or through personal intuition or through immediate personal contact. So, it is, hmm... [*Pause. Mumbles in German.*] So, it is not first and foremost directed to the beauty of forms. What otherwise... [*Pause.*] What would a, hmm... [*Hesitates*] a flower, a spring, a stone with moss, the song of birds, the humming of the bees and so on — why are they so striking for us? What could give them a claim on our love? Well, it's not those [*Stressing*] objects, the natural objects [*Page flipping. Very quietly to himself in German.*] Mm-hmm, it's not that natural objects that we love for themselves, it is the idea, the transcendental idea that comes through them. That's what we love. We love in them a life of... [*Cough in the audience*] emergence and creation, the calm, hmm... [*Hesitates*] hmm... [*Pause*] the calm... [*Looks for words*] the... the calm production of itself, so to speak, and beings that follow their own laws, their inner necessity that has a kind of eternal oneness with itself.

[*Long pause. Cough in the audience.*]

> They are... [*Quietly*: and this is the famous part.] They are what we were [*Pause.*] They are what we ought to become once again. We were nature like them, and our culture should take us back to nature by way of reason and freedom. They are, at one and

> the same time, the representations of our lost childhood, which remains the dearest to us, and thus they feel us with a certain sadness; and at the same time, they are representations of our highest completion in the ideal and thus they arose in us a [*Stressing*] sublime feeling.[13]

Okay. So that's one of the ways in which beauty in this period functions — by nature. [*Pause.*] Now, as this representation of a transcendental ideal, which is also in some much more general sense a political ideal, right, that is to say... [*Quietly*: we have to get back to that state somehow, and if it's not through revolution, then through aesthetic education.]

[*Long Pause.*]

Okay, so now let me, hmm... [*Quietly:* let me give you a rather different version of all of this.] This is in one of Sartre's very best books, which is his book on Genet, as it tries to deal with the natural and the unnatural, hmm... [*Hesitates*] and Genet being for Sartre the poet of the unnatural — the anti-natural. And you have to take this in the modern context in which, for example... [*Quietly*: the famous line by... (*Cough in the audience*) "I hate nature," and that's what this is. And then, in Sartre, there are stories about him and de Beauvoir vacationing in Spain or somewhere, and then some nature enthusiast says, "look, a very weird natural formation over there," to which Sartre says: "I will go as far as I can to see man-made things but no natural curiosities, I have nothing to do with those."] [*Chuckles.*] So, this is Sartre's discussion of nature in his Genet book... [*Begins reading.*] Hmm...:

> Will he at least have commerce with the great natural forces? Is not Nature precisely the region of being which man has not yet been able or never will be able to reduce to the state of tool? Since men have driven him out, it is for the inhuman solitudes to welcome him. No. Nature is a utensil too. And it is social.[14]

And so on, and he then reads from Marx's German Ideology. [*Pause.*] Hmm... "The cherry tree, like almost all fruit trees, was, as is well known, only a few centuries ago transplanted by commerce into our zone" — that's Marx — "and therefore only by the action of a definite society in a definite age provided for the evidence of Feuerbach's 'senses.'"[15] Feuerbach's materialism is a materialism of the senses and of contemplation; most Marxists say, "look, if you just contemplated, if you"... [*Quietly*: here is a famous passage in German Ideology] if everybody stops working and is contemplating for a year, a month, even a few weeks, this countryside you're looking at — the Roman Campania, for example — will completely disappear. All of, all of human history will disappear if you go back into the swamps. [*Softly.*] Only production perseveres us over time. This is Marx's critique of Feuerbach's contemplative and aesthetic materialism. Alright, so that's... [*Words indistinct.*] Well, okay, so Sartre goes on:

> That's exactly how the just man... [*Quietly*: the righteous man, the bourgeois] usually sees nature, that is, when he is a city dweller and read statistics in his newspaper. "Landscape" is viewed as "land." Land is defined by its resources; its configuration is accounted for by the property system and agricultural techniques [and so on and so forth.] But several times a year the urban communities of honest folk decide in common — taking into account the necessities of economic life — to change their attitude towards big farming areas. On a given date, town society expands, plays at disintegration; its members betake themselves to the country where, under the ironic eyes of the workers... [*Quietly*: these are the peasants] they are metamorphosed for a while into pure consumers. [*Pause.*] It is then that Nature appears...[16] [*Quietly*: nature with capital "N."]

And you must know France a little bit to know that the French will shoot out even to some piece of grass about this big at every chance, at every weekend to go... [*Chuckles.*] So, the connection of Germany to nature, and France's is quite over... [*Words indistinct*] I mean [*Quietly*: there is an absolute French passion for the countryside and la campagne and so forth.]:

> It is then that Nature appears. What is she? Nothing other than the external world when we cease to have technical relations with things. The producer and the distributor of merchandise have changed into consumers, and the consumers changed into mediators. Correlatively, reality changes into a setting; the righteous man on vacation is there, simply there in the fields, amidst the cattle; reciprocally, the fields and the cattle reveal to him only their simple being-there. That is what he calls perceiving life and matter in their absolute reality. A country road between two potato patches is enough to manifest Nature [*Chuckles*] to the city dweller. The road was laid out by engineers, the patches are tilled by peasants. But the city dweller does not see the tilling, which is a kind of work that remains foreign to him. He thinks that he is seeing vegetables in the wild state and mineral matter in a state of freedom... [*Chuckles*.] If a farmer goes across the field, he will make a vegetable of him too.[17]

[*Audience laughing*.]

There are very interesting histories of landscape. You know The Dark Side of the Landscape, this is one of the great books by John... [*Chalk strokes on the blackboard*] B-A-R-R-E-L-L.[18] If you're interested in the history of art, this book is about the English and, I believe, Dutch landscape of the eighteenth century... [*Quietly*: and what that was supposed to do or what it was supposed to conceal and so forth, so you turn the peasant into a piece of nature this way.]

[*Page flipping*.]

> Thus, Nature appears at the horizon of the seasonal or weekly variations of our society; it reflects to the just their fictive disintegration, their temporary idleness, in short their paid vacations. [*Pause*.] They wander through the undergrowth as through the damp, tender soul of the children they once were; they

> consider the poplars and plane trees planted on the roadside; they find nothing to say about them since they do nothing about them, and they are astonished at the wonderful quality of this silence. If they seek Nature on the outside, they do so, in reality, in order to touch their own depths. The quiet growth of the forest reflects to them the image of a blind and sure finality; it makes them feel that social life is a surface disturbance.[19]

... and so on and so forth. [*Softly*.] Well, that's almost a reply to Schiller here. And it could also alert us to historical differences. Mm-hmm. Lukács, in his essay on Schiller,[20] which is a very important major piece in which he sees Schiller's aesthetics as a kind of a forerunner of dialectics and of Marxism, he says, [*Impersonates Lukács*] "Look, you gotta be very careful what nature you're talking about — there is the nature of the [*Stressing*] manufacturing period, then there is the nature of the industrial period." Then, presumably, hmm... [*Hesitates*] there is another nature today, of the cybernetics period, even though I'm not sure if we have a notion of nature at all. You see, if you have genetic engineering and biotechnology and editing techniques, where is nature then? What could possibly serve as nature... [*Quietly*: can be trees... (*Words indistinct*) it's a long history.] So where would you find this form of otherness that could still be available in the industrial period, and also available in a different way in the manufacturing period?

[*Long pause*.]

This is why, says Adorno, it is worth looking at what it is that nature is supposed to be; that natural beauty is supposed to be the opposite of ugliness, because then, at that point too, we will find various kinds of ugliness. There could be, for example, the incom... [*Footsteps*] the incompletely formed, the raw, the sort of magma, or what is that called, the khôra of this material that has not yet come into creation. [*Pause*.] But it could be, hmm... [*Hesitates*] it could be the ugliness of technology and the industrial landscapes. And he is relating this here to dissonance in various ways, and to the function of musical dissonance.

[*Pause.*] So, you've got the ugly in society, and landscapes resembling the medieval relationship to all of these people who are crippled and all of these things that are grotesque, and in which apparently nature reveals itself. You have even… [*Quietly*: there is this wonderful anecdote about a soldier in Wilhelminian Berlin who is sent out by his… (*Pause*). He was sent out to the zoo for some reason by his commanding officer, and he could not believe what he saw, and when he returned he said, "animals like that don't exist," they're too grotesque, there cannot be such things.][21] And then you have that wonderful thing in Claudel about a Spaniard on his way to the new world, who was observing all the grotesque beings of the sea, whales and all of these bizarre and exotic fish, and denying that God could possibly have created such grotesque things in the Order of the Universe.][22] [*Enthusiastic.*] And that would be one notion of nature, and of ugliness versus beauty.

[*Long pause.*]

Then, later on, as I said, with industry, you get a rather different nature and presumably a different use of dissonance as well, not wrong notes maybe, or noise, but a more productive principle of musical dissonance. Where does this come from? [*Pause.*] What's the difference between these two periods, hmm… [*Hesitates*] the "manufacturing" and the "industrial" periods… [*Quietly*: I tend to keep nature separated into periods and I think that Adorno doesn't always respect that.] Well, you could say, I think that… [*Creaking floor*] industry represents the moment in which human beings overtake nature and begin repressing it. Manufacture… [*Pause.*] Mm-hmm. In the manufacturing period, the human beings don't yet have too much power over nature. Obviously, the further you get back in time, then nature becomes the truly sublime, and that is the form of overwhelming power in a primitive society, in a tribal society… [*Quietly*: there is almost no control over the thunderstorms and all of those other forces] but with industry you arrive at the moment when the story of the repression of nature begins; the harnessing of nature, which [*Stressing*] humanizes nature and at the same time exploits it. So, here we get to two sides of production, right: we get production by the turning of everything natural into the human, and a praxis philosopher like Sartre always in some ways celebrates this moment, but for the Frankfurt School, and I think for the ecological movements that follow, that power of production is somehow abhorred by the kind of repression that it must entail. [*Page flipping.*] So here we have, right away on page 46:

> The impression of the ugliness of technology and industrial landscapes cannot be adequately explained in formal terms [...] The impression of ugliness stems from the principle of violence and destruction. [...] Violence towards nature is not reflected through artistic portrayal, but it is immediately apparent. It could be transformed only by a reorientation of technical forces of production that would direct these forces not only according to desired ends but equally according to the nature that is to be technically formed. After the abolition of scarcity, the liberation of the forces of production could extend into other dimensions than exclusively that of the quantitative growth of production.[23]

And you find this dilemma also in Marcuse. There is an ambivalence here. [*Pause.*] We have, Marcuse who says that the productive power to transform nature has some positive impact, but on the other hand, we must also observe the ways in which all of this production is based on the destruction of nature, on its instrumentalization and subordination to the needs of capitalist production.[24]

[*Long pause.*]

Now, this is one of the main [*Stressing*] features of the Frankfurt School. I've tried to show that there is certainly a characteristic synthesis of these notions in the Frankfurt School. There is, hmm... [*Hesitates*] there is a style in which all of these themes come together. But these themes are relatively overdetermined, and the notion of domination is at certain points very important here. And that's a philosophy of power, really, if you like a more Nietzschean philosophy than it is a Marxian one... [*Quietly*: because in Marx, it is production that comes first, and the economic determines power, but not the other way around.] Whereas in the philosophy of Nietzsche or Foucault, power comes first, and production is only... [*Mumbles indistinctly*.] So here we have a more power-oriented feature of the Frankfurt School. [*Page flipping*.] "This bourgeois indignation" about the ugliness in the industrial landscape is itself "part of the ideology of domination. Ugliness would vanish if the relation of man to nature renounced its repressive character, which perpetuates — rather than being perpetuated by — the repression of man."[25] [*Pause*.] So, power relations of human beings are double reinforced, even produced by the power of the exploitation and domination of people over nature... [*Quietly*: and out of this then comes all kind of all possible political movements, I mean, animal rights for one... (*Cough in the audience*) there is a relationship to feminism, where women are imagined as a nature that's repressed and so on and so forth.] I mean, this can take all kinds of different forms, either in Frankfurt School... [*Quietly*: I think you get a better individual sampling of this in Adorno's Minima Moralia, which deals with all of this in much more existential terms, but it's there in some permanent way.] Or you can follow this theme in some of their followers. There is a book by William Leiss that a lot of people used in the old days, with stories about the domination of nature and environment.[26] Well, you can certainly see the Frankfurt School and Adorno as steering centrally towards... [*Short, sharp noises*] whereas other people would say, "no, nature is not identical, and so forth," and other people like myself will read this in a more Marxist and political way, but these are all here somehow.

[*Long pause*.]

So, the ugly can be the sign of repression, whether it's natural repression, physical repression, psychic repression, social repression, or whatever. [*Pause*.] Mm-hmm. Or it could also be the sign of the archaic and this is a more curious way of looking at things. Remember, I said the other day that myth had a very specific meaning for Adorno, that it is this ur-Jungian kind of thing — this shapeless, formless sort of element, which reason tries to tame. Now, of course, reason then tries to dominate this and the dialectic of enlightenment is sort of the ironic price reason has to pay... [*Quietly*: because it ends up dominating itself, and reason produces its own irrationality and so forth.] But underneath all this, there is still the archaic, and the archaic... [*Page flipping*.] "The concept of the ugly," see the same page, 47...:

> The concept of the ugly may well have originated in the separation of art from its archaic phase: It marks the permanent return of the archaic, intertwined with the dialectic of enlightenment in which art participates. Archaic ugliness, the cannibalistically threatening cult masks and grimaces, was the substantive imitation of fear, which it disseminated around itself in expiation. As mythical fear diminishes with the awakening of subjectivity, the traits of this fear fell subject to the taboo whose organon they were; they first became ugly vis-à-vis the idea of reconciliation, which comes into the world with the subject and his nascent freedom. But the old images of terror persist in history, which has yet to redeem the promise of freedom, and in which the subject — as the agent of unfreedom — perpetuates the mythical spell, against which he rebels and to which he is subordinate. Nietzsche's dictum that all good things were once dreadful things may well have had their origins in the experience of art.[27]

And he'll go on later in this chapter to show that beauty — hmm... [*Hesitates*] what we normally call "beauty" in art — has this secret dimension, which is that of terror and death. [*Pause.*] You have, I suppose, the passage here that he has in mind, is the moment, probably the archaic, or human if you like, and it's the moment in ancient Greece... [*Quietly*: I guess, in the sixth century, when the first smile appears on a Greek statue, and from our world, this is the sign of the emergence of the human, in the smile.[28]] [*Pause.*] In archaic statuary, and in art before that, you don't have a smile — you have the fearfulness of the mask, which is caused the lack of any discernible expression, making it difficult to read the wearer's feelings or intentions. For Adorno, what he insists on is not so much the smile, but... [*Quietly*: I think this is a misnomer because all these statures were painted] but his way of explaining it — and he uses these figures all the time — is the blankness of the eyes, the "empty eyes" in the Greek statues. [*Pause*.] Now, as I say, all of these sculptures were thought to have been painted, so the eyes might have been painted too, but the way we have them, they're blind... [*Pause*] and this blindness of the eyes is Adorno's conviction in the fearfulness that's present in beauty. For him, this is the archaic remanence that is still there in the work, which is supposed to repress them. And this is a kind of a Hegelian thing, I mean, in order to repress something, it has be there; if it isn't there, you don't have to repress it and you just forget it. So, for beauty to have its tension as a reconciliation... [*Chair scratches the floor*] with the world and as suppression of this terror... [*Quietly*: the terror has to be there in order to be managed and controlled.] And so, the tension in there is that you can still sense its presence, and that's the terror of the archaic and of the repression into one of those things, in the blankness of the eye and the archaic smile.

[*Long pause*.]

Mm-hmm. Now, hmm... [*Long silence. Paper shuffling*.] I wanted to read you also... [*Pause*.] How many people... [*Quietly*: we did this in some other course maybe.] How many people know anything about Peter Weiss's great novel, The Aesthetics of Resistance...? [*Quietly:* Just one, okay.] I wanted to show you because I think it has some relation to what Adorno is trying to say here... [*Mumbles indistinctly*.] This is the dramatist Peter Weiss, about whom we don't know very much, about his novels over here. This is a huge novel, and it is very central to the Germany of the 1970s and 1980s, the impoverished class; he wrote it right before he died. Mm-hmm... [*Hesitates*.] It is a novel about aesthetic education; it's also about the [*Stressing*] resistance during the Nazi period. It begins in Berlin in 1936, and it's about workers who are about to either go into the underground, or flee Germany and join the Spanish Civil War, then there is flight after the fall of Spain to Sweden... [*Quietly*: Peter Weiss grew up in Sweden, and Brecht was also in Sweden, so there is a long section about Brecht.] And then, in the final section, the return to Germany and the execution of these resistance fighters in the last year of the war... [*Quietly*: there is a historical reference here, maybe you've heard about the White Roses, a small resistance movement consisting of students and professors in Munich, a non-violent group, they distributed leaflets calling for peace... (*Mumbles indistinctly*).] But this novel is also an aesthetics of education, like Schiller's, and he constructs themes on the relationship between art and politics, on oppression and resistance, and collective... [*Pause*.] There is a famous episode there, which is a kind of an illustration of Benjamin's proposition that all of the monuments of culture and civilization from the past are also monuments to barbarism, because they all come out of class society and out of violence. And therefore, what is going to be with all those monuments of the past [*Pause*.] Well, from one point of view... [*Quietly*: and this is not exactly the point of the Taliban, but let's say of the anti-Confucius red guards in the Chinese Cultural Revolution, that they wanted to destroy all of that past.] There are also a certain kind of iconoclastic moments in other revolutions, in the English Civil War, or in the French Revolution when the mob knocked off the tombs and the heads of the kings and the statues of the saints for all of that was associated with tyranny. You destroy the works of the past because you couldn't work through them somehow... [*Pause*.] How can you deal with this inheritance of blood, which we call "culture"? Well, that's the question that this whole novel, The Aesthetic of Resistance, seems to me to want to answer, and next time, if I can find it, I will give you the first few pages, which are about the visit of these kids... [*Quietly*: on their ways to form a resistance] to the great Island Museum in Berlin to see the Pergamon Altar, which shows the battle of the Olympian gods and the Giants. The massive Altar, which is all in fragments, and it is basically a partial reconstruction in the museum of these frieze fragments, shows the Gigantomachy, the mythical battle for the supremacy of the cosmos... [*Cough in the audience.*] But it is also a monument of repression, and these first pages of The Aesthetics of Resistance try to show you what you do in order to derive from the study of the Altar a [*Stressing*] productive cultural value... [*Quietly*: instead of simply being mesmerized by the sense of sheer power.] Mm-hmm. Adorno obviously didn't know Weiss's work yet... [*Quietly*: but Peter Weiss knew Adorno, so there is another sort of connection there.]

[*Long pause.*]

Okay, let me see now... [*Talks to himself.*] Now, therefore, we have to say, and this is, as I said, essential in this chapter, that he says on page 50: "...it is beauty that originated in the ugly, and not the reverse."[29] [*Pause.*] Beauty is conquered from ugliness, and reconciliation, in a sense, is conquered from repression... [*Page flipping.*]:

> The definition of aesthetics as the theory of the beautiful is so [*Stressing*] unfruitful because the formal character of the concept of beauty is inadequate to the full content [Inhalt] of the aesthetic. If aesthetics were nothing but a systematic catalogue of whatever is called beautiful, it would give no idea... [*Cough. Cough.* Excuse me] of the life that transpires in the concept of beauty. In terms of the intention of aesthetic reflection, the concept of beauty is but one element.[30]

... and so on and so forth. Now...:

> With all the ambivalence of triumph, what subjugates expression — the formal character of beauty — is transformed into expression, in which what is menacing in the dominating of nature is wed with a longing for the vanquished, a longing stirred by domination. But it is the expression of suffering under subjugation and subjugation's

> vanishing point, death. The affinity of all beauty with death has its nexus in the idea of pure form that art imposes on the diversity of living...[31]

I am not sure if you can see what kind of argument this is. [*Pause.*] This is somehow, hmm... [*Hesitates.*] The very idea of art that's inherent in this historical notion of beauty, which can't really be ours anymore as such, it comes out of a situation of tension where it cannot but be somehow tainted by the suffering and the violence that's inherent in it. But in modern times... [*Reads from* Aesthetic Theory.] "Because totality ultimately engorges tension and makes itself fit for ideology, homeostasis itself is annulled."[32] [*Pause.*] It becomes harder and harder — with the way of, let's say, humanization, the domination of nature, power, bureaucracy, and everything else — it becomes increasingly difficult to achieve this momentary, let's say, foothold and victory over repression, which beauty used to do. And therefore, Adorno says, there is a crisis of beauty.

[*Long pause.*]

And today, beauty, [*Whispering*] in some ways, has to come through ugliness. So, dissonance has to be the mark of suffering and come up in some negative sense as happiness. [*Pause.*] Ugliness has to be the mark of repression and violence and yet to mean beauty. Because beauty by itself, happiness by itself, in the old sense, are what these people contemptuously called [*Stressing*] affirmative... [*Quietly*: that is to say, they are ideological, humanistic, sentimental, kitsch, and so on and so forth] and this is due to this overwhelming and overpowering development of the powers of production and repression over the individual human being. [*Pause.*] So that can't be held in balance in this aesthetic homeostasis, which was beauty in the older period. Now, as he says himself, this is history that remains to be written, hmm... [*Page flipping*] page 56: "Following an internal logic whose stages will need to be described by an aesthetic historiography that does not yet exist..." We haven't looked at the history of aesthetics from this standpoint at all, and Adorno is not proposing anything like that here, but I think I introduced… [*Quietly*: because it comes in and out here] this other moment of the fin-de-siècle, of symbolisme, Jugendstil, and so forth. That is the moment, I think at one point of, let's say, monopoly capitalism stage, in the late nineteenth century, and this is the moment in which beauty really is used against the status quo… [*Quietly*: against the industrial ugliness and the machine.] Mm-hmm. The fin-de-siècle, the decadence, as it is sometimes called, is the moment in which the aesthetic — whether it's in Wilde, Ruskin, William Morris, or whatever — is used as a critique of this industrial business society. But this is a very unstable moment because, precisely, it tries to be substantive, it tries… [*Quietly*: as in Morris or Ruskin] to sort of build up a dream image of the perfect beautiful society in which we should be really living in; and this turns into a fantasy and then it is swept… [*Zipper zipping up*] away by the second moment of modernism. So, you have that moment of very early beauty-of-nature moment in modernism, and this in symbolism or fin-de-siècle, and then you have the machine-like moment of modernism, the ugly moment, which is the true modernism, and that's from futurism on. That might be part of this kind of history. If you wanna go through further, I think it's always very interesting in film, for example, you've got in Godard all kinds of images of beauty all the time; then you've got in other people who use classical music in this way… [*Quietly*: I'm thinking of, hmm… (*Tries to remember*) of Kubrick, for example.] These are not only ironic references, I think, but it is as though, in the history of film, there is also some seeming balance in which an impression of beauty can be used in a [*Stressing*] critical way… [*Quietly*: but maybe that doesn't last.] Certainly, if it's nothing but beautiful travelogues, it's a rather different kind of image… [*Quietly*: I think the great image of this is, anybody seen that science-fiction picture… (*Words indistinct*).] Mm-hmm, they have a euthanasia institute, and your final minutes are spent looking at this National Geographic, images of an Earth that doesn't exist anymore… [*Quietly*: I can't recall what that picture is called.][33] Well, that's an interesting intervention in the whole discussion about beauty.

[*Long pause.*]

Okay, I think we'll try to finish this chapter... [*Footsteps. Audience noise*] a little more adequately next time, then we'll go on to the next part. But keep walking away through this... [*Chairs scratching the floor. Footsteps. Zippers zipping up.*]

Audience stands up. Objects drop on the floor. Door creaks open. Students return chairs to other classrooms. Some form a line to discuss their assignments with Jameson. General noise. Screeching microphone noise.

[*Microphone turns off.*]

CURTAIN

LECTURE NINE

FEBRUARY 20, 2003

NATURAL BEAUTY (CHAPTERS) — THEMATIZATION — AESTHETICS AND POLITICS — MIMESIS/ EXPRESSION/CONSTRUCTION

CURTAIN RISES

Moving chairs, squeaking door, coughs, other sounds filling the noise environment of a large classroom in the Literature Department at Duke University. A few students are exchanging jokes about the "end of nature." The exchange started when a newly arrived graduate student complained about her cat Benjamin, who is exhibiting fits of wild and erratic behavior. The student sarcastically explains the sudden change in her pet's conduct as one of the side effects of this seminar, or perhaps the need for neutering. The cat, she says, is repeatedly urine-marking and constantly growling, wailing, and snarling — interfering with the student's concentration and the large amount of reading required for this seminar. A few other students respond with witty comments about the suppression of nature under capitalism, one underlying theme of Adorno and Horkheimer's Dialectic of Enlightenment, *to which Jameson so often refers in this seminar. The grad students' exchange has a few nearby undergrads roaring with laughter. One foreign student with a thick Eastern European accent says that he finds vivid illustration of this theme of the subjugation of nature when he visits the garden section at the local Walmart, Kroger, or Lowe's. Students continue joking about "subjugated" flowers, trees, and shrubs.*

Jameson enters the classroom carrying a few books, his scattered notes and the red pen in the chest pocket of his western shirt.

[*Microphone turns on.*]

JAMESON: [*Screeching microphone.*] This is a draft... [*General noise. Microphone distortions.*] Somebody say something? Uh-huh? [*Audience noise. Footsteps. Zippers unzipping.*]

[Long pause].

Mm-hmm... [*Pause.*] This is a draft of a translation that we are trying to get together for publication here at Duke... [*Chairs scrape the floor.*] As I said, this is a book that's been translated into any number of languages... [*Hands over copies*]; it was published simultaneously in East and West Germany. It was not translated into Russian, although... [*Quietly*: as some of these Germans put it to me, "They could have used it back in the days of the Soviet Union."][1] It is very much, I could say, one of the major books in East Germany... [*Footsteps*] of the 1980s. It was a, hmm... [*Hesitates.*] It is very much about history, about the history of the Third International... [*Clears throat*] of the Comintern, which as always is very complicated and has to do with resistance, and so on and so forth. Lots of history in it. However, this opening part is more contemplative, and as I said, it takes place in the famous Pergamon Museum in Berlin. This is only the first ten pages of what must be a forty-page discussion of these statutes — hm-mmm, and these are not statues, but they are friezes... [*Pause.*] And what they've done — they were all broken into fragments and the curator put them on a blank wall in such a way that you get an idea of what the whole altar was, and you also have drawings in your... [*Creaking floor*] museum guide of what it might have looked like, but of course, only the found broken pieces are there... [*Pause.*] And obviously the Turkish government would like the Pergamon frieze back, and the Greek government would like these marble fragments back, and so forth. I'm not sure, there were negotiations with... [*Door creaks open*] the Germans after the reunification... [*Cough in the audience.*] I don't know. I don't know what happened... [*Quietly*: but I'm sure they won't give it back.] Anyway, look at this because it's a very fundamental aesthetic lesson and it belongs really right about this point.

[*Long pause.*]

Now, today I wanted to finish up with this third chapter and I wanted to point out that, hmm... [*Hesitates*] that in a way... [*Pause.*] In a way, it's obvious that Adorno has to point out that the whole end of the chapter, far from being an attack on [*Stressing*] subjectivism — which is what we've seen sort of recurring in the current ways, and we will see it over and over again here — is also an attack on [*Stressing*] objectivism, or Sachlichkeit. Mm-hmm. Because there is here some pressure, or need, for some kind of balance... [*Words indistinct.*] Therefore, we will use this word... [*Chalk strokes on the blackboard*] T-H-E-M-A-T-I-Z-A-T-I-O-N. Mm-hmm, for example. You think that Derrida is about ... [*Zipper unzipping*] and frames of reference, or it's about writing, right? Deconstruction: it's a philosophy of writing, of... [*Chalk on the blackboard*] É-C-R-I-T-U-R-E, and so on and so forth. Well, he says that's not true; it's not about anything. [*Pause.*] To assume that it's about writing is to [*Whispers*] thematize some of the formal movements of one of the books of this philosophy, maybe several, and to turn it back into content. I've already talked about this by using some other language, but this is the idea. Mm-hmm... [*Pause.*] Thematizing means taking a movement of thought, which could be a dialectical movement, or some kind of relational oppositional movement, and freezing it over, or "reifying" it — I guess this would be my view of describing this process — into a... [*Chalk on the blackboard*] T-H-E-M-E. Mm-hmm... [*Talks to himself.*] And a theme, by definition, is something static because it's a form of content. So, if we reify Adorno and we say, "oh, yeah, he's for objectivity and against subjectivity in art," then this is what we do, we thematize — because he is not for anything. If Adorno is talking about subjectivity, he wants to make sure we understand that it's objective, and it's not really subjective at all; and on the other hand, if we get carried away and start to polemicize about objectivity — that is to say, this Sachlichkeit or Neue Sachlichkeit or whatever — then that's thematization too, and it has to be also criticized. However, remember this other thing, and I will read you again this page that I believe I quoted before from this important paragraph: "The definition of aesthetics as the theory of the beautiful is so unfruitful because the formal character of the concept of beauty is inadequate to the full content [Inhalt] of the aesthetic..."[2] [*Quietly*: and you have this excellent footnote on Inhalt and Gehalt.] But this means that, what aesthetics really means is that it cannot be covered by the mere concept of beauty. [*Page flipping*.] "If aesthetics were nothing but a systematic catalogue of whatever is called beautiful..." [*Quietly*: oh, as when you say that a work of art has to be harmonious, it has to be balanced, pleasant, colorful, and so on and so forth] "it would give no idea of the life that transpires in the concept of beauty in terms of the intention of aesthetic reflection, the concept of beauty is but one element. The idea of beauty..." and then this is very important: "The idea of beauty draws attention to something essential to art without, however, articulating it directly."[3] So, thematization would be using beauty as a concept rather than as a clue or a symptom. And there is the other paragraph that I read you from a later part, on which we will of course stumble later on, where he talks about categories. He says here, the thing is that these categories used to measure beauty... [*Quietly*: expression, taste, harmony, form and whatever] they may be all wrong in themselves, and yet you have to keep using them. If you decide that an aesthetic category is bad or useless, you cannot simply get rid of it, because once you got rid of the categories, you are left with an empty space which has no content. So, it's by the clash of these aesthetic categories, which in and of themselves are false, that something is able to develop. And obviously this is very Hegelian as well. One has to proceed by error, because it is only error that gives the content of the work its structure, or what Slavoj likes to call it... [*Chuckles*] the "stupid first impression," he says. Everybody has to have their stupid first impression, otherwise you're not doing anything, you're not even connected with the work. But then you go through the stupid first impression and you start correcting that and climb up and do other things, and so on and so forth. Mm-hmm, and I think that's in a sense what is at stake here... [*Mumbles indistinctly*.]

[*Long Pause*.]

Now, we talked a little bit about violence and horror and so forth, hmm... [*Hesitates*] and the way in which this expresses the domination of nature. Mm-hmm. There is a... [*Pause*.] And also, as we're passing here, I don't want to get into it yet because we will have an exposé later on, but there is this constant struggle against Benjamin's notion of "aura." Because Adorno feels that aura too is a kind of thematized notion, and in fact, if you look at it closely, maybe it's more or less the same as beauty. There is beauty from some... [*Door creaks open*.] You know that this modern notion of beauty has evolved against industrial ugliness... [*Cough in the audience*] and aura has something to do with that too, with originality and what has remained un-industrialized, so to speak. It is connection to immediacy, to the thing in its presence, and the material... [*Zipper unzipping*.] But insofar as it is a thematized concept, it has no opposite — it's a value in and of itself — and this then is somehow misleading. And it is indeed a confusing concept, I happen to think. So, Benjamin says... [*Impersonates Benjamin*] "You know, we produce works of art that do not have aura," referring to film as opposed to paintings. Okay, but these great paintings in the museums, I mean, you're there and the painting is enormous, and you're in the presence of it. But you don't want to know that these curators have probably repainted it over and over again and that you are not looking at an original... [*Quietly*: I have a friend who is an art historian, and after my first trip to the Getty, he asked me,

"So do you like this thing?" And I replied, "Yeah, it's stunning, what a great painting, you know." "Well," he says, "they are all fakes, every new curator is repainting and restoring them..." (*Words indistinct*) and so on and so forth.] [*Audience laughing.*] But I take his point, hmm... [*Hesitates.*] I'm not sure that I believe that entirely... [*Laughter continues*] though that could be true, but these paintings are so stunningly repainted; I mean, they stand up with such freshness that you know they can't be original. I mean, layers of curators' re-painting have gone into these works... [*Pause.*] Anyway, let's forget about that, and let's just assume that we are in the presence of the real thing. Mm-hmm, and there it is and it's a one-time experience and it's only there in the Rijksmuseum that you can see and so forth, and the movies supposedly don't have that. Okay, but now... [*Pause.*] But you see, I think it's dialectical and that in the age of mechanical reproduction, that is to say, in the age of the video, when you are at that point of first seeing the artwork — and I don't care whether it's mechanically reproduced or not — that is what the moment of aura is. And it doesn't matter if it's a bad copy, that brings out the materiality of it, or if it's a redone copy or that it is a stunning new printing of, I don't know, of Vertigo or something like that. I mean [*Stressing*] that thing of seeing it for the first time on the big screen — that is aura. And your VHS video, hmm... [*Hesitates*] not video, whatever that other thing is called, it's not a CD but a...

STUDENT: DVD?

JAMESON: Right. And that's because now the movie screen has something to negate, because I believe aura is a form of negation. Anyway, we'll come back to this.

[*Long pause.*]

Now, when he comes to here on page 56, this is very interesting: "Following..." [*Pause.*] I think I have said this already [*Starts reading*]: "the principle of montage therefore became that of construction."[4] That's very interesting, hmm... [*Hesitates.*] That's a very interesting historical proposition that we need to follow out. You'll see later on that Thomas Mann also uses this idea of construction and montage, but in a rather strange way. Mann wants to say, "Look, montage is when you put elements of the real into fiction in such a way that you can't tell if it's fiction or not." For example, lots of Doctor Faustus... [*Loud screeching noise across the floor*] is really lifted from Nietzsche's life. Mm-hmm. And indeed, Thomas Mann points out that there are even pieces of Leverkühn's writings and letters, which are really by Nietzsche, from his letters and correspondence. So, he says... [*Pause.*] And, and of course, the principle there is that since Nietzsche has become Leverkühn and there can be no mentioning of Nietzsche in this novel... [*Quietly*: but I think there is one mentioning, although I am not totally sure about that and I may be wrong.][5] Because since there is no Nietzsche anymore, he is here, in the fiction. But this combination, this way in which... [*Cough in the audience*] the way in which he mixes real events with fictional ones — this is what Thomas Mann calls "montage." And I think that it is not what the artists, and people like Eisenstein, actually meant by that; it is an interesting thing in itself, but it's not quite that technique. But the idea that montage can then lead to a kind of constructivism where you abandon nature entirely, hmm... [*Hesitates*] I think that's an interesting one.

[*Long pause.*]

Now, the point is that we start out with this mythical view of history that these people, the Frankfurt School, authorized. We start out with mimesis. Mimesis is the fundamental drive. Mm-hmm... [*Pause.*] This is the strange anthropological concept that they had; and as I said, one is perplexed by this... [*Quietly*: because they bring it in very often, but it's never really explained.][6] I frankly believe that the two famous fragments of Benjamin on this matter about mimetic faculty and language, and mimesis and similarity, are unrelated and of no help at all here.[7] Although it seems quite possible that Adorno got this [*Stressing*] theme of mimesis from Benjamin. There was a famous meeting... [*Quietly*: they ran into each other in the mid-1920s.[8]] Adorno was working in Vienna, where he studied with Alban Berg, hmm... [*Hesitates*], and he was also running a music magazine, Anbruch,[9] then he came back to Germany. Frankfurt was the center of all this... [*Quietly*: in those days, the newest, most modern of the German universities... (*Cough in the audience*) the most socially oriented and so forth, and where the so-called Institute for Social Research was developed. Horkheimer was able to become, as you know... (*Quietly*) endowed by a very wealthy German Jew from Argentina... (*Mumbles indistinctly*).] Mm-hmm. This story of the Frankfurt School could have been told from many directions. One would be related to what Bertolt Brecht, and what a bunch of people called ... [*Chalk on the blackboard*] T-U-I-S. This is an acronym... [*Audience murmuring*] from the German word Intellektuelle, and you get this new word "tuis" and even a way of writing in Brecht that you could call "tuella."[10] Mm-hmm. These were his references to the mandarins and the intellectuals, and the idea was derived from a Chinese legend, which posed the same problem that the Frankfurt School also had. The legend is about a great mandarin, a very wealthy man who, on his deathbed, wished to do something good for society. And so, he summoned all of his great intellectuals, because in China the intellectuals were the bureaucracy... [*Quietly*: and you know how the Chinese exams work, which are literarily exams that test and assess you] so he summoned all of the great Mandarins around and asked them to use his fortune to study the origins of evil [*Pause*]... not understanding, says Brecht, that dass das war er selber, (it was he himself) or that "evil is the origins of evil." His wealth was the evil. So, you can see that there is a difference of opinions on the relationship of the intellectuals and the study of evil, and this is explicitly Brechtian... [*Quietly*: Brecht and the Frankfurt School, they hated each other, I think Adorno met Brecht in some musical circumstances.] But out in Hollywood, Brecht didn't like Thomas Mann either, and the feelings in all these cases were mutual... [*Chuckles*.] Mm-hmm. But... [*To himself*: I lost my train of thought.] Where was I? Oh yeah... [*Pause*.] The history of... [*Pause*.] So, Adorno and Horkheimer ran into

Benjamin in the late 1920s and they had some memorable, for Adorno even mythical talks; they spent a few days in an idyllic suburb of Frankfurt called Königstein. Mm-hmm. Nothing was recorded from this conversation, but apparently this was a real spark that radically... [*Pause.*] I don't say it pushed Adorno's work into new directions; in his later work, you can see elements of the earlier work — but this was a real spark that released a lot of productivity. It was also very important for Horkheimer, even though... [*Quietly*: we now know that Horkheimer was responsible for one of the most traumatic events of Benjamin's life, namely refusing the authorization of his thesis... (*Mumbles indistinctly*) and Cornelius, who was Benjamin's thesis director.] The thesis was supposed to be about the Origins of the German Baroque Drama, which was published, but it was not accepted as an academic thesis, and therefore Benjamin did not get a degree, and therefore he couldn't get a university position, and therefore he broke up with his family and he had to make... [*Quietly*: a difficult kind of living, for the rest of his life, partly relying on these subsidies from the Frankfurt School.] And that was a very nasty situation. A lot of people relied on Horkheimer. The Institute was very heavily endowed, and already with the first Nazi victories in 1932, I guess — this was the first election when this insignificant party of creeps and oddballs and weirdos, hmm... [*Hesitates*] suddenly became a serious party in the Bundestag. Already at that time, Horkheimer sent the money out of the country... [*Quietly*: hmm, I think he sent the funds to Switzerland, or maybe first to Amsterdam and then to Switzerland, something like this.] So, when they all fled in 1933 and '34, they were not penniless, hmm... [*Hesitates*] and the money was then transferred over to the United States. When they arrived in the US, Horkheimer got a distinguished position at Columbia, and they all moved out to... [*Words indistinct.*] But the... [*Pause.*] But the document for the Institute's endowment was written in such a way that Horkheimer's salary had to be paid first. After that, the money could be used for other projects. So, in a way, Horkheimer was in this position of really helping out these people or, you know, and always having people around him. If you read their correspondence, the letters are very respectful... [*Quietly*: Marcuse's letters to Horkheimer are really filled with a kind of respect that Herbert, I don't think he would have... (*Words indistinct*).[11]] Well, they all depended on him. And Benjamin, it's very sad that Benjamin, hmm... [*Hesitates*] but it gave them power over him and over his publications. Benjamin had to write and rewrite whole sentences in "The Work of Art" essay, and they didn't like the Arcades project, which is... [*Cough in the audience*] expressing the conflict... [*More coughing*.]

[*Long pause*]

But anyway... [*Pause*.] Benjamin's approach to things was very important for Adorno, and I think that is very clear. As I said, this notion of "mimesis," I don't see it in any way... [*Pause*.] What you have here is a kind of... [*Quietly*: natural history of humanity] an... (*Spells*) a-n-t-h-r-o-p-ological history and not a [*Stressing*] historical or social history. Maybe when we come to the next chapter, I will say a little bit more about that, because I think this is fundamental here. So, the idea is that mimesis emerges in order to meet some basic human need. [*Pause*.] Mm-hmm. And for them, this is the notion of mimesis. There is mimesis in the animal world, and for that, I refer you to the opening chapters of Doctor Faustus... [*Quietly*: the butterfly, and all these windblown petals that imitate each other, it's a whole marvelous natural catalog of m-m-ma... (*Stammers*) of the mimesis in nature.][12] The chameleon is just one banal version of this. The person they mostly draw on, in case any of you is interested, is Roger... [*Chalk strokes on the blackboard*] C-A-I-L-L-O-I-S — a French, sort of transplanted Argentinian, an idiosyncratic author who was instrumental to introducing Borges and others to the French... [*Mumbles indistinctly*.] Roger Caillois wrote some interesting essays about mimicry,[13] and there are several books on natural imitation that they found very interesting, but he did not anthropomorphize or anthropologize this theory of nature. So, this process is a process of imitating nature and getting power over nature by imitation. It goes back to the "golden bough" by Frazer.[14] The Golden Bough poses two relationships to, hmm… [*Hesitates*] to objects, and it does so by distinguishing two kinds of magic, one should say: there is… [*Pause.*] Well, these are really, hmm… [*Hesitates.*] Jakobson would say that these two forms of magic are really "metonymy" and "metaphor." There is metonymic magic… [*Quietly*: I don't remember now what Frazer calls it, "sympathetic magic" or something, and the other kind is something-something else.] Anybody knows anything about this? How does Frazer call the second kind of magic… [*Raps his knuckles on the desk.*] What is the expression… [*Quietly*: hmm, but to The Golden Bough it means this great, great… (*Mumbles indistinctly*).][15] Let's call it metonymic magic, that's when… [*Pause*] you get an object from a person, someone's lock of hair, for example, and use it in spelling rituals in order to influence or gain control over them, or when you, you stick a pin in a doll of the enemy to get his death and that's the… [*Pause*] that's… [*Audience laughing.*] The other form of magic would be metaphoric — that is mimetic. And that's when you paint the bison on the wall of the cave in order to get some power over it, so that the hunters could hit and kill the bison. And the opposite, I guess the metonymic one, would be taking a piece of the bison's hide and doing something to that, so there are these two paths. Well. So, mimesis is this second path of imitation and, for them, in the Dialectic of Enlightenment, magic is a form of rationality and of Enlightenment, because it aims to control the world; and in some cases, maybe it does — the hunters imitate the bison, they try to think like the bison, and so on and so forth. But that means that there are some elements of knowledge involved in these practices and that it helps train some skills and so on. In another, in a later stage, that would be canceled by a new level of rationality for which the older level of rationality would have become superstition. So, alchemy is the exploration of the elements, but once you get the chemistry, it's no longer proto-scientific, it's pre-scientific. That's what the dialectic of enlightenment is: this constant cancelation of the… [*Pause*] of the previous stage of rationality. And mimesis, which manifested in what today we call "art," plays an important part in the early stages of human reason.[16]

Auguste Comte...

[*Long pause.*]

Auguste Comte — the father of positivism. [*Pause.*] Well, positivism, the belief in the empirical, scientific observation and quantification of knowledge. Yeah, but it itself becomes a religion.... [*Quietly*: Comte turned his mistress into a kind of Virgin Mary of this strange new religion.] And he is still all over South America, the Brazilian flag is this positivist slogan, "Ordem e..." what is it...? "Ordem e Progresso." This is Auguste Comte, right? Mm-hmm. And you find little backwaters of positivism also in France; you find people from older generations that study Comte. So, so, hmm... [*Hesitates*] Comte was very progressive in certain moments... [*Quietly*: let's get rid of metaphysics and religion, and let's only have science] but in a later generation, suddenly Comte himself becomes completely superstitious, religious, and metaphysical. What Adorno and Horkheimer say in Dialectic of Enlightenment is that modern science, which started as this new and different way of acquiring knowledge by negating older so-called "magical" or "superstitious" forms, turns into a new myth of the modern age through a sort of reversal that is, in essence, mimetic. And, of course, as you remember the final... [*Finger snapping*] stop on this train is that what Adorno calls "positivism," and that is the complete elimination of the subjective, of the negative and critical, and so on, this sort of new, hmm... [*Hesitates*] how would you say it... [*Reluctantly*] this spell cast by the logic of affirmation of what-is. Only what negates [*Stressing*] what-is is true, says Adorno. Now, remember also though that he can't say that too often... [*Door creaks open*] because that would be a thematic statement, right? And thematization, as we said earlier, offers a reified picture of existence that doesn't negate but supports what-is. But I mean, this is also the dialectic of culture, for what negates what-is also [*Stressing*] is, in some sense. A cultural critique of something is also an existent part of a body of knowledge or system with its own privileges and benefits that it tries to preserve. It is another kind of affirmation. So, these are, if not lapses, then moments of enthusiasm for the negative in Adorno, which we can't altogether endorse, and which is not even in the spirit of Adorno to endorse fully. And the same with the pessimism, I think we have to... [*Door slams shut*] we have to allow for other possibilities and that's historical. Remember Schoenberg's remark about harmony... [*Quietly*: maybe we will do it again sometime in the future, but right now harmony is not on our agenda.] And the same goes on with suffering, happiness, the positive — they are not right now on the agenda. Oh, but that has to be taken strongly... [*Mumbles indistinctly.*]

[*Long pause.*]

Okay, hmm... [*Pause.*] So, this notion of mimesis in itself, I would think, would split into two possibilities. One would be that of construction, and one of expression. [*Pause.*] So, mimesis. When you're trying to control nature... [*Quietly*: this fearful and forbidding thing] you start representing it, or you start making masks, and I don't know if you can understand how terrifying these masks are in... [*Stammering*] in.... in the so-called primitive cultures. These masks are really sources of fear... [*Quietly*: you can read, there are some nice accounts of these, hmm... (*Hesitates*) in Amos Tutuola, the Nigerian storyteller, and other people who write historical novels about Africa.] And this is also true in the American experience. The people in the great... [*Taps on the desk with his finger*] in the great rituals, when they put these masks on, they are not people anymore — they have been visited by the gods, and you are terrified. And everyone runs in fear, because they seem so real, and they are very frightening. If you ever seen, for example, the Thunderbird on the West Coast, in Northwest Coast Indian rituals, hmm... [*Hesitates*] in the totems, and so on — this is a terrifying animal. Okay, so what does it do now? From one hand, these masks or sacred object imitate the power of nature, but from another they also [*Whispering*] <u>express</u> our fear and our emotion and terror in front of nature. We're seeing here a split between expression — the expression of terror — and construction, in the mimetic rendering of nature... [*Quietly*: or, as is with these totems, they can have other functions related to power structures in the community.] And as these two things, expression and construction, are getting further and further apart... [*Back-chair creaks*] then they begin to oppose each other, and we have this ongoing struggle between subjectivity and objectivity. Then it certainly seems as though the way to deal with mimesis is to divide it into these other drives... [*Quietly*: expression and construction] to take it apart, and then put it back together again in some new way. And then, later on, we have what is then [*Stressing*] pure constructivism, which now deals only with pieces of the world, with colors from the world, and so on, but now those colors are not any longer attached to objects — we are refashioning the world in some new, human way, and of course, in some sense, we are dominating it. So, all of these things can come in if you follow out the paths of mimesis. Mm-hmm...

[*Long pause.*]

And then there is also the so-called "mimetic taboo," which is... [*Quietly*: in the Old Testament, the Second Commandment, "thou shalt have no other gods," you shall make no graven images.] This thought raises a very interesting cultural question: why is Islam, hmm... [*Hesitates.*] Where did this ban on images come from in Islam? [*Pause.*] Mm-hmm. And... [*Pause*] certainly you cannot completely repress the mimetic drive, and you can see mimetic representations going on in the way in which the Arabic script, for example, is used as decoration. [*Exhales deeply.*] Well, nobody really does know... [*Pause*] and it seems that it is not really something that Muhammad taught. But it seems as though they understood very early that they shouldn't adopt the dominant... [*Cough in the audience*] figurative forms of their great enemy, namely Byzantine, the Roman Empire, or the Eastern Roman Empire. Ah, and we know what those representations looked like, finally the great icons, you know... [*Qui-*

etly: which end up in Russia with Christ, hmm... (*Hesitates*) the Victorious Christ rather than the suffering Christ, and all these images that... (*Mumbles indistinctly*).] Well, Islam then attempted — according to some of these theories[17] — to completely differentiate itself culturally from this high civilization that it came in contact with. And one of the most fundamental forms of differentiation was the ban on graven images. Ah, and this is very clear, I mean: nobody can mix up Islamic art with, hmm... [*Hesitates*] with... [*Pause*] with Western art.

[*Long pause.*]

But for Adorno, the ban of graven images is deeper than that, and that is to say — it represents a [*Whispering*] fundamental impossibility of expressing. So now we are on the other side of this dialectics... [*Cough in the audience*] where expression now says: "No, these masks are stupid," "No, your novel about suffering is stupid," "No, your song about your misery is stupid," because "you can't really represent these things." We are on our way to Beckett now. And therefore, the law of art must be a ban on graven images. And for Adorno, as we'll see... [*Quietly*: when we'll see that, I don't know that... (*Mumbles indistinctly*)] the aesthetic law of Beckett's Endgame is a ban on graven images. [*Pause.*] Endgame is what you see after graven images have been banned, after figures have been banned, and when we get to this complete emptiness [*Pause.*] And if you still see something going on in Endgame, if you treat it as representations that you are trying to interpret, then you are not reading it right. So, we have again here this movement back and forth between expression and construction. Now, as I say, at the end of this is, hmm... [*Choo-choo-choo. Amtrak train whistle in the distance.*] "By means of construction, art desperately wants to escape from its nominalistic situation, to extricate itself by its own power from a sense of accidentalness and attain what is overarchingly binding or, if one will, universal." This is on page 57. Yes, but I think then... [*Choo-choo-choo. Amtrak train whistle closer*] that we can look at it in a somewhat different way, as being hmm... [*Pause.*] Mimesis is always a second guess, a reaction, a... a... a situation of weakness with respect to the outside world... [*Quietly*: hmm, you have to respond to the frightening nature and if not... (*Words indistinct*) people will make up their own stories, lines, and colors and so on.] Mm-hmm, but with construction,[18] it is as though human beings invented all those things, the pictorial elements, and so construction is an attempt to substitute its own praxis for nature, and thereby to escape from this... [*Stressing*] contingency, which is always present in our dealings with nature: to escape from accidents, powerlessness, disasters, disruptions, and so on. Mm-hmm, but it can't go much further in this. What happens is that the subject becomes alienated, bottom of the same page: "The subject in its quasi-logical universality is the functionary of this act, whereas the self-expression of the subject in the result becomes a matter of indifference."[19] Okay, this is one form of alienation. Subjectivity has now been split into private emotions and this supreme act of construction. But you notice the word that he uses, and I assume the German is very explicit too: "functionary," which means bureaucrat. The subject has simply to become [*Stressing*] an administrator of this constructional process. So, we come across a path in art which looked as though, if you're gonna reinstate, hmm... [*Hesitates*] reinstate some control over the outside world, and re-make it in some new way, you must simply become a sort of engineer. [*Pause*.] And, if you think of architecture... [*Cough in the audience*] well, you see that there is a difference between the demiurge, that is Le Corbusier, and his multiple followers, who were just administrators of these various forms of modern space and techniques that he proclaimed and initiated. There is a dialectic of the subject that takes its revenge here. And this whole last part on... [*Pause*] on Sachlichkeit is a denunciation of it. "As was not infrequently the case in modern movements after World War II," this is very important, on page 59, "whenever aesthetic technology strove for the [*Stressing*] scientization of art rather than technical innovation, art was dazzled and went astray." Mm-hmm. As science itself develops tremendously during the

Second World War, and then the artists get mesmerized by these innovations, you get these forms of art and music, for example, which uses all kind of machinery, and computers and scanners and whatever, all of these, hmm... [*Raps his knuckles on the desk*] images and fractals, and mathematical algorithms, and so on. There you have some fine form of this alienated subjectivity. [*Pause.*] Mm-hmm. You see, because the work of art has to express something negative with regard to the world, and the problem with the engineer is that it has to be all positive, tangible, real: the raw material is positive, the natural laws and your techniques are also positive, and you as a functionary of a building, you are also positive. So finally, the work has to do this thing, which is on the top of the page, and which I quoted many times before: "only what does not fit into this world is true."[20] [*Pause.*] "By their very existence artworks postulate the existence of what does not exist and thereby come into conflict with the latter's [*Stressing*] actual nonexistence."[21] Mm-hmm... [*Hesitates.*] The work of art is imaginary, and the imaginary is a form of negativity... [*Quietly*: this is also Sartre's version of the imaginary, it's a way of negating the world.] And that is true. Let's say you have a painted canvas, and if you look at it like an engineer, then you look at it as something that exists in this world: you are looking at a painting and you're seeing a canvas stretched on a frame, some paint, a piece of wood, a label... [*Cough in the audience*] and so on. You are seeing an object in this world. But in order to have any sense of this as a painting, you need the imaginary... [*Quietly*: its negativity has to come forward... (*Words indistinct*). And where does this negativity come from?] Well, that's the whole question of aesthetics, and that will be the main question in some of these later chapters. Ah, what do we call that? We can't just talk about it in some ways of being art and culture as opposed to reality or whatever — I mean, it must be something in this thing in relation to which negativity is possible, distance from being, or being out of the world of [*Stressing*] what-is, or positivity, and this relation is indeed very mysterious. How, hmm... [*Hesitates.*]

How would you... [*Pause.*] Where.... [*Pause.*] Where would you invent this possibility of looking at paintings and being outside the world; you're not looking at a piece of wood, a piece of canvas, you're not in a museum, you're not in a room; you're not standing and so on — when you're looking at a painting, you are somehow somewhere else. Well, that's what the work of art does: it sends you on an imaginary journey somewhere else. So, this is the definition of the imaginary in terms of negativity — it negates what-is, it takes you away from the actuality of the present or whatever you want to call this — and without an understanding of this relation, none of these questions of aesthetics work. Alright, so much for this... [*Hesitates*] hmm, for this chapter. Now...

[*Long pause.*]

Now we come to natural beauty, and this is a very interesting, hmm... [*Hesitates*] proposition. And in fact, as he points out throughout the book... [*Quietly*: people don't talk about natural beauty very much anymore.] Natural beauty is scarcely even a topic of theory today... [*Cough in the audience*] whereas in Kant's times this was very important; it takes up, I think, over half of the third Critique, or rather half of it is basically a theory of nature. [*Pause.*] Why is nature beautiful? Why do we think that? Well, evidently, we don't think that anymore because it is not something we discuss, and it's certainly not part of modern aesthetics... [*Quietly*: like why nature is so and so beautiful, and why does it attract us, I mean, this is not the most standard understanding of our aesthetic relation to nature.] Mm-hmm. I don't know if we still, hmm... [*Hesitates.*] I believe it's kitsch when artists today tell you how much they love nature, or how beautiful it is. Isn't it so? I mean, this is... [*Words indistinct*] or... [*Pause*] or... even Joyce Kilmer, or whatever, I mean this is... [*Sighs*] this is not serious stuff.[22] Mm-hmm...

[*Long pause.*]

So where has nature gone... [*Sniffling sounds near the microphone*] and how can one talk about it without falling into the kitsch trap? Now, Adorno makes fun of this, as did Sartre in a passage I've read you the other day, about these city bourgeois admiration for nature. But Adorno has great difficulty in saying something positive without himself falling into kitsch, because anybody would... [*Quietly*: ah, I remember in some conversations of Robert Craft with Stravinsky, he was saying something about Schoenberg's First Quartet; there was a great unison passage where the quartet sort of picks up a theme and does it like Tchaikovsky; and Stravinsky says, it always made me "squirm," a word I believe he used, the English word, which is very odd... (*Words indistinct*) especially for a foreigner.][23] Mm-hmm, well... [*Pause.*] So, this means that to discuss natural beauty today is to make people squirm. I think what Adorno says here, and the German is much more explicit than this: "The gesture of stepping out into the open is shared by these theoretical sentences with the artworks of their time"[24] — that is to say, Kant's discussions of nature. Well, even the fact of evoking the sort of freshness and relief of stepping out into nature is perilously close to a notion of nature that makes us squirm; even though I think lots of people believe that, maybe not everybody, but, hmm... [*Hesitates*] lots of people still have some kind of relationship to the outside, to being in the woods, to going on a walk, and so on and so forth. But why, and how is this, hmm... [*Pause.*] How is this to be spoken of? And this next chapter is very unusual, because I think like some of the stuff you get at the end of Negative Dialectics, this is one of the few moments when Adorno, or any modern philosopher... [*Quietly*: I can't imagine Derrida telling us about his feelings about nature... (*Laughter*) and I'm sure he may have some, but it is not part of his... (*Laughter continues*).] As for Heidegger... [*Pause.*] Yeah, if you talk about Being rising up, hmm... [*Audience laughing*] and the clear end, and then also the woods and the clearing — there is a lot of nature in Heidegger, but somehow his nature is not so... [*Pause.*] He's got a language that allows him to touch that without doing it into a manner of kitsch. You could sort of do a seminar... [*Pause.*] I think it would be a very interesting course, and maybe some of you will teach it one day, a course about the changing function of nature. You would begin with Rousseau and then Wordsworth, but then Tolstoy, for whom nature is the peasantry that's… [*Car honking outside*] the relationship to this… [*Honking continues*] peasants, which is sort of very touching, and then, after all of that, probably comes Heidegger, because Heidegger, I think, is really… [*Quietly*: late Heidegger is really very much in this tradition of nature.] But it's also not just a historical matter of what it can mean for them, and what it is able to negate, which is what's of interest for us here, but also what kind of linguistic invention allows you to talk about nature in the right way, and Heidegger's linguistic invention comes as a very different type from Tolstoy's or the early ones.

[*Long pause.*]

Now, we have in Adorno all the same things that I pulled out of Schiller. "Genetically…" page 69. "Genetically," he says… [*Pause*] "aesthetic comportment may require familiarity with natural beauty in childhood and the later abandonment of its ideological aspect in order to transform it into a relation to artifacts." Well, what he's saying here is not so different from the famous passage in Schiller that I read to you the other day. There is a relationship to nature in childhood, by the very, hmm… [*Hesitates*] by the very experiences of childhood and this is a form of relationship to nature which we lost. Ah, even in surrealism you know… [*Exhales deeply.*] Mm-hmm. In surrealism, there are three ways of getting back to the unconscious, or three forms of a primordial relationship to the unconscious, which we've lost… [*Quietly*: surrealists are not so far from these nostalgic anthropologists either.] One is the dream, the second is laughter, and the third is childhood. The art of childhood, naïve and outsider art, or the recapturing of something childish through the dream, which is in effect a kind of more primitive moment of thinking, this is also present there. So, as city-oriented as the surrealists were… [*Cough in the audience*] and as sophisticated as they might be, they are also maybe another part of this tradition. But in all of these traditions — and I think Adorno is perfectly right — the experience of nature is the… [*Pause.*] Or the experience of nature has the function of [*Stressing*] negating the existing experience: the experience of adulthood, the experience of work, the experience of an alienated society, capitalism, oppression, and so on and so forth. Now, for Adorno, it's also something else. Nature is the one... [*Pause.*] And I do think this is one place where this notion of "non-identity" that people like Martin Jay want to claim as the fundamental theme of Adorno's philosophy comes from... [*Quietly*: I don't really think that, but it is the place where one has to talk about that, and indeed... (*Zipper unzipping*).] Where is it? Ah, here... [*Page flipping.*] "Natural beauty is the trace of the [*Stressing*] nonidentical in things under the spell of universal identity."[25] Universal identity is what's happened to the universal, what's happened to the world, which is now standardized, mass-produced, humanly controlled, hmm... [*Hesitates*] it is capitalism as a system of identity. And nature is the one reminder that there is something beyond the system and beyond human subjectivity. [*Softly.*] Nature, it's the reminder, it's the symptom of this existence of, let's say, nature, it's the thing-in-itself... [*Quietly*: although this is not what Kant meant by this term.] Without nature, we're sort of confined... [*Door creaks open*] to the nightmare of solipsism, and the eternal present, including conspiracy theories, because we made everything, and so we're trapped in ourselves in some way. Everything is us, whereas nature says, even if we can't even find it directly anymore, it says there is an outside to this process. The... [*Raps his knuckles.*] The argument, I think, it's a little... [*Cough in the audience*] like the argument I made, or rather the argument Adorno makes about the aesthetic in the very beginning of Aesthetic Theory: in order to feel an aesthetic work aesthetically, you have to feel it more than aesthetic, there has to be an outside to it.[26] Because if you want to apprehend the work of art directly, like, for example, Beethoven's Eroica, which is inspired by the ideas of the French Revolution and Napoleon, then you stop listening to the symphony and you go read the biography of Napoleon, or read the history of French Revolution. But that's not right. You have to feel that the Eroica... [*Quietly*: or the David painting of Bonaparte, or whatever] that they have a relationship to the whole world of political and revolutionary context. But it's not a relationship of representation. It is their outer dimension — their [*Stressing*] external dimension; they have a dimension of externality, just as the thing-in-itself in Kant is the dimension of externality of the phenomena of the things for us. We can't ever have an immediate relationship to those things because they all come to us through representation, right… [*Quietly*: I mean, you have to stop listening to that and read something else, some facts or something, ah, history books or something like that.] There is no immediate relationship to history, hmm, or, hmm, or… [*Words indistinct.*] And there is no immediate relationship to these contacts, but the work of art has to have that outside. But I think that nature plays the same role, and in all of these experiences, it's this ex… [*Stammers*] exter… externality of reality that is, that we are being reminded of, even though we can't look at it directly. Mm-hmm, I think that's really the theory.

[*Long pause.*]

Now… [*Pause.*] Mm-hmm, and there are other connections between nature and history. What is this so-called "cultural landscape," Kulturlandschaft, that he talks about… [*Quietly*: where is Kulturlandschaft, hmm… (*Leafs through the book. Talks to himself*).] Well, think of the places that you think are beautiful… [*To himself quietly*: where is that page?][27] Or let's call it "monumentality." Yeah, but how can we possibly have an immediate experience of monumentality that is not saturated with images and history, right? Hm-hmm, Britain… [*Pause.*] King Arthur and everything else, I mean, there is not a single place in the landscape of Britain, which you would think it's beautiful and it's wild, and is sort of how people would descri… [*Cough in the audience*] which is not saturated with all of these other ideas. Mm-hmm… [*Door creaks open. Footsteps*] the German forest and Geist and millions of other associations. Or Italy, hmm… [*Hesitates*] and even the desert of Sahara. There is not any of those places that is not a Kulturlandschaft, that is to say, it's not already a cultural landscape. The only true unmediated contact with the landscape would be the moon, and even the moon now is pretty well saturated with cultural associations. So, that really seals the connection between nature and history here. The experience of nature, hmm... [*Hesitates.*] Adorno is not saying that those experiences are inauthentic necessarily, but that those experiences are always not without history, and are mediated by history. So, it is very hard to separate natural beauty from these other problems that are historical and social, I think.

[*Long pause.*]

Now, mm-hmm... [*Sighs.*] Then we come, I think, to one of the main features. We've already seen in the previous chapter, I believe, that he says... [*Quietly*: and I think we'll break it here for today... (*Mumbles indistinctly as he is leafing through the book*).] Nature is speaking the language of silence, nature is speaking the language, hmm... [*Hesitates*] not the language of flowers, but the idea is that the landscape is mutely saying something to us but without language.[28] That would be the end of this chapter. But what I wanted to remind you of is, in the previous chapter, what he says about the domination of nature... [*Exhales deeply*] ugliness is the domination of nature. Therefore, natural beauty is some glimpse of non-dominated nature, that is to say, the end of domination and this is Adorno's vision of utopia. [*Firmly.*] For him, utopia... [*Door creaks open*] is the end of the instinct of self-preservation. It is the instinct of self-preservation that makes for the evil and violence in the world, because if I am to stay alive, then it doesn't matter what I do. That's the fundamental excuse, or force — the Darwinian force, if you like — for violence, evil, domination, power and all the rest of it. And therefore, utopia would be the moment in which the situation is such that you need no longer exercise this instinct of self-preservation, and the minute when you don't need to exercise that, then death doesn't matter... [*Quietly*: because you're not constantly obsessed with preserving your life.] Mm-hmm, I think this is a very interesting and beautiful notion of utopia. Well, later, he has something to do with that, bottom of page 65: "The sloughing off of the aims of self-preservation

— which is emphatic in art — is carried out to the same degree in aesthetic experience of nature. To this extent the difference between the two forms of beauty is hardly evident." And that's also an interesting idea. I'm not sure whether we wanna follow him on into this notion that it is the... [*Pause*] that the work of art is also this, hmm... [*Hesitates*] is this... [*Searches for words*] ...ah, "sloughing off of the instinct of self-preservation." But it, maybe it is. In another place, he defines music as what amounts to live without anxiety. Music is the moment when — if you can hear it right — you are outside the world of survival, of clinging to life, of anxiety, of all of those things. And I think that's connected to his notion of utopia too, hmm... [*Hesitates.*] In some sense, what we think of this is some kind of acceleration that the work of art... [*Quietly*: which doesn't have to be Dionysian, or Apollonian, or has to do with constellations, or whatever] is somehow connected to this momentary release from the principle of self-preservation.

[*Long pause.*]

[*Firmly.*] Anyway, self-preservation is another one of these basic themes in the Frankfurt School, in Adorno, and some others. Okay, so we will get back to it next time... [*Chairs scraping the floor. Zippers zipping up.*]

Audience stands up. Objects drop on the floor. Feet shuffling. Door squeaks. Students return chairs to other classrooms. Some students form a line to discuss their assignments with Jameson. General noise. Screeching microphone noise.

[Microphone turns off.]

CURTAIN

LECTURE TEN

FEBRUARY 27, 2003

ART BEAUTY (CHAPTER) — DEARTIFICATION — FIREWORKS — *APPARITION*

CURTAIN RISES

Moving chairs, squeaking door, coughs, other sounds filling the noise environment of a large classroom in the Literature Department at Duke University. Some students discuss the situation around Iraq, and the increasingly belligerent rhetoric of the Republican President George W. Bush. They try to guess the possibility of a new war. One student is arguing with two others: "C'mon! They're all in bed with the military-industrial complex and big oil, of course. All of these slogans like 'Remove Saddam' and 'Iraqi Freedom' is only a pretext to profit from war and secure new oil fields." Another student does not believe that war with Iraq will happen. "They were not involved in 9/11, and there is no proof of WMDs yet." A third student joins the conversation. He is attending the Slovenian seminar in the Union Building and is now telling the other two how Žižek said the other day [imitates an Eastern European accent]: *"I will eat my shoes if Bush dares to invade Iraq." Žižek says that today Americans like only coffee without caffeine, cream without fat, and beer without alcohol, and that Colin Powell prefers warfare without casualties (on the American side, of course). To him, the days of naked, ruthless violence and pure Otherness are gone. He had been talking about anxiety in Lacan, and how the Oth-*

er today is deprived of its Otherness, illustrating this with the situation around Iraq and insisting that George W. Bush is not going to attack Iraq. "No, Mama. There won't be war. Relax."

Jameson enters the classroom carrying a few books, his scattered notes and the red pen in the chest pocket of his flannel shirt.

[Microphone turns on.]

JAMESON: [*Chair legs scraping the floor*] ...they will show their project at two o'clock on Saturday, which will also be sort of a joint seminar with... [*Footsteps.*] Mm-hmm. Are there other announcements, questions, comments... [*Thud. Heavy object falls on the floor.*]

[*Long silence.*]

Alright, let's try and make a little more progress here, but also... [*Chair leg scraping the floor.*] This will sort of prepare us for... [*Door creaks open*] and we will also have a few exposés in our next sessions. Remember that our idea was that, after this, hmm... [*Hesitates*] we would go on to Doctor Faustus, and this will happen after the... [*Pause*] after the break.

[*Long pause.*]

And, hmm... [*After reflection.*] I think you will find this novel very interesting; it is a very engaging text, and I will give you a few extra readings before the break. Some of the compositions that are involved... [*Footsteps.*] Mm-hmm, some of the texts that are involved... [*Loud cough in the audience*] and maybe I was also hoping... [*Addresses a student.*] If you could have your presentation on music before the break too, so we could get a sense of what is at stake here? Mm-hmm... [*Pause.*] I will also indicate a few things. That's to say, I will show you some connections here, if we could get to the sixth chapter, and then we'll go back to this. I think we'll do some Beckett after Thomas Mann because, in a way, for Adorno, that has to do with... [*Chair scraping the floor*] contradictions in art and so on.

[*Long pause.*]

Alright, I think that the... [*Looks around.*] Mm-hmm. Are there questions from the last few days? [*Softly.*] Because it seems to me that I have been talking too much and we didn't have too many discussions... [*Door creaks open.*] You still find Aesthetic Theory interesting? You find it difficult, or tiresome, or boring? Well, if you don't have any questions about it, then it's all obvious and clear. I asked you to write down some of the questions you may have with Adorno's aesthetics. Which is... [*Pause.*] Did any of you write down any questions? You can send them to me by email or print them and leave them in my office... [*Quietly*: if you are too embarrassed to bring them up here.]

[*Long pause.*]

I do think that we should think about Aesthetic Theory as finished. Because there are many of these ideas circulating around that it's an incomplete work, but I don't think that Adorno would have changed a lot if he had the time... [*Pause.*] He might have moved a few parts from one place to another, but I think that essentially the book is finished... [*Quietly*: unless he had another ten years, but again I don't think he would have produced anything more substantial than what we have here... (*Mumbles indistinctly*).] You have the notes at the end of the book, and also some earlier drafts, and the editors' introduction or afterword, and other historical texts, which gives you an idea about the various stages of Aesthetic Theory.

[*Long pause.*]

Well, I think that this book shows, in a way, his mode of thinking, which unfolds in these short fragments. His mind is the kind of machine that, once you push the topic of that particular fragment or paragraph, then all of the associated contradictions and antinomies come into presence and engage with each other. And we find out that something is quite impossible and also doable, or that the truth doesn't always lie between both... [*Cough in the audience*] sides of these engaged oppositions. And yet this is, for him, the only way to go. I suppose that that is both a stylistic idea and a, hmm... [*Hesitates*] and an intellectual one. This is the case I think where Adorno's style and his... [*Quietly*: I'd like to call it "method" but... (*Words indistinct*) and that is to say, the way he thinks about things] is the same as the way he writes these sentences. So, if you find the right sentence to sum everything up, then you really get the whole treatment of these thoughts. And his thinking [*Stressing*] necessarily has some self-canceling categories, which keep going on, in order for what he wants to say to survive. You can illustrate this with the way he talks about these key aesthetic categories, as if he is saying... [*Impersonates Adorno*] "Oh well, you can't think of the work of art only in terms of construction, and you have to think about it also as expression..." [*Cough in the audience.*] Well, that doesn't mean that you just get rid of those categories and try to think of other ones, but it means that you have to use both of them, expression [*Whispers*] and construction, as insufficient as they are. So, the categories survive... [*Chair-back creaks*] but what's underscored by the movement of these categories is their radical insufficiency. Mm-hmm. And so, where the movement seems to aim towards the elimination of these categories, in fact they have to be preserved in order for the idea to have some content. And this is exactly what he says about the work of art. The good work of art can too successfully overcome all of these oppositions — because if it doesn't, it is just mush. It has to keep the traces of these categories; it has to keep what he calls their articulation and... [*Mumbles indistinctly.*]

[*Long pause.*]

Okay, now. Mm-hmm, regarding nature. I hope you can see that these shadowy things called "nature" are things that we can't apprehend directly. I guess this is somewhere in between Kant's thing-in-itself, and the noumenon, and something that has to do with the distant past. [*Door slam in the distance.*] Adorno seems to be very, hmm ... [*Hesitates*] ambivalent about this notion of the past. That is, certainly we don't expect a kind of full-blown celebration of the past in the way that we get in Schiller, for whom... [*Quietly*: as we discussed in one of our past lectures] childhood is related to nature and they are somewhat the same, and that only in some distance past we understood what nature really was, and so forth... [*Chair scraping the floor.*] On the other hand, I read you a sentence the other day where he says, [*Impersonates Adorno*] "Look, maybe there is some connection between a child's experience of nature and the relationship to art." So, nature is somehow there, but it is also inaccessible — but not as inaccessible as the thing-in-itself. Because the contradiction in Kant is that, if it's a thing-in-itself, then how can we even talk about it... [*Quietly*: and this was Hegel's objection. If you can name it, form an idea of it, say that you can't get to it because you are constantly perceiving it through human categories, well, then this means that we do have some access to it. Right?] [*Pause.*] Mm-hmm. And that would be, I think, a little closer to Adorno's position, for whom nature is not an enemy, nature is otherness, but it's... [*Cough in the audience*] not otherness in any of the interpersonal sense. That is, it isn't like in Hegel's master and slave dialectic, it isn't the otherness of the Other, in the sense of other people. It's not master and slave, it's not Sartre, hmm... [*Hesitates*] it's not Lacan, and it's not Levinas either. [*Pause.*] This otherness is the otherness of the world of Being, so... [*Quietly*: it might be even closer to Heidegger, except that you never have these ecstatic moments in Adorno where Being somehow appears.] And besides, Adorno would really hate it if you compared him to Heidegger; although people have done that, and I think it's quite silly, because if you take the critique of technology in Heidegger and say, "Well, isn't that a little bit like the critique of 'instrumental reason' in the Frankfurt School?" Well, and the point is that, if it is the same, then both of them are uninteresting, right? If you reduce them to that point of what these critiques have in common, hmm... [*Hesitates*] then Time magazine can also do it. [*Chuckles.*] So, I think it's better to expect that Adorno's loathing for Heidegger... [*Quietly*: and I suppose of Heidegger's position for a bunch of them would be similar, but it doesn't involve his relationship to Marxism... (*Mumbles indistinctly*) and so on and so forth.] Ah, so... [*Pause.*] So... [*Pause.*]

[*Long pause.*]

So, this [*Stressing*] otherness of nature is the otherness of the world of Being, from which we are separated, and which we can never get at. All right... [*Clears throat*] we can't get back to it except in one form, which is abominable, namely its repression and its domination. It is through domination that we can only get to nature, but we get to it in such a way that it isn't there for us anymore, right? Why? Because we destroyed it. [*Pause.*] So, those are traces of nature, but they are not a positive experience of nature. So, nature is this thing which almost seems to appear, it almost seems to mean something; it is the other side of the artwork, and the artwork gives us this big sense of the otherness of nature without really being able to do it... [*Cough in the audience*] because, after all, the work of art is made by people, and nobody has this immediacy or access to nature. And then art is there in that form of otherness.

[*Long pause.*]

But what about the [*Stressing*] other other — the social other that I mentioned in connection with the master and slave, the Sartrean look, the big Other or the Levinasian other that you must respect, and so forth? I think that's soaked up in the "social" in Adorno, and I must also add that there is a tremendous enlargement of the social to the point where everything is social in Adorno. [*Reflects.*] Mm-hmm. There may be some personal exce... [*Achoo. Sneeze in the audience*] but even those are social, they are also defined against the social. So, everything else really is... [*Quietly*: Goethe said once that nobody was ever original, that every thought you had was somewhere or is somebody else's, it was in history and so on.][1] Well, that doesn't mean that there can't be any art or originality in that sense, it simply means that we have nothing that is private; that everything we are and think and so forth is [*Softly*] historical, or social. So, I would say that the category of the social is so vast in Adorno that it really replaces any dialectic of the other person, or even of the big Other, who is the person but not there that we find in these other figures. Is this some... [*Pause.*] Is this a, hmm... [*Hesitates*] a flaw, a weakness, or is it characteristic of all of this dialectical... [*Quietly*: but the other is dialectical too] of a certain kind of Hegelian theory? The struggle with the other in Hegel is just a moment really, and then you get to the social. And in Heidegger, we don't have the other at all, except of some very tense sense of inauthenticity and conservative anti-populism, I mean the mob, inauthentic thinking, and so on and so forth. But authentic thinking in Heidegger is this... [*Quietly:* heroism, being-towards-death, the soldier, anxiety, and so forth.] So, in Heidegger, I think this plays a part in the turn towards the pre-Socratics... [*Chair leg scraping the floor.*] This is obviously in Deleuze too. I would say, you don't have a dialectics of otherness in Deleuze in particular... [*Pause.*] I mean, there are great movements of things but, hmm... [*Hesitates*] the focus of these people — at least in Heidegger, Deleuze it seems to me — it's the return of the pre-Socratics, which means a return to the [*Stressing*] forces of the Universe, and the belief in the cogito, which was the source of this reflection on the self, the other and so on and so forth. So, it's a going back to more primordial forces, which are not particularly permanent in Deleuze, but maybe they are in Heidegger, I don't know. [*Absorbed.*] Mm-hmm. I would say that, in a way, for Adorno, there is also no obsession with the cogito, that of which we call the modern, and modern philosophy. [*Pause.*] It's sort of sociological, psychological — the psychology of the authoritarian personality, and so on and so forth, but it is not really... [*Door slams shut*] it is not really this individual struggle... [*Quietly*: and I don't know whether one has this in Benjamin either, I don't think so, I don't think so.] Now, whether one wants to divide the currents of modern philosophy in Deleuze into branches, I am not sure, but I think it does matter at least for the moment to find this strange place of nature in Adorno.

[*Long pause.*]

Now, the next chapter will then return out of this whole meditation on natural beauty to art beauty...[2] [*Quietly*: and that is supposed to turn us to questions of Kunstschöne... (*Looks at his notes. Mumbles indistinctly*).] That is to say, having gone through the way in which this category of beauty that seems to be a natural one, as we've seen in chapter four and chapter three, also poses problems in a purely philosophical way. And here then we have a different kind of reflection on the work of art. And I think the first part of chapter five is quite accessible... [*Quietly*: and then we get into some really specific problems that I think we will not get today... (*Mumbles indistinctly*).] Here, hmm... [*Hesitates*] we're still... [*Pause.*] We're still facing the crisis of the situation of art — this business of what this translator calls the "deaestheticization of art,"[3] or Entkunstung, but which would however be better translated as... [*Chalk on the blackboard*] D-E-A-R-T-I-F-I-C-A-T-I-O-N. That is the moment when art is "de-artified," so to speak, as the prefix de- indicates a negation or separation. It is the moment when art ceases to be art and becomes mass culture. Mm-hmm, but once again we read it in a very peculiar way, that is to say, not only is Entkunstung part of the crisis of art... [*Quietly*: we could also imagine it as the spirit of the culture industry... (*Cough in the audience*)] as well as the future of art. It is the direction of progress in art. [*Pause.*] Page 79: "...the deaestheticization of art [Entkunstung] is not only a stage of art's liquidation but also the direction of its development." And when you think about it, it's obvious. If... [*Pause.*] If the most advanced art is the best, if the whole reason of modernism is to apply the most advanced production techniques and remain at the level of increased production and increased technique... [*Quietly*: in some economic sense] then obviously this has something to do with addressing the increasing crisis of art. And therefore, as art is more imperiled by this process of [*Stressing*] de... [*Pause*] deartification or deaestheticization, the techniques made in response to that will be more advanced than the earlier ones. Or you can put it the other way around. You can't use some of the earlier artistic techniques to solve these new problems because it is much more intense. So, you can't use the older kinds of harmony and triads, and so on, to address the specific crisis in music to which we will come to later, hmm... [*Hesitates*] because they don't work anymore. And therefore, the mode in which you address that crisis has to be far more complex... [*Quietly*: and thereby ambiguous and sophisticated... (*Words indistinct*) the rest of them.] [*Loud metal screech. Opens the window.*] But we still don't know quite what that means.

[*Long Pause.*]

But I mean some of these themes we can understand. Mm-hmm... [*Pause.*] Beckett's is then the most advanced of these responses because it involves falling mute. [*Pause.*] On page 79: "Aesthetic transcendence and disenchantment converge in the moment of falling mute." So, the specific crisis of language is solved by silence that comes [*Stressing*] after the crisis of language, not in the sense of the old silence — I mean, that was Rimbaud's silence... [*Cough in the audience*] where he writes all these books and then he stopped writing poetry. [*Pause.*] That's not the kind of silence Adorno means.[4] Or this is Lord Chandos, which is a similar kind of silence, but maybe that's a silence before we could even get around writing any works.[5] Rimbaud wrote his works and then stopped. Lord Chandos sees that new works had to be written and stops before he gets to them. In Beckett, the silence has to be constructed by the work itself, because only then does it have meaning. Obviously, the sound... [*Reflecting.*] Everything in art has a meaning from the system it is imbedded in, and this silence will only have the value of a, hmm... [*Hesitates*] of a powerful gesture if it's understood to be a response to a situation, which has been, hmm... [*Hesitates*] which has been... [*Pause*] created by the work. So, the possibility of speaking, of saying anything, not just communication but expression and all the rest of it... [*Door creaks open*] that has to be laid in place by the work in order for the silence to have this quality. Now, going back a little before that, he talks about Brecht [*Page flipping.*] "One need only compare good poems by Brecht that are styled as [*Stressing*] protocol sentences with bad poems by authors whose rebellion against being poetic recoils into the preaesthetic."[6] Mm-hmm. You all know what protocol sentences would be?

[*Long silence.*] [*Raps his knuckles on the desk.*]

STUDENT: [*Words indistinct.*]

JAMESON: You know what protocol means in a...? [*Quietly*:

I guess this has something to do with the legal language and the language of the police.] It means you set down the facts. A dream protocol... [*Quietly:* I mean, that's a little bit more literary, so maybe we will come to it later, but a "dream protocol" means that you write your dream out; you quickly write it out before you forget it.] But a "police protocol" is just... [*Door creaks open*] when you say: "at 8:55, the car ran a stop sign, and so on, and there were three people there and so forth." That's a protocol. It simulates objectivity, obviously. I mean, it seems to rely on the reality of facts, on objectivity. [*Exhales deeply*.] Now, hmm... [*Hesitates*.] Ah, Brecht's poems are very simple... [*Quietly*: I should have something to read for you here, but... (*Chair scrapes the floor*) I read you William Carlos William the other day and that would be also very simple, like: "so much depends upon a red wheelbarrow glazed with rainwater beside a few white chickens."] In any case, these are sentences seemingly without people, without speakers, without subjects, without subjectivity, they are a kind of objective protocols. I think Adorno's point about Brecht, whom he is not attacking here — as opposed to the reversion into the preaesthetic, which would be this kind of attempt to express something in the simplest, most naïve way — is that these are very sophisticated senses that are designed to respond to the crisis of the work of art by getting rid of any trace of subjectivity [*Pause*.] As symbolic gestures they are radically different from the seemingly objective sentences... [*Quietly*: like someone who doesn't even know that there is such a problem.] Mm-hmm. Once again, the work of art has to be... [*Pause*.] You have somehow to reconstruct the situation it comes from, but that's not... [*Reflecting*] you know, that doesn't mean the historical or sociological background of the artist like... [*Quietly*: when William Carlos Williams was born in such and such a year, and that he was a doctor and he had a house in New Jersey, or that kind of stuff.] It means to reconstruct the [*Stressing*] situation of art at that moment. It means the situation of, hmm... [*Hesitates*] the whole poetic language at the moment when the poet wrote this. And it must be understood here that a "situation" means crisis. Situation has to be a crisis, and this also refers to the title of the second chapter of Aesthetic Theory. And Brecht's procedural poem is then a response to a crisis, and the moment when something either objective like silence or whatever, or... [*Excited*] or, or something overly florid and overly expressive, like an Italian opera or something like that, none of these can be read as symbolic gestures capable of solving a modern crisis in art. Then suddenly, Brecht's poems take on a meaning... [*Pause*] they take on a value, let's say... [*Quietly*: and since Adorno doesn't like the term "meaning" either] they take on a value that they don't have if you just look at them as some spontaneous... [*Reflects*] as a heap of language or something that... [*Mumbles indistinctly*.] So, I think the notion of the crisis situation, and of the work of art as response to it... [*Distant cough in the audience*] or as solution to these antinomies or crisis that can't be solved, is central here. The work of art can be a success, but it is a success insofar as it recognizes the solution and recognizes the crisis. And you must understand that you have to go, hmm... [*Hesitates*] you have to deal with it in a very intense way; you have to go to an extreme to deal with this crisis... [*Quietly*: there is another place I think you've seen already] where he says, [*Impersonates Adorno*] "Look, art can only be extreme, or interesting art, there isn't any normal or average art." Now, you still have to remember that this is modernism. Modernist art is [*Stressing*] only interesting if it goes to the extreme. That's less visible if you deal with earlier periods like Wordsworth, or something like that, because we've already passed that period and this is why it's not so obvious. But that's also an extreme. All of these things which... [*Pause*.] All of these works which react to a crisis situation in art are doing that in some very extreme ways. And if their reaction is ordinary, then they just... [*Quietly*: they, I suppose, they are simply part of the culture industry or advertising... (*Mumbles indistinctly*).]

[*Long pause*.]

Okay, now where do we go with that? I think I've already mentioned the static and dynamic state in the work of art, on page 80... [*Pause*.] Mm-hmm. This is gonna take us deeper into the "Art Beauty" chapter, and there is a long development on temporality. And I guess that it will continue into the next... [*Page flipping*] yes, it will continue into the next section. The crucial category of temporality here... [*Pause*.] So, this is gonna be one thematization of what the work of art is, and how it could be described. But it's only one thematization. If you weren't interested in temporality, we would talk about the work in some other way. So, none of these aspects of the work of art have a stable definition, they are never final, they are always in some tension with their opposites, and so forth. The problem of the next sixth chapter called "Semblance and Expression ... [*Quietly*: which I hope that we get to it today] is, hmm... [*Hesitates*] is this word which is really untranslatable... [*Chalk on the blackboard*] S-C-H-E-I-N, and which here was translated as "semblance," even though it also means "appearance"... [*Cough in the audience*] and it also means a few other things.[7] Mm-hmm... [*Quietly*: I think, in Heidegger, well, we will see that maybe in the next chapter, but in Heidegger, it also means "to shine" in the literal sense, and that's a cognate.] But unfortunately, we can't translate it and the translator should have just left it in German, because it's a word that really has several English counterparts, but not a specific one. But it means the [*Stressing*] surface of the work, or the appearance of the work. So that would be another framework from which we try to define the work of art here and in the next chapter. In this one, however, we are dealing with time... [*Pause*] and we're dealing with the work in a way in which is both static and dynamic. Mm-hmm, it is static because artworks are objects, and they can't disappear completely; and it is dynamic because they are not only objects — they are also somewhat closer to events.

[*Long pause*.]

Okay. [*Addresses the audience*.] So, what's the category that he invents in order to talk about this process? [*Pause*.] Something that holds this being together with whatever its opposite is, or it's supposed to be... [*Mumbles indistinctly.*] What's the crucial word in this first part of the chapter?

[*Long pause.*]

STUDENT: Sphere?

JAMESON: That's later on, that's a big problem. We'll get to that. I meant in the early part of the chapter.

[*Silence.*]

JAMESON: And he wants to use, hmm... [*Pause.*]

STUDENT: The pregnant momen...

JAMESON: Sorry?

STUDENT: The pregnant moment?

JAMESON: Well, that's close, but that's not the word. That's sort of the idea. Mm-hmm. That's not the word he uses. [*Footsteps.*]

STUDENT: Apparition?

JAMESON: [*Pronounces in French*] Apparition. Yes, and I think that he is using the French word here because... [*Quietly*: the German also doesn't exactly have this word in the same form.] It is not apparition, which in English would refer to something unexpected or ghostly, but the French apparition. He doesn't want to use Erscheinung, because Erscheinung still has too much of those overtones that have to do with... [*Mumbles indistinctly.*] Apparition is, I believe, a word that he brings from a poem by Verlaine, and which Adorno likes... [*Mumbles indistinctly.*] And the point here is that... [*Pause.*] How is the work of art...? Hmm... [*Hesitates.*] What is the work of art compared to? And he quotes somebody and then he says, [*Impersonates Adorno*] "Look, what is the closest thing that you should imagine when you see a work of art in the outside world?"... [*Quietly*: not in the world of high culture, like a museum or something.] What is the closest equivalent that the work of art possesses? What is it really supposed to be like?

[*Long pause.*]

Mm-hmm. Where he gets this from, I don't remember, but I think it's crucial for this discussion and this is... [*Whispers*] fireworks.

Paul Valéry = DANCE 12 – Jameson (2)

FIREWORKS CONTINGENCY

Episode is important in the modern because a construction is made up on ~~etc~~ details.

Montage of attractions of Eisenstein

• Realistic novel – temporal continuity

• Modernistic – (Joyce i.e.) what is going on right now, the sentence is analised (individually)

Classical art – fixations on one moment

Crisis of temporality, Deleuze schizoph.

Nominalism in Adorno

~~Mann~~ Wagnerian leitmotiv Mann

Roland Barthe: Camera Lucida dedicated to Sartre's "L'Imaginaire"

Zeitkern

Page from student's seminar notes.

[*Audience murmuring.*]

The work of art is supposed to be an apparition. It's supposed to suddenly explode, turn into this absolutely dazzling and mesmerizing thing, and then disappear. [*Pause.*] Now, when we talk about aesthetics, that doesn't really happen, although I would think maybe ballet would have some closer connection to this, and I don't think that he talks much about ballet. Ballet, and dance, you will find in a writer who is very close to Adorno, and I would say this is the one essayist whose thoughts on aesthetics Adorno comes back to again and again, and which he appreciates. It's a writer of the preceding generation, and that's Paul... [*Chalk on the blackboard*] V-A-L-É-R-Y. Any of you who are with a French background and who are interested in these things, must know Valéry's essays on architecture, on all the arts, but especially the one on dance. [*Softly.*] Do any of you know what his famous essay on dance is called?[8] [*Pause.*] The art of dance would have some of this quality of the fireworks, and the point about the fireworks is that it is absolutely de-corporealized. In dance, you still have the body of the dancers and so forth, but here in principle... [*Quietly*: we always see fire from a distance, because you don't look at a piece of exploding firework close up and see that it has some material traces, because it's not there at all.] So, with the fireworks, you ask yourself, "Is it physical or non-physical?" Because this is an instant in time which produces bright flashes of light, sparks, and smoke and then it disappears. Page 81: "Fireworks are apparition... They appear empirically yet are liberated from the burden of the empirical, which is the obligation of duration." This analogy underscores the temporality of the work of art and, hmm... [*Hesitates.*] And I would like to say that perhaps happenings, except that he is very skeptical of the latest inventions in American art. Happening, as you all know, is this idea that emerges in America in the 1950s and 1960s as another answer to the crisis of the work of art... [*Chair scrapes the floor.*] With happenings, the artist declares that we don't need scripts anymore, we don't want to stage things, we want to... [*Cough in the audience*] create a pure event which is spontaneous, unscripted, and interactive, and it must also involve the audience. Well, Adorno thinks... [*Quietly*: and he is not seriously drawn by this possibility] but I think it is as an event that may be close to what they called "happenings" that he is looking at the work of art in the moment of crisis. Mm-hmm... [*Pause.*] Hmm, and... [*Absorbed.*] So, the question is, can we then look at a work of art in terms of its [*Stressing*] eventness? Well, in a way, that almost solves the problem of aura, because fireworks have this aura, but then their aura disappears or turns into kitsch, becoming mass culture, or something like that.

[*Long pause.*]

Now, this is also close to something else. You know that you get these things in Adorno, and you think that this is not very funny... [*Quietly*: although Adorno can be funny or even smashing in his sarcasm, and what he does to people who generally deserve it, I think, hmm... (*Chuckles*) I don't know, or maybe not always.] Mm-hmm, but... [*Pause.*] But there is an admiration for certain kinds of humor in Adorno and that's above all the slapstick. Mm-hmm, they went... [*Pause.*] You can't underestimate the experience of movies for all of these people. I like to quote an episode in Sartre where he remembers as a child... [*Quietly*: we are talking about 1905 or 1906, his mother was taking him to the early movie theaters, and he said "coming out of the theater back into the streets of Paris..." (*Cough in the audience*) there are cars already, and the film triggered in him the fundamental experience that later becomes existentialism, Sartre says, because it enabled this notion of contingency.] What's in the theater, what's on the screen, it's somehow necessary and meaningful... [*Pause*] no matter what kind of detail this is. Once you go out in the world again, then everything is contingent. Mm-hmm... [*Reflects.*] And that's a central experience of existentialism — the absence of certainty. All the other people... [*Pause.*] Well, I think that the role of film in other people is very interesting too. And it seems certain that, in Hollywood, these Frankfurt School people went out to movies all the time. Adorno's great admiration — most of what passes for humor in Hollywood — is for him an object of disgust, even though he must go see all this stuff. But what really works for him is the Marx Brothers and zaniness, because zaniness is beyond bourgeois humor.[9] This is somehow related to forces of nature, which are really to be admired for their energy.

[*Long pause.*]

So here, on this page or two when he talks about apparition, fireworks, I think you have to find a really authentic relationship to the preaesthetic — and this is not the preaesthetic in our terms — but to a [*Stressing*] genuine popular culture, as opposed to a bourgeois culture or a culture industry. And this is then... [*Pause.*] If you're talking about events, if you talk about fireworks, the primordial form of culture is the circus. And the experience of the circus is crucial in many ways. First of all, it's le numéro, it's the circus act...[10] [*Softly.*] You go to a circus and the first thing is the clown, then you have the elephant, and then you have the trapeze, dancers, and so on and so forth. And these are always separate, unrelated and self-contained acts, which are part of the larger spectacle. Now... [*Cough, cough*] they all exist in terms of apparition in some sense: suddenly they burst out of nowhere, do something or other, and then they disappear behind the curtain, and then there is another act. The whole temporal succession is very important here. And they also bring into being this logic of the episodes that is so important in the modern. Because remember, one of the features of this crisis... [*Quietly*: or maybe not remember because I don't know whether we got to this] it's the increased difficulty of [*Stressing*] constructing a large work. We can also think of philosophy, as I am talking about this book too, because this is Adorno's own problem of putting together a large philosophical work, right...? [*Quietly*: Well, Aesthetic Theory is also a circus in some sense.] Here is a paragraph on apparition, here is another paragraph on the circus, here is another one on fireworks. This is a set of philosophical episodes, of philosophical numéro, and in the modern work of art this is also the case. Mm-hmm...

[*Pause.*] The person who will theorize all of this in a fundamental way is Eisenstein. One of his earlier essays is called "The Montage of Attractions."[11] And the montage of attractions means the circus. The first play that Eisenstein puts on, in what's going on in the great period of Soviet modernism, and then even his films are these "montage of attractions" — one thing after another, one thing after ano... [*Pause.*] And in Eisenstein, montage is this sort of admiration of the clash between two images. But he is not the only one. I mean, there is a whole... [*Reflects.*] Most of the great traditions of moderni... [*Cough in the audience*] can be looked at in terms of the episodic, as something more than the categories, as some deeper necessity of the work, and then the strange temporality of appearing. If you think of... [*Pause.*] Think of the realistic novel as opposed to something like Joyce, or I suppose Proust. In a realistic novel, you have a temporal continuity, right? You are in a scene. The scene is gonna go on for twenty pages or so, and you know that there is a basic question whether that hero will get the money or not, or whether the hero will get the lover... (*Words indistinct*) or not, and that scenes are part of a larger framework that you're working through. There is a kind of temporal process going on here, which means that your attention has to be divided. You've got to be looking at what they're doing and saying, but then another part of the mind must be thinking, "Well, how does this fit into the whole...?" [*Cough in the audience*] "Why do they say that and what's that gonna mean for the end of the chapter, and then the later developments?" Right? [*Pause.*] Now, in the modern work, I think in Joyce, for example, hmm... [*Hesitates*] it is always different because you wanna know what's gonna happen, what will happen later on in the day, but that's not the same kind of interest. Instead, what you wanna know is "what is this sentence?" "What's going on [*Stressing*] right now?" And then, I think, in the logic of the thing, the modern work — if viewed from a certain angle — falls apart into these separate sentences. The modern artwork is broken into these separate presences, separate numéros if you wish, and then they become like a montage of attractions. [*Pause.*] And how do you hold those acts together? Well, in Joyce, hmm… [*Hesitates*] it's a drag, I mean, you take the book of the Odyssey, and you say, okay, well, in this sentence, we gonna be doing Ulysses and Nausicaä, or something like that. And then you think, okay, well then… [*Quietly*: I understand there is a unity here and that I don't have to pay any attention to it anymore… (*Words indistinct*) in the literal sense.] If you only had individual sentences, you would be in big trouble, I think, and the work would be exceedingly boring, and this happens to some modernists and also to some postmodernists. But in general, the ratio of the instant of the apparition to the length of time, and the attention to time changing, has been radically modified from the previous aesthetic regime.

[*Long pause.*]

Now, if you read your Auerbach, and if you want to go back to Homer, that's how Auerbach describes the epic… [*Sighs*] the epic in the classical sense. Because in Homer, Auerbach says, it looks as though the narrator, or whoever, is just focused on this sentence.[12] The narrator is not remembering this episode, hmm… [*Hesitates*] he is not referencing anything that went on before, or anything after. Classical, hmm… [*Hesitates*] classical art is this absolute fixation on the [*Stressing*] present in time; it is something marked by the use of the concrete detail, and the focus on the here and now. You take a moment and then you line it up with another moment and so forth, and the example he gives is the scar on Odysseus…[13] [*Quietly*: remember when Odysseus goes back to Ithaka and they are bathing him, and the maid finds the scar that he had… (*Mumbles indistinctly*).] And so the question is then, why wasn't this narration prepared somehow in advance? Because in a modern novel, this scene would expand in time: you'd have to introduce the bath earlier, then there is a door to… [*Clears throat*] and then you would have to say something else, and then any habitual reader of the novel understands that, when the maid is mentioned in chapter one, she is gonna reappear in chapter five in some significant way, and so on and so forth. But in Homer is nothing like that, here you have just this separate presence [*Pause.*] But that's not what I think it at stake here, and that's not indicative of a crisis of temporality — that's something else... [*Quietly:* and what is that called, we don't know.] Anyway, but this is not our first problem.

[*Long pause. Footsteps.*]

Mm-hmm. But here I think is a crisis of temporality [*Pause.*] And you can connect it up with the Deleuzian schizophrenia. I mean, we are living in the present. We're not really, hmm... [*Hesitates.*] Not only we are not interested in the past and the future, but we certainly have lost the habit of doing that. So, it had to be linked only to this here and now. Mm-hmm, I think that's obviously not part of Adorno's primal reference, but what he calls "nominalism" is, and it means that... [*Thud. Backpack falls on the floor*] there are no general ideas, there are no general categories. This doesn't fit under something else in such a way that it's an example of that — it's all by itself. [*Whispers.*] It's a singularity. And then there is another one. And then there is another one. And if you start getting bored with that, then either you or the artist must do something... [*Words indistinct.*] This is somehow addressing some kind of crisis of, hmm... [*Hesitates*] of... of... of universals, [*Pause*] and some kind of crisis of temporality, and I would also say of the biographical universals. Mm-hmm. You just want this moment of life, right now, even though it doesn't fit into anything. Whereas we think that people in other periods had a longer attention span and they understood that this unique present fits into other larger categories, like destiny or fortune, or a lack of fortune or bad luck, and something like that. In the old narrative, the here and now is assumed to be part of a larger whole. And they were able to think in these larger categories, which one would call "universals," because these particulars were subsumed under them. But once you got nothing to subsume a particular under, then you are in nominalism, and you are just... [*Cough in the audience*] fixated on these orphan singularities. Anyway, it seems to me that all this is part of this reflection on, hmm... [*Student raising hand.*] Yes... [*Pause.*]

STUDENT: [*From the back of the class*] Can this be applied to Thomas Mann...? [*Words indistinct*] Because in his novel, he used to introduce some motive that he will develop later. His insistence on such temporality plays through music in Thomas Mann. So, can this be applied to Thomas Mann, and I am also thinking of Proust? Because Proust played, what he did in his novel in the last... [*Words indistinct.*]

JAMESON: Yeah, I think the answer has to be "No," but for two different answers. I think, in Proust, there is absolutely this fixation on a certain moment of the past, but that moment gets to be so huge... [*Pause.*] You know, he's about to have dinner with these horrible... [*Quietly*: nobles and snobs of the Parisian upper class and... (*Mumbles indistinctly*).][14] And that moment is gonna take him fifty pages because someway everything will go into it. [*Pause.*] So, I would say that rather, hmm... [*Hesitates.*] I mean, is Proust supposed to be about time? Yes, and yes, and so forth, but I think that it's rather coming very close to something like a universe in a grain of sand in a Blakeian sense, where everything is in [*Stressing*] <u>that</u> moment. And then it's also episodic, because Proust has to bring that off somehow, generally by way of a... [*Pause.*] There is a certain kind of falling cadence in the Proustian paragraph that signals the end of that, and then somehow everything has to be around so he can pop to another one, and this is also what is called "spatial form" in Proust, because if you remember early into the novel, hmm... [*Hesitates*] he used to take these walks. Alright. First, we see the author... [*Cough in the audience*] walking beneath the tress. Ah, episode one. Then, as he went on, we met mister so-and-so. A huge episode. And so spatial form allows you to line those things up in what is really not a temporal way. I mean, maybe the walks were a continuity of time, but that's not the principle that allows you to get from one to the other. Anyway, I think the Proustian answer would be like that.

[*Long pause.*]

For Thomas Mann, you're talking about the Wagnerian leitmotif? [*Walks to the blackboard.*] And this is... [*Chalk on the blackboard*] L-E-I-T-M-O-T-I-F. [*Pause.*] I think this is the great lesson that Mann learned both from Wagner in one way, and from Zola in another. Because, in Zola, you have some sort of similar play with the thematics... [*Door creaks open.*] So, the leitmotif... [*Footsteps.*] Mm-hmm. Does it really connect up these temporal parts? In the beginning of the Ring,[15] obviously Wotan the god has its music. Then there is Alberich's curse, which has to do very importantly for Doctor Faustus with the renunciation of... [*Quietly:* well, "love," it's called, but of sexuality, and castration, and that you get also in Parsifal and so on and... (*Mumbles indistinctly*).] Mm-hmm. Okay, so later on, the curse, it's a very ominous kind of motif. Well, then we go on a couple of operas and, at a certain point, Siegfried is about to do something rather, and there is again the curse, right? Alright, now what does this have to do to the past? That certainly holds Wagner's music together in some way, but is it really a continuity with the past or is it... [*Pause.*] Does it replace this older form that the eighteenth century and Beethoven invented, which was the sonata kind of unity of music, which is already breaking up by the time of Wagner? I mean... [*Pause.*] I mean, I think that's a really basic question of the leitmotif: what it does to temporality? Whether it's not a substitute for temporal continuity rather than the expression of it? And I tend to think the, hmm... [*Hesitates*] the latter, ah, sorry, I mean the former.

[*Long pause.*]

But how it works, certainly we get a whole set of these motifs... [*Pause.*] This was... [*Pause.*] I mean, it's not just Thomas Mann, although that is a very visible tactic in Thomas Mann, but it's also part of contemporary criticism. You know the whole Image School... [*Quietly*: what's that, maybe the... (*Pause.*) It came along with the New Criticism, but it wasn't exactly New Criticism.] If you read any of this old Shakespeare literary criticism in books like, what's his name, G. Wilson Knight... [*Addresses audience.*] Anybody still read G. Wilson Knight?

[*Long pause.*]

JAMESON: Nobody?

[*Long silence*]

It's a thematic kind of criticism, which somewhat vaguely comes out of the Jungian school, I suppose. So, Wilson Knight says, look, every play of Shakespeare is a constellation of images...[16] Mm-hmm. Hamlet is full of images of disgust and vomit. [*Pause.*] Mm-hmm. Coriolanus is metal and gleaming, and so on and so forth.[17] And then he takes these plays and goes all the way through and, indeed, finds all of these motives. Mm-hmm... [*Pause.*] Why is this...? [*Looks around.*] I mean, they are really there, but on the other hand, are they meaningful? Mm-hmm. Empson said that the actors have to do things over and over again. So, maybe these motifs are not there for the public, because this is like Schoenberg when one cannot hear some things that are going on in his music; the public doesn't follow these various motifs, and they are really for the actors... [*Quietly*: to keep the actors amused, because they go back in the green room and talk about it.][18] I'm not sure if that's possible either. I think it's closer to what, hmm... [*Hesitates*] to what Freud called "overdetermination." It is a secondary elaboration. It's a way of tying everything together. So, once your mind said so-and-so, something, a very important motif, is discussed in Hamlet... [*Quietly*: which is like the motif of the mother's marriage that is a recurring theme in Hamlet. The marriage of Queen Gertrude to his uncle shortly after the death of his father is a central event ... (*Words indistinct*) and the horrible things that Hamlet feels, and which cannot be expressed is all that he... (*Mumbles indistinctly*).] Then those images get picked up and they pop up everywhere. I mean, they occur to Shakespeare, and he then just sows them into everything, in the play. But then, in another play, they are gone and something else takes place. Now, that's a... [*Pause.*] I'm interested not in the truth of this image criticism, or thematic criticism, but only in the fact that this emerges in literary criticism as well as in other disciplines... [*Cough in the audience*] like Thomas Mann and other writers. It's not just critics who work with image-finding, representations of characters or themes and so forth... [*Quietly*: like you can write your thesis on the imagery or this or that author... (*Words indistinct*) by going through all of them and find all kind of meanings... (*Footsteps shuffle across the floor*).] But then this phenomenon is part of what Adorno would call the breakdown... [*Clears throat*] of artistic form, that becomes a secondary wave, despite the elaboration of the dream. You've got an initial dream content, which is this wish, and then the unconscious says, oh, but let's, hmm... [*Hesitates*] let's make this like a story, let's put all of these things together in time in some way — in some [*Stressing*] autonomous way — so even making a complete dream is a little bit, you know, like the autonomy of the work of art. And so... [*Pause*] this becomes a different way of doing it, but I think we should wait, when we get to Doctor Faustus we will have a better idea of how this process works.

[*Long Pause.*]

Other quest...

[*Silence.*]

Okay. Um... [*Pause.*] Now, I think I already jumped ahead to the army joke about the lieutenant and the soldier who came from the zoo saying that such animals do not exist,[19] hmm... [*Hesitates*] solche Tiere gibt es nicht. Okay. In every genuine work of art, page 82: "...something appears that does not exist. It is not dreamt up out of disparate elements of the existing. Out of these elements artworks arrange constellations that become ciphers, without, however, like fantasies, setting up the enciphered before the eyes as something immediately existing." Mm-hmm, yeah. So, you can say almost that these [*Stressing*] themes we were talking about, these thematic constellations are more like ciphers; that is to say, they're encrypted markings that you think you might be able to unravel... [*Cough in the audience*] like the enigma code, or something, but you can't figure them out. But Adorno thinks that figuring things out, it's not right, and we don't have to do things like that in the work of art. The work of art is not something to be decrypted... [*Quietly*: except in very special historical circumstances where a composer or a poet runs certain letters through all the time, and you are supposed to figure out the first letter of how this is spelled... (*Mumbles indistinctly*) or Doctor Faustus, where Mann used the letters of Adorno's name.] This is not what Adorno is talking about, this is not about "truth content." That's something else. This is not the story of the centaur. You know, who was the philosopher who said that nothing can be in the mind if it's not first in the senses...? [*Quietly*: Was it Descartes? I don't remember now who said that... (*Mumbles indistinctly*).] But then another philosopher came along and said, "Look, these phantastic things, the centaur, it didn't come out of nowhere: you have a horse, you have human beings, you just put them up together, and that's what the mind does."[20] [*Pause*.] All of those ideas were in the senses before and now they are just combined. What Adorno wants to say in that earlier sentence is that what's non-existent, and what lies beyond the work of art, which is somehow non-existing, is its, hmm... [*Hesitates*] its negativity, or its imaginary quality because [*Stressing*] even representations of existing things, like landscapes, portraits and so forth, they have some portions of the non-existent within them. Otherwise, they wouldn't be called... [*Dull muffled sound*] they wouldn't be works of art. And then, I think, in this context, the interesting question to ask is... [*Quietly*: and for which I don't exactly have an answer, but I think it's historically more appropriate for us than it was for Adorno] and that's the question of photography. Photography has become one of the great arts now... [*Quietly*: I mean, it's not any longer this sort of lesser, or... (*Hesitates*) secondary art.] Now, photographic art is also considered among the predominant arts of our times. But then, we should ask, what is the relation between photography and the non-existing? [*Pause*.] And also, what is the relation between photography and objective reality...? [*Quietly*: We know there is a relationship with the past, but is that the only one? That's certainly one of the sources... (*Words indistinct*) as it comes out of the moment of the past.] But I think that's also what Adorno means here, and I think that he is talking about an object which is imaginary — the work of art is a real physical object, but it is also imaginary. I'm using Sartrean terms now, something that he called L'imaginaire, which, in Sartre, is a very fundamental early work before Being and Nothingness.[21] Barthes's book on photography, for example, is... [*Pause*.] You know how most books are dedicated to names, right, or to the memory of people? But Barthes's book on photography is dedicated to Sartre's book L'imaginaire.[22] And since Sartre was iced during the whole structuralist period, this marks the return of something interesting... [*Quietly*: because all of these people who were Sartreans and who... (*Mumbles indistinctly*) before Levi-Strauss, which was also one of the markers that structuralism was coming to an end at that particular moment.] So, to use Sartre's language, it is the [*Stressing*] imaginary dimension of not being of a physical object, and that is not exactly Adorno's terminology to discuss something that does not exist. Because remember that what doesn't exist also calls into question [*Stressing*] what-is, or that what exists, as we talked the other day. So, this imaginary thing that isn't in the world could also be — and is necessarily also — a critique of this world. What doesn't exist in these artworks... [*Cough in the audience*] throws into question everything that does exist. This is the first, almost ontological level of the critical and [*Stressing*] negative nature of the artwork... [*Quietly*: and that it appears in other ways as well.]

[*Long pause*.]

"If," see page 83, "If..." [*Page flipping*.] Mm-hmm... [*To himself*: I'm trying to see; where is that place where he talks about "exchange."] Ah, "...that of exchangeability. What appears is not interchangeable because it does not remain a dull particular for which other particulars could be substituted..."[23] Exchangeability is, of course, already quantification, and it has to do with this critical capitalist notion of... [*Chalk on the blackboard*] E-X-C-H-A-N-G-E. If you can exchange one thing for another — they have a common value. In other words, when you manage to exchange, you produce the abstraction of value which is already commodified. The numbers don't have to mean money. But the very fact that they are numbers and that you could say... [*Points to the water bottle in front of him*] this bottle of water is really worth... [*Pause.*] Or three of these bottles of water is worth the same as this book [*Holds up* Aesthetic Theory] and if you are capable of saying that, then we are already in the world of the commodity. Anything that's exchangeable means that, even though things may not be the same, the act of exchange sets up an identity between them; a sameness has been constructed for them, which has nothing to do with the individual properties... [*Quietly*: and this is the chapter on commodities in Marx's Capital, Volume One... (*Words indistinct*) exchange as a central theme that refers to the value of a commodity in terms of its exchangeability for other commodities.] Okay, so exchangeability [*Page flipping*]: "What appears is not interchangeable..." the moment of the fireworks are not interchangeable because they are a product of a specific instant in time "...because it does not remain a dull particular for which other particulars could be substituted, nor is it an empty universal that equates everything specific that it comprehends by abstracting the common characteristics,"[24] which is some kind of Platonic idea. "If in empirical reality everything has become [*Stressing*] fungible..." that's a nice word in Adorno that I never read in anybody else's books, but it means that suddenly things are replaceable, and you can replace or do anything with anything. Mm-hmm... [*Quietly:* fungibility is sort of one of the ways in which he describes exchange-value in capitalism, this activity where everything is mutually interchangeable, and you can substitute ice cream, or books, or bottles of water, where everything has become everything else. You're sort of swept away in this scene of exchangeable value.] Mm-hmm. "If in empirical reality everything has become [*Stressing*] fungible art holds up to the world of everything-for-something-else images of what it itself would be if it were emancipated from the schemata of imposed identification."[25] That is, just as the work of art gives you a glimpse of nature, um... [*Pause*] free from domination, so it also gives you a glimpse of what things would be like if they were not dominated by identity. And, in Adorno, identity means commodification — it means capitalist commodification...

[*Long pause*]

So, what would a world look like or be where things are... [*Quietly:* where things cannot be reduced to each other, where everything is unique and individual, everything is — to use this Deleuzian word again — a "singularity"?] That's what art would allow you to do and that's what somehow just temporality of the... [*Cough, cough*] of the apparition allows you to do. [*Page flipping.*] "The telos of artworks is a language whose words cannot be located on the spectrum; a language whose words are not imprisoned by a prestabilized universality."[26] And then he talks about colors and then passes into science fiction, hmm "... science fiction credulously and therefore powerlessly make[s] a fetish of such themes."[27] Okay, well... [*Quietly*: well, maybe not that... (*Words indistinct*).]

[*Long pause.*]

Regarding his reference to spectrum and colors, I wanted to read you a section from the novel by... [*Quietly*: no one knows anything about this man named David Lindsay... (*Pause.*) I think he had some connections with the conservatives like Tolkien and C.S. Lewis, and all those people. But Voyage to Arcturus is more of an agnostic novel, it's a fantasy novel and not really science fiction. Um, Harold Bloom admires him.] Anyway, the novel itself is about a planet where strange things happen... [*Pause*] and I mean, if you are an agnostic, I don't think you'd wish to figure them out. But these strange things are really interesting and relevant for our reading of these parts in Aesthetic Theory. In the novel, the main characters land on Tormance, and this is an imaginary planet orbiting Arcturus sun,[28] and they, hmm... [*Hesitates*] and they encounter these peculiar beings with their unique views, and this planet also has colors that don't exist in the Earth's spectrum — these are colors that don't exist. [*Page flipping.*] "What was peculiar about was its color. It was an entirely new color — not a new shade or combination, but a new primary color, as vivid as blue, red, or yellow, but quite different. When he inquired, she told him that it was known as ulfire." That's the new color. "Presently he met with a second new color. This she designated jale." [*Spells letter by letter.*] J-A-L-E. "The sense impressions caused in Maskull by these two additional primary colors can only be vaguely hinted at by analogy. Just as blue is delicate and mysterious, yellow clear and unsubtle, and red sanguine and passionate, so he felt ulfire to be wild and painful, and jale dreamlike, deverish..." [*To himself*: deverish? This must be "feverish"] "...and voluptuous."[29] Well, now you can say, if you think that these are interesting or not. And is it enough to point to these colors that do not exist? But the whole thing on art in some of Adorno's paragraphs, I think it's inscribed here. If something doesn't exist... [*Pause*] then how can you refer to it, right? If you can refer to it, you already know what it is and therefore it [*Stressing*] does exist... [*Quietly*: again, it's like Hegel's critique of Kant's limit.] Anyhow, I think that some of the things that you find in science fiction are in the spirit of these remarks about, hmm... [*Hesitates*] about art and what doesn't exist, and these are also interesting things to look at them in that way.

[*Long Pause.*]

Okay. I want to get now to a part... [*Whispers.*] Page 85: "The instant in which these forces become image, the instant in which what is interior becomes exterior, the outer husk is exploded; their apparition, which makes them an image, always at the same time destroys them as image." And then below, towards the end of the same paragraph:

> What appears in the artwork is its own inner time; the explosion of appearance blasts open the continuity of this inner temporality. The artwork is mediated to real history by its monadological nucleus. History is the content of artworks. To analyze artworks means no less than to become conscious of the history immanently sedimented in them.[30]

There is something here that he discusses in this whole chapter in terms of the impregnable or the pregnant moment... [*Words indistinct.*] That is to say, hmm... [*Pause.*] History is in the works of art — but precisely in them and not outside them. Artworks have an inner temporality and then there is also the temporality of history, and this is what lies outside the work of art. This is when you discuss a work of art by saying, well, this novel was written on the eve of World War One... [*Quietly*: and this was the period of the rising tensions among the major European powers... (*Words indistinct*) of empires like Austro-Hungary and the Ottoman, and so on and so forth.] We have a kind of historical temporality, which is external, because it comes from other books, right? It's other history books that we read about or memoirs or something about this period when Europe was... [*Paus*e] the old Europe before the explosion of World War One. And when we are applying such knowledge to art, we are just transferring this stereotypical temporality that you've read about in history books to the work of art. Whereas Adorno is saying, no, no... [*Pause.*] There is a connection between art and history, but that lies inside each artwork; it's the Zeitkern... [*Chalk on the blackboard*] K-E-R-N-E-L O-F T-I-M-E, and this is what is historical in them, and which appears and gives us this inner sense of history, or the moment of history.

[*Long pause.*]

And this inner time form is also collective and so maybe we end with this...[*Pause.*] See page 86, it's a long passage: "Subjective experience contributes images that are not images of something, and precisely they are essentially collective; thus and in no other way is art mediated to experience."[31] It doesn't reproduce experience. The experience is collective in and of itself, and it's, hmm... [*Hesitates*] and it's inside the work. "By virtue of this experiential content, and not primarily as a result of fixation or forming as they are usually conceived, artworks diverge from empirical reality: empiria through empirical deformation."[32] Then he goes on and talks about the dream, and so forth. It's another attack, to a certain degree, on, hmm... [*Hesitates*] on Freud... [*Quietly*: but it's political.] [*Student raising hand.*] Yeah...

STUDENT: [*Far from the microphone.*] Is he trying to say that all social antagonisms are collected in the form of the work of art... [*Words indistinct*] and that the artistic form contains within itself all the social contradions...? [*Words indistinct.*]

JAMESON: [*Agitated.*] Well, I think you have to keep this... [*Pause.*] He doesn't want to you to... [*Words indistinct.*] We all know that the opposition of form and content is bad, but on the other hand, you have to keep it for a moment because, in the modern work of art, the contradiction is always of form, whereas in empirical reality... [*Quietly*: and this is how we normally think about reality] the contradiction is always one of content. The historical, political contradictions in the social world are... [*Quietly*: and this is, I think, one of the basic doctrines of this text, namely that]: contradictions are reproduced in the work of art not because it [*Stressing*] <u>represents</u> them, but because they manifest in the work of art in terms of their own technical problems and challenges of productivity. [*Cough in the audience.*] It's a technical contradiction of artistic form, which reproduces the social contradiction, or which it mediates in its own way. Now, does that get out of this separation or out of the mind/body problem, or the problem of levels of homologies and so on and so forth? Hmm... [*Hesitates*] I don't know. I mean, in other words, is this relation between artistic form and social content a proper philosophical solution and does it sound convincing? I am not sure. But we will have to keep our eye on this because it keeps coming back. That's the crucial mediation, that what in a... [*Pause.*] In other words, you've got a workers' strike going on, and this is a true social antagonism. but social antagonism gets into the work of art, not by painting a picture of the strike, but by virtue of... [*Reflecting*] of, let's say, problems of representation, of pigment and form; it must be an artistic "strike," if you wish, such as cubism or other similar Isms, that the work of art has to make sense of its own material conditions. You see what I'm saying? So, there is this basic... [*Cough in the audience*] what Breton would call "communicating vessels," and this is a basic channel of communication between things... [*Door creaks open*] or mediation between the inside and outside, in which content on the social outside is transferred into artistic form.[33] Now, this is Adorno's argument with the political artists, and that's why whenever he gets a chance, he reinterprets Brecht... [*Quietly*: because he says, "Look, Brecht thought he was writing about these contradictions, showing the true path to emancipation and so on, but in fact, he was just an artist and the emancipation was going on in Brecht's poetic form," right? It's not what the protocol sentences say, it is that neutral style that Brecht invented first of all... (*Mumbles indistinctly*) which is the solution to the social contradiction.] So, whenever we approach [*Stressing*] representational political art, Adorno wants to push that away, like commitment or [*in French*] engagement, any of these things, he turns to the modernist notion of form. It's a politics of form rather than a politics of content. [*Agitated.*] But to do it justice, you have to remember this other thing that he says, which is that, up to 1927 or something like that, nobody thought modernist art had any incompatibility with modernist politics... [*Quietly*: that is to say, with revolutionary politics.] And then, after the late 1920s, what all of these people were doing — from Malevich and many other crazy people — this was all ending. And the advanced artform is revolutionary content; their aesthetics, it's the same as radical politics. So, what is he trying to do in this book from 1969, I guess, or something like that, is an attempt to revive that kind of connection between art and politics that existed before Stalin's so-called "great turn" in 1929... [*Quietly*: that was, hmm... (*Hesitates*) sort of the end of that interconnection between art and politics that existed in the years from the turn of the century to the Soviet Revolution... (*Door screech. Footsteps*).] Now, I'm just saying this is not... [*Pause*.] He is not some weird antipolitical aesthete... [*Quietly*: or maybe he is that too] but, I mean, he is really trying to reinvent a tradition from the past when art and politics went together.

STUDENT: [*Far from the microphone. Indistinct*.] But isn't this kind of boring... [*Words indistinct*.] If the artwork is produced through this process, wherein it can't help but already contain a social truth in its form. This is not like going to make a difference for the social... [*Door creaks open*.]

JAMESON: You mean all these crises are gonna be the same as we look back into the past, or how is the past gonna be...?

STUDENT: More like all artworks already contain everything social in them, so why bother making new works... [*Words indistinct*.]

JAMESON: Mm-hmm... [*Long pause*.] Yeah, but, hmm... [*Hesitates*.] But I don't see that as an objection. I could see it if you said: "Look, what can art's relationship to the past possibly be since the past is gone..." [*Quietly*: and we don't have the same contradictions that we had.] Or I could see this as a perspective on the postmodern, where this doesn't seem to be going on anymore, as nobody knows what the contradictions in postmodernism really are, and all seems very strange and distant to us. Mm-hmm... [*Reflects*.] No, I think it's the articulation of the work of art as a social or political contradiction that's crucial for him. If it doesn't articulate that in its form, well, then the work is just mush, or culture industry, kitsch, something worse or whatever. So, the articulation is absolutely essential to him, and that's what is producing the technical problems too. Because if you thought, "Oh, I'll just write more sonnets like Shakespeare or somebody else," then it would mean that we don't understand anything about the current situation, either politically, socially, or artistically... [*Quietly*: I mean, we don't understand why people can't write sonnets, why this sonnet can't be written, and so on and so forth.] So that has to be this moment of crisis, which is embedded in the work, or rather it must be reconstructed through the work, and which is the nature of society for him, right? [*Pause.*] All of these historical moments are moments of crisis: the crisis is, as Benjamin says, that things just go on like this... [*Quietly*: hmm, there are no moments that are not crisis, but if the work of art doesn't make it happen then... (*Mumbles indistinctly*).] But keep working on your question, I think there is something very important that you're asking that I'm either not getting or you're not saying it right.

STUDENT: It is just that he seems to be differentiating between artworks that reveal some contradictions, and those that don't...

JAMESON: [*After prolonged reflection.*] Yeah, but if some works of art don't point to contradictions, then they are not any good. Only the extreme ones do, and the ones that are not extreme are not interesting. That's just how, hmm... [*Hesitates.*] He makes fun of Lukács's idea of the [*Whispering*] normal work of art, which is like saying "normal science," right? You have the great scientific discoveries and then you have normal science. [*Chuckles.*] So, the normal work of art, for him, this is a horrible vulgar notion. [*Audience laughing.*] I mean, this is... [*Agitated*] that's just culture industry. That's what he would call a normal work of art. For him, good or authentic art cannot be normal. For him, art, to be of any interest at all, it has to be extreme and... [*Mumbles indistinctly.*]

STUDENT TWO: What if... [*Pause.*] What if the nature of this contradiction is somehow embodied by the artist, as if he sees this conflict and then, you know, he ruminates and cogitates on it, and then he is reproducing it or he gives it knowingly artistic form? Or it is that the artist is just a medium of the context? As he is coming in conflict with his environment, he reproduces the contradictions naturally, as it were... [*Pause.*]

JAMESON: Ah, well, there you have all of these people... [*Quietly*: like Pound and... (*Words indistinct*) who were sort of registry apparatuses.] Mm-hmm. It's like saying you have to be able to do something to the ego, in such a way that you become a receptacle. It does not make this into... [*Pause.*] Or let's look at it like Freud and say that the work is not to be a private wish-fulfillment. Any bestselling novel, all of these three hundred or four hundred pages of airport literature, they are all wish-fulfillments... [*Quietly*: and you know that everybody reads them, thinking how will the hero find all the money, and how will they find love and happiness, and so on, or these power struggles that are so exciting, and we all know that all of that, it's just junk, because it's clear that that's a wish-fulfillment.] So, what the artist has to do is find a way of turning himself, or herself, into a registering apparatus that they just receive all of these social vibrations. That's one way of talking about it. Mm-hmm, but the personal... [*Pause.*] I would say that the life or the personality of the artist... [*Pause.*] It's in Hegel's ruse of reason... [*Self-corrects*] hmm, ruse of history.[34] Here is an artist who is particularly... [*Zipper unzipping*] selfish, cruel, misanthropic, and everything else. Yeah, but that's all part of the masterplan, because it's precisely those qualities that allow that artist to pick up these kinds of vibrations that go into the world. So, this is, hmm... [*Hesitates.*] I mean, it does matter that the biography says that the artist had these or those qualities. And it matters only because those are part of the antennae or part of the artist's registering apparatus. Maybe only with those qualities can the artist pick the social vibrations up... [*Quietly:* and somebody else would overlook what only this artist could see... (*Mumbles indistinctly*).] So, I think it's... [*Door creaks open. Footsteps.*] Is this going back to the idea of genius in Kant — I am not sure. I mean, obviously... [*Pause.*] But... [*Quietly*: I don't think this has to do with regressing to... (*Words indistinct*) all of that Christian stuff about grace and the hand of God and so on.] I mean [*Stressing*] predestination plays some part in this, right? But this is après la lettre, for it is only afterwards that you realize how fortunate it was for this artist to be, like Thomas Mann's Hans Castorp, and be a tubercular in a sanatorium, and what great luck it was for Joyce to have been lied to, and so on and so forth, but presumably that's, hmm... [*Hesitates*] that's the kind of... [*Pause*.] Mm-hmm, so there are artists without concept, and there isn't any concept involved, and this might be one way... [*Agitated*.] Or... [*Pause*.] Or there are artists who are politically very astute, and they see what's really going on and understand it. It could be that too, for it is nothing that is ruling out concepts.

STUDENT THREE: So, this would mean interfering with the form...? [*Door creaks open. Students leaving for other classes*.]

JAMESON: No, it means producing a very interesting form of political art, of which I think there isn't very much. I think The Aesthetics of Resistance[35] is a very astute form of political art. I think, hmm... [*Pause*.] In Mann, he's astute about the politics of art... [*Quietly*: with a certain kind of political intent somewhere in there, and the way things are interpreted with regard to the broader historical situation.] Political astuteness is generally about assessing the situation. This force wants to do that, but there's a counterforce, and so on... [*Quietly*: like, for example, Lenin's assessment of the situation in "What Is to Be Done?" where he argues that a vanguard revolutionary party is needed in order to lead the working class, and later he again assesses the situation during... (*Mumbles indistinctly*).] And art could be made that way too, I think, but it's just that it too often does not tend to be so. Mm-hmm. So, there is no reason... [*Pause*.] And artists could be like philosophers, I mean... [*Softly*] if you think of people having fine philosophical minds, well, there are many of them. But they don't use it to write philosophy, or they play dual roles and dual existences, like Sartre who was both an artist and a philosopher. So, there is no recipe for... [*Pause*.] I think the whole point of this kind of analysis is that there is no formula in advance to grasp this relation between social contradiction and artistic form; you can't really define it a priori and only maybe interpret it after the fact. You can't define a crisis in advance until someone is trying to respond to it, and then you can say what happened.

[*Long pause*.]

Okay, listen, we will be going with this... [*Pause.*] What I want to say is that the last chapter is very troublesome, because we have a word here, which is Geist. It is a very popular and important German word, which is untranslatable. It isn't English "spirit"... [*Quietly*: what's spirit, it's like you're talking about ghosts.] Mm-hmm, and in French... [*Pause.*] What is Geist in French?

[*Long silence. Door creaks open. Zippers zipping up.*]

JAMESON: What is spirit in French? Anyone?

AUDIENCE: [*In unison.*] L'esprit. L'esprit. L'esprit. L'esprit.

JAMESON: L'esprit. Yeah, but that means "wit." [*Pause.*] I mean, The Phenomenology of Wit?[36] [*Audience laughing.*] You know, it doesn't make any sense. Mm-hmm, so spirituality, this must not be understood in some religious way. Geist... [*Pause.*] The whole next section here is very difficult for us, because we will have to do something with this word Geist, which is not in our... [*Quietly*: specially not in our American parlance.] We'll set a race to that, then we will get to the next section. And Tuesday we will have the... [*Words indistinct.*]

Audience stands up. Chairs scratch the floor. Door squeaks. Students return chairs to other classrooms. Zippers zipping up. Some form a line to discuss their assignments. General noise. Screeching microphone noise.

[*Microphone turns off.*]

CURTAIN

LECTURE ELEVEN

MARCH 4, 2003

SEMBLANCE AND EXPRESSION (CHAPTER) — *SCHEIN* — HEIDEGGER, "THE ORIGIN OF THE WORK OF ART"

CURTAIN RISES

Moving chairs, squeaking door, coughs, other sounds filling the noise environment of a large classroom in the Literature Department at Duke University. Two students sitting next to each other talk about the circumstances that brought them into this seminar. The undergraduate girl confesses that she is attending the seminar by chance. "My best friend Ann enrolled because this course met her requirements for her Literature degree." She asked me to join her for this course because she was too afraid to come alone to a seminar for very smart grad students. I'm only here because she asked." The girl then confesses that everything in this seminar seems very strange and different to her. Sometimes it is very complicated to understand what Jameson is talking about. The same goes for Aesthetic Theory. *"It's like an unclimbable wall of text." She then explains that she grew up in a conservative family of Southern evangelicals and this is not the type of book that she's been used to. The grad student says that, before coming to Duke, he was an artist and heard the name "Jameson" in artist circles. He adds that he comes from a former communist country, and he finds this version of American Marxism very different from the one he used to read in Russian. "In America, you can make even Marxism profitable," he says, chuckling at his own wit.*

Jameson enters the classroom carrying a few books, his scattered notes, and the red pen in the chest pocket of his flannel shirt.

[Microphone turns on.]

JAMESON: ...Doctor Faustus went through several editions and... [*Footsteps. Door creaks open*] he moved to North America. This was a second life for Thomas Mann as a writer, because normally... [*Chairs scraping the floor*] given the connections which you will observe between his work and the German language, once you lose that connection with language, it starts to change you. The writers who had to flee Hitler... [*Pause.*] I mean, hmm... [*Hesitates.*] Benjamin, for example, wanted to become the greatest literary critic of his age, but... [*Quietly*: you can't do that in Paris. I mean, as a German critic? He wrote some pieces in French, of course, but that is not... (*Mumbles indistinctly*).][1] What I mean is that your role as an intellectual and as a critic and so forth, or as a novelist like Mann, is to be there, in your home language and with your people. And this brings us to the issue of translation.

[*Long pause.*]

Mm-hmm. Thomas Mann didn't want to hear any criticism of Miss Lowe-Porter, even though he must also have known that there were many moments that were weak.[2] Well, I think this is a great translation... [*Holds an edition of* Doctor Faustus *translated by Lowe-Porter.*] You will see that the variety of styles is really comparable only to Joyce in a lot of ways. [*Softly.*] You have this medieval style, and she manages to do that very well.[3] I don't know who else would have done it... [*Quietly*: we'll see how this new guy is gonna translate Doctor Faustus and how well he does it.[4]] In any case, I think it's nice to have... [*Pause.*] You know, it's like the old Constance Garnett translations of Dostoevsky, hmm... [*Hesitates*] they have a certain kind of old-fashioned flavor of their own, which is very distinct. You recognize Constance Garnett's translations at once, and the same is true with Lowe-Porter's translations of Thomas Mann. And somehow this is in a way that's desirable, I mean that gives a [*Stressing*] distinct English style to these books. These translations, they should be good — whatever that means — but also remember Benjamin's essay on translation.[5] He says, [*Impersonates Benjamin*] "Look, you don't want it to be simply switching words from one language into another. What you want is that it [*Whispers*] does something to your native language into which the work is translated." A good translation must ensure that the language is not colloquial; that it is not really natural, but it does some violence... [*Quietly*: we're talking about English now] that it does some violence to English and somehow another language, another kind of English language appears. [*Softly.*] And Lowe-Porter does that, and it's both strange and wonderful. Anyway, as you'll see, it's a remarkable novel which, like Proust, you need a while to get into, but once you're in... [*Pause.*] People would now say that The Magic Mountain was supposed to be the greatest of Thomas Mann's books... [*Quietly*: that's how he got the Nobel prize and so on, and indeed, it is very remarkable novel] but I think now maybe people feel that this one is the, hmm... [*Hesitates*] this is his greatest book. I don't know whether people still read The Magic Mou... [*Achoo. Sneeze in the audience.*] The Magic Mountain is post-World War One, and many debates in Doctor Faustus — one may call them "Cold War debates," in a way — are also not any longer so relevant, hmm... [*Hesitates*] or contemporary, or maybe they are... [*Quietly*: not that the devil is particularly contemporary either.] [*Chuckles.*]

[*Long pause.*]

Anyway, okay. So now today we gonna also switch gears to, hmm... [*Hesitates*] to Heidegger. But first, I wanna make a...

[*Quietly*: that's why I brought up Doctor Faustus and the issue of translation anyway] I wanna make a little... [*Floor creaking*] connection with the beginning of chapter six, and this thing on "appearance" in Adorno.[6] Because I want you to see that there is a bit in Thomas Mann which deals with appearance more sharply, and to give you an idea of both what Adorno means and then how Thomas Mann borrowed all of these ideas... [*Quietly*: not from Aesthetic Theory, of course, which was written in the 1960s, but from some earlier manuscript that he used] borrows it and turns it into his own narrative. It's a very interesting kind of process.

[*Long pause*.]

Anyway, the point about appearance... [*Mumbles indistinctly*.] How... [*Addresses student*.] How much time would you need for your presentation on Heidegger?

STUDENT: Fifteen...

JAMESON: Uh-huh? How much?

STUDENT: Fifteen minutes.

JAMESON: Fifteen minutes, hmm... [*Quietly:* well, we may need more than that] but let me just... [*Pause*.] It'll take me just a few... [*Mumbles indistinctly*.]

[*Long pause*.]

The point about it is that "appearance" is not enough of a word for Schein. [*Exhales deeply*.] Schein is the whole, hmm... [*Hesitates*] ah... [*Looks for words*] hmm, and... ah... [*To himself:* hmm, what was that word I was gonna use?] Mm-hmm. Ah, Schein involves an [*Stressing*] experience, insofar as you experience the appearance of the work of art. And when we're dealing with music, but also with literature, this experience is temporal. That is to say, there has to be a web of temporal being in this experience to give you the density you need for it to be... [*Pause*] for one to compare it to... [*Pause*] for one to [*Stressing*] feel that it is a full kind of object. Schein, or appearance, as they translated it here[7]... [*Chalk on the blackboard*] A-P-P-E-A-R-A-N-C-E. [*Quietly*.] I think they should stick this word in parenthesis whenever they use it in order to remind you that it is more than that. Schein is the real of the work of art. [*Pause.*] It's what makes up the reality of the experience of the work, or the aesthetics. Now, what Adorno is talking about here is [*Softly*] the crisis of appearance... [*Quietly*: the crisis of Schein.] And this crisis takes all kinds of forms, but among other things... [*Quietly*: we'll talk about the truth of the artworks later on, and about aesthetic nominalism] but mainly, it takes a temporal form. That is, we're going from ordinary life into the closure of another temporal continuum, which is that of the work of art. I don't care whether you're reading a novel, or you are listening to music, or you are looking at a painting, whatever it is... [*Pause.*] You have to enter that other time, which is the work of art. Now, what would be suspicious about that? [*Pause.*] Why should that go into crisis? This is the big question. And for Adorno, modern art as such can only be understood in reaction, or as a reaction to, this crisis. Modernism is a reaction to the crisis of Schein. Because the crisis, hmm... [*Hesitates*] finally affects the very fact of art itself. Art without what's been called here "appearance" or Schein, or whatever else you wanna call it,[8] is nothing. It's only an empty mark, it's completely hollow, it's like looking at some notes, I mean, nothing is happening. This has to be a substitute world, for the kind of density that allows you to go into it and feel it somehow. So, if that's under, hmm... [*Hesitates*] under threat, what would the experience of the work be? And of course, the analogy to aura is part of this, and that's a very important theme of this chapter... [*Quietly*: chapter six, because, mm-hmm... (*Raps his knuckles on the desk*) well, we'll come back to that.]

[*Long pause.*]

Now, mm-hmm. [*Footsteps.*] Can we then talk about appearance in relation to meaning? [*Pause.*] That is to say, the idea is that there is something immanent in the work, something that means something, there is a coherence to it, which is meaningful. Well, just as appearance and your experience is threatened so, little by little, meaning itself is also threatened. [*Pause.*] And then we come to what's the opposite of time and of meaning... [*Quietly:* and what's the opposite of this? Well, silence is the opposite of meaning, right?] The meaningless is the cancelation of meaning and so on and so forth. So, you can see how we're moving from the crisis of appearance to what, in shorthand, we can just call "Beckett." [*Pause.*] Right? And we will look at Beckett after Thomas Mann, because Thomas Mann somehow only registers this crisis and then — it seems to me, if we're doing an Adornian history of all of this — Beckett somehow then doesn't just register, but really invents another solution to which is not exactly the one we'll get here.

[*Long pause.*]

Okay, now there is a guilt involved in this crisis, and this guilt, as you'll see — or maybe I'll read that passage first — you'll see what that comes from. Mm-hmm... [*Page flipping. Talks to himself.*] Well, let me now read you the section in Thomas Mann which has to do with this crisis. This is the great central chapter which, like Dostoevsky, involves the dialogue with the devil... [*Quietly*: mark the moment of temptation because that's already happened, but it is the moment when the devil appears to Adrian. And the devil takes, as you see, several forms; he changes form, and it has been suggested that the central form in the dialogue is Adorno.] Mm-hmm, Adorno neither affirmed nor denied this, hmm... [*Hesitates*] and in fact, we have here a nice reply to an earlier impersonation of this kind, and this is the character of the Jesuit communist Naphta in <u>The Magic Mountain</u>, who was supposed to have been physically modeled on Lukács... [*Quietly*: because the arguments draw a lot on Lukács, actually, so Lukács was the Adorno of <u>The Magic Mountain</u> and Adorno was the Lukács of <u>Doctor Faustus</u>.] So, they asked Lukács whether he recognized himself in <u>The Magic Mountain</u>. Well, he said, [*Impersonates Lukács*] "At least Thomas Mann gave me well-cleaned and ironed trousers." [*Chuckles.*] Mm-hmm... [*Quietly*: because he looked like a vagrant wandering around in old clothes and so on and so forth (*Chuckles continue*).] So, presumably, Adorno said something similar. This is all written in a kind of old German or medieval German... [*Quietly*: which, as I said, the translator has managed to render, and which remains quite remarkable.] Anyway, this is what the devil, hmm, says... [*Page flipping*] explaining music to Adrian who was already a composer:

> Why should I not find some pleasure in the sickness which has attacked the idea of the musical work? Don't blame it on social conditions. I am aware you tend to do so, and are in the habit of saying that these conditions produce nothing fixed and stable enough to guarantee the harmony of the self-sufficient work. [*Quietly*: here he brings in the autonomous work of art, of course.] True, but unimportant. The prohibitive difficulties of the work lie deep in the work itself. The historical movement of the musical material has turned against the self-contained [autonomous] work. [*Quietly:* Now you'll begin to recognize some of these themes as we also find them in Adorno.] [*Continues reading*] It shrinks in time, it scorns extension in time, which is the dimensions of a musical work, and lets it stand empty. Not out of impotence, not out of incapacity to give form. Rather from a ruthless demand for compression, which taboos the superfluous, negates the phrase, shatters the ornament... [*Quietly*: Adolf Loos and "Ornament as Crime"] stands opposed to any extension of time, which is the life-form of the work. Work, time, and pretence... [*Quietly*: but that's Schein, appearance, which Lowe-Porter translated as "pretence."] Work, time, and [Schein], they are one, and together they fall victim to critique. It no longer tolerates [Schein] and play, the [*Stressing*] fiction, the self-glorification of form, which censors the passions and human suffering, divides out the parts, translates into pictures. Only the non-fictional is still permissible, the unplayed, the undisguised and untransfigured expression of suffering in its actual moment. Its impotence and extremity are so ingrained that no seeming play with them is any longer allowed.

[*Softly*: Then Adrian's remarks:]

> Touching, touching! The devil waxes pathetic. The poor devil moralizes. Human suffering goes to his heart. How high-mindedly he shits on art! You would have done better not to mention your antipathy to the work if you did not want me to realize that your animadversions are naught but divel-farting.[9]

[*Audience laughing.*] Anyway, this is very much what Adorno has in mind here by the crisis of the work of art. The appearance of the work is a matter of guilt because it's fiction. Outside the artwork, there is suffering, and this is inexpressible.... [*Quietly*: I mean, obviously Thomas Mann wrote this after Auschwitz, although this is taking place in the 1920s. But after the First World War, that was suffering too, but of a different kind... (*Mumbles indistinctly*).] So, you have genuine suffering about which there is already a problem of expression. Mm-hmm, too fu... [*Pause.*] It's sort of futile to address all that... [*Words indistinct.*] But this is sort of a new version of the famous objection to art, that it is all, hmm... [*Hesitates*] the... the... that art is the pastime of the privileged classes, of those who can afford to engage in this, at a time when poor people suffer. You can see this kind of objection to the frivolity of works of art and culture, and in poetry, and in the excesses of other arts. But here, this crisis is something that is somehow picked up by the very raw material of the work. The very process of extending art in time, of repeating phrases, of building up affects, of, hmm... [*Hesitates*] all of this is no longer tolerable. It's not externally or socially imposed, but pertains to the internal logic of the work. We don't want that fiction; we don't want that kind of leisurely elaboration of time — we want something else. So, as you'll see, next time, there is this tremendous... [*Pause.*] I think that there are actually two solutions to this crisis, that is to say, one is the tremendous extension in time, and that you get in Mahler, and indeed in Thomas Mann, who says... [*Quietly*: in the preface to The Magic Mountain, I think, hmm... (*Hesitates*) it's a phrase I always liked] "only the exhaustive is truly interesting."[10] You see this in The Magic Mountain, which is the story of a vacation that was to have lasted seven days and it ends up lasting seven years. And the novel is describing slow time in very detailed accounts in this tuberculosis sanatorium, which is also a mirror of the European society... [*Pause.*] So, that's another response to this extension of art in time; it is the Proustian response... [*Quietly*: you know, you make it... (*Pause*)] you expand it to infinity and then you never finish it, like Musil.

[*Long pause.*]

But the other one is the absolute compression of time. So, what happens then to the work? You don't have... [*Quietly*: we'll look at this some more] but instead of having an extended representation of something, like feelings and sufferings, you only have one sort of outburst, and which is reduced to nothing, but that... [*Door slams shut.*] And this could be the cry, or the shock. But with the cry and pain in art, hmm... [*Hesitates*] how do you tell that from real life? I mean, how's that reconcilable with art? It's a very much a period objection... [*To himself*: where is this thing?] hmm, which is also discussed in this chapter — the way in which these things become, as he says, Adorno, sort of like electrocardiographs of shock... [*Quietly*: shock in old Baudelairean and Benjaminian notion.][11] But the way you express shock is not to elaborate it and lead people up to it or to represent it, [*Softly*] but you just give it to them like that, and all you have is just the experience of shock. But then, is this just a document of psychosis or something, or neurosis? What is artistic about this anymore? That's the problem. [*Long silence.*] That's essential... [*Zipper unzipping*] the problem that is in this crisis of appearance. And although the devil tells us he doesn't want social explanation, in effect he gives us one. [*Softly.*] We can't tolerate fiction anymore, we feel guilty — we don't want that. And all you have to do is to think first of the nonfiction novel and now... [*Quietly*: what is it they call this thing on television] reality television. I mean, you have there in reality television, hmm... [*Hesitates*] a beautiful dialectical development of the crisis of Schein, of people who can't come to have the patience to read novels... [*Quietly*:

if we want to put it this way] or people who think that novels are not a worthy occupation. There have been many moments in the history of the novel, in particular in the feudal period, when the novel was thought to be this very low-class occupation, because the greatest thing was poetry, of course; I mean, you read a sonnet, but you don't mess around with novels... (*Door slams shut*) Quixote was the moment of some kind of transition there.] But here again with all of this: does it produce a realism, or does it simply produce...? [*Pause.*] Like TV shows with cops, where the camera simply goes around to record real life, and then we somehow consume it as we once used to consume fiction. But the fiction is no longer satisfying. That isn't only... [*Pause.*] I don't think that's only a... [*Pause.*] The other side of this would be some kind of sadism and delight in violence and such things, but it seems to me that this is a fair way to talk about this crisis of appearance, fiction, Schein, using examples from our contemporary popular culture.

[*Long pause.*]

Anyway, you will see this for yourself when you start reading Doctor Faustus. So now... [*Slams his palm on the desk*] we'll pass on to a very different cup of tea, Heidegger, who is not writing this in [*Stressing*] that period of the 1920s, but rather in the 1930s. [*Addresses student.*] Matthew, you can go ahead! [*Loud. Chair scratching against the floor. Footsteps.*]

Student Presentation: Heidegger, "The Origin of the Work of Art"

STUDENT ONE: That's not going to... [*Student starts reading his presentation on Heidegger's "The Origin of the Work of Art."*] What, for Heidegger, does it mean to theorize aesthetics? In the epilogue to his essay, "The Origin of the Work of Art," which was first published in 1950 in German, based on a lecture delivered in 1935 and 1936, he is critical of the field of aesthetic inquiry. Reading aesthetics or aisthesis as another technology, a technology of the subject. I quote from the Epilogue [*Page* *flipping*.] "Almost from the time when specialized thinking about art and the artist began, this thought was called aesthetic. Aesthetics takes the work of art as an object, the object of aisthesis, of sensuous apprehension in the wild sense. Today we call this apprehension experience."[12] [*Pause*.] The way in which man experiences art is supposed to give information about his nature. Experience is the source and the standard not only for art appreciation and enjoyment, but also for artistic creation. Everything is an experience. And perhaps experience is the element which art does. [*Pause*.] This subjective technological apprehension of the work of art marks, for Heidegger, the logic of Western metaphysics, and specifically an empirical notion of "truth." In this case, truth manifests its judgment at work "assigned to cognition and science as a quality in order to distinguish from it the beautiful and the good, which function as names for the values of nontheoretical activities."[13] In Heidegger's project against metaphysics, this notion of aesthetics is problematic and unsatisfactory. It merely rehearses metaphysics and fails to grant its access to the truth of the work of art or with its origin and definition of art itself. Rather, this reading suggests that art dies when it becomes equated for subjective experience... [*Chair leg scrapes the floor*.] That art stands in a very different relationship to the subject, that as the self-sovereign subject performs the genius and it suggests something living in art, something active that stands apart from the subject, but not merely as object. [*Pause*.] This is where Heidegger begins negotiating this subject-object problem, which he opens by interrogating the circular logic of the origin of the work of art as it is commonly understood: as a set of relationships between the artist and the work, and then the work itself and the very nature of art. [*Quietly*: And I'm gonna read this.] "The artist is the origin of the work. The work is the origin of the artist. Neither is without the other."[14] Although this should be inferred from the work, but the work of art must be derived only from the nature of art. [*Explains*.] The fact that the artist is the maker of the work, and the work has its origin in the artist — everyone can easily see here that we are moving in a circle. In this hermeneutic circle that Heidegger enables, and in the course of this investigation according to the circle, is a departure from the ordinary understanding which demands that this circle be avoided because it violates logic. The question then becomes not how to avoid such logic, but rather… [*Cough in the audience*] how to interrogate it successfully, how to disrupt the circularity of the argument.

[*Long pause*.]

His way in is with his analysis of the thingly element in the work of art. All works of art are things of some sort… [*Door slam in the distance*] where "thingly" is here used to designate what we might call "materiality," the raw materials of the works. According to Heidegger, this "thingly" character is self-evident. There is, however, something else that contributes to the work of art, something that is not exactly a thing. This opens to the analysis of the being of the thing, and in a section entitled "The Thing and the Work," Heidegger leads us to several possible and competing definitions of what it means to be or describe a thing. In a first example, we understand a thing is something around which its properties have assembled. This is a stabilized notion of thingness, represented of Western tradition… [*Page flipping*] and it is here that Heidegger invokes the translation from Greek into Latin and the impulse of such an understanding — hardly the innocent process as it is considered to this day. [*Page flipping*.] What is evident in this description is the extent to which this understanding endures specifically at the level of grammar. [*Quietly*: And I quote here]: "No wonder that the current attitude toward things — our way of addressing ourselves to things and speaking about them — has adapted itself to the common view of the thing. A simple propositional statement consists of the subject […] and the predicate, in which the thing's traits are stated of it."[15] So we read that the subject describing the thing assigns traits to it. The root of this divide takes place not only at the level of language, in terms of the sentence structure and again to matters of translating

Greek into Latin, but in the division between subject and object as it is understood as the thing's structure. What is at work here, according to Heidegger, is a forgetting of the source when these two qualitative understandings are derived. [*Pause.*] If we were to begin to remember, then to realize that the propositional way of understanding... [*Achoo. Sneeze in the audience*] denies us the ability to lay hold of the things as it is in their own being, we might take account that something is freed up when we grasp the thing, as it were, and free feel to display its "thingly" character directly. This is the next possible definition of the thing, or "thingly," where the situation always informs our sensual perception. Again, to quote: "The thing is the aistheton, that which is perceptible by sensations in the senses [...] Hence the concept later becomes a commonplace according to which a thing is nothing but the unity of a manifold of what is given in the senses."[16] This is too subjective for Heidegger, too close to us, pressing too hard upon us, even if the propositional definition is too stable and colonizing the notion, whenever at arm's length. The thing itself rather must have some constancy; it must be accepted in its own constancy. The traits of the thing, then, are derived directly from its matter, which, according to its need for constancy in the analysis, corresponds directly to its form. [*Page flipping.*] Form is imposed upon them. This distinction informs the conceptual schema for all of our steps. It seems so common and so obvious, which leads one to question why Heidegger waits so long before he introduces this. But coming to this distinction serves the purpose. It's because the distinction in the corresponding analytics is so enduring, especially when coupled with the subject-object and rational-irrational oppositions. This is form occurring in matter — thingness as form-matter. [*Pause.*] To know these definitions of things is inadequate for Heidegger. The latter, however, opens to further analysis after considering the form-matter distinction, which concerns usefulness or equipment. [*Explains*: It becomes an assault upon the thing, he turns this critique of the third notion of thingness.] And he goes as far as to say:

> The self-contained bloc of granite is something material and indefinite on its shapely form. Form means here the distribution and arrangement of the material parts in spatial locations, resulting in a particular shape, namely that of a block. But a jug, an ax, a shoe are also matter occurring in a form. Form as shape is not the consequence here of a prior distribution of the matter. The form, on the contrary, determines the arrangement of the matter. Even more, it prescribes in each case the kind and selection of the matter impermeable for a jug, sufficiently hard for an ax, firm and... [*Excuse me*] firm yet flexible for shoes.[17]

[*Explains*: So, he's turned it around, and this introduces "usefulness" or "equipmental being" into our discussion.] Thingness here is defined by use, or usefulness mediates between thing and work. A "...piece of equipment is half thing [...] and; at the same time, it is half art work and yet something less, because lacking the self-sufficiency of the art work."[18] And Heidegger develops this through a reading of a painting by Van Gogh. If the character of equipment is to be discovered through usefulness, it's the use of the shoes in the painting that's important...

JAMESON: You've all probably seen this painting that, it's a... [*Pause.*] It's a, hmm... [*Hesitates.*] It's a... [*Pause.*] Are you going to describe it? It's a... [*Pause.*] What do you call that kind of chair... [*Tries to remember*] in his bedroom? Hmm... [*Hesitates.*] What's that kind of material that the chair was made of? In any case, you have this chair on which two... [*Quietly:* well, there are several versions of this painting] but you have two peasant shoes on a chair. Okay, go on.

STUDENT ONE: [*Continues reading.*] If the characters... [*Quietly*: I should have brought a picture.] If the character of equipment is to be established through usefulness, is the use of these shoes... [*Cough in the audience*] that appears in the work. The being of equipment is organized around this notion of use, which Heidegger translates into reliability, which in turn unites the terms of work and world, and the equipmental being of peasant woman... [*Quietly*: and I'm gonna bracket "peasant woman" for a second.]

JAMESON: [*Shows to the audience a reproduction of Van Gogh's painting* A Pair of Shoes, *1886.*] Here, you can look at... [*Mumbles indistinctly. Students laughing.*]

STUDENT ONE: [*Continues reading.*] Okay, I just look at the language here, which speaks of class and toil... [*Pause.*] And this is him reconstructing the... [*Pen drops on the floor*] painting.

[*Page flipping.*]

> From the dark opening of the worn insides of the shoes, the toilsome tread of the worker stares forth. In the stiffly, rugged heaviness of the shoes, there is the accumulated tenacity of her slow trudge through the far-spreading and ever-uniform furrows of the field swept by a raw wind. On the leather lie the dampness and richness of the soil. Under the soles slides the loneliness of the field-path as evening falls. In the shoes vibrates the silent call of the earth, its quiet gift of the ripening grain and its unexplained self-refusal in the fallow desolation of the wintry field. This equipment is pervaded by uncomplaining anxiety as to the certainty of bread, the wordless joy of having once more withstood want, and trembling before the impending childbed and shivering at the surrounding menace of death. [...] But perhaps it is only in the picture that we notice all this about the shoes. The peasant woman, on the other hand, simply wears them. If only this simple wearing were so simple. When she takes off her shoes late in the evening, in deep but healthy fatigue, and reaches out for them again in the still dim dawn, or passes them by on the day of rest, she knows all this without noticing or reflecting.[19]

[*Explains quietly*: he ties into this notion of use, and when something is in use or at hand, it becomes less conspicuous, but you see how he reconstructs that from the artwork... (*Words indistinct*).] What is immediately important is, in terms of inclusion, Heidegger draws from the readings of this work of art. "The equipmental quality of equipment was discovered." Then he asks: "But how? Not by a description and explanation of a pair of shoes actually present; not by a report about the process of making shoes; and also, not by the observation of the actual use of shoes occurring here and there; but only by bringing ourselves before Van Gogh's painting. This painting spoke."[20] Something is set to work in a work of art and Heidegger names it... [*Chair-back creaks*] as truth, but then he comes back and names it [*Stressing*] explicitly as "truth" later. And his truth is aletheia — the Greek unconcealing of beings, the truth of being setting itself to work of art.

[*Long pause.*]

This is a departure for Heidegger, and from aesthetics as it has been understood. And then he says, "until now art presumably has had to do with the beautiful and beauty, and not with truth. The arts that produce such works are called the beautiful or fine arts, in contrast with the applied or industrial arts that manufacture equipment."[21] The "Origin of the Work of Art" here marks a shift, where art has to do specifically and explicitly with truth. This truth does not rise from art's mimesis, grants things are reproduced, but rather, it is a reproduction of the things' general essence. [*Quietly*: And this is a point he actually begins invoking this notion of "essence."] This gives Heidegger an aspect of the basic assumption of the thing, particularly in relation to the work of art, that it belongs to a substructure. [*Explains*: And this again, he begins again to talk about general assumption and common understanding of the work of art, not just as a form or matter, but as a substructure as something built on that.] The work of art, for him, cannot belong as such, because this "thingly substructure" as science characterize equipment. But the artwork is not a piece of equipment, but it's rather truth itself setting itself to work.

[*Long pause.*]

To this point in the text, Heidegger is willingly performed a failure — the failure of an adequate analysis of the character of art, according to the traditional aesthetic problematic. What follows in the text is a detailed analysis of the work of art according to the terms introduced in the... [*Words indistinct*] where the artwork sets itself to work and where artists' truth is setting itself to work. What is used to be explored is the origins as process. This activity having established the steps of artworks unreserved — hanging in collections or exhibitions or resting on shelves as objects of the art industry — and also having established the status of art-historical science, as rendering the artworks as calculable materials, objects of a science, what needs to be thought is the encounter of the work of art itself. [*Pause*.] The encounter is a phase in taking the artwork from its own world. But even if the artwork remains preserved, never leaving its place and material origin, the world of the artwork perishes. We must take the world as an effort to read the question of origin, but first we think world as something akin to situation... [*Quietly*: but sort of a situation outside of materiality.] Moreover, "World-withdrawal and world-decay can never be undone." This is a statement he makes. "The works are no longer the same as they once were. It is they themselves, to be sure, that we encounter there, but they themselves are gone by."[22] What we perceive in this is the object of being not the work... [*Page flipping*.] This is related to the notion of historicity in Heidegger, one that is also linked to the question of origin. We have this, the origin of the work of art, that is the origin in both the creators and its preservers, that is to say, of the people's historical existence as art. This is to say that art is, by nature, an origin; a distinctive way in which truth comes into being that it becomes historical, returning to the notion of world as moral decay. We understand world here as an open relational context... [*Explains*: and if I'm correctly reading the historical context... (*Words indistinct*).] "The Greeks," he says, "early called this emerging and rising in itself and in all things phusis. It clears and illuminates, also, that on which and in which man bases his dwelling."[23] [*Explains*: so, if we want to think dwelling as in relation to, but I'm reluctant to say "opposed" to world.] "We call this ground the earth."[24] As Heidegger develops this relationship between earth and world, the latter [*Stressing*] world opens to and clears the former, illuminating part of it, unconcealing it, according to the notion of truth as aletheia — a notion of truth as process, or art set to work. Earth is the act of refusal shattering "...every attempt to penetrate into it."[25] These are not opposites uninterested in one another, but rather are intimately related through strife. [*Explains*: I do not necessarily know that the work would correspond to the ideas of, say, oppositions like ideology or materiality respectively, I don't know if it's global versus local; it's difficult to think the relationship, but the opposition you can think in terms of holding and opening, where the earth sheltering and concealing always draws the world into itself in order to keep it there.] The world rather is an attempt to overcome the earth. This is conflict of clearing and concealing, but the work in relation to this strife does hold open the world as it is grounded in the earth, it clears it, it provides a space for beings that... [*Choo-choo. Amtrak train in the distance*] kind of truth, according to aletheia, that be known. And then we ask how truth happens to receive an answer to this primal conflict, truth happens is the work-being of the work. "Setting up a world and setting forth the earth, the work... [*Page flipping*] is the fighting of the battle in which the unconcealedness of beings as a whole, or truth, is won."[26] [*Explains*: so, the work is situated in this rift between this conflict between the world and earth... *Choo-choo. Amtrak train approaching.*] The work is then located in this rift between world and earth, but this is not to totally discount the role of the artist. On the contrary, having established in part the nature of the work of art in the happening of truth, what now needs to be interrogated by Heidegger is the mere process of creation. Work is not equipment, as we have seen. The difference is that bringing forth works of art is a matter of creation, while the bringing forth of equipment is a matter of making. The latter manifests as handicraft, and although Heidegger is vague and elusive in this section in particular, regarding the crisis in terms of handicraft. [*Explains*: he says that creation comes out of handicraft, but at this point, it is difficult to follow precisely where handicraft ends and creation keeps going, and where is the departure.] But nevertheless, we reach a point in which creation is now attributed to clearing, but also to the establishment... [*Door slams shut*] of some truth, setting forth in that opening. This is not actually exactly a form of making, but rather a form of knowing, for example, of phusis, the open relational context. The nature of the work as creation is known through the journey of work into the world, the latter can mean an attempt to overcome what the earth offers as a refusal. The rift is where art is located and it is also in this conflict between the terms of world and earth that the nature of art in fact reveals itself as a work as a process, unconcealed itself in the opening, it has itself created. Art is, for Heidegger, the becoming and happening of the truth.

[*Long pause.*]

Returning to the opening question, what it means for Heidegger to theorize aesthetics, there is a great deal at stake. The aesthetic tradition until Heidegger, at least as he frames it, as he takes it, is the disinterested humanist technology. An industrial man rests on assumption that disable his ontological thing. For him, beauty in the work, as it is truth at work, is the illumination of the self-concealed being. This unconcealedness, and to end with a quote from him: "Light of this kind joins its shining to and into the work. This shining, joined in the work, is the beautiful. Beauty is one way in which truth occurs as unconcealedness."[27]

STUDENT ONE: Thank you.

[*Applause.*]

JAMESON: I mean, der Schein, scheinen, Erscheinen and all that is part of this complex, which is translated in Adorno as aesthetic appearance or semblance. Mm-hmm. Questions. How many people read this essay...? [*Raps his knuckles on the desk.*]

[*Audience murmuring. Chuckles.*]

JAMESON: Okay.

STUDENT TWO: I sort of... [*Words indistinct.*] I wonder if you could say a bit more about what Heidegger is saying here about art in terms of revealing, unconcealedness or disturbance of...? [*Cough in the audience.*] How can this be understood in light of other forms of modernist thinking, like defamiliarization...?

STUDENT ONE: [*Long silence.*] My own take on this... [*Quietly*: I can't speak for other forms of modernist thinking] is that, for him, art is a mode of revealing the world and the truth about the world. It is not just representation or imitation of reality, or expression, as in the most common understanding of art. Art reveals the truth of being, it disrupts the everyday perception of the world, like in his example with Van Gogh's Shoes, which sort of reveals another world beyond the simple utility of these shoes; the painting is a kind of disturbance of everyday reality, because it shows something about the world, like the bitterness of hard peasant labor. That's... [*Door slams shut*] how I understood it, as a challenge of representation, but turning to the present... [*Words indistinct.*]

[*Long pause.*]

JAMESON: Well, that was very informative... [*Pause.*] I appreciate that. Mm-hmm. I would say that this is a very interesting question about defamiliarization because... [*Pause.*] You know, Heidegger was not a modernist, particularly... [*Quietly*: Van Gogh is as far as he gets, I think, in modernism; I don't know what he thought of music, but I think he quite disliked Wagner, which, for a Nazi, this is very strange (*Chuckles*).] Well, you know Hitler's people didn't like Wagner's either... [*Chair scraping the floor.*] There is a new book on culture in Nazi Germany and there is an episode where Hitler is opening a new museum in, hmm... [*Hesitates*] I don't remember where. And at that opening, there were various museum and culture people, and then the author says, "you notice that there are no Nazi party members present, as Hitler considered them culturally challenged."[28]

[*Chuckles.*]

Anyway, I would say rather... [*Cough in the audience*] that this essay is an effort to make defamiliarization into an ontological matter. [*Pause.*] And, in fact, what this translation calls "unconcealment," I would translate as [*Stressing*] deconcealment, because it seems to me it is an event. It's a moment when... [*Quietly*: you have similar things in Sartre as revealing and unveiling] but this term here has an ontological vein, that is — it does something to open up Being. So, I think if you could isolate... [*Pause*.] For the formalists, all radical art involves an act of defamiliarization.[29] But if you could isolate only those words in which you could make defamiliarization by getting rid of habits, getting rid of the humdrum sort of relationship to things, into this experience of the opening of beings, then you could connect to the truth of Being. Whereas the way defamiliarization is used with Brecht, it is more political, and for the formalists, it is more from an artistic standpoint... [*Quietly*: like a constructivist position.] But here with Heidegger, we have defamiliarization, or deconcealment, from an [*Stressing*] <u>ontological</u> perspective. And I think that is what is meant in the difference between ontic and ontological because, all of a sudden, you're among things all the time... [*Quietly*: I'm talking about philosophy, mm-hmm, general philosophy, not aesthetics.] You are among things all the time; you have these habits, which the proponents of defamiliarization wanted to explain in aesthetic terms, and then, all of a sudden, there is this clearing... [*Quietly*: <u>Lichtung</u>.] There is a space of disclosure of Being, where the truth of Being is made manifest — an opening that allows you to see things in a different light, and this is this moment of deconcealment. Suddenly, you realize that everything [*Whispers*] <u>is</u>. This is then the moment of the revelation of Being. And I think this disclosure comes and goes in Heidegger. In Sartre, of course, it's also, hmm... [*Hesitates*] it's also Being, but for him this is nausea. [*Softly*.] In Sartre, there is a very different relation to nature than in Heidegger. In Heidegger, I would say even the definition of being is as... [*Tapping his thumb on the desk*] — what's both there all the time and not there all the time... [*Quietly*: so, in that sense, it can be located and... (*Mumbles indistinctly*).] But this has to be an experience.

[*Long pause*.]

Now, what we have here, this is one of the early works after the so-called... [*Chalk on the blackboard*] K-E-H-R-E. The word means "turn," Kehre, but in Heidegger studies, this word is used for the alleged great moment of transformation of Heidegger's philosophy, hmm... [*Hesitates*] and that's when he ceases to be an existentialist. What do existentialists usually talk about: despair, death, freedom, choice, angst, anxiety... [*Quietly*: you know, all those awful things, like authenticity and the self.] He ceases to talk about that, he ceases to interrogate the [*Stressing*] subjective in human reality, and in Heidegger's German, that is called... [*Chalk on the blackboard*] D-A-S-E-I-N. Suddenly, we get a movement towards the so-called "being-there" and human beings situated in a particular time and place... [*Quietly*: but even this gets to be too subjective, too Cartesian, Western and so forth, starting out from the individual consciousness] and we get this new move all the way back to pre-Socratic philosophy. Mm-hmm, that is to say, forget about consciousness — now we're talking about Being itself. So, the Kehre is this move from an existential philosophy to a philosophy of Being. Now, there are some very nasty, hmm... [*Hesitates*] analyses of this Kehre, which takes place, to be sure, after he steps down as rector of the University of Frankfurt and... [*Chair screeching across the floor*] an active Nazi... [*Door slams shut.*] That was his moment of political engagement. Both Habermas, briefly, but Bourdieu in a far more extended analysis, called The Political Ontology of Martin Heidegger — a book that I admire... [*Quietly*: except that, as with Bourdieu, it's unremittingly hostile, but that's okay, you don't have to adopt that side of it.][30] And their point is that what Heidegger was trying to do was an operation... [*Quietly*: I mean, in Bourdieu, it's always about your profession right.] How I'm gonna carve a place for myself that is not anybody else's; we have a crisis of the profession; all that has been done, all that has been done, how can I make a special place for myself? [*Pause.*] Well, in Heidegger, you do it — says Bourdieu, and Habermas in another way... [*Student blows nose into tissue*] — by adopting a language of being which sort of effaces all kinds of inherited philosophical problems, at the same time that it purports to solve them. So, you heard about in the beginning of this essay — it has to do with form and matter, the subject-object relationship and so on and so forth. These are the traditional problems of philosophy. [*Exhales deeply*.] What Heidegger wants to do is to get rid of those, to mark them as "bad" Western metaphysics... [*Quietly*: you see the Derrida connection here] but also to overcome them, in a sense, and solve them and replace them all at once. And the language of Being, and the event, will be a replacement for these bad Western dualisms. And these dualisms are called — those "subject-object," "form-matter," and all the rest of it — are called in Heidegger [*Stresses*] representation. [*Long silence*.] What happens in the West, with the fall... [*Quietly*: when is the "fall," that's always the question] probably one of them is with Socrates, as with Nietzsche, another one is with Descartes, and so forth, but all of the falls are falls of the Western metaphysics into the subject-object problem. [*Pause*.] And the reason this is representation is because, hmm... [*Hesitates*] that's a relation of the subject to object, right? To handle the object, you gotta somehow represent it somehow, that's what that is. Is Adorno's mimesis another attempt to get around that? Mimesis is not exactly Heideggerian representation; anyway, that's another topic.

[*Long pause*.]

Okay, so, mm-hmm... [*Pause*.] Heidegger then invents this new language of Being, with all of the various word plays... [*Addresses Student One*.] Did you quote the "world worlds," I mean, Welt weltet?

STUDENT ONE: No.

JAMESON: What you do is you take the noun "world," and you make a verb out of it. And what does the "world" do? It makes... [*Door slams shut*] it brings the world into being, it points to the process of [*Stressing*] worlding, or self-manifestation and self-concealment of the world, and it is not anymore a passive but an active process... [*Quietly*: and there is a lot of language like that in Heidegger.] Now, what Bourdieu and Habermas say is: this is very convenient in the mid-1930s. If you wanted to put yourself on the... [*Pause.*] If you wanted to carve your own space and place, you squash all the other philosophers and make your own philosophy. But at the same time, it means that your political responsibilities become absolutely unclear. Why are you talking about "the call of conscience," and the "being-towards-death" — and I think his militarism is pretty tangibly present, right... [*Quietly*: this is the experience of World War One, and the trenches and the hope for a sacrifice, and all of these demands its own language because he spoke about "sacrifice" and his own experience as a soldier, who was cast in the First World War, and so on.] The minute you turn that into this evocation of Being, politics, the battlefield, militarism, Hitler, none of those things are present anymore, right? So, this is a very nice way of weaseling out of your political guilt or something. I think there is some truth in this; this is exactly what it does, but it also does a lot of other things, so I wouldn't necessarily wish to abandon it. Of course, Adorno takes a very dim view of these ideas and of Heidegger in general.

[*Long pause.*]

Okay, so "The Origin of the Work of Art" comes in this period of shift that occurs in the mid-1930s, and I think it's the most substantial presentation of Heidegger's themes. It's a little bit like Adorno's Aesthetic Theory, in that sense that you have this closed area of the aesthetic, and here is where all of these themes suddenly can come back in some interesting ways. Whereas if you haven't talked about subject-object, like God... [*Quietly*: which he does of course] then you have to take on the whole history of philosophy, and one book wouldn't be enough. But here in this closed microcosm of art and aesthetics, we can get a lot of Heidegger's late philosophy. That's why... [*Pause.*] And the essay is accessible, it's readable, and that's why this is an important text, which you should all eventually read. It is also itself a kind of event. That is to say, this is this solemnity of a lecture style that Heidegger developed, in which the whole point of this lecture is like... [*Achoo. Sneeze in the audience*] — he is taking you through this argu... [*Pause.*]

But it no longer has the feeling of philosophical argument; it has the feeling of this movem.... [*Pause*] almost musical movement in time, where you have moments in which the realities are conveyed as you say poetically when you read the passage about the shoes and so on and so forth. Then you have other things laid in place. And it really is a very special way in which the lecturer, the philosopher, is somehow [*Stressing*] leading you to truth in some way. Now, obviously... [*Pause.*] Although a lot of Adorno, especially the Notes to Literature are also oral... [*Quietly*: that is his Radio stuff] pretty obviously, that's a very different use of language. Mm-hmm. And I think Heidegger is giving you, hmm... [*Hesitates.*] He is showing you the truth in its unveiling or its appearance in deconcealment, showing you why the work of art is one of the modes of truth... [*Footsteps*] and he is laying in place a kind of language suitable for this. When Adorno talks about any of this, anything having to do with aesthetics, you see at once that he is aware that there is always a terminological problem. That any term you use — "matter," "form," "subject," "object" — has to be dealt with as... [*Door slams shut*] any possible opposition that you have to take a distance from and do some kind of metaphysical... [*Pause*] or philosophical reflection on it. So, Adorno is not so much about aesthetics as he is about the various languages in which aesthetics, the aesthetic experience of the work of art, who knows [*Stressing*] has not been able to be expressed. [*Pause.*] And his dialectic is that of a "second reflection," if you like, which then allows him to say something about art or aesthetic experience. Whereas in Heidegger... [*Pause.*] What's utopian about Heidegger is that he assumes that we can put the fallen language of Western metaphysics behind us and have this new utopian language that he invented. And when you come to the later offspring of this in deconstruction, then you're returning to a situation in which it's clear that for Derrida... [*Chair-back creaking*] you could do neologisms, and sort of break into it that way, but there is really no possibility to invent a new language... [*Quietly*: and he says that in Of Grammatology, that we may need a new language, we have to have a whole new system and a revolution of words. But he critiques the idea that it's possible to invent a new language, which would be free from the problems of existing languages. You can't ... (*Pause.*) The utopia is not possible. You would reproduce a new system with the same hierarchies and differences.] Here in Heidegger not so much. And here there is an idea that the system itself can be... [*Determined*] can be or maybe has been changed.

[*Long pause.*]

[*Addresses Student One.*] Now, what you didn't read is this important section on... [*Mumbles indistinctly.*] Mm-hmm. It is where he talks about the various ways in which truth can exist. And I think this is [*Stressing*] fundamental for understanding what Heidegger means here and why this is different from... [*Quietly*: what Adorno could possibly have thought in the West Germany, in Frankfurt, in the 1950s and 1960s, and what Derrida may be thinking today.] [*Page flipping.*] "One essential way in which truth establishes itself in the entity opened up or disclosed by it is the setting-itself-into-work of truth."[31] Alright, what that means is there is a mode of truth which is philosophy [aesthetics.][32] Okay then... "Another way in which truth exercises its being is the deed that grounds the state,"[33] and that is the political state. [*Softly.*] That's revolution. This is about origins; he doesn't not believe in origins — he thinks that truth is in origins, and that what its effect finally is, in all of these respects — is [*Stressing*] foundation. The foundation of the whole new... [*Cough in the audience*] the transformation of the world. So, the founding of the political state, of the original state, and not just somebody new coming to power... [*Quietly*: American revolution, French revolution, Russian revolution, the Nazi revolution] these are the moments of emergence of the new state. And that's a form of truth. "Still another way in which truth comes to shine forth is the nearness of that which is not simply an entity, but the entity that *is* most of all."[34] Okay, what does that mean? [*Pause.*] I think that means religion. So, while this is religious and solemn and full of all religious kinds of things...

[*Quietly:* Heidegger went to a seminary, he broke with Catholicism at the same time that the Nazis did; and Nazis were radically anti-religious and radically anti-Christian.] But this is sort of ter... [*Pause*] hmm, and... [*Hesitates*] and his philosophy is that all of these different ways of truth, enumerated by Heidegger, are distinct modes. Religion could be that one mode. It isn't all the time, philosophy could be that, and it isn't all the time, but under certain circumstances the philosophical act, the political act, the religious act — those are moments of the revelation of truth. "Still another way in which truth grounds itself is essential sacrifice."[35] Opfer. [*Softly*.] That is warfare, that's death... [*Quietly*: and that is his own experience of war... (*Mumbles indistinctly*) soaked in blood and so forth.] "Still another way in which truth becomes, is the thinker's questioning which, as thinking of being, names the latter in its question-worthiness."[36] Fragwürdigkeit, we would say "questionable," and fragwürdig is something that is worthy of being questionable. Now, maybe that's philosophy... [*Quietly*: so, what was the first one, I don't know.] The setting-itself-in-the-work of truth... [*Raps his knuckles on the desk.*] Mm-hmm, hold on... [*Agitated.*] Actually, now wait a minute...

[*Long pause.*]

Yeah, the "setting-itself-in-the-work of truth" — I'm sorry — the first thing I've read to you is aesthetics; it's the making of the work of art. This is now philosophy that is distinct from religion, politics, and art. On the other hand... [*Quietly*: and here is your reservation] science is not part of... [*Starts reading.*]

> By contrast, science is not an original happening of truth, but always the cultivation of a domain of truth already opened, specifically by apprehending and confirming that which shows itself to be possibly and necessarily correct within that field. When and insofar as a science passes beyond correctness and goes on to a truth, which means that it arrives at the essential disclosure of what is as such, it is philosophy.[37]

So, science... [*Pause*.] This is the anti-modern side of Heidegger... [*Quietly:* we want to go back to the Greeks, we don't want Galileo, that's the moment of the "fall," right?] This is his moment of the [*Stressing*] anti-modern. Science is not the revelation of Being, and not the right path. And to this will be attached his reflections on, hmm... [*Hesitates*] technology, which is another aspect of the "fall." A lot of his later writings on technology really sets out from this point. [*Cough in the audience*.] Germany is bad, modern civilization is bad, this is classical conservative... [*Quietly*: this joke from the 1920s, you know, where the masses are bad, well, in Heidegger, they are inauthentic, you know; hmm, science is bad; this is... (*Pause*).] When you strip away everything that's original about Heidegger's language, you see some very familiar pictures appear, which are... [*Quietly:* the denunciations of the modern world, of the revolt of the masses, of modern industry and the press, of workers' politics, and of everything else.] Now, the one interesting thing here... [*Pause*] — I mean, if one is interested in this anti-modern strain in Heidegger — you have several other things. [*Addresses Student One*.] Did you mention... [*Pause*] because that's very important in this essay: have you talked about "dwelling"? Well, there is a famous essay... [*Quietly*: all the architects read it nowadays] called "Building, Dwelling and..." [*Quietly:* building, dwelling and something... (*Finger snaping*).]

STUDENT ONE: And thinking...

JAMESON: Uh-huh?

STUDENT ONE: Thinking

JAMESON: Ah, yeah, "Building, Dwelling, Thinking," obviously.[38] And that's his essay on space, and in effect, on architecture. There are the technology essays, then there is a lot of stuff on poetry... [*Quietly:* Die Sprache ist das Haus des Seins.] Language is the house of Being.[39] And it is in these places that you'll find this Heidegger of Being, and finally the enormous book on Nietzsche, which is a description of how Western repre... [*Pause*] or only a part of it is a description of how Western representation, subject-object stuff, comes into being.[40]

[*Long pause.*]

Now, in all of this... [*Pause.*] Okay, so what's... [*Pause.*] What's interesting about this, I think... [*Pause.*] First of all, this is a real aesthetic, although once you get to it — and this is very characteristic of Heidegger — is that he doesn't wanna call it an "aesthetic." If you call it "aesthetics" — that's for specialists. For Heidegger, this a mode of truth. [*Pause.*] So, art... [*Chair scrapes the floor*] is a mode of truth. Mm-hmm. It is ontological, it's about Being. And I think the whole business of the... [*Addresses Student One.*] You didn't mention the... [*Pause.*] Did you mention the "rift"?

STUDENT ONE: I did.

JAMESON: Mm-hmm... [*Door slams shut.*] Rift is Riss in German, and it has all kind of complicated meanings. But when it comes to this rift, you see... [*Quietly*: one has to say these things, you know.] You mentioned in the very beginning the "fall," and for Heidegger, the first "fall" happens when the wisdom of the Greeks, that is to say, of the Greek language, falls into Latin. [*Pause.*] Latin is the language of power, of the Empire, of debasement, and so on and so forth. So, when these Greek terms are being translated into Latin, they become substance, properties, or accidents, and all the philosophical terms that we know. Well, for Heidegger, that translation is the alienation of all of the Greek relationship to Being into what's already a debased modernity. And that's why, for him, all of those words are bad. Now, hmm... [*Hesitates*] the nice thing about Greece is... [*Pause.*] You see, for him, German is like Greek, because it is one of those unmixed and uncontaminated languages. French... [*Door cracks open*] but especially English, is this mixture of French and German, you know; and French is full of Latin and Gaul and Celtic and other kinds of stuff. But German is pure. So, you get the Heideggerian Nazi-type of false etymology [*Self-corrects*] of folk etymology — you take a word and then you take it apart and find out what it was in ur-German, and then you have a relationship all the way back to before, to the Great Forest or something, right? As with Greek, the very language itself is a connection back to a mode of living in the world which the West doesn't have. You have to understand that, for Germans... [*Softly.*] Germany is not the West. The West is France and Britain... [*Quietly*: we'll see this when we get to Thomas Mann.] Mm-hmm, there is a moment in there when these... [*Quietly:* it was before the First World War, you know, when all these student movements... (*Words indistinct*) and they went out in the country and had these long philosophical discussions.] And one of the famous moments is when these German students are talking and they say [*Impersonates students*] "Well, look, you know..." [*Raps his knuckles on the desk*] "the whole point is that the French have form but not content, and the Russians have content but no form. Only we Germans have the two of these things, the profundity and the surface."[41] And this is profoundly anti-Western. And to understand Germany up until the Bundesrepublik, I think you have to understand that there is a strong relationship of inferiority... [*Door slams*] towards the West. The Germans are latecomers, they are not cultured, they, hmm... [*Hesitates*] they don't have the culture of the French; they don't have the Empire of the British; they are latecomers to machinery and industry... [*Footsteps. Door creaks open*] and this leaves them with a profound sense of inferiority. We'll... [*Pause.*] We'll talk about that, because it's very central to Thomas Mann, so we'll talk more.

[*Long pause.*]

Now, the thing about art, and about Germany, hmm... [*Hesitates.*] I assume people still read this novel, and the students also read it... [*Door slams*] despite all the historical changes. I mean, it is the great novel of the German twentieth-century situation, and you also get this situation in Heidegger. So, there is a theme of... [*Quietly*: which is sort of a reflexive theme of language and how it's only by replacement.] [*Exhales.*] Bourdieu is right, in a way — Heidegger knew that you had to replace this fallen Western kind of language with this other one... [*Loud laughter and chatter comes from the corridor*] that included this new relationship to Being. We'll come back to this next time. And the whole business of the world, I think Heidegger is absolutely right. World means history. [*Pause.*] Mm-hmm. Earth means nature. [*Pause.*] And the artwork... [*Zippers zipping up.*] And in human experience, there is always this war between nature and history. History wants to destroy nature and produce the human. Nature, in its strongest form, probably wants to get rid of people and of history and so on. And then the tension of the work is in this gap or Riss and rift, which is the holding together of world and earth or of history and nature. And that holding together allows you to see Being and, in a sense, to replace, to show the relationship of human beings to this double existence that we lead as being in history, in the human world and in nature, in the material world... [*Footsteps.*] So, this goes very far... [*Pause.*] I mean, the work itself must be this experience of this thing that brings being into deconcealment and it must also produce this being in this ori— ... hmm... [*Hesitates*] in this original act. The recovery of Being is always an origin — it is an original act by which life, and everything in the universe, begins again.

[*Long pause.*]

Anyway, mm-hmm, I think "The Origin of the Work of Art" is very useful as it gives you a sense of the real importance of Heidegger, but it also gives you a sense of how different he is... [*Chair-backs creaking*] from Adorno and Aesthetic Theory. The one with the aesthetic... [*Loud. Chair screeching the floor*] next time... [*General noise. Footsteps.*]

Audience stands up. Objects drop on the floor. Door squeaks. Students return chairs to other classrooms. Some students form a line to discuss their projects with Jameson. General noise. Screeching microphone noise.

[*Microphone turns off.*]

CURTAIN

LECTURE TWELVE

MARCH 6, 2003

TWELVE-TONE MUSIC — ABSOLUTE AND PROGRAMMATIC MUSIC — SCHOENBERG VS. STRAVINSKY

CURTAIN RISES

Moving chairs, squeaking door, coughs, other sounds filling the noise environment of a large classroom in the Literature Department at Duke University. Students are talking about transportation. It all began when one international student complained about her lack of a car in Durham, NC. "It's very difficult for me, you know, to come every day to campus and walk through parts of the town with no sidewalks. It feels like I'm walking along a highway. Giant cars drive by very fast and the drivers stare at me like I'm a criminal or something." Another student is kindly suggesting learning to drive and getting a car, but the foreign student resists, insisting that she does not want to contribute to pollution or to support the status quo of the chronic lack of public transit, which mainly affects the poor. "Well, this may be your only option," says a local. "Being in America without a car is like having no legs." Then students shift their discussion to Jameson. "I saw him the other day — he was driving a red Volkswagen." Another student adds, "Yeah, he is often com-

plaining that that car is a lemon, it breaks often; he once almost missed a class...."

Jameson enters the classroom carrying a few books, his scattered notes and the red pen in the chest pocket of his flannel shirt.

[Microphone turns on.]

JAMESON: [*Chatter. Audience hubbub. Zippers unzipping*] ...I encourage one of you to make a short presentation on Ernst Bloch's essays... [*Door creaks open.*] One essay is about the detective story, and the other one is on the Künstlerroman, or the artist novel. [*Hubbub fades away.*] He draws on the mass popularity of the detective novel and the relation between solving a crime, collecting evidence, and analyzing a modernist novel, and the Künstlerroman deals with the interest in lives of the artists, with the literary form that portrays the life and struggles of the artist.[1] [*Pause.*] It would be important to discuss them in the context of our seminar... [*Footsteps shuffle across the floor*] what Bloch is talking about, and to also consider his relation between art and utopia. We don't have the class yet, but come talk to me about the presentation if you are interested. Something short. [*Pause.*] So, I just need to work... [*Addresses students standing in the back.*] Anybody needs a chair... [*Chairs scratching the floor.*] Okay, okay. Well, listen, we'll make some more copies of Bloch's texts... [*Quietly to his Student Assistant*: If you could make copies from his The Utopian Function of Art? You can pass by, I'll give you the book.]

STUDENT ASSISTANT: I have it... [*Door creaks open.*]

JAMESON: Ah, you have it, okay. Okay, we gonna do music today in order to get a little bit of sense of what is twelve-tone music... [*Addresses student near the door.*] And maybe you can close the door over there, this would allow us to make a more intimate atmosphere in here ... [*Chair scraping against the wooden floor. Door creaks open.*] We will have this music presentation… [*Turns towards Music Ph.D. student.*] Do you want to come forward…?

Student Presentation: Arnold Schoenberg and Twelve-Tone Music

STUDENT ONE: Okay, I will start by playing for you a short piece of music. [*Inserts music CD. Presses "Play" button on the CD player.*]

[*Presses "Stop" button.*]

STUDENT ONE: [*Deep sigh.*] Nothing more than a moment, really, and yet, to my ears at least, that was the first of Anton von Webern's Fünf Orchesterstücke, or Five Pieces, Op 10. [*Pause.*] Today, I will play for you some of the most known of these pieces, talk about atonal music, and present to you a vision of Webern's teacher, Arnold Schoenberg. I will treat Schoenberg

ANTON WEBERN

FÜNF STÜCKE

für Orchester

OP. 10

I.

Anton Webern, "Fünf Stücke für Orchester op. 10," (Fragment). Copyright 1923, 1951, Universal Edition. Public domain.

very briefly, as an historical next... [*Self-corrects*] nexus to which one can understand one side of the rise of modernism in the twentieth-century Western art music.

[*Long pause.*]

We begin, however, in the mid-nineteenth century. [*Pause.*] The Viennese music critic Eduard Hanslick... [*Zipper unzipping*] contributed to the controversy that was to become the basis of the historical construction of Western romantic music, and this is the divide that emerges between the so-called "absolute" and "programmatic" music.[2] Actually, the division was initially sparked by the rebellious and... [*Cough in the audience*] as usual, untactful Richard Wagner, who coined the term "absolute music" in his public denouncement of the young conservative, Johannes Brahms. Hanslick, however, preferred more traditional, early authors coming on the side of Beethoven and Brahms rather than Mahler, Strauss, or again, Wagner. Because of Hanslick's public role as a music critic, the lines were drawn.

[*Long pause.*]

I will make a diagram for you. [*Walks towards the blackboard.*] So, imagine we have emerging after 1850 the figure of... [*Chalk strokes on the blackboard*] B-R-A-H-M-S. And Brahms is considered this conservative classicist, and then we also have... [*Chalk strokes*] W-A-G-N-E-R, who is the revolutionary figure, and then Hanslick is here, the critic, sorting these people into camps. So, immediately, everyone else falls into place. Here, we later have... [*Chalk strokes*] S-T-R-A-U-S-S, and up here we have... [*Chalk strokes*] D-V-O-R-A-K.

One other consequence of this division into programmatic and absolute was that it reached and arranged some other previous musicians. And so, we have here... [*Chalk strokes on the blackboard*] S-C-H-U-B-E-R-T, and then the ones that came later... [*Chalk strokes*] S-C-H-U-M-A-N and... [*Chalk strokes*] C-H-O-P-I-N — all of them on the side of absolute music. And of course, what's interesting in this part is that they pledge allegiance to... [*Chalk strokes*] B-E-E-T-H-O-V-E-N, who is the icon of the nineteenth-century music. Now we have two sides.

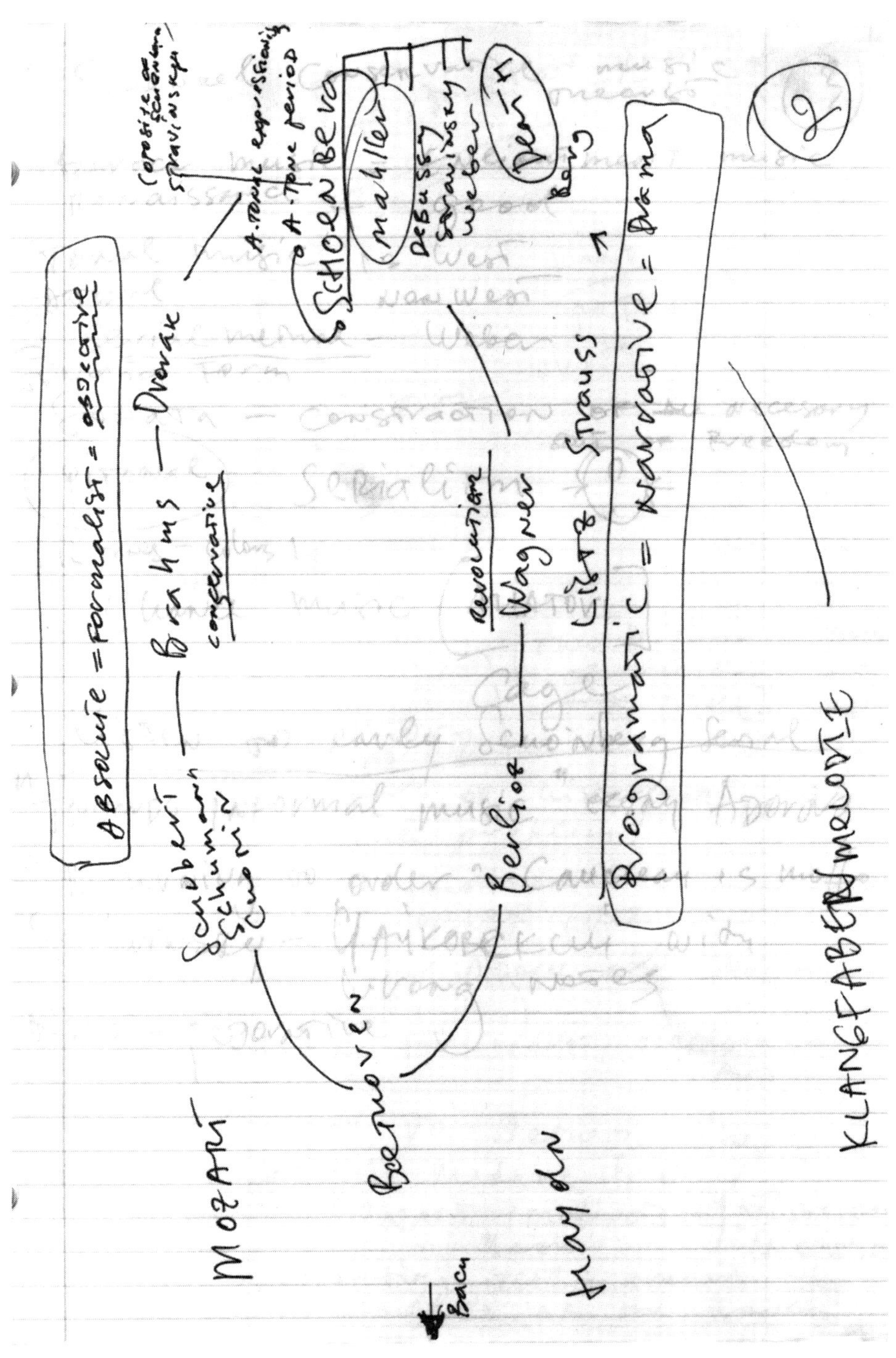

Presentation diagram on the blackboard. Page from student's seminar notes.

This one here is... [*Chalk strokes*] A-B-S-O-L-U-T-E and this one down here is P-R-O-G-R-A-M-M-A-T-I-C.

[*Long pause.*]

This one is called "absolute" because it's music that is understood in the mind. [*Pause.*] It's music that is not "about" anything, it is music that is interested in form, or as Hanslick would put it, it is music that has no other subject beyond the simple combinations of the notes that we hear. And then this one, on the other hand... [*Knocks on the "Programmatic" on the blackboard*] is music that is interested in drama; it is interested in the extramusical narrative and the connection to the body, insofar as it is interested in tone-color and extreme gesture. So, we could say that absolute music here is... [*Chalk strokes*] O-B-J-E-C-T-I-V-E and the programmatic one below is... [*Chalk strokes*] S-U-B-J-E-C-T-I-V-E. But you can look the other way around and switch Objective and Subjective depending on how you treat the relation of the musical material to... [*Indistinctly. Talks facing the blackboard.*] Then, speaking about genealogies, you could probably go here and say, before Beethoven... [*Chalk strokes*] M-O-Z-A-R-T and H-A-Y-D-N, that the precursor of them all is certainly... [*Chalk strokes*] B-A-C-H.

[*Long pause.*]

So, by the end of the nineteenth century, hmm... [*Sighs*] this divide existed for thirty or so years, and at this point, Wagner is dead, Brahms is dead, and many stopped caring about the divide. Well, one person did not stop and that was... [*Chalk strokes on the blackboard*] S-C-H-O-E-B-E-R-G.

JAMESON: [*Corrects spelling*] Schoen... You left out "N."

STUDENT ONE: Ah, yeah... [*Chalk strokes*] S-C-H-O-E-N-B-E-R-G.

[*Long pause.*]

Schoenberg positions himself as a synthesis in this divide. So, you get on one side those who find, in Beethoven, form and formal development, and this is the absolute music. And the programmatic side saw in Beethoven an interest in narrative, and for Wagner... [*Words indistinct*] there is the metaphor of the "forest melody,"[3] which was Wagner's first move towards Gesamtkunstwerk — the total work of art, which, as we all know, was his vision of the art of the future. [*Pause.*] Schoenberg sees himself as the completion of these two categories. Schoenberg's teacher was Alexander von Zemlinsky, who had among his supporters Johannes Brahms, and so Schoenberg was profoundly aware of himself as a historical figure and part of a histori... [*Door slams in the distance*] lineage. Later on, Schonberg will write about the relation between Brahms and the modernists.[4] Since atonality was a natural development of compositional technique, he proved himself to be a messianic figure. However, Schoenberg denied thinking of himself only as an end of the historical epoch... [*Points to the blackboard*] but also as the beginning of a new one. He gave enormous importance to his formulation of the serial technique, and his marvelous discovery of serialism, and I quote: "Today I have made a discovery that will ensure the supremacy of German music for the next hundred years."[5] And there is another quote by him that I couldn't find, where Schoenberg is imagining, in the future, boys doing their homework in twelve-tone tonalities, which is totally ridiculous...

JAMESON: [*Laughing loudly*] ...there is another remark by Mencken,[6] who was one of the great critics of early music journalism, and who once made the remark, [*Impersonates Mencken*] "There are two kinds of music: German music and bad music." [*Jameson and audience laughing.*]

STUDENT ONE: [*Presses "play" button on CD-player.*] Okay, here is another part of Webern's Fünf Stücke.

JAMESON: This is still Webern, not Schoenberg, right...

Webern, "Fünf Stücke für Orchester op. 10," (Fragment). Public Domain.

STUDENT ONE: [*Presses "Stop" button.*] Although Schoenberg may have viewed himself as a revolutionary rather than a conservative, one finds in his music many familiar terms inherited from the traditional German romantic aesthetics. [*Pause.*] His reliance on themes of nature and organicism, for instance, did little to separate his thought from contemporary music theories, even from those who were violently opposed to atonality and Schoenberg's radical aesthetic ideas. Mm-hmm, so let me now talk about Schoenberg's aesthetic ideas. Schoenberg regarded musical tonality as an artificial product, as a product and technique of art.[7] In fact, he does not like the word "atonality," and preferred instead the term "pantone," because he felt that his music was not renouncing tonality but rather embraced all tones equally. Another way for us to see the idea of nature in Schoenberg is this concept of "genius." For Schoenberg, genius was something that existed in the mind but was not conscious of itself, or that the man of genius learned from his own nature, and he also says in one place that the human mind will produce things that we can't take credit for them. Then, there is the notion of organicism, which of course takes us back to Goethe, at least. You see this in his defense of Brahms,[8] where he first creates this idea of developing variations... [*Chair scratches the floor*] in Brahms' music. The two compositional processes that are talked about in the nineteenth century would be [*Stressing*] development and variation. With variation, you're taking something and repeating it by keeping the same basic structure and changing it, and development is taking something and changing it into something else. For Schoenberg, he combines this into one complete idea of [*Stressing*] developing variation, and here we have the standard German totality at work. [*Pause.*] Also, under the category of organicism falls his concept of the "musical idea," which is not merely a melodic theme but rather the piece as a whole. There is a sort of adequacy between musical form and content... [*Chair dragged along the floor*] the idea controls the larger structure... [*Loud chair noise continues*] as all if the parts are interconnected...[9] [*Loud thud. Object falls on the floor.*]

[*Long pause.*]

But the truly innovative feature of Schoenberg's theoretical work, however, is his concept of the [*Stressing*] motif. He writes in an essay entitled "My Evolution"... [*Page flipping*], "Coherence in classic compositions is based — broadly speaking — on the unifying qualities of such structural factors as rhythms, motifs, phrases, and the constant reference of all melodic and harmonic features to the center of gravitation — the tonic. Renouncement of the unifying power of the tonic still leaves all the other factors in operation."[10]

JAMESON: What was this? Oh, yeah, motif.

STUDENT ONE: Mm-hmm, so this is... [*Pause.*] I mean, this is another political move to, hmm... [*Hesitates*] to rescue himself from his critics that complained about his atonality. But his idea was that tonality was a form or a unifying principle, and he was saying that we don't need this anymore, because there are other things that we've learned from Beethoven, and way back from Bach, all these great masters. It wasn't just tonality that held music in place, it was also rhythm, harmony, pitch... [*Door creaks* *open*] other features which unifies the work, held it together and made it work. So, Schoenberg's aesthetics can also be said to be historical in nature. As he remarks in "The Problems of Harmony," an essay that he wrote in 1934: "In no art, properly speaking, can one say 'the same thing,' the same thing which has been said once before, least of all in music."[11] For Schoenberg then, aesthetic categories are contingent on history; tonality was not wrong, rather it was outdated — free of tonality and then serialism will possibly be the aesthetic of the future.

[*Presses "play" button on the CD-player. Plays another part from Webern, "Fünf Stücke für Orchester op. 10." Presses "Stop."*]

Now I will talk about Schoenberg and his contemporaries. [*Pause.*] Schoenberg was certainly not the only composer of the period, and certainly not the only one who could have claimed to be the inheritor of this position. Mahler comes immediately to mind; he was ahead of Schoenberg... [*Quietly:* as a precursor of expressionism, and then Strauss as well, until at least 1906, when he retreats from the extremity of his chromaticism.] Then you have the French, and the most known is Debussy, who was also regarded as one inheritor of late Romantic tonality in service of modernism. And of course, we have Schoenberg's students, Webern and Berg, and then you also have this figure, Igor Stravinsky, who attaches himself to... [*Cough in the audience.*] And what was most apparent with all of these musicians is the issue of temporality. During the early atonal period and Schoenberg's first pronunciation of atonality, you get also these extremely tiny pieces with extraordinary motivic and intense moments of emotional concentration. [*Pause.*] So, these brief pieces written by Schoenberg and his pupils are compacted as tight as possible. Schoenberg had plenty of short pieces... [*Words indistinct.*] With Mahler, you get these gigantic symphonies that take an hour and a half, almost two hours to perform... [*Cough in the audience*] and these are works that present an entire world in often pragmatic and some sort of quasi-spiritual sense... [*Quietly*: Mahler was Jewish, but was also influenced by Catholic mysticism.] You know, in Mahler's symphonies, you're gonna have this situation of a temporal space that is gigantic and infinite, in a way, because it attempts to extend to some point of resurrection or redemption, hmm... [*Hesitates*] the end of history.

[*Long pause.*]

The spatial force of the atonal system is different. They make no such attempts at resurrection, and they are almost not to engage... [*Achoo. Sneeze in the audience*] in their own demise as quickly as possible. These are works that are often interested in [*Stressing*] death, pain, and suffering. This is also associated with the expressionist phase in Schoenberg, and a lot of music and texts written — especially after Mahler's death, which was interpreted as the death of tonality — is very dark and macabre. And the aesthetics is a very different one, between Mahler and Schoenberg. Then we get to... [*Chalk strokes on the blackboard*] S-T-R-A-V-I-N-S-K-Y [*Pause.*] Stravinsky is very important here because, for Adorno at least, he is the very opposite of Schoenberg. And this is because Stravinsky presented his own version of modernism, which is certainly unlike Schoenberg's. Whereas Schoenberg worked so much to position himself as a sort of continuation of all these... [*Points to the diagram on the blackboard*] nineteenth-century processes, trying to show himself as following on the footsteps of Beethoven and Wagner, as a synthesis of absolute and program music — Stravinsky claimed no such thing. By the time Stravinsky wrote The Rite of Spring, he was thinking of himself as completely revolutionary, because he was making a music that relied on folk or folk-like melodies. And in this music, he offers no development at all, and not really any variations. [*Pause.*] Stravinsky's music is based on sections, it is very sectional and repetitive, and it is interested in dividing up time... [*Words indistinct.*] So, this is a very different aesthetics from Schoenberg's. Schoenberg was interested in totality and a sort of organic aesthetics, whereas Stravinsky was sort of already denying all that. And in Stravinsky, his radicalism comes in the early 1910s, a few years after Schoenberg and probably in response to Schoenberg.

[*Presses "Play" button on the CD-player. Plays another part from Webern, "5 Stücke für Orchester, op. 10." Presses "Stop" button.*]

I must also add that Schoenberg's historical position, as I try to describe it today, was created by Schoenberg himself. It can be said now at least... [*Cough in the audience*] to be real. Generations of composers have developed atonality and the serial method. For instance, there was Pierre Boulez and Karlheinz Stockhausen and the rest of the Darmstadt composers, and George Perle in America. This group came to be known as "integral serialism" because they saw Schoenberg's technique applying not only to pitch-ordering, but to ordering of all other elements in music, or at least those that were containable: articulation, dynamics, timbre, orchestration, register, and rhythm, to name a few. Then, from Eastern Europe, we have the school descended from Béla Bartók, who never wrote serial music exactly, but his use of motifs shares much with Schoenberg's atonal period. Polish composers, such as Witold Lutosławski ... [*Words indistinct*] and a few others, and even the American composer Aaron Copland, wrote a more melodic form of atonal music. Even Stravinsky — Schoenberg's nemesis — eventually utilized the technique in 1954, although he waited until Schoenberg was firmly in his grave... [*Clears throat*] Schoenberg died in 1951.

[*Long pause.*]

Thus, serialism became the dominant progressive paradigm in twentieth-century music, and this was also due to its entrenchment in academia... [*Quietly*: and this also happens ironically because of the Nazis.] As the Nazis came to power, and their ideas of aesthetics became enforced, a lot of musicians from Germany and Europe in general fled, a lot of them came to the United States. Mm-hmm. After World War Two, when the United States emerged as the dominant producer of new musicians, you have all these German composers who are teaching the serial method sitting in different American academies. So, you have this tremendous output and this enormous volume of serial music being produced. Another phenomenon from World War Two is the entrenchment of German critics and historians of music in the American universities, which is probably why I am standing here taking about Schoenberg as the most important composer in the twentieth century, and this becomes clear why he is more important than a lot of others of his contemporaries. And the fact that Adorno establishes himself as a preeminent aesthetic theorist and philosopher is also related to him being able to come to... [*Words indistinct*] America and then return to West Germany. This is probably also one of the main reasons why we have this great interest in Schoenberg today. There is obviously lots of politics behind the history of twelve-tone music, and its theorization, of course, which no one wants to talk about... [*Chair leg scrapes hard against the floor.*] So, I guess that's it. I will play the last part...

[*Presses "Play" button on the CD-player. Plays another part from Webern, "5 Stücke für Orchester op. 10." Presses "Stop."*]

So, hmm... [*Clears throat.*] Does anyone have any questions? If not, then I'm gonna play some more music. Questions, if you have any.

STUDENT TWO: [*Far from the microphone.*] Were there other theories of music emerging at the same time in opposition to serialism or atonal music as put forward by Schoenberg and his pupils...? [*Words indistinct.*]

STUDENT ONE: Yeah, there were other theories. There was this critic called Heinrich Schenker, a conservative music theorist in early twentieth-century Vienna, and he developed gradually this idea of the early fundamental structure he called Ursatz, which is this large-scale structuring thing that happens in tone music. But the way he developed it... [*Chalk strokes on the blackboard.*] So, we have N-A-T-U-R-E here, and then from nature you get this nominal tone, which is... [*Words indistinct*] the Urline. From these springs the real tone and all the notes in the harmonic scale. And based on the hierarchy of... [*The student walks further away from the microphone as his voice becomes less* *discernible, but in this part of his presentation, he talks about the so-called Schenker-Schoenberg polemic. The dispute between the two musicians was often described in terms of conflicting paradigms for the analysis of tonal music. Their debate built upon German-Austrian music theories from the eighteenth and nineteenth centuries, revolving around the origins and fundamentals of tonality. Both Schenker and Schoenberg embraced a form of totality, or organicism, with regard to music harmony, but each relied on a different philosophical system that various interpreters have described as "vitalism," "repetition," "imitation" and "procreation" for Schenker, versus that of "variation," "production," "organization" or "geometric construction" for Schoenberg.*[12] *Schenker has often been regarded as more "conservative" given his insistence on the natural roots of music. Their conflicting views regarding the origins of tonality often clashed in their attitude toward* new *music. Schenker built his theory on the concept of archetypal* Ursatz *(fundamental structure) and* Urline *(the fundamental line) that produces the musical motif or musical form through repetition. Schoenberg argued that musical form is like a living organism, in that it is organized. Schoenberg also argued that new music was difficult to understand because it avoided "repetition" (unnecessary today) and that good music was based on the principle of variation.*[13]]

JAMESON: And you should realize that these debates are still going on... [*Pause.*] What we call "postmodern music" today is a reaction against all these Schoenbergian ideas. I saw a crazy article in the Times, I don't know, a few years ago, some journalist was saying, you know ... , [*Impersonates* New York Times *author*] "Our latest scientific research has shown that tonality really is rooted in nature." He didn't seem to know that these debates have lasted throughout the entire history of music, wanting to say: "Thus we should be happy now that we have science, and that we got rid of all these unscientific twelve-tone people like Schoenberg, and all the rest of them, and in its place, we have postmodern music." But we can also turn it around and talk about globalization and world culture — tonal music is the West. [*Pause.*] Adorno even says so, that music is only this one great moment in the history of the West, so now, in this age, we are going back to the kind of music that existed in Greece, and Arabic countries, and in China, and so on and so forth: we are going back to these non-tonal traditions. So, this can also be played out in some other ways, you know.

[*Long pause.*]

JAMESON: Any more questions? [*Addresses Student One.*] Can we then say that the sonata is a problem for twelve-tone music?

STUDENT ONE: Well, actually, later, the integral serialists — what's their name, people like Boulez and so on — actually renounced Schoenberg, because he was too traditional for them. Schoenberg, his approach to serialism was to use the order of pitches to maintain these traditional forms of music. So, he would write sonatas and then he would also write a suite, which is actually a baroque form, so he would do these antiquated forms. But he is using these forms as what is structuring and holding together these pieces with this new harmonic dimension... [*Words indistinct.*] But for these later integral serialist musicians, this was insufficient because of his cut-out old forms coming out of Schoenberg instead of something radically new... [*Pause.*] The integralists wanted to establish total control over the musical material. Later in the twentieth century, in the 1950s and 1960s serialism, it is Webern, in fact, who becomes their icon because... [*Police siren in the distance*] the serial movement is much more connected to the form, and it is more [*Stressing*] formalist, whereas Schoenberg is more traditional in his reliance of musical forms.

JAMESON: And in principle, the sonata is related to tonality, right, because... [*Pause.*]

STUDENT ONE: [*Trying to interrupt*] Well, that's... that's...

JAMESON: Because of the keys... [*Pause.*]

STUDENT ONE: Well, that's really arguable. I mean, for Schenker, sonata, as we know it, when it takes this name, was something that was constructed in the mid-nineteenth century. Mozart was doing it, and Haydn, you know, and Beethoven was already extending it. So, all the ideas about form and developing form are really lined up in the nineteenth century, and then, right around Schoenberg's time, sonata detaches itself from traditional harmony — and... [*Pause.*] I would say, hmm... [*Hesitates.*] I wouldn't say that sonata is necessarily connected to tonality, or [*Stressing*] essential to it, but that's something... [*Words indistinct*] of a conflict between serialism and tonal elements in the sonata form, especially for the later serialists, who thought that not only should the pitch-ordering be determined by the row, but also by the pleasure of the form.

JAMESON: Mm-hmm. Adorno's sociology of the sonata is interesting because he says, [*Impersonates Adorno*] "Look, what the bourgeois wanted to do was to combine freedom and necessity." So, here in the sonata, which you have is some opening of something or other, which is some kind of melody, but it's completely arbitrary because it comes out of nowhere, and what the sonata is trying to do is to... [*Chair scratching the floor*] that into various places in such a way that, when you come back at the end, it has become [*Softly*] necessary. So, the whole form of the sonata is this [*Stressing*] construction of the necessary out of the arbitrary. It's an... [*Cough in the audience*] interesting idea; and I think you can see why... [*Pause.*] I mean, you can hardly feel that the Webern pieces pause necessity for anybody... [*Quietly*: economic necessity is happening anyway... (*Mumbles indistinctly*).]

STUDENT ONE: Another weird thing about this is, as what I was saying earlier about Schoenberg, that he preferred the term [*Stressing*] pantone, and pantonality. I mean, there are lots of people — I've met a few of them — who will hear music that we've heard, the twelve-tone music, and hear it [*Stressing*] as such. And I don't think they are so far off, because I get a sense of tonal movement in a lot of these. Some people claim they can hear all of Schoenberg's works as tonal or immaterial works, I think that is a much sillier claim, I don't know if you can do that.

JAMESON: But let's push that a little further and talk about how art is supposed to be revolutionary, and it is supposed to change habits. You see this with film, hmm... [*Hesitates*] how opinions, history, morals, beliefs, all of those things are changing, right? So, tonality is perhaps also a sort of [*Stressing*] <u>habit</u> in the Western society, and this atonal music revolution was supposed to, hmm... [*Hesitates*] not maybe expand it, maybe transform music, or maybe get rid of traditional tonal music. But tonal music is still around. Right, I mean, so we don't seem to be able to shake this habit off. So, what does this mean... [*Looking around.*] It's, hmm... [*Hesitates.*] It's like a... [*Pause.*] It reminds me about David Bordwell talking about cinema in the 1960s.[14] During the 1960s, there was this explosion of new cinematic ideas with Godard and all these new cinematic techniques and perceptions, but as he says now, we can see that Hollywood absorbed all of them and there is no revolutionary cinema anymore, and perhaps there never was. I mean... [*Pause.*] It was folded back. [*Excited.*] Well, remember that Schoenberg also taught us a lot about music, even through film music, because those guys were all his students in LA.[15] So, I mean, is it then fair to think that this other argument, which claims that tonality is natural, is right? No, it's not Western, it's not bourgeois, it is... [*Pause.*] You will never get rid of it somehow; we will always have to oppose or deal with tonality when we're listening to music, and so on. It's an argument that has more consequences than just... [*Police car siren far in the distance*] purely musical and stylistic.

STUDENT ONE: I mean, the funny thing is that Schoenberg himself, after the 1920s, when he reaches this point of [*Stressing*] <u>extreme</u> rebellion, when he proclaims serialism as the way of the new, is hmm... [*Pause.*] But then, later on in the 1930s, he writes tonal music again. So, he wasn't really committed to this, and he didn't think that tonal music was gone or worthless anymore. And he may have felt that tonal music will always be around, at least in popular music. Like when he was in LA, there are pictures of him playing tennis with George Gershwin... [*Clears throat*] of all people, so one can imagine, given the way Schoenberg has been presented by these German music historians, as someone uncompromising and radical... [*Words indistinct.*] He didn't think this at all, he thought he definitely was self-important, but he was also fairly flexible... [*Door cracks open.*]

[*Long silence.*]

STUDENT THREE: I found that the pieces you were playing are very colorful when compared to Wagner... [*Pause.*] They sound pretty colorful.

STUDENT ONE: To Wagner?

STUDENT THREE: Yes, compared to Wagner. Because they are colorful. And like, they make this basic connection between the twelve tones and color, because it seems to me that the tones are increased in color somehow. Is that correct, or would you agree with that?

STUDENT ONE: I don't, hmm... [*Hesitates.*] I don't think that's... [*Pause.*] Well, I think there is probably a connection between his atonal period, from 1908 to 1921, and color. A lot has been said about the relation between Schoenberg and Kandinsky during this period. But once he gets through this period, I think this relation changes. I find it interesting that you don't think Wagner is colorful...

STUDENT THREE: I think Wagner is colorful, but compared to this...

JAMESON: And Beethoven is much less colorful compared to even Brahms or the later ones... [*Pause.*] But you should know, this is a key concept derived from Schoenberg... [*Chalk strokes on the blackboard*] K-L-A-N-G-F-A-R-B-E-N-M-E-L-O-D-I-E.

STUDENT ONE: This is tone-color melody...

JAMESON: Timbre-color melody. Timbre is... [*Pause.*] I mean, each of the instruments has its own color, and this is a melody made out of these various colors.[16]

STUDENT ONE: Yeah, with Klangfarbenmelodie, the idea is that you have all these different instruments, and each has its own sound quality, and then Schoenberg figured out that you can basically create something that had melodic direction without even necessarily having to change pitches; you can do this just by changing your instrument [*Pause.*] So, this is certainly something that you are hearing in Webern, and why you are hearing it as colorful, it's because Webern's clarinet, trombone, flute, drum... [*Cough in the audience*] they all are responding to each other, he uses timbre as a component of his composition.

JAMESON: And the series of the instruments, it's sort of the melody; it doesn't matter what the notes are. If you have clarinet, trombone, violin, I don't know, piano and drums — I mean, that's a melody, whatever it's playing, right?

STUDENT ONE: Well, well, of course, this would be true except for this...

JAMESON: Yeah... [*Pause.*] Yeah. So, when you say that the later people like Boulez and so forth, or the integral serialists, that they included all kind of things like this...

STUDENT ONE: Right...

JAMESON: ... some horrendously complicated mathematical system? So, these integral serialists, they were denouncing Schoenberg?

STUDENT ONE: Yeah, and they would, hmm... [*Hesitates.*] The reason they are called "total" or "integral serialists" — I think, but I'm not sure — these are people who convened in Darmstadt in the early 1950s, and which include composers like Boulez, Stockhausen, and others who were inspired by the later work of Webern. They did not like Schoenberg; Boulez even wrote a very harsh article called "Schoenberg is Dead."[17] These people applied the ideas of twelve-tone technique to other musical variables, often even using mathematical formulas. [*Pause.*] So, they made music determined by some sequence, and it has some articulation, and then everybody started making music like this... [*Student One chuckles.*]

JAMESON: So, it takes Schoenberg further? Schoenberg wanted to move everything, but now this is really big and serious, and this problem also raises issues which come out in Doctor Faustus: is music only just what you can hear, because people say, "Oh, you can't hear after all these things that come out of Boulez." [*Pause.*] I mean, your ear doesn't pick these complex relations and your mind doesn't pick them either. It's on paper, you can maybe read it somehow, but you can't hear it. Well, but isn't music, doesn't music also include the things that you can't hear? [*Pause.*] The things that are only on paper, isn't that sort of a graphic, can't music also be one of the visual arts? I think those are all part of these problems of modernist aesthetics.

STUDENT ONE: Yeah, there are these crazy avant-gardists of the twentieth century who made music that totally exists on paper. Music became this thing that was abstracted from... [*Cough in the audience.*]

JAMESON: Well, you should think of it as "paper architecture." A lot of architects in the contemporary period, they couldn't build their projects anymore, although some of them are buildable, so their projects existed only on paper as pure architectural concepts... [*Stomp-stomp-stomp. Heavy stomping across the floor*] and this is not totally different from music...

STUDENT ONE: Here is another composer. [*Shows CD cover to the audience.*]

JAMESON: Ah, this is Babbitt...

STUDENT ONE: This is Milton Babbitt, who is a totally different kind of music... [*Inserts CD in the player. Presses "Play" button. Plays a fragment from Milton Babbitt's* Concerto for Piano and Orchestra *(1985). Presses "Stop" button.*]

JAMESON: And things like this that could last five or six hours?

STUDENT ONE: Yeah, and except that it sounds like it's a... [*Pause.*] There is a point in serialism at which you can hardly distinguish it from chance music...

JAMESON: Aleatory mu...

STUDENT ONE: [*Interrupts.*] Aleatory music, which, on one hand, is a complete lack of control, and then the total control of everything. John Cage is famously known for introducing chance music, or maybe I should say... [*Stressing*] re-introducing it, as some pre-war dada members already played with chance compositions.

JAMESON: Wasn't he also in contact with Boulez and Stockhausen and all of those people...?

STUDENT ONE: Yeah, he was. Cage also come to Darmstadt, only later in 1958... [*Pause.*]

JAMESON: But the aleatory music, you know... [*Pause.*] How many people heard anything by John Cage? [*Silence.*] I mean, you have, for example, the concerto for... [*Cough in the audience*] eight radios. There are eight people, and they turn their radios on and off, or down and up, or something like this. There are directions, right? Like radio one turns on or moves the dial selector to a prescribed station.[18] There is a lot of stuff like this in Cage, like the prepared piano, where he sticked nuts and bolts and screws, mutes inside the piano to alter its sound,[19] and then played it by a score... [*Audience chuckles.*]

STUDENT FOUR: I heard a piece once, and all I heard was only the beginning. Have you heard of pieces of music based on something that is called flicker noise...?

STUDENT ONE: Flicker noise?

STUDENT FOUR: ...It is different from white noise that combines different frequencies, or brown noise would be really very low frequency, and then flicker noise would be based on some other frequencies and power density or something. I am not sure how it works, but...

STUDENT ONE: I don't know that term, hmm, it's not pink noise?

STUDENT FOUR: No, it's not pink.

STUDENT ONE: Is this electronic music?

STUDENT FOUR: But I think it's more like this aleatory kind of music, except that it keeps going like this... [*Rustling sound*] this is sort of a repeating pattern that has been used for composing. Like, you know, you look at the pattern of traffic during the rush hour, or when you're standing in the middle of an intersection and look at the waves people cross, and then you try to compose with these...

STUDENT ONE: I don't know anything about this, but it sounds like it is conceptually the same thing as Cage's radios and radiators and altered pianos. I don't know. [*Pause.*] Okay, I'll play for you some songs by Schoenberg. This is an early Schoenberg, I mean [*Stressing*] early atonal music from 1908, and one of the first songs he was writing, and I thought I'd play some songs because they are pretty easy to appreciate, they could be very emotional.

[*Inserts CD into the player. Presses "Play" button. Plays a fragment from Arnold Schoenberg,* Das Buch der Hängenden Gärten (The Book of the Hanging Gardens)*, Op. 15. 1908-1909. Presses "Stop" button.*]

STUDENT ONE: So, I don't think this music is specifically complex. Mm-hmm... [*Tinkers with the CD player.*] Maybe I'll play for you another part of Schoenberg's early serial music and you could maybe hear why the integral serialists were objecting to it so much. [*Pause.*] Because, hmm... [*Inserts CD into the player. Presses "Play" button. Plays two notes, then presses "Stop" button.*] This is Arnold Schoenberg's Suite für Klavier (Suite for Piano), Op. 25, which is a twelve-tone piece he composed in 1921. I don't know if this piece will mean anything to you, but the rhythms are gonna be regular and the patterns are a very traditional kind of rhetorical gesture, even as the pitches and the harmonies are serial... [*Presses "Play" button. Plays fragment. Presses "Stop" button.*] So, these later integralists would have not approved of something like this... [*Words indistinct.*] And I think this is why Adorno likes Schoenberg so much, because he seems sort of a wonderful combination of knowledge and intuition, and I don't think Adorno was a big fan of these later integral serialists, although he recognized that this is the general direction of new music and, hmm... [*Hesitates*] of progress.

JAMESON: Mm-hmm. Let me just mention this because I just read about it... [*Pause.*] There is this book called Quasi Una Fantasia that Verso published and the long essay by Adorno, which in French is called Vers une musique informelle, "Towards an Informal Music", and it's all about Darmstadt.[20] And here Adorno says ... , [*Impersonates Adorno*] "Well, I'm not sure, on one hand, I don't really quite understand some of this new stuff, but on the other hand, I believe that there is progress in music," and so on and so forth. And then he goes through Stockhausen and Boulez, and I think, overall, he is quite sympathetic to them. So, this book would be the place to see his mixed feelings about Darmstadt and the direction of new music after World War Two.

STUDENT ONE: Adorno was also a student of Berg, who was in turn a student of Schoenberg, and this I find interesting — the differences between Berg, about whom I didn't talk very much, and Schoenberg... [*Pause.*] Adorno thought that Berg, when compared to Schoenberg or Webern, was more traditional, he was working within this tension between radical innovation and tradition. If compared to Webern, Berg preserved a link to the past, in other words... [*Quietly*: Wozzeck is a good example, given its traditional form, but this is also an early work by Berg.][21] Here is another serial work by Webern... [*Shows CD cover to the audience.*] I'll just play from the beginning. [*Inserts CD into the player. Presses "Play" button. Plays a fragment from Webern's* Symphony Op. 21 *(1928).*]

STUDENT ONE: [*Speaks over music.*] So, I guess I will stop here then. [*Presses "Stop" button.*] That's an example of Webern's music, this one is very tiny, only ten minutes in total. Webern was known for his attention to detail and organization of structure. Adorno valued Webern for his pure expressivity, and the ability to take atonality to new expressive heights. [*Pause.*] He thought Webern has attained pure lyricism... [*Cough in the audience.*][22] But Berg was his teacher, and these are... [*Shows CD Cover to the audience*] Altenberg-Lieder or "picture postcards" by Berg. Peter Altenberg was a Viennese poet who wrote these tiny aphoristic poems on the back of postcards and scraps of paper, and then these were collected into volumes of prose poems called Neues Altes. So, Berg set on music five songs on picture postcards by Altenberg, known as Altenberg-Songs. This is an early song from 1912 by Berg, but the aesthetics is very different, it's very romantic and with a lot of thick, dramatic and expressive gestures. [*Inserts audio CD. Presses "Play" button. Plays a fragment from Berg's* Altenberg-Songs. *Presses "Stop" button.*]

[*Long pause.*]

So, you notice these dramatic explosions, and there is also a changing relationship between the singer and the... [*Words indistinct.*] Anything else?

JAMESON: Do you want to talk a little bit more about Schoenberg and Stravinsky?

STUDENT ONE: Mm-hmm... [*Pause.*] Well...

JAMESON: And Adorno's Philosophy of Mo...

STUDENT ONE: Yeah, in the Philosophy of Modern Music, Adorno presents Schoenberg as the artist who imposes an objective structure on the musical material. He says that modern society controls music not from outside... [*Quietly*: by forbidding the artist to do certain things] but from within. Society urges the artist to follow musical conventions, which is false, and for Schoenberg, music has to do with truth... [*Achoo. Sneeze in the audience.*] Schoenberg resists society by imposing his own ordering universal principle on the musical material, by introducing his own [*Stressing*] objective structure that of the twelve-tone music. Now, Stravinsky also proposes an objective structure, but to Adorno, his is, hmm... [*Hesitates*] of a conservative nature, because he is bringing back neo-classical forms from the past. Whereas Schoenberg is offering pure negation by proposing a truly new musical universal that is atonal music, and therefore he is progressive, Stravinsky is affirmative, for he relies on the music of the past, which is tonal. So, for Adorno, it is Schoenberg who is the creative genius, although he also recognizes that Stravinsky is also a significant composer. But Stravinsky's music is more conformist because it seeks to restore tonality, and it is also concerned with authenticity — it is also a form of construction or montage, but of "dead material."[23] He sees Schoenberg and Stravinsky as the most important figures in modern music, precisely because they stand at its extremes as two dialectical poles. And other composers like the French Debussy, they are essentially undialectical... [*Pause*] and they're not getting any credit at all, because they are not extreme enough for Adorno. But ultimately, Stravinsky is the positivist and conservative extreme of modernism, and Schoenberg is the one who projects the future of music.

JAMESON: Everybody knows The Rite of Spring? [*Silence.*] Well, Adorno had several things against Stravinsky. One is that Stravinsky went through a sort of neo-classical period in the 1920s, which was part of a wider reaction... [*Clears throat*] and it happened not only in music but also in painting, literature. It was a movement that was called after Jean Cocteau's famous slogan of "rappel à l'ordre"[24] — a return to order, which, for Adorno, was a very reactionary move... [*Pause.*]

STUDENT ONE: And that's a post-World War One phenomenon with this return to classicism...

JAMESON: Yeah, an interwar cultural history where classicist trends emerge as a reaction to modernism. And Stravinsky, he was like writing music with wrong notes... [*Laughs to himself*] deploying triads and components of music that were independent of technique...

STUDENT ONE: [*Interrupting.*] I don't know if that's anti-modernism, or maybe it was... [*Cough in the audience*] but another way to think about Adorno... [*Pause.*] He was criticizing neoclassicism and was praising Schoenberg, but Schoenberg was doing some of the same things. When you write a piece called "suite," and that's a baroque piece, that's a genre that's three hundred years old, and Schoenberg is writing this thing and using these rhythms and using these melodic forms; and it's not like he came up with a whole new way of approaching the pitch or harmony. Certainly, Schoenberg was not outside of the classical forms, but he didn't really do it as much as Stravinsky did, or Prokofiev and many others... [*Words indistinct.*]

STUDENT FIVE: I don't want to interrupt, but...

JAMESON: Oh, go ahead...

STUDENT FIVE: I was wondering about the relationship or

the definition when you were talking earlier on about noise, like brown noise and white noise. What's the actual definition of, hmm… [*Hesitates*] noise, or what something must depend on to be called noise? And what's the relation between music and noise? Is noise the opposite of music? Is it the space that appears in music… [*Cough in the audience*] and how important is noise, especially for these modern musicians? I don't think I have a musical ear, but when I listen to a lot of this twelve-tone stuff, this serial stuff, the first thing that comes to mind is noise versus music in the classical sense. And I'm wondering is there, hmm… [*Hesitates*] is there… [*Pause.*] Is noise sort of a serious concept in music theory business?

STUDENT ONE: It is not till later in the twentieth century, but noise was always around in music. Noise was the anthesis to music, and music was the art of ordering sound. Noise used to be defined as sound lacking organization, and until the early twentieth century, it looked like the role of music was to get rid of all noise… [*Chair scratching across the floor*] to eliminate the unpleasant, or any trace of irregular sound. [*Pause.*] But then dada and the futurists came along, and they said that new technologies and machineries demand new sounds, as in Russolo's manifesto.[25] Later, with people like Cage and Fluxus, noise turned from being in opposition to… [*Stressing*] becoming musical material. Now, to what extent is the term "noise" appropriate to what we have been talking about here today, that I don't know. After all, both Schoenberg and Stravinsky, they were proposing new [*Stressing*] organizing principles for sound material…

STUDENT FIVE: So, in a way, modern music, as you are defining it, is sort of dealing with what other people call noise…

JAMESON: Well, you must try to remember that if noise is discussed in the context of music, then we must call it dissonance, and then it has a historical dimension, for there are moments of different kinds of dissonance. That would be what Adorno…

STUDENT ONE: Precisely, and that atonality and dissonance is not the same, as dissonance is sounding apart of several notes, versus sounding together as in consonance. [*Pause.*] You have dissonance in Bach, Mozart, and Beethoven, but here, dissonance is introduced in order to be shown how it is resolved or turned into consonance. And with Schoenberg, he didn't view consonance and dissonance in oppositional terms, but for Adorno, dissonance is, hmm... [*Hesitates*] is a term for what ordinary people call the ugly,[26] but which has more liberatory potential than tonality or consonance. With Schoenberg, hmm... [*Hesitates*] he is taking it to an extreme, because he is taking dissonance as a way of creating the sublime and its ugliness and bringing the emancipation of dissonance. But the thing is, once you get to Schoenberg, you cannot even call it dissonance anymore... [*Door cracks open.*] The idea that consonance and dissonance have changed in early, early, early church music and the only things that are constant are perfect fifths and octaves... [*Stomp-stomp-stomp. Heavy stomping across the floor.*]

STUDENT SEVEN: Are there examples of perfect consonance?

STUDENT ONE: No, no, no — I'm talking about the very early forms of music, like the Notre-Dame school of polyphony... [*Pause*] where you had rules, like you had music based on pure intervals. And that's exactly what consonance and dissonance, that's how these categories were created. I mean, inclusion — that is consonance, and dissonance is what is left unresolved. But by the time you get to chord music... [*Words indistinct.*] That's what I'm saying is that consonance and dissonance are categories that are constantly changing...

JAMESON: They are historical, that's how they get their value...

STUDENT ONE: Yeah, and so by the time you get to Schoenberg... [*Pause.*] I mean, from Schoenberg's point of view, the idea of dissonance doesn't exist anymore. He didn't want to recognize this music as dissonant because he wanted to make it [*Stressing*] expressive. And this was not only with

Schoenberg, but there were other artists and painters who, at the time, engaged in this disruption of harmonic order and sort of liberation of subjectivity through expression...

JAMESON: [*Handles music CD to student.*] Please, put this on... [*Pause.*] Well, what I wanted to bring up about the Schoenberg-Stravinsky polemic is that, for Adorno, Schonberg is progressive whereas Stravinsky is reactionary. Stravinsky goes back to the atavistic, you can hear people stomping their feet, and these are references to the primaeval history in The Rite of Spring. And then, that's the ultimate point of Stravinsky, it seems to me; that, after all, it is all pastiche of music history, concluding with — [*Looks at Student One*] as you said — a pastiche of Schoenberg himself... [*Quietly*: this is when Stravinsky himself starts writing twelve-tone music, after Schoenberg's death.] This is probably... [*Pause.*] I don't think Adorno would have... [*Pause.*] I mean, he would have been a little bit more embarrassed by his absolute judgment that he made in the 1940s, because later in the 1960s, he slightly changes his tune about Stravinsky... [*Quietly*: not entirely, of course, but he now considers Stravinsky an example of expression in a totally alienated society, and so forth.[27]] So, now, why Schoenberg is progressive, we can talk about when we get back next time... [*Addresses Student One.*] Let's listen to the last piece...

[*Inserts audio CD into the player. Presses "Play" button. Plays Stravinsky's* The Rite of Spring.]

JAMESON: [*Talks over music.*] Okay, this is all for today. Let's all thank Ben Cro... [*Audience applauding*] for this great presentation on twelve-tone...

Audience clapping. Objects drop on the floor. Feet shuffling. Door squeaks. The Rite of Spring *continues playing. Students return chairs to other classrooms. General noise. Screeching microphone noise.*

[*Microphone turns off.*]

CURTAIN

LECTURE THIRTEEN

MARCH 18, 2003

CONCEPTS IN ADORNO — THE STRUCTURE OF *AESTHETIC THEORY* — MANN, *DOCTOR FAUSTUS*

CURTAIN RISES

Moving chairs, squeaking door, coughs, other sounds filling the noise environment of a large classroom in the Literature Department at Duke University. Students talk about their spring break, which usually takes place in March. A few of them took a trip to Asheville, a small city in western North Carolina. Asheville, on a plateau in the Appalachians, is commonly regarded as a liberal "oasis" in the conservative desert of rural North Carolina. It is a tourist hub with seasonal music festivals, a local art scene, and other entertainments that attract students from across the state. Asheville is also important for students of modern art and culture, as it once hosted the Black Mountain College, a hotbed of the post-World War Two North American neo-avant-garde. Two students share their memories from a spring break trip: mountain hiking, unexpected snowfall, an unforgettable night at the local hot springs, and a disappointment (the Black Mountain College Museum was closed).

Jameson enters the classroom carrying a few books, his scattered notes, and the red pen in the chest pocket of his flannel shirt.

[Microphone turns on.]

JAMESON: Regarding your papers and... [*General noise. Footsteps shuffle across the floor*] it is not my decision, it is the Registrar's, and I hasten to explain to you that... [*Door creaks open*] incompletes are being enforced now and I need to keep track of the people who are taking incompletes. I don't really care if you're taking incompletes, hmm... [*Hesitates*] just let me know, give me a piece of paper when the time comes that says: "I want an incomplete." [*Zipper unzipping.*] If you give me your paper later on in the month, I will turn your grade in, and I think your incomplete gets removed, I believe... [*Quietly:* am I right about that?] [*Addresses front row student.*] Is it within a certain period of time that you can submit your paper, is that right?

STUDENT: They changed the rules now, I don't know.

JAMESON: And after a certain amount of time, you'll get your grade, but I don't know how long it takes for the system to process it... [*Mumbles indistinctly.*] So, what I'm trying to tell you, if time is too short for you, and if you are doing an ambitious project — which I hope you do — you can certainly have more time, but I need to know in advance, as I have to turn in these "incompletes." The other thing is, I want your papers for this course, or notes of "incomplete" or whatever, delivered here by... [*Chalk strokes on the blackboard*] 1-2pm, because they will have to be FedExed to me, so that I could get these grades sooner rather than later. And there will be a little box either in the library or in Joan's office where you can leave your papers. Obviously, if it's done beforehand, and if you give me your paper earlier, that is much better.

[*Long pause.*]

That's that. Now, I want to, hmm... [*Knocks lightly on the desk*] begin with <u>Doctor Faustus</u> today, if we can... [*Looks at his *notes. Talks to himself*: let me see what else we have here... (*Chair scratches the floor*).] And that means that it will probably take us two weeks to deal with Thomas Mann. As you already know, the novel is a collaboration with Adorno, it was written with Adorno's notes, so this gives us an opportunity to look at Adorno's modernist aesthetics from the perspective of literature and of art itself. And then, that will give us three more weeks to finish the rest of Aesthetic Theory... [*Page flipping*.] There is a total of twelve chapters, and I think we are up to six at the moment. Last time, we did Semblance and Expression... [*Quietly:* and that is if we discount, as we agreed we would, the "Paralipomena," the "Theories on the Origin of Art" and the "Draft Introduction."] So, I hope everyone is okay if we take a break and do a little bit of Thomas Mann, and then, beginning on April 1st, hmm... [*Exhales*] we will return to Aesthetic Theory and finish the rest of those chapters. Obviously, you have an interest to try and finish it as soon as you can.

[*Long pause*.]

Mm-hmm, are there questions about anything?

[*Silence*.]

Alright, now we've been reading this up very close, Aesthetic Theory, and it is indeed difficult to take a step back and try to see it from some distance. So, in order to see the overall pattern of this book, I invited one of your colleagues... [*Quietly*: Where is Fabio — ah, there he is] he just defended a brilliant thesis on the subject with a lot of new ideas about Aesthetic Theory. I invited Fabio to come to our seminar today and say something about the book, and about Adorno as a whole, before we move on to Thomas Mann. [*Addresses Fabio*.] You want to stand here in front of the class or you wanna sit? What do you want?

STUDENT: I'll stand... [*Chairs scratching the floor. Stomp-stomp. Footsteps across the floor*.]

Student Presentation on the Role of Concepts in Adorno

STUDENT ONE[1]: [*Clears throat.*] There are perhaps two ways of reading Aesthetic Theory, which is the thing I wrote about and which I think offers a productive manner for dealing with this text. One way of approaching this book is to think first about how Adorno relates to his titles. I must say, I really like Adorno's titles, because they are very inconspicuous... [*Chalk on the blackboard*] M-I-N-I-M-A M-O-R-A-L-I-A and then P-R-I-S-M-S or N-E-G-A-T-I-V-E D-I-A-L-E-C-T-I-C-S and others. These titles are very interesting to compare with current ones. They are very unlike the structure of the titles that we usually get in academia... [*Pause.*] It is common today to have one part of the title with something that is very abstract, like "The Weight of Fire"... [*Audience laughing*] and then after a colon comes something very specific like, "The Role of Women in Nineteenth-Century Welsh Short Stories" [*Laughter continues.*] So, this first part... [*Jameson laughing*] is supposed to be the creative one, and the second part of the title is the pragmatic one, which is supposed to make the book circulate and sell. And this disjunction here around the colon... [*Strikes the blackboard with his chalk*] is the total opposite of what happens in Adorno, and that's why I like his titles, because Adorno is not concerned with this structure of thematization or with circulation and promotion of his books. Adorno's titles point rather to their inside, and that's also related to the way in which he composes his texts.

[*Long pause.*]

So, when we go to... [*Pause.*] I don't like to talk about this without context, I'm not following the course, so I would like to avoid repetitions. When you come to the title... [*Chalk hits the blackboard*] A-E-S-T-H-E-T-I-C T-H-E-O-R-Y, there is an ambiguity here. You can read this title as Aesthetic [*Stressing*] Theory, or as [*Stressing*] Aesthetic Theory. And the transition or emphasis from one word to the other is what I think the title and the book means. Essentially, we have two different ways of reading this title, which are the two ways I mentioned before: as an Aesthetic Theory, or as an Aesthetic Theory. It is either a theory or an aesthetic gesture. And the way of reading it as an Aesthetic Theory — where the emphasis falls on the theoretical — it is to go after concepts. And then it's important to think about how Adorno deals with his concepts... [*Door creaks open.*] In his Philosophische Terminologie lectures,[2] in the second volume, hmm... [*Hesitates*] I am not sure if they have been translated into English...

JAMESON: [*Exhales deeply.*] Neither am I...

STUDENT ONE: They have translated some of Adorno's seminars, like metaphysics, sociology, aesthetics...[3]

JAMESON: Are they translated?

STUDENT ONE: Yes, some are... [*Pause.*] His Kant and Hegel seminars,[4] for example, they are really interesting, and we see in them a totally different Adorno than the one we find in Aesthetic Theory. In these seminars, it is like Adorno is talking directly to you... [*Pause.*]

JAMESON: This is true. I am thinking of Heidegger, but I am also thinking of Derrida's seminars. There are ten thousand pages of recordings of Derrida that people have made where you can hear Derrida responding and engaging more fully... [*Mumbles indistinctly.*]

STUDENT ONE: Yes, and the thing with Adorno is that you see this man who is making an effort to be more didactic, right, so he had to repeat many of his thoughts. And then he had students coming to his office hours, and then he addresses some of the conversations he had in the office hours in the next sessions of the seminar, and so on. So, the seminar is a very different form of discourse from what you see when you are reading Aesthetic Theory. And then he also has this thing about concepts. He says that whenever... [*Cough in the audience*] a problem crystalizes, you have a concept, so the concept is the crystallization of a particular problem. And in a certain sense, concepts, for him, are like scars of historical suffering.

[*Pause.*] This is why Adorno does not abandon tradition; this is why Adorno insists on using, hmm... [*Hesitates*] you know, "subject-object," "metaphysics," all of these old concepts, because they have a history of their own; they are imbedded in history; the history of a problem is something inside the concept... [*Pause.*] That's why Adorno is very different from people like Deleuze, who says in What is Philosophy?[5] that the task of the philosopher is to create new concepts; it is to come up with new concepts and... [*Pause.*]

JAMESON: With new concepts?

STUDENT ONE: Yes, new concepts, and Adorno is like... [*Pause.*]

JAMESON: And new names? Neologisms and so on...

STUDENT ONE: Yeah, new names and neologisms. So, Adorno makes it clear in several places that he is for tradition and for continuing using old philosophical concepts.

[*Long pause.*]

So, the first thing about Adorno and concepts is that he is sticking with traditional concepts. The second thing is... [*Pause.*] You see, concepts in Adorno are always contextual. He says the same thing about Kant in his lectures on Kant. If you go for a concordance to see what a concept in Kant means, you won't get too far — Adorno has this very nice definition of a definition. He says that definitions are like a moment of luck, and the most beautiful thing is when a philosopher comes up with a nice definition, but they are in no way absolutely essential to the making of philosophy. Therefore, Adorno always discusses concepts [*Stressing*] in context, so that when you say... [*Pause.*] If you want to write a paper on the concept of "subject" in Adorno, you have to read all over and try to figure out the context in which the word "subject" appears, or the concept of "metaphysics" and all the other ones. Concepts emerge as part of the texture of the text in Adorno. [*Pause.*] This also calls attention to Adorno's use of proper names, and these are especially visible in Aesthetic Theory. Proper names for him work differently... [*Pause.*] They don't relate primarily to something like a body, for when you think about a proper name like "Kant," "Hegel," "Nietzsche," you think about a body of works, or texts on their own, and then these names relate to the texts. And that's not the way they work for Adorno. For Adorno, the names are categories, so when he says "Hegel," this means, hmm... [*Hesitates*] this is a category which works according to the logic of the text. And this category has [*Stressing*] a place in the text, which can work very differently, because it is subjected to the text's movement, to the categorial progression. Therefore, proper names acquire meaning in relation to the place they have in Adorno's texts. So, I think it's a nice idea... [*Door cracks open*] to think of names in terms of categories and not so much as a stable body of theory or philosophy, right? So, this is then always about his relation to concepts.

[*Long pause.*]

On the other hand, and this is very smart of Adorno, he makes all these arguments... [*Door slams shut*] about the preservation of tradition and he views concepts as having history imbedded in them, and tensions, and in sum, these concepts are not equal to themselves. But on the other hand, he is also creating new concepts... [*Cough in the audience.*] So, in Aesthetic Theory you have, for example, "fireworks," "enigmaticalness" or "the enigmatic character of art," and what else... [*Tries to remember*] or something like "Entkunstung" in the beginning, which was translated as... [*Looks at Jameson*] "deartification"?

JAMESON: De-... [*Hesitates.*] Wait, "deaestheticization" is how they translated it, but I think it's more like "de-arting" or "des-arting" or something like that... [*Pause.*]

STUDENT ONE: Yeah. So, it is interesting to see that if, on the one hand, Adorno always defends the usage of traditional concepts; on the other hand, he is also always producing his new concepts. But he uses these neologisms as if they were already part of the tradition... [*Words indistinct*] he never calls attention to them for their novelty, he doesn't parade or advertise them or something. This is something then that points the way to what I was trying to get at in my dissertation... [*Cough in the audience*] that opposed to this conceptual reading, there is one which looks very different. That if you read the book as an [*Stressing*] Aesthetic Theory, then the text can yield a strong reading and you're going to end up seeing it as an aesthetic artifact... [*Door cracks open*] with its own theory. Philosophy hasn't taken notice of this because philosophers only look for definitions and truth claims... [*Pause*.] One example of this could be Zuidervaart's book, you know, The Redemption of Illusion,[6] which is one of the best introductions to Aesthetic Theory in a sense, as a set of propositions; then there is also one by Marc Jimenez[7] and many others, but Zuidervaart, he makes a big deal of this Wahrheitsgehalt concept, what is it, the, hmm... [*Hesitates*]

JAMESON: Truth content.

STUDENT ONE: Truth content, yes, and he organized the book to explain what truth content means. And Zuidervaart then uses this whole argumentation to say that Aesthetic Theory is all about propositional truth, in the end to prove it wrong. A lot of people do that. By the way, there is an interesting formal argument to be made about how people take pains to read Aesthetic Theory, or read Adorno's thought as a whole, in order to prove that Adorno should not be read, like the saying, "Do what I say, don't do what I do"... [*Cough in the audience*.] Why so much effort on the part of Habermas, of Wellmer and others, just to say in the end that Adorno is wrong? Why not just go about doing their own business, you know? They interpret and contextualize in order to see how much they could integrate Adorno's theory of art into their own projects, but maybe they could do that without trashing Adorno... [*Words indistinct*] like Wellmer especially.[8] But then against it, my contention would be that there is [*Stressing*] an expressive side of Aesthetic Theory... [*Pause*.] Oh yeah, and the thing about Wahrheitsgehalt is that Zuidervaart makes the whole point about the truth content of artworks and how artworks are political because they absorb into themselves historical processes, but in a non-conceptual way, like in a monad. But then, as Zuidervaart analyzes this, and when this is competently done, he forgets that the enigmatic character of art is in opposition to the truth content. Zuidervaart deals with concepts as transparent and stable entities, but when we pay attention to this component of the concept of truth content, which is in dialectical opposition to the enigmatic character of artworks, we realize that truth content enters a relationship with time, because as artworks age, they reveal new layers of meaning. There is a part in the beginning of Aesthetic Theory where Adorno says that, for Flaubert, Madame Bovary is just a great work because we don't pay attention to adultery anymore. It's the waning of this moral problem, of adultery as a theme, that made the novel's style become more visible; as long as the subject matter impacts you, you can't distance yourself to enjoy the style. So, there is a whole relationship between truth and time, which Zuidervaart forgets about. And then, if you start to think about this... [*Pause.*] That's the idea, like the more you go into Aesthetic Theory to look for concepts, for a chain of concepts, or the organization of concepts, the more you start to realize that there is an aesthetic principle of organizing... [*Cough in the audience*] the whole book.

[*Long pause.*]

And then, the next step, the next thing to do is to investigate how discontinuity can be seen as the main element in the structure of Aesthetic Theory. [*Pause.*] Even if it's a book which was published posthumously, as lots of commentators say on strategic points, "Oh yeah, it's complete but still unfinished"... [*Words indistinct.*] The fact that it was published posthumously, and it didn't have Adorno's last touches, is not a reason for not trusting its structure. And then... [*Pause.*] So, how does this discontinuity play in the book? I guess that we usually say that the different parts of the book are like constellations, and that they express. It's like they are surrounding the object and express it through the tension that they create around it. But constellations are normally taken as not formally strict, and I would like to argue that they are mixed in the book with more traditional dialectical reversals. Negation through juxtaposition and opposition coexist. And then, if we think of the organization of the book in terms of these discontinuities, then we can see four, at least four different levels of these discontinuities. First, it is between the big blocs that constitute... [*Pause*] how do you call these things, they are not chapters, but...

JAMESON: I wouldn't call them chapters either and I don't know how to call them; they have no name... [*Pause*.]

STUDENT ONE: Yeah. The first thing, like the book is a...

JAMESON: They've been added afterwards, I believe... [*Quietly*: I have the first edition, I should have a look at... (*Words indistinct*) if it was already there. Tiedemann, I suppose, wrote those things up... (*Mumbles indistinctly*).]

STUDENT ONE: Yeah, but... Right, right — the introduction was started by Adorno himself.

JAMESON: That's right, yeah, Adorno wrote it.

STUDENT ONE: So, you can say that Aesthetic Theory is organized in circles. There is a sort of circularity in it, in the sense that the book starts with "Art, Society, Aesthetics," the so-called Chapter or Bloc 1, and it also ends with "Society," in Chapter or Bloc 12, and this is if we ignore the last three appendixes that were added later... [*Quietly*: "Paralipomena," "Theories of the Origins of Art," and "Draft Introduction."] And then you have levels of discontinuity between these huge blocs: "art, society, aesthetics," "situation," "on the categories of the ugly," "natural beauty" and whatever. This is like a first level of discontinuity. [*Decisively*.] Then, there is a sort of, hmm... [*Hesitates*] it is like a progression from the most concrete to the culmination or germination of the most abstract. Because if you start with the concrete situation of art, as Adorno saw it, and then he goes through this situation to history and the historical categories, as Adorno comes to terms with Hegel and... [*Thud. Object falls on the floor*] Kant — hmm, Kant and Hegel — then he does a sort of appropriation of these things, revisiting all these traditional concepts like "semblance and expression," through "enigmaticalness," which I mentioned already, and then you go to more philosophical Adornian concerns, like "subject-object," "toward a theory of the artwork," after that "universal and particular," and then you end with "society" again.

[*Long pause.*]

So, this is the first level. Then, inside each of these blocs or chapters, there are moments of breaks or discontinuity, and then inside each paragraph, and sometimes inside each sentence, there are places in which you have a semicolon or something else that marks a turning around in the argument. So, these are the units... [*Pause.*] And I think that these discontinuities are not static, and you cannot map them. They are also subject to time; to the time of reading as well as in connection with the process of aging of the Aesthetic Theory itself. The, hmm... [*Hesitates.*] Mm-hmm, Shierry Weber Nicholsen registers that. Perhaps hers, we have one of the most beautiful books on Aesthetic Theory, which is called, hmm... [*Tries to remember*] Exact Imagination[9] or something like that. She deals with how Aesthetic Theory itself, hmm... [*Hesitates*] she deals with what is happening to the book, and how the book is self-aging, and this acts like one other theme in this book. And so, up to a certain extent, in a sense what Adorno is saying about art can be also said about Aesthetic Theory itself. And then there is the thing of what one could do with... [*Student raises hand.*] Yes...

STUDENT TWO: Could you repeat the name of Nicholsen?

STUDENT ONE: Of Nicholsen?

JAMESON: [*Chair-back creaks.*]She is the translator of the Notes to Literature, and of many other books. [*Chalk strokes on the blackboard*] S-H-I-E-R-R-Y and W-E-B-E-R. She translated Prisms with Sam Weber under the name [*Chalk strokes*] N-I-C-H-O-L-S-E-N.[10]

STUDENT ONE: And then... [*Door cracks open*] I guess, given all of this, the problem is what we should do with Adorno's, hmm... [*Hesitates*] "end" of this book, if we can say that. [*Pause.*] He says that the book is paratactically organized in a way to express a Mittelpunkt, a middle point, which is not present. So, the book organizes itself around an absent center. This idea which is, hmm... [*Looks for words*] I think there is a reference in Minima Moralia about this too — an idea which comes from Benjamin, of course — but then, which becomes a true ideal for Adorno to pursue. And there is a conscious compositional aim in Aesthetic Theory, which was the closest he reached with this ideal of paratactical organization. And then, I guess the question to ask is what would this sort of empty center represent in the book? [*Pause.*] It is an absent center that is made out from all of these discontinuities, and all of these breaks and turns are then pointing to this, hmm... [*Hesitates*] to this thing in the middle of the book that is empty? And then Shierry says that this empty middle point could be mimesis, and Gerhard Schweppenhäuser, who was here this term, he said that it could be tradition. And this postmodern German philosopher, what's his name, mm-hmm... [*Tries to remember*] Wolfgang Welsh claims in his study of des Erhabenen that it is the sublime.[11] So you can see how many possibilities there are to interpret this book aesthetically. But it is important to observe that this middle point is not a thing, but is rather constituted exactly by the discontinuities in Aesthetic Theory, by this... [*Pause*] by the fact that it is not the result of an argument, for it doesn't work like a proposition. So, you can see that these empty middle points disrupt the whole book or the other way around, that these discontinuities form an absence in the center. This is why I contend that the middle point stands for the Revolution; it points or gestures towards rebellion, and here are some arguments for that. First of all, among all these options, it is clear that a satisfactory one should not be present in the book as such, and one can't find the concept of revolution used in this strong sense there. The revolution... [*Sighs*] is there, but not as an event, there is no resolution for the revolution there... [*Jameson laughing.*] But for Adorno, as for Benjamin, the revolution is the, hmm... [*Hesitates*] you know, of course, a concrete event, but it is also an epistemological ideal, it's a point from which things acquire a different character; from the messianic light, things appear differently. And of course, there are critics who say that the revolution is just a regulatory concept, like in Kant, that you can never get to it, but just measure yourself against it. I disagree with that, because the revolution is something that might be started at any moment as a concrete event, just like the Messiah may already be here now. But at any rate, and then I guess it... [*Audience murmuring.*]

JAMESON: Well, utopia could also be a word for revolution.

STUDENT ONE: Right. Well, for Adorno... [*Pause*] *Versöhnung.*

JAMESON: Mm-hmm... [*Exhales deeply.*] Have we come to that yet? Reconciliation? Yeah, I don't think we had, and it's a very important concept to introduce here... [*Chalk strokes on the blackboard*] V-E-R-S-Ö-H-N-U-N-G or "reconciliation." What else, what other similar words are there to discuss? [*Decisively.*] We'll get to it. Are there questions?

[*Long silence.*]

STUDENT THREE: May I?

STUDENT ONE: Yes.

STUDENT THREE: When you were speaking about center and discontinuity, and also before that, when you spoke about concepts in Adorno and how proper names work as concepts, so what I gathered from this is how much movement is implied in his thinking. The idea that arguments and claims revolve around this absent center of *Aesthetic Theory*, which I think is what you mean when you talk about the book's expressive character, and that they create and are created by discontinuities, is this also connected somehow to tension? Do you think tension and movement are concepts that can illuminate the idea of constellation...?

STUDENT ONE: [*Enthusiastic.*] Oh yeah, yeah, yeah...

STUDENT THREE: ...where everything is moving and you have these pictures of discontinuities always there and of reconciliations, or whatever. Can this be a way to interpret this book...? [*Words indistinct.*]

STUDENT ONE: The idea also of constellation, and also of what Benjamin calls dialectical... [*Tries to remember*] *Stillstand*, or something...

JAMESON: Mm-hmm, "dialectic at a standstill."

STUDENT ONE: Yes, standstill, dialectic at a standstill... [*Chuckles.*] So, there is this idea also that you have one point at which the present and the past converge into the future, or converge into one point, this also happens here, but it is much more interesting because this convergence can only be activated by the process of reading...

STUDENT THREE: [*Interrupting.*] By what? But how does this...? [*Words indistinct.*]

STUDENT ONE: By the process of our reading. So, it's not simply that you can conceptualize or deal with concepts outside of this process of reading. And that's, I guess, why it is productive to start with concepts as the units, which are then to be subjected to the play of negativity [*Pause.*] Again, the first thing to reject is to, hmm... [*Hesitates*] to reject solidified concepts, as if they could be extracted from textual discontinuities. This form of reading, moving away from the organization of concepts and sentences, involves a kind of practice in time. Because time... [*Excited.*] Time itself is also a component in the book. There is also a sense by which time is [*Stresses*] <u>inside</u> the book itself, which in turn is only embodied in the process of reading, which is an act in time. It's sort of a double process... [*Looks for words*] the text receives the reading, but it also reacts to it; reading takes place in a specific time, but it also enacts the time in the book, that's why time is also a category inside the book.

[*Takes a deep breath.*]

JAMESON: Other... [*Raps his knuckles on the desk.*] Other questions?

STUDENT FOUR: I'm curious about this play between using traditional concepts, but also using new ones, like neologisms. You mentioned that there are these passages where Adorno gives some kind of arguments of why we still need traditional concepts, why it has to be traditional concepts, including this essay with... [*Words indistinct.*] What exactly, or how does the argument go, I mean, why we should use traditional concepts and why we shouldn't use any of the new concepts?

STUDENT ONE: Mm-hmm. [*Nods.*] Well, Adorno is explicitly programmatic about this, but we can say first because of their relationship to history; because they solidify historical problems… [*Pause*] and for Adorno, history is a history of suffering, which is registered in language. Basically, what unifies human spirit or experience is suffering, and in a certain sense, these concepts can be seen as scars, like sedimentations of suffering. Let me add as a parenthesis that this could look like a moral position. [*Agitated.*] But this is also interesting, just as I tried to argue here, the thing with Adorno is… [*Pause.*] One can ask, is Adorno a moral philosopher? He taught a course on moral philosophy in 1963, and then he also had plans to write a moral theory, but then nobody knows exactly what it would have looked like. Because his writing is so much imbued with what one could term as moral concerns, hmm… [*Searches for word*] with injunctions, right? And one can sense throughout his work something resounding in the background, like "life shouldn't be like this," and it is an interesting thing to see how there are some many rhetorical figures… [*Pause*] one of the figures is exaggeration. When Adorno is discussing Alban Berg, for instance, or I don't know, people like Schoenberg in his Philosophy of New Music, one quite often has the impression that it is the [*Stressing*] fate of humanity that hinges on the right appreciation of these artworks. Right? And it's really curious to see how some enthusiastic readers of Adorno take him to the letter, they attach themselves to the text and they… [*Giggles*] like, truly believe in these exaggerations and lose the point. Adorno deals with exaggerations as moral interjections, as it were. On the other hand, however, this negative morality coexists with conceptual flexibility; as we saw, concepts are not equal to themselves. So, when you get almost any concept… [*Pause.*] And that's because Adorno subjects concepts to a textual economy; again, he doesn't deal with the concepts in the abstract or on a purely definitional way. And so, if concepts are not equal to themselves, or identical to themselves, then Adorno can stick with them to make them work in opposition.

And that's how their truth content emerges too. Just like art, hmm... [*Hesitates*] concepts may also have truth content... [*Cough in the audience.*] There is a philosophical-literary program there, retrieving the truth content's potential in the concept itself. The... [*Pause*] the... [*Excited*] the big topic which people discuss all the time has to do with the subject. Adorno doesn't want to let go of the subject... [*Stammering*] over... over... over, he doesn't want to surrender strong subjectivity which, he thinks it is, like, totally necessary to enable political action and anything like praxis. And from this, a lot of people say that this is elitist, outdated and so on...

STUDENT THREE: But do you think that this is ultimately compatible or reconcilable with someone like Deleuze, for whom, you know, the emphasis is more on the invention of new concepts, or you think of them as totally different projects?

STUDENT ONE: I think they are totally different projects...

JAMESON: Yeah. Of new works... [*Quietly:* the model is in the works; so, there will always be new works, which Deleuze also maintains, you know (*Mumbles indistinctly*).] Any other... [*Pause.*] Questions?

[*Long silence.*]

JAMESON: [*Addresses Student One.*] Well, listen, that was very helpful. It is very good for us to draw back from the details of Adorno's aesthetics... [*Cough in the audience*] and try see the bigger picture. Ethics, I think you haven't mentioned the word "negate." Adorno's ethics would be [*Stressing*] <u>to negate</u>...

STUDENT ONE: Right... Right.

JAMESON: ... and if you want to know what <u>Versöhnung</u> is, well — our relationship to formed reality is to negate it. That's why it has to be what you're calling a "strong subject." That won't be Ego stuff, in the Lacanian tradition, I think, but it would be taking a position from which one can negate and refuse. [*Pause.*] The great refusal from Dante was also one of the things that Marcuse liked to talk about. Mm-hmm... [*Pause.*] So, and if you [*Whispering*] <u>affirm this reality</u>, then we're in positivism and you fall prey to different forms of conformism, social commodification and so on and so forth. If you could live in a world without negating it, that would be reconciliation or Versöhnung, but that's only possible in the utopia. Or maybe utopia is a regulative idea, as you say… [*Quietly*: unless it's the work of art, which is the utopia.] Now, that's when all of that comes into decline, hmm… [*Hesitates.*] Take the historical concept of "beauty," for example. This is an impossible concept for which there is no use anymore — although there are people who try to resuscitate it, and I'm not gonna give you names…[12] [*Audience chuckles*] — hmm, beauty is historically marked and therefore it is the [*Stammers*] ssss… symptom and the crystallization of a concrete historical experience. That's the "truth content," as you… [*Looks at Student One*] discussed it. Well, just because beauty is wrong, we can't get rid of it, because if we get rid of it, we get rid of history, and we get also rid of the "truth content" of that particular historical experience… [*Quietly*: I don't know if you wanna call that in the eighteenth century.] So, all you're left with is to preserve and cancel, and we have the Hegelian moment here. You have to keep it, but… [*Cough in the audience*] but also leave it behind, keep it in the back of our mind. Now, the way I would put this, maybe this is a crazy… [*Chair scratching the floor*] way of putting it: we should go through all of these concepts, and it's a whole world of them, and they are all wrong, but they're all also indispensable. [*Pause.*] And in general, these concepts, they come in pairs, so that they cancel each other out. So, you always would get two of them. If you held on to one, hmm… [*Hesitates*] you would be in that one expression that I used [*Stressing*] thematizing it, and maybe we can think of it this way… [*Quietly*: at least in Adorno's version of the twelve-tone system, or of the atonal system] that if you held on to one of these concepts, then you can say: "well, Adorno is really all about this," then you would be re-establishing a tonal center, right: you would be turning the work back from atonal into a tonal work, and thus undoing everything that you were trying to do. [*Softly.*] But that's very hard not to do that. [*Looks at Student One.*] You mentioned an absence of the center, that's exactly what they're doing, and you are obviously right. So, if you say: now it's really all about "mimesis," or maybe it's all about "non-identity"... [*Quietly*: and that's the favored post-structuralist version of this] yes, of course, but it's also about anything else, and if you do that, if you try to thematize and establish a tonal center or theme, then you are wrong about him. [*Excited*.] I would have said myself it's about [*Whispering*] production and objectivity. Mm-hmm. I mean, that may be also wrong, but I do think that there is something here in Adorno that people overlook, and that in a lot of these bourgeois fixations... [*Chair scratches the floor*] they are overlooked, and that this is really fundamentally a productionist... [*Quietly*: and he says that over and over again] aesthetics. So, one would have to...

[*Long pause*.]

The other way to deal with this would be maybe if you could do something like Hegel's Logic and say: "Take all of these concepts, and if you could hope to show as each one of them breaks down, forming its own opposition, and something else takes its place, and that one is a little better, but then it also breaks down," and so on and so forth. I mean, that's sort of the structure and the layout of Hegel's Logic. With all each of these categories sort of proving unequal to the totality, as they are breaking down, and then another concept is taking its place and so on. Maybe that would give you something... [*Pause*.] It would certainly give you Aesthetic Theory as a work in time, but if it's a work — I like your idea about reading the title in two ways — if it's an [*Stressing*] aesthetic theory, then it is a work in time and it is also an object, and finally you can't do that. So, I mean... [*Pause*.] But I mean, I think we have to also, once in a while, draw back and we'd be doing that more and more hopefully as we get to the end of this. But we have to think of the overall project, which you can't just look at individual things, even though we also have to look at individual things in order to get to the overall project. So, it's, hmm... [*Hesitates*] so, it's a very... [*Pause*.] But I think that's the proof that this is in a way...

[*Quietly*: this is Adorno's most successful book.] If philosophy gets to be a failure anyway, then this is his most successful failure.

[*Door creaks open.*]

I mean, because, in Negative Dialectics, when he comes to the end, he gives you what he calls "models." That's a very bad word, because he can't... [*Exhales deeply*] that's the worst moment, I think, of Adorno's theorizing. He can't just give us illustrations of what is the soul, what is the... [*Quietly*: I forget now what they are, like a model of freedom, model of reason... (*Mumbles indistinctly*).] You can't just extract something and then think about that in isolation. And the greatness of Adorno was to realize that one can't go on doing this kind of illustration, so this is then one book in which you really get this [*Stressing*] sequence, this never-ending sequence, and yeah, maybe it's a circle, or he is going in circles of some sort, as you said, refusing to set a theme or give us models...

STUDENT ONE: Just to clarify something about history. What makes Adorno different from Hegel is that, for Hegel, historical progress is somehow constantly aiming at this one goal of reconciliation in Absolute Spirit and...

JAMESON: [*Interrupts.*] Yeah. Yeah. You can't do that with Adorno. For Adorno, remember, this leads to regression, progress, and domination of nature, so, hmm... [*Exhales deeply*] so you have to find a way to reconcile somehow with nature. But then again, when Hegel gets to the end, and you think, "Oh, thank God, he finally got somewhere," then it turns out you have to go through the whole process all over again, so it's not also like you got somewhere... [*Mumbles indistinctly.*]

STUDENT ONE: Yeah. Right... [*Chuckles.*]

JAMESON: And on another plane, with Hegel, you are always caught within his system. I mean, you get to the Science of Logic, then you've gotta go through his philosophy of Nature, and then to Spirit, and then, within Spirit, you have subjective, objective, and absolute, where art, religion and philosophy belong. Whereas in Adorno, all you have to go through is history, and that doesn't stop... [*Quietly*: but unfortunately, maybe that it also cancels... (*Word indistinct*).] So, it's a question of how we read their relation to history. I always liked Schoenberg's remark after he wrote his violin concerto and when he sent it off, he said, [*Impersonates Schoenberg*] "Now they will have to invent a completely different way of playing the violin." [*Chuckles.*] What I think that he meant is that, when a radically new work of art is made, it also brings about other radically new forms of perception, of listening, or even maybe new forms of community and collectivity.[13] Thomas Mann likes to quote... [*Pause.*] He couldn't read James Joyce, really, he used to say, [*Impersonates Mann*] "It's really too rich for me and I can't make any..." [*Cough in the audience.*] But he read Harry Lavin's book on Joyce[14] that was sort of the kickoff book for modernism — a book that nobody reads anymore, I think. Anybody read Harry... [*Chalk strokes on the blackboard*] H-A-R-R-Y L-A-V-I-N?

[*Silence.*]

That's what I thought. It's in the "New Directions" series that was the vanguard. It was our Suhrkamp in those days, as they published Pound, William Carlos Williams, and many others. And it was in their critical series, this book just called James Joyce, with a very short introduction that became the sort of defining moment of what came to be called "modernism"... [*Pause.*] This is, hmm... [*Hesitates.*] This is obviously already in the early 1940s, I think, and this was Lavin's first book... [*Quietly*: he never got a Ph.D., he was a junior fellow and they didn't get Ph.D.s in those days.] So, Lavin's James Joyce was published in 1941 maybe, or something like that, and I don't know whether Joyce was still alive... [*Quietly:* I think Joyce died in that same year.] But anyway, as Lavin was suggesting... [*Looks around*] the thing about Ulysses is that it makes it impossible to write novels in the old way. You can't do it anymore. And in a sense, one could say something similar about Adorno's philosophizing, that it sort of canceled out all kind of traditional ways of philosophizing. I think the main thing is... [*Quietly*: it's not the only main thing, of course] but this business of the historicity of these concepts.

You know, you think about these philosophers, and maybe this is a good place to say something here about Marcuse... [*Quietly*: I mean, it was clear to me that Marcuse, unlike Adorno, did not deal very much with the historicity of the concepts that he was using.] You had to feel that these concepts are coming out of a place there, that they are marked, that they are breaking down, or that they are like punctured or something. And traditional philosophers normally don't do that — they know what their concepts are, they are distinct, and these are words, and they try to do something with them, by clarifying or proving them. We will touch on this later on, when we will talk about Adorno's essay about essay. But in traditional philosophy, there is no history of the becoming of these concepts, and maybe one could say with Marx that they, hmm... [*Reflects*] that they believed that once there was history, but there isn't one anymore. And if you read Marcuse, for example, you see there is much less historicity in the use of his concepts... [*Pause.*] But here, what makes Aesthetic Theory remarkable and self-referential is that, with Adorno, you can't really tell the difference between whether he is talking about the reality of the concept or about reality itself... [*Door cracks open.*] Both are historical. So, his is a way of how words are changing, and when you notice that things are happening to these words, then this happens at the same time with changes in historical reality. These things are happening at once. And how to use these concepts... [*Cough in the audience*] as they've been evolving all the time, I mean, how would you pin them down, that is the problem for true philosophy or theory. That, I think, is one of the things that Aesthetic Theory gives us as a concrete example of, concepts or knowledge and reality evolving or developing at the same time.

[*Long pause.*]

Incidentally, I haven't said that, but a few people turned... [*Pause.*] You remember when I asked you at the beginning of this seminar to make a glossary, an index or a lexicon of concepts or issues in Aesthetic Theory? And the few people who turned in those pages are very good... [*Looks at one student.*] I think you gave me one, right? They are excellent, and it's a pity that, hmm... [*Pause*.] I mean, those of you who are doing it should go on because I think it is really a fun way of re-organizing Aesthetic Theory, and I guess I would almost be tempted to take one of those indexes as a substitute for the seminar's paper if anybody wants to do it... [*Quietly*: but you can also come talk to me... (*Indistinct*).] Mm-hmm, okay. Do we have any further questions or thoughts on concepts in Adorno's Aesthetic Theory?

[*Silence*.]

Okay. We'll suspend Adorno for a little bit and turn to Thomas Mann. Now, they have Doctor Faustus in the university bookstore, right? Everyone got a copy of it? [*Pause*.] How many people have their copies? [*Counts raised hands*.] Mm-hmm. Bring them in next time. How many people have read it? [*A few students raise hands*.] Good. Good. How many people have read it halfway? Okay. Okay. Mm-hmm. There is a new translation of this book and I'm trying to get a hold of it. I would prefer if you can use this one[15] [*Holds book up*] because it has the same pagination, which comes in very handy... [*Quietly*: even your paperback is just a miniaturized version of this.][16] Mm-hmm. But obviously, if you read German, it would be wonderful, and you should read it in German because there is a lot of... [*Mumbles indistinctly*.] You know, Gide in the 1920s, when he was writing what he decided was to be his great novel, The Counterfeiters, he also kept a diary. So, Gide is writing a novel called The Counterfeiters, which is a novel-within-a novel, and a sort of an author diary or journal about the novel he is writing called "counterfeiters." And on top of all that, Gide himself kept a diary of his writing of the diary of... [*Audience laughing*] The Counterfeiters.[17] Well, this is all very entertaining as these are not very... [*Quietly:* Gide's own diaries are not terribly interesting; I mean, there are some important parts, but overall, they... [*Mumbles indistinctly*.]

[*Long pause*.]

Thomas Mann kept a diary throughout his life, and he began writing Doctor Faustus, well, he gives you the exact date, I believe, in 1943. I think the Russians, hmm... [*Exhales deeply.*] When was the surrender at Stalingrad...? [*Looks at the class.*] Anyone? [*Quietly*: Was it in 1943? I believe so. It's right before the great Russian counter-offensive in the east... (*Mumbles indistinctly*).] Mm-hmm, but that's not when Zeitblom begins to write his biography, but when Thomas Mann begins to write the novel, and it was concluded, I think, in 1945, I think, at some point. And it may well be that it came out in English before German because, after all, Mann was here in the US. The stuff they printed in German at that point was in New York with a German press, and there was also stuff printed in Sweden, and of course in Switzerland. So, and I'm not sure when those... [*Achoo. Student sneezes*] were first published. Anyway, Mann thought this novel was the most difficult thing he'd ever done... [*Takes a sip of water.*] But he couldn't let it go, and so then he wrote up his account and it's called Die Entstehung des Doktor Faustus.[18] I don't know if it was translated into English, but you can look for something called the "writing" or the "genesis" of Doctor Faustus...

STUDENT: It has been translated as The Story of a Novel...[19]

JAMESON: The Story of a Novel? Ah, okay, well, that's very enlightening and you get a wonderful sense of Thomas Mann there as he uses his own diaries. And yeah, somewhere in there he also talks about Adorno. So, the Story, which came out in 1949, in German first, is a useful adjunct to this as it gives you a little more of the material and context. Now, I guess the main question is... [*Quietly*: maybe that's his own question really]: Is this novel a national allegory? [*Pause.*] I think yes, it's a novel that is very much about Germany. Mm-hmm... [*Looks at the audience.*] How many of you read German...? [*Quietly*: I think I've already asked you several times.] [*Counts.*] Okay, one, two, three... oh, that's not very many. How many of you have some special interest in Germany?

[*Silence.*]

How many of you have a special interest in World War Two?

[*Silence.*]

Or in the Nazi period?

[*Silence.*]

Mm-hmm... [*Gently slams his palm on the desk.*]

[*Audience laughing.*]

How about music? Well, music we've already covered.

[*Long pause.*]

I think what you have to understand about this novel is how to come to terms, in some sense, with this question of "Germany" and "German identity," "German guilt," "German exceptionalism," "German uniqueness," and so forth. It's a book about the war and this is maybe not a bad moment that Doctor Faustus starts in 1943, since it gives voice to those feelings that Zeitblom describes in terms of losing the war, or those feelings that all Germans had at that moment in their history. Mm-hmm, again, and maybe that people can understand both sides of this... [*Quietly*: that is what you do when your government is responsible for a war like this] and then, what would you do on the other side when you're losing, as it happened in 1945, when he alludes to the Werwolf units...[20] [*Stomp-stomp-stomp. Footsteps.*] Anybody knows what that was? These were just kids who were... [*Door cracks open*] supposed to organize guerilla resistance behind the enemy lines, just children fighting in this Germany that was stormed on both sides by the Americans and the Soviets. Berlin was the city in which there was ferocious fighting, not nearly as... [*Quietly:* I just heard on the radio the other day that the only cities that the Americans have been involved in real city warfare since World War Two were Huế in Vietnam and Mogadishu; both of which were disastrous defeats for the Americans. But it was the Soviets who took the Reichstag.] So, these forms of urban resistance, they are also somewhere in the background here in the novel.

[*Long pause.*]

Now... [*Cough in the audience.*] On German modernity, I think you have to understand that, since World War Two, Germany is just another sm... [*Hesitates*] relatively small European country with a sort of a provincial cast. West Germany — or if you consider it still West Germany — is a rather provincial place. [*Takes a sip of water. Screws-in water bottle cap.*] I don't think you can understand the sense which is being conveyed or alluded to in the novel, of this specific German national sense of inferiority and isolation. First of all, you have a country that only comes to unification very late; it's very interesting if you follow up Wagner's path through this. Wagner's patron was the King of Bavaria... [*Quietly*: this is a whole different story] but the French wanted to try to preserve Bavaria as an independent kingdom and you can see why. Because it means that this enormous Prussian entity next door would not have been unified anymore, and there would have been a counterweight. Bavaria, if you look at the map... [*Quietly:* Bavaria has always been a sort of loose cannon in all of its relationships between Austria and the other kingdoms.] And this is a novel about Bavaria, by the way, so this extraneous information, most of it takes place in Munich. That is the city of the, hmm... [*Hesitates*] of the German revolution, outside of Berlin, of the German Soviets, so to speak, Räterepublik Bayern; it is the Red Republic that lasted maybe a month or two. Munich is also the city of Hitler's Beer Hall putsch... [*Quietly*: in twenty, when was it, 1923?] Munich is also the capital of Wagner's patronage and it's, of course, where Thomas Mann... [*Raps his knuckles on the desk*] himself lived. His house was on an island across the river, and it was destroyed. He describes what that house was when he went back to look at it after the war and saw in what condition it was. And much of the intellectual background is also that of Munich as the artistic capital of Germany, the... [*Hesitates*] or it was once the artistic capital. Munich was the center of fin-de-siècle Germany, whereas Berlin was more of the capital of the Weimar period. So, this Munich that he is describing here for the most part, in the pre-World War One period, and then in the 1920s, it's still this bohemian Munich world... [*Pause.*] If you're interested in this history... [*Quietly*: for the Bavarian period, I'm not even sure, but there is... (*Mumbles indistinctly*).] There is one movie that you can watch which is based on a novel by Thomas

Mann's brother, who was also a novelist as famous in his day as Thomas... [*Quietly*: well, maybe Heinrich Mann wasn't as famous as Thomas, for no one gave him the Nobel prize] but there is an East German movie based on his novel that is called [*Chalk strokes on the blackboard*] D-E-R U-N-T-E-R-T-A-N, and that means the S-U-B-J-E-C-T.[21]

[*Long pause.*]

But of all that, if you want to pick up the story after the war, in the immediate post-war period, and this ends with Germany's year zero. I mean, that's the final thing, and nothing in the book foreshadows any of that. So, then you can also look at The Marriage of Maria Braun. This is Fassbinder's film, who gives you another great historical view on the [*Stresses*] immediate post-war German period, and finally there is the great series by Edgar Reitz... [*Quietly*: this was a TV series] and it is a very remarkable historical panorama called... [*Chalk strokes on the blackboard*] H-E-I-M-A-T or Homeland.[22] This one is about a family in a fictional Rhineland village from 1919 to the present. The first Heimat series ran from 1919, or the end of World War One to Bitburg... [*Quietly*: that's when Reagan visited the SS cemetery in Bitburg, Germany.] That was not one of our finest moments... [*Chuckles.*] Heimat is about this family and how various brothers go off, and one of them, Hermann, becomes a musician. And then there is a second Heimat series, Heimat 2,[23] in which you follow the music of Hermann to Munich in the 1960s and there is a lot of stuff about music and film and so forth. [*Pause.*] And then there is supposed to be a third Heimat,[24] which would be about the fall of the Berlin Wall, and this one takes place in Berlin. It is very remarkable and... [*Cough in the audience*] I highly recommend that, just for you to get some sense of what Germany and Munich was like. Now, to come back to the monarchy, Germany has a very late unification, and a very fast, very impressive indeed, modernization. The French and the British got all the colonies, so Germany had to scrabble around and find something in Africa, and I think it was Burundi, Rwanda must have been German colonies, or was it Tanzania...? [*Mumbles indistinctly*] and a few other places around the world. There wasn't much left for Germany in terms of colonial territories. The Kaiser, hmm... [*Hesitates*] is the central figure of this whole period and the relationship to the Kaiser is sort of the relationship to Germany... [*Quietly*: this very bombastic, upstart... (*Pause*) that's the nephew of Queen Victoria, I believe.] You will find the Kaiser quoted in the great final scene of Leverkühn's Lamentation, I think, but his famous remark is attributed to God, about the mistake: "I didn't mean this," that is God's creation of the world. These are in fact the Kaiser's words at the end of World War One ... , [*Impersonates the Keiser*] "This is not what I had in mind, all this horror." But this is then translated into the divine creation in this final work of Adrian.[25]

[*Long pause.*]

So, this Germany is not... [*Exhales deeply.*] It would be very wrong to imagine that Germany thought of itself as "Western," or that it was a Western country. In those days, there was a concept called Mitteleuropa, "Middle Europe," neither Western nor Eastern, and Germany, up until 1945, was that. The West was France, and England, and England — as Hegel thought — was essentially, there is an English phrase, "a nation of shopkeepers,"[26] you know, a nation of businessmen, and France was the homeland of culture... [*Quietly*: but the Germans were not really cultured, not really modern.] So, there is still sort of inheritance of a "third world" or "subaltern" mentality in Germany, and both World Wars can, in a sense, be seen like this kind of psychology, as historical attempts to break out of their geopolitical and cultural isolation. [*Pause.*] One of the fundamental themes of this book is the "breakthrough"... [*Chalk strokes on the blackboard*] D-U-R-C-H-B-R-U-C-H, but if you follow it carefully, you'll see that it is also about fighting the enemy. And then, part of the allegory that's been arranged is this [*Stressing*] isolation of Germany, and these spasmodic violent attempts to break out of this subaltern isolation and to become European, or to become liberal, or to become something or other [*Whispering*] except German.

[*Long pause.*]

Thomas Mann himself wrote about the suffering in the First World War.[27] It is very amusing to see... [*Quietly*: I think this is not only amusing] his brother was very much a liberal. After the war, Heinrich went to [*Stressing*] East Germany and became their great writer.[28] Thomas Mann himself actually returned to Germany through the East and gave a lecture on Schiller in Weimar, which was in the socialist Germany rather than in the West. At that point, he also turned against the United States, even though, by that time, he was already an American citizen... [*Quietly*: he became an American citizen in the early 1940s or something.] Anyway, in the First World War, Thomas Mann is a patriot, so to speak, who was for the German war effort. You know, I mean, we are brainwashed by our kind of historiography... [*Door creaks open.*] I don't think that anybody... [*Quietly:* except maybe some Croatian extremists or others, who have suggested that it may have been good if Hitler took over and made a united Europe.] But this idea that Germany winning the First World War wouldn't have been altogether bad is, hmm... [*Hesitates*] is still around. There is even a new type of historiography that does this new genre of counterfactual history — these are sort of speculations as "what would have happened if..." [*Pause*] if Germans had won the World War One. Well, of course, for counterfactual history, the great thing is that there wouldn't have been a Russian Revolution; hmm, because there would have been enough police power to contain Russian revolutionary groups... [*Loud. Chair scrapes against the floor.*] But the bad thing is that it wouldn't have changed political thinking in Western Europe... [*Mumbles indistinctly.*] Anyway, this book the Reflections of a Nonpolitical Man... [*Quietly*: "man" spelled as M-A-N, of course] which I think is now also translated, contains Thomas Mann's arguments for German supremacy. And they are very much like some of these discussions of the schoolboys in here, where they say that only we Germans have both form and content or depth and purpose.[29] The Reflections are one long conversation with his brother Heinrich. The brother is pro-

French, pro-liberal, pro-Western, universalizing and so forth, and these themes are starting to... [*Quietly*: this is a book of four hundred pages.] So, there is very much a kind of strange imaginary investment of Thomas Mann in all of these themes. [*Pause*.] If you read The Magic Mountain, you see what that turns into, but at that point, Thomas Mann had himself become Western and pro-liberal and all the rest of it, and then the Joseph tetralogy, which he wrote in exile and finished in early nineteen... [*Exhales deeply*] 1940s, I guess... [*Quietly*: before he started Doctor Faustus] is a tribute to President Roosevelt.[30] The figure of Joseph is Roosevelt, and Mann made this explicit and this is Thomas Mann's idea of Western democracy... [*Quietly*: which then, immediately after the war he began, in the McCarthy and Cold War period, he began to have second thoughts about it... (*Mumbles indistinctly*).] Mm-hmm. So, these are some of the existential things; they are an exercise in a kind of political imaginary in which these named countries are really characters in this psychodrama. And, as I said, in order to see what's going on here in this novel, you have to also engage with the history of modern Germany.

[*Long pause*.]

Now, the question we can ask is... [*Quietly*: we can ask it eventually but not right away] the question revolves around the parallel between Germany's failed attempt to break through and this modern music of the musician Adrian Leverkühn, who sells his soul to the devil. Well, you can also understand it in terms of Germany selling its soul to the devil, I mean, that part is easy. [*Softly*.] But what does it have to do with genius? Why is Adrian having to do that? Does he have to do that? Isn't this theologically wicked? What kind of an explanation is Nazism to this question of art and music, in other words? And what kind of investment in, hmm... [*Looks for words*] what kind of political theory does this book give us, in the attempt to account for fascism? Does it demonize fascism, precisely Nazism, precisely in a way that glamorizes and celebrates it? Anyway, these are questions I think we want to keep in mind for... [*Door cracks open.*] And as I said, this is still the great historical novel of recent times; it's the modern novel about the war and what is to come after it. And you can almost say that Thomas Mann was the greatest German novelist, both of the nineteenth century and of the twentieth century, in the sense that Buddenbrooks... [*Quietly*: his first novel, which he wrote when he was twenty-five and published it in 1900[31]] is still in this nineteenth century that doesn't really end until 1914. Buddenbrooks is the great summary of the German bourgeoisie in the nineteenth century, and Doctor Faustus is the great book of the twentieth century... [*Quietly*: of the Second World War and what has led to it, but also... (*Mumbles indistinctly*).] Mm-hmm, and so people have also said "you know, hmm..."

[*Long pause.*]

They say, hmm... [*Loses his train of thought.*] Many say that the last things that Thomas Mann wrote were not that great, like, mm-hmm, Der Erwählte,[32] which he wrote after 1945. He published it when he was seventy. You would wish to also look at Adorno's little essay called "Late Style in Beethoven," which is about the maturity of the late works of significant artists — a theme that has been picked by other critics.[33] So, people started losing interest in his late work, it was too heavy-handed, and it was very German-oriented. Now, I think the question is to what degree today in globalization is this emphasis on the [*Stressing*] national still valid, and I think, hmm... [*Pause.*] Well, let me put it this way. To what degree is the national question unavoidable in literature or anything else, and in specific literatures around the world? I think much depends on the way in which modernization and whatever governmental evolution... [*Quietly*: it doesn't have to be parliamentary democracy, but that's the way that we are taught to think about it now] have been connected to nationalism. I think that, in France, in England, in the United States, democracy and nationalism are [*Stressing*] not connected... [*Quietly*: and I would have a long argument to make about American nationalism, and that is because, as some people have argued, the United States is not a nation state, but that's a totally different issue.] But once you get out of the core so-called "third world" countries, then it seems to me that nationalism — whether we're talking about socialism or capitalism or whatever — has been a fundamental component of modernization, and therefore the [*Makes quotation mark signs in the air*] "national question" is always fundamental to their literature, art and the political debates of the period, or for the most part.[34] You have to go to other countries to see... [*Pause.*] I don't know if this is still the case, but it used to be that I had to go to Mexico City and you look at any library and you will see [*Whispering*] shelves of books about mexicanidad and what it means to be a Mexican, and the essence and sense of pride in Mexican culture; and they would go from the psychoanalytical to cultural and all the way to I don't know what. So, I mean, this obsession with the [*Stressing*] national, this is not something that you would encounter everywhere. You don't find this here in the US... [*Quietly*: you may find Scotsmen, Welsh, and certainly Irish talking about their roots, I would guess, but you won't find many asking, "What is to be an American or an English in the US?"... (*Raps his knuckles on the desk*).] I don't think you will find this happening in France either, and I certainly think that it would be nice if we did that in the States, but we don't. [*Pause.*] But in other countries, the "national" has been an important category of cultural production, and I think that Mann's interest in the "German" is very instructive for us, and in ways that are not strictly limited to Germany but to the relation between culture and the concept of the "nation" in general. And this interest in Germany was not only in Mann. There is this great poem by Brecht, "O Deutschland bleiche Mutter", which goes [*Begins reciting*]:

O Deutschland, bleiche Mutter!
Wie sitzest du besudelt
[*Pause*]
O Germany, pale mother!
How soiled you are

As you sit among the peoples.
You flaunt yourself
Among the besmirched.

[*Exhales deeply*.] And the "national" goes beyond this generation of Brecht or Mann and remains a central concern well into the 1960s, when these kids who formed the Red Brigades and the Baader-Meinhof understood that their parents were basically Nazis. This notion of Germany as this weird place out of which all these horrors came, I mean, this is, hmm... [*Hesitates*.] This is very present in a later period. And I think all of that is part of the approach to this novel.

[*Long pause*.]

Now, but there are many other things to say about Doctor Faustus. Let me... [*Pause*.] Let me say two more things and then we'll wrap it up. Why do we need to have, hmm... [*Hesitates*.] Why does Adrian need to make this pact with the devil? If you watch Heimat, you'll see that the Nazis were the main force of modernization in Germany. Historians have said, "Look, the bourgeois revolution in Germany — that's Hitler..." [*Quietly:* that hasn't and doesn't happen before.] And the way they learned, in this little peasant village depicted in Heimat, that the Nazis had come to power is that electricity arrives in the village. Hitler pioneered electrification, the Autobahn, the Volkswagen, the radio, all of these techniques of modernity. And then we have Nuremberg, and all the mythical stuff with Wagner and all that other business... [*Cough in the audience*] and Germanic anachronisms come to the surface. Well, the modernity that we're talking about in Adrian is that combination of the [*Stressing*] absolutely modern and the archaic... [*Footsteps. Door cracks open*.] The return of polyphony in the novel is... [*Quietly*: a return to the fifteenth century.] A bad harmony is the nineteenth century, the bourgeois period, but going back to polyphony means going back to the past, so this combination is this mix of modernity and the archaic. Why does this have to be done? Well, I will just jump ahead here and read for you this remark by Adrian in his final... [*Quietly*: his final secret manuscript.] Towards the end of chapter twenty-five:

> So my desperate heart hath trifled all away. I had I suppose a good toward wit and gifts gratiously given me from above which I could have used in all honour and modesty, but felt all-too well: it is the time when uprightly and in pious sober wise, naught of work is to be wrought and art grown unpossible without the divel's help and fires of hell under the cauldron...[35]

It has become too hard to make art. It has become hard, and beyond the force of the individual to do things in some normal conventional way. And therefore, some [*Stresses*] supplement has to be found, and this is one of the ways to understand the devil's pact. You need to bring the devil in, in order to produce radical change. The other way is, of course, hmm... [*Hesitates*] a more materialist one. Here is a book, I clipped this one the other day from a newspaper... [*Rapid chalk strokes on the blackboard*] the book is called: P-O-X and then Genius, Madness, And the Mysteries of Syphilis.[36] And it is a book about the importance of syphilis in the history of art and of the world. Her parade of likely or possible syphilitics includes Beethoven, Nietzsche, Flaubert, Van Gogh, Schubert, James Joyce, Goya, and Abraham Lincoln now... [*Audience laughing*] and then Ivan the Terrible, Columbus, and Hitler. [*Laughing continues.*] Anyway, I recommend this... [*Pause.*] Actually, I don't recommend it, but here is an example of a document that makes an abusive reading of the relation between art and this bacterial infection, and where syphilis is presented as the "work of the devil" that was moving forward modernity.

[*Long pause.*]

The other thing to stress is the writing. Zeitblom is writing of all this in the middle of the war — as is Thomas Mann — and the war is breaking [*Stresses*] into the artwork constantly. So, there is something about... [*Quietly*: I think maybe écriture would be the wrong way to put this, because that gives it a flavor that isn't quite right] but there is both the excitement of how my hands are trembling and then also he is wrapping himself in this whole long second sentence in which he is constantly interrupting himself; obviously, for a second, it gives you most of the themes of the novel and what's going on, but that's not nearly the psychological process. You have to see... [*Quietly*: page 31]:

> I would not even suppress my suspicion, held on psychological grounds, that I actually seek digressions and circumlocutions, or at least welcome with alacrity any occasion for such, because I am afraid of what is coming. I lay before the reader a testimony to my good faith in that I give space to the theory that I make difficulties because I secretly shrink from the task which, urged by love and duty, I have undertaken.[37]

What's coming, of course, is the final breakdown. What's coming is both Hitler and Nazism and the destruction of Germany at the end of the war, for which Zeitblom longs and wishes, but which on the other hand also means the end of Germany... [*Zipper zipping up*.] So, all of that is sort of embedded in the structure of the novel. [*Pause*.] The other thing we have to say about the form of this novel, which is very interesting and much more modern than it looks, it is the alterations in the styles of writing. This is quite remarkable with all of this medieval demonology, and when Adrian is speaking... [*Words indistinct*.] I think that Lowe-Porter does a great job of translating this for us into English, and her choice is remarkable. Mann's imitation of other styles is also, hmm... [*Hesitates*.] Look, Proust used to do some imitation as well... [*Quietly*: he would imitate people, other styles, individuals, voices, to a degree that one could even talk about pastiche... (*Feet shuffling*).] In Mann, the side of imitation is different because all, or let's say some of his characters are real people, except for the devil, of course... [*Chuckles*.] Some think that the image of the devil in this novel is modeled on Adorno. I mentioned to you the other day that Lukács was believed to have been the model for the Jesuit communist Naphta in Mann's Magic Mountain, and it is believed that Lukács said, [*Impersonates Lukács*] "He can have as much of me as he wants, it's a great honor and I'll be pleased to be of service." But some other people were not so pleased to recognize themselves in Doctor Faustus. Mm-hmm, what time is it? I think our time is up. So, we will get back to this next time... [*Feet shuffling. Chairs scraping the floor.*]

Audience stands up. Objects drop on the floor. Zippers zipping up. Door squeaks. Students return chairs to other classrooms. Some students form a line to discuss their papers with Jameson. General noise. Screeching microphone noise.

[*Microphone turns off.*]

CURTAIN

LECTURE FOURTEEN

MARCH 20, 2003

DOCTOR FAUSTUS (NOVEL) — TEMPORALITY OF THE NOVEL — ADRIAN LEVERKÜHN AND SERENUS ZEITBLOM

CURTAIN RISES

Moving chairs, squeaking door, coughs, other sounds filling the noise environment of a large classroom in the Literature Department at Duke University. "I was a smoker for a long time and didn't realize until recently that this town was a major point of production and distribution in the American tobacco industry. As I walk around town, I see buildings named by the brands of cigarettes that I used to smoke." Two students discuss the history of the town and of the university in relation to the American Tobacco Company and its founder, James Buchanan Duke, whose name the university has carried since 1924. Another student replies: "Well, yes, it used to be big until ten or so years ago when tobacco was still very strong down here. But yeah, you should keep smoking, that way you'll be contributing to your education." Other students are laughing. They continue chatting about J.B. Duke's monument on campus, and how he was quick to purchase the revolutionary cigarette-rolling machine that turned Durham into a prosperous town in the South. That machine permitted him to establish the Duke Endowment Fund in 1924.

Jameson enters the classroom carrying a few books, his scattered notes, and the red pen in the chest pocket of his flannel shirt.

[Microphone turns on.]

JAMESON: A few announcements... [*Thud. Backpack falls on the floor. Footsteps*] will be this week's main event. Those of you who wanna do it, let's try to meet at twelve, but also keep in mind that we have to leave... [*Addresses student looking for a chair*]. Over here, there is one chair for you. I will have to leave at twelve in order to take Mr. Balibar over to the Franklin Center, and therefore we will try to break off at quarter to twelve. I have some handouts here, ignore these little things, the machine started to staple it all of a sudden... [*Quietly*: so, some of them... (*Mumbles indistinctly*) made by the machine.] Does everybody have a copy of Kleist's short story, "On the Marionette Theater"?

[*Silence.*]

STUDENT: I don't have it... [*Words indistinct.*]

JAMESON: This is a very famous and notorious short story, which is a conversation about the nature of beauty by comparing movement in these mechanical puppets, or marionettes, and the human mind, or mental powers... [*Chair scratches the floor.*] It's a philosophical reflection on grace and beauty in how these dancing marionettes compare to the human dancer. The story is considered a key text of Romanticism and modernism, and I think that Paul de Man talks about it somewhere... [*Raps his knuckles on the desk*] but I can't remember where. In some of his later essays maybe, do any of you know...? [*Pause.*] Nobody knows. Okay, I will try to find it and bring it to you next time, along with a few other references.[1]

[*Long silence.*]

Okay now, I am little perturbed because I was talking about this whole business of translations, and none of you have told me that you have the new translation of Doctor Faustus. [*Pause.*] I've got all my references from Lowe-Porter's version, and I was talking, in fact, about the old translation of this book. Let's put this a little bit off so that I could take a look at the new edition for a while. [*Talks to student in front row.*] Can you give me your copy...? [*Pause.*] You have the new edition...

STUDENT: Uh-huh. [*Nods.*]

JAMESON: [*Holds up the new edition of* Doctor Faustus *translated by John E. Woods.*] I haven't even opened this new translation yet, and I realized today that you could only buy the newest translation of Doctor Faustus in your university bookstore. It would have been nice to coordinate this sort of thing... [*Mumbles indistinctly*] because this is gonna be sort of a mess. [*Pause.*] Mm-hmm. Okay, now, one other thing I forgot to mention when I was talking about, hmm... [*Hesitates*] mm-hmm, the... [*Looks for words*] about the... [*Zipper unzipping.*] I was talking the other day about the drop in Thomas Mann's stock since his death, and this is a normal matter, I mean... [*Quietly*: the same thing happened to Gide and to many other writers.] On the other hand, what I wanted to say is that I believe... [*Quietly*: sorry for keeping interrupting myself, it's like the narrator of this book (*Audience laughing*).] There is a long review by Michael Wood in the latest London Review of Books,[2] which talks about the old and the new translation of Doctor Faustus and about the merits of each translation. Wood also talks about a new companion to Thomas Mann, which just came out, and it is about his life, relation to music, politics, film, life in America and so on, as well as a new biography of Mann... [*Quietly*: I mean, the biography is not new, but it has been recently translated into English.][3] It is quite interesting to read this review if you want further reflections on Mann or the translations of this book. Anyway, I think Wood makes the point there that, although Thomas Mann's reputation was supposed to have dimmed as a result of changes in taste, hmm... [*Hesitates*] or the eclipse of modernism as such, or maybe that it's not modern enough, nonetheless there has never been so much published of Thomas Mann, as it is now. This partly has to do with the German academic industry... [*Sound of tearing page*] and that there are literally pounds and pounds of books written on Thomas Mann, I mean, theses and all the rest of it in the last years. It has been a tremendously flourishing industry.

[*Long pause.*]

If you think about differences in national forms of literary criticism, then I think that the Germans still work a lot with source criticism. It seems to me that these recent and older studies on Mann are made for source criticism, and that a lot of these secondary sources are written in such a way that... [*Achoo. Sneeze in the audience*] you can go back and look around for the originals. For example, to illustrate this to you; it's on page... [*Page flipping.*] It's on page 10... [*Quietly*: in my edition, but you may also find it in your new translations] where Zeitblom is talking about the Nazis and about his own family... [*Pause.*] You understand, from what Zeitblom is saying about, his family... [*Quietly*: "My sons served their Führer," well, the sons were obviously in the youth organizations and were estranged from the father, who was himself fired by the Nazis from his teaching job.][4] He was put on retirement. Well, one reference here is a very malicious and nasty portrait of a Jewish intellectual... [*Starts reading*]: "I need only to think of the private scholar Breisacher in Munich, on whose dismayingly unsympathetic character I propose in the proper place to cast light."[5] Well, this Breisacher was a real person, Oskar Goldberg, who was sort of, mm-hmm... [*Searches for words*] he was obsessed with various currents of speculative thinking. Goldberg was a thinker and medical doctor and a well-known figure in the Germany of the 1920s and 1930s... [*Door cracks open.*]

FACULTY MEMBER: [*From the doorway.*] Oh, I'm sorry, I thought this was my class...

JAMESON: Oh yeah, please come in. [*Audience laughing.*]

Mm-hmm. So, as I was saying, Goldberg was something like a, hmm... [*Cough in the audience*] a Jewish-German religious thinker and philosopher and a very controversial figure in Weimar. At some point, he came in contact with Benjamin, Brecht, Mann, and all of these people we are dealing with, and he had these very provocative ideas about mythical religious speculations and different races… [*Quietly*: later, they distanced themselves from him, as did Mann, who called him at some point a "Jewish Fascist" or something like that.] Goldberg wrote these obsessive books about the mythical Jewish past, which was very much in the spirit of what the Nazis were writing about the German past. Clearly, the original for this figure Breisacher was an extremely, hmm… [*Hesitates*] how can I say it, a very ambiguous character, but on the other hand, it is also a very nasty portrait, and Mann was worried about his depiction because he was wondering whether people would accuse him of anti-Semitism. But you can see that… [*Pause*.] Now, what I was gonna say is this. Someone has naturally written a whole book on this topic, that is to say, on Oscar Goldberg's work and personality and on his relationship to Thomas Mann.[6] But as I try to speculate here, German criticism tends to be about tracing back sources; it is about traveling back and finding some precedent, or historical figures on whose personality these literary characters have been built. [*Pause*.] French criticism, I would say [*Quietly*: and you may or may not agree with me] but French criticism would be much more of a semiotic kind; and the American one is still based on "close reading," I think… [*Quietly*: and a lot of the old type of New Criticism.] And the English one… [*Softly*.] Well, English criticism is always very theological, I mean, that is a very English way of talking about high morality and religious virtues, and ideology, and so forth. [*Chuckles*.] And finally, the Irish criticism is always about Ireland… [*Audience laughing*.] I mean, there you have a genuinely national obsession [*Laughter continues*], or so I think. But there are national forms of criticism and it's hard to say whether Thomas Mann is being revived, or whether the machine is simply turning out more and more books on this subject. Or he may have also become a school classic, because Buddenbrooks is very accessible and very much a nineteenth-century novel, and in that case, everybody reads it in high school, but that doesn't exactly relate to his later, more ambitious engagement with modernism.

[*Pause.*] I mean, when it comes to the classics, you wouldn't consider Dickens... [*Looks for words*] part of an intellectual vanguard... [*Quietly*: or maybe he was seen like that in his time, but this is not anymore the case in our day and age.] So, Mann may be still widely read, but not in that sense in which Doctor Faustus deals with the new and the modern, and... [*Chair scrapes the floor*] it seems to me that it may also be possible that there is a break at the end of this novel, which impacts our understanding of modernism. And you may ask yourself if this book really has no further posterity of this kind. And that's that about Mann's place in contemporary criticism.

[*Long pause.*]

Now, this is a problem that we would want to deal with, since the whole point of... [*Cough in the audience*] the temporal structure of this narrative is to put us into the picture. We have something that's happening in this novel in the early twentieth century, up to about 1932, and if you want to amuse yourself, you can make a chronology of all of these dates. Mm-hmm. Adrian, in the early 1930s, enters into this deep night from which he passes into the deepest night of all, at the time, and that's the beginning of the Great War. So, his life is, to a certain degree, chronologically patterned on German history. [*Pause.*] Meanwhile, as we are made to understand over and over again, as the book is being written in the moment in which Fortress Europa is being broken down; that is, when the Soviet troops are advancing from the East, and the allies are... [*Raps his knuckles on the desk*] they are at first in North Africa, and then they open the second front and you follow the whole course of the war up to the very end with Germany's, hmm... [*Hesitates*] capitulation. This series of historical events is chronological, and it aligns itself with the alleged writing of the book. Mann creates a double... [*Chair-back creaks*] chronology using the figure of Serenus Zeitblom. First, Zeitblom, is reflecting on the life of his friend, Adrian Leverkühn, and the broader historical and cultural context; and Thomas Mann himself writes the novel more or less at exactly that time. He finishes the book in 1946, but nonetheless, the chronologies are pretty close, and the writing begins for Zeitblom on the very same day that Thomas Mann begins writing the book... [*Quietly*: that is to say, in 1943, at this moment when, after Stalingrad, the German fortune in the war are about to change.] Now, meanwhile, we're reading it in the present, and I think that you can't... [*Microphone distortions caused by electrical interferences*] read something in which this chronology is so... [*Zipper zipping up*] on these multiple temporalities. The interplay of these multiple temporalities — between Mann's writing, and Zeitblom's narrating and German history — is very strongly emphasized. What is relevant is not only about the history or the story of this musician, but the history of Germany, and the novel is also about this interpretation of the history of Germany. And it seems to me that one isn't doing justice to the work unless you re-introduce these questions into it... [*Cough in the audience*] and as I said the other day, it seems to me this is the right thing to do, especially now, when we have another war going on. But the novel also involves the question of the temporality of the modern, and as I said, hmm... [*Hesitates*] and I think I said that the other day, the whole point about this view of the modern... [*Quietly*: at least of Adrian's music and presumably of Schoenberg's, because Mann says this about Schoenberg at several points in his diaries] is this very strange combination of the archaic and the technologically up-to-date. [*Pause*.] Now, for various reasons that we will look at more closely, the technologically up-to-date is not to be achieved unless you go back into the relatively distant past to draw materials, inspirations, and forms from that past.

[*Long pause*.]

That distant past in musical history is that of, hmm... [*Hesitates*] polyphony, as it flourishes in the sixteenth century. But then, if you look at Adrian's ideological development, it is really the sixteenth century of Protestantism, and this weird way in which Luther emerges as both a medieval figure and the beginning of modernity in Germany. How many of you know anything about Martin Luther, about his personality... [*Chair scratches the floor*] and his place in history...? [*Quietly*: It would be great to have a presentation on him in this seminar.] Luther is a major figure in German history of the period. Mm-hmm. Lutheranism in German history, as it starts to emerge in the sixteenth century as a reformation movement within the Catholic Church, has been linked to the whole issue of guilt and punishment, faith, and salvation, but it was also a major cultural event. Hegel gave great importance to Luther and to Protestantism, acknowledging his role in modern philosophy, especially in light of that fact that Luther was a simple monk who has inaugurated such a mature stage of the spirit, hmm... [*Hesitates*] and that takes place a century earlier than Descartes. And then there are many other German historiographies, which have been written with this periodization in mind. You can also say that about the modern German language, which is the moment of its so-called standardization, and here Luther also has played a key... [*Floor creaking*] with his translation of the Bible. [*Pause.*] Nietzsche once said that there were only three great German books, hmm... [*Hesitates*] Luther's translation of the Bible, Goethe's Conversations with Eckermann... [*Quietly*: and of course, his own works (*Chuckles*).] Mm-hmm, but there is much truth in this; that is to say, the functioning of a more expressive and somewhat less heavy-handed kind of German would have greatly contributed to all of those things. So, Luther is central. And you have all these interesting psychobiographies... [*Pause*] Erik Erikson, does anybody read him anymore? He wrote Young Man Luther, and that's a book that I think is still worth reading and is quite interesting. Lacan used to, hmm... [*Chalk strokes on the blackboard*] E-R-I-K E-R-I-K-S-O-N. Lacan used to have these debates with Erikson... [*Quietly:* it had to do with the origins of Western civilization, and whether it was constituted though primal parricide, as was Freud's position, or if it was matricentric, as many of the deviationists from Jung to the French feminists... (*Mumbles indistinctly*).] But at any rate, Erikson has been involved in the development of some of these psychoanalytic biographies, and what he wants to say is that the power of these seemingly charismatic individuals... [*Quietly*: he wrote about Hitler, Gorky, Luther[7]] is to be explained by the way in which, in them, a whole collective neurosis related to the family structure of the period comes to an end. And when these individuals find an original solution to their neurosis, it then becomes available for the collectivity in whatever form... [*Clears throat.*] So, Luther's Oedipus complex, his anxiety, these fits that Luther had — the famous episode of the lightning bolt that almost kills him when he is a monk and so forth — mm-hmm, all of this is somehow transformed into Luther's act, into this whole new revival of the archaic, of the scripture, of pure original Christianity that he has been associated with. So, for all of that relation to collectivity and religion, Luther's story is very interesting, but for our purpose, you have this theologian Dr. Kumpf who throws a... [*Quietly*: I think it's a roll in this book[8]] he throws a roll of bread at the devil, whereas in Luther's case, he threw ink at the Devil, which you can still see if you go to... [*Quietly*: I think it's in the Wartburg Castle, where Luther took refuge.] If you travel to Wartburg, you can still see on the wall the mark of the inkwell that Luther threw at the Devil. And obviously, a medieval diabolism is included in this seemingly modern Protestantism, which then also shows a revival of the superstitions... [*Achoo. Sneeze in the audience*] practices rooted in the Middle Ages. One interesting book on all of this is... [*Tries to remember*] Eisen... [*Pause*] Eisenstein I believe is her name, who has this major book on the development of printing in the early years of the printing press.[9] And she points out that, although, you know, one is tempted to say that the invention of the printing press is a remarkable instrument for Enlightenment, over half of what came out of these new printing presses during that period were revivals of all these old medieval superstitions about magic, and witches, and witchcraft, and astrology and so on. So, history does not always proceed in an absolutely linear way, where progress in technology and printing and so forth lead on to further intellectual processes. Sometimes, this involves regressions and leaps back before they go forward. At any rate,

Luther as a person is associated with dramas like that and what he does in the Table Talk... [*Quietly*: which is a collection of informal conversations and reflections recorded by his followers, and which are full of scatological comments, crude language, and jokes.][10] And in Doctor Faustus, all of that, the archaic and the medieval, is sort of conveyed in the scenes with that one theologist and professor, hmm... [*Hesitates*] Dr. Kumpf, that Adrian was studying with in Leipzig.

[*Long pause.*]

This regression to, hmm... [*Pause.*] So, the sixteenth century is both polyphony in music, and these other layers of the mythical and the archaic that are still around. And you remember the portrait of Kaisersaschern, the little town that they are in. And this is a very... [*Quietly:* Thomas Mann uses that in some of his other novels and essays too, where he tries to explain Germany using these genuine medieval settings, because some of them... (*Achoo. Sneeze in the audience*) have a gate or are surrounded by walls, and some were completely destroyed in the war.] There are few enough of these genuinely medieval sceneries in Germany after the war, but it is very interesting that he associated these with the archaic and rural. And you have to also think in terms of what Marx says about the peasants, about the rural poor, or what I called "provincialism" the other day. The Germany of this whole period is provincial in its relationship to the so-called "West," and "progress." But this German provincialism has much more sinister or darker characteristics, and you remember that Zeitblom talks about these semi-crazy people who were wondering around in the streets. I mean, these are people that we would associate today with homelessness and drug addicts, but this is in a period in which, presumably, you don't yet have drugs, and the whole issue of "homelessness" — I frankly don't quite know how that fits in a medieval city or not — but where nonetheless this provincial isolation breads all kinds of psychic experiences, hmm... [*Hesitates*] of psychic disorders. These original "characters," these eccentric and "half-crazy souls," as he calls them,[11] there is something more sinister than that, I think, in this picture of the medieval as it emerges in Kaisersaschern. And this is nineteen-what... [*Quietly*: one of these years when Adrian was going to school, in 1910 or something] and the depth of antiquity is still there in the so-called Wilhelminian Germany, which is the epoch of economic and industrial growth, of rapid cultural and social modernization. Now, the question about Thomas Mann for us is whether whatever we call "modernity" today, whether it still includes this layer... [*Quietly*: of the medieval and the archaic.] And if the archaic is still there, then this brings us also to the question of nature.

[*Long pause*.]

Remember we talked about nature and whether nature survives in connection with Adorno. We talked whether there still exists anything that could function as nature, as otherness, as the... [*Quietly*: you wouldn't call nature "archaic," I guess] but as the most primordial form of otherness that's available to our experience. So, if that's not there, and if this archaic dimension of history, it's not really there anymore... [*Pause*.] I mean, look at anthropology and look around the world. Levi-Strauss says somewhere that thousands of so-called "primitive languages" have disappeared, hmm... [*Hesitates*] in the last twenty or thirty years, maybe fifty years. And this is very much a catastrophic form of progress in which even the archaic of tribal society is being both assimilated into the, hmm... [*Hesitates*] into the contemporary, like the Aboriginals in Australia, or when the tribal is simply wiped out, hmm... [*Exhales deeply*] and destroyed. So, this combination of the new and old, for Thomas Mann, seems to characterize [*Stresses*] that modernity, which involves its relation to the past, and to its opposite and this, this... [*Pounds the desk*] also involves art, as with Schoenberg, or politics, as is the example of Hitler. The question to ask is whether the modern carries with itself the archaic. And do we have a true modernity without the archaic? It's like the question about the disappearance of the unconscious, do we still have a... [*Zipper zipping up*] do we still have that unconscious, at least in the senses in which both Freud and Jung talked about it? Well, and since we are here, I would say that that's what is called "postmodernity," which is the disappearance of the archaic, of the medieval and all of those things.

[*Long pause.*]

If you look at, hmm... [*Hesitates.*] If we leave behind modernism, and if we turn to so-called... [*Pause*] "contemporary music," and to people who followed on the footsteps of twelve-tone music, and these are people like Boulez... [*Quietly*: I don't think that there is anything archaic in Boulez; I don't know what your feelings are on this matter] but it seems to me that, with postmodernism, there is no return to these older archaic elements that we see in modernism. Instead, there is rather a sort of heightening of scientificity, as manifested in the use of number theories, and very complicated mathematical models, or of different technologies in order to figure out the succession of notes in a composition. We discussed this in one of our past lectures, this transition from the twelve-tone system of the Vienna School to the postwar contemporary music from Darmstadt. And here we don't see that combination of the archaic and the up-to-date that we saw in the modern. So, that leaves us again with another question about Adrian's posterity after year zero, or about, hmm... [*Hesitates*] or about this book's posterity and its influence on the theories of modernism.

[*Long pause.*]

Now, I wanted to draw your attention in that connection to several words here... [*Talks to himself*: let's see where they are... (*Leafs through the two editions of* Doctor Faustus), or maybe I should go this way.] Hmm, yes... [*Pause.*] Mm-hmm... [*Pause.*] As I said, all of this is... [*Footsteps*] clear, and in the first chapters, he is gonna lay over the themes in place as he stops and starts and so forth. [*Starts reading*] "...my overhasty differentiation between pure and impure genius" and so on and so forth, and then, "I have been frightened by the notion that in so doing I am being carried beyond an appropriate and wholesome level of thought and am myself experiencing an [*Whispering*] 'impure' enhancement of my natural talents..."[12] This was the new translation, whereas Lowe-Porter translates this part as: "an 'impure' heightening of my natural gifts."[13] Well… [*Pause.*] This word "heightening" is… [*Chalk on the blackboard*] S-T-E-I-G-E-R-U-N-G, and it is a very important word, to which we will return. I think it's not so insistent a leitmotif, but it's a very crucial word. I will try to give you from Dostoevsky another time the description of the, hmm… [*Looks for words*] of the correlative, hmm… [*Tries to remember*] of the correlative physical experience, which is the experience of the epileptic fit. The condition is central in Dostoevsky, where you have this sense of a linking of a mental or other powers and then dashing out of them. But I think something similar is being expressed here in truly physical terms as the result of a… [*Quietly*: I am not sure of the medical process] but I think the whole point of Adrian's visits to these doctors is the most Kafkaesque moment of this book. Remember, he goes to a doctor to have his syphilis treated and the doctor gives him an injection… [*Quietly*: whatever that was, but it is before penicillin] and suddenly, the night of his next treatment, the doctor is being led out by the police, and the second doctor is lying in a coffin. Some power or other has interrupted his treatment. But it has allowed him the beginnings of the treatment so that he doesn't… [*Pause*] so that, in effect, hmm… [*Hesitates*] some of the most catastrophic effects of the disease have been holding it, allowing this artificial… [*Door creaks open*] or maybe natural kind of Steigerung, this heightening tremendous capacity for visionary experience, for all kind of mental excitations, and escalation of tension and emotion that has allowed him the moment of that, before syphilitic eruptions appear in the final stages.

[*Long pause.*]

Steigerung and heightening is also connected to what here is called the "demonic." And I think you also have to know that it's not just [*Stressing*] demons, but that it is the… [*Chalk strokes on the blackboard*] D-A-E-M-O-N. A daemon was a kind of intermediary spirit between gods and humans, like, for example, in Socrates, who believed that he had an inner voice that guided him. So, for Socrates, this voice of presence warned him about things that could go wrong and so forth.[14] But in this case, it is Goethe who talks specifically in passages of... [*Raps his knuckles on the desk*] his autobiography, and in some of the poems, about the way in which he is governed by a kind of inner destiny, a kind of guiding spirit that helps him develop his artistic goals... [*Quietly*: which is the daemon.][15] So, demonic is both of these things, and particularly in German, it is also this suggestion of some heightened power. But if one wants to talk about the historical allegory, you can certainly say, if you think of the purely technological, hmm... [*Hesitates*] power, not excluding industrial development... [*Achoo. Sneeze in the audience*] then you can also talk about the importance of Steigerung in German history. You'd be getting that before the Nazi period, as it is certainly much more visible after the Weimar crisis and inflation. Under Hitler, in the great days for the Nazis, as it was around 1936 or so, the Weimar economic depression has been completely overcome. Germany had full employment, everybody was very prosperous, and the popularity of the Nazis was at the height. So, you can talk about the same kind of thing in the allegorical subtext of this novel, and the question, I think, between the two meanings of this word: the "daemon," which is, hmm... [*Hesitates*] both pure and impure. There can be a pure kind of heightening of your gifts and then also an [*Stressing*] impure heightening of them, which relies on... [*Cough in the audience*] — I called it a "supplement" the other day — but I meant an artificial stimulation, either from illness and from whatever other form, or in terms of the scrupulousness of the Nazi ideology. How does one distinguish between those two things... [*Quietly*: it seems to me that it is very much the question here] that this book raises, and again that leaves the evaluation of Adrian's music in a very peculiar place. I suppose... [*Pause*.] This obviously... [*Words indistinct*] has also to do with Schoenberg, and Schoenberg was very furious, because Mann's portrayal of this new music in the novel seemed to say, "this music of Leverkühn is evil, it is demonic, just like Hitler." I mean, this what it was assumed, but this is not exactly what Thomas Mann meant to say.

[*Long pause.*]

The other crucial, hmm... [*Clears throat*] crucial scene in this first chapter is the one at the end of it: "All around him lay coldness."[16] Mm-hmm. This is, I think, the point, at least the characterological point, which announces Adrian's relationship to things; it is one of the themes that takes multiple forms. It is, first of all, the idea of isolation. [*Pause.*] And you remember later in the novel when he does meet the devil, the physical sensation is that of immense... [*Quietly*: of an immense cold, hmm... (*Hesitates*) and the devil says to Adrian, go and get your overcoat in the other room... (*Mumbles indistinctly*) this tremendous frigid coldness.] Now, let's see what level that is operating on. So that's both... [*Pause.*] First of all, it is on the level of affect, for this would turn into a Wagnerian theme of the renunciation of love. At the very end of this whole scene, the devil says, you remember ... , [*Impersonates the devil*] "And of course, by the way, you will have to renounce love," which means sexuality. So, like the way Alberich, in the beginning of The Ring,[17] after he is, hmm... [*Microphone distortions caused by electrical interferences.*] In order to steal the ring in the first place, he must renounce sexuality... [*Student raises hand.*] Yeah...

STUDENT: I have a question. It seems to me that Adrian and his friend Zeit...

JAMESON: Zeitblom.

STUDENT: Yes, Zeitblom, represents the Apollonian and... [*Door cracks open*] Adrian is the Dionysian, if we follow the Nietzschean distinction. But the connection is sort of more nuanced when it comes to the demo...

JAMESON: To?

STUDENT: To the demonic...

JAMESON: Ah, ah... [*Pause.*]

STUDENT: If... [*Pause.*] If this is true, and if Adrian is the Dionysian type, which has this connection to the demonic, then how does this work with religion? Because, as you said, there is a very strong religious or archaic element in the modern...

JAMESON: Mm-hmm. [*Nods.*] Uh-huh. Well, first of all, we can think about the distinction between these two main characters in terms of Catholicism and Protestantism. [*Pause.*] Zeitblom is Catholic...

STUDENT: Uh-huh...

JAMESON: Yes, Zeitblom was a Catholic humanist, and the image that is transmitted here is precisely that of Renaissance humanism and its values... [*Cough in the audience.*] One research that's been done on the relationship between antique motifs and religion, it's a famous thesis by Jean... [*Chalk strokes on the blackboard*] S-E-Z-N-E-C, who wrote a book called The Survival of Gods or something like that,[18] where he looks at art, thinkers, and various symbolisms, and argues that the many elements of pagan thought persisted and even thrived in Europe, despite the rise of Christianity. What happens is that the Greek gods become demons, or devils, hmm... [*Hesitates*] in the Middle Ages. So, this whole classical tradition is taken over, but they are all made to represent forces of evil. Now, when you get to... [*Quietly*: I think he mentions at some point, hmm... (*Hesitates*) and this is very beautiful too, when you get to the Renaissance, he talks about Minerva and The Virgin Mary, where pagan divinities are interpreted using moral... (*Mumbles indistinctly*).] So, suddenly you get a transformation of the Christian symbols back into these classical motifs. And I think that the idea here is that it's not Protestantism that is responsible for countering up these images of the devil and of evil, but Catholicism... [*Loud page flipping*] which is built on a theology for which evil cannot be a positive force, right? Evil is just privation, absence, and lack of good. [*Pause.*] In all of the struggles of the early church, I mean, if you endow evil with anything positive, you slide towards Manichaeism... [*Quietly*: because then you have... (*Pause.*) I mean, the Manichaeans are the great enemies of classical Christian theology.] So, for Zeitblom, evil must not be endowed with positive characteristics.

[*Long pause.*]

And I think that you are quick to identify these two characters in these Nietzschean opposites, but... [*Pause.*] Well, first of all, the novel asks a deeper question, namely, [*Softly*] who is the hero of this novel? Is it Adrian or is it Zeitblom? [*Pause.*] Mm-hmm. And I think Thomas Mann obviously thought of himself as being both of these figures, but probably for us reading this... [*Cough in the audience*] it is Zeitblom who is Thomas Mann. [*Pause.*] So, when Zeitblom says: "I'm not a creative type. My life energy is that of admiration..." [*Quietly*: and not in the kind of creativity that Adrian had.] Well, but then one would be tempted to endow that with some kind of creative force too, and make of it a sort of creative opposition that would respond to Adrian's form of creativity. [*Pause.*] You could also say that for Zeitblom, that is, philology, in the larger sense of the word, as he concerns himself with the relationship to the past. And then I think that certainly reading this is supposed to invoke some notion of pedagogy, which is involved, as we'll see, maybe not today, but there is a great chapter where this is very much a theme. Zeitblom is a pedagogue... [*Quietly*: Adrian doesn't talk to anybody.] Mm-hmm... [*Pause.*] Hmm... [*Hesitates*] and this is very much, I think, some of the pleasures of reading this — as opposed of reading what it's about — these are philological pleasures, and that's the whole pleasure of the style, it seems to me, and its relationship to these... [*Loud nose blowing near the microphone.*] So, I think you could divide two Weltanschauung in here that are at least juxtaposed. Whether that's altogether Apollonian and Dionysian in Nietzsche's sense, I'm not sure, but that's a very odd opposition in Nietzsche anyway... [*Quietly*: since it's resolved by Wagner... (*Mumbles indistinctly*).] And then the other opposition here, which I think is a very important, but which is not worked out in a very consecutive way, and this is the Quixote...

AUDIENCE: [*Audience murmuring.*] Who? What? [*Whispering.*] Don Quixote.

JAMESON: Is Don Quixote about its main hero or is it about Sancho? [*Pause.*] This is a double novel in which you have, first of all, the heroic figure, and then you have the servant, the one who is devoted, who is always there, who helps to write and translates the librettos for him, who is the critic and editor, his confidante and promoter. Mm-hmm. I think it's very much that relationship and it parallels two different kinds of... [*Exhales deeply*] two totally different kinds of systems. What I wanted to reach today, which I don't think we will, but I'll mention it anyways, is this very important conversation at the end of chapter eight... [*Quietly*: which is the great chapter of the last piano sonata] where Serenus says... [*Page flipping. Talks to himself*: let me find it... (*Pause*) where is it, hm-mmm; it's not here.] Nobody has Lowe-Porter's translation, right? [*Silence*.] Okay, I could have given you the page number for that translation, hmm... [*Sighs*] mm-hmm... [*Pause*.] Ah yeah, page 76:

> "A gift of life," I responded, "if not to say, a gift of God, such as music, should not have the mocking charge of paradox leveled at it for things that are merely evidence of the fullness of its nature. One should love them."
> "Do you believe love is the strongest emotion?" he asked.
> "Do you know any stronger?"
> "Yes, interest."[19]

Mm-hmm. And you have to understand this as the passion in this isolation of Adrian, who is then cut off from other people, and from any kind of affective relationships, but whose passion is a purely intellectual one. Well, [*Whispering*] what is interest? "By which..." and this is Zeitblom's definition: "By which you probably mean a love that has been deprived of its animal warmth..."[20] [*Pause*.] So, this is another form of Steigerung and also the mind and the body, the warmth of the animal, the creature, and then this colder thing, which is... [*Looks for words*] which comes out of it, and from which, hmm... [*Hesitates*] the body has been removed. The discussion of music consistently goes back and forth, so whether this is music in the Dionysian sense, or something else, it is always this debate over music. Is it an art of warmth and spiritual intoxication, or it is some purely mental intellectual exercise? If you read another very important book on music, I think I mentioned it the other day, by a former advisor of the president Mitterrand in the last decade or two, by Jacques... [*Chalk strokes on the blackboard*] A-T-T-A-L-I, and it's a book called Noise or Noises, Bruits in the plural but the English translation, I think, is just called Noise.[21] He divides the history of music in several periods, defining each period as "Sacrificing," "Representing," "Repeating," and so forth. This is a kind of history of music in which he says, [*Impersonates Attali*] "Look..." [*Quietly*: he has several very interesting ideas; first of all, he asks] "does art reflect the social context?" [*Pause*.] Well... [*Cough in the audience*.] Sometimes it can even anticipate the social context, so the various forms of music in the West have been not only reflective, or let's say residual, coming from the past... [*Door slams shut*] but it actually anticipated forms of economic organization that didn't yet exist... [*Quietly*: Attali is an economist.] So, the very organization of the musical notes themselves foretells something to come in the economic system, as a sort of abstraction which anticipates the things to come. And his point is that music, and let's say mathematics or economics, these are the two, hmm... [*Hesitates*] disciplines, if you like, that are the furthest from lived experience. These are the most abstract of all the arts, and therefore they have something to do with each other, and that, if you knew anything about mathematics, which unfortunately I don't, you could probably look at, I don't know the state of music in a... [*Words indistinct*] or something like that in the early nineteenth century, or some other things that were going on in music at that time... [*Quietly*: and you may find all sorts of interesting parallels with the world of economics and the social... (*Mumbles indistinctly*).] But it's a very, very interesting book.

25

Doktor Faustus

existing simultaneous dimensions at once, about temporality & history

conversation btw Adrian / Rudy "not there"

passage to tertiary state, passage to Nazism

show how that experience is key

日曜日 月火水木金土 literal = writing

thinking subjectivity in Frankfurt school. possibility of negation

thus & then problem of music — how can you 'do' anything

"Germany" — analogical

introduces ethical prob. war/nazism — moral-soul

Adrian — life of Christ allegory

literal = writing — literal - writing

brought in new way

'breaking out of paradox'

adrian's coldness

ch 28 diminishing of individualism, [indifference]

— Adrian's music — return to form

今日はあの日
今日はあの日
今日あれ忘れ
知っている?
東西南北飯
緑園都市
緑園都市
教会
二俣川池
学校学校
行交客行

04/3/03 Schelling — before creation of world there was no other, so we are his other

Ernst Bloch

empty place — work of art, is whole universe of non alienated labor

Balzac's unknown masterpiece

Kant - subjective experience of aesthetic experience

Hegel - objective history working itself out

Supplement
supplementary

Nietzsche / Deleuze - critiquing system of representation (unless you do this there is no thinking)

b/c subject of thought to requirements of representation

"new"

liberate thought from ...

*Is aesthetics possible? & indeterminate possibility

WHY? precisely its relation to philosophy

Page from student's seminar notes.

[*Long pause.*]

Mm-hmm. This question of coldness is then opposed to that of animal warmth. Did I quote you this... [*Quietly*: where he is talking about Adorno's... (*Words indistinct*) the other day, right? I don't remember if it came up because we went reading Negative Dia... mm-hmm, Aesthetic Theory, as far as I recall.] Adorno's other definition of the ethics... [*Quietly*: we talked about the negativity as the most radical or dramatic one] but there is another one that states that human beings should live like good animals.[22] That's what people should try to be... [*Quietly*: mm-hmm, be good dogs, that they should behave in their material... (*Pause*) in their material animal warmth.] Well, that one could much more closely be associated with Zeitblom, with Catholic theology, mm-hmm, with the orga... [*Pause*] the organization of the church, in confession and absolution, and things like that, and then the sense of coldness, it seems to me, is more appropriate to describe this Protestant sense of individualism, and anxiety, guilt, hmm... [*Hesitates*] and all such things. Anyway, those are some of the ways I think this opposition plays itself out here. Mm-hmm, I... [*Pause.*] Hmm... [*Hesitates.*] And I... [*Pause.*] It's one thing to imagine that this is a characterological, hmm... [*Hesitates*] form that Adrian has long before the temptation scene. Mm-hmm, is one to make a social explanation of this, as he comes out of a farm, farming family; you must also ask yourself, it's very interesting... [*Quietly*: what are we dupli... (*Pause*) what is the theme of repetition.] Thomas Mann just read Kierkegaard the first time when he was writing this... [*Quietly*: but you remember that when Adrian confronts the devil, he was reading Kierkegaard.] Mm-hmm. At any rate, one needs to ask oneself whether that repetition, which destiny has in store for him, namely that he finds a retreat for his years of composition, which is identical almost in all ways with the place he grew up. Now, what does that mean exactly... [*Quietly*: mm-hmm, and one can ask this on two planes: what it really means and what does Thomas Mann think it means.]

[*Long pause.*]

But there is one important thing that you have to notice. You remember that, at the end, when the real mother comes to take him back to the real place of childhood, hmm... [*Hesitates*] the dog is dead, of course, but there is the farm, the little hill, everything else is the same... [*Quietly*: he is furious, and he doesn't want to go and then he tries to kill himself.] One doesn't assume... [*Quietly:* Lukács says somewhere that he hated his mother, but maybe he lied... (*Mumbles indistinctly*) people usually hate their father, of course, and we even have a theory for that, but why he would hate his mother, I'm not sure.] [*Audience laughing.*] But... [*Laughter continues.*] But it seems to have some meaning here, unless it corresponds to the very nature of repetition that it is not really a going back... [*Zipper unzipping*] and if you go back to the first thing without any change, that means absolute sterility and the death of everything that is creative. This is the thing with repetition. But I'm not sure, I am just throwing this out, and it seems to me that it's very important to think about that, because clearly this is part of the structure of this novel that is underlined over and over again.

[*Long pause.*]

Mm-hmm. Okay, I think we will hold the family and the father, the mystic alchemical father, and all these wonderful transformations of the natural until... [*Pause*] until next time, and then... [*Looks at the audience.*] Did everyone get this? [*Holds up a book.*] This is one more piece in your collection of the originals of, maybe it's... [*Chairs scraping the floor*] in the Dante section, and here you have the quite... [*Footsteps shuffle across the floor.*] Okay then, we will continue next time with...

Audience stands up. Objects drop on the floor. Door squeaks. Members of the audience talk among themselves. Students return chairs to other classrooms. Some students form a line to discuss their assignments with Jameson. General noise. Screeching microphone noise.

[*Microphone turns off.*]

CURTAIN

LECTURE FIFTEEN

MARCH 25, 2003

OPPOSITES IN *DOCTOR FAUSTUS* — BEETHOVEN, THE PIANO SONATA NO. 32 IN C MINOR, OP. 111

CURTAIN RISES

Jameson enters the classroom carrying a few books, his scattered notes, and the red pen in the chest pocket of his flannel shirt.

[*Microphone turns on.*]

JAMESON: Questions? Are there any questions for me? Mm-hmm... [*Pause.*] Regarding your papers... [*Door creaks open. Footsteps.*] If you are undecided about your paper, come talk to me, and if you can't think of anything, also come talk to me by next... [*Chalk strokes on the blackboard*] T-H-U-R-S-D-A-Y. You must have been thinking about your papers by now, I hope, and if not... [*Door slams shut. Zippers unzipping.*] Your project can take many forms in relation to modernism and aesthetics, music, art, literature, theory... [*Sighs*] and so on and so forth. I want to help you start thinking about your papers soon, because if you're not, then this may be in... [*Mumbles indistinctly.*]

[*Long pause.*]

Alright. That is that. [*Pause.*] Now, are there questions that you wanna ask regarding what came up last time?

[*More footsteps.*]

Okay, give me a list of some of the key oppositions in Doctor Faustus.

[*Silence.*]

We talked about Sancho Panza and Don Quixote last time, in terms of the character's relation... [*Quietly*: between Zeitblom and Adrian.] What else?

STUDENT: Nature-human; archaic-modern... [*Pause.*]

JAMESON: Okay, okay, that could be immediately in the next section, and we will take a look at it. Alright, hmm... [*Pause.*] What else?

[*Silence.*]

JAMESON: Okay, let's talk about the archaic and the modern, which, as we agreed last time, it's so crucially important for modernism. What's archaic and what's modern in this novel?

[*Silence.*]

STUDENT: Maybe folk art is archaic?

JAMESON: Uh-huh? Sorry?

STUDENT: There are many references to folk in the novel, so maybe folk is archaic and modernist art is... [*Pause.*]

JAMESON: [*Interrupting.*] Yeah, yeah, if you like folk, that's okay, but keep in mind that folk, Volkskunst, or Volk in Germany is very suspicious, as you all know. I mean, Hitler's newspaper was called Völkischer Beobachter [People's Observer] and the word had always this quite sinister right-wing ring to it. Words like these are complicated as they translate into ideological terms. What would be, in this book, one of the manifestations of the historical... [*Chair scratches the floor.*] We are thinking of oppositions here.

STUDENT: Tonality?

JAMESON: Uh-huh? [*Breathes on the lenses of his glasses and begins to polish them with his handkerchief.*]

STUDENT: Tonality?

JAMESON: [*Determined.*] No. No. You see, that's modern.

Mm-hmm... [*Hesitates*] when you talk about music and tonality, you're generally presupposing modernity. Max Weber, for example, wrote a little book on tonality. It is quite amazing for a sociologist of religion, political economist, and everything else, to write a book on the sociology of music. But for him, it is quite clear — or at least this is what he says, and his position is very Eurocentric — that there is only one kind of tonal music in the world, hmm... [*Exhales deeply*] and that's the kind that comes into being in Europe in the... [*Pause*] well, essentially, it is in the eighteenth century. I mean, it is evolving before that, but Bach's preludes from The Well-Tempered Clavier[1]... [*Zipper unzipping*] where Bach abandons the modal elements, embracing the modern tonal system, and where the tempering process is so important for musical tonality. But this process is also central for rationalization and thus for capitalism.[2] It is a form of rationalization that is instrumental for modernity. So, what is it that comes before tonality? It is not atonality, but... [*Looks at the audience.*]

STUDENT: Modality.

JAMESON: Uh-huh?

STUDENT: [*Loud*] Modality.

JAMESON: The modes, yeah... [*Pause.*] I think here in Doctor Faustus, what gets dramatized in this way is polyphony. Mann uses musical polyphony as structure of the novel to reveal the diversity of themes and motifs running through the book, and these are the kind of themes that he talks in the book through Adrian. In the immediate chapters that we were reading about Adrian's childhood, what's the great manifestation of this? [*Looks at the audience.*]

STUDENT: Is it the milkmaid or...?

JAMESON: The milkmaid, yeah. What about it?

STUDENT: Hanne, the milkmaid, where she... [*Pause.*][3]

JAMESON: Yes, that's right, but all of that... [*Pause.*] What's the difference between [*Stressing*] that kind of experience of music and this nineteenth-century harmonic kind? There is a long description of this on page... [*To himself.* Where is it?

Where is it? *Page flipping*.] Mm-hmm, page, hmm... [*Hesitates*.] Yeah, page 32: "None of us was aware that under the direction of a milkmaid we were already moving on a comparatively high plane of musical culture, a branch of imitative polyphony, which first had to be discovered in the fifteenth century before it could provide us with amusement."[4] I think that if you re-read this section on page 31 and 32, you will see that the reference to polyphony also takes the social dimension as well, for in polyphony each of these voices are doing something meaningful. If you were a voice in an orchestra... [*Walks towards the blackboard*] in a nineteenth-century orchestral composition, then your role is different than if you were part of a pre-modern musical group. As probably most of you know, in orchestral music, not all the voices have the same importance. Usually, the orchestra has a sophisticated structure; it is a construction where what you would be doing would have no musical meaning at all, except in relationship to what the composer is trying to put together in orchestrating a single melodic line — a totality. So, maybe... [*Door slams shut*] the main line of the orchestra, let's say the violins, would be playing the melodic line — that is what I mean by musical meaning and that is something that has some coherence in itself, temporally — and then everyone else is just filling in, right? They are adding up to the notes of the main work. [*Pause*.] Whereas, with polyphony, each of these voices have an intelligible musical meaning that is individually unique among the others. Now, I wouldn't say that this is exactly an allegory of social life... [*Cough in the audience*] but it does correspond to some practices and human relationships, and that is very different from the modern orchestral as well as modern social organization of life.

[*Long pause*.]

Now, if you want, you could talk about this musical difference using the sociological categories of Gemeinschaft and Gesellschaft.[5] In a sense, maybe you can. In the Gemeinschaft, or let's call it "community," all of these independent human activities are meaningful in themselves, and they are all intertwined and inseparable... [*Quietly*: because if you cease one activity, then you don't have anything, since it is the combination of melodies that matters, like in polyphonic music... (*Cough in the audience*).] And that would be what's called the horizontal dimension of music. Whereas, in harmony, it is the vertical dimension or relationship of notes in chords, which, if you like, is the analogy of the worker's role in the modern factory. You're doing one little thing, which in itself is not significant; it's only meaningful in terms of the finished result, hmm... [*Reflects*] of the overall finally assembled product. So, there is a fundamental difference in the logic of these two principles of organization of musical, social and productive forms, and I think one of the great themes in Mann is precisely about this.

[*Long pause.*]

But what else is archaic here? So, if we're going back to the sixteenth century, called the late medieval period, you have the waning of the medieval forms. [*Pause.*] Anyone of you knows the Dutch writer... [*Chair scratching the floor*] he was very influential at one time... [*Chalk on the blackboard*] H-U-I-Z-I-N-G-A, whom Thomas Mann certainly read and was influenced by. One of Huizinga's books is called Homo Ludens,[6] which was about play... [*Quietly*: it's a sort of follow-up on Schiller, really, and it's a more philosophical work.] But he wrote a few other books that became very famous... [*Quietly*: they are not philosophy exactly, but rather history of ideas; I would call them anthropological or cultural theory.] One of these is called The Waning of the Middle Ages,[7] and this is a book that is very much appropriate to the treatment of these historical oppositions of the archaic and modern. It is an excellent portrayal of the moment of hysteria that you get at the close of the medieval, as he is famously talking about the decline of these medieval ideals and customs. It portrays the waning of the medieval period, which he describes in terms of play and symbolic ritual, and the emergence of the rational and instrumental modernity.

[*Long pause.*]

So, what would you consider to be archaic from that standpoint?

[*Silence*.]

[*Softly*.] Well, it's the devil and all of that kind of stuff, which, as Zeitblom says, is associated with theology. As in theology, he says, the devil is always there somewhere, and you can't really do theology without the devil. And then... [*Choo-choo. Amtrak train whistle loud*] when Adrian gets to Halle, to do his theology studies at the University of Halle, there are very sophisticated theological arguments that they discuss... [*Choo-choo. Amtrak train whistle fading away*.] For example, felix culpa... [*Quietly*: that's already in St. Augustine. In order to prove our freedom, people have to exist in sin, and that unfortunate events eventually will lead to a happier outcome.] So, evil is somehow [*Whispering*] necessary for human freedom, and it is somehow behind everything in life — it is like Oedipus in Freudian interpretation. And insofar as the devil is concerned... [*Quietly*: the devil is the personification of evil in various mythologies, and it has not only mythological but other connotations in Doctor Faustus, through the Nazis and so forth.] But then this would be somehow re-combined here. What I mean is that Thomas Mann was a Protestant, his mother was Catholic, but he was baptized into the Lutheran religion of his father. So, we have here another opposition of Protestantism and Catholicism, and Protestantism is the demonic and the archaic here. Luther was not the beginning of German modernity — as Hegel says, and a lot of other people have said — but rather, he was a sort of the return of the repressed and the worst features in medieval Germany. And it is Catholicism, which, on the other hand, is the humanistic worldview. The theological opposition is played out here through these two main characters: Zeitblom is the Catholic humanist and Leverkühn is the ascetic Protestant, like Mann himself.

[*Long pause*.]

There are some other oppositions involved that we could also think of. He talked about, or believed in, hmm... [*Hesitates*] what he called "children of light" and "children of darkness." [*Pause*.] The children of light are Goethe and Tolstoy, as two... [*Quietly*: Goethe was technically not an aristocrat] but I mean, these are two figures whose destinies are somehow wondrously fortunate and lucky, despite Tolstoy's early misfortunes in life, like gambling or his participation in the Crimean War. And I think people who read such authors, they can understand why this might seem to be the right way of talking about them in opposition to the forces and the children of darkness, who are Dostoevsky and Nietzsche. These two are thinkers whose work really involves, hmm... [*Exhales deeply*] in the case of Dostoevsky, it involves a secret crime of some sort, which appears in his writings, as, for example, the child rape confessed by Stavrogin in The Possessed.[8] And then, in Nietzsche's case, there is not one specific thing, but certainly his expression of misery and physical suffering... [*Quietly*: because Nietzsche really had these migraines, headaches and eyestrain, infections, insomnia that he talks about them most of his life] as well as the secret guilt, and we will come back to that, because there are some new ideas in Thomas Mann himself. And this opposition — between the children of light and the children of darkness — is also clearly present in this book through these two figures of Zeitblom and Adrian, of the Catholic-humanist and the Protestant-demonic...[9] [*Achoo. Sneeze in the audience*.] These major oppositions then lead to, or break into multiple, smaller opposites, like happiness, family, humanism, and so forth, versus... [*Quietly*: misery, diabolical pact, the Protestant angst, theology, and all of the archaic... (*Mumbles indistinctly*) and then all that other business, like distance and isolation in Adrian, or his difficulties to make human contact, or even him not wishing to make any contact, and his surrounding by coldness and a certain indifference to everything and absence.] And let's mention one other major opposition that comes up: animal or "bovine warmth" and sensuality as opposed to coldness, asceticism — these are very much part of these main themes in Doctor Faustus.

[*Long pause*.]

Mm-hmm. Now, in terms of the, hmm... [*Hesitates*] of this first chapter about the father speculating on the elements, this is quite a wonderful chapter which lays in place this whole notion of mimicry or mimesis... [*Clears throat*] through this butterfly called Hetaera Esmeralda. As you know, the German musical notation is unlike ours and they call a B... [*Quietly*: a plain B, not a B flat; not a black key, but a regular B] they call it, in the German musical nomenclature, H, and that's how a B is; on another hand, a B flat, I believe, right... [*Looks at a music graduate student.*]

STUDENT: [*Nods.*] Yes.

JAMESON: Mm-hmm. And therefore, you can have things that make... [*Door creaks open. Footsteps*] like the famous B-A-C-H in Bach, where German musical letters correspond to pitches. We have here other motifs like that, and this is the series H-E-A-E-Es, starting with H being a B in Anglo-Saxon annotation, and it ends with Es, which is an E flat. And you can play with it; it is an interesting theme that runs through the entire work, like a rune standing for the name and which is associated with this butterfly, Hetaera Esmeralda...[10] [*Quietly*: and the name he had associated with this syphilitic prostitute that Adrian had... (*Mumbles Indistinctly*).] Mm-hmm... [*Pause.*] Now, that starts out being the question of beauty and disguise and the whole business of mimetism in nature, stuff that I think that, in a lot of these people — and I assume Thomas Mann as well — borrowed from Roger Caillois, who wrote on the subject of... [*Chalk hitting the blackboard*] M-I-M-E-S-I-S and mimicry. Caillois was also an influence on Benjamin and Adorno as well, and we've already talked about mimesis in Adorno's chapter on "natural beauty." But I think the most interesting reflections for our purpose come when Adrian's father, the amateur naturalist, talks about those insects that mimic their environment. Of course, the figure of the father, we must also take notice, as it is part of the archaic German tradition, as every country has its own way... [*Cough in the audience*] of telling these nationalist stories, as you know. You've got at the very moment of Lutheranism, this recrudescence of medieval superstition, and Luther's language, and the devil, and all of that are all part of this whole process. You also have the figure who is the most, I suppose, gloomy... [*Chair screeching the floor*] and melancholic and not only the greatest German visual artist, and the only one who is equivalent to Leonardo or Michelangelo or something like that, hmm... [*Hesitates*] and that's Albrecht Dürer. If you know Dürer's famous self-portrait with the blonde hair and the beard, resembling Christ — that's the father and that's very clear. And Adrian's father is described as fitting into this pure German tradition. Later, Adrian will set to music some of the Apocalypse that comes out of Dürer's series of woodcuts, and I think Adorno was right when he said that, hmm... [*Exhales deeply*] that these, Dürer's series on the Apocalypse, are too beautiful; even Bosch's and Bruegel's are more terrifying — especially Bosch's[11] — than Dürer's. And so, Adorno recommended... [*Quietly*: what Kant has done][12] that Mann should have researched the entire apocalyptic tradition and bring in all kinds of horrible legends, fallen angels and other such things into this process and not rely only on Dürer, which at that stage is almost too pure or too beautiful. I will show you Dürer's Apocalypse series next week when we get there.

[*Long pause.*]

Now, when we get to the end of this section... [*Quietly*: on mimesis and the father's speculations on nature and the temptations of nature, so to speak] we come to what some of you have mentioned here, which is the opposition between the organic and the inorganic. That is the imitation of the organic by the inorganic...[13] [*Looks at the audience*: Or is it vice versa?] Well, I think, in these works, which wish to be, in a modernist sense, a book of the world, there is a moment at which this whole human story must open onto the cosmos. [*Pause.*] Mm-hmm. And the parallel to this is the Divine Comedy, this is the original and ultimate book of the world, let's say, and more so than is Homer's Iliad or the Odyssey. With Homer, the first allegories turn Homer into both psychomachia, that is to say, where the great fights, not only between these bloody slaughters, between all these various Greeks and Trojans, becomes an allegory of the emotions (in the Christian period) but also of the elements. [*Softly*.] And some of the first allegorical readings of Homer admit that into an allegory of the physical world. But once you get to Dante, you really have the physical world built into the poetic... [*Quietly*: the whole business with Jerusalem as the central point and the Mount Purgatory] all this stuff is worked out absolutely, according to the Ptolemaic system, so that the physical structure of the cosmos is inscribed in the Divine Comedy. Here, in Doctor Faustus, this, I think, it's a little less obvious. In The Magic Mountain, this merger between the poetic and the physical happens when Hans starts to read scientific books as he is sitting out in the chill area of the sanatorium in the Swiss mountains as tubercular patients used to... [*Quietly*: as he sits wrapped in a blanket in a reclining chair doing his air cure by breathing mountain air, and as he does that, he begins to look at plates of the body, and since this is a tuberculosis sanatorium, then there is a lot about the body in The Magic Mountain.] There are other things about the cosmos itself, so there the cosmos is sort of drawn into this world by way of his readings, which become symbolic in a lot of ways. Here, in Doctor Faustus, I would say it's in this section about the father, Leverkühn, that suddenly the whole matter of imitation of nature seems to go into the very pores of the physical universe and absorb everything else in it... [*Cough in the audience*.] You can then later notice the strangeness of Adrian's compositions, which is the one about the... [*Quietly*: sort of Jules Verne oratorio set, on the tale of the descent in a diving bell and the creatures under the sea and so forth.][14] That sort of draws a different kind of nineteenth-century science-fiction speculation into this ultimate view on the world. But along with the theological speculations, all of these physical speculations are part of the way in which this book, hmm... [*Hesitates*] makes its effort to be the supreme work. And you all know that "work" is a word also used in alchemy... [*Quietly:* as in the turning of lead into gold is the work; it's like the philosopher's stone.] Well, all of that is in here somewhere... [*Clears throat*] and I think it's necessary to emphasize the cosmic natural dimension of this book.

[*Long pause.*]

But the other thing I wanted to point out is... [*Pause.*] I wanted to point out how all of this is told in a new kind of way. Mm-hmm. You understand that normally as the novel develops... [*Quietly*: and this is true of Buddenbrooks and The Magic Mountain as well] hmm, you have this moment in which the novelist is passing into a scene... [*Quietly*: the scene is set, and then suddenly the curtain rises] and you are faced with characters who speak to each other or describe events. Now, I think you have to notice that, with the exception of certain important conversations in Doctor Faustus most of those are given to us in the form of secondhand reporting. [*Pause.*] So, for example, the scene when Inez Rodde talks about her love affair, we don't really hear her speaking — as I recall, maybe just a phrase or two — but most of it is Zeitblom telling us what [*Stressing*] she said. So, I propose that, rather than an opera... [*Cough in the audience*] which at least after Wagner and a certain moment in Verdi... [*Zipper unzipping*] everything is sung and you hear everything, this is still more like an oratorio in which you have orchestral storytelling, and then, at crucial moments, you have one of the characters singing an aria of some sort. [*Pause.*] And I think you should watch how this is varying throughout the novel. One of the ways Mann manages to do it is quite wonderful... [*Quietly*: I would call it using perhaps a word associated with Brecht and this is "gesturality"] that is the moment of a single gesture, or a single remark that sums everything up.[15]

[*Long pause.*]

And this one I always liked... [*Exhales deeply*: and I really wish we had the old Lowe-Porter's translation, I don't think he does it very well here... (*Mumbles indistinctly*).] When the father is explaining how all of these various chemicals, which of course come from father Leverkühn's pharmacy, how all of these inorganic compounds mimic nature. We are back in mimesis. [*Starts reading*]: "the whole dubious crew-mushrooms, phallic polyps, tiny trees, and algae meadows, plus those half-formed limbs bent toward the pane of glass through which the light was falling, pressing forward with such longing for warmth and joy that they literally clung to the pane and stuck fast there."[16] [*Quietly*: these are like the tropisms.] This is a book by… [*Chalk on the blackboard*] S-A-R-R-A-U-T-E, and I believe it was her first novel called [*Sound of chalk*] T-R-O-P-I-S-M-E-S,[17] which is informed by a natural phenomenon of plants and other biological organisms that respond to environmental stimulus. So, something similar is taking place here. And then the father says, with tears coming into his eyes, "but they are not alive," and so he shows respect for these growths because, remember, he already said, [*Impersonates Jonathan Leverkühn*] "No, no, they are not plants, they only pretend to be, but don't think less of them. The fact that they give their best to pretend preserves all due respect."[18] We must respect this Pinocchian attempt of the inorganic to become organic, of animals to become humans, of these chemicals to become plants. But in this final part, hmm… [*Hesitates*] in this final moment, to be moved by these "woeful imitators of life," as he calls them with tears in his eyes, that's again the question of mimesis, for even though they are dead, they cannot escape these forms of tropisms and the directional growth in response to light, as in plants, for example… [*Mumbles indistinctly*.] And then, I think this is a marvelous way of stating it, "'And even though they're dead,' Jonathan said, and tears came to his eyes" but then, for certain reasons, Adrian "was shaking with suppressed laughter."[19] And you understand that Adrian's laughter is the demonic here. As Baudelaire says about laughter, it is the sign of the principle of evil, it's the, hmm… [*Hesitates*] I mean, laughter is always at other people's expense or suffering … [*Cough in the audience*.] And when you get to Wyndham Lewis, you can have a theory that laughter is the grinning of the teeth of the animal who is meeting its enemy, right?[20] This shows us that my laughter means that I am very dangerous and I must be watched out for… [*Quietly*: of course, it doesn't go that far here] but Baudelaire's essay on laughter is absolutely essential, as he explores the nature and significance of laughter in human experience, concluding that it can also be a destructive force, or that laughter is the sign of the original sin.[21]

[*Long pause.*]

But for Adrian, I think the laughter is part of what will become the whole musical problem of the novel, namely that nothing is natural anymore. Composition is more and more difficult, that's one thing; it's not natural, hmm... [*Hesitates*] music doesn't come spontaneously and nothing that we do in this new technological society comes naturally. Mimesis is not possible anymore. And therefore, anything that everybody does, it's all been done already, if you prefer it that way. Anything that anybody does seriously nowadays... [*Quietly*: turns into parody] and at best [*Stressing*] into self-parody, and we must distinguish between the two. With self-parody, it means that you at least know what's going on, and you are not taking it seriously, but it's all that you can do. Now, remember that, in Adrian's case, the devil will give him this little additional supplement to overcome this problem, and this will allow him to make self-parody into something that is higher than that. Thomas Mann is always associated not only with parody... [*Quietly*: I mean, it's all these styles of writing that he is using and also what he calls "montage," which we've already spoke, and we'll get back to it] but also with irony. Now... [*Addresses the audience*] I don't know, but do you think this is an ironic novel?

[*Silence.*]

Mm-hmm. I often wonder about that. And certainly, the role of parody is very important, and hence Adrian's laughter — this is the deeper meaning of Adrian's laughter in that ending part of chapter three. He is laughing because he sees that nobody can do anything anymore, that his pride in accomplishing things nowadays — mainly musical ones — can only simply be the production of parody. And so, this laughter is demonic, and it is indeed a very crucial moment in the novel, as it also avoids, hmm... [*Sighs*] — it is a way of avoiding the question of authenti... [*Quietly*: not exactly in terms of avoiding the tru... (*Mumbles indistinctly*).]

[*Long pause.*]

Now, we know that Wetzler was a real person...[22] [*Pause*] and indeed, they have recorded some of his music... [*Addresses the music graduate student*.] Have you ever seen any of his music?

STUDENT: No.

JAMESON: I wonder if they have anything by him in the library. Because, at one time, people were suddenly interested as this book aroused a lot of interest in all of these side matters, and Wetzler's compositions... [*Loud cough near the microphone*] were actually resuscitated and recorded.[23] So, I think Doctor Faustus is also a marvelous pedagogical effort; it shows us to what degree pedagogy is deeply inscribed in this work. I wouldn't say it's didactic though... [*Pause*.] I mean, this is a Bildungsroman, as they call it in Germany, a novel of formation or education that involves a coming-of-age, and the psychological and moral growth of the protagonist. Alright, but here the formation is a very strange one indeed, hmm... [*Hesitates*] and has to be this principle of Bildung in it, as Adrian gets this formation from some place. And I think the idea that this German-American Wendell Kretzschmar comes over from the United States and gives lectures — and this is another feature of it — not because he thinks... [*Door slams shut*] but because he wants to teach something, he wants to instruct people. His lectures are not very popular, only ten people are attending, and then his unfortunate stutter, but his method of pedagogy is that you don't look for other people's interest. It's your own interest that you follow and that, if you are interested enough, then other people will also be. That is the pedagogical motif of the lectures, it seems to me, and that's exactly what happens. Remember this word [*Stressing*] interest that becomes crucial for Adrian... [*Cough in the audience*.] It is, I quoted to you the other day towards the end of chapter eight, where they talk and he says, "yes, interest"[24] is the stronger emotion than love, it is love that has been deprived of the bovine, or animal warmth. [*Addresses music graduate student*] How long is your presentation?

STUDENT: Thirty minutes?

JAMESON: Okay, let's make it ten more minutes or

something like that, because I just wanted to say something about Beethoven's thirty-second Sonata, which is indeed a very weird thing... [*Quietly*: I think everybody but... (*Words indistinct*), who wrote a big attack on Adorno, would have agreed on that... (*Mumbles indistinctly*).][25] And this is indeed a funny and wonderful topic that comes up in Doctor Faustus when Kretzschmar devotes an entire hour to the question of why Beethoven didn't write a third movement for his last piano sonata, Opus 111.[26] Because, you know, in the sonata, you generally have three movements. [*Pause*.] Well, a lot of this stuff is derived from Adorno — this is Thomas Mann's indebtedness to Adorno, but the ideas of this account of Beethoven is from an essay by Adorno called "Beethoven's Late Style"... [*Quietly*: which I don't seem to find it in English, I think I referred you to Notes to Literature, but it's not in there... (*Mumbles indistinctly*).][27] For Adorno, Beethoven's late style is marked by its episodic character, and this general impression of the unfinished, which ultimately boils down to a very simple idea: objectivity vs. subjectivity. [*Pause*.] What people have said in the standard... [*Exhales deeply*] in the official narrative of modernism is that, when you move from realism to modernism, you're progressing from the objective to the subjective. The objective is what the realists describe... [*Quietly*: houses, what everybody wears, what they do, and so on and so forth.] Once you get into the modern, you are much more into the realm of deep subjectivity... [*Quietly*: Dostoevsky, and the guilt, internal suffering, angst, self-hatred, and all of these things in their various ways.] What Adorno says is very much a Žižek kind of dialectic — everybody wants the positive and nobody wants to tarry with the negative — and the late Beethoven is the bypassing of the illusion of freedom from objective reality, which manifests in the crisis of aesthetic experience and what Adorno will associate with nominalism and construction.[28] So, the late style of the master is not profoundly subjective in the opening of the work but it's profoundly objective. It is the [*Whispering*] absolute eclipse of subjectivity. Mm-hmm. In

Beethoven's middle period of the "Appassionata",[29] you have this combination of subjectivity that's really energizing all of these conventions, in a way he is melting them down into something that's, hmm... [*Hesitates*] that's a... [*Pause*] that's a real event. In the late style, on the other hand, the self is eclipsed. In Thomas Mann, the eclipse is by death... [*Quietly*: I think that might not be Adorno's way of dealing with objectivity] but at any rate, here the self is purged, the ego is purged away, and the late composer or writer is confronted only by objective conventions, and the entire work is made out of these objective rules, hmm... [*Sighs*] formulaic trills, rhetorical flourishes, all of these things become suddenly the absolute essence of music. [*Pause.*] It's a very interesting and dramatic idea on late style, and this is exactly what Kretzschmar is explaining among other things. We talked also about the visual and how a lot of things are going on in a rhythmed score that you can't hear, but it's nonetheless there, and the parts... [*Clears throat*] of the music, and I forget now what the other was... [*Pause*] hmm, cosmologies as well, the description of Wagner, The Ring (of the Nibelung),[30] the primal elements coming out and so forth. This is another way of inscribing the cosmos itself in music, as music is this emergence of Being from absolute nothingness, like the beginning of The Ring... [*Quietly*: where you hear the Rhine, the sounds of Rhine coming out of... (*Pause*) before the creation of the world, because I think it means greatness, it's the moment of the human age, it's the coming into the human age.] But, hmm... [*Hesitates.*] But, mm-hmm... [*Pause.*] But in each moment, you have this emergence, this absolute emergence, and yet you have... [*Cough in the audience*] a musical possibility to begin this dialectic between what's gone before and the creation of modern subjectivity.

[*Long pause.*]

[*Exhales deeply.*] Okay, let's look at this... [*Page flipping*] on page 87, you can make a test if you like. There is the description of a piece of music at the end of that chapter nine, where Adrian is describing it, and which is not identified... [*Raps his knuckles on the desk*] and therefore, you can try to figure out what it is — it's very well known — and you will put it into a little envelope, a sealed envelope, and give it to me and we will award a prize to those who gets it right. Apparently, Thomas Mann didn't know very well... [*Mumbles indistinctly*.]

[*Audience chuckles*.]

Okay, let's hear now Ben's presentation on Beethoven's thirty-second Sonata, because I want you to have a sense of... [*Chairs scratching against the floor*. *Footsteps*.]

Student Presentation: Beethoven, The Piano Sonata No. 32 in C minor, Op. 111 (by Music Ph.D. Student)

STUDENT: This presentation is on Beethoven's thirty-second Sonata... [*Chair screeching across the floor*.] This is his last piano sonata that he wrote in 1821 and 1822, and it is his most famous work among musical professionals and critics. I thought I would do what Fabio did last time with Adorno's titles by starting to look at some of Beethoven's titles, although there are no really titles for works like this. Beethoven did not give titles to his sonatas, and some were nicknamed only after his death, like the Moonlight Sonata and others, where the "moonlight" came from a description that a critic gave and then it just got stuck with it... [*Pause*.]

[*Long pause*.]

So, first I'll talk about the key. The key is C minor, and this is significant for Beethoven, because of the other big works. C minor has been associated with the dramatic and the heroic and he uses this key in some other of his works. I'm also thinking of other famous musical compositions set in C minor, like Mozart's Piano Concerto No. 24 in C minor, and then Mozart's Adagio and Fugue in C minor for strings, which is also considered one of the most dramatic creations... [*Words indistinct*] and then, of course, Beethoven's Fifth Symphony, where there is this very famous motif [*Sings*] "ta – ta – ta — TA," which opens the symphony. I am sure you all know it. And then there is Beethoven's Sonata No. 8 in C minor, Op. 13, also called sometimes "Pathétique," one of his early sonatas, written in 1798-99,. [*Sings*] "Ta–ta–ta–ta–ta–ta–ta — ta." But now back to the thirty-second... [*Pause.*] The last and second movement is in C major, and this is the sort of the transformation that goes on within this sonata from minor into major, which has been interpreted variously as expansion into luminous tonality, spiritual enlightenment, and so on. But another thing about C minor, it is often associated with a certain kind of feelings, with expressions of pathos. And I'm thinking now of some fugues of Bach from The Well-Tempered Clavier, and if you look at some of these pieces from The Well-Tempered Clavier... [*Achoo. Sneeze in the audience*] if you look, for example, at Bach's second Prelude and Fugue in C minor from the first book, he is working out the C minor tonality as part of Bach's early attempts at equal-temperament tuning. You have this because, by now, we've reached the point of rationalization and standardization of our tonal system. I don't know how many of you know but, in the Renaissance, before modern music, you had scales that were not equally tuned. Now we have scales, so that the intervals between the notes are equal all the way, it is an equal division of the octave. In the Middle Ages and the Renaissance, this was not the case, because these were tuned to pitches that only approximated the relations between the overtones. I mean, this gets very complicated, and this is not even our subject, but before modern music, tuning was based on pure mathematical intervals, and so that the music that we know today and listen to today is actually not... [*Pause*] I mean, it's not consonant in the physical sense, but with respect to the... [*Words Indistinct*: ...combination of frequencies.] [*Stresses*] But, the point of this being that, for Bach, writing The Well-Tempered Clavier, well-temperament was not quite equal temperament, as the latter only comes into use in the twentieth century, and in the eighteenth and ninetieth centuries, we still have the well-temperament. There was that different keys would have different relationships, and each tonality had different flavor and feel to it. If any of you ever heard the organ in the chapel, before each organ was tuned differently, and therefore you had to know the particular organ, and even now they are built for particular spaces and may sound differently. So, before the organ player came to perform, he would come to know the specificity of that organ and how it was tuned... [*Door slam in the distance.*] So, there is actually a difference between C major and something like F sharp major, as this could be a very different kind of music when instruments were not yet equally tempered. And it was in fact one of Bach's sons, C.P.E. Bach, who is often credited among the early writers of keyboard sonatas, and as a transitional figure between the baroque music of his father and the classical musical age.

[*Long pause.*]

Now I will talk about the sonata, which is probably the fundamental, or one of the fundamental, words in Western musical tradition. I say "words" because, in the case of the sonata, we're talking about a genre of officially solo instrumental work. [*Chair-back creaks.*] Sonata originally means anything that was instrumental music, as opposed to song or cantata, which is a sung thing. The word "sonata" comes from the archaic sonare and suonare and whatever else it means in Italian, but which basically means "to sound," or something "played." And then, in the early baroque, you have sonata da camera and sonata da chiesa, which are genres of instrumental music that are for the chamber or the court, and then the sonata da chiesa is for the church. [*Pause.*] And then, by the time, we get to the high baroque period, we also have the trio sonatas, which are a genre of music usually consisting of three movements — fast, slow, fast — like the most known to us are by Vivaldi. So then, by the time we get to... [*Chair legs screech along the floor*] Beethoven, sonata means pretty much a solo instrumental work, which also would include a piano and cello, or violin sonata. Sonata evolved to become the... [*Stresses*] fundamental genre for instrumental works... [*Quietly*: and it usually has three movements — this one, Op. 111, has only two.] Sonata also means it's... [*Stresses*] a musical form or a structure which appears in the first movements of piano sonata, trios, symphonies, concertos, and string quartets... [*Quietly*: it's probably more complicated than this, but I am trying to make it pretty simple for the sake of this presentation.] I mean, sonata form was used not only in the first movements of sonata pieces, but also in the first movements of symphonies and of pretty much any kind of musical work in the Classical, and then goes on also into the Romantic period. Beethoven is the transition phase between classic and romantic music. What's interesting is that sonata form was just done at some point. [*Pause.*] Haydn is in fact often regarded as someone who played a key role in establishing the sonata as a form to compete with the symphony. Historically, sonata is also related to the European tradition of playing music at home, and it was often considered semi-private, as its development is sometimes explained by the emerging bourgeois market for musical instruments. And around the middle of the nineteenth century, theorists and composers engaged with the sonata form as both musical composition and intellectual tool.

[*Long pause.*]

The idea of sonata is a combination of... [*Pause.*] I mean, sonata is very much related to tonality — but the idea of sonata is a combination of the thematic arrangement of music and the tonal arrangement of music. Also, sonata usually has a fixed form, so what you get is this fast-slow-fast... [*Begins drawing on the blackboard.*] There are three sections in the first movement of the sonata form: the exposition, development, and recapitulation. And here the "exposition" is little bit like a debate... [*Rapid chalk strokes. Drawing a diagram on the blackboard*] where you have a sort of fundamental dissonance created.

You have your first theme, let's call it "A," which is presented in a tonic key, and so, in the case of the thirty-second sonata, this is C minor. This is the so-called "home key." Then you have a little modulatory section or transition, and then you have your second theme "B," which is presented in another key, usually the dominant. But here, Beethoven is doing something different, he is not going to the expected tonality. [*Pause.*] Then you have the... [*Stressing*] <u>development</u> section, sometimes called the "argument," which key-wise is modulatory and theme-wise is a

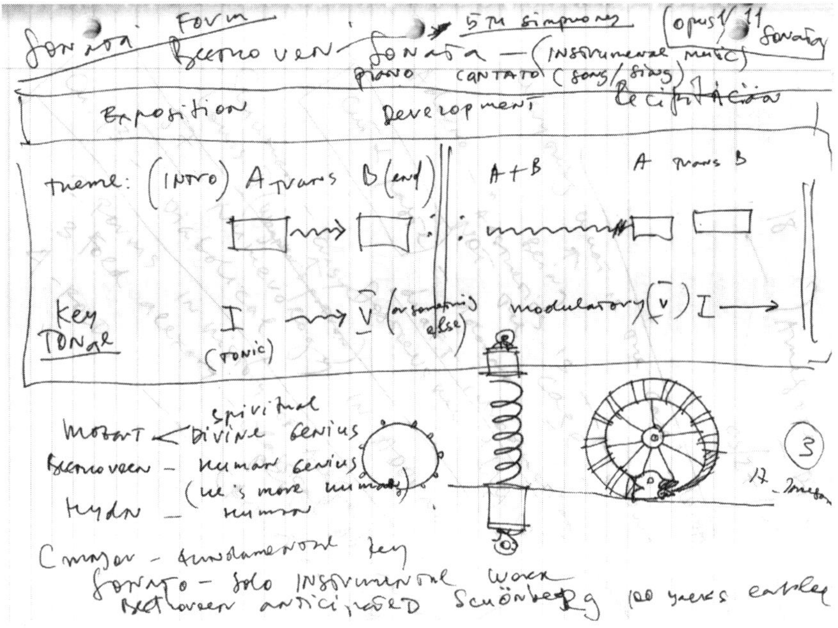

Presentation diagram on the blackboard. Page from student's seminar notes.

development of the material you've started with. The A and B themes introduced in the exposition are being reworked, often in a dramatic way, and contrasted in the development part. So, you gonna have... [*Chalk strokes on the blackboard*] a fragmentation of themes, and working out the motifs and gestures, and then this sort of culminates with a return back... [*Strikes the blackboard*] <u>here</u> to a tonic recapitulation where the themes are replayed in the home key with a form of finality. This last part of recapitulation is sort of the big resolution of this whole business. And this is a sort of a canonic description and probably you and me may find many sonatas that do this in some other way, but what we have here... [*Knocking the chalk against the blackboard*] it's sort of a basic principle of the sonata form. You can maybe bring in the term... [*Showing quotation marks with fingers*] "dialectical," by saying that this is the thesis, and development is the antithesis, and then here, with recapitulation, we have the synthesis where everything gets wrapped up back to the place where it... [*Door creaks open*] started and this opposition gets unified. And as I said, this has a lot to do with the idea of tonality and the opposition between the tonic and dominant, and what comes out of that.

[*Long pause.*]

Regarding its form, critics have sometimes suggested that the sonata is a sort of utopian genre that introduces conflict, and then it pushes it to reconciliation and happy ending. Pretty much any single work in the Classical and Romantic period, you can have sonata in the work. But I think, and I have to be cautious here... [*Cough in the audience.*] Like recapitulation in the sonata form is similar to the exposition, as it seeks to resolve the argument. I wonder if this might be something like those categories that are close to each other, and what I mean is that you have this tonic here... [*Strikes the blackboard at "Exposition"*] and you have a tonic key here and you have this tonic key here [*Strikes the blackboard at "Recapitulation"*] and I wonder if they are really the same thing, they are physically the same pitches. But the question is how it made the journey here after you come to this process. Are you at the same place? They are like what the Deleuzians sometimes like to talk about, a sort of folding, or self-folding and repetition. I mean, but is it the same place, and I don't know if that's... [*Pause.*] Again, like in Deleuze's Difference and Repetition,[31] we may ask ourselves: if you repeat the same thing over and over again, is it the same or there is deference? You certainly would have to start with the sonata as just going up somewhere, but which is not the same place; it's a combination of this, but it is also a temporal movement away... [*Looks at Jameson.*] You talked about this...

JAMESON: The other figurative metaphor of this sort of movement is the spiral... [*Chair legs screech along the floor*] where you come back to the same place but it's not the same place anymore, it's a higher moment. [*Draws a spiral on the blackboard.*]

STUDENT: Right. I don't... [*Pause.*] I don't know what visual metaphor would be better to apply to the sonata form, but it has been said, also by Adorno, that sonata form is a sort of an allegory of the bourgeois society, as this closed totality and sort of illusory bourgeois freedom, which in fact is only a replay of the same elements within a confined or already established rules.

[*Long pause.*]

Finally, I will talk a bit about Beethoven, and sort of the image of Beethoven. I think he was the first human genius, and what I mean is, if you look at Mozart, hmm... [*Hesitates.*] Mozart was this figure who was endowed with some sort of divine genius. If you look at his manuscripts, the way he wrote his works, it is prematurely straight up; he saw this music in front of him or had it in his head and he was just recording it in the heat of inspiration and ecstasy. [*Pause.*] Beethoven, he worked on his manuscripts with pain, writing and rewriting till the last minute, and you can see the intense labor he puts into his work, and how he agonizes over each individual piece of music, over each individual note. And I think it's a much more... [*Pause*] I think Beethoven's music is much more down to the human level, human character. I said this last time, something that Haydn was a much more human kind of music and Mozart being a more spiritual kind of music, and I think that Beethoven is a combination of Mozart and Haydn, of divine genius and spiritual human. What marks Beethoven as a genius, it's his humanity. You can imagine, he was writing this sonata in about 1819 and 1820; I mean, this is the man who has been deaf for nine or ten years and he was losing his eyesight too; someone who had so many illnesses, from headaches, chronic abdominal pain to rheumatism. He hasn't figured his family situation, he had romantic failures; his health and many people have been asking how could he write music if he couldn't hear? Well, he could hear for a good part of his life, so he knew how voices and instruments sound, so most of these late compositions are from his imagination. And these are absolutely fantastic pieces of music, something about his late style that is... [*Door creaks open.*] But what's interesting, I went and looked at some other people's analogies of the Opus 111, to see what they would say about it, and so one commentator says that Beethoven was very transparent working out this form, whereas before Beethoven was constantly pushing and fighting the form, now he is sort of embraces it. Another contender, Plantinga, he says that Beethoven dissolves the sonata form as he refuses to follow the rules of the sonata form, and he is exposing its conventions. I'll read you something that a critic wrote to the editor, telling the editor why he would not review one of Beethoven's sonatas [*Shuffling paper. Starts reading.*]

> Perhaps you, dear editor, can establish a position from which criticism and the commonly accepted rules of aesthetics can be defended against these novelties, these attacks on first principles. For when the primary conception of a work of art is divorced from reason, when feeling alone provides the basis for judgment, when works that scorn all our rules gain such passionate admirers — then I must be silent."[32]

I think this is a funny quote; this is the same kind of things that you can take that, hmm... [*Hesitates*] and you can imagine that being said about the works that Schoenberg wrote earlier in his career, when he wrote his early atonal works, or even the serial works. And I think... [*Pause.*] I'm not sure I agree with Adorno's description and the return to the objective in Opus 111, but that's probably a longer discussion.

[*Long pause.*]

But as far as Beethoven's thirty-second Sonata is concerned, I think what happens here, in the first movement as the sonata expands, you see something that already anticipates Schoenberg, and that is the same type of intense motific development that we already see in Bach. It is from Bach to Beethoven to Schoenberg. When you hear this... [*Starts singing the famous motif from* <u>*Sonata 32*</u>] "Bum-bum-bum-ta-ta-ta-ta-ra-ra-ra-ra-rum," and so then, this first raw: "Bum-bum-baaaam," so then you'll get it all over the place as the sonata unfolds. And really the movement becomes much less about working out the tonal oppositions or working out the thematic oppositions... [*Pause.*] I mean, at first, I don't even know if one could see it as a second theme, I wonder if anyone else can find a second theme, but it's almost as if the movement becomes less about organic form and more about the development. The first Allegro movement in C minor, somewhat typical of Beethoven, and the second movement... [*Quietly*: this sonata has only two movements that form a kind of opposite, like allegro/adagio, C minor/C major] and the second movement is really where I think this sonata is incredible as a theme variation. So, in the second movement, he starts up a very slow Arietta, a little aria, and then gradually the notes become faster with intense syncopation, and it all starts to dissolve or culminates into these... [*Exhales deeply*] wonderfully sublime trills that keep intensifying. And there is a moment, I think, where you could almost say... [*Cough in the audience*] that it's not working anymore, because you've reached this point where there is just a fantastic chasm of space and there is this sort of infinite, but it is focused too. [*Words indistinct.*] So, I guess that's it, I don't know how much I should be playing it?

JAMESON: Mm-hmm, maybe a little bit from the second movement, as this is the part which he does with the names, that open with the notes C, G, G, hmm... [*Pause*] "meadowland," the syllables of Adorno's name, Wiesengrund... [*Quietly*: maybe a little bit of that, if we can find it there.]

STUDENT: Okay, I'll try. [*Presses "Play" on the CD-player.*] This is the beginning of the first movement... [*Pause.*]

STUDENT: [*Presses "Stop" button.*] Now, I will play you the part where you can hear the famous "Boom, boom-voom, voom-throom, throom."[33] I will skip as I'm trying to find the part where... [*Presses the "Forward" button.*] Ah, here it is...

Ludwig van Beethoven, *Piano Sonata No. 32, Op. 111*, Breitkopf und Härtel, 1862. First Movement. Public Domain.

Beethoven, Sonata 32, Op. 111, First Movement. Fragment.

STUDENT: Okay, this was the first movement, and I'll go now to the beginning of the second movement. [*Presses "Forward" button. Talks over skipping sound.*] Okay, this is now the beginning of the second movement, an Arietta in C major. We have a theme in two parts, a C major, then A minor, then goes back to C major... [*Presses "Play" button.*]

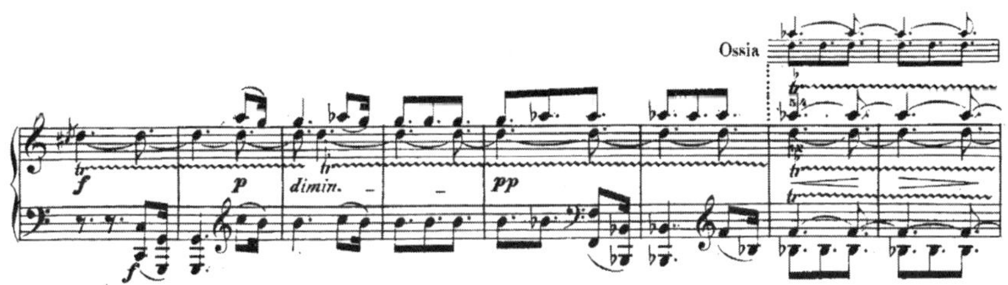

Beethoven, Sonata 32, Op. 111, Second Movement. Fragment.

JAMESON: Here it is [*Intones*]... W-I-E-S-E-N-G-R-U-N-D...

STUDENT: [*Talks over skipping music.*] You can hear different accompanying textures, and this is where he starts speeding up... [*Pause.*] The movement proceeds as a set of variations, each one speeding up... [*Words indistinct.*]

JAMESON: [*Addresses student.*] So, you have slow movement, the trio, and the tonalities — is that what you mean?

STUDENT: [*Talks over music.*] Yeh. There is... [*Music stops.*] Yeah, usually, your first movement is gonna be fast, or slow, or something fast like that. But this is definitely slow, and it

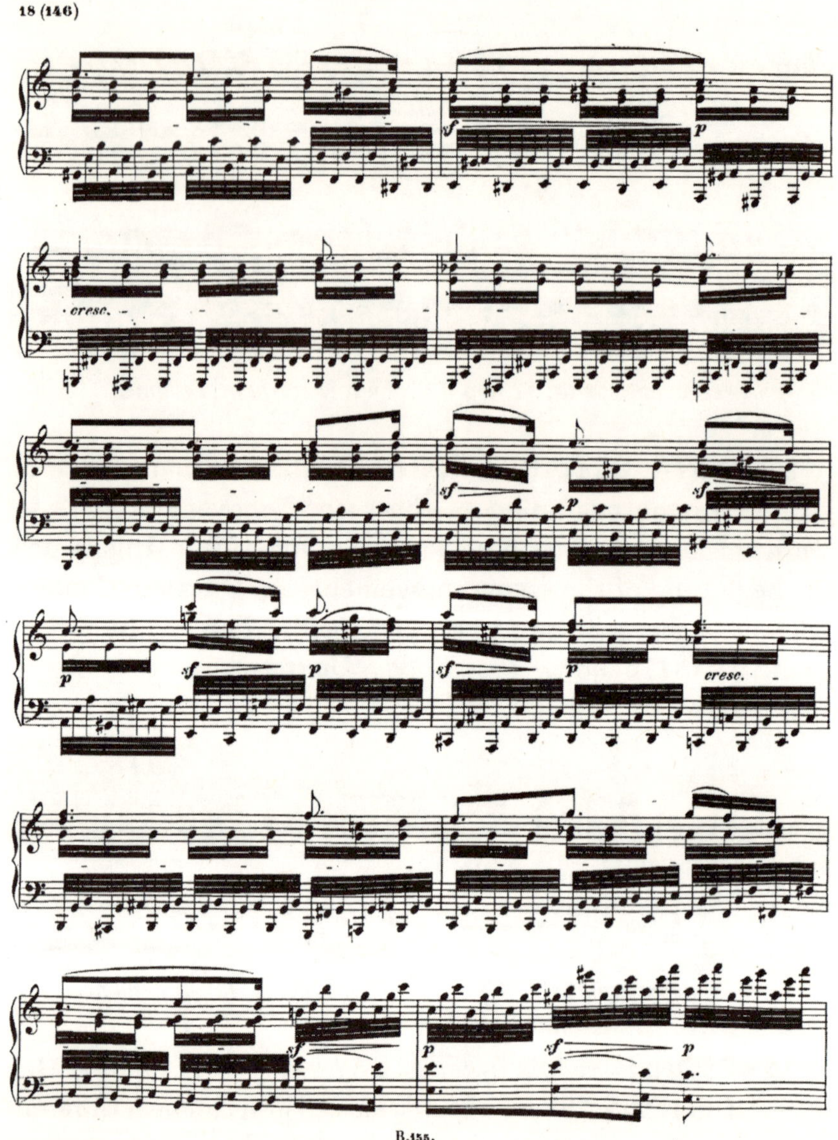

Beethoven, Sonata 32, Op. 111, Second Movement. Fragment.

is interesting if you look at how he keeps the same tempo, but speeding the variations till he reaches syncopations and going into the trills, which is the most extraordinary.

[*Presses "Play" button.*]

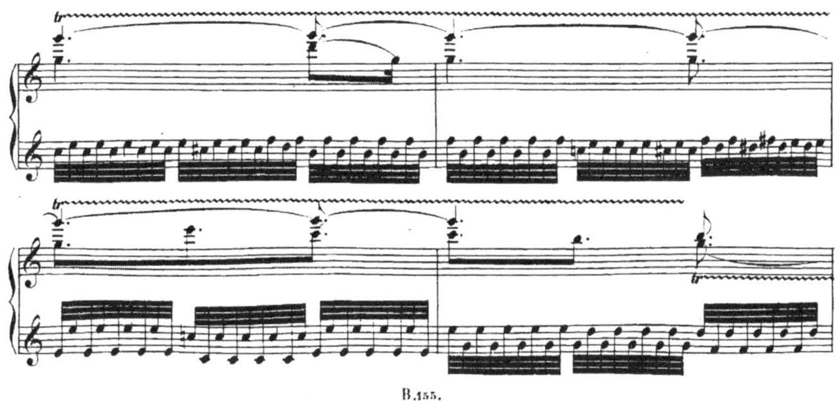

Beethoven, Sonata 32, Op. 111. The trills part. Fragment.

[*Skipping music.*]

STUDENT: Here... [*Pause*] and then we go towards the end.

JAMESON: Mm-hmm, the trills are really what Adorno means by objective, I mean, all of these rhetorical things going into it; it's not embedded... [*Stressing*] expressive stuff, but it's construction. [*Pause.*] The other opposition, as I understand it here, is between development and variation, right?

STUDENT: Well, and that's the thing. I mean, if I was gonna say how is Beethoven dissolving the sonata form... [*Pause.*] I mean, if I was a very pedantic German, I'd say, well, in the first movement, he is destroying sonata, and the second movement, he is destroying variations, and these are the two sort of paradigms for musical technique, the idea of theme variation and the idea the development. After all, Thomas Mann says that Opus 111 was a farewell, hmm... [*Hesitates*] to the sonata form. The idea of theme variation and the idea of development in sonata form is done, and by the time we get to Brahms, we have developing variations [*Pause.*] Brahms actually adopted

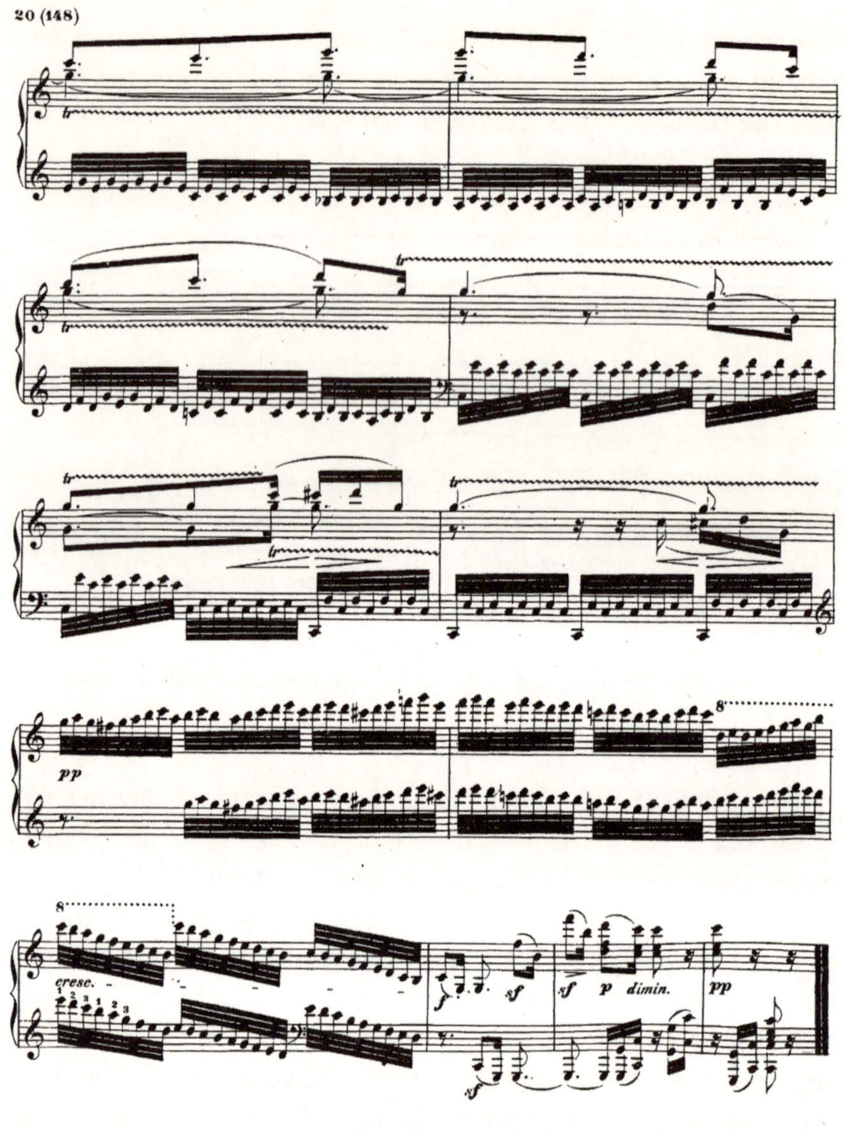

Beethoven, Sonata 32, Op. 111. Second Movement. Fragment.

and modified Beethoven's ideas by taking a small theme and expanding it, turning developing variation into a principle where there is nothing but the endless reshaping of the same theme, hmm... [*Hesitates*] and Schoenberg then works with the same serial material. Once the series is set, you cannot get out of it...

JAMESON: There are a couple of other things to say about these thoughts on Beethoven, which you can find throughout Aesthetic Theory anyway. One is that, and Adorno comes back to it... [*Pause.*] This is a re-confirmation of necessity; it is not just coming back to the same key, but that a key is then made [*Stressing*] necessary again. Another idea is that, as you can see here, you don't have themes anymore, I mean, they are broken up atomically into smaller elements, and then you have all kinds of combinations that are no longer really melodic... [*Quietly*: that I think is another thing that is going on here.] Mm-hmm... [*Raps his knuckles on the desk.*] Ah, yes, and then when Adrian writes his quartet later on, hmm... [*Quietly:* I forget what composition that is] he says, and I think this is very interesting [*Impersonates Adrian*] "I did not wish to write a sonata... but a novel."[34] And Thomas Mann talks about the way in which these things sort of move in the completely unrelated areas, as a wandering through dimensions of being that are unrelated to each other, and so forth. [*Pause.*] And I think that this is also key in this notion of variations. Anyway, we'll come back to some of those things... [*Chairs scratching the floor*] and remember to bring and talk to me about the first ideas for your papers... [*Words indistinct.*]

Audience stands up. Door squeaks. Students return chairs to other classrooms. Zippers zipping up. Some in the audience form a line to discuss their assignments with Jameson. General noise. Screeching microphone noise.

[*Microphone turns off.*]

CURTAIN

LECTURE SIXTEEN

MARCH 27, 2003

FOUR LEVELS OF ALLEGORY AND *DOCTOR FAUSTUS*

CURTAIN RISES

Students are discussing their papers. One student is talking about how difficult it is for her to choose a topic. "Aesthetic Theory *is just too hard for me." Another student replies: "Maybe you make the index, as he suggested?" "Are you kidding me? I can barely make it through the first chapter, and you're talking about indexing the whole book. I'll ask for an incomplete, and then I'll think about it." A third student enters the conversation to talk about the many meanings of the word "incomplete." "The other day," he says, "I was in the Office of the Registrar, and they asked me if I had an incomplete. But what they said was, 'Are you incomplete?' At first, I thought maybe they were saying 'in Comp Lit,' like in the Literature department. Or then, that they were asking if I — as a person — were not complete somehow, like a fragment or something." Students are laughing.*

Jameson enters the classroom carrying a few books, his scattered notes, and the red pen in the chest pocket of his flannel shirt.

[*Microphone turns on.*]

JAMESON: Mm-hmm, this is a volume made from Dürer's illustrations of the Apocalypse ... [*Holds a facsimile edition of*

Dürer's Apocalypsis cum figuris.][1] You can pass it around and take a closer look at Dürer's engravings...

STUDENT: [*Words indistinct. Feet shuffling. Chair legs scrape hard against the floor.*]

JAMESON: Sorry, what's that?

[*Long silence.*]

JAMESON: I haven't given you any secondary readings because I think that they all, hmm... [*Hesitates.*] None of them can really be very rigorous when compared to you working with the primary source. I think it is more important for us to learn how to read Adorno, rather than get his thoughts thematized for us by his numerous interpreters. In a way, this is like looking very closely at these Dürer engravings... [*Quietly*: instead of reading about them from some art historians, you take a look at how the lines are made.] Such an approach would be somehow more in the spirit of this book... [*Quietly*: I mean of Aesthetic Theory] because I hope you've understood by now that, for Adorno, there are no [*Whispering*] disembodied thoughts. People's opinions are of no interest at all to him... [*Quietly*: they are generally ideological: you like art or you don't like art, or you like Bartók more than you like Schoenberg, and so forth — none of that is of any interest to Adorno.] Mm-hmm... [*Pause.*] What is important for him is the way in which concepts get connected to each other, and how these concepts interact in order to create a reading context, a forcefield of meaning... [*Exhales deeply.*] So, therefore, plot summaries or secondary literature are not so crucial when it comes to engaging with Adorno. [*Absorbed.*] However, I did ask a student to make an up-to-date list of the most recent works on Adorno, and we may just profit and be informed on the research that is going on in this area. A lot of it is in German, of course, but there are a few important books in English as well. [*Looks at a paper. Page flipping.*] The student put down only those sources that he thinks are... [*Pause.*] This book... [*To himself:* would something simply called "Adorno" be in English or in German?] Mm-hmm. I assume that's in German... [*Cough in the audience.*] I also assume that some of the books included here in this list may also be in some other language. Obviously, a bibliography on Adorno is not quite as enormous as one on Thomas Mann, but there is nonetheless already an “Adorno industry,” if you like, and it has reached by now to all kind of themes... [*Clears throat*] that normally involves everything you could imagine written about Adorno but the essential.

[*Long pause*.]

You may not recognize it in English, but in German the word for “case” is der Fall, as in “alles, was der Fall ist,” and this is obviously Wittgenstein’s famous conclusion to his Tractatus. “The world is everything that is the case,”[2] and this is Wittgenstein’s way of getting out of this philosophical field called “ontology.” If you call something an “ontology,” then it’s a philosophical discipline that studies alles, was der Fall ist, or “whatever is the case,” and that’s what being is, right... [*Looks at the audience*.] To this, Adorno responds in a, hmm... [*Hesitates*] in a chapter of Aesthetic Theory that I am about to recommend to you: “aesthetics has to do with ‘alles, was nicht der Fall ist.’” Aesthetics deals with everything that is [*Whispering*] not the case, and by this he means that aesthetics or art have to do with the negative and the nonexistent, with what is not there, with what is imaginary or what’s an image, and what is not real and a non-existent world. This Adornian quote comes from the... [*Sighs*] from the “Draft Introduction,”[3] to which I hope we will dedicate a full session one day. We haven’t gotten to the end of Aesthetic Theory yet, but you will find three chapters there. One is called “Paralipomena,” and this one contains his various aesthetic observations and fragments that the editors decided to compile into one chapter added at the end. Given the way Adorno worked, I suppose all of those... [*Door slams in the distance*] thoughts, ideas, dispersed notes have been incorporated somehow in there. I don’t think you will find anything new in this chapter, but you may always find some marvelous formulations... [*Quietly*: apparently, Adorno was very good at that] and these are formulations that you may not find in the main text. Presumably, these fragments assembled by the editors in the "Paralipomena," he would have gone through them and have them organized. I assume he worked a bit like, hmm... [*Hesitates*] maybe what Žižek has described as being his method, which is to say a sort of cut-and-paste... [*Quietly*: that is, you rant on and on and on, and then you stop, print this all out, and start figuring out what is the right way to organize the material.] This is not what Adorno necessarily did, but we may imagine him doing something like that... [*Mumbles indistinctly*.] All of these additional thoughts in the "Paralipomena" chapter are quite optional for you to browse through. Mm-hmm, some people like to read fragments, I mean, a lot of Nietzsche is fragments and there is a special kind of pleasure, I guess, in reading fragmentary prose.

[*Long pause*.]

Then there is the other chapter at the end, which is called "Theories on the Origins of Art," and that is the only section which Adorno really deals with other works. Mm-hmm... [*Pause*.] The whole business of the [*Stressing*] *origins* of art is obviously anthropological. That is what they found at Lascaux in those caves, what do those paintings tell us about early art, or what is the origins of art, and here Adorno turns to a number of anthropological theories...[4] [*Clears throat*.] All of these theories of the origins of art and the sources he gives at the end of that chapter... [*Quietly*: and whether the beginning of art is in ritual or mimesis] they may be right or wrong, and I think this may not be a very interesting debate for us to have, because we don't know anything about these anthropologies. But in pursuing the question of the origins of art, the chapter does connect a little bit to his and Horkheimer's *Dialectic of Enlightenment* and therefore... [*Quietly*: if any of you are working on the questions of art's origins, then this chapter could be of interest] but if not, then I don't think you need to read it. Next comes the "Draft Introduction"... [*Pause*.] I think that, over the years, I have underestimated this chapter because I think that it's quite a, hmm... [*Hesitates*] it's quite a good introduction to the whole *Aesthetic*

Theory. This early "Draft Introduction" forced Adorno to put a lot of thoughts together, which of course was very helpful later during the execution of this very complex project. For our next time, as we are trying now to go back to Adorno... [*Cough in the audience*] I will ask you to read the "Draft Introduction," which might or might not have been discarded when he went back to the book as a whole. Because I think... [*Zipper unzipping*] now that you know how to read Adorno and have sampled a lot of the thematic things, I think that this early introduction will be much, hmm... [*Hesitates*] it will be much stronger and more meaningful than if I asked you to read it at the beginning of our seminar. One can extract from it a history of aesthetics... [*Quietly*: he doesn't give you one as such, but you could find it there] in the Kantian and Hegelian poles, then the issue of nominalism, the genres, truth content and all that is central to Aesthetic Theory. And I think that this would be the best way to work our way back to these... [*Raps his knuckles on the desk*] other chapters and to the book as a whole.

[*Long pause.*]

But before we do that, there is some loose business for us to finish in Doctor Faustus. I wanted to read for you a passage... [*Pause.*] You know that Prince Myshkin, the main character in Dostoevsky's Idiot, had a condition that in French is called le grand mal, or the "falling sickness," and in modern medical terminology, it is a form of epilepsy. People with epilepsy may experience alterations in consciousness during a seizure, but it may also involve an altered form of consciousness and a very [*Stressing*] special kind of state — a Steigerung, as we discussed this term in one of our previous sessions. This intensification of mental activity and Dostoevsky's use of epilepsy is analogous to the way syphilis is used in Mann's book. And we can find a description of this state in various places, but the one paragraph in Dostoevsky's Idiot, I think, is very striking in this respect. [*Page flipping. Starts reading.*]

He fell to thinking, among other things, about his epileptic

> condition, that there was a stage in it just before the fit itself (if the fit occurred while he was awake), when suddenly, amidst the sadness, the darkness of soul, the pressure, his brain would momentarily catch fire, as it were, and all his life's forces would be strained at once in an extraordinary impulse. The sense of life, of self-awareness, increased nearly tenfold in these moments, which flashed by like lightning. His mind, his heart were lit up with an extraordinary light; all his agitations, all his doubts, all his worries were as if placated at once, resolved in a sort of sublime tranquility, filled with serene, harmonious joy, and hope, filled with reason and ultimate cause. But these moments, these glimpses were still only a presentiment of that ultimate second (never more than a second) from which the fit itself began. That second was, of course, unbearable. Reflecting on that moment afterwards, in a healthy state, he had often said to himself that all those flashes and glimpses of a higher self-sense and self-awareness, and therefore of a "highest being..." [Quietly: this is in quotation marks] were nothing but an illness, a violation of the normal state, and if so, then this was not the highest being at all but, on the contrary, should be counted as the very lowest. And yet he finally arrived at an extremely paradoxical conclusion: "So what if it's an illness?" he finally decided "Who cares that it is an abnormal strain, if the result itself, if the moment of the sensation, remembered and examined in a healthy state, turns out to be the highest degree of harmony, beauty, gives a hitherto unheard-of and unknown feeling of fullness, measure, reconciliation, and an ecstatic prayerful merging with the highest synthesis of life?[5]

Well, I think this is very much in the spirit of the book we are looking at, as it gives you, in... [*Stressing*] existential terms, a sense of the tremendous burst of creativity that Adrian Leverkühn shows in Mann's novel. You remember in Doctor Faustus that, at the end of World War One, Adrian is almost paralyzed by these headaches, by complete immobility, but out of which also emerges this tremendous excitement and burst of creativity from which the Apocalypse comes, and then it is renewed in the final Doctor Faustus oratorio. [*Pause*.] But I think existentially this is, hmm... [*Hesitates*.] And this is obviously all an allusion to Dostoevsky, as well as to Nietzsche's manic and prophetic moments. The final scene of attempt to suicide at the pond,[6] I believe that part may have been inspired from Robert Schumann... [*Quietly*: if anybody knows the musical history of this... (*Mumbles Indistinctly*).] Schumann also went crazy, and he tried to drown himself, I believe...

STUDENT: He jumped off a bridge...

JAMESON: Sorry?

STUDENT: Schumann, he jumped off a bridge into the Rhine...

JAMESON: [*Excited*.] Yes, yes, and they picked him out of the water and committed him to an insane asylum. But it was also Ludwig the Second of Bavaria, who was Wagner's patron... [*Quietly*: he is also said to have drowned himself in a pond, right?] But I think he didn't die though...

STUDENT: He did.

JAMESON: He did die? Okay, then...

STUDENT: There are speculations it was murder...

JAMESON: Ah, okay, but here again we have this principle of what Thomas Mann calls "montage," and which we have talked already... [*Quietly*: the mixture of fiction with historical facts... (*Mumbles indistinctly*) some of the words come out of Nietzsche's letters.] I personally don't think this is a very good word for this of writing, and I don't think that this is what Eisenstein meant when he explained cinematic montage as a new principle of composition, but, hmm... [*Looks for words*] but this is what Mann preferred.

[*Long pause*.]

We were talking the other day about... [*Cough in the audience*] the way in which some modern works of literature wished to be... [*Quietly*: if not universal or cosmological in the scientific sense] then a sort of the "book of the world." In Joyce's Ulysses, if you recall, there is this dense symbolic world where each chapter is dominated by a variable, be it a color scheme, a symbol, an organ of the body, an art and so on and so forth. There is, in the organization of Ulysses, a reference to the entire world, and this is what Joyce allegedly told... [*Sighs*] Stuart Gilbert about various levels of reference, which are tied to the structure of the book, and then Gilbert published his schema.[7] Examples of such symbolism and references to deeper meanings and truths of the world... [*Takes a sip of water*] may also be found in Doctor Faustus, and they can be numerological too, although I'm not sure whether numerology is worth mentioning here. [*Softly*.] How many chapters do we have in Doctor Faustus? It is forty, hmm...? [*Hesitates*] Forty-seven, and I don't know if this is a meaningful number of some sort... [*Quietly*: does this number has any diabolical numerological significance?] But in the past, many books have deployed astrology and numerology, like Dante's Divine Comedy is organized around numbers and theological or numerological medieval traditions considered sacred... [*Quietly*: like the significance of number three in the Inferno, with the three beasts.] I think you may find similar things structurally inserted in Doctor Faustus as well, and indeed, it's not unlikely that some German scholar has already written about it, and we shouldn't perhaps worry about it. But I think this may be a clue to us, and we could talk about the cosmological order in a somewhat different way... [*Chair scratching against the floor*.]

[*Long pause*.]

We can try interpreting Doctor Faustus in a different way. It is through what I call "allegory."[8] [*Pause*.] In the history of allegory, there are two forms, in the West at least... [*Quietly*: and I don't know if there is any non-Western theory of allegory, but that's another discussion.] There is the three-fold allegory, which is that of the pre-Christian or Alexandrian period... [*Cough in the audience*] this is the Hellenistic allegory centered on myth. And then, with Christianity, this three-fold system becomes four-fold, and we get something that is called... [*Chalk on the blackboard*] Q-U-A-D-R-I-G-A. This one has four levels:

Literal, Allegorical (also called sometimes Mystical or Typological), Moral, and Anagogical. The quadriga is an innovation of Christianity as it becomes the central part of Biblical exegesis and was used for reading the scripture... [*Quietly*: at the moment when Christianity introduces its greatest innovations, as when Kierkegaard calls it "Christianity's modernity."] With this change in the interpretative innovation, you can see what Christianity does to the ancient world, among many other things. For the Alexandrian tripartite allegory, Homer's epic poems constitute the main source material where this type of interpretative method is practiced. What you had was, hmm... [*Hesitates.*] Let me write it this way, you have a... [*Chalk on the blackboard*] L-I-T-E-R-A-L level. This level is, of course, the Homeric story itself... [*Quietly*: in the Iliad, this is the account of the Trojan War, between Greek states and Troy and the rest of it.] And as you know, in the Iliad there are just these innumerous confrontations between heroes from all over the known world, as the story is told... [*Quietly*: I don't know how many hand-to-hand combats are there, but there are a lot of them.] So, in the pre-Christian allegorical model, as I said, the Literal level is [*Stressing*] physical, in the sense of physics, astronomy and of the elements, like Zeus is the air and Kronos was time. This would be a sort of "scientific" level... [*Quietly*: I'm not sure we can use this word here] or let's call it a "materialist" level, because that would be a little bit more... [*Hits blackboard with chalk*] consistent with Lucretius's interpretations. The second level would be the... [*Chalk on the blackboard*] M-O-R-A-L level, and this level is dealing with virtues and vices. [*Pause.*] You could have Diomedes fighting a lost Trojan opponent, and that would take place in reality, but that would also mean... [*Quietly*: now I will have to make this all up] mm-hmm, that here, at the Literal level, it is interpreted as the struggle of oil with water, and here on the Moral level, it would mean fortitude versus bravery. These are all battles between the virtues and the vices. And with Odyssey, the entire journey is allegorized and interpreted in terms of virtues and challenges that humans encounter in the course of their lives. [*Pause.*] Then we also have the last… [*Chalk on the blackboard*] S-P-I-R-I-T-U-A-L order, which lies beyond the other levels, and this is the cosmological level where the Homeric characters represent the planets and the atoms as they collide in the universe.[9] And this is — in a very short and simplified way — the way that the classical Alexandrian allegory functions.

[*Long pause.*]

Now, I think that we could just apply these old Alexandrian levels to interpret Doctor Faustus as well. That is to say, we have the option of reading the novel in such a way that it… [*Door slams in the distance*] incorporates what I called earlier the "literal" as the cosmological order of physics and the elements. And then we can move to the "moral" order, and here we talk about the so-called virtues via the opposition between Catholic and Protestant, as they appear in the novel. But I also think that there is another way of reading it, which is much more complicated and interesting than this Alexandrian model… [*Knocks the chalk against the blackboard.*]

[*Long pause.*]

Now let's look at the Christian layers. In the Christian system, you have four levels of allegory, and this is because another feature or narrative then enters the picture — and this is the life of Christ. [*Pause.*] The minute that you understand the presence of that narrative level of allegory, you can see that everything starts to change because all of a sudden history is here. Things are happening. There is an end of time and a redemption, and this new presence then changes the interpretative model. Alright, so now, with the four-fold Christian allegory, you have first of all the [*Stressing*] Literal level, and now let me give you the most obvious example that everybody uses. And by the way, the main book on this — and there are many special books — but I would say is the book by one of the Jesuit cardinals of Paris named Jean… [*Chalk strokes on the blackboard*] D-A-N-I-É-L-O-U. [*Softly.*] You may know that the theologians have an immense publishing industry with big libraires and books you've never seen or heard of. This is a book called From Shadows to Reality, or something like that in its English title,[10] and it gives you a history of Christian allegory. The other name I would also like to mention in this context is that of Henri de... [*Chalk strokes on the blackboard*] L-U-B-A-C, but this one is very, very formally researched material, as he is thinking in historical types.[11]

[*Long pause.*]

Now, the Christian allegorical levels... [*Draws a line on the blackboard*] addresses problems that are different from that of Alexandrian allegory. The problem that classical Greeks, and to a lesser extent the Romans, was that they just wanted to deal with the myth. Homer is certainly the great book, it is the source of all education, it is the place where you learn about virtues and justice, about the elements, but it appears at times that Greek allegorization is completely arbitrary and based on a loose body of legends and myths. The Christians did not want their interpretations to be frivolous, and therefore they wanted to turn it into something more serious. In addition, the Christians already have a book... [*Quietly*: in fact, they have two of them.] So, here the first question arises as what do we do with the Old Testament? Hmm... [*Hesitates*] something has to be done to the Old Testament. In late antiquity, there is this new ideological strategy of assimilating the Old Testament to the New, which is a sort of rewriting the Jewish textual heritage to make it usable for Gentiles.[12] So this is then the... [*Chalk on the blackboard*] L-I-T-E-R-A-L level of Christian allegory where the Old Testament constitutes the point of historical originality of Christianity as this [*Stressing*] midpoint between Judaism and... [*Cough in the audience*] the world. It is the attempt of Christianity to negate both of them and balance them into a synthesis. And for this, something had to be done with the Old Testament, and the Literal level is simply that book — the application of the Old Testament. The next level of Christian exegesis is... [*Chalk strokes*] A-L-L-E-G-O-R-I-C-A-L, and it is called "allegorical" because, hmm... [*Hesitates*] because history itself is above all written by God and therefore it can be interpreted... [*Door slams in the distance.*] Let's take an event of human history, a fact from the Bible... [*Cough in the audience*] an illustration from the Old Testament about the Hebrew exodus from Egypt and their ultimate escape through the Red Sea. What is that? The descent of the Hebrews into Egypt, their captivity there, then their rescue out of Egypt through the Red Sea and into Sinai — this is the death and resurrection of Christ.[13] Christ dies, descends into Hell, and then you can see the rifts in the rocks where Christ has gone through into hell and he stays there... [*Quietly*: What the period would be, from three in the afternoon on Friday until Sunday morning? I'm not sure.] Mm-hmm, and then he rises from the dead. This literal or historical fact from the history of the Hebrews has as its allegorical meaning, and this... [*Achoo. Sneeze in the audience*] the moment of redemption in the life of Christ. So, the second Allegorical level is then the life of Christ. Alright. But now there is a third moment. This is the... [*Chalk on the blackboard*] M-O-R-A-L level, and then the fourth one which is the... [*Chalk strokes*] A-N-A-G-O-G-I-C-A-L. Now, this is... [*Points to the word "Moral" on the blackboard*] the life of the individual soul, and the Anagogical one deals with the universal and political or the fate of the human race. So, these levels turn into something which is the fall of the individual soul, "myself," in other words, into sin and my conversion and [*Stressing*] separation from sin. [*Pause.*] And on this level... [*Points to "Anagogical"*] clearly it is the degradation of history and the Last Judgment, and thus the Apocalypse precisely and the separation of the blessed from the damned, and so on and so forth. So, this little [*Stressing*] true fact from the Exodus... [*Quietly*: because the Old Testament is sometimes considered as a set of facts] is inscribed in it all of these levels of meaning. So here we have the levels [*Points to the blackboard*]:

A-N-A-G-O-G-I-C-A-L (history, the fate of human kind)
M-O-R-A-L (the fate of the individual subject)
A-L-L-E-G-O-R-I-C-A-L (the life of Christ)
L-I-T-E-R-A-L (the text itself in its first application, the Old Testament).[14]

[*Long pause*.]

Now, the Church fathers concluded that maybe one could think of even more layers of allegorical interpretation, of up to seven... [*Quietly*: and this is another special kind of number, like four... (*Mumbles indistinctly*)] but then they decided that four was enough. The layers could also be linked to the history of the Church, but since the history of the Church and the life of Christ is the same, then you could merge them into one layer. And there are other similar options that can be reduced or superimposed, so the issue over how many layers of interpretation are required does not need to be seen as a completely cut-and-dry affair, but there are possibilities for other kind of meanings on top of these four layers. But then, one must also consider very carefully what the relationship of these levels to each other are. Overall, this is the interpretative formula that became predominant, and Dante talks about it in a Letter to Cangrande, which is allegedly his explanation of the Divine Comedy... [*Quietly*: although many people are very doubtful whether he could have done this, I mean... (*Mumbles indistinctly*).][15] Here Dante describes his journey and the characters and people he encounters along the way through the afterlife, and also explaining these four levels, which made it into a famous letter.

[*Long pause*.]

Okay, but then what does that mean for us? I want us to remember that Doctor Faustus involves the tremendous interrelationship — we talked about this already — of time schemes. [*Pause*.] We are constantly... [*Cough in the audience*] being reminded that we are not at the same time all the time, right? Or rather, that we are existing, and this text is existing [*Stressing*] simultaneously in a number of temporal dimensions all at once.

[*Pause.*] Mm-hmm. It seems to me that a central part of this book is this sensation that it is impossible to escape this state of simultaneously inhabiting several temporal dimensions. The book is about temporality, it is about history, and as I say, history is, hmm... [*Hesitates.*] Did I tell you the story about the Pope?

AUDIENCE: [*In unison.*] No.

JAMESON: Once, the Pope... [*Quietly*: and that is well before he became John Paul II, when he was still the archbishop of Krakow] he had many meetings with the officials of what was back then socialist Poland. So, he had a whole set of interesting anecdotes from that time, and one was this one. The Pope... [*Quietly*: remember, he is still the archbishop in Poland, not yet the Pope] was debating the communists and he begins by saying, [*Impersonates future John Paul II*] "One thing I don't wanna hear that you people say is the word 'history.' We invented history, the Christians. History belongs to us." [*Chuckles.*] Well, I think that this is part of this four-fold scheme, and the first genuinely historical eschatological thought that... [*Cough in the audience*] history is going somewhere, that history means something, that it has its own laws, that is, not just a series of births, populations, and deaths. All of this is a Christian idea. I don't think you can find it in... [*Pause.*] You don't find it in Judaism. For those who read Benjamin, you know that the Messiah is [*Stressing*] not the combination of anything. I mean, in Benjamin, the Messiah just happens when it is least expected, and nothing is moving towards that, but then suddenly the Messiah is there as a sort of a "side door" that he comes in. [*Pause.*] And in the other religions, presumably the same takes place. Mm-hmm. Islam... [*Raps his knuckles on the desk*] that would be a whole other discussion. But what I wanted to mark at this point is not only Thomas Mann's concern with history, but also let's say the role of exile in sharing these different temporal dimensions... [*Door creaks open. Footsteps.*]

[*Long pause.*]

As you know, Doctor Faustus ends before reconstruction, and I think I've recommended to you Fassbinder's The Marriage of Maria Braun, which is the first part of Fassbinder's postwar trilogy that gives you a little idea of what happens after the war... [*Quietly*: in the period right after the war and the beginning of the making of the so-called "German economic miracle."] World War Two is really the end of something, and I think that you have to read into this novel the problems of exile that are less often talked about. It's not just the painfulness of exile for not being in your homeland, but it's the fact that when you have been living in exile, you no longer have a relationship with your people at home, and therefore you can't speak for them, they resent you... [*Cough in the audience*] you have missed out on the national experience. And there are a number of people who left... [*Quietly*: in France, this question of exile is also very striking.] Breton left, hmm... [*Hesitates*] as did Levi-Strauss. But Levi-Strauss was Jewish, and that's a different matter. Breton was not, and when he decided to leave France, he had some very interesting experiences with Trotsky in Mexico, with the Indians of the Southwest tribes, in Quebec, Haiti, and all of these other places. But when Breton decides to go back to France, he is utterly without authority. Surrealism is almost fully dead, and this is because he left. [*Pause*.] The same is true... [*Quietly*: there was a little Surrealist group that are still doing things, but it never reached the prewar level.] But that group that Breton reconstituted around himself... [*Quietly*: people of whom you never heard of, particularly] was the first to denounce the French imperialism. Breton had a very keen sense of imperialism, and he was well in advance, but nonetheless, after his exile, his career in France was finished.

[*Long pause*.]

With Thomas Mann, it's very interesting, as later on you'll see in the novel that Zeitblom says, [*Impersonates Zeitblom*] "Look, I'm giving you the conversation between Adrian and Rudi, I'm giving you the conversation between so-and-so, because I wasn't there." But what does that mean, [*Whispering*] I wasn't there? In such places, "Zeitblom's absence/presence is that of Thomas Mann himself,"[16] and one could infer that

Thomas Mann was thinking about Germany, but he was not there. [*Addresses student.*] You wanna close that window? [*Chair scraping against the floor. Windows creaking.*] Mann is absent; he was on a trip to Switzerland, and he didn't come back, hmm... [*Hesitates*] although Goebbels was very insidious in trying to keep some of these bright intellectuals in Germany. The famous case is that of Fritz Lang. Goebbels was well aware of the power of film... [*Quietly*: it is said that he admired Eisenstein's Potemkin[17] very much and that he showed it to all of these Nazis all the time telling them, "Look, this is the kind of political film that we should be making here, Potemkin."] Goebbels wanted Fritz Lang to head the movie production industry in the Third Reich, and Lang said... [*Quietly*: you can find this in Lang's memoirs], [*Impersonates Lang*] "But you know my mother was Jewish," to which Goebbels replied, "We will decide who is a Jew!" And then, the next morning, he was gone, to France or Switzerland. These were obviously dangerous offers, but he never went back. So, during the whole Nazi period, which is central here for the book that he is writing, Mann was not there. He is telling this story from exile. And this aspect then becomes very problematic, for how can you speak for the people? How can you write the national novel when you haven't even lived through the national experience?

[*Long pause.*]

But Mann has lived it up to the 1920s. In other words, he's lived the national experience that Adrian has lived, and Adrian's passage into the stage of madness is the moment when Nazis came to power, and this is also the moment when Thomas Mann left. So, in a sense, he can say, [*Impersonates Mann*] "Yes, I did experience everything, and this gives me a right to tell the story. How would the novel had been different if I stayed, if I was part of Germany's history?" But we know that, hmm... [*Hesitates*] that Mann lived for a long time abroad in Switzerland and in America. He even died in Switzerland. When the American McCarthyism began, Mann went back to East Germany, where he gave these famous Schiller lectures, and at this point, he turns relatively pro-Soviet, maybe not a communist, but let's say he becomes a fellow-traveler liberal-democrat. Mm-hmm... [*Pause*.] But I think that he really never... [*Quietly*: I am not sure, I must look that up, but I am not sure if he set foot in West Germany after the war.[18]] But this is... [*Hesitates*.] At this point, when he finally detaches himself, as it were, from Germany, his work is over, and everything that he does after Doctor Faustus is a kind of [*In French*] divertissement. There are several other books, including Der Erwählte, where he tells the story of Pope Gregory the Great and his illegitimate son, and where you come across characters like the giant, a bear... [*Mumbles indistinctly*.][19] There are a few other odds and ends that he completed, but Doctor Faustus is the end for him, in many kinds of ways.

[*Long pause*.]

Alright, now what do we do with all of this? It seems to me that there are several levels of meaning here... [*Chair-back creaks. Walks towards the blackboard*.] Let's apply the four-fold allegorical schema discussed earlier to the novel. What is the Literal level in Doctor Faustus? [*Pause*.] Well, we would be tempted to say that the [*Stressing*] literal level is very obvious here: it is, of course, the story of Adrian Leverkühn, his biography. [*Softly*.] But I don't think so. I think that the Literal level here is the act of writing of the book called Doctor Faustus. I think it is Zeitblom who is sitting there and writing it chapter after chapter, and everything in it brings us back again and again to the act of writing. And it's very interesting that there should be this theme of writing, given what happens later on with the emergence of structuralism... [*Takes a sip of water*.] But if this is an example of écriture exactly, or I don't know, maybe the novel gives us some difference between the French and the German positions in structuralism, hmm... [*Hesitates*.] Writing Doctor Faustus has to do with history insofar as it involves the German sentence, its emergence out of a kind of... [*Quietly*: you know that the Medieval sentence is not very well established with its reliance on inflected endings, and it was not till the Renaissance that German language developed more standardized sentence structure, which you can still see some of those here... (*Mumbles indistinctly*).] There is a remark on this process of language here... [*Page flipping. Talks to himself*... I hope I can find it now.] It is in Adrian's final... [*Quietly*: page 520 in Adrian's final public confession, as it were.] [*Starts reading*] "...he used a kind of antiquated German, which given its defects and incomplete sentences, had always had something dubious and careless about it — and indeed, how long has it been since out tongue outgrew its barbaric stage and has to some extent obeyed both grammatical and orthographic rules."[20] It is the emergence of the law, the emergence of a national culture, it is the moment of Goethe, and therefore we get this paradigm of the inchoate and the archaic and whatever forms of order and repression modernity builds on.

[*Long pause*.]

Then we talked the other day about anticipations. Am I jumping ahead in the novel because I have all of these thoughts in my mind and I want to anticipate what's going to happen, or are these delaying tactics? [*Pause*.] And is this delaying a signal that... [*Door creaks open*] I don't want to go to the end? Or is it both? Is there any difference between them...? [*Pause*.] In this excitement that Zeitblom talks about in writing, is there any difference between anticipating the end, wanting to arrive at it and not wanting to arrive at it? All of that becomes allegorical as well, and it seems to me that is also part of the first Literal level of allegory and that process of writing. Why talk about chapter breaks, and then what is all this fuss about...? [*Quietly*: Now I've started a new chapter and all of this should have gone in the previous chapter, because now this is too long and so on and so forth.[21]] I think that all of this is done in order to draw your attention back to the, hmm... [*Quietly*: since we're talking about allegory] to the scriptural level of writing. I mean the way in which this has to do with a humanist tradition, in which writing and language are the fundamental things in the discovery of the great languages... [*Quietly*: whether it's Greek or Hebrew and then the translations of all these languages.] So, allegory would be a kind of translation, like in the great image of Saint Jerome, who is sitting at a wooden desk and is translating the Vulgate.[22] Translation is a saintly activity [*Pause*.] All of this, it seems to me, is part of this first level, which is inscribed in Zeitblom's act of narrating.

[*Long pause*.]

Okay, but then, with Adrian, we come across another level, which I will call "existential," and that allows us then to advance further in the interpretation of the novel. It has to do with the life of Adrian, and there is a lot of stuff, especially when we come to the end. "Watch with me," these are the words of Christ to his disciples in the garden of Gethsemane before his arrest,[23] and then this counter-thing of Dr. Faustus, "go home and sleep, don't worry about me."[24] [*Pause*.] All of this is part of what makes Adrian's life — the fatal gamble and the pact itself, the business of production versus paralyses, suffering, the transmutation of consciousness, either in the sense of Dostoevsky's epileptic fits... [*Quietly*: which we talked about above] or that of the Little Mermaid, who is ready to give up her life in the sea for being made into a human being at the cost of these terrible suffering... [*Quietly*: that she is ready to take... (*Mumbles indistinctly*).] All of that is sort of the figure of Adrian's life, the whole notion of buying some advantage at tremendous cost, and that would be one way of putting it. [*Pause*.] But this is also about the whole history of music, and this whole drama of the interrelationship between the archaic and the modern, and it is also about whether it's possible to do anything.. [*Cough in the audience*] new nowadays, when so much has been done after this comfortable nineteenth century. [*Softly*.] Remember that Adrian says in the novel what a wonderful century the nineteenth century was, because they were still able to do everything, and how hard it is to be at break with it. [*Quietly*: Where is it? (*Page flipping*).] Ah, here: "even as a student he once said to me that the nineteenth century must have been an uncommonly cozy period, since never had it been more painful for humanity to separate itself from the views and customs of the previous epoch than it was for the present generation."[25] Now, once you get to the end of the nineteenth century and the end of the great middle-class period, it becomes harder and harder to do anything. We can also translate this into economic terms. It is a great difficulty for entrepreneurship that — as Adorno says somewhere — what we call "consciousness of the subject" — it's simply... [*Takes a sip of water*] a, hmm... [*Hesitates*] it's not a reflection, but an after-image of the economic. So, you have, in the nineteenth century, the great subjectivities that were still possible, the great freedoms, and the heroic robber barons as the emblems of free-market entrepreneurship, when people could have an idea, start a business, make a fortune. [*Exhales deeply*.] This is the moment in which subjectivity also feels the vast potential and that immense possibilities that are still possible... [*Quietly*: that certain kinds of strengths and innovations are possible.] Then, little by little, as Adorno says, great conflicts start to take over, even in the space where individuals have made those fortunes, and we have the initiation of trusts, monopolies and conglomerates controlling most of economic activity. It is no longer possible for [*Stressing*] isolated individuals to make money... [*Quietly*: all of the money is increasingly now made by corporations.] Well, this is the stage in which free... [*Quietly*: well, seemingly free] subjectivities enter the constraints of an increasingly total system, and which you have to be — to use this famous phrase from the 1950s — an "organization man," who is a cog in the wheel of the system. [*Pause*.] You can see there is a kind of parallel of notions of shrinking freedom, of shrinking subjectivity, that really played a very important part in the views of the Frankfurt School on, hmm... [*Hesitates*] on subjectivity itself, on the possibility of negation, on the freedom to criticize things by standing outside this "totally administered world," as Adorno calls it.

[*Long pause*.]

This very problem then reemerges in music. How can you..? Hmm... [*Hesitates.*] How can you make new great music after Wagner, and after the late Wagnerians and the late Brahmsians and the other great composers of the nineteenth century? [*Pause.*] And if you are doing something in a special way, is this indeed [*Stressing*] new or it's just parody? And it is very important to understand that Adrian's work is not parody... [*Quietly*: parody is what everybody else does, and it's the only thing that is left for them to do.] But Adrian is breaking out of parody and, of course, this term "breaking out," or "breaking through," is one of the crucial leitmotifs of high modernism. The notion of "breaking through" is an absolutely recurring theme that has to do with the question of how to operate in this society that Adorno calls of "total administration"... [*Door slams shut*] a society based on complete control, and where individuals are forced into these roles that are defined by the free market. A society where there are no, hmm... [*Hesitates*] where there can't be individuals in this society, where there isn't room for individuality. A lot of these contradictions are then made part of the thematic of Adrian's life.

[*Long pause.*]

Now, above these Literal and Allegorical levels, we have two other degrees of interpretation. We have the Moral level, which works differently than the existential one. [*Exhales deeply.*] I don't know if we can really experience Adrian in the existential way... [*Quietly*: we can't have sympathy with him, we don't know what is going on in his mind, we only know what Zeitblom is telling us.] In other words, we can only see him from the outside, and it's only in the letters and this strange archaic language of the last sections that we're getting a glimpse of what goes on in his mind. [*Pause.*] So, existentially, this is not at all a first-person possibility for us. And the same would be true of the Allegorical level too... [*Cough in the audience.*] The life of Christ is certainly a set of events and a narrative form, but we don't know anything about the existential or the interior life of Christ. [*Pause.*] That takes place here... [*Points to "Moral" level on the blackboard*] with respect to ourselves, and I suspect that, at that point... [*Quietly:* keep in mind that all of these are my conjectures on how to put these interpretative levels together.] Remember that we have at least two kind of times going on in Doctor Faustus: there is the time of Adrian's life, which takes place mostly in the 1920s before World War Two, and then from Adrian's birth on... [*Quietly*: after the first pages of Doctor Faustus in the biography] there is the time of the war, which is running from the high point of the Nazis' advance to take the whole world, so to speak, to the breakthrough with the Soviet advance and the opening of the second front. So, I think that this Moral level also includes the fate of the individual in the war and against the Nazis. And it seems to me that that's the level that introduces the ethical problem here. [*Pause*.] For the First World War, as I said the other day, hmm... [*Hesitates*.] When it comes to the ethical judgments of the World War One, one cannot single out one evil — [*Whispering*] all of those governments were monstrous. I mean, the way they sent their people into the machine-gun fire... [*Pause*.] The... [*Stammers*] the... [*Pause*] the most... [*Exhales deeply*.] It was the most horrible of all wars because, before that, only... [*Quietly*: the Civil War, the Crimean ones had started exploiting the use of mass-produced rifles and some early kinds of machine-guns.] But it was during World War One that all of these European governments put their soldiers into the most modern form of machine warfare... [*Quietly*: when some colonel would decide, well, next week, let's have a successful counterattack and order all of his people in these trenches to get up and run into the machine-gun fire.] There is no possibility of judging the Germans or the Austrians as worse than the English or the French or the Russians — these are all horrible governments who were fully responsible for all those deaths. As for the rest of it, it's not clear — did Germany really start the war? Did the Serbians start the war? I mean, all of this goes back into the Balkans somewhere, back to Sarajevo. [*Decisive*.] Therefore, I think that you can't talk about a Moral level of interpretation with regard to World War One.

[*Long pause.*]

But World War Two, that is a very different story. And so, the source of moral judgments that you're gonna be asked to make, hmm... [*Hesitates*] and not conclusively, because you cannot make a definitive moral judgment, but only so that you are aware about the nature of good and evil, and the diabolical, and the heavenly and theological, and so on — all of that I think finds its place here on this... [*Chalk hits the blackboard*] Moral level. It's in the question of Nazism, and this is because it's a given that the fascist ideology is so stupid... [*Pause.*] There is a point where Mann reminds himself of the Duce and the Führer walking through the Uffizi garden in Florence, and he says, [*Impersonates Mann*] "Look, if it's a matter of the dictatorship of the lower classes and the hegemony of some over the others, as is with Bolshevism, then I will opt for Bolshevism."[26] This is part of the discussion about the German revolution after World War One... [*Quietly*: you know that there was a council in Munich of the Bavarian Soviet Republic for a few months, and there is a page that describes a lot of these events. You can also look at Flaubert's Sentimental Education, talking about the events leading to the 1848 revolution, where masses of people get up together to demand what they want to have, what is their view of the future utopian state.[27]] In Mann, this is the point at which Bolshevism comes into the picture. This is a given that has been prepared specially for intellectual thought and the whole scene of Weimar itself. [*Pause.*] Then there comes these reflections about the revolution... [*To himself*: Where is it...? (*Page flipping*)] The discussion of a council meeting and the "Revolution and Brotherly Love," where the revolutionary moment brings to the light of day all sort of types [*Starts reading*] "confused discussion among those outlandish sorts who emerge into the light for a brief moment only on such occasions: buffoons, maniacs, specters, nasty obstructionists, and petty daydreamers."[28] Zeitblom then states that revolutions bring two different kind of things: either new freedoms or new forms of tyranny. And these are articulated by right-wing intellectuals who are for a new kind of strength, a new kind of authoritarianism, who are saying that the age is demanding a whole new kind of mass culture, which will be dominated by power and essentially by [*Stressing*] indifference to... [*Door creaks open*] by a sort of Darwinian, hmm... [*Hesitates*] overcoming of sympathy and pity. It's a kind of new indifference to the suffering of other people. And remember that indifference here means a number of things: it means Adrian's coldness, his indifference to various things in life, and it is also used oddly for the fact that his friend, the translator Rüdiger Schildknapp, had the same color of eyes, so they are [*Stressing*] indifferent in the sense that there is no difference between them.

[*Long pause.*]

Now, these motifs, they are all as changeable as notes in the tonal system itself. A good deal was made earlier about the role or relationship and relationality in music, where a single note is meaningless by itself. [*Pause.*] A note takes on meaning only in a tonal context, and in another one, the same very note could mean something else. Something like that is also at work as the main principle of relating these themes. There is a very funny section, and even the later part of the novel with the murder of Rudi is a sort of... [*Door slams in the distance.*] Now that Adrian is settled out in the country, there is not much that one can do with him in a narrative way, so we have to add on the stories of these other people around him as their destinies are connected to his. But that's the raw material of the novels. Mm-hmm... [*Cough in the audience.*] And I may have already said that a lot of the portraits of pre-World War One Munich or Weimar-era upper-class types that you find in the novel were taken from a satirical project that he once worked on and never finished, and which, during World War Two, he had incorporated into Doctor Faustus.[29]

[*Long pause.*]

But in terms of what I said earlier about the way this novel is composed, this is also like Adrian's music — a return to an older kind of form. I said the other day that there was a kind of oratorio-like structure where you don't have scenes, you have a kind of, hmm... [*Hesitates*] interactive scores, and then suddenly a gestural, almost pictorial moment, which of course can be seen as a verbal gesture... [*Achoo. Sneeze in the audience*] "though they are dead!"[30] The other thing to remember is the role of the [*Stressing*] portrait or the caractère in pre-bourgeois literature. [*Pause.*] There are some magnificent portraits here. That's a form. It's not yet a novelistic form, but the novel comes out of the collection of portraits, and those other pictorial moments, but it's as though this is now returning after that, and you get these brilliant satiric portraits of all these ridiculous people. [*Pause.*] This is, I think, Zeitblom's combination of the archaic and the modern, going back cannibalizing those forms and using them. [*Decisively.*]

[*Long pause.*]

And then here... [*Points to the Anagogical level on the blackboard*] at the level of history and fate of the humankind, I think the first word for it would be... [*Chalk hits the blackboard*] G-E-R-M-A-N-Y probably, but this is on condition that we see that as a larger matter of the destiny of the nation. [*Pause.*] The whole point of these breakthroughs... [*Quietly*: if you wanna be completely banal about it] is the attempt of Germany as this latecomer to economics, politics, and nationhood, to find... [*Quietly*: as he says] an appropriate political form for itself. So Germany tries them all: it tries monarchy, democracy, dictatorship, fascism, which, in the early twentieth century, was the new political form that excited so many people... [*Quietly:* allegedly, Gandhi, when he was invited to visit Italy, they asked him what he was particularly interested to see in Europe, and he supposedly said, "Oh, I want to see Mussolini." Mussolini represented this whole new kind of political form, so there was interest, of course.] So, Germany too, it tries them all and they all turned out to be disastrous. And of course, this ends without any conclusion, and I think our conclusion can be that... [*Quietly*: this ongoing search for the most appropriate political form ceases to be an issue for Germany.] West Germany finds its destiny in the European Union, and the era of military confrontation with all those former nation-states is over. Something else begins to happen, which... [*Very quietly*: I don't know if you know him, Hans-Magnus Enzensberger, he became more conservative lately, and I heard a funny joke that he said, which was that he believes that the most important thing for Germany today is to remain mediocre.] And that is because when we Germans try to be "interesting..." [*Quietly*: that's a word Goebbels liked to say] the world then regrets it and suffers. Let's be ordinary and not try to impress anyone, hmm... [*Mumbles indistinctly*.]

[*Long pause*.]

And I think that the whole focus on Germany, we can see in this business of Gemeinschaft and Gesellschaft, which we have also discussed. The word Gemeinschaft or "community" comes up a great deal in these proto-Nazi discussions in the Weimar period of the 1920s. [*Pause*.] Because what these people were saying is that, primarily... [*Door creaks open*] the collective consciousness of the Gemeinschaft is much more important than individualism. All this is already moving towards the Nazi mass-mobilization and the fascist state. The Gemeinschaft is the archaic. Mm-hmm. And the individual, equipped with technological power, is the modern Gesellschaft, and our main question now is: How can one put them together? [*Pause*.] Hmm... [*Hesitates*] Can we go back to this old form of... [*Quietly*: Gemeinschaft is often translated into English as "community"] which is characterized by strong, intimate, and face-to-face relationships between its members leaving in these rural small-scale communities built on strong family ties? Can you somehow find ways for the Gemeinschaft to be amalgamated into technological modernity? Heidegger thought... [*Quietly*: in the 1930s, when he was still more or less a Nazi] that the Nazis had really been able to invent a historically original relationship to technology. Back then, he was still very optimistic. But at the end of the war, he starts to write all of these texts on technology, which are now profoundly anti-modern, and here he says,

[*Impersonates Heidegger*] "The greatest problem is technology. We can't master this modern technology, nobody can, even Nazis could not do it..."[31] You have a decidedly [*Stressing*] anti-modern turn in all of Heidegger's discussions of technology, which end with the famous... [*Zipper unzipping*] posthumous interview where he declared that "Only a god can save us now."[32]

[*Long pause.*]

But in Thomas Mann, you still have this confrontation of what to do in our technological modernity with the social relations... [*Electronic distortion causing high pitch whistles in the microphone.*] It seems to me those are, hmm... [*Hesitates.*] That's the ultimate form in which one would attempt to universalize this Anagogical level as being the story of all nations and of humanity as a whole, and not merely this exceptional matter of Germany. But remember that the universal and particular is one of the great themes here. And in Adorno, nominalism versus the general... [*Quietly*: we will come back to all of this later] and this is also very much what is going on still in Thomas Mann. Is the German case [*Stressing*] absolutely exceptional, or is it characteristic of the problems that other nations are also facing? Or is this not what all of the other countries face in one way or another when confronted with technological modernity? And once again the ending breaks off... [*Footsteps.*] So, it seems to me that such questions that are very relevant for our age could be grouped in accordance with the medieval system of allegory.

[*Long pause.*]

I'm sure there is so much more to say about Thomas Mann, and these levels of allegorical interpretation. Mm-hmm. Any thoughts? Questions? [*Pause.*] Yes...

STUDENT: How can we talk about the contribution of Christianity to our modern historical consciousness...? [*Words indistinct.*]

JAMESON: In the sense of conceiving the notion that human history has a telos, that it is going somewhere, that there are historical laws, yeah, I think that is the most obvious. Clearly, the notion of the Last Judgment as a historical idea comes out of Christianity, along with other historical thoughts, like the interaction between the cosmic and the social orders... [*Quietly*: you can think of Fourier, or there are many other utopian socialists that have appropriated Christian ideas, trying to achieve harmony based on brotherly love, mutual cooperation and other Christian values.] All of those are part of historical thoughts infused with Christian sentiments. You can look at Collingwood's idea of history, where the primary purpose of history is not to record what happened in the past, but to understand the actions of individuals and groups, as the study of history allows us to gain a deeper understanding of human nature and the world.[33] [*Pause*.]

[*Long pause*.]

Other questions? [*Silence*.] Okay. Next time we will get back to Aesthetic Theory, and we will start from the end with the "Draft Introduction," and then we will go back to where we were — I think it was chapter six... [*Door creaks open*] and we will then start asking... [*Foot shuffling*.] I hope I will have... [*Chairs scraping the floor*] everybody's topic here, and if you don't have it yet, come talk to me... [*Zippers zipping up*.]

Audience stands up. Feet shuffling. Objects drop on the floor. Door squeaks. Students return chairs to other classrooms. Some in the audience form a line to discuss their assignments with Jameson. General noise. Screeching microphone noise.

[*Microphone turns off*.]

CURTAIN

LECTURE SEVENTEEN

APRIL 1, 2003

CONSTELLATIONS — SECOND REFLECTION

CURTAIN RISES

Moving chairs, squeaking door, coughs, other sounds filling the noise environment of a large classroom in the Literature Department at Duke University. A few students discuss the music scene on campus. One of them has started DJing at the college radio station, WXDU. She talks about her experience with programming, and what music she likes to play, saying that, in the past, the station was mostly known for country, bluegrass, and folk music. "It was even in the news for that," she adds.

Jameson enters the classroom carrying a few books, his scattered notes, and the red pen in the chest pocket of his flannel shirt.

[*Microphone turns on*]

JAMESON: ...they got it from Shakespeare, I think... [*Footsteps. Door creaks open*] and each of these themes in Berg's opera is organized around... [*Chairs scraping against the floor.*] One theme would be scherzo, another would be a rondo, another is sonata form and so on and so forth — all kinds of smaller forms are embedded, which, naturally, you can't exactly hear, but you can study them from the score. [*Pause.*] Schoenberg said, when he heard about this project, he said... [*Impersonates*

Schoenberg] "Listen, this is a very cultured man and he will never be able to do something that is wrong and proletarian."

[*Long pause.*]

Now, Woyzeck, as you all know, is the story about a schizophrenic, a poor and simple-minded solider who does these different extra jobs, like shaving the captain, cutting wood or being a sort of walking medical case study for the doctor. [*Pause.*] Finally, after being driven to madness by his superior, and infidelity, he kills... [*Quietly*: what used to be called, in these circumstances, his common-law wife, Marie.] Then his little boy runs with other children to find his mother's body at the pond. Deleuze was very interested in the piece by Büchner, which is a novella based on documentary evidence about this poet called... [*Chalk strokes on the blackboard*] L-E-N-Z,[1] who is also a participant in this proto-romantic movement called Sturm-und-Drang — the radical angry youth of the period. Lenz was a friend of Goethe, and at some point, he went... [*Takes a sip of water*] he went insane, and the story is about him wandering in the mountains and coming into the care of this very progressive pastor called Oberlin, who had a very calming effect on the terror-stricken Lenz... [*Mumbles indistinctly.*] Mm-hmm. So, there is this prose piece by Büchner purporting to be a day in the life of Lenz, so to speak, a kind of schizophrenic promenade, which is remarkable, and to which Deleuze explicitly refers in some of his writings. [*Pause.*] Deleuze and Guattari, as you all know, have been interested in the relation between the schizophrenic delirium and the unconscious processes, so their connection to Lenz is not an arbitrary one. But Woyzeck is Büchner's other story and this... [*Shows DVD cover*] is Alban Berg's opera Wozzeck which I brought for us to watch the first scene, which is very short, where he is shaving his master, the captain, who is the very opposite of the crazy soldier, and here you get a sense of how remarkable this works out. It's very unlike Thomas Mann... [*Police siren in the distance*] and unlike Adrian, I should say, and Adrian's music, but it's a great classical work that comes out of the First Vienna School. [*Pause.*] It has been more successful than

Lulu,[2] which you saw earlier, but which was a completely different project that shares some of the same organizational patterns... [*Quietly*: with all of these very complicated forms going on under the surface.] [*Handles DVD to student.*] Can you insert this into the player...? [*Pause.*] Just to give you a little idea of what's going on here...

[*Long pause.*]

STUDENT: Got it. But where is the...? [*Pause.*]

JAMESON: Oh, the plug, you mean, or the socket?

STUDENT: Both...

JAMESON: Ah, okay, plug it in here... [*TV static.*] Let's see if we can get it to work now... [*Talks to himself. Decisively.*] Mm-hmm. The other article I've given you is the famous "Late Style" piece by Adorno. It's very short, hmm... [*Hesitates*] and it comes out in a book, of which I didn't know until now, which is not complete, but it's a collection of his musical essays, which you can take a look at it if you are interested...[3]

STUDENT: I found the plug...

JAMESON: You did... [*Footsteps.*]

STUDENT: Should I turn off the lights?

JAMESON: Yeah... [*Pause.*] But it doesn't seem to work, for some reason it's not playing. [*Jameson and Student fiddle with the video equipment.*] And where is the sound...? [*To himself:* maybe we move along and not play it today.]

STUDENT: I could set it on "video," but I don't know how to...

JAMESON: Something was happening here yesterday when we tested it... [*Quietly*: maybe we should call the technician.]

STUDENT: It should work now. [*Faint sound of* Wozzeck *opera.*]

JAMESON: Yeah, but now there is no picture. Ah... [*Technician walks in.*] Ah, okay... [*To himself*: and where is the sound?] Oh, do we need to push something here? [*Audience chuckles. Footsteps.*] No... No... Yeah, here you go... [*Sound of music.*] Oh, thank you. [*To the audience.*] Please pay attention. The whole schizophrenic aspect, the expressions, the silence, all of that is very important here.

[*Presses "Play" button. Audience watches Act One, Opening scene from* <u>Wozzeck</u>, *opera by Alban Berg.*]

JAMESON: Okay, that's enough. You wanna push this back? Thank you. [*Footsteps. Technician walks away.*]

[*Long pause.*]

Alright. Mm-hmm, now let's talk about your topics. The ones I received are satisfactory, but I don't know about the other ones that I haven't received yet. Now, I think maybe we should begin this session with the exposé. [*Addresses student.*] You wanna do that now?

STUDENT ONE: Sure.

JAMESON: Okay. And then we will go on after that. Do I have the...? [*Choo-choo. Amtrak train whistle in the distance.*] Am I correct in thinking that we got through the sixth chapter of <u>Aesthetic Theory</u>, and that we are at the seventh section, page 118, section called "Enigmaticalness, Truth Content, Metaphysics"? Is that right? [*Silence.*] Okay, good. [*Addresses student.*] Are you planning to read something for us?

Student Presentation: Constellations and Second Reflection

STUDENT ONE: [*Nods.*] Yeah, I propose to focus in my presentation on one paragraph from <u>Aesthetic Theory</u>, which is on page 26-27, the paragraph at the end. I would like to talk today about "constellation" and "second reflection" in Adorno, based on the readings from this paragraph. [*Starts reading from* <u>Aesthetic Theory</u>.]

> The truth of the new, as the truth of what is not already used up, is situated in the [*Stressing*] <u>intentionless</u>. This sets truth in opposition to reflection, which is the motor of the new, and raises reflection to a second order, to second reflection. It is the opposite of its usual philosophical concept, as it is used, for instance, in

Schiller's doctrine of sentimental poetry, where reflection means burdening artworks down with intentions. Second reflection lays hold of the technical procedures, the language of the artwork in the broadest sense, but it aims at blindness. "The absurd," however inadequate as a slogan, testifies to this. Beckett's refusal to interpret his works, combined with the most extreme consciousness of techniques and of the implications of the theatrical and linguistic material, is not merely a subjective aversion: as reflection increases in scope and power, content itself becomes ever more opaque. Certainly this does not mean that interpretation can be dispensed with as if there were nothing to interpret; to remain content with that is the confused claim that all the talk about the absurd gave rise to. Any artwork that supposes it is in possession of its content is plainly naïve in its rationalism; this may define the historically foreseeable limit of Brecht's work. Unexpectedly confirming Hegel's thesis of the transformation of mediation into immediacy, second reflection restores naïveté in the relation of content to first reflection. What is today called a "message" is no more to be squeezed out of Shakespeare's great dramas than out of Beckett's works. But the increasing opacity is itself a function of transformed content. As the negation of the absolute idea, content can no longer be identified with reason as it is postulated by idealism; content has become the critique of the omnipotence of reason, and it can therefore no longer be reasonable according to the norms set by discursive thought. The darkness of the absurd is the old darkness of the new. This darkness must be interpreted, not replaced by the clarity of meaning.[4]

STUDENT ONE: So, this is the paragraph that I would like to discuss. [*Student One proceeds to explain this paragraph by drawing a diagram on the blackboard. She marks the key concepts in the paragraph connecting them into a shape that resembles a constellation of stars.*]

[*End of presentation. Audience applauding.*[5]]

JAMESON: [*Staring at the blackboard.*] Thank you. Questions?

STUDENT TWO: I have a question regarding the way you talk here about "intentionless" and how you connect that to culture industry. When you say that culture industry has no intentions, what do you exactly mean by that?

STUDENT ONE: [*Points to the blackboard.*] Well, because point A is presence of intentionality and point B is a way of saying that you have no intentions because you cannot see your intentions, you see what I mean? So, the culture industry is... [*Pause.*] The intention of culture industry is not to have intentions, so to make that real, they will erase the intention of reflection, or the intention of negation and any intentionality. Like when you say in Kant that beauty is without interest, so the culture industry is similar, for it has these various dynamics but with no intention to it.

JAMESON: More questions?

[*Silence.*]

JAMESON: Well, it is very instructive, this paragraph you chose. I also thought there is a sentence which you skipped where he talks about "message." What is today called "message," whenever we speak of it, that is, not in the German version, or not in this paragraph anyway...

STUDENT ONE: Oh, I didn't know that... [*Pause.*]

JAMESON: Yeah so, I mean, you were quite right. I don't know if you used the German, but then I don't understand, there must be something about the text here... [*Quietly*: you've been using an older translation or something?] I mean, that is perfectly consistent with everything Adorno says, and right, and it could be a sentence in some other place that may have been transferred in this edition, hmm... [*Page flipping. Talks to himself.*[6]] Now, I think this paragraph that you chose to analyze from the chapter called "Situation" is a very good introduction to the "Draft Introduction" that we are going to read and discuss next time. We have everything there: there is Hegel's opposition and mediation in there, then the whole business about the new, and the intentions. However, "constellations," I think it's not quite the, hmm... [*Hesitates.*] Constellations: it's an idea to which Adorno pays homage, but it is actually Benjamin's idea... [*Chair scraping the floor*] and I'm not sure I would read it exactly the way you do because you tend to use constellations... [*Points to the blackboard.*] Is this a picture of a constellation of stars that you have over there?

STUDENT ONE: Yes.

JAMESON: I see. [*Pause.*] Well, look, I don't think that constellations mean exactly individual propositions or concepts linked to form the illusion of a pseudo-totality... [*Pause.*] It is not arranging concepts like "truth" versus "reflection," where reflection is one star and truth is another star, and then "second reflection" is another one, and then you add "intention" and the "new," and "Hegel" and so forth, and you get a constellation. For Benjamin, constellations are something messianic, they have to do with Platonic ideas and, hmm... [*Hesitates*] and relations between essences, and not so much with individual concepts, which are individualities. [*Pause.*] I also think it's easier to see constellations by looking over a larger textual terrain than just picking up a few concepts from one paragraph as you did here. For example, mimesis and construction. Okay. Here are these two modes of representation that, in modernity, become opposite to each other. Then we have mimesis and expression, with all the system of concepts and the tensions that exist between them, and so we have another constellation in the way you put it together here with all these points and stars. [*Looks at the blackboard.*] So, I think it's over this larger... [*Pause.*] It is all of that, the key categories of the aesthetic like mimesis, expression, the tragic and so forth, which are the ideas, or the Ideals, that convene and reject each other to constitute a constellation. It is about the mode of philosophical Darstellung and the way ideas and concepts relate to objects, as Benjamin puts it, "ideas are to objects as constellations to stars"[7]... [*Clears throat.*] So, constellations are not simply a range of concepts, which you weave like a spider web in an attempt to ensnare the truth,[8] but rather a unity of essences, the Idea as the system of concepts, or a mosaic of groups of concepts that are constantly re-arranging and dis... [*Achoo. Sneeze in the audience*] dissolving or re-forming over and over again. Think of it as discontinuity. Constellations are sort of unstable constructions, because these stars or ideas that gather concepts are constantly moving, so to speak, and the constellation gets dissolved again. This is the way I read it in Benjamin, hmm... [*Hesitates.*] His discussion of constellation, which is dense, Platonic, idealist, and finally very undecidable, you will find it in the preface, or his "Epistemo-Critical Prologue," to the German Tragedy book.

[*Long pause.*]

So, Adorno then takes this idea from Benjamin and tries to historicize it by returning to Hegel. In Negative Dialectics, he calls constellations a "model," which is a very awkward term to use, but for Adorno, this is a musical term that he gets it from, hmm... [*Hesitates*] he gets it from Schoenberg and turns it into a sort of twelve-tone philosophy. [*Exhales deeply.*] Now, with Adorno, constellations have a different meaning; it is not anymore these Benjaminian timeless Platonic Ideas, but it deals with networks of causes and is more in line perhaps with Althusserian structural causality.[9] Another thing that one has to take into account is that, while we are getting this very different positions between groups of concepts, as you very well say, and [*Stressing*] pushing is a good word for it... [*Pause.*] In Hegel, you come to point A, and then somehow you get a contradiction generated out of that point B. [*Walks towards the blackboard.*] It's a little bit different here, I think. [*Knocks on the blackboard.*] Here, point A is right, but not quite right because it implies something about reflection, and then, as we get to point B, which is in contradiction with A, time is passing and this relation between A and B in your diagram has already changed, and we have to restart it again. It is a bit like playing twelve-tone music, right? One has to deal with all of these positions: we've got Kant, then Hegel, and that's evolving underneath of this too, until other so-called "notes" in the history of thought come along. His hint to Schiller's version of sentimentality... [*Quietly*: of the naïve versus sentimental, I think we talked about that before] and what Adorno is referring to where he is saying that, in Schiller's doctrine, reflection means burdening artworks down with intentions... [*Pause.*] But then we have the history of drama from Schiller to Beckett, because, at the end, if you remember, he says... [*Exhales deeply. Looks for the right passage in the book*] "content can no longer be identified with reason as it is postulated by idealism."[10] So, evidently, at one point, maybe Schiller's ideas of poetry being descriptive — that is, mimetic — and the other one sentimental or reflective, and so identifiable with reason, makes sense, but by the time we get to Beckett, this division in art does not work anymore. Underneath all of this, it's not just that the argument is progressing, history itself is changing, maybe bringing up more to the argument or maybe not. Now, one thing I don't understand though... [*Staring at Student One's diagram on the blackboard.*] I have two criticisms to your reading of this paragraph, and the paragraph talks about it, but you don't mention it, and this has to do with the notion of the "new." How does all of this... [*Points to the blackboard*] define the new? We never get to it, hmm? [*Pause.*] And the second criticism is what happened to the "second reflection," which is so crucial in Adorno's own methodology, and you don't mention that either.

[*Long pause.*]

STUDENT ONE: Yeah, reflection of the second order, I wanted to talk about it, but I ran out of time... [*Giggles.*]

JAMESON: Yeah, and what would that mean here?

STUDENT ONE: It means that we first have the idea of truth, and the idea of truth is possible, and there is only one way of putting it in circulation, but then behind that idea of truth, we have a "second reflection," and we have the responsibility to correct the idea of truth that we have and that cannot be something fixed and immobile.

JAMESON: And that's in your schema? But that's then here somehow... [*Knocks on the blackboard*] when he talks about "the darkness of the absurd," right?

STUDENT ONE: Yes, in content... [*Continues drawing her diagram on the blackboard.*]

JAMESON: Oh, content, you mean it's becoming more opaque, and I think that means the absurd. Is it because you can't understand the content anymore?

STUDENT ONE: Yes, but for him, for Adorno, the absurd, which is not a slogan, is there to keep reflection alive...

JAMESON: [*Looks at to blackboard.*] But not on this first level, but on the second level?

STUDENT ONE: Yes, on the second.

JAMESON: Okay, alright, then I accept that. Sure. But since the paragraph is about second reflection, we probably are... [*Pause.*] I mean, did you read those crucial slogans out for some specific reason...?

STUDENT ONE: Yeah, because...

JAMESON: So, in a way, you are living out of the "new" and "second reflection," because you are taking a second reflection on it. [*Audience laughing.*] Mm-hmm. I don't think this is what "second reflection" is, though. Now, there is one other point that I also think it's not quite right, and that is your take on the culture industry stuff. [*Softly.*] How do you get from blindness to the culture industry?

STUDENT ONE: It is here on page... [*Page flipping.*] Ah, sorry, I can't find it, but you go from culture as something without intention to something that is just for entertainment...

JAMESON: Yeah, but see, I don't think this is what's meant here. [*Reads from* Aesthetic Theory.] "Second reflection lays hold of the technical procedures, the language of the artwork in the broadest sense, but it aims at blindness."[11] [*Pause.*] I mean, here, "it aims at blindness" is identified with second reflection, because second reflection [*Stressing*] wants to be blind... [*Floor creaking.*] It does not want to see intentions but do something else. It is the [*Stressing*] first reflection that wants to see, and to understand conceptually, all about collective energies, labor and the forces of production, or the technologies and so forth. But the second reflection wants to do something else. If second reflection wanted to be culture industry, that's rather a negative thing, right? So, that's not what Adorno means here. The blindness is elsewhere, and I think it means that second reflection does not want to think [*Stresses*] conceptually about the work in the way the first order reflection does. [*Pause.*] First order reflection wants to think about the artwork's intentions: what did the author have in mind here, what is meant here, what is the work doing, and so on and so forth. With this, it wants to substitute the answers it has found for the work of art. What is the meaning and how can we analyze the significance of this work, what does it express or represent — that would be the task of the first reflection. The second reflection rises above that... [*Cough in the audience*] and does not want to see the work in those terms anymore. That's... [*Pause.*] So, I think second reflection is blind, in the sense that it wants to maintain a distance with the work, without identifying itself with the work.[12] But maybe this will be clearer when we come to the "Draft Introduction," where this comes up again in greater detail. I'm not sure, but I really think the notion of "second reflection" is a successful one in Adorno, as one can get a better sense of what it means in relation to the work of art. [*Addresses Student One.*] But I do not think it means regressing to the level of the culture industry, it is the opposite...

STUDENT ONE: Yeah, but he mentions Kant there...

JAMESON: Sure, but I don't think Kant is the theoretician of the culture industry. Adorno may think that Kant is productive in the way that it would lead to this situation, as we will see, but it's not altogether accurate to link Kant to the culture industry. [*Pause.*] Kant does not and could not have... [*Door creaks open. Footsteps.*] If you are referring to the part in the Dialectic of Enlightenment where Adorno and Horkheimer talk about Kant as anticipating Hollywood ... [*Quietly*: where they say that, for Kant, the object is determined a priori in a way, mass culture is determined in advance according to some logic of profit... (*Mumbles indistinctly*).][13] But [*Stressing*] intentionless, in this context, means, hmm... [*Hesitates*] you don't want to do anything with it. The intentional work is the one that wants to do something to you, and the notion of the "message" that a work of art must deliver, I don't know what the history of this is, but "message" comes out in the 1920s or so, and it is some sort of vulgarized form to speak about the intention of the work of art. But this is not about the culture industry because the culture industry doesn't want messages; this has more to do with the didactic and political, with commitment, and that's why he mentions Brecht, or "the historically foreseeable limit of Brecht's work."[14] [*Pause.*] Brecht thought that he was making art with intention, he wanted his art to have a political impact, whereas Adorno says [*Impersonates Adorno*] "Okay, all of this is great, but it is against art's own will, because the artwork is not in possession of its content or intention." So, it is intentionless in this regard, and any time that art becomes didactic, or... [*Excited*] for some other purpose, like it likes to move us or to teach us... [*Quietly*: what are the three forms of traditional art in rhetoric?] Hmm... [*Tries to remember*] ah, yeah, to teach, to move and to please. So, all of these have an "aim" in mind, and any art that wishes to make you experience any of these, like an art that wishes to make you weep or laugh — all of [*Stressing*] <u>that</u> is culture industry. [*Pause.*] It is a kind of art that wishes to manipulate the audience, by wanting to make you think something or do something, and these are some basic forms of intention. And speaking of Kant, he is very good at getting rid of aesthetic intentions when he states that a work of art is purposeful without a purpose... [*Quietly*: for it does not make you do anything.] Now, intentions are also things that operate at a higher level of criticism, and I think this should be part of this too. Like, what exactly Joyce meant by such and such a thing? Why did he put these things in here? That's all appealing to some authorial intention which, for Adorno, is... [*Chair-back creaks.*] Well, let's put it this way: intention is not to organize the work, or deliver a message, but it is... [*Stressing*] <u>part</u> of the artwork itself. For Adorno, the authorial intention is part of the form. So, if instead of reflecting on it and seeing that as "Oh, this artist intended this and that one intended that..." [*Cough in the audience*] and at the first level reflection, you acknowledge that there was an intention... [*Quietly*: like we may know now from personal correspondence what Joyce, Pound or Lawrence really meant with this or that passage or poem] but you as a critic must rise above that and try and see that intention was itself part of the work of a... [*Door slams shut.*] Then you've reached the second reflection... [*Quietly*: I think something like that is what is going on here.]

STUDENT ONE: But to come back to "message," Adorno always talk about the jargon and the message of the radio, but then you said like three minutes ago that message has nothing to do with culture industry...

JAMESON: Ah, well, okay, I take that back. What I mean was that there is a sublimated... [*Raps his knuckles on the desk*] critical use of message in terms of literature. [*Pause.*] So, the critics of the 1920s, for example, would be judging all these texts and saying, "Well, the main message of this novel is a certain kind of idyllic pastoralism, and the other novel is a criticism of modern warfare," and so forth. I mean, a message is something that could move up and down, but rhetoric and propaganda, of course, those are messages too, and they...

STUDENT ONE: So, we could also make a constellation from message and... [*Words indistinct.*]

JAMESON: [*Softly.*] Perhaps, perhaps, but I think probably Adorno's intention is not to talk in this passage about the culture industry, as he does in many other places...

STUDENT ONE: Yes, no, of course, but...

JAMESON: But you may have a similar kind of movement in places that does talk about culture industry. [*Pause.*] I mean, what you have given us here is a diagram or a form of Adorno's thought, right? But now the big problem is that, ideally, this back-and-forth relation between these concepts should not be reified or arrested into a "positive" doctrine, and therefore we must turn to the new. [*Softly.*] The "new," or the Novum, is central to modernism because of its relation in Adorno to the productive forces, to technology, machines and so forth, which, in modernity, are constantly shifting and changing.[15] So, we cannot erect the new as a doctrine because it always changes, and therefore we need the second reflection, which seems to be his method to keep the critical mov... [*Achoo. Sneeze in the audience.*] You can make a critical method out of it, but then it has escaped from the process of dialectics and becomes something else. You sort of did it yourself when you were talking a while ago about the concrete, hmm... [*Pause.*] I think you cannot say that Adorno is the philosopher of the concrete either, because the concrete is only one of these parts and bits of a constellation, and the minute you start to say, "Oh, it's obvious, here is his message," so to speak, "and here is the concrete, and this is the basic proposition...

STUDENT ONE: [*Tries to interrupt*] Yes, but..

JAMESON: ...in Adorno," then something else begins to happen and that soon gets negated too. That would be the [*Stressing*] ideal picture of Adorno's method. And why are constellations... [*Cough in the audience*] constantly turning? And why it must even be a constellation, because it's not a single sun, so to speak; all those stars, or sets of stars, as the Latin term "constellation" suggests, tending to form a certain pattern ... [*Quietly*: there can't be a single dominant star, and the Sun has no constellation.] So, any thematization, any attempt to freeze the moment and set some concrete... [*Achoo. Sneeze in the audience*] all of that is not allowed in his system, even though, once in a while, Adorno does it, as we all know it... [*Raps his knuckles on the desk.*] For it is impossible not to...

STUDENT ONE: [*Interrupting.*] So, how do you get to the constellation then...?

JAMESON: Ah... [*Exhales deeply.*] I think the point is that you get to the picture as you gradually go through these different basic categories, and then you re-organize them in a [*Stressing*] historical manner, because these constellations are historical too. [*Pause.*] Just as they say that, thousand years ago, the "North Star" was not called the "North Star," and back then stars were not mapped according to our modern astronomical principles, regarding physical nature of the planets or knowledge of the sky. These categories that we are using here with regard to modernism must be considered historically variable from... [*Quietly*: say from the seventeenth century up to the present.]

STUDENT ONE: So, we are getting waves in here, as most of history are like waves...

JAMESON: Well, no, because we are getting both of that here. You are getting movement. [*Walks towards the blackboard.*] Let's say you insert the drama from Schiller to Hauptmann in this process, and on the other hand, we are also judging this from the standpoint of the present, that is to say, from the point of Beckett... [*Door slams in the distance.*]

STUDENT ONE: In other words, we are making a constellation as something that is always in progress, as something that is constantly moving, right? So, if now I am making a constellation... [*Turns towards the blackboard*] of this paragraph here would then be the "new," and the "absurd," "Beckett," and here is the "second reflection," as a reflection on somebody else...

JAMESON: Well, I don't think constellations, in the view of Adorno or Benjamin, work this way. [*Pause.*] Again, I don't think you can arrest all these words into a diagram and call it a constellation — this will just have an opposite effect to their proposed mode of radical thinking. [*Decisively.*] Second reflection is a way of getting [*Stressing*] <u>at things</u> which don't necessarily benefit from ordinary or first reflection of facts... [*Quietly:* like works of art, where ordinary contemplation fails to help us grasp the complexity of the sensory and conceptual experience.] But you could talk about many other things as forming constellations: you could talk about the absurd, theater of the absurd, as opposed to the new, the history of theater and so forth. And then, one other thing to keep in mind is that this one paragraph you chose doesn't have everything in it, you would need to have at least a chapter, one would like to hope.

[*Long pause.*]

JAMESON: Are there other questions...?

STUDENT TWO: Looking at all of this, it seems to me that under certain circumstances, or at any given time, or maybe context of the circumstance which doesn't have anything to do with it, there is some cycle of possibility of communication between all of these points, and maybe even thousands more, as argued by Adorno. Like, if you take the first sentence where he says that, "The truth of the new, as the truth of what is not already used up, is situated in the intentionless." [*Pause.*] And then the very next sentence calls reflection, "the motor of the new," that raises reflection to the order of second reflection. So, truth is, on one hand, in opposition, and you can't communicate with it; there is a stoppage there, but then the reflection is the motor of the new, of which, as per first sentence, the new is related to the truth. What Adorno seems to be saying here is like cutting off the possibility of trying and figuring it out what exactly he is talking about here. Because, hmm... [*Hesitates.*] It seems to me that a constellation just cannot be drawn up, it is just like the kind of music that cannot be heard, it exists only on paper but cannot be played... [*Quietly*: we talked about it in a previous class.] The same goes for a constellation — it's like you can intuit it, but you cannot... [*Cough near the microphone*] give it fixed form as, I guess, it's some dialectical entanglement and tensions that I don't see how it can be done, or ultimately visualized...

JAMESON: Okay, let's see, let's see. [*Pause.*] I mean, the point is that the new will be different every time, there is no historical difference, so what's new in Racine or in Rousseau is not going to be new in Berg or Thomas Mann, or whatever? So that's gonna be constantly changing.

[*Long pause.*]

But now, I think what second reflection also means here, hmm... [*Leafs through the book.*] He is also talking about it in critical terms, referring essentially to those people who think that a powerful artwork doesn't need to be interpreted or talked about. [*Decisively.*] It is like this fear that talking about an artwork will destroy its aesthetic effect. For some of these people, all they want is to enjoy or [*Stressing*] experience this artwork and they don't want critics coming and telling them [*Impersonates a critic*] "Oh, look over here, the artist did this because he needed a second character in order to reach the climax more dramatically," and so on and so forth. So, ordinary reflection would be bad for this kind of people... [*Quietly*: because it sort of demystifies the work of art and turns it into an ordinary everyday experience... (*Mumbles indistinctly*).] Now, when you get to the new though, the new is owing to reflection, presumably because the artist is thinking in terms of... [*Zipper unzipping*.] It's what Benjamin calls the raison d'état; you know what that means in politics as it was invented by people like Machiavelli, and what is at stake is the following: you would think today that George Bush's politics has an intention, but it is the American state that has its own [*Stressing*] reasons for acting the way it does. It is part of the state's self-preservation. And that's the raison d'état. [*Pause*.] Machiavelli is proposing a politics which is the politics of the interest of the state, and not of particular players. So, Benjamin says that Baudelaire — or modernism — has its raison d'état,[16] because he had to figure out how to be a great poet without turning into a Victor Hugo, a Gautier, a Lamartine, not be one of the romantics but become something new and special. Therefore, reflection has to do with knocking at the right doors, so to speak. Reflection also seems to have something to do with the new, but what that process of criticism, whether it's being done by the artist who tries to figure out the new, or by the critic who is trying to figure out what's going on in the work. What Adorno wants to do is to oppose that to... [*Quietly*: truth content.] Mm-hmm. And it's only in [*Stressing*] second reflection that you pick up truth content. Second reflection is not opposed to truth content, but this first kind, or ordinary reflection, is opposed... [*Quietly*: well, they are not the same.] So, when you go through a work and you say to yourself, "oh, this is what it means, the novel is dealing with this problem as this is the author thinks about it, and so on," that's not the truth content. [*Softly*.] So where is the truth content then? [*Pause*.] The same holds true for music; you are listening to a piece of classical music and then you go and say, "oh, this is a sonata form, but it deviates from the traditional structure of the sonata and so on" — this means you are thinking about the music, but that again [*Stressing*] is not the truth content either. [*Pause*.] You can arrive at the truth content only by doing what he calls a "second reflection," that's essentially what is going on here. [*Long pause*.] Now, I guess I don't understand your question...

STUDENT TWO: No, I think maybe you did because the answer has something to do with the new, which is, in a sense, unknowable except through reflection, but then reflection makes it old. So, you've got the new, and then you have the definition of the new, which is defined by commentary, criticism, historical data, but the ultimate newness — the truth content — is at first glance... [*Clears throat*] unknowable, and according to Adorno, it can only become known through this second reflection, which is totally different from ordinary reflection. I guess, it makes sense to me now how...

JAMESON: Take immanence and transcendence, for example. [*Exhales deeply*.] There is a certain school of criticism, which we will look at when we get into his "Draft Introduction," that believes in the work's immanent criticism... [*Quietly*: a bit like the New Criticism.] Here, you can only talk about what's [*Stressing*] immanent in the work, nothing extrinsic, only the intrinsic qualities. So, the extrinsic are what is transcending the work of art, that is to say, these were the ideas of the artist, his biography, these was the ideology of the period... [*Quietly*: something like formal and social analysis.] I think that what Adorno tries to do is to find some kind of a pole position from which the experience of the work unites both those perspectives. [*Pause*.] And you can say that, in this way, I think he says it very strongly in the "Draft Introduction." Mm-hmm... [*Page flipping. To himself*: now, where, and how does he say that exactly?] He is saying it somewhere around here... [*Pause*.] The work of art is autonomous, and yet it has a connection with what is not the work of art. Therefore, your experience of the artwork must have both, it must engage with the work immanently, but also to transcend this immanence of facts through an emphatic critique of interpretation that he calls "second reflection." You must be able to experience the work both from the inside and outside, you have to see it from the inside and yet understand both what it negates... [*Quietly*: in what situation it was made, the context and so on and so forth.] And if you don't do that, you are reading it in a [*Stressing*] purely aesthetic sense... [*Zipper zipping up*] that is to say, you just engage phenomenologically with art's properties and sensations... [*Raps his knuckles on the desk.*] This would be what we may call traditional literary or artistic criticism, and even formalist criticism, but on the other hand, there are these bad Marxists and they read art exclusively for what's outside of the work of art, for the so-called social critique. They talk about how, in this historical period... [*Door creaks open*] the working class was threatening the middle class and the latter got anxious and they started producing or demanding artworks that express middle-class anxiety for the workers, who are trying to take control of the means of production and so forth. [*Pause.*] This is social criticism, right? Well, Adorno doesn't want to get rid of these two forms, but he wants to combine them in some way, because he also thinks that the outside is important, but he wants to see it in the work and [*Stressing*] feel that outside from the inside in a certain sense. So, that's one of the things that is going on here. But that is not necessarily all going on in this very important paragraph that we discussed today...

[*Long pause.*]

Because, after all, if you say that second reflection has its own constellation, that would be precisely the situation with mainstream criticism we have today, and then we have to move around and find another angle, then move around and find another angle, and so on and so forth. It's not just your arbitrary decisions, history is involved in the way we... [*Door slams shut*] these constellations, and the options you have, are deciding for the one or for the other, and we are not going to be reading artworks the way they did it in the eighteenth century... [*Quietly*: although Kant, in some ways, anticipates things with his Critique of Judgment.] But that's no longer our set of constellations; we would look back and we would see, "Oh yeah, they put these things together." They had an idea of beauty that we can't have anymore, but clearly for us today we know that this is what was available to them, and it's not wrong because the other ideas: the truth content and history are connected, and something that is over and done with, that has passed out of being, that's extinct, can still get truth content, or still be true. [*Pause*.] So, the aesthetic experience of the feudal period, that's all gone, and we have nothing more to do with that, but its content is still in some way with us. You can look at it through Nietzsche's eyes... [*Cough in the audience*] Adorno does so by stating that what is in becoming can also be true.[17] Whereas the philosophers of the past were saying that, if something was changing, then it could not be true, right, because truth is what is hard and stable... [*Pounds his fist against the desk*.] Well, anyway, we will come back to very similar sets of thoughts next time with the "Draft Introduction," because there is still this opposition between Hegel and Kant, and this is a lasting opposition of subject and object in aesthetics. Next time, let's get to Benjamin's aura, anyone's interested to talk about the aura... [*Footsteps. Door creaks open*] if yes, come talk to me after class... [*Chairs scratching against the floor*.]

Audience stands up. Objects drop on the floor. Door squeaking. Students returning chairs to other classrooms. Zippers zipping up. Some in the audience form a line to discuss their assignments with Jameson. General noise. Screeching microphone noise.

[*Microphone turns off*.]

CURTAIN

LECTURE EIGHTEEN

APRIL 3, 2003

BLOCH, "THE DETECTIVE STORY" AND "THE NOVEL OF THE ARTIST" ESSAYS — "DRAFT INTRODUCTION" — NOMINALISM — BENJAMIN, "THE WORK OF ART IN THE AGE OF MECHANICAL REPRODUCTION"

CURTAIN RISES

Moving chairs, squeaking door, coughs, other sounds filling the noise environment of a large classroom in the Literature Department at Duke University. A few students discuss Bea's party coming up on Friday. One student recalls the last party stating: "I hope this time it will end differently, with no cops showing up at four in the morning to send us all home." Bea's parties are legendary among grad students.

Jameson enters the classroom carrying a few books, his scattered notes, and the red pen in the chest pocket of his flannel shirt.

[*Microphone turns on.*]

JAMESON: ...mm-hmm, what else, what else... [*Chair legs screech along the floor.*] How are your papers coming? [*Door creaks open. Footsteps.*] When you are doing your papers, for example, on Kafka, or whatever... [*Zippers unzipping. Door slams shut.*] Adorno wrote a great deal, and you should look those things up or check with me because there are a number of other Kafka essays, and in some cases, essays by some other people... [*Quietly*: obviously, some of these references you're not going to find in Adorno.] Okay, at any rate, I will be here right after class if you need come talk to me about your papers, sources, and so forth.

[*Long pause.*]

Now, regarding Ernst Bloch, that's a good deal more complicated, and your work on him needs to be resituated in his whole philosophy of the future. [*Pause.*] In The Principle of Hope, Bloch talks about an ancient grammarian who once wrote a complete grammar of Latin case forms, but who omitted the future tense...[1] [*Zipper unzipping.*] This way Bloch draws attention to philosophy's lack of interest in the future. According to his hermeneutics, we know a lot about the past, about the sufferings and all the failures that humanity once had. [*Pause.*] We also know a lot of things about the present, which it also contains latent possibilities, or it gives us signs and sense of direction... [*Clears throat*] to proceed further. But the future, hmm... [*Hesitates.*] The future, which is linked to our wishes and dreams, we somehow systematically evade... [*Door slams shut.*] So, Bloch has this idea that there is another kind of unconscious, which is the "not-yet," or "anticipatory consciousness"; it is like a tidal influence that exerts some unconscious influence on us. This "not-yet" of existence is like another form of ontology, which is an ontology of the future utopia, the unrealized dreams, and achievements.[2] Bloch's The Principle of Hope is an immense three-volume book written in the late 1930s and through the 1940s... [*Quietly*: and it's been translated into English now.] It is a compendium of whatever form the utopian impulse could possibly be imagined: from the official utopia to the utopian thinkers, but then fairytales, bodily drives, daydreams, erotic dreams, advertisements, medicines, medical utopias, like patent medicine or now, of course, prescription medicine. All of these forms of utopian thinking are not just to cure some incidental conditions but are part of his principle and anticipatory consciousness. Bloch's utopian aspects are somewhat eternal, which have prompted many to call him a Christian-Marxist, and a sort of "theologian of the revolution."[3] [*Pause.*] One could also locate in his utopian thinking some religious overtones that are then mixed or transfigured into most modernistic technological promises, and progress... [*Cough in the audience*] method of detecting positive impulses within the negative ones.[4] His hermeneutics is a bit like that of Northrop Frye in Anatomy of Criticism,[5] which builds on some medieval hermeneutical modes... [*Quietly*: we talked about four-fold levels of allegory in one of our past sessions] that he adopts for criticism. Bloch works around with these levels of what the Christians would call "hope," but in his case, he is more specifically invested in artworks of literature, fantasy, and its potential for the horizon of the future and utopia. [*Pause.*] Bloch was very close to Lukács at some point, when they both attended Max Weber's seminar. He was very pro-Soviet and an early anti-fascist, so when the Nazis came to power, he fled Germany, first to Switzerland, then to a few other countries, and finally to the United States. His Frankfurt School colleagues often found him too mystic and prophetic in nature, as you could imagine. Whether he was a party member, I'm not sure, but after the war, he went back to East Germany, taught there for a long time, he was named professor at the Philosophical Institute in Leipzig. When the Berlin Wall was erected, he was in West Germany and he decided to stay in the West, but he wanted it to be clear that it wasn't a defection, but he was just old and tired, so he retired... [*Quietly*: I think it was in Tübingen where he settled down and died, when he was about ninety-five or something like that... (*Mumbles indistinctly*).[6]]

[*Long pause.*]

But The Principle of Hope is an immense work, very difficult to translate, very idiosyncratic in German, hmm... [*Hesitates.*] It is not difficult like Heidegger is, it is not difficult in that sense, but it wants to approach this folk language, and the difficulty here lies especially with foreigners, in that it adds some strangeness. [*Pause.*] His other important work is a collection of observations, aphorisms, peculiar experiences that came up in 1930 and is called Spuren, or Traces in English.[7] So, the hermeneutic of the future, the utopia, and the presence of utopian elements make themselves known to us via these signs, marks, and traces or Spuren.[8] In this process, art plays a central place for Bloch, and here we should also mention these two extraordinary essays... [*Quietly*: there is a full collection now of his aesthetic writings] and he had this great idea of juxtaposing the detective story with the artist novel. Mm-hmm. The detective story explores the time before time, it deals with something that happened long before the story begins... [*Quietly*: it has happened before the creation of the world, so to speak... (*Clears throat*).] This is also part of the changing nature of the legal system, which now demands proofs and investigation. Bloch gives us a sort of the pre-history of the genre by talking about various precursors to the genre and hinting on various cosmologies. There is the part about Schelling's cosmology... [*Quietly*: I don't know if you ever heard Žižek talk about this, but for Schelling, you can find everything in heresy, you know.] Anyway, Schelling believed that God created the world [*Whispering*] because he was insane. [*Chuckles.*] Before the creation of the world, there was no [*Stressing*] Other, and therefore God had no sense of who He was, or what He was, so He had to create this form of otherness in order to free himself out of this state. There is a little science-fiction story that dramatizes this, I don't recall now who is it by, but it is a man mumbling things to himself and then he can't decide, and the final words are, "Okay, yeah, I'll do it. Let there be light." [*More chuckles.*] That is the story, but that, in Schelling's cosmology, the time before time is this time of immense disorder, and insanity and chaos and the rest of it, and in order to be cured of this, God had to bring in order. So, that's a little bit like this here as well. And Bloch holds that too, as part of this whole form from which the detective story is somehow coming, but these are the secrets that are hidden, things hidden from the very beginning of time... [*Chair dragging across the floor*] and the detective story then produces this kind of fixed narrative form, in which you narrate the search for the clues, the Spuren, the traces, these are all the traces of what might have been before, and they must be re-constructed, and finally, the detective is the great hermeneut who will bring these tracks back to light. [*Pause.*] And it's a nice little history, the detective story, which begins, as we know... [*Quietly:* at least according to our official... (*Mumbles indistinctly*)] with Edgar Allan Poe, but he mentions a few other earlier authors, such as Hofmann, Schiller.[9]

[*Long pause.*]

Now, the detective story introduces an interesting new thing for us. Something happens before the beginning of the story and the reader was not present. A crime was committed and now there is this suspense created by the process of reconstruction of the chain of events. With the detective story, we have an archetype, a sort of Oedipal construction, where everything in it draws its ultimate value from an event that is external to the work.[10] But then there is another blind spot, and that is the future. [*Pause.*] Could there be... [*Quietly*: since we are talking about the detective story] could there be that something that corresponded to the past, a misdeed that the reader and the detective are trying to solve, is now somehow in the future? So, Bloch turns to the Künstlerroman or the artist novel. The detective story and the artist novel stand in some form of juxtaposition as both deal with something missing. [*Pause.*] Because, at the center of all these artist novels, there are some imaginary works that the artist is supposed to have painted, composed, written and so forth. [*Page flipping.*] Here is what he says: "Whereas the detective novel requires a process of collecting evidence, penetrating backward to a past crime, the novel of the artist requires recognition of and interest in the creative person who brings out something new instead of something past."[11] So now, the center of this construction is not anymore a missing event from the past, but the empty place of an imaginary work of art. Because, if the writer was going to compose those works, we could talk about a secondary dimension that has to escape the plane of language, so you have the artist bringing up the new, bringing in the utopia, but these are sort of empty spots that haven't come into... [*Achoo. Sneeze in the audience*] a failure to represent the new. It is a sort of emptiness of the work within a work, the blank canvas at the center and the very locus of the not-yet-existent itself.[12] And if you think of it this way, then we can also bring in the whole tradition of aesthetic or artistic production that wishes to be part of non-alienated labor... [*Quietly*: in a non-alienated society.] That is to say, art is an activity which is taking place in an atmosphere of non-alienation, an activity that is satisfying and is not oppressive or repressive or any of those... [*Takes a sip of water*] and you can see how, beyond this notion of empty place, which is the work of art, in these artist novels what's really in there is the whole universe of non-alienated labor. Now, I suppose you could say, well, the successful one is really Balzac's Unknown Masterpiece... [*Quietly*: how many of you know this story?] Le Chef-d'œuvre inconnu is about a colleague of Poussin in Rome... [*Corrects himself*] no, no, it's actually in Paris. It is about this fictional character named Frenhofer who is obsessed with reaching perfection and finishing his masterpiece, which is the portrait of a woman. He works on it for many years, revising it and trying to find the perfect technique, and to "breathe life" into the canvas, so to speak. It's been the only thing that he paints for ten years. So, when the time finally comes to show it to his colleagues and they steal a glimpse of it... [*Quietly*: they see this complete chaos, confused colors and confused lines, all lost in search for absolute perfection ... (*Mumbles indistinctly*).] He ruined the painting by trying to make it into such a masterpiece that it... [*Choo-choo. Amtrak train whistles in the distance.*] This is then one realization, by way of the negation of these processes in modern art, where there is a clash between intention and result, between expectation and search for the essential technique... [*Quietly*: as illustrated in this story by Balzac.] So, when you have the description of a work, you don't exactly have the processes of work... [*Clear throat cough near the microphone*] maybe that's what's missing. In detective stories, there are occasionally examples... [*Pause*] and Sherlock Holmes is the best example of this, when you reach the great moments of investigation showing the great detective's mind at work. I mean, you can't really see Holmes' mind at work, but he explains it to us.. [*Cough in the audience*] as in his famous inductive method when he explains to Watson how he does it. [*Impersonates Holmes*] "Oh, that's because, on his shoes, there was this yellow sand, which means that he came from such-and-such place," or "You have a little callus on your hand, and I can tell by scratches on your watch that you just arrived from India or something..." [*Audience laughing.*]

[*Laughter continues.*]

So, here in the detective story, you have these radical examples of going back into the past in order to seize the past. Does anything like this correspond to the artist novel with regard to the future and the work of art? Anyway, I think these are wonderful essays that involve the work of art in regard to temporality, time, utopia, which I think must be read in the context of Bloch's other work, namely that of utopia, of Noch-Nicht, of the "not-yet-existent," but also to that of anxiety of the past and the longing for utopia.

[*Long pause.*]

Now, I feel we are running out of time here in several ways, because we have still so much to cover in Aesthetic Theory. It's a little bit like we are trying to do some fast-forwarding, but I guess the technique does not work equally well in every medium of art. You can certainly do that with videos, by jumping to different scenes, but as you heard the other day, when we tried to fast-forward some of that twelve-tone music, that was a little harder to do, and that is because music cannot be broken into scenes the way film is constructed. [*Pause.*] Now, can we do some fast-forwarding with Adorno's <u>Aesthetic Theory</u>? It is not yet clear to me if we can really do that, but what I would propose is, hmm... [*Hesitates*] is that we shift today to the "Draft Introduction"... [*Quietly*: and let's see how far we can get with it] then I think there is a moment when we will have to talk about Benjamin, so you can do your [*Refers to student*] presentation on the aura?

[*Long pause.*]

[*Bang. Softly slams the palm of his hand on the desk.*] Okay, now there is one way to start talking about Adorno's "Draft Introduction," and that is by returning again to the two great pillars of modern aesthetics, which are... [*Chalk strokes on the blackboard*] K-A-N-T and H-E-G-E-L. This opposition runs all the way through the "Draft Introduction," and it's very clear what the opposition is: Subject and Object. [*Pause.*] Kant has insisted on the [*Stressing*] <u>subjective</u> nature of aesthetic experience by describing the experience of beauty and that of the sublime, as well as the relationship of the individual to the universal. It is as if he wants to say, [*Impersonates Kant*] "By calling this 'beautiful,' I wish that everyone admires this work." [*Pause.*] Hegel, on the other hand, believes that art is part of the [*Stressing*] <u>objective history</u>. For Hegel, it is history of the Spirit that is working its way out in the artwork, and in particular, in the historical changes of styles. It doesn't matter what we think of the pyramids or of the Greek statues or of Shakespeare. The artistic form has been evolving from what he calls... [*To himself*: let's see what are his three systems] the symbolic, which is the pre-Greek society, so to speak; then we get to the Greek work of art, which is the classical form in its aesthetics of the democratic polis; and finally, the modern work of art that Hegel calls romantic... [*Quietly*: but keep in mind this must not be confused with Romanticism of his age.] Romantic here, for Hegel, means, as with Schiller's "Sentimental Poetry"... it means the presence of reflection. [*Pause.*] Mm-hmm. The Greek statue is beauty without reflection, it's somewhat non-intellectual, in the sense that it is not the primary product of reflection but of the superior senses. The symbolic works of art, the Pyramids are indeterminate content, it is part of the pagan world... [*Quietly*: religion is key for Hegel, as with Christianity, the trinity is really dialectic, (*Sighs*) there are all kind of weird religious metaphors in Hegel, and they have been explored at great length.] So, in pre-romantic art, there is sensuous expression but there is no reflection, and one may wonder how, in those pre-philosophical cultures, could have been anything rational... [*Quietly*: and knowing Hegel's Eurocentrism, all of this must be taken with a grain of salt, there are things that are only discovered these days and the whole history of the pyramids as seen by Napoleon, or of the Sanskrit in the context of British colonial project in India.] This "world culture" is only arriving in Europe during the Romantic period, and his philosophy of history can raise a lot of questions, especially when looked at from the position of today... [*Door creaks open.*] But anyway, that is what is going on in the works. For Hegel, artworks don't need people to judge them or agree upon, as is presumed with Kant. Whereas, in Kant, it is in the reception of the work, and Kant doesn't seem to care very much about the individual works themselves; I mean, it never really gets clear, I think, whether beauty or the sublime is a merely natural thing, whereas with Hegel this is very clear, that only the products of mind are part of aesthetic experience.

[*Long pause.*]

Now, somewhere in Aesthetic Theory, Adorno has this saying, which I find quite hilarious, and it goes something like, [*Paraphrases Adorno*] "These were the last two great aesthetics that were written by people who knew nothing whatsoever about art."[13] After Kant and Hegel, it is either different philosophers who write their aesthetics, or these are practicing artists, critics and dilettantes. [*Pause.*] So, we have two separate things: we have... [*Pause.*] Or let me put it to you this way: mm-hmm, the main question here is, hmm... [*Hesitates*] "Is aesthetics possible?" [*Long pause.*] And I think you should guess it right away that the answer is "No," but this is a determinate impossibility, which is to say that we can't really know if it's impossible until we go ahead and try to do it, try to write an aesthetic. We have to try and make it possible, and then we will know when it fails in some interesting, specific, historically determined way. And then we should also ask why has aesthetics fallen out of favor? [*Pause.*] Why is nobody in this period... [*Quietly*: and we are talking about the 1950s and 1960s] or even today, a course on philosophical aesthetics is not possible or it is very rare? One of the questions or challenges that are related to aesthetics is [*Stressing*] precisely its relationship to philosophy. Is it true, as Schelling thought, and I was also trying to suggest here in connection to Adorno, that there is a way in which aesthetics is the organon of all philosophy, that is, philosophy as a failure. One can see what philosophy is doing better, if you look at it through aesthetics rather than through logic, metaphysics, epistemology... [*Raps his knuckles on the desk*] and that was what Schelling's position was about.

[*Long pause.*]

But what is the relationship between modern philosophy and aesthetics? [*Pause.*] I would say that, of the modern philosophers, it's only John Dewey whom Adorno admires because... [*Quietly*: as in his earlier remark about Hegel and Kant] he knows nothing about art. [*Audience laughing.*] Their pronouncements on the matter of art and aesthetics are completely abstract and irrelevant to anything, or let's say irrelevant to [*Stressing*] particular aesthetic or artistic experience. Okay, so what is the relationship between aesthetics and philosophy, what are the philosophizing categories of aesthetics? This is the first question. Then, what is the relationship between aesthetics or an aesthetic theory and an individual work of art? [*Long pause.*] Well, for the most part, there is no relationship. Most of these aesthetic theories are completely irrelevant when it comes to the individual work of art, and the only discipline that encourages such a relation, I suppose, we could call [*Stressing*] criticism. Because nowadays we practice particular literary, artistic, musical, and so on criticism when we have to deal with individual artworks. [*Pause.*] There are generalizations you can make, but nonetheless, you do hear about studies of an individual text, or maybe studies of the whole corpus of a particular writer, but to jump out of that and leap into some universal speculation about aesthetics... [*Chair-back creaks*] seems difficult or less common in our times, it seems to me. So, on the one hand, we have these absolutely abstract treatises going on here with elaborate reasonings about beauty, taste, and art and so forth, and on the other hand, you have [*Softly*] studies of Kafka, or Manet, or Borges, or Joyce, or whatever you like. There is the individual work of criticism. [*Pause.*]

[*Long pause.*]

Then we also have art, and that's something different. [*Pause.*] The relationship between aesthetics and art is very different from the relation between aesthetics and an individual work of art. Because, with art, we have all kinds of people and very often the artists themselves are the ones who are telling us things about art... [*Quietly*: like what art is, what art should be, for example, if you think of Duchamp, who has most recently been celebrated for raising the question of what art is.] Modern artists do this by means of manifestos... [*Door creaks open*] and I did at some point say that Adorno hated the Isms and their manifestos. Well, I think he did, but on the other hand, this is not what he says, and what he says it's quite interesting. [*Pause.*] He says, hmm... [*Hesitates.*] He says, there are situations in which an Ism... [*Quietly*: surrealism, for example] makes it possible to project the notion of art through a manifesto that corresponds to no individual work of art, and yet which is more important and has more truth than any of those individual artworks. Take the surrealists, after Breton wrote these incredible manifestoes, they went home and started practicing their surrealist techniques: sleepwalking, automatic writing, Cadavre Exquis... [*Quietly*: you know what that is, right? "Exquisite Corpse," in English, were these collaborative games that were so popular among surrealist artists.] You take a paper, and you fold it over, and then I write a little line above the fold, then I fold it over and pass it to somebody else to write another line, or you can also do visual arts, and so on. The result was a sort of collective work which was surprising and unpredictable. [*Excited.*] Well, yes, sure! That's putting into practice the manifesto, but is it interesting... [*Quietly*: I mean, all of these exercises in the liberation of the unconscious have their place in surrealism, and some great poets came out of surrealism, maybe not Breton, but Éluard and maybe a few others.] But that's not important, Adorno says. [*Pause.*] It is not important that the individual works correspond to the manifesto. It's the great manifestoes, like futurism, surrealism, or even, I suppose, with Hugo's preface to Cromwell, in which he defends ugliness as a necessary component in art that must be embraced, not avoided... [*Door slams shut*] and of Romanticism...[14] [*Mumbles indistinctly.*] What comes now is a vision of art, a new vision of art, which doesn't need individual works of art to support it, but can rest solely on these generalized radical views about beauty, ugliness, place of art in society and so on.

[*Long pause.*]

At that point, aesthetics, which is busy talking about art in general terms, has to come to terms with some of the things that the actual makers and producers or the artists have to say. And it does not look that such a dialogue is going to happen, because the artists are very distrustful of academic discourses and philosophies... [*Tapping his thumb on the desk*] about art. It is not just the manifestoes, which highlight the complex relation between academic aesthetics and art, but the complex relation touches upon other elements... [*Cough in the audience*] history of philosophy, the history of individual artworks, history of styles, history of the manifestoes, all of the things that define what we call art. This also brings into view something else that art raises for aesthetics, namely the culture industry. [*Pause.*] Mm-hmm. If... [*Quietly*: according to an Ism, a manifesto or a philosopher's aesthetic theory] art is defined as this particular mode or way that art can only exist as, then what is that other thing, what is culture industry? It's not what Adorno calls "easy art," like light music, or leichte Musik. Easy music, that's often Bach, and that could also be regarded as part of the great classical music. And "easy literature," you know there are some great popular writers who can bring to their work very high levels of artistry... [*Quietly*: I mean P. G. Wodehouse has been universally admired by everybody, including by Brecht, he wrote Brecht's favorite novel.[15] I mean, I don't read this kind of literature myself, but this is not to be classified... [*Cough in the audience*] as what Adorno calls the "culture industry."

[*Long pause*.]

So, how do you define the culture industry even when you know what art is? What do you do with the large number of products of culture, do you just say that's not "serious" art? [*Pause*.] Do you just dismiss it by saying: "Oh, that's not art, that's junk"? Yeah, but by saying that, this means that you are avoiding coming to terms with a wide range of cultural products, and at least Adorno, he tried to come to terms with the culture industry, by saying that the culture industry is everywhere and that sometimes you can't even tell whether we're dealing with "serious" art or with the culture industry. The relationship can even be more problematical today and more of a [*Stressing*] philosophical problem... [*Quietly*: this is what I think he wants to say] than what was before. This is what he says in the "Draft Introduction" about the culture industry, which is the result of the logic of calculation and the totally managed world. But then, there is also something else: is the culture industry non-art or bad art? And then there are other aspects which seem to have nothing to do with the culture industry, but which is also a real problem, and that is the problem of the so-called [*Whispering*] philistines. This is a term one comes across very often in their language, and it refers to people for whom art doesn't exist.[16] [*Pause*.] They don't have an ear for music, an eye for painting, any sense for whatever artistic is out there placed in front of them. In their world, art does not exist, because their world is completely taken by money, or by serious business, or by facts and science, and they have nothing to do with art. But how is that even possible? [*Pause.*] Where does philistinism fit into the picture, and how are we supposed to deal with it? Because, hmm... [*Exhales deeply*] because the great aesthetic theories were busy telling us all this time how art was universal, and then when you look at some people, it turns out that art is not universal at all. [*Pause.*] And out of this then comes... [*Takes a sip of water*] and in various forms the manifestation of... [*Chalk on the blackboard*] R-E-S-S-E-N-T-I-M-E-N-T... [*Quietly*: "resentment" in English is not a good translation.] So, for some people, modern art provokes this intense violent feeling of [*In French*] ressentiment. They cannot stand it or agree with what modern art stands for. For the most part, that is a class feeling, and it could well be that and it has to be analyzed. It's not just the Amusische, as Adorno calls them, the non-, hmm... [*Hesitates*] the non-musical-oriented, the non-artistic or artistically insensible. And it's not just that entertainment is culture industry or reified art... [*Achoo. Sneeze in the audience*] it's also that this process of commodification also affects serious or... [*Showing quotation marks with fingers*] authentic art. You can see then, from the very beginning, how all of these many things are involved and how they must be made to work out.

[*Long pause.*]

Now, what happens then to aesthetics properly? Are we going to get to some answers by the end of this "Draft Introduction"? Adorno, he's going to tell us... [*Impersonates Adorno*] "Oh, aesthetics has to be philosophical!" [*Pause.*] Aesthetics has to give into philosophy, let us do it, philosophy has to give into aesthetics, this is an important problem, maybe more important than metaphysics, or any of other subdisciplines of philosophy, and therefore philosophers should take art into their hands... [*Quietly:* of course, he doesn't want... (*Mumbles indistinctly*).] Does this mean that aesthetics is to be shoved back into the discipline of philosophy? The history of aesthetics shows that it was the crisis after Kant and Hegel... [*Pause.*] With the death of Hegel in 1831, little by little you have Büchner in the 1930s...

[*Quietly*: we watched some Wozzeck the other day] then you have Wagner, Melville, and everybody else in the 1850s, and Baudelaire… [*Pause.*] The death of Hegel and his notion of the "end of art" coincides with the beginning of this crisis and with the beginning of modernism as such.

[*Long pause.*]

Alright, now modernism, which is advanced culture that corresponds to modern society, capitalism, industrialization, is characterized by something which is deadly for both art and aesthetics… [*Words indistinct*] as a philosophical discipline. This is what Adorno starts to call "nominalism." Do you all know who Benedetto Croce was? [*Silence.*] I am asking because I remember in the past people used to read Croce, but it seems to me that this is not the case anymore. Croce was a great thinker who wrote on history, politics, aesthetics, he was also an important political figure… [*Quietly*: he was still in his eighties after World War Two.] Croce was the supreme philosopher at the end of nineteenth-century Italy, he was in a way what Bergson was in France, and then Sartre in the immediate postwar period, and what Hegel was for a while in Germany. These are the so-called "Absolute spirits" under whose shade nothing can grow, so to speak. Gramsci came directly out of Croce, that is to say, Gramsci's arguments are all in one way or another debates with Croce. [*Pause.*] And Croce is essentially a historicist thinker. I am not sure to what degree other traditions read Croce, I know that in the 1920s and 1930s they did, but nowadays, hmm… [*Hesitates*] I can't think of any new book on Croce published today. Does anyone know?

[*Silence. Long pause.*]

So, according to Adorno, what Croce stands for is very important. Let's add that this phenomenon, which is happening in the 1870s and 1880s, is something that we've touched upon and have mentioned many times in our past sessions, but we never really came to terms with it, and this is… [*Chalk on the blackboard*] N-O-M-I-N-A-L-I-S-M. Croce believed that you could only talk about individual artworks, and that you could not talk about universals. Now, what does that rule out? [*Long silence.*] What are these universals in art and the theory of aesthetics? [*Long silence. Cough in the audience.*]

STUDENT: [*Softly.*] Genres?

JAMESON: Yes, above all, or let's say, below everything, at some basic level, the aesthetic universals are the genres, and the history that you write of the genres. Mm-hmm. Tragedy. [*Pause.*] Well, it's earliest manifestations are dated back to the fifth century BC, and then it is developed by Sophocles, who has written over one hundred and twenty plays, and then with Euripides, who gives an innovative approach to storytelling, tragedy enters a state of decadence, then it is revived again, and so on and so forth. This is a sort of a standard literature history, which Croce rejected absolutely. His dictum that "all art is one" is a rejection of genres or the treatment of each work of art as a genre of its own. For him, there is no such thing as tragedy — there is only this play by Sophocles called Oedipus Rex or Antigone. [*Pause.*] I think Adorno adds to that by assuring us, and I think it's very useful, because anybody who writes on novels tries to do something with the novel as a genre, and Adorno says... [*Cough in the audience*] novel, it's what happens in a nominalist age. [*Pause.*] That is to say it looks like a genre, but it isn't. Each form of the novel is contextually rooted and that makes it unique and non-universalizable [*Pause.*] Then we have beauty and the sublime, we have all the abstract concepts of the aesthetics, and all of them are parts of the universals, and it is all of these universals that fall into decay once nominalism takes over. [*Softly.*] Now, I think you could see, hmm... [*Pause.*] You know that the great political debates today are precisely about universals: is American freedom, consumerism, democracy, and voting, is that a universal right? And then human rights, are they also universal? Should we not impose them on everybody else, on other countries, because after all, we are liberating them by imposing these universals called "freedom," "liberty," "democracy," and so forth. Or "no," there should not be universal values but treat each culture as different; we have a variety of cultures, and each has its own traditional norms. [*Pause.*] All of the political fights today are around this question of the universals. It didn't come up during the Cold War because, in that period, there were two universalizing sets of principles confronting each other — communism and capitalism — but now these debates are everywhere in all of the political discussions when you turn on the TV... [*Loud. Chair screeching the floor.*] This nominalism then is not a purely aesthetic matter, and if we need to deal with other forms of ethics, for example, for how can one have an ethics without universals? We saw this idea that there is only this unique individual experience that came out of existentialism and gradually settled and became mainstream.

[*Long pause.*]

So, this notion of [*Stressing*] nominalism is a very powerful description of what history has done under capitalist modernity, that is to say, the gradual atomization of everything and the destruction of.. [*Achoo. Sneeze in the audience.*] Nominalism is sometimes linked to the nature of money... [*Quietly*: it comes out of Aristotle's Nicomachean Ethics, where he talks about the nature of money.] Money is this weird thing that is neither universal nor particular; it is essentially a solvent that destroys any form of universal group, class, value, norm, but without substituting it and thus leading to the fragmentation of knowledge, morality. So, going back to aesthetics, this is the crisis of aesthetics, and this is the moment with Croce that this crisis is identified and named. Then, after Croce, the "Draft Introduction" goes back to Hegel and Kant... [*Quietly*: where he is saying that these two, they knew nothing about art] and then our old friend the subject-object split. Adorno is absolutely against reception theories. Anything which talks about effect in the audience, for example, as is in Kant with the universal feeling, or in Aristotle with the power of art to evoke strong emotions, such as pity or fear, is not, hmm... [*Hesitates*] is not... [*Pause*] is not satisfactory for him. Why is he rejecting reception aesthetic theories? Well, the problem with these theories is that it gives you recipes, as when Aristotle is giving you a recipe not just for producing the regular tragedy, but for how to produce a kind of speech... [*Quietly:* if you look at the Rhetoric of Aristotle, which Heidegger called a great phenomenology of social relations.] It is a handbook to use for your intentions, it is giving you practical advice on how to deliver an argument. [*Pause.*] Now, Kant, as we know, is more complicated than that, and that's what saves Kant from being purely receptive or subjective... [*Cough in the audience.*] The minute Kant starts to reason about the judgment of taste, beauty, the agreeable, and the sublime, we get some extremely reflexive accounts of the difficulties of all these aesthetic notions. And so, for Adorno, in that way, Kant is somehow still very productive for us, because it is unfinished, and all of these paradoxes are still there. Whereas Hegel, he says finally, he had the immense historical merit on insisting on the primacy of the [*Stressing*] objective, and of art as spiritual and intellectual principle, but his views on art are somewhat too optimistic. [*Pause.*] Mm-hmm. His analysis of the object and its meaningfulness presuppose that the object was already meaningful, and that art has fulfilled its mission, incarnating experiences, and social forms... [*Footsteps. Door creaks open*] and the embodiment of the Idea. So, in a way, Hegel appears here cruder and more debased than Kant in this great dialogue of positions..

[*Long pause.*]

Now, hmm... [*Page flipping*] at this point we've talked a little bit about second reflection already... [*Door slams in the distance*] so we don't have to go through it again in this section of the "Draft Introduction." But what this is going to arrive at is again our old friend "truth content." There are some problems here with pagination... [*Page flipping*] and I'll just tell you in a moment what the translator has done. He's missed a few breaks here, hmm... [*Hesitates.*] There are two breaks in the original version of the Frühe Einleitung... [*Quietly*: the "Draft Introduction"] which sort of end these long reflections. One is on our page number 345, and if you look at the German original, you will see that the end of that part where he talks about Hegel's master and slave dialectics, it ends with a space, which the English translation didn't preserve.[17] Then, the translator or the publisher... [*Quietly*: I don't know who did that] has made a break on page 353, and there is not one in the German version. And then, at the very end, on page 357, there is another break before the end in the German version, which the English edition totally ignored. This is important for the phrasing and structuring of the argument, let's say, and I just wanted to draw your attention to it.

[*Long pause.*]

Now, you may have already noticed how often Adorno engages with Benjamin's notion of the aura throughout Aesthetic Theory. I think we'd better... [*Pause.*] You could imagine then that his repeated critique of the aura has to do with the notion of... [*Exhales deeply.*] It has to do a little bit with the critique of Hegel and how both of them presupposed to have resolved the subject-object split [*Pause.*] But obviously, Adorno was also very inspired by Benjamin's work... [*Quietly*: and so, there is a lot more mixed feelings going on in here, when Adorno makes these references to Benjamin and especially to the notion of the aura.]

[*Addresses student.*] Maybe now it's a good time to talk about Benjamin and the aura. Are you ready to present?

[*Loud. Chair screeching the floor. Footsteps.*]

Student Presentation: Benjamin, "The Work of Art in the Age of Mechanical Reproduction"

STUDENT ONE: [*Starts reading his presentation.*] Mm-hmm. This presentation will focus on what Benjamin calls "aura" and its relation to a politicized aesthetics. I will first briefly examine the history of his aura essay; next, the majority of the presentation will focus on the notion of aura as developed by Benjamin in "The Work of Art in the Age of Mechanical Reproduction." [*Pause.*] I will conclude by examining some of the premises that underlay Benjamin's aesthetic theory and will draw some preliminary conclusions as to the utility of this essay for our consideration and the contemporary relation between politics and aesthetics.

JAMESON: How many people here have read this essay by Benjamin? [*Counts to himself*: one, two, three, four...] Oh, that's not too bad.

STUDENT ONE: [*Continues reading.*] "The Work of Art in the Age of Mechanical Reproduction" is the last of the three essays that Benjamin wrote as marginal notes to the larger Arcades Project, where he considered the effects of mechanical reproduction on the work of art. The previous essay, where he studied the impact of film and photograph on the reception of art, was entitled a "Little History of Photography" and the "Paris Letters" of 1936. In "Little History of Photography," written in 1931, the concept of the "aura" made its first full-blown appearance as an element of early photography. He compares an early photographic portrait of Kafka aged six to the early-nineteenth-century photographs, suggesting that, in the early photos, people did not yet look at the world with such profound sadness as witnessed in Kafka's child photo. [*Pause.*] "There was an aura about them, a medium that lent fullness and security to their gaze even as it penetrated that medium."[18] Then Benjamin provides what is considered by... [*Door creaks open*] as the first definition of aura, where aura is defined in relation to... [*Footsteps*] an object of contemplation as fixed in time and space. He asks: "What is aura, actually?" and proceeds to define is as "a strange weave of space and time: the unique appearance or semblance of distance, no matter how close it may be."[19] [*Pause.*] This definition moves aura closer to the discipline of aesthetics, but not without other meanings invested in this concept, meanings that place aura in relation to Hollywood stars or the mass spectacle of fascist politics. The auratic work of art is in turn understood as an attempt to deny the finitude of the work, an attempt to internalize the present and deny the future, a future that, according to Benjamin, technological reproduction in general and photography in particular forces one to recall now more than ever. In Benjamin's words [*Page flipping*]:

> No matter how artful the photographer, no matter how carefully posed his subject, the beholder feels an irresistible urge to search such a picture for the tiny spark of contingency, of the here and now, with which reality has (so to speak) seared the subject, to find the inconspicuous spot where in the immediacy of that long-forgotten moment the future nests so eloquently that we, looking back, may rediscover it.[20]

[*Long pause.*]

These preliminary considerations, attempting to tack together politics, technology and art, have been more fully developed in "The Work of Art" essay, which, it should be noted, Benjamin wrote three drafts. The first draft was completed in 1935... [*Quietly*: I think this is considered the unpublished version and I am not sure if it ever got translated into English.] The second draft was completed in the spring of 1936 and Benjamin submitted it for publication to the Institute for Social Research, where it was published in French with a translation by Pierre Klossowski.[21] This draft has been very heavily edited by the Institute, and they also made him add references to Marx. [*Pause.*] The third draft was produced between 1936 and 1939, and it was this version that eventually made its way on the pages of Benjamin's Schriften, supervised by Adorno, and I think it is also this draft that was translated into English and included in Illuminations.[22]

[*Long pause.*]

My presentation concentrates primarily on the last draft, which Benjamin begins by reminding the reader that Marx perceived the future of capitalism not simply as an increasing exploitation of the proletariat, but also as maturation of conditions that would make it possible to abolish capitalism itself. [*Pause.*] Benjamin then contemplates on the changes in the superstructure and the future implications for the art of the proletarians. According to Benjamin, any thesis on the work of art that takes into consideration the development of tendencies of the present conditions of production is a weapon that forcefully brushes aside such obsolete concepts as "genius," "creativity," "eternal value," and "mystery." The latter are concepts that Benjamin believed have been perfected by fascism in order to encourage a monumentalized notion of the present, reducing the masses to passive observers charged with the task of simply processing data. [*Clears throat.*] It is the job of the critic, in Benjamin's essay, to enter in the struggle over the prevalence of concepts into superstructure... [*Chair-back creaks*] in this case, art that would accurately express the changes that have taken place in the base, an idea that I will return to in my concluding remarks.

[*Long pause.*]

The effects of the mechanical repro... [*Pause.*]

[*Page flipping.*] Oops, sorry, wrong page! In the first line of the essay, Benjamin acknowledges that art has always been reproduceable, but he insists that the mechanical reproduction introduces a new element that changes the nature of art itself. In the past, manual reproduction lacked the technology to reproduce the uniqueness of the original — that is, it was not able to replicate its presence of the original in time and space. Consequently, the original was able to preserve its authority in the face of reproduction to which it was always able to lay the charge of forgery. The situation changed drastically with the invention of mechanical reproduction, and now the original itself was put in question, due to the fact that the reproduction could now take place without, or independently of, the original. [*Pause.*] New technical means have the ability to extend the reach of the copy, to place it into social situations where the original could not be placed. [*Footsteps.*] As a consequence, the value of the presence of the mechanically reproduced work of art depreciated the original's authenticity — defined here as "all that is transmissible from its beginning, ranging from its substantive duration to its testimony to the history which it has experienced"[23] — was now jeopardized... [*Door creaks open.*] With the elimination of this historical testimony for authenticity, what is put in question, according to Benjamin, is the authority or [*Stressing*] the aura of the object.

[*Long pause.*]

[*Page flipping.*] "That which withers in the age of mechanical reproduction is its aura of the work of art."[24] The withering of the artwork's aura is a symptom of a much larger change taking place beyond art — it is the effect and the success of a technique of reproduction in detaching the work of art from the realm of tradition through the production of such a number of copies that the unique existence of a work of art becomes obsolete. [*Pause.*] Yet this process is not one-sided with regard to the object. By bringing the artwork closer to the beholder and opening it to multiple uses and identities, this process also reactivates the reproduced object. Both the decline of aura and the reactivation of the object are, Benjamin believed, tied to the mass movements of the time: fascism and communism. Each of these political movements responds accordingly to this new situation, with fascism glorifying war and art-for-art's-sake gratification, as in the saying, Fiat ars — pereat mundus ("Let art be created, though the world perish"), to which communism responds by politicizing art... [*Quietly*: this is from the famous final paragraph of "The Work of Art."]

[*Long pause.*]

For Benjamin, this change in the organizational experience and the ensuing dislocation of the object is centered on the contemporary character of perception. Perception, in Benjamin's account, is not only the product of nature, but it is also enlarged and molded by social circumstances. If it is a decline of aura — for which Benjamin provides the definition from his 1931 "Little History of Photography" as "the unique phenomenon of a distance, however close it may be,"[25] while resting on a summer afternoon — it signals a change in perception and it also provides an understanding of the social cause of this change. Benjamin concludes that these changes are due to the increased importance of masses in daily life, and their desire to bring objects closer spatially and humanly, and to overcome the uniqueness of every reality. The new character of changing perception in the masses... [*Achoo. Sneeze in the audience*] "pry the object from its shell, destroy its aura," and rid itself of the unique through the application of reproduction is linked to the wish for "universal equality of things."[26] It is important to know that, by making references to the masses and their attacks on distance and uniqueness of phenomena, Benjamin is simultaneously attempting to disrupt and reformulate the Kantian forms of intuition, according to which space and time assume a leading role in formulating both experience and perception. The unique value or authenticity of the work of art, its aura, which mechanical reproduction now places in question, had its origin, according to Benjamin, in ritual. [*Page flipping.*] In fact, he believes that aura cannot be separated from the ritual function: aura is a representation of distance and of the inapproachable, both of which are qualities of the cult image. This ritual function that is at the origins of art, however, has survived the secularization of art through the promotion of the cult of beauty. When art senses demise with the rise of first revolutionary means of reproduction... [*Door slams shut*] which, for Benjamin, is photography and film, art pursues its own course or teleology, resulting in the doctrine of "art for art's sake."

[*Long pause.*]

We have to conclude that, through mechanical reproduction, the work of art is for the first time liberated from its reliance on authenticity and ritual, thus allowing now for art to be based on the practice of mass politics and entertainment. Under prior regimes, the regime of ritual, the work of art was valued solely for its secular cultic value of beauty that developed with the Renaissance. With the rise of mechanical reproduction, when the work of art is liberated from the cult of ritual, art is made to fit public presentability. The latter increased to such an extent that today there is an absolute emphasis on the work of art's exhibition value. [*Pause.*] This change then creates a situation in which the previous function of art — its cultic function — is superseded and replaced with the artistic function. The supersession of the cultic function should lead us to recognize the equally incidental nature of the artistic function of the object.

[*Long pause.*]

That being said, Benjamin acknowledges that the cult value of art will not disappear without a struggle. For example, in early photography, the cult value of art finds refuge in the portraits of human face, serving the cult of remembrance of the lost loved ones and giving the manifestation of incompatible melancholic beauty. [*Chair scratches against the floor.*] The survival of aura vanishes quickly though with the disappearance of the human figure from the photograph, which is most visible in Eugène Atget's photos of deserted Paris streets that look like scenes of a crime. These deserted pictures serve as evidence of historical occurrences and hidden political significance. Consequently, pictures must now be accompanied by the captions, which attempt to guide those looking at the picture, for a correct and incorrect medium of the occurrence. In short, the appearance of deserted pictures, and the emergence of captions in the age of mechanical reproduction, has separated the work of art from its basis in the cultic function. Now, simple contemplation becomes impossible. Mechanical reproduction contributes to the separation of art from its basis in cult, and with this, any semblance of art's autonomy also disappeared.

[*Long pause.*]

Benjamin also considers the role of film and what he considers to be the most powerful evidence for the progressive effects of the introduction of mechanical reproduction for the work of art. [*Clears throat.*] According to Benjamin, the film and the use of the camera puts the viewer... [*Door creaks open*] in the position of the critic. The special angles, close-ups and various other positional views of the audience subject the film actor to a series of what Benjamin calls "optical tests," in which "the audience's identification with the actor is really an identification with the camera."[27] With the introduction of the camera, the film actor loses the opportunity to adjust his or her performance, as does the stage actor before the audience... [*Page flipping.*] Before the camera, the film actor is forgoing their aura because the camera replicates the actor, reducing them to an image. The aura, which could not be separated from the theater actor due to the presence of the public, now disappears due to the singularity of the shot in the studio, where the camera takes the place of the public. This puts the film actor in a vulnerable position... [*Loud cough near the microphone*] the authority of the aura that was held in classical theater, with its direct relationship to the audience, allowed for a degree of improvisation and spectator reaction. In addition, filmed behavior lends itself more readily to analysis, because — as Benjamin argues — this behavior can be isolated more easily, especially when compared to a painting or to theater. The close-up allows us to explore time, slow motion allows us to extend movement, contributing to a deepening of apperception and comprehension of life's necessities. The film's use of the shock effect makes the cult value recede by turning the public into a critic and observer, yet one who is absent-minded.

[*Long pause.*]

These characteristics of film... [*Cough in the audience*] what Benjamin believes are the two post-auratic functions of art. First, the play with time and distance allows for what Benjamin believes will be a better understanding of, and experimentation with, the new nature of experience that mechanical reproduction has made possible. Second, through the fusion of enjoyment and the positioning of the audience as critic or expert, the film allows for the unprecedented exploration of the optical unconscious a process that would allow the masses to enrich perceptual experience, which could be analyzed using Freud's method of exploring the unconscious mind. The spectator is now involved in a new sense of participation, of mass distraction, which some would lament as the masses' inability for concentration... [*Page flipping*] but which Benjamin believes is in fact a sign that, in the age of mechanical reproduction, it is not the work of art that absorbs the spectator but rather that "the distracted mass absorbs the work of art."[28] The new function of post-auratic art allows the spectator to simultaneously enjoy and appropriate the objects, as is the case with architecture, where distracted masses of spectators consume it collectively. Spectators are able to interact with the object through both site or perception and habit or technical appropriation. They inhabit the object... [*Door slams in the distance*] without the contemplation or tension that was previously required by the cult value of art.

[*Long pause.*]

Capitalism attempts to deny the death of aura through what Benjamin calls "the spell of personality" or the allure of the superstar... [*Thud. Object drops on the floor.*] Yet, as Benjamin notes, even this effort cannot revive aura — it simply replaces aura with the cult of the commodity. Moreover, the film industry in the West is increasingly forced to promote illusion-promoting spectacles and speculations in an effort to steer the masses away from their demands to participate and their rights, as experts of the mechanical age, be reproduced.

[*Long pause.*]

Last but not least, Benjamin concentrates on the reaction of fascism. Fascism has the advantage over Western capitalism of simultaneously responding to the demands of the masses for self-expression while preserving the existing structures of property relations. Accordingly, fascism sought to place the entire technical apparatus — the newly created devices, the newly required abilities for speed and energy — to use in the glorification of war. This is the main means through which fascism integrates the masses in accord with the most technologically advanced material, while maintaining the existing property relations. In addition, war has the advantage of simultaneously integrating aesthetic pleasure to geometrical formations of light, the metallization of the human body, the smooth architecture of large tanks, all of which, in Benjamin's view, were the consummation of art for art's sake. Humanity, Benjamin claims, has now reached a stage where it can experience its own self-destruction as an unsurpassable aesthetic pleasure, a situation which causes Benjamin to end this essay with a following enigmatic line: "This is the situation of politics which Fascism is rendering aesthetic. Communism responds by politicizing art."[29]

[*Page flipping.*]

If we summarize Benjamin's notion of the death of aura, and the subsequent function of art in the age of mechanical reproduction, I would like to conclude with an examination of the main theoretical premises of Benjamin's essay. [*Pause.*] For Benjamin, the fundamental role of the critic can be also explained by what he once termed "dialectics at a standstill," where the dialectical image temporarily raises above what is "always the same" to form a new constellation or an awakening... [*Quietly*: to quote from a famous paragraph in the Arcades.[30]] Although the notion of "dialectics at a standstill" was already present in Benjamin's earlier works, after his encounter with Brecht, Benjamin believed that with this redemptive operation, the critic actually partook in communist action within the superstructure that paralleled the transformation of the working class. That is, by entering into a struggle with the ruling powers or potentially ambiguous interpretations of critical social phenomena, the critic fulfills his commitment to the class struggle. [*Pause.*] On the surface, such an approach seems attractive, and potentially provides us with an aesthetic theory. Many critics, however, found some aspects of Benjamin's aesthetic theory insufficient in light of its weak understanding of the autonomy of the work of art, as was the case with Adorno's critique, or that Benjamin applied some redemptive methods, which I believe effectively neutralized both his interpretations and its positive effect for political aesthetic... [*Door creaks open*] practice. Specifically, Benjamin adapts what I believe to be a form of technological determinism: the belief that the changes in the economic base nearly produce a technological restoration, which is both developmentally linear and inherently progressive. [*Pause.*] And consequently, the application of the most advanced technical material to art will have a progressive outcome. This developmentalist premise stands in total opposition to Benjamin's previous notion of natural history and it can undermine the possibility of political action. As Benjamin himself says, "The development of productive forces which includes, besides the proletariat, technology, has led to a crisis which pushes towards the socialization of the means of production."[31] This crisis is above all a function of technology; it is as if technology precedes and renders crisis... [*Zipper unzipping*] redundant. This critique is necessary, despite the fact that Benjamin does identify new forms of possible collective resistance, which is the role of the expert, and his version of the optical unconscious. In addition, Benjamin's technologism leaves him to see aura as a purely one-dimensional concept that simply represents outmoded forms of technological material. Here Adorno provides the usual corrective. In a 1936 letter to Benjamin, Adorno agrees with Benjamin about the increasing destruction of aura within contemporary art, but he correctly points out that aura cannot be conflated with the autonomy of art as a whole. [*Page flipping.*] That is, one cannot simultaneously delineate art's social place while still showing that the elaboration of the technical laws of art, as evidenced in Schoenberg's twelve-tone system, has the capacity to resist... [*Door slams in the distance*] freedom to the elaboration of the consciously produced work. In a second critique that can prove equally to the Benjamin's developmentalist premise surrounding the death of aura, Adorno points out in Aesthetic Theory that, to the extent that the work of art is intended for subjective appreciation by men, it is itself a reproduction of itself, placing in doubt the linear relation Benjamin has described between the introduction of technology and the impact of mechanical reproduction on art. Regardless of its limitations, Benjamin's theory of art also contains numerous concepts of what continues to derive material for the continuous elaboration of a politicized aesthetics.

STUDENT ONE: That's it.

[*Audience applauding.*]

JAMESON: Questions?

[*Silence.*]

JAMESON: [*Addressing Student One.*] Is there really...? [*Pause.*] Have you, or can you see the aura at work here?

[*Long silence.*]

STUDENT ONE: I'm not sure I understand.

JAMESON: In other words... [*Chair-back creaks. Footsteps.*] See, I think the big problem that everybody has with Benjamin's notion of aura is that it looks like a positive notion, like something affirmative. [*Pause.*] I mean, you quoted one of his definitions, hmm... [*Hesitates*] "a distance, however close it may be," and it has to do with the branch of the tree, the flowers, or mountain range "that is both close and far away." This seems to be a very idyllic account of some kind of aesthetic experience, defined in terms that are quite unique. I mean, they are certainly not that of beauty nor of the sublime in Kant's sense, but they are part of some other aesthetics. And it seems as though this defines, for Benjamin, a certain kind of aesthetic, a certain way that art could be or has been once or something, and this is a [*Stressing*] positive theory of aesthetics. [*Pause.*] And yet, everything he then does go on to say about it is negative, right, like it isn't there anymore, or "No, no, we don't want this," and so on. [*Addresses Student One.*] Mm-hmm. How do you deal with that? Isn't this very odd? Maybe this is a dialectic or maybe it isn't a dialectic for Benjamin... [*Quietly*: the posit has been posited, and then he keeps negating it, so you can't adopt it as a positive aesthetics.] See, I think Adorno, he doesn't really go through with his critique of aura, but it is everywhere — he constantly comes back to aura and makes his hints and qualifications. [*Pause.*] One of the things he is afraid of is that these speculations about aura may be taken for a complete aesthetic. Just as there used to be an aesthetics organized around beauty... [*Quietly*:

and now maybe there are aesthetics organized around the sublime] there could be an aesthetics organized around aura, which would argue that true great art is defined by its ability to create, possess, or evoke an auratic experience. And the minute you go that way, you may see one other reason Adorno keeps criticizing Benjamin, and this is because it seems to be an aesthetic of effect, like Kant's. Benjamin's aura seems to define an aesthetic effect — you can't say, hmm… [*Hesitates.*] Can you tell from this definition of aura what an artwork would look like that did that? I think it's like Kant in that sense, that when a certain kind of artwork or experience meets certain criteria, then it will produce effects like this. But on the other hand… [*Door slams in the distance*] in another moment, he seems to be saying… [*Impersonates Benjamin*] "Well, this is just when you are in the presence of the original." If you manage to see the, hmm… [*Reflects*] The Taking of Christ by Caravaggio, if some of you really see that with your own eyes, that's different from what you would see in a reproduction. [*Whispering.*] And that is aura. But then we are not talking about aesthetics at all, are we? [*Pause.*] We are talking about relationship to an object, handicraft, and the opposite of industrial reproduction… [*Quietly*: very much the… (*Mumbles indistinctly*).] But the point is that there are many and various lousy attacks on the aura, which seem to have been coming from very different places. [*Looks at Student One.*] I don't know if you have this sense while working on Benjamin…

STUDENT ONE: Maybe this has to do with the issue of political representation, and the crisis of political representation, which I think we can call "sovereignty." If you look at it as sovereignty, then you could never say that the crisis would equal the death of sovereignty or sovereign representation. I think we would talk about the exception and how sovereignty recuperated itself, so there isn't a mirror here, where there is only one side in the death of aura as work of art, but there are all these other notions like sovereignty that goes in parallel with aesthetic notions. I don't think he would see it in a linear...

JAMESON: Mm-hmm. That's very interesting that you should have brought that out. So, in a way, this is what Carl Schmidt calls the "state of exception," and that is when a political order is suspended, allowing the sovereign power to restore order. So, this would be then a political equivalent of aura in art, or something like that?

STUDENT ONE: I think it could be, yeah. I think it could be because this would be the definition of what sovereignty has been, right?

JAMESON: Other questions?

[*Long silence.*]

JAMESON: See, the other thing that struck me... [*Pause.*] You did very well to go back to photography, as certainly some of this aligns with what other thinkers have said about photography. How many people have read Roland Barthes' book on photography? The... [*Pause*] the, hmm... [*Tries to remember.*] What is it called?

AUDIENCE: [*In unison.*] Camera Lucida.

JAMESON: Yes, Camera Lucida it's called, and that's a wonderful book where Barthes has his theory of the punctum. A punctum is this element in the photograph that you notice; it is this weird thing that shoots out at you.[32] It is not the center of the photo at all, but something that marks historical time in some sense. It seems to me that punctum is somehow very close to what Benjamin is saying here, and whether Barthes has read about Benjamin's aura, I don't know... [*Pause.*] It took a long time for Benjamin's essay to be known. The two German volumes came out in the 1950s, and then Illuminations, if anybody has a copy, it came up in the 1960s. As for the French translation... [*Quietly*: I mean, yes, they had it with that version translated by Klossowski that was published in Zeitschrift, but I don't think in France this Frankfurt School stuff was very well known for some... (*Mumbles indistinctly*).] So, I am not quite sure when this essay started to be widely read in France, but

I doubt it that Barthes was aware of it when he wrote Camera Lucida... [*Door slams shut*] but to some extent, it's a similar idea. Then I also think in this context about Bloch's ideas of "traces" or Spuren that we talked earlier, that the punctum and aura maybe are like traces or marks pointing to history, where some mysterious past is hidden, and it only stands out in the trace. [*Pause.*] But what strikes me is that all or most of this is about time, whereas the actual [*Stressing*] official definitions of aura that you read us earlier, and several of them, about the distance and the mountain and the tree branch and so on, there is one of space. And this is very odd because, if you put it in terms of time, then you could see why maybe these newer arts, even photography, as well as film, could do something with this that the older arts wouldn't. And incidentally, since we've been talking about nominalism, it is clear that, beyond the novel then, film and photography are the more nominalist arts for our times than the novel, for they are even less generic in many ways. Mm-hmm, but it seems to me there is something there too that needs to be worked out, and I hesitate to think of this as confusion in Benjamin; I think that these are references to a central thought which was never laid down anywhere. But your reference about sovereignty, that is very interesting, that might lead us somewhere. [*Tap, tap. Taps his thumb on the desk.*] From what you said, you've got several things going on here: you've got aura, which is associated with cult value, that is religious art, right? Then art becomes secular, so this is sort of the after-effect of the cult that's lingering on in the work of art. [*Pause.*] Then you have reification, which is presumably the way the bourgeois commercial century takes over all of this, packages it and tries to sell it. Then, with the Nazis, you have something which I think Adorno would have called... [*Quietly*: and Benjamin as well, and that's another reason this concept of the aura does not always work out so well] the myth. [*Pause.*] This is the Arcades, like going back to the archaic and mobilizing... [*Mumbles indistinctly.*] Then you can think of art and fascism in terms of Triumph of the Will...

[*Quietly:* there is a new book on Hitler and his relationship to art and it's just astounding, I mean, he designed everything practically. Speer was there, of course, but Hitler designed the standards, he re-designed the swastika, he turned it around and tried different colors, all of that is the product of Hitler's imagination.] I think somebody was proposing a topic... [*Slams lightly his palm on the desk*] a topic that would be connected to this... [*Looks at student.*] Oh, it was you, right, who mentioned the remark that Stockhausen made after 9/11, when he stated something regarding the collapse of the twin towers ... , [*Impersonates Stockhausen*] "Oh, this was the greatest work of art in the century." [*Long pause.*] And with that, he became an instant pariah, as other artists and institutions all over the cultured world stopped playing his music, and his daughter declared that she is going to change her name... [*Chuckles.*] But the precursor of all this, are these ideas on the relation between modernism and totalitarianism, where some have claimed that Hitler was a great artist because he shaped the human masses, and then there is also a Soviet version of this with Boris Groys, who stated that Stalin was the greatest of all modernists, as he created the total modern work of art, which was the Soviet Union with its Gulag system, the forced collectivization, the reign of terror, industrialization and so on.[33] So, there is a follow-up of Benjamin's instant diagnosis of Nazi aestheticization in some of these more recent ideas, and they have to do with the modernization of myth.

[*Long pause.*]

And then, finally, we come to production, and that's the essay that the Sixties adopted... [*Quietly*: there is this strange little essay by Benjamin called "The Artist as Producer," which has a very Brechtian title.] And, by the way, this is one other reason that Benjamin had to change his "The Work of Art" essay for the Frankfurt School so many times — it was because they thought there was too much Brecht in it. They let him understand... [*Door slams shut*] he had to get rid of all of this Brecht stuff, he had to clean it up, to remove everything that was remotely Brechtian in there, which he did dutifully. So here he says, look... [*Quietly:* and we are still getting this in Adorno] this is a productionist view and the artist is like the worker because he uses the most advanced forces of production. Now, you... [*Looks at Student One*] criticized this as "technological determinism," and that's fine, but that's in Adorno as well, and Adorno says the same thing: the artist must use [*Whispering*] the most advanced modes of production. Now, where do we stand with such statements since we don't believe in the most advanced modes of production, for this is all modernization theory, and ideology of progress, exploitation, and conquest of nature and so on. Or, if we do, then... [*Pause.*] The most advanced modes of production today are computers, as you find them already in every industry. And of course, in music, as you recall, we talked about Boulez and other Darmstadt musicians who, after the twelve-tone system, produced a kind of music organized by computers. I mean, no individual mind could put all those complicated rows and musical sequences the way these computers did... [*Pause.*] But then this is a kind of music that is totally organized by machines, and this is very much Adorno's nightmare vision of late-capitalist society, which is this bureaucratic — as Weber thought — form of organizing everything and turning it into commodities. It is the totally administered society, this is at work in these musical works; in a way, they cannot escape it, or maybe this is how they respond to these social processes. But is this then the most advanced mode of cultural production? [*Pause.*] Where do we stand with this now? Mm-hmm. And I am not sure... [*Addresses Student One*] and I'm not sure I would call Benjamin's aura "technological determination." Well, there you could really talk about the whole period changing, and you could say that the kinds of perception that we have with film or photography are part and parcel of larger changes of perception in general. But finally, they all come back to machines, and Marx also came back to machines too... [*Quietly*: and Heidegger, with the question of technology.] We are facing the most radical question, and that is what technology does to human reality...

STUDENT ONE: What's interesting to me is that it would seem ahistorical, because there is no instance in which Benjamin would say that class struggle can actually intervene into the technological crisis, and that the technological crisis faces the capitalist form of property relation, but not the actual class struggle. [*Pause.*] So, you could see how I think like maybe "technological determination" or "technological change" is an expression of that antagonism...

JAMESON: I think that the utopian ideals — as they are shown in some early Soviet avant-garde — is that the property relations are holding back technology. We could go on and produce all kinds of new things, we could conquer space and liberate all planets and so on, if it wasn't for the profit money-making greed of the corporations that hold us back from technical progress and the utopian future. So, I think that's the way that this is being thought of, and this is certainly still according to some teleological notion in some sense, and that's also there in Adorno...

[*Footsteps.*]

Okay, listen, next time let's get back to chapter seven and eight of Aesthetic Theory... [*Door creaks open*] because I think they can be approached together ... [*Chairs scratching against the floor.*]

Audience stands up. Objects drop on the floor. Door squeaking. Students returning chairs to other classrooms. Zippers zipping up. Some in the audience form a line to discuss their assignments with Jameson. General noise. Screeching microphone noise.

[*Microphone turns off.*]

CURTAIN

LECTURE NINETEEN

APRIL 10, 2003

ADORNO, "THE ESSAY AS FORM" — TRUTH CONTENT

CURTAIN RISES

Jameson enters the classroom carrying a few books, his scattered notes, and the red pen in the chest pocket of his flannel shirt.

[Microphone turns on.]

JAMESON: Okay, I want us to talk about these two chapters, but maybe we will do this after we listen to a short exposé on Adorno's essay about the essay, or whatever it's called... [*Addresses student*.] You have it in the Notes to Literature with you?

STUDENT ONE: Yeah.

JAMESON: Okay, do you want to step up in front here and talk about Adorno's essay piece? [*Chair legs scrape hard against the floor. Footsteps.*]

Student Presentation: Adorno, "The Essay as Form"

STUDENT ONE: I didn't know what the best way was to prepare for this presentation, so I decided I will simply retell Adorno's "The Essay as Form" using as much as possible my own words... [*Quietly*: or at least some of my words.] It's a simplified summary of a process by which I am trying to make sense of what I think he is saying here. I will talk using my notes, so please don't be shy to interrupt me. In a way, today's presentation is my interpretation of this famous essay...

[*Long pause.*]

I will start with some background information... [*Pause.*] Adorno wrote "Der Essay als Form" in the 1950s as a sort of introduction to his larger collection of essays called Notes to Literature... [*Looks at Jameson.*] It deals with what is considered Adorno's preferred form of writing. Adorno begins the piece with the observation that the essay form was not very liked in the German academic circles of his day... [*Quietly*: that is, in the 1950s, and maybe earlier or later.] Although there have been many great essayists in the past... [*Quietly*: he names Simmel, Lukács, Benjamin, Kassner[1]] his contemporary academic circles were generally distrustful towards this form of writing... [*Quietly*: it was not considered serious or a very scholarly way of writing.] Adorno explains this distrust by the limited impact of the historical Enlightenment in Germany, hmm... [*Hesitates*] adding that, even today, in conditions of Western democracy, the situation did not change. The essay is different from other forms of writing in that it does not surround itself with limits, which it then tries to fill up, but remains open and flexible; it is a preferred medium for those with imagination or who tackle serious problems in a playful and leisurely way. The essay does not start from boundaries or from points of origins, but from what the author... [*Quietly*: the essayist] is mostly interested in. It does not classify or communicate existing facts, which Adorno believes is the main aim of dominant thought, but it seeks to [*Stressing*] interpret phenomena, and for this alone the essayist is... [*Quietly*: and I quote] "is marked with the yellow star."[2] Throughout his essay on the essay, Adorno resorts to multiple metaphors in order to highlight the difference between the essay and other forms, mainly the scientific writing. He compares the essayist to the "man with the head in the cloud," rather than the one with their "feet on the ground"... [*Quietly*: and later on, I will give you some other of his metaphors.] To some, the essay may resemble art... [*Door creaks open*] but then Adorno insists that the essay is different from art in that its main concern is not that of aesthetic appearance... [*To herself*: Schein] but that of seeking the truth. The medium of the essay is not sensuous form and materials but concepts, adding that even such great essayists as Lukács have often failed to see the difference. The essay still has more in common with art than with other forms of writing, and this is due to the honesty of the writing subject vis-à-vis the object... [*Cough in the audience*.] Unlike positivist writing, which pretends that the cognitive subject has no impact on the object, or that the cognitive subject is capable of wiping off any trace of subjective expressions... [*Quietly*: thus, allowing truth to present itself in its full splendor] the essayist, like the artist, believes that subjective presence cannot be fully eliminated.

[*Long pause*.]

In the modern age, the essay has degenerated, or it has been misused to name various forms of banal and superficial writing. In such instances, ready-made concepts are taken for granted... [*Cough in the audience*] reified to new levels. The light, informal and often humorous tone of the feuilleton may serve as an example of such corrupted modern forms used to affirm the status quo or to serve commercial interests. The essay can trace its origins to the days when science and art have not yet been separated; when intuition and concept, sign and image, have not been estranged from each other. Any attempt to restore this lost unity... [*Quietly*: if it ever existed] would be a disaster. We see the failures of these attempts in Lukács's equation of essay and art, in Kant's intellectual intuition (intellektuell Anschauung), and most clearly in Heidegger's fusion of the literary and the philosophical, in the [*Stressing*] poesis of Being ... [*Quietly*: what Adorno famously denounced as the "jargon of authenticity."] Such attempts only play into the hands of positivism, which seeks every opportunity to denounce the essayistic thought as feuilletonic, fantastic or arbitrary. The essay must seek inspiration in art, and together they could resist dominant positivist methodology. But the essay thought also borrows from science

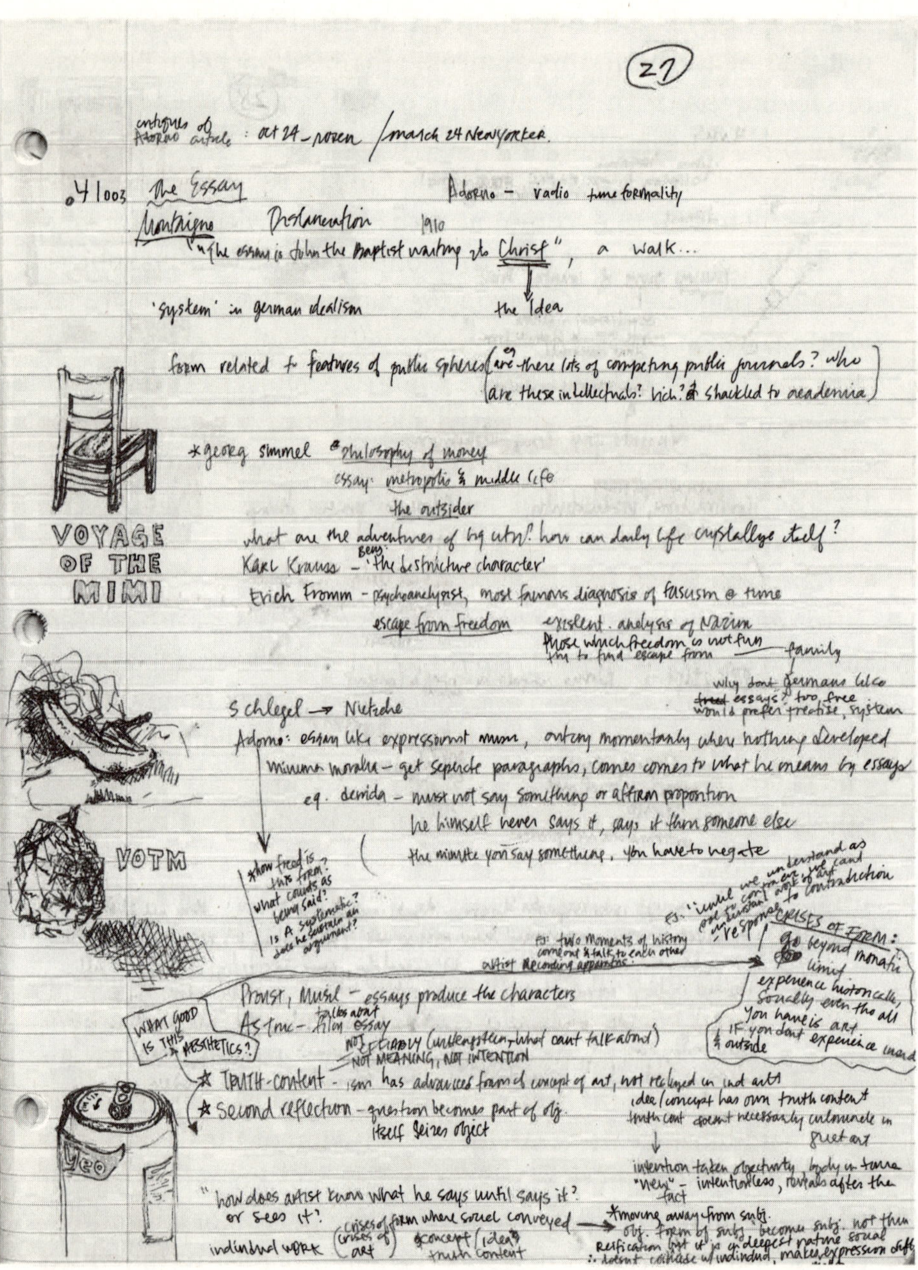
27

critiques of Adorno article : oct 24 – rosen / march 24 New Yorker

4/1003 The Essay
Adorno – radio time formality

Montaigne Dislimention 1910
"the essay is John the Baptist waiting to Christ", a walk...

'system' in german idealism → the Idea

form related to features of public spheres (eg are there lots of competing public journals? who are these intellectuals? rich? shackled to academia)

*georg simmel @ philosophy of money
essay: metropolis & middle life
the outsider

what are the adventures of big city? how can daily life crystallize itself?
Karl Kraus – 'the destructive character'
Erich Fromm – psychoanalyst, most famous diagnosis of fascism @ time
escape from freedom

Schlegel → Nietzsche
Adorno: essay like expressionist music, ...
Minima Moralia – get separate paragraphs, comes to what he means by essays
eg. derrida – must not say something or affirm proposition
he himself never says it, says it thru someone else
the minute you say something, you have to negate

Proust, Musil – essays produce the characters
Astruc – film essay

WHAT GOOD IS THIS AESTHETICS?

★ TRUTH-content – ... has advanced from concept of art, not realized in ind arts
★ Second reflection – question becomes part of obj.
itself seizes object

CRISES OF FORM:
go beyond monadic limit
experience historically, socially even the all you have is art
if you dont experience ...

"how does artist know what he says until says it? or sees it?
individual WORK
crises of form where social conveyed → *moving away from subj.

Page from student's seminar notes.

by investing itself in technique... [*Quietly*: or construction] but in doing this, it must remain fully aware of the subjective pole of expression, which does not only act as opposite but also as main force and motivation. When art and essay make claims to be in possession of scientific truth, they risk losing their power of negation.

[*Long pause*.]

The historical separation of art from science has led to a compartmentalized culture in a modern society, which lost interest in the "whole truth." [*Pause*.] In an internally divided culture — where philosophy is in charge of "eternal values," science delivers the "unquestionable truths," and art is the realm of "aconceptual intuition" of the senses — the free crossing of borders is forbidden. Such a culture is repressive, for it rests on the belief that other forms of knowledge... [*Quietly*: art and philosophy] can be converted into science, while the opposite conversion is not possible or advisable. The division of modern culture, which is the result of the division of labor, also reveals itself within each individual sphere, as is the case with the existing unbridgeable gap between academic aesthetics and art. Practicing artists do not find useful the range of abstractions provided by academic aestheticians, while the latter are not often knowledgeable of the most recent formal innovations in art. But these internal divides are not the fault of philosophers or artists, and they certainly cannot be overcome by rational planning... [*Quietly*: like today when everyone calls for "interdisciplinary" or "multidisciplinary."] The cause of the cultural divide is to be sought in the mode of material production, based on the guilt of exploitation and domination of nature, which modern consciousness seeks to conceal by putting forward new methodologies that repress each previous stage of development on its way to the "promised future," and thus keep further and further apart each realm or mode of knowledge.

[*Long pause*.]

The essay is critical of such forgetfulness or privilege of new methods. It refuses to embrace methods put forward by scientific theories, seeing in them ideological preconditions imposed on knowledge... [*Shuffling paper.*] The essay prioritizes the consciousness of non-identity without insisting on it, because if it did, this would mean imposing a principle which is against the very spirit of the essay form. In its refusal to embrace a method of thought... [*Quietly*: deduction, induction, and so on] the essay resists the Spinozian parallelism between the order of things and the logical order of ideas. It also rebels against the old philosophical postulate that what is transient is unworthy of thinking, and it does not accept the conviction that truth and history are incompatible. [*Pause.*] Instead, the essay directs its attention to the fragmentary, contingent, and temporary. But it does not seek to find the eternal in the transient, but tries to render the transient eternal. The essay criticizes the existing split between a primary philosophy — which is presumable in possession of some valuable age-old categories — and a secondary philosophy of culture that must rely on the said categories in order to exist. In going against the divide, the essay ignores pre-established categories, revealing instead its utopian nature, powered by the excess of intention over its object. The essay does not see its role in reducing the order of things to the order of ideas... [*Quietly*: this is science's task] but in penetrating as deeply as possible into its object, which it does by analyzing the object in relation to various forms of mediations... [*Quietly*: social, historical, political, cultural.] The essay does not proceed from origins but submits itself to the study of immediacy... [*Quietly*: what is initial, given, un-related, simple] and mediation... [*Quietly*: what is developed, complex, or related.] There is nothing in this world, says Adorno, that is not mediated. The essay refuses to subscribe to the dogmas and illusions of its time, to the illusion that nature and culture are reconcilable, or that human life is still part of the natural order, or that Nature is still alive or meaningful for the human race.

[*Long pause. Page flipping.*]

In working out its form, the essay refuses to see its main task in terms of providing definitions to its concepts. While modern philosophy has criticized definitions for some time, scientific thought still relies on this scholastic practice. Science still sees its role in pre-critical terms of providing conceptual definitions, thus lagging behind philosophy... [*Cough in the audience*.] Since Kant, philosophy substituted the habit of compiling conceptual definitions for the practice of critically investigating the process through which concepts are being produced. The essay treats concepts unceremoniously, or in their immediacy... [*Quietly*: that is, loosely defined or ambiguous] and this approach is in accordance with the essay's concerns for mediations... [*Quietly*: as I said, the essay does not try to define, but to place instead concepts in a relation to each other.] In essay thought, the concept acquires precision not from its precise definition... [*Quietly*: this is what gives scientific discourse its authority] but from the successful placement of the concept within a force-field where they become part of a constellation. It is their place within chains of signification and relations that gives meaning to the concepts, making them useful for reflection.

[*Long pause*.]

In its relation to the concepts, the essay seeks the perfect balance between scientific writing and phenomenological interpretation. If the former is primarily concerned with providing definitions, the latter goes into the opposite extreme and fetishizes the relation between concepts and language, which is often done at the expense of truth... [*Page flipping*.] The essay does not treat its concepts as mere tools, whose precise definition would secure a firm grasp of the object, neither does it fetishize the language base of the concept in a pretense for literary quality. Fully aware of the dialectics of form and content, the essay is attentive to the manner of expression... [*Quietly*: or presentation] most fitted for the penetration of truth of the object. The form of the essay is not organized in linear fashion, but instead it resembles a woven fabric or a carpet, whose quality depends on the density of its texture. The woven pattern is inspired by the mode of unfolding of everyday experience, which proceeds... [*Quietly*: I quote:] "methodically unmethodically." Adorno then uses another metaphor, comparing the essay thought to a traveler in a foreign country who is forced to speak the local language in the way that comes from direct experience rather than relying on grammatical rules learned in school. [*Pause.*] Certainly, this kind of practice is prone to error, and scientific thought fears it like death, but the essay knows that this is the price it must pay for a more immediate… [*Achoo. Sneeze in the audience*] spontaneous and interesting intellectual experience. With this, the essay proves that it rejects the idea of "indisputable certainty." Rather than erecting scaffoldings and methodological structures suitable for the generation… [*Quietly*: in a linear fashion] of [*Stressing*] indisputable definitions, the essay form weaves itself into a forcefield resembling a dense constellation where the truth content emerges from the relationship between concepts… [*Quietly*: which is somewhat similar to the truth content and art.]

[*Long pause.*]

In part two, Adorno is careful to state that the essay [*Stressing*] might be interpreted as a protest against Descartes' Discourse on Method, which stands at the origins of modern Western science, knowledge, and theory. [*Pause.*] The essay thought, says Adorno, gently challenges the main criterion of Cartesian truth, defined in terms of clara et distincta perception… [*Quietly*: clear and distinct perception] and unquestionable certainty.

[*Long pause.*]

Adorno talks about the second rule of the Discourse on Method, which stipulates that, in order to find an adequate solution to a problem, the object of inquiry should be broken into as many parts as possible. To this, Adorno responds that artifacts, which constitute the main subject matter of the essay, cannot be broken into elements. Since Kant and the Romantics, artifacts have been considered indivisible, like monads, or like living organisms that cannot be torn apart without being destroyed. Therefore, the essay thought does not tolerate the idea of disjoined elements, but looks instead at its object as the product of reciprocal interaction between elements, where the whole takes precedence over the parts... [*Chair-back creaks.*] The essay thought treats the whole like a monad (and not a monad) by pursuing not only the object alone, but also the moments that are in proximity or are mirrored in the object. [*Quietly*: In other writings, Adorno talks about artworks resembling monads, that is to say, forms that reflect and mirror other forms.]

JAMESON: [*Interrupts.*] Yes, monads, we will talk about them — this is very important in Adorno...

STUDENT ONE: The essay does not focus on the broken parts of the object... [*Quietly*: as prescribed by Descartes] but on the auratic proximity of all the moments reflected and refracted in some monadic way from the object, on mediation and immediacy.

[*Long pause.*]

Adorno then... [*Page flipping*] discusses the essay in relation to Descartes' third rule, which requires that one should start with the simplest problems and proceed in an ascending manner to the more complex ones. The essay, however, does not want to start with what is easy... [*Quietly*: what is already known, reified, or infused with ideological interests] but it proceeds in the opposite direction, starting from the most difficult or unknown. The essay thought is similar to the student of philosophy who refuses to begin her study of philosophy from simplified questions... [*Quietly*: like we have today in the well-known series of books called Plato for Dummies or Descartes for Beginners (*Chuckles*)] but who jumps instead into the most complex problems of philosophy. This student, says Adorno, is clearly in the possession of philosophical wisdom, for he or she does not believe in the illusion of graspable certainty and unquestionable truth. By contrast, the student who proceeds from simple truisms lives in a state of continuous postponement of knowledge... [*Quietly*: says Adorno.] And it is the dominant thought that encourages this state of continuous postponement of knowledge, which it does by presenting truth as a [*Stressing*] product of casual relations to which one arrives gradually by postulating a state of "comprehensibility."

The essay thought wishes to destroy the idea of a simple and graspable world constituted of multiple causes — a world that, when properly or [*Stressing*] methodically grasped, releases the concealed truth.

[*Long pause*.]

Finally, he takes aim at Descartes' fourth rule, which again prescribes breaking up complex problems into steps that need to be examined through exhaustive enumeration. [*Pause*.] The fourth rule aims at creating a "general view" by enumerating what could be then grasped in a deductive manner. To this, the essay responds that there is no such thing as exhaustive… [*Quietly*: or all-inclusive enumeration] as the object may be encircled by an infinite number of aspects, and it is up to the cognitive subject to choose which of these aspects are to be given priority. Such enumerations, which are often called "frame of reference," "methodology," "general view," and which are announced in advance, appear arbitrary, given object's unlimited collection of immediacies and forms of mediation… [*Achoo. Sneeze in the audience*.] Adorno then states that the essay opposes fragmentation on aesthetic grounds, for the essay form sees inspiration in the mode of operation of the mind… [*Quietly*: the mind cannot be broken up into parts.] But the aesthetic mode of the essay also relies on the fragment, even though it does not use fragments as building blocks… [*Quietly*: like to construct a whole from multiple fragments] but it looks at the fragment inwardly, through self-reflection and by promoting a form of [*Quietly*: I quote:] "anti-idealist motive in the midst of Idealism." The essay form is fragmentary just as human consciousness or external reality is fragmentary. In its special monadic way of relating to the fragment, the essay form is like a construction that may collapse at any moment, and this is because the essay form maintains its balance by relying on inter-fragmentary discontinuities and breaks. The essay resembles a conflict which has been brought to a temporary standstill.

[*Long pause*.]

Adorno's description of the essay-form production process

often brings to mind the idea of constellation. Like constellations... [*Quietly*: we discussed constellations in another session] the essay form derives its meaning from a field of forces, or of conflicts and standstills in which concepts... [*Quietly*: or stars] participate. The meaning of the essay rests in its German word, Versuch, a word that is translated into English as "essay," but also as "attempt," "experiment," "test" ... [*Quietly*: French essai has a similar meaning.] Such meanings express the essay's utopian attempts "to get at the truth of things," despite the provisional, fragmentary, and fallible character of consciousness. The utopian aspect also manifests itself in the idealistic belief that, when the ongoing internal conflict reaches a standstill, it produces a bright flash of light capable to illuminate for a very short moment a feature of the totality. This utopia is what the essay secretly hopes to achieve on its own or in a mosaic-like combination with other essays. [*Pause*.] Adorno cites Max Bense's Über den Essay und seine Prosa... [*Quietly*: I'll read the full quote:]

> This, then, is how the essay is distinguished from a treatise. The person who writes essayistically is the one who composes as he experiments, who turns his object around, questions it, feels it, tests it, reflects on it, who attacks it from different sides and assembles what he sees in his mind's eye and puts into words what the object allows one to see under the conditions created in the course of writing.[3]

[*Quietly*: End of quote.] Unlike the treatise, the essay does not rush to arrive at a conclusion — and this refusal serves as that a priori from which the essay derives its energy. Adorno insists that the essay is both more open and more closed than the treatise: it is more open because the essay allows parts of the system that it seeks to negate to enter its own structure... [*Quietly*: like philosophical prose that is often part of literary criticism] but it is also more closed because of the attention the essay pays to its form of presentation. The essay must constantly question the theory it is producing, for the more it pretends to act as if it is in the possession of truth, the more disastrous are the consequences. To create conditions for the object to appear in a new light, the essay must remain committed to the idea of experiment, and in order to create such conditions, it must constantly devour its own opinions and theories, including those that the essay has started with. The essay seems to be lacking a "point of view," and this is because it maintains its balance by resting on discontinuities and breaks or on something outside itself. Nothing is fixed or trustable for the essay. And when the opponents accuse the essay of lacking a secure point... [*Quietly*: of view] the essay reminds them of the Hegelian logic which states that the singularity of individual judgments ... [*Choo- choo. Loud Amtrak train whistle*] on the multiple dimensions of truth. The essay form is woven of multiple details, but... [*Quietly*: and I quote:] "the untruth in which the essay knowingly entangles itself is the element in which the truth resides..."[4] [*Quietly*: End of quote.] The essay's main concern is the culture-nature opposition. It addresses this relation by treating cultural phenomena as immediacy... [*Quietly*: as a sort of "second nature," because nature is unmediated] and it does it in order to reveal what is false or constructed about society. The essay freely chooses its object and interprets it not from the point of view of its origins, but that of mediation across key categories... [*Quietly*: culture/nature, individual/society, immediacy/mediation.] It addresses modern cultural phenomena the way medieval exegetes read the scripture, but unlike the latter, the essay is critical as it seeks to confront the dominant texts with their own concepts. [*Pause*.] The essay challenges culture by pointing to its primordial untruth... [*Quietly*: this is ideology, basically, that runs deep and counters everything that culture proclaims.] The main task of the essay is to reveal the foundation of modern ideology, which is the process of complete domination of nature that constitutes the "second nature" of culture to which the essay thought also belongs.

[*Long pause*.]

The essay shares its origins with scientific writing in ancient rhetoric, something that science has been working hard to conceal. Giving in to the demands of the age of Enlightenment, modern scientific thought rid itself of concerns it still had when it was part of rhetoric... [*Quietly*: imagination, play, or Schein, truth] turning, as a result, into an [*Stressing*] instrument for registering and managing what-is... [*Quietly*: or that what-is or which-is the case.] Dominant thought embraced the basic principles of ancient rhetoric, which is the concern for the immediate, or providing instant gratification to its listeners, incorporating them into modern communication. For the sake of delivering the message, dominant reason is ready to sacrifice everything... [*Quietly*: form of the presentation, commitment to truth.] The essay, on the other hand, has sublimated the rhetoric's main source of satisfaction, which is the delivery of the message, into a heightened concern for the preservation of the autonomy of its presentation... [*Quietly*: and I quote:] "and [its] happiness in freedom vis-á-vis the object..."[5] [*Quietly*: End of quote.] This is another major difference between the essay and other forms of thought, as the latter are primarily ruled by the reality principle... [*Quietly*: the accommodation to the demands of the external world.] This makes them hostile to happiness. [*Pause.*] The essay, on the other hand, remains committed to happiness, although it silently grieves the fact that even its most esteemed philosophies... [*Quietly*: Kant and Hegel, and I quote:] "truth has betrayed happiness and itself along with it..."[6] [*Quietly*: End of quote.] The essay infuses rhetoric's main devices, which serve the purpose of enslaving the listeners, with truth content. The essay appears to its multiple critics too vague and ambiguous, especially in the way it uses words to refer to objects. But this ambiguity is mainly due to the fact that the essay wants to remain truthful to the complex web of significations and meanings associated with objects, events, or actions — a mission that the essay form tries to accomplish by following the logic of music. The latter translates its relation to the world not by discourse argumentation, but aconceptually or by means of subjective acts of expression.

[*Long pause.*]

The essay's opposition to science is not necessarily in terms of resisting discursive logic. The essay obeys the laws of logic but only insofar as they agree with its efforts to coordinate the conceptual elements and energies generated from the ongoing conflict of addressing immediacies. The essay does not build on principles of deduction and neither does it draw its conclusions based on empirical observations. [*Pause.*] When it comes to logic, the essay acknowledges it only in relation to its content, but not in relation to the form of presentation. The main task of the essay, insists Adorno, is that of coordination and not subordination... [*Quietly*: it is science that seeks to subordinate concepts according to principles, laws, frames of reference, general views, or methods.] In the essay, the act of coordination rests on the ongoing internal dynamic or tensions which the essay tries to achieve in order to reach the standstill or the truth content. Unlike traditional thought, the essay affords itself a more elastic form, which it does in order to give more space for the dynamic tension to contract and expand, allowing for the most accurate reflection or intense expression of contradictions in empirical reality.

[*Long pause.*] [*Quietly*: I will conclude now.]

Today, the essay form is under threat, as it has been caught in between the concerns of science and scholarship... [*Quietly*: concerns that have to do with enumerating what already exists] and that of contemporary philosophical thought. The latter is also adopting scientistic concerns, picking up empty concepts or that what has been dismissed by science. Adorno ends the essay on essay with a quote from Nietzsche, which reaffirms that the search for happiness is the most sacred goal of knowledge, but then he adds that, since the essay is suspicious of any form of affirmation, it appears that heresy remains the only law of the essay thought.

STUDENT ONE: [*Deep sigh.*] That is all, thank you.

[*Audience applauding*.]

JAMESON: Questions?

[*Long pause*.]

Well, it is paradoxical, hmm... [*Hesitates*.] I would think that, for most people, the essay is something like a, hmm... [*Chalk strokes on the blackboard*] V-E-R-S-U-C-H in German is "essay," but it also means "attempt," as we saw in the presentation. This meaning is not only in German but in French too, where the term "essai" means "the attempt" or "the trial." So, when Adorno titles another of his essays "Attempt to Understand Endgame," it almost reads like [*Stressing*] the essay to understand Beckett's Endgame.

[*Long pause*.]

Montaigne, who is regarded as the originator of the essay form during the French Renaissance,[7] started with a kind of chapbook or commonplace book. [*Addresses the audience*.] You know what that is, right? [*Silence*.] It's a notebook where he kept records of quotes and sentences collected from various classical texts. Montaigne wrote down the most memorable... [*Chair scraping the floor*] quotations, and then gradually he started adding his commentaries. The collection grew into little units, which were later published... [*Quietly*: I don't remember the exact story of this, but it has to do with him leaving the city due to the plague outbreak and settling in the countryside where he completed his Essais in order to cope with isolation.] He then completed several publications during the plague. The first was a relatively short one, then when it came to republish them, he began adding things, so that the later editions were different from the earlier ones. This is also a little bit the way Proust used to work. He would take a notebook... [*Shows a notebook*] something like this one and write notes, and as his thoughts or commentaries grew, he would then attach another paper... [*Quietly*: these were notebooks with loose sheets of paper that he referred to as "carnets" or "cahiers" ... (*Words indistinct*) paper folded out and attached to the margins, like expandable margins. This may be debatable, but some also used the term "palimpsest" ... (*Mumbles indistinctly*).] In his case, we have a form of writing with a very distinct physical form... [*Zipper unzipping*] and Montaigne's editions are indexed with letters A, B, C to indicate these various textual strata.

[*Long pause*.]

This form certainly suggests something about the nature of the essay, which, as we saw in Adorno, is supposedly free or must have no pre-established boundaries. [*Pause*.] But the essay also tells us about the nature of the writer. Lukács wrote a lot of essays. Already in his early socialist period, he was active in the cultural circles of Budapest... [*Quietly*: he was engaged in avant-garde theater at some point, this is the moment that has a lot of symbolism... (*Mumbles indistinctly*).] Lukács' famous line about the essay is that of John the Baptist awaiting his savior.[8] But we may wonder, who is the savior here? [*Softly*.] It's the idea... [*Quietly*: and you don't have this in Adorno's view on the essay] but what would this idea be? It would be some form of the idea, right, or of a, hmm ... [*Hesitates*] a system. "System" is another interesting and related concept. System, in German thought, goes back to... [*Cough in the audience*] the key moment in the very early lives of Hegel, Schelling, and Hölderlin, who went to school together. Together, they wrote a document, and we don't know exactly who the author was, because it looks like it was written by one person. It's called the Systemprogramm and came out sometimes in the 1790s...[9] [*Quietly*: this is the moment of the French Revolution and other political reforms] and which is the product of their conversations. The discovery of the idea of system was very important for German objective idealism, as it makes a statement about some fundamental unity underlying all reality, seen now as a dynamic process of becoming and self-development... [*Quietly*: and this is opposed to Kant, for we don't have a system here.] There seems to be this opposition between system and... [*Microphone distortions*.] The system, in its German tradition, is older than the essay is... [*Takes a sip of water*] and that is something that I suppose Lukács is indicating: that the essay is just a probe, which eventually must become a truth. The canonical way in which German philosophy imagined this process was in terms of a system... [*Quietly*: Hegel is a good example. His is a system in which everything is connected to each other in triadic form with the Absolute at the top.]

[*Long pause.*]

The other important question here is who writes these essays. This is not philosophy, and it isn't even the oldest form of philosophy which is the treatise; it isn't the kind of articles we write either... [*Quietly*: what most of us write today, those are not exactly essays.] It's like a talk and that's also something that is of rather distinct form. You could think of Heidegger's lectures, which are very meditative, and you can see how time was also involved, as he is slowly taking the audience through his meditations. A lot of Thomas Mann's lectures were in the form of essays. [*Pause.*] Now, it is not irrelevant that most of the essays written by Adorno were initially radio talks. They were not written for any old purpose. He didn't just say [*Impersonates Adorno*], "I have an idea and I will write a little essay about it." These radio talks were very specifically... [*Quietly*: hmm, I don't want to say timed, that doesn't sound right] but the fact that you have to think about the time when you are on-air adds a degree of formality and openness to this form of writing. Now, the historical form of the essay is also related to the social role of the person... [*Cellular phone rings*] who is producing them. Essays are... [*Cellular phone continues ringing*] we use the phrase "public intellectuals." In the former days, this was Sartre, or Lippmann here in the US,[10] but nowadays we lost this tradition, as we are all called "academics." The point about these public intellectuals is that many of them were great essayists. They were... [*Exhales deeply*] cultural commentators, who were able to freely communicate complex ideas to broad audiences. I don't want to use the word "journalism" exactly, because I think nowadays this word means something else, but they had their periodicals and journals in which they published these essays. What we call "essays" today may be indeed a matter of intellectual degradation, as we've seen with Adorno, for the term had a different meaning in the past. They were not exactly "columns," and "reviews" is also not exactly the right term. Benjamin wrote a lot of book reviews, but I wouldn't call those "essays" exactly, as they have a different form.

[*Long pause.*]

You have to think of the essay form as connected to the public sphere, and how was this public sphere organized. Is today's public sphere still a place where you have a lot of competing intellectual ideas? [*Pause.*] Mm-hmm, and if it is not, then what is the mode of circulation of ideas? Is it constrained like samizdat under socialism, or something circulating among the upper classes under the ancient regime of the eighteenth century? And the same goes for the intellectuals: were they free, like the wealthy dilettantes who used to engage in a field of study as a pastime… [*Quietly*: as the Italian term "dilettare," which means taking delight in things, suggests?] These are the sort of questions we address with regard to the history of the essay form. [*Softly.*] The figure of the essayist is then of someone who is both independent and not; someone who has the luxury to write these essays without being constrained by an academic position, which demands a certain kind of writing or form of scholarship. They respond to this demand or compulsion to constantly write… [*Quietly*: Michel de Certeau used to send every year his updated bibliography to his friends. The Jesuit intellectuals had to write, just like the Communist intellectuals used to write a lot. They knew that writing was their main business.] So, their form of production may be a little bit different, but those were the times when the form of writing was connected to the professional position. This is the position of the essayist as someone who is both autonomous and not, and that is what distinguished them from the wealthy dilettantes who were not bound by such things. We can see this relation again in the case of Montaigne. [*Pause.*] He served as the mayor of Bordeaux, which was not really an administrative position exactly… [*Quietly*: more like hereditary] and he had the luxury to pursue his intellectual interests. This condition then becomes part of the idea of the essay — you are on a walk, which is not predetermined, and you follow the turns as they come.

[*Long pause.*]

But this is Montaigne's notion of the essay. In the German modern tradition, there were a few intellectuals who served as mentors for these people... [*Quietly*: Adorno, Lukács, Benjamin.] One of them was Georg... [*Sound of chalk hitting the blackboard*] S-I-M-M-E-L. How many people read anything by Simmel? [*Silence.*] Ah, he wrote some very important... [*Achoo. Sneeze in the audience*] and you gotta read some of his writings. Simmel was very important for Benjamin's generation. There was a private seminar in Berlin organized by Simmel, and I believe Benjamin, Bloch and Lukács attended it a couple of times. Simmel did not get a professor's position for some time... [*Quietly*: because of his Jewish origin, which in Germany of that period was a great impediment.] I believe it was only very late in his life that he became a professor somewhere in Strasbourg. Simmel wrote a few books, which are very essayistic. One is called The Philosophy of Money,[11] and what you will find here is something that is even more fragmentary than Aesthetic Theory. [*Pause.*] But in his main body of writing are a few little essays, and the great one that everybody reads, and which was especially important for Benjamin, is called "The Metropolis and Mental Life."[12] Here Simmel talks about the modernist city, which was Berlin in the nineteenth century, and about money and speed and distraction... [*Cough in the audience.*] Nervousness, as it manifests in the city, plays an important part in modern culture regulated by the money economy, and the kind of thinking that people do. These are some of the motifs in Simmel's essays that you will later find in Benjamin's work... [*Quietly:* like the reproducible work of art, or the idea of social figures like outsiders and the flâneur.] Simmel was a sociologist, and he wrote on sociology, but his way of writing was very different from that of professional sociologists. [*Softly.*] Sociology as a discipline was only coming into being at that time, and if you read Weber, you can see what a [*Stressing*] professional sociologist was supposed to look like. They were not much fun to read, as they did not have this aesthetic dimension that the essay form offers; instead, they dedicated themselves to the invention of endless typologies and nomenclatures. [*Pause.*] Simmel was quite unlike that, and his essays are very enjoyable. They appeared in various collections... [*Quietly*: I can never remember the one that is in the American translation] but his writing is something between what we call "theory" or "philosophy" and belles lettres, which is a type of writing that is aware of the aesthetic qualities of language. His essays are about [*Stressing*] figures, and adventurers and the adventures of psychic forms as a form of life. This is the moment of what in the late nineteenth century was called Lebensphilosophie, or vitalism and the philosophy of life. One of these forms... [*Achoo. Sneeze in the audience*] you can see in Lukács' early writing, which is titled Soul and Form.[13] One of the forms in which — what we would call the "existential" — is able to express itself, and you could see that an adventurer... [*Quietly*: what would be the adventurers in these big cities, how would their lives crystalize itself amidst these new modern structures.] By looking at Simmel, you can get an idea of what kind of essay is prevalent in this period, and of course, in the big cities, there were the journals that published these essays. [*Pause.*] Karl Krauss was the other figure, very famous in Vienna, and he wrote everything: journalism, essays, poetry, plays, and he founded his own newspaper, Die Fackel; he also did cabaret shows. Krauss was the satirist and humorist with an extraordinary style, and he is the thinker whom Benjamin associates with the destructive character.[14] Because what is satire? [*Pause.*] It is this rage to destroy; it is this sense that everything is going down; it is someone who has a deep dissatisfaction with the status quo; it is someone for whom language is being debased. Krauss has been such a major figure, a kind of immovable reference point, a sort of independent speaking tradition for the intellectual life of these German intellectuals.

[*Long pause.*]

But the point that Adorno wants to make in the "Essay as

Form," when he states in the beginning that the essay is not well-received in Germany, is because Germany lags behind these processes of liberalization. It is a sort of fear or escape from freedom — a diagnosis that was pioneered by one of the Frankfurt School psychoanalysts who was momentarily connected to them, and that is Erich... [*Chalk on the blackboard*] F-R-O-M-M. He published a number of writings in the Frankfurt School journal, but then, little by little, separated himself from them. Fromm has produced the most famous... [*Cough in the audience*] diagnosis of fascism in that period, which influenced many of his colleagues. Adorno worked during the war on a book called The Authoritarian Personality,[15] which argued that conformity, obedience, and aggression are somehow correlated. In this book, they all invented a psychological test that you could take in order to see how close you are to being a totalitarian... [*Quietly*: by counting how many times you wash your hands, or something like that (*Chuckles*).] I think this book was the least interesting of anything that Adorno has worked on and is certainly not typical of him... [*Quietly*: the only book he published in English, and which was probably a sideline project for an American university or something.] But this idea of authoritative personality is derived from Fromm, who tried to determine personality types, their situations, and actions. In the case of Fromm, this is however a little bit different, and his famous book... [*Quietly*: I don't think that people read this anymore] is called Escape from Freedom.[16] [*Pause.*] The book was a kind of existential analysis of Nazism and of people for whom freedom provokes a state of anxiety. These people do not wish to be free, and they seek escape in authoritarian regimes or leaders who would give them a sense of security. The various forms of fascism have responded to this need, and then from the psychoanalytical point of view, this goes back into the family, and notoriously into the German family, which is a very patriarchal and dictatorial form, organized under the rule of the father. [*Pause.*] It seems to me that Adorno's analysis of the essay, and asking why the Germans don't like the essay form, is moving into that direction. Why don't the Germans like the essay? What is it that makes them nervous about it? [*Softly*.] Is it because the form is too open and free... [*Quietly*: and they don't want freedom, they are still authoritarian, they're still trained in the securities of a fixed form?] And therefore, the minute something like this practice of freedom becomes a possibility, they get nervous, opting instead for an official treatise on something, or a philosophical system, or whatever.

[*Long pause*.]

Now, this points the essay in the tradition of another form that is imported from German Romanticism on... [*Quietly*: in Schlegel, for example, and then Nietzsche] and that's the form of the... [*Chalk on the blackboard*] F-R-A-G-M-E-N-T. Much is still made of the fragment in one book by Nancy and Lacoue-Labarthe called The Literary Absolute or something like that.[17] Here, they make the fragment central to the understanding of German romantic literature, linking the fragment to the aphorism, so that the two appear as key forms of literary expression, hmm... [*Hesitates*.] But I think one would have to draw some distinction between the fragment and the aphorism. Certainly, much more than Adorno's essays, all the fragmentary writing in Nietzsche, his collections of aphorisms in a given text of Nietzsche — those would be the anti-German practice of freedom, in some sense... [*Quietly*: because there, it's not only the form but also the content that strikes at the system, especially at the philosophical system and especially at Hegel... (*Mumbles Indistinctly*).]

[*Long pause*.]

I guess with Adorno, mm-hmm... [*After prolonged reflection*.] You could take any paragraph of Aesthetic Theory and say that it is an essay on its own, which is open, and it wanders around in order to return and start all over again. But I don't know, and I ask myself whether this is not... [*Agitated*.] You see, Adorno is thinking about the essay a little bit in terms of expressionistic music, right? [*Pause*.] The essay would be this momentary expression, like one outcry of Schoenberg or Webern that would last for a minute — something in which nothing would be developed, something in which you would... [*Door creaks open*] something out. There is a nice word in German, which we don't have in English: "Einfall," which means... [*Pause.*] It means "inspiration," and you perhaps know this famous sonnet by Valéry... [*Quietly*: where he takes a predetermined line, and then the other lines have to sweat out and produce the form... (*Mumbles Indistinctly*).][18] Einfall is that kind of inspiration, but it would be a musical theme or melody that produces a little crystallization, and then you would have to work out and develop by putting a lot of things in it. With this expressionistic work, development reduces itself to the Einfall, this is one thing that is said and that's it, it is gone. [*Pause.*] Now, my sense is that it's a little bit [*Whispering*] like that that Adorno is thinking about when he talks about the essay form... [*Footsteps shuffle across the floor*] because he wants to make that sort of the description. And this is very different from the people who, on the contrary, want to have something formally developed... [*Quietly*: this is my Einfall, my first draft, then I'll make another draft, then I'll put it together, and finally, after some time, it is been sealed and delivered.] Whereas, with this momentary outburst, we don't have anything that follows a plan or course of action. So, the question now is whether Adorno actually corresponds to this form. [*Pause.*] In Minima Moralia, you do get these separate paragraphs, and for that reason they are... [*Exhales deeply*] they are Adorno's most entertaining book. And I guess those paragraphs come close to what he means by "essay." [*Softly.*] Those are the essays. He has an idea, it is part of a set of things, it is part of his themes, but on the other hand, he will develop it only for itself and then break it off. And then you have some more.

[*Long pause.*]

But here, in these actual essays, in the... [*Tap, tap. Taps his thumb on the book*] in the Notes to Literature, it seems to me that it is really much more a matter of organization. I think that here there is an aesthetic involved and a kind of, hmm...

[*Hesitates*] conceptual writing as well. An aesthetic means that you set up some rules and you cannot do certain things, and you have to figure out what you can do; it is what Adorno sometimes calls "the canon of what is forbidden,"[19] and this is a kind of stylistic aesthetic that means that there are certain things that are permissible and other things that are not. In Derrida, for example, that's very easy, as you can see that what is forbidden is to make any kind of a statement, to emit or [*Stressing*] affirm a proposition, right? The philosopher must not state anything. [*Pause.*] There is a lot that is being said in Derrida, but he himself does not make any statement that could reinforce existing assumptions, values, and power dynamics, and I think this is very problematic and requires a very difficult form... [*Quietly*: but then he occasionally nods, and then says something, but that's okay for he has transgressed himself... (*Cough in the audience*).] For those of you who read the Specters of Marx,[20] there is a chapter where Derrida decides to tell us what he thinks is wrong with the world today. But that's not Derrida anymore, for he is saying things and he is not supposed to make statements, because that's very unlike what deconstruction is. The same goes for Adorno, I think. In a sense, that's the comparability of these two aesthetics. [*Pause.*] In Adorno, you can say something, but the minute you say something you have to negate it and say the opposite. And the whole writing has to move back and forth between these two opposed operations. And then I also think there is the themes and variations side of this... [*Quietly*: we talked about it in our music session] or if you want to call it "constellation," and there you need to look at Benjamin and the notion of the "treatise," which is in his Prologue to the German Tragic Drama book... [*Quietly*: it is very mystical, but there you have the discussion of constellations.] Here, if it's about constellations, then I think it's thematic, or it also changes with regard to, hmm... [*Hesitates*] to aesthetic modes like construction, expression, mimesis. They shift and move constantly, depending on the intention of the author. And the paragraphs in Aesthetic Theory are also like pieces of music, in which one of the themes comes forward and is... [*Quietly*: I don't want to abuse the musical terminology] a sort of the dominant which is the fifth note in the scale. One theme comes forward while others are standing by in the background, and then next time they come forward while this one retreats.

[*Long pause.*]

And then one other question is: How free is the essay form? Or, how free is Adorno, who likes to talk so much about freedom? [*Pause.*] What does it mean to talk about freedom of the subject, or to criticize the Germans for their lack of freedom... [*Quietly*: which is all fine] or to work in a form that may not really be that free? This is not Montaigne wandering around through the countryside observing the world around him, hmm... [*Reflects.*] Adorno's essays have some very strict rules, which are aesthetic in principle, and which are based on this canon of what is forbidden. What you can say is very... [*Raps his knuckles on the desk.*] What counts as being said... [*Quietly*: or let's put it this way.] I think that what counts as what is theoretically being said must be very precisely defined. And I wonder whether Adorno is not, hmm... [*Hesitates.*] When you read Lukács, although Lukács is transgressing his own ideas, or Lukács is caught in orthodoxies... [*Quietly*: according to Adorno] but his ideas of freedom are more thoughtful than the ordinary sense of freedom that Adorno's essay seems to raise. [*Softly.*] Adorno's writing falls into the kind of contradiction that he himself talks about when he criticizes twelve-tone music... [*Zipper unzipping*] he himself is caught up in his own genre, so to speak... [*Quietly*: which is the problematic of the essay as form.] In modern music, the question is: When you get rid of tonality is everything still free...? [*Achoo. Sneeze in the audience*] Or as it turns out, nothing is permanent once you move into the twelve-tone. There is a dialectic of freedom and constraint here. The great aesthetic question here to ask is: If you give yourself your own harsh laws, are you free or are you constrained? [*Pause.*] You freely adopt those laws, but they are much more difficult to obey than anything that was called "freedom" in some older dispensation. I think this is the kind of issues that the essay, and Adorno's aesthetic in general, raises.

[*Long pause.*]

Now, one other thing is the whole notion of the essayistic, and I don't think Adorno touches on this, although there has been a lot of discussion. For example, Musil. [*Addresses the audience.*] How many people here have read some Musil? [*Silence.*] How much of that is essay? Is there something like the essayistic digression, I mean, there are pages and pages of Proust that are not novel-writing anymore, but they are really essays. His famous attack on Sainte-Beuve,[21] or his translations of Ruskin.[22] And what's odd is that the essays in early Proust then produce the characters, when the essay begins by talking about "Sainte-Beuve and Balzac,"[23] or when it criticizes Saint-Beuve's method... [*Quietly*: his literary criticism that relied heavily on biographies] and then Proust's novelistic characters emerge from these essays, but as readers and writers of the essay. [*Pause.*] And in Musil too, you have the emergence of these long essayistic passages — are those still essays, or what are they?

[*Long pause.*]

And then consider film, and the New Wave in France. [*Pause.*] Alexandre Astruc, I believe, he was the one to talk about the "film essay,"[24] and I don't think that he meant the documentary... [*Quietly*: I mean, you could say the documentary is to fiction-film what an essay would be to the novel.] But then, within the film, you could have a kind of essayistic movement line in Godard, who is often classified in this way. For example, when Godard is looking at inexpensive migrant workers' housing, well, how much of that is part of the story... [*Quietly*: or his other older film about white-collar prostitution, or occasional prostitution of housewives, and polygamy[25]], how much of that is part of the story or only the background? Every new critic would ask what is the unity of this work, and is the whole digression on the low-cost housing necessary? Or is that only the background for the characters? Well, it is not clear, maybe the characters are there only to allow these digressions, and you get more and more of these marks of freedom of form. The form is immensely free in Godard, because he does anything he wants — he can pause and show you graffiti, or words and images, or he can break the fourth wall by commenting into the camera, and all other kinds of deviations and digressions. [*Pause*.] But then, the question is to what degree... [*Takes a sip of water*.] I guess for us here today, the real question is to what degree is this related to what Adorno calls Entkunstung... [*Quietly*: you remember we talked about this word that Hullot-Kentor translated as "deaesthetization," but which is not good.] I would say "dearting," which is often understood as the blurring of the distinction between art and life, or the disappearance of the artistic form.. [*Door slams shut*] and the way in which, now, artistic freedom consists not in imposing laws on yourself, like in the twelve-tone system, but rather in this form of spillage, when you can move into another medium, or into another genre, or into whatever other... [*Smacks his palm on the desk*.]

[*Long pause*.]

Since this question of freedom is very central for the essay form, and for Aesthetic Theory, we could also ask: Is Adorno systematic? This is another important question. We know that Adorno is not capable of a... [*Exhales deeply*.] He is not unrigorous, you certainly cannot refuse him in lack of rigor but, on the other hand, does his work withstand what traditional philosophers would call... [*Quietly*: I remember this question once addressed to me by a philosopher.] Can you sustain your argument? [*Pause*.] For philosophers, this is a big question; philosophers are not just about thinking, but they are also about [*Stressing*] sustaining an argument. Does or can Adorno sustain an argument? [*Pause*.] Maybe not so much. If you look at the end of his Negative Dialectics, where he comes up with all those models... [*Quietly*: we talked about this and I am repeating myself here] but he's got a model for metaphysics, he's got one for being, and so on. Well, I would say that they are long essay digressions on these themes, but they are not arguments because they don't aim to sustain a set of propositions. [*Pause*.] What is in crisis in Adorno, and in deconstruction, is the philosophical proposition; it is the idea that you could make a statement and defend it once and for all because, out of this defense, something very important comes.

[*Long pause.*]

Okay, now let's try to go back to what I think becomes our major question in this seminar. You've read enough of Adorno by now to have some thoughts about these two things called "truth content" and "second reflection"... [*Two students whisper indistinctly near the microphone.*] But what are these things? [*Pause.*] Can somebody tell me what you think, or what comes to your mind, when you read this expression "truth content"...

[*Long silence.*]

[*Agitated.*] Oh, you may have misunderstood me — there is no one correct answer. [*Chuckles.*] These are the two enigmatic ideas that Adorno thinks he knows what they mean, but on the other hand, the very constellation method suggests that they could look quite different in different places. If you decide to follow these two ideas through, you may not necessarily find a definition... [*Quietly*: there is a famous reference in Nietzsche, I don't know where, where he attacks the very idea of definitions.] How could you define something, Nietzsche says, unless you knew what it was ahead of time? [*Pause.*] What would a definition in philosophy be, right? It could only be a starting point... [*Quietly*: it is like development in music] it changes and acquires greater conceptual richness from a starting point. Definitions are not, hmm... [*Hesitates*] but nonetheless, we need to have some basic notions. [*Softly.*] So, what do you think is "truth content" and "second reflection" in Adorno?

[*Long silence.*]

STUDENT TWO: Could "truth content" be something like a Socratic gesture? In Socrates, definitions are about the nature of something, of virtues, or about essences...

JAMESON: Right, yeah, hmm... [*Hesitates.*] I think something like that may be going on here to some degree, but we've already seen that truth content, it's not about meaning exactly, or the essence of things. It is not, hmm... [*Hesitates.*] What else it is not? It's not about intention, not about meaning. There is a whole series of things, or these so-called definitions that the truth content, it's not... And we know also that Adorno is very much opposed to the philosophers of ineffability, that means people who say that the most important things are things that escape language. [*Pause.*] You have two of those, and they are quite different: one is Heidegger, where truth somehow appears but language is certainly not capable to articulate it; and the other... [*Quietly*: or at least a part of the other that's reserved for ineffable] is Wittgenstein of the Tractatus, with his famous what you cannot talk about you must remain silent.[26] Adorno is certainly opposed to the idea that there are things that you can't say or talk about. Why does he say this? [*Long pause.*] Let me put it to you in another way. Adorno says himself here that the problem with aesthetics has always been that it is not good for anything practical. Philosophers can write books about questions of aesthetics, but when it comes to artworks themselves, what good are these aesthetic questions for the artist...? [*Quietly*: Who said it? One of the famous artists who once said something like "aesthetic is for me like ornithology is for birds."[27]] So, then I repose the same question to you about this piece of aesthetics: What is "truth content" good for?

STUDENT THREE: I was under the impression that part of the "truth content" of art has to do with the author's intentions, insofar that it constitutes a part of the work. [*Pause.*] Adorno sees the "truth content" of a work of art as something that is embedded in the production process, and everything that is involved in that: the artist's intentions, the actual objective materials, the historical intentions that the artist raises in the work. I think that this is what inspires the artist to do that. I kind of see what Adorno is getting at here, but the truth content maybe is something which, as we discussed when we talked about the "new," only reveals itself to consciousness [*Stressing*] after the fact, and too late to be fully understood.

JAMESON: Yeah, but you said, "part of the work," and so you don't answer the question. But yes, sure, all those things you've mentioned are part of the truth content, but what is it that they are part of? [*Pause.*] I think this sounds a bit like Forster's lady, who says: "How do I know what I think till I see what I say?"[28] Right? The artist thinks he has a thought, but how does he know what he really thinks until he says it... [*Whispering*] until he makes the artwork? And then once the artist made the work, it may be rather different. Hmm... [*Hesitates.*] Yeah, I think you are absolutely right, but that doesn't tell us what truth content is, or what good is its aesthetics in practical terms? That's what I'm trying to answer...

[*Long silence.*]

STUDENT FOUR: Can we say that the truth content gives you some validity about the world, or that it enables some truth about history, culture, and all those things...? [*Pause.*]

JAMESON: But how? How would that take place? Is this validity in your own reaction to the artwork? [*Pause.*] It allows you to discover things, hmm... [*Hesitate.*] But wouldn't that just bring us back into something very subjective, which is not even the [*Stressing*] effect of the work, like I find Beckett very funny, or I find him very depressing. That's more like a viewer's response in some Kantian effect, but... [*Softly*] what good is it otherwise? That makes the work of art look like an instrument of self-knowledge, or like a Litmus test that would respond to the question: "How do you react to?" or "How do you react to that?"

STUDENT FIVE: Maybe it brings in the distinction between particular works of art, and art as a concept, or universal form, which, per Hegel's terms, is in charge of the consciousness and truth?

JAMESON: On the concept of art? Well, I think this is one of the most interesting things in Adorno, the distinction between the concept of art and the individual work. He seems to imply that there is a gap between them. [*Pause.*] So, whereas art itself is in crisis... [*Quietly*: art as social institution] no individual work can save it from that crisis nor, hmm... [*Looks for words*] nor disprove it, hmm... [*Hesitates.*] I think that you are right, and this distinction would have to play a role in this, yeah, hmm...

STUDENT SIX: I don't know if this helps, but can we think about the truth content in terms of the ancient Greek sculptures... [*Words indistinct.*] It's like when every philosophy has its material presuppositions that it tries to dress up without getting at what's underneath, you know what I mean?

JAMESON: Mm-hmm... [*After prolonged reflection.*] Not quite. You're using various kinds of inherited languages, which have their own philosophical connotations, to put into words something that is in fact antagonistic... [*Footsteps. Door creaks open.*] But that's also negative, and we are looking for a positive notion, like a... [*Mumbles indistinctly.*]

STUDENT SEVEN: Maybe it has to do with the crisis of art, and the social crisis in modernity and how difficult it is for the content of art to represent it. Maybe this notion of "truth content" has to do with this relationship between art and social crisis in the modern age, and the difficulties or even impossibilities for art to put into form the social material, or the contradictions of this age? Could that be something like that...? [*Pause.*]

JAMESON: I think that makes some sense. I get the feeling most of the time that what Adorno is saying is that there is a general social crisis out there... [*Quietly*: the society doesn't function as it used to, and so on and so forth.] But we can't grasp that crisis [*Stressing*] immediately, through the content of the work of art, but only through its form and through the increasing difficulty for the form to express this crisis of the social. [*Pause.*] It is through the crisis of the form of the work of art that the social crisis is mediated and conveyed. That sort of brings us to the inside and the outside of the artwork... [*Quietly*: and this is a long discussion in one of his chapters about the monad.] What's the matter with the monad... [*Cough in the audience.*] Isn't the monad this idea of a windowless ontology where everybody and everything is a kind of monad?

The indivisible entities that are the basic building blocks of life and where everything, even a stone or a rock, has a kind of life. These monads are immaterial and have no spatial extension, yet they overlap somehow. And why is a monad windowless? It is because everything is included in it — the entire cosmos is part of my monad, so what would I need a window for... [*Quietly*: if everything is already included in my world and there is no outside?] And so often Adorno is saying that the work of art is the windowless monad, right? [*To himself*: What page he is talking about this] yes, page 180, or actually page 179. [*Starts reading*.] "As an element," I think that's how... [*Raps his knuckles on the desk*] this translator is translating "moment"... [*Quietly*: which is a very funny Hegelian word, it's not the same word as a moment of time, it's a different term... (*Mumbles indistinctly*) and it means sort of an aspect of something.] "As a [moment] of an overarching context of the spirit of an epoch, entwined with spirit and society, artworks go beyond their monadic limit even though they lack windows."[29] Well, this is something that he's been saying all along — that you can't understand the inside unless you posit an outside, that is the outside of... [*Pause*] even though you can't see this outside of it. Does this make any sense? [*Silence*.] You have to experience the work historically, socially... [*Quietly*: this is the outside] even though all you have there is the inside, or the aesthetic. I think some of this is involved in this crisis of form — the social crisis of the outside. Inside, all we have is the aesthetic crisis of form, but that's the outside, that monadic crisis of form inside the monad [*Stressing*] <u>is</u> the outside. And if we don't see the two together, we don't experience the work. This is the way I understand it... [*Chair-back creaks*] and why is it such a problem is because it will be different with each work of art. Each artwork... [*Quietly*: but it must be a real work of art and that's an important category too, where Adorno says, (*Impersonates Adorno*) "Look, are there bad works of art? You can't accept that."] Because, if we say there are bad works of art, then it means that it does not work as a work of art. If it's bad, it means it doesn't work as art. Every successful work of art is a work of art and otherwise it's mush. This is a little bit like de Man's notion of the text, because, for de Man, not everything is a text — only those things are text which do what he says texts do [*Softly*] — they deconstruct themselves. And if they don't do that, then it's not a text but mush. It's ideology... [*Door slams shut.*] So, this is a very basic problem for any aesthetics; should an aesthetics deal with good and bad works or does it just [*Stressing*] assume the good works and leave the rest of them out. Remember, we had a similar sort of question answered in a different way, when we talked how an aesthetics should deal with, hmm... [*Looks for words*] not only deal with people who can experience works of art, but also with people who are resentful of art, people who hate art and people who are philistines, that is, they have no sense of art. [*Pause.*] Those evidently are aesthetics terms that are meant to deal with everything [*Stressing*] but the bad works of art.

[*Long pause.*]

Therefore, every work of art has its truth content... [*Quietly*: by definition, that's what this means, and that bad works of art are those that have no truth content.] Only good or real art has truth content, or only what has truth content is art for Adorno... [*Quietly*: you can turn it either way, if you want.] Now, I think that means that truth content also means the [*Stressing*] right kind of experiencing a work of art. But we must also learn to distinguish truth content from the existential experience, so it has to be a slight gap between me listening to this piece of music, or reading this book, and its truth content; it has to be something that I do to this experience, but I don't do things to it far enough to turn it into examples of my philosophy, or into my ideology... [*Quietly*: like when you say that the experience of this work of art shows this or it proves that, and so on.] You don't translate the work into a different language. It must remain in the language of art, but it must not exactly be the work of art anymore or its effect... [*Quietly*: does this make any sense?] [*Silence.*] I think the easiest way to think about it is that, in a work of art, the aesthetical and the historical situations have to come together; we have to understand our experience of the work of art as the response to a situation, as the solution of a contradiction which is always historical. The work of art is not [*Stressing*] <u>about</u> that history, it is not [*Stressing*] <u>about</u> that contradiction, but until we understand our immediate experience of the work of art, until we frame that as a solution to a situation, we haven't found its truth content. And that's where the idea of art comes, because that would be another way to talk about contradictions; it's gonna be the social contradictions that have to be solved and the contradictions in the very idea of art itself, that the social contradictions are mediated by and that the work tries to solve... [*Quietly*: it doesn't matter if it fails or not] and nor does it matter if it's ideological... [*Quietly*: because Adorno says, and we know that a lot of great artists are reactionaries...]

STUDENT THREE: So, the historical contradictions are part of the moment of experiencing the art, or the moment of art's creation?

JAMESON: [*Softly.*] Now you've asked a very embarrassing question. [*Audience laughing.*] Well, it certainly has to do with the time. You see, all these people are telling us, "Oh, Baudelaire is the first great modern poet." That means all kind of new things happened in that time with which we don't have anything to do with, for [*Stressing*] <u>that</u> historical moment of Baudelaire is all gone anyway, right? But when we read Baudelaire, do we reinvent that moment? [*Pause.*] And can we understand the things that are new again, or is that a purely philological or archeological thing, where you try to figure out how did the artist do it, and how did the readers of the period feel about it...? [*Quietly*: That's what they do in art history by trying to figure out what was going on, or "the way it really was."[30]] Or is Baudelaire's spirit still alive, and if it's still alive, does it still contain the historical moment in it? I think Adorno would say

... [*Impersonates Adorno*] "Look, there were a number of things that were new that we can't even feel anymore." Take radio, for example... [*Quietly*: do you understand what kind of experience that could have been, or the electric lights to begin with.] There is a passage in Lacan's Seminars where he talks about Socrates on his way to the symposium, and it's getting dark and he says to his companion, "Go ahead, I will meet you there," while he stands there in the dark.[31] Then Lacan says, [*Impersonates Lacan*] "But we can't know what the dark was, we have never lived in a world in which we did not have this possibility of lighting things up at night." So, electricity, radio, these are positive innovations which we lose the sense of, but the negative taboos, maybe we don't lose, and we can still understand why in Baudelaire you had to say it this way — because it was not possible to say it another way. [*Pause.*] It seems to me this is the way one recreates the situation you are talking about, and the moment in which this is alive. But obviously, then you gotta involve some kind of Benjaminian notion that there is a connection between our moment and that moment in the past, or that there is a force that Benjamin calls blasting open the continuum of history.[32] There is some sort of elective affinity and there are parts of the past to which we are closer than the others, or that there are things like that in which your possibilities of connecting up with the situation is transformed, but this does not seem to be a part of what he is reflecting on here.

STUDENT THREE: But doesn't the "I," or the personal experience of the work, compromises or prevents the work of art from being accessible across periods of...?

JAMESON: No, no... [*Agitated.*] Okay, but then we get to the question of subject and object. This is the... [*Door cracks open. Footsteps*] of the object; remember, he keeps saying it over and over again, the "I" is no longer a personal subject. It is this moment when the personal subject is sort of blasted out of existence by the moment of astonishment. [*Pause.*] And I think what you are talking about is the personal experience of the individuals reading it, and you are also talking about the historical situation. That's there fully as much as with the artist and the readership in that period. [*Pause.*] So, in a way, maybe you can say that it's not that an individual reads another individual, but the first individual, the reader, comes out of a moment of history, or situation of history, the writer comes out of the moment of history, and these two moments of history talk to each other through the medium of the two people involved... [*Chairs scraping across the floor.*] Adorno will say here in one of these chapters that the artist is an instrument of these two moments... [*Door slams shut*] the artist is a recording apparatus for the time, or for the main contradictions of the period in which the artist lives. When we talk about genius... [*Quietly*: and this is a long discussion about this notion, as many of them are ideological, no doubt] but it also probably refers to somebody who is depersonalized enough to pick up all of these vibrations. Genius is not somebody... [*Footsteps shuffle*] who has a powerful artistic personality, which needs to be expressed, but somebody who has no personality at all, perhaps. Or you could think of it in terms of artistic subjectivity being an instrument for registering objectivity, and that would be as true of the reader... [*Zipper zipping up*] as well as of the writer. Anyway, what time is it, I think we went well beyond our time...

STUDENT: It's 12:45...

JAMESON: 12:45, oh, that's late, let's break it for now... [*Chairs scraping against the floor.*]

Audience stands up. Objects drop on the floor. Door squeaking. Students returning chairs to other classrooms. Zippers zipping up. Some in the audience form a line to discuss their assignments with Jameson. General noise. Screeching microphone noise.

[*Microphone turns off.*]

CURTAIN

LECTURE TWENTY

APRIL 15, 2003

NIETZSCHE, *THE BIRTH OF TRAGEDY* — SCHOPENHAUER — THE ARTWORK (CHAPTER)

CURTAIN RISES

Moving chairs, squeaking door, coughs, other sounds filling the noise environment of a large classroom in the Literature Department at Duke University. One graduate student entertains his friends by reading a front-page article from the University's daily, The Chronicle. *The article reports on this year's rankings for the best American graduate schools.* [Starts reading.] *"The School of Law, after falling out of the top 10 last year, stayed put at No. 12, while the School of Business slipped a spot to No. 7... 'We are very surprised that the law's school rankings did not improve this year,' said the Dean of the School of Law..."*[1]

Jameson enters the classroom carrying a few books, his scattered notes, and the red pen in the chest pocket of his flannel shirt.

[Microphone turns on.]

JAMESON: ... [*Footsteps. Chairs scratching against the floor.*] A few words about your incompletes. If you're planning to graduate, I will need your papers by the end of April, because I might not likely be here during the summer, and I don't want any last-minute emergencies. I can give you another prolongation, if you tell me I need it till fall, but I would need to know that beforehand... [*Door creaks open. More footsteps. Zippers unzipping.*] I'm telling you that because there are people, and I've met quite of few of them, who suddenly wake up in the middle of the summer to realize that they have incompletes and cannot graduate, and then I have to deal with... [*Mumbles indistinctly. Chuckles.*] So, remember, for those of you who plan to get incompletes, keep track of your timing, because a lot of things are going on and it's not always possible for us to pay attention to these things. Do we have anyone who plans to graduate this year?

STUDENT: I am graduating...

STUDENT: Me too... [*Zipper unzipping.*]

JAMESON: Oh, so only you two are graduating. Let's talk after class. Come see me... [*Pause.*]

[*Long pause.*]

Okay, we are approaching the end of this course and we still have several exposés. We have one on Nietzsche, and then we also have another one on film, as far as I remember...

STUDENT: I will present on film next time.

JAMESON: Ah, okay then. So why don't we go ahead with Nietzsche today. [*Addresses student.*] Are you coming forward?

[*Chair legs scratching against the floor. Footsteps.*]

Student Presentation: Nietzsche, The Birth of Tragedy

STUDENT ONE: I wrote something on The Birth of Tragedy, and I really wanted to also say something about Wagner, because he was a very significant figure for The Birth of Tragedy.

[*Page flipping. Starts reading.*]

In 1886, when Nietzsche was intensely working on his later books... [*Quietly*: Beyond Good and Evil, On the Genealogy of Morals] he had a chance to make a critique of one of his early works called The Birth of Tragedy. [*Pause.*] Nietzsche wrote

"An Attempt at Self-Criticism" as a prefatory essay to the new edition of The Birth of Tragedy... [*Quietly*: the first 1872 edition was called The Birth of Tragedy Out of the Spirit of Music, and this one from 1886 with a new introduction was called The Birth of Tragedy, Or: Hellenism and Pessimism.] In "An Attempt at Self-Criticism," he writes that the book was the product of a young mind... [*Quietly*: Nietzsche published it when he was only 28 years old, working on it during the Franco-Prussian war while he briefly served as nursing assistant.] He calls the book questionable and premature because it was... [*Quietly*: I quote:] "constructed from nothing but precocious and underripe personal experiences."[2] [*Pause*.] The Birth of Tragedy, he continues, is a book for artists... [*Clears throat*] that delves into the intricate connection between morality and science; it is a book that considers the problem of science from the position of art... [*Quietly*: I quote:] "Already in the foreword addressed to Richard Wagner, art — and not morality — is established as the real metaphysical activity of man; in the book itself the suggestive proposition that the existence of the world is only justified as an aesthetic phenomenon recurs several times."[3] Later, Nietzsche continues that, after fifteen years from the date of first publication of The Birth of Tragedy, the book appears unpleasant to him, due to the way he handled it, although he also adds that his eyes did not grow colder, nor was his interest for looking at science from the perspective or optic of the artist, and at art from the perspective or optic of life.

[*Long pause*.]

Although The Birth of Tragedy was primarily an essay on aesthetics, it was also Nietzsche's early attempts to overcome nihilism, which, according to Heidegger, was a failure. Heidegger discusses Nietzsche's nihilism through his main themes, which are the death of God, the transvaluation of all values, the eternal return of the same, and the will to power... [*Door creaks open*] arguing that Nietzsche did not succeed in overcoming nihilism but instead intensified it.[4] [*Clears throat*.] In The Birth of Tragedy, art and philosophy not only have parallel histories, but they also share the calling to represent the truth. Nietzsche writes in The Case of Wagner... [*Quietly*: I quote:] "one becomes more of a philosopher the more one becomes a musician."[5] Nietzsche's artistic perspective on life, the tragic wisdom and art are represented through the tremendous figure of the Dionysian artist. Following Friedrich Schlegel's concept of the Dionysian and the Apollonian, Nietzsche develops the opposition between these two drives or gods of Greek attic tragedy. The Apollonian represents reason, order, and restraint, and was associated... [*Achoo. Sneeze in the audience*] with sense of order and clarity in art. The Homeric Apollonian artist is using the power of reason to create beautiful images, and this is an interpretation of life, as the Apollonian is associated with the dream, the clarity of illusion and the image of reality. [*Pause.*] By contrast, the Dionysian, which is typified by the lyric poetry of Archilochus... [*Quietly*: a seventh-century BC poet] and the odes of Pindar... [*Quietly*: fifth century BC] is using language to imitate music and the primordial pain that is part of musical origins, and is associated with the chaotic, irrational, and emotional side of art. This distinction between these two forms of art... [*Quietly*: the Archilochus, which is lyric and Homeric, that corresponds to the Greek epic] draws on Schopenhauer's difference to suggest two forms of artistic expression. One is will, or expression of pain, as is the case of music, and the other is the Platonic idea, which draws on the principle of individuation. Instead of the dream and longing for beauty, the Dionysian drive is presented through the analogy of intoxication. [*Pause.*] The Dionysian drive also embodies the collective bonds, represented in the chorus and the orgiastic, or the dancing and singing of people under the influence, or the spell of Dionysus, and we have the association between emotion and representation. Whereas Homer's heroes belong to the ground of individuality, the Dionysian Archilochus poetry is part of the folk songs... [*Sound of blowing nose*] collectivity and the chorus. The Dionysian sense of tragedy is the ultimate way of revealing the truth, a way of having access to the will, which is beyond the phenomenon. As

Nietzsche writes... [*Quietly*: I quote:] "the chorus already expresses in allegorical form that original relationship between thing-in-itself and phenomenon."[6]

[*Page flipping.*]

But beyond the rather schematic, and in many ways old-fashioned dualities, Nietzsche finds in The Birth of Tragedy his voice, which is the Dionysian voice... [*Chair-back creaks*] the voice of Zarathustra. This new voice... [*Quietly*: I quote:] "should have sung, this 'new soul' — rather than spoken. What a pity that I did not dare to say what I had to say then as a poet: I might have managed it!"[7] From this Dionysian point of view, morality and Christianity... [*Quietly*: "Christianity" is Nietzsche's later word, for he barely mentions Christianity in the initial 1871 version of The Birth of Tragedy, but later Christianity emerges as his main target] so, morality and Christianity are signs of decline and sickness. [*Pause.*] Similarly, science and scholarship only appear as a kind of fear, and escape from pessimism, "a refined means of self-defense against — the truth."[8] [*Clears throat.*] The duality of the Apollonian and the Dionysian is young Nietzsche's view on the historical development of art, with "Apollonian spirit" leading to decline. The Apollonian principle still persists, but now somewhat in a weaker form, that of concept, form, or logic, whereas the Dionysian one is unrepresentable and unintelligible. [*Pause.*] Apollo is sometimes associated with appearance and, as for the German Romantics... [*Quietly*: like Schiller or Goethe] it has to do with aesthetic illusion that one could say holds a veil over the natural phenomena associated with Dionysus. In the Attic tragedy, the chorus is immersed in life to the point that, according to Nietzsche... [*Quietly*: I quote:] "there was at bottom no opposition between public and chorus."[9] In contrast, Euripides... [*Quietly*: who is one of the key culprits responsible for the decline of tragedy] he limits the role of the chorus and brings the spectator to stage. Euripides's heroes are human beings — they are no longer faces of gods hiding behind the masks of actors, but instead a naturalistic display of human weakness. [*Pause.*] To Euripides, drama corresponds to Socrates's formulation, "everything must be understandable in order to be beautiful.... "[10] [*Page flipping.*] Socrates was to philosophy what Euripides was to tragedy. With Socrates comes the decline of the ancient tradition of anarchic instinctive force because, from now on, we have the arrival of the [*Stressing*] theoretical man. For the theoretical man, there is no realm of knowledge beyond knowledge, and his optimism is sort of mindless... [*Footsteps. Door slams shut.*] The theoretical man, like the artist, takes an infinite satisfaction in the present, but while the artist, in his relation of the truth... [*Quietly*: I quote:] "remains perpetually fixed on the truth which has been unveiled but remains even now a veil, the theoretical man derives delight and satisfaction rather from the discarded veil and finds his greatest pleasure in a happy process of unveiling which always succeeds through its own efforts."[11] [*Quietly*: end quote.] Therefore, with the new way of understanding the world, the great culture becomes more superficial.

[*Long pause.*]

This is now the moment in which Wagner appears in Nietzsche's writings... [*Stops reading. Explains.*] Nietzsche was thinking about Greek tragedy in terms of the German nation, because Nietzsche thought that Germany was different from the Western civilization, from what he called sometimes as "Socratic culture" and "Alexandrian culture," of the theoretical man. [*Pause.*] He saw in Wagner's music, which relied on Nordic myth and primordial rites, the opportunity of reviving the tragedy, in the sense that, for Wagner, the chorus and the orchestra, hmm... [*Hesitates*] and the orchestration was like going back to Aeschylus. He saw in Wagner an embodiment of the Dionysian spirit, and a power capable to restore art to its ancient tragic form and thus reverse the decline. But this was still in his youth when he was writing The Birth of Tragedy. Gradually, his relationship with the Wagners... [*Quietly*: also with Wagner's second wife, Cosima, with whom Nietzsche was in love] soured when he published in 1876 the essay "Richard Wagner in Bayreuth," and later he also published some other anti-Wagner books, like Nietzsche against Wagner, and then another one was The Case of Wagner.[12] Here he complains about Wagner, whom he found very close to Christianity, and Nietzsche at this point is against Christianity, and so he complains that Wagner was strongly Christian... [*Pause.*] Nietzsche recognizes in Wagner the skill for expressing suffering, which is very important for the Dionysian... [*Chair scrapes against the floor*] artist, or for pure artistic creation, but at the same time Wagner was very, hmm... [*Hesitates*] megaloman... [*Quietly*: is this an English word...?]

JAMESON: Megalomaniac.

STUDENT ONE: Yes, Wagner was very megalomaniac, especially the late Wagner, so Nietzsche was against it. [*Pause.*] That's it. It's very short. I'm done.

[*Audience applauding.*]

JAMESON: Okay, how many people have...?

[*Applauding continues.*]

JAMESON: Okay, questions?

STUDENT TWO: I have a question. Could you very briefly tell us how do you think Nietzsche's overall aesthetics in The Birth of Tragedy relates to, hmm... [*Hesitates*] or parallels Adorno's aesthetics? I was wondering if you are thinking about that, I mean, that would be very cool because I couldn't myself see a relation...

STUDENT ONE: Neither do I...

[*Audience laughing.*]

STUDENT ONE: I'm sorry, I've been reading Nietzsche for some time, but I only encountered Adorno in this class, and haven't spent enough time with him to be able to answer your question...

JAMESON: Other questions?

[*Long silence.*]

JAMESON: Okay, that was very useful, because we haven't talked much about Nietzsche here, and obviously he was very important for Adorno. Nietzsche was also very present in

Thomas Mann, as we've seen in... [*Quietly*: you remember that the figure of Adrian Leverkühn was modeled on Nietzsche] and there too, there is this combination of opposites moving back and forth throughout the novel: the Apollonian humanism of Zeitblom and the Dionysian darkness in Leverkühn... [*Mumbles indistinctly*.] With Wagner too, this opposition is very present, as is this notion of the Total Work of Art, that is... [*Chalk on the blackboard*] G-E-S-A-M-T-K-U-N-S-T-W-E-R-K, which manifests in Wagner's opera, for example, in how the visual and the imagery in the staging, and the lighting is opposed to the musical. In some sense, the Apollonian and Dionysian, the plastic and the sonorous, meet in the Total Work of Art. This divide runs deep, and in Germany, you may often come across this division between an "eye person" and an "ear person." Everybody is divided into these categories of Augenmensch and Ohrenmensch, that is, those who are primarily visual and those who are phonic, acoustical... [*Quietly*: sometimes they also use the term "aural"] — and that is also part of this central Nietzschean opposition, I think.

[*Long pause*.]

And indeed, this is a very funny book... [*Quietly*: The Birth of Tragedy] and I would encourage you to consider that the Apollonian and the Dionysian here are not very symmetrical oppositions. Too often you have combinations, so that, within each one, there could be an "Apollonian/Dionysian" or "Dionysian/Dionysian" and vice versa. But overall, it is a very odd book to read if you try to think about these oppositions in symmetrical terms. Mm-hmm. I think you are right about Christianity, that is important, but it is also important to go back a little bit, hmm... [*Hesitates*.] Well, let's talk about that. In Nietzsche's vision of history, there are two great villains. One is Socrates, and you said it quite rightly that the moment when knowledge appears... [*Quietly*: logic, self-knowledge, rational thought, knowledge of other things] we are beyond this primal realm of purely irrational, intuitive, and chaotic behavior. Now, alongside the emergence of knowledge, there is also the figure of

Christ, who, for Nietzsche, is the second great villain, because with Christianity then comes the domination of the weak over the strong. How is this working out? And is this really fascist? [*Pause.*] I take the position that if it could be used for fascism, then it's pre-fascist, whatever Nietzscheans will tell you... [*Audience chuckles.*] Nietzsche was not an antisemite like his horrible sister...[13] [*Quietly*: who used her brother's work to promote her own political beliefs; she established the Nietzsche archives in Weimer, or was also involved with her husband in setting up the nationalist settlement "Nueva Germania" in Paraguay.] Nietzsche was not an antisemite... [*Quietly*: he hated the new German Reich, founded by Bismarck in 1871] and he thought that the German bourgeoisie was the worst among other kinds of bourgeois; he was a Francophile; he had a passion for the French moralists, like Pascal and Stendhal. Finally, even after the whole Wagner infatuation, he comes to something, which is maybe a little strange for us, namely, he abandons Wagner for Bizet's Carmen [*Chuckles.*] It's a little bit like when Stravinsky said that he would give all of Schoenberg for one melody of Tchaikovsky, and I think you could interpret this as a sort of negation of negation — it's not just philistinism, but it must be something else.

[*Long pause.*]

But what you need to understand about him, and the fact that Nietzsche ends up in Switzerland... [*Quietly*: he was a classics professor in what became the great age of classics at the University of Basel.] You remember that Switzerland also plays an important part for Thomas Mann, who escapes from the Nazis. The Swiss are the Western Germans, and therefore they are considered the cultured ones, the French ones, and thus free from the original sin of the other Germanic... [*Quietly*: Lutheran, diabolical, irrational... (*Mumbles indistinctly*).] So, this relation between West and East is also in Nietzsche, and it is very difficult to give this up. And like Mann, I would also think that Nietzsche would have thought that the Nazis were crude and boorish... [*Microphone distortions*] and would not share Hitler's taste, expect maybe in the matter of Wagner. Now, regarding the domination of the weak over the strong: what does this mean? [*Pause.*] I think the most persuasive re-working of Nietzsche for us is Deleuze, and in Deleuze this becomes the active and the reactive force. The weak is whenever your position is [*Stressing*] reactive on another one, that is when it is passive and reactive to the world around you, hmm... [*Hesitates*] that is to say, there is a certain kind of subconsciousness in which you are positioning yourself as the Other of some vital life... [*Cough in the audience.*] Deleuze's book on Nietzsche is a great book,[14] and I recommend it to you very strongly. [*Exhales deeply.*] And for Heidegger, on the other hand, The Will to Power is simply Aristotelian energeia, that is, the actualization or being-at-work of a force in the world — it is the realization of the thing's full potential... [*Quietly*: it's not power in the sense of a particular willing or... (*Mumbles indistinctly*) authority.] Therefore, I think there are ways of looking at Nietzsche which are quite different from the most critical interpretations of him... [*Quietly*: but the critical is there too; you can't really get away from that entirely, I think.]

[*Long pause.*]

But where does all of this come from...? [*Door creaks open.*] It is Schopenhauer. You know that Schopenhauer was Hegel's great enemy... [*Quietly*: Schopenhauer used to schedule his classes at the same time as Hegel's, because anybody who would go to Hegel's classes meant that he didn't want them in his... (*Audience laughing*) but unfortunately, the result was that Schopenhauer only had like three students.] Even before Kierkegaard, Schopenhauer was the great anti-dialectician, the anti-Hegelian, and the main source of this is to be found in what the European intellectuals of that generation and the previous one was only discovering, and this is namely Eastern Buddhism. Now, the... [*Pause.*] Hmm... [*Hesitates*] the... [*Pause*] and... [*Loses his train of thought.*] Oh yeah, and on top of these Oriental spiritual influences, you also have the [*Stressing*] absolute glamorization of music in Schopenhauer. Here, music is the great philosophical art; it is the source of the unconscious reality of the world. Well, before Nietzsche, it was Schopenhauer who expressed this connection between music, intoxication, the unconscious, and a genuine philosophy of music... [*Quietly*: I think Schopenhauer preferred Beethoven, but he was in touch with other people of his time, with Goethe, for example. Goethe, on the other hand, admired Mozart, and he thought that Mozart should have really written an opera called Faust. Goethe, on the other hand, was very suspicious of Beethoven, because he thought the emotions were too extreme, too stormy, and violent, so he felt that this paused some kind of danger, and I think I quoted one day this famous remark, which is very complicated but... (*Pause*). "Romanticism," Goethe says about this younger generation of people, "romanticism is the sick, and classicism is the healthy,"[15] because, as you know, Schiller and Goethe called their neoclassicism classicism.] Well, I think there is something there — Goethe suspected Beethoven of being too romantic, whereas the classical composers were different. So, in some way, we get the same musical opposition, like Mozart being the Apollonian and Beethoven the Dionysian force. We can also connect the Apollonian/Dionysian to Kant's opposition of the beautiful and the sublime. [*Pause*.] Adorno makes this point over and over again, but I think it's important for us to realize that Kant did not make a place for the sublime in art. He thought that the business of art was with the beautiful, and that the experience of the sublime was an experience of nature. Adorno then points out that one of the great evolutions in the history of art, beginning with romanticism and going on into modernism, is that now the sublime becomes possible in the work of art. I think that, with modernism, the sublime takes over and leaves no place... [*Quietly*: or only very little place for its opposite — the beautiful.] You could also think of the Apollonian and Dionysian in that way too, or as a kind of reworking or adaptation of beauty and sublime.

[*Long pause*.]

But the Apollonian/Dionysian opposition is also present in

Nietzsche's relation with Wagner. Nietzsche followed Wagner as a young disciple and had to suffer the usual fate. I think that Wagner appreciated having somebody that smart around him, and he certainly treasured the reviews... [*Quietly*: The Birth of Tragedy, in its original publication, was a book dedicated to Wagner.] In their relation, the personal, the political and aesthetic was running side by side, and I am not sure if it's the Ring that distanced Nietzsche from Wagner, but it was certainly Parsifal. [*Pause.*] I don't think Nietzsche objected to the Ring,[16] but Parsifal, with its religious ethos, was... [*Zipper unzipping*] for Nietzsche an absolute abomination, as he saw in it the full ideology of Christianity. Now, there is a twofold irony in this. It's that actually, hmm... [*Hesitates*] despite Hitler's Wagner idolatry... [*Quietly*: and this is very funny how Hitler used to force his party members to sit through these long operas, and the party members, I think we would be doing them too much credit to say that they didn't like Wagner, they were all philistines; they didn't like any of these and to have to sit through a whole Wagner opera... (*Chuckles to himself*) was not a pleasant task for this kind of people.] But Parsifal was never played during Hitler times, as the Nazis were officially anti-Christian, hmm... [*Hesitates*] Christianity was their main competition. There is a wonderful film of Parsifal by someone called... [*Chalk hits the blackboard*] S-Y-B-E-R-B-E-R-G. He is a very controversial filmmaker, who is better known for a film about Hitler, where he was trying to purge the German psyche of Nazism. In his Parsifal film, Syberberg[17] is trying to connect and disconnect the opera to Nazism, but as a matter of fact, the opera was declared ideologically suspicious and was never played under the Nazis. Wagner's journeys to Italy, to Siena, I believe, where he saw the Siena Cathedral, left a deep impression on him and on the scenography of Parsifal. But one other thing that he wanted to write later on was the life of Buddha, and then you could also make the case that the religious in Parsifal is not even Christian but Buddhist. [*Pause.*] And this drives us back into Schopenhauer in some way, because Wagner was also profoundly Schopenhauerian; he shared this interest with... [*Achoo. Sneeze in the audience*] Nietzsche, but then Nietzsche got rid of it, as he went somewhere else... [*Mumbles indistinctly*.]

[*Long pause*.]

And then we need also to think about the traces that these thinkers left on Adorno and the Frankfurt School. [*Pause*.] I think you can see it better in Dialectic of Enlightenment than in Aesthetic Theory. One must recognize Nietzsche as the third major strain in the critical theory of the Frankfurt School... [*Quietly*: the other two are Freudianism and Marxism, or Freudo-Marxism.] You have a Freudian strain right through it, hmm... [*Hesitates*] and there wasn't one until after the war with Wilhelm Reich, then Fromm, who I mentioned the other day. Fromm was already working with them in the early 1930s till they split, and then after the war, it is Marcuse who will become one of the leading exponents of Freudo-Marxism... [*Raps his knuckles on the desk*.] Their reading of Freud, hmm... [*Pause*.] Adorno was always very sharp about the [*Stressing*] use of psychoanalysis, and what it signifies, but I think he tends to... [*Quietly*: especially if you come to Frankfurt School people from Lacan] he tends to have a very simplified notion of what Freud was all about, which I think is essentially organized around the idea of repression, of the repression and the ego. Their use of Freudianism is a kind of social Freudianism, in which Freud's language and models are useful for describing the decline and disintegration of the European bourgeoisie. We have the notion of a rising class conquering a unified psyche in the triumphant moment of the French Revolution, and then we have the gradual reification and disintegration of this psyche... [*Quietly*: a return of repression, although the word "repression" had a very different use in their vocabulary... (*Mumbles indistinctly*).] As for Marxism, it is clear that the notion of "commodity form" is absolutely central here, along with the Marxist notion of capital and how it functions. In their Marxism, they followed one of their first collaborators, a man named Pollock,[18] whose notion of Marxism was not fully dominated by economic pictures coming out of the Soviet Union, and the so-called "Soviet Marxism" of which Marcuse later wrote a devastating analysis.[19] [*Pause.*] Pollock's idea was that of a total reification of society, and this is what Adorno calls sometimes "a totally administered society," a society in which everything is [*Stressing*] subsumed... [*Quietly*: and that's a very important word] under the commodity form. I would then say that, since World War Two, this idea has become the most powerful and widely appreciated picture in the Marxist analysis of capitalism. The notion of subsumption... [*Thud. Backpack falls on the floor*] you will find it in the unfinished and unpublished last section... [*Quietly*: what is it, chapter six of Capital, Volume One?] which is now reprinted in the Penguin edition... [*Clears throat.*][20] The notion of subsumption was adopted by many people... [*Quietly*: for example, Negri and other Italians] to show that it isn't just a working class that is subsumed under the process of commodification of labor, but everything in capitalist society is subsumed under capital, and therefore you can pass this notion to a much larger social strata than that of the working class... [*Quietly*: that's the basics of many of the great uprisings.]

[*Long pause.*]

Subsumption is certainly very strong current that inflects Adorno's Marxism. My point in mentioning all of this in this section is that there is a third current in Frankfurt School that one should not ignore, and this is the Nietzschean current, which has to do with [*Stressing*] power. One has to also understand that the other two currents are radically distinct from this one. [*Pause.*] Marxism [*Stressing*] is not a philosophy of power; it's a philosophy of production, of labor, of alienation, but not of power... [*Quietly*: obviously, power is implicit here, but that's not what Marxism is about. It is economics rather than politics.] And Freud is also not a matter of power, even though, in the Superego, the Father, the primal horde and so forth, power is certainly involved, but I still think that that's a little bit different — it is a kind of libidinal authority based on castration more than simply a notion of power... [*Quietly*: and obviously, you could turn them into questions of power too. You find it in certain ways in Foucault, whose work has been associated with the notion of power and who likes to... (*Door creaks open*) Marxism out of it.] [*Footsteps.*] It is in Nietzsche where you get a tradition of thought invested in power, and the whole notion of domination, which is very noticeable in the Dialectic of Enlightenment and to an extent in Aesthetic Theory. This has its roots in Nietzsche. Now, I think that when people are trying to make a synthesis, they often like to talk about the Freudo-Marxist roots in Adorno and the Frankfurt School, but maybe they don't talk enough about Nietzsche. This is relatively distinct matter, as though the question of power domination were somehow semi-autonomous, and rather different from the matter of commodification. The thing that Frankfurt School anticipates is a notion of how power functions, hmm... [*Hesitates.*] It has nothing to do with micropower, not very much to do with biopower, and things like that, but certainly with the idea that knowledge is a form of power, and this is very much already present in the Frankfurt School. And this is really in Nietzsche, I mean, Socrates wants to know things, well, that's a way of having power over things... [*Quietly*: to know something is first and foremost to have power.]

[*Long pause.*]

Then, take the visual. To possess things visually is to have power over them, and the Frankfurt School gives us a way of talking about this form of knowledge... [*Raps his knuckles on the desk.*] It is in the ambiguity of the work of art, which has to [*Stressing*] dominate the material in order to resist domination... [*Quietly*: this is certainly a Hegelian dialectical method.] The work of art has to be seen as itself a form of domination, but it does that not to continue with domination but to resist it, and we will look at how this works in an Aesthetic Theory chapter in a bit. Their whole idea is that knowledge is... [*Quietly*: and this is pre-Foucault, certainly; the Frankfurt School was not known in France for a very long time... (*Very quietly*) maybe in the late 1960s, and then it becomes an anti-Marxist instrument... (*Mumbles indistinctly*).] In the Dialectic of Enlightenment, all forms of knowledge are forms of domination. Initially, people are absolutely powerless in the face of nature, and the first thing they are trying to do is to achieve some local power, and so enlightenment is figuring out how to control nature. Mastering fire, for example, this is one of the secrets of nature. [*Pause*.] One can speak from the very beginning of a dialectic of domination at work in knowledge and enlightenment. Magic is first of all enlightenment. You paint the bison on the wall of the cave because you gonna hunt it down and the painting gives you magical [*Stressing*] power over the animal. And the reason it becomes a dialectic of enlightenment... [*Cough in the audience*] is because, with each new stage of knowledge, the earlier stage is canceled out. The minute more sophisticated instruments and weapons are devised, the older ones are dismissed; you don't need your magical paintings anymore as they are no longer enlightenment but superstition [*Pause*.] Therefore, religion cancels magic, and science cancels religion, and then methodologies within science cancel each other, like alchemy gets canceled by chemistry and so on, it becomes a progressive movement towards... [*Quietly*: well, towards what... (*Pause*).] Towards positivism, which is our current relation to the world and nature, but also towards what Nietzsche calls the "death of God," which you can interpret as the end of traditional values, and the emergence of purely secular and manipulative social behavior.

[*Long pause*.]

This dialectic of enlightened thought, although understandable as the source and motive of power in human history, is moving towards a position of absolute domination over nature. [*Pause*.] The natural world is alienated, and these forms of domination are transferrable. In that sense... [*Quietly*: and whether you like it or not] it seems to me that you could trace in their work some early forms of current liberation movements, like a form of proto-feminism. The domination of women is borrowed from the domination of nature, and other forms of liberation too, like animal rights... [*Quietly*: and ecologism, or cruelty to the animals that we're eating, and so many other horrible things that we are doing to nature] this is all part of this narrative. The Dialectic of Enlightenment can be seen as some early form of ecological conscience and movement. [*Gloomily*.] It offers a very powerful vision of history which, in a way, ends up not in a class privilege, as in Marxism, but in some of these other movements that affect everyone else. At this stage in the Frankfurt School, it seems to me, these are all very harmoniously blended into the narrative of nature domination, and you have to understand that this is a very different vision of history than the one based on class conflict. Now, you can also say, "sure, but production is a way of dominating nature," because in order to produce, you have to dominate other people, to make them slaves, or to wage workers and subtract from their labor surplus value, and so on and so forth. No doubt, the political concept of domination is capacious enough to include forms like "class," "production," "alienation," "exploitation," but it is a different concept, and I think that there is some kind of ambiguity there.

[*Long pause*.]

I think that some of the most beautiful things that come out of Nietzsche and Schopenhauer here is the utopian moment... [*Quietly*: I may have mentioned this before, and I will mention it again... (*Takes a sip of water*).] It is that domination comes from self-preservation, from our instinct for self-preservation. I have to dominate nature in order to stay alive [*Softly*.] And therefore, I think that Adorno's utopia would be a utopia in which the instinct for self-preservation no longer exists. Now, what does that mean? That means that... [*Clears throat*] "I'm not worried anymore that I may be killed; I'm not worried that I gonna starve." It's all of these and it essentially means: "I don't care about death." [*Pause*.] The reason that death is so horrible is because of the instinct of self-preservation; it's the things that you want to avoid and everything in your own existence and in human society is predicated on [*Stressing*] not-dying. But in a utopia, this does not matter. And I think that this is the most beautiful picture of a different relation to death, which goes back to Schopenhauer, because Schopenhauer's Buddhism accentuates this instinct of self-preservation in relation to religion. For him, what Buddha teaches is that the cause of suffering is desire, is the ego, which needs to be rejected by reaching enlightenment, and then this, of course, will tie him up with Freud. [*Pause.*] You want to get rid of this urge to... [*Cough in the audience*] create an "ego fortress" and the illusion that it will help you defend against the unconscious desires, and the external world of...

STUDENT: What's the role of...?

JAMESON: The role of? Can you repeat?

STUDENT: What is the role of the death drive in all of this...?

JAMESON: Ah... [*Quietly*: let me see, how can one talk about Thanatos here? That will be a long deviation from our...]

[*Long pause.*]

Mm-hmm, the death drive is the species... [*Quietly*: the return to the inorganic, the return to the inertia, as in Freud, or this immortal-like vampire force of negativity, rooted in a sense of dissatisfaction and desire to escape our limitations, and that would be Žižek's readings of Lacan.] We would then float with it, I suppose. Most of these people do not think that the death drive is about death, but is certainly something about the nonhuman, and you could imagine a world of people who don't care about their own survival. They would be then post-human, right? [*Pause.*] I mean, those would not be the humans that we are familiar with, or what humanity means. There are all kind of speculations that you could make from this idea of the death drive, but it seems to me that it's a very, hmm... [*Hesitates*] it resembles art, perhaps. That's why the work of art or beauty is somewhat utopian because, remember, it is purposeful without a purpose, as Kant tells us, and therefore it has no interest in it. Because [*Stressing*] interest means self-preservation — self-interest. And if there is no interest in the work, at that point the ego is suspended. We will see more of that today when we look at some of the sections of Aesthetic Theory… [*Quietly*: there is a long section in the concluding part where he talks about the eclipse of the subject.] The work of art does not want to have the ego around; the work of art wants to abolish the ego; and that's very Lacanian too… [*Quietly*: you know that he was very much opposed to all that ego psychology and the whole idea of psychoanalytic cure that was to (*Stressing*) assure you, to build up and enforce your ego or your interest.] Lacan then says, you're building more and more fortresses around yourself, and instead you need to tear all of this down and be vulnerable and not have these ego defenses. [*Pause*.] Are there other thoughts?

[*Long silence*.]

In Mann, the figure of Nietzsche appears in both fictional and his other writings about Nietzsche. The fictional is Adrian Leverkühn, and the complex relationship between Nietzsche and his older sister is translated in Doctor Faustus through the relation between Adrian and his mother. The real Nietzsche in Thomas Mann is also very different. Is he pre-fascist or not? Mann was a wonderful essayist, and there is a late essay on Nietzsche in which he reflects on all of this since he went back to Europe.[21] [*Softly*.] Here Mann also makes the claim that Nietzsche is not a pre- but rather a [*Stressing*] product of fascism — it is fascism that created Nietzsche and not the other way around. Mann's Nietzsche is this sensitive instrument of history that expresses the new rising dangers of fascism, which we are still seeing in a modified form in our days. [*Pause*.] The guilt of fascism is the guilt of Adrian Leverkühn; they are both the guilt of Germany in some sense, but they are not exactly the same. The German people have sold their souls to the devil, to the Nazis, but the sales processes were very different, and in some way, we can read Germany's tragedy in terms of Nietzsche's collapse. [*Gloomily*.] They say that Nietzsche's collapse, which Mann also featured in Adrian, has been attributed to syphilis, but most recently I heard that… [*Quietly*: I haven't verified this and nobody I know knows anything about this] but apparently he went to Italy a lot, as Italy was, for a lot of these people, a great place for culture and... [*Raps his knuckles on the desk.*] In Italy, in those days, and I think this is true in a lot of other countries, you could get any drug, for there were no prescriptions, as prescriptions come up only later with drug companies... [*Quietly*: there is an excellent book on the history of American drug companies showing how doctors, drug companies, prescriptions have all been tied together... (*Mumbles indistinctly*).] So, in Italy, you could buy anything, and Nietzsche did. There are apparently some records one researcher found in some of these little Italian towns of the drugs that he bought, and this is what that report is saying...[22] [*Quietly*: a little bit like Sartre's abuse of amphetamines.] So, Nietzsche's breakdown could just as easily be attributed to drugs, as to any kind of third-stage syphilis.

[*Long pause.*]

Okay, now let's get back to Aesthetic Theory... [*Door slams shut.*] I think we have gotten to chapter number ten, which is called "Toward a Theory of the Artwork," on page 176. I'm not gonna try to walk my way through this chapter; I don't think at this point in our course this is possible, but if you have specific questions about this, let's hear them, because that would be a way of picking something out and looking at it more closely.

[*Long pause.*]

No questions? Okay, I think that here we've already seen how, hmm... [*Hesitates.*] There is, in all of the Aesthetic Theory, a dialectic at work between art in general and the individual work of art. They don't run side by side — they're in a... [*Achoo. Sneeze in the audience*] tense interaction with each other, which is something comparable to the dialectics of art and society. Later on, Adorno will comment on the relation between art and society, taking Marcuse's famous 1937 essay on affirmative culture as point of departure and reflection. Adorno would say it all the time ... , [*Impersonates Adorno*] "Yeah, the artwork resists society, but it is also a product of society." The very experience of art, it's a social encounter... [*Quietly*: buying tickets for a concert, which is an incredibly bourgeois habit that enforces the structure of the capitalist order] and this goes hand-in-hand with the things that are going on [*Stressing*] inside the work of art, and which is part of the autonomy of art, which continues to challenge society. Therefore, you cannot really separate the two. [*Exhales deeply.*] And for that reason, modern art is also critical of itself, because it feels deeply complicit in the social order that it denounces. It is not enough for art to attack the social... [*Softly*] it has to attack the social in itself; and it has to [*Whispering*] feel the guilt of its own privileged condition. Art, then, is caught in a dialectic here as well, because now art understands that it is itself part and parcel of the social inequalities... [*Quietly*: of the poverty, misery, ordinary people can't afford art] which it often seeks to expose. In order to rectify that, art must feel its own guilt as a work of culture and inscribe that in some way within its very form. And increasingly, this is an intensifying contradiction as industrial capitalism produces more and more inequality of this kind, so the artwork gets guiltier and guiltier about itself, about its own sin, so to speak, and finally wishes to abolish or cancel itself. You have either the complete renunciation — the gesture of Rimbaud — or we have Beckett's famous sentences, those minimalisms that are also suggesting that the work of art would rather speak without saying anything, or not be a work of art in the traditional... [*Quietly*: but yet, it still has to be one in order to be able to make these very statement and denunciations.]

[*Long pause.*]

All of this is in Adorno. [*Pause.*] Marcuse is different, I can recommend to you... [*Quietly*: I think Marcuse, it's not that fun to read, Herbert's style is too... (*Mumbles indistinctly*). In this sense, Adorno is much more interesting to read.] Marcuse's essay, I mentioned it in the beginning of our seminar, is called "The Affirmative Character of Culture," and you can find it in Negations. It is a great dialectical piece of writing about how culture separates from society in order to create a space for critique and change, but then it has to give it up due to the demands of capitalism. But Adorno's objections to this are very interesting; he says, look: [*Impersonates Adorno*] "Yes, this is true of art, but the individual work of art is not the same as Art." The work of art may be reproducing all of these social contradictions, but it also challenges them along with the very notion of art itself, and in a different way. [*After prolonged reflection.*] The artwork does not only challenge its individual status, but it wants also to challenge the general concept of "art." It gets out of being sheer artifice, sheer art, or privileged culture or whatever, by attacking the very notion of "art"... [*Chair-back creaks.*] It tries to make a place for itself outside itself, but then, of course, time moves on, and what previously was avant-garde art has been absorbed into the culture industry. This would be the way I think of what one would find in a more complex way in Peter Bürger's Theory of the Avant-Garde, because he is quite right to see that the distinction between the avant-garde, and the non-avant-garde, is that the latter wishes to fetishize art — that is their main business — whereas avant-garde wishes to destroy art... [*Quietly:* the general notion or institution of art.] But then, the avant-garde attack is itself part of art in some way. This is similar in some way to, hmm... [*Hesitates.*] Breton wished to steer a line between the left-wing deviations, those were people who tried to join the communist party, and the right-wing deviations, and those were the people who tried to keep a place for surrealism that was politics and art... [*Quietly*: but they did politics, no art.[23]] So, I think you can see some kind of similar divide... [*Quietly*: I once mentioned that I was wrong to say somewhere that Adorno hated the avant-garde.] He makes a place for its moment of truth too, which is the attack on art as such — art has to be attacked, but at the same time, it has to be practiced in some way. And this is the main task of the individual artwork, which is somehow distinct from the... [*Takes a sip of water*] let's call it "art as such," or the "institution of art." If aesthetics is too crude in its way of thinking about itself, it is because it is split into these two parts, which we've seen in the "Draft Introduction"; we have a pure aesthetic theory of art on one side, and a practical criticism of art that deals with individual works on the other... [*Quietly*: you may recall Adorno's remark about poor Hegel and Kant, who were writing about aesthetics without knowing anything about art.] This is then what Adorno wishes to bring together... [*Decisively*.] The aesthetic must be the place where you address the individual works as well as the general notion of art. This is what I think Aesthetic Theory is also about.

[*Long pause*.]

Now, at the center of this chapter ten, called "Toward a Theory of the Artwork," is the individual work of art, and the part that I think is the most interesting here is... [*Quietly*: there is a long section on spirit, that is, Geist.] I don't think that the English readers have any great attachment to the word "spirit," but you understand that spirit in German philosophy is a much more powerful word than in English. [*Pause*.] Some of that is part of the argument that we don't necessarily have to fight about German Idealism, but when it comes to this notion of the spiritual dimension of art, hmm... [*Quietly*: and it doesn't have anything to do with religion.] The Geist dimension of art is what we would call the "imaginary." [*Pause*.] Spirit is the part of the work of art that [*Stressing*] is not in it — and that's all of it, really. If you look at a painting, you think you're seeing something, but you're just looking at pieces of material, at canvas and paint. There is something on the surface which is not really in that painting, and that's what the word Geist stands for. Mmhmm, that's the imaginary, and then that's the important thing for art, which I have been quoting several times in this seminar, and that is Alles, was der Fall ist — that's the Wittgensteinian famous definition of the world as "everything that is the case." Art then is what [*Stressing*] it's not the case, the non-world, the non-existent, the illusion, and appearance. Schein.

[*Long pause*.]

The interesting thing that I would like to focus on, in these last few minutes that we still have, is on page 186. Here he deals with unity... [*Page flipping*] and here we have to go back to Schopenhauer. One of the most powerful things that Schopenhauer said was about Kant's categories, and how they make up a lot of what we see in the world. Yes, with Kant, we see the world not only in terms of time and space... [*Quietly*: the transcendental aesthetic] but also thanks to the categories of "relation," "modality," "causality," "quantity," "quality," and all the other ones. But then, as Schopenhauer says, Kant omitted one fundamental category, which is that of the [*Stressing*] <u>thing</u>. We see the world as a collection of things. And why do we do that? Remember that, before any of these things materialize, there is a sort of pre-human world of sensations, a world that is... [*Quietly*: this is William James's famous phrase] of a "blooming buzzing confusion."[24] That means that there is no articulation in this world, it's just all these... [*Agitated*.] If you think about some super-scientific theories of perception; they use this notion called the "sense-data," and that's what is given to the senses as meaningless sensation — the perceiving experience that is prior to when the act of judging, affirming, or recognizing the world as things starts to appear. This data is hammering away at our organs of perception, and then something in there is reorganizing into perceptions, and finally we see that that is not just a blotch of this color or that color... [*Quietly*: but it's a person, a chair, an apple.] I mean, this is a form of mythology, but it's a very productive mythology, because out of it comes impressionism... [*Quietly*: all of those painters who read the books that were in the beginning of experimental psychology] and so they decided they would paint paintings which were depictions of sense-data. [*Pause*.] Seurat,[25] as silly as it may sound, it's a great art with all those little dots swarming and swirling around there... [*Quietly*: what do you call that kind of impressionism...? (*Mumbles indistinctly*).]

STUDENT: Pointillism, chromoluminarism?

JAMESON: Pointillism, yes... [*Quietly*: and for the phenomenologists, something like that may be totally clueless, as they may not see psychological sense-data in the same way.] So, if you imagine this world with its various masses of sense-data that are unorganized, you may be asking yourself:

what will, or what can organize all of those? [*Pause.*] It is not Kant's categories, but it is by combining them into things, into objects... [*Cough in the audience*] and that's where Adorno's notion of "unity" comes in. The work of art also imposes itself as a unity or a thing. It has to take all the stuff from the outside world... [*Quietly*: words, pieces of paint, sounds, notes, and so on] and it assembles them into things. Above all, it puts them together and separates them from what's around. It is not because of a Derridean frame of some kind, but because they are supposed to be part of [*Stressing*] a thing. [*Pause.*] There is a history, then, of the theory of the thing... [*Quietly*: which you may know Heidegger has a famous essay on this, and Lacan also has this very enigmatic notion of das Ding, which is derived from Freud.[26]] And of course, "thing" was also oddly, if you go back to the old German tribes... [*Door slams shut*] "things" were called governing assemblies or tribal meetings, a sort of parliament... [*Quietly*: they were legislatives assemblies that met to elect chieftains and kings] and it is very interesting how the modern meaning of "thing" in English, and in other languages, has been changed to mean not a gathering or collectivity, but an object. [*Pause.*] You can almost read a social and political meaning into the strange philosophical and etymological development that has taken place in the word and idea of the "thing"... [*Quietly*: but we don't have to go that far, and Adorno doesn't go either.]

[*Long pause.*]

To impose unity, then, is to make a thing out of all... [*Loud sniffing sound*] the scattered sense-data. And therefore, this process is also a form of domination. It takes the multiple... [*Quietly*: now we're almost in Deleuze]; it takes the multiple, which ought to be good, and it imposes unity, which is the bad. It takes difference and makes it into identity, right? [*Exhales deeply.*] This is now also [*Whispering*] a primal form of domination that the work of art has, and that aesthetics has to address. And you can't have a dialectic, because if you think of modern art, contemporary art, aleatory art... [*Quietly*: it goes as far as John Cage] you could have a... [*Door slams shut*] you could expand the notion of the aesthetic and the artwork to the point where the work challenges itself, as do most interesting forms of contemporary art. Look at installations, for instance... [*Addresses audience*.] You know what installation art is, right...? [*Quietly*: These are three-dimensional environments or experiences that have been installed within a gallery or museum; there is a room with all these objects laying around.] And its main message is: "I do not wish to be an easel painting." [*Chuckles*.] Easel paintings are those bad form of old bourgeois unity, and I don't want a be such a form of unity anymore. And happenings is another new form of that refusal... [*Quietly*: they may seem old-fashioned to you now] but, they also seem to say, "I don't want to be a play, I don't want to be staged like in an old-fashioned theater; I just want to be this moment, this event in time and space, and then I want to disappear." It is about the spontaneity and ephemerality of the moment. The same holds for concrete music, where you get rid of musical instruments and pick instead sounds from the streets, put them together with these synthesizers, and then we have something which is aesthetic but not an artwork in the traditional sense anymore. Okay, so why do we have to have all of these, hmm...? [*Hesitates*.] Because they go and challenge that form of domination, which is the traditional form of unity, or the traditional work of art. But is the new art still a work of art? Well, if it wasn't a work in some form, we couldn't talk about it, right? You wouldn't be able to write our reviews for the museums' greatest exhibits about installations and happenings. [*Pause*.] So, the minute it gets identified as an "installation," or "happening," then it's another form of unity, and it's all over and we have to go on and find something else, find new forms for unity. But how long can we do that? Then Adorno writes on page 186-187 that Penelope's weaving of the web is an allegory of art...[27] [*Quietly*: but I think this translation isn't quite right... (*Mumbles indistinctly*).] "Ever since," page 187... "Ever since Homer's verses this episode is not the addition of rudiment for which it is easily mistaken..."[28] I think Adorno here means a category of the episode, that is, how can you break the work or the unity down? What could an aesthetic be without being a work anymore...? [*Footsteps. Door creaks open.*] Anyway...

[*Long pause.*]

Okay, I think that will be enough for today... [*Door slams shut*] and so our next time, we will talk about film, and then we will finish with this book. And I want to see those who plan to graduate in my office... [*Chairs scratching against the floor. Footsteps.*]

Audience stands up. Objects drop on the floor. Door squeaks. Students return chairs to other classrooms. Zippers zipping up. Some students form a line to discuss their assignments with Jameson. General noise. Screeching microphone noise.

[*Microphone turns off.*]

CURTAIN

LECTURE TWENTY-ONE

APRIL 17, 2003

ADORNO AND FILM — CONSTRUCTION — SOCIETY (LAST CHAPTER)

CURTAIN RISES

Moving chairs, squeaking door, coughs, other sounds filling the noise environment of a large classroom in the Literature Department at Duke University.

As the semester draws to a close, students are excitedly chatting about their summer vacation plans.

Jameson enters the classroom carrying a few books, his scattered notes, and the red pen in the chest pocket of his flannel shirt.

[Microphone turns on.]

JAMESON: I wanted to announce to you... [*Footsteps. Chairs scratching against the floor.*] In the latest issue of the New Left Review... [*Quietly*: there are two journals that you should be only reading] one is Critical Inquiry and the other one is New Left Review. These are the journals where you can find out what happens in the areas that interest us, in English, of course. In the latest New Left Review, there is an article on Thomas Mann and Adorno by Michael... [*Chalk on the blackboard*] M-A-A-R. He is a kind of literary detective, who goes around to find out all sort of interesting things about writers, theorists. So, this article...

[*Quietly*: called, I believe, "Teddy and Tommy"[1]] is a study of their relationship. [*Pause*.] Adorno, as you already understood in this course, was very close to Mann; he truly admired and loved Thomas Mann. But the relation was not reciprocal, and Mann did not have the same enthusiasm for Adorno. Maar's article will tell you more about the nature of this relation; it has a lot of literary gossip and is ostensibly based on the exchange of letters between the two that I already mentioned.[2] [*Sighs deeply*.] Maar wrote another book, which is also a sort of forensic analysis... [*Quietly*: apparently, it's coming out in English, and I thought it would be a longer version of this article, but it is not.] The book is called Bluebeard's Chamber, and here he argues... [*Quietly*: and you may think about it whatever you want] that all the guilt in Thomas Mann's novels comes from a crime that he supposedly witnessed during one of his visits to Italy, to Naples.[3] He insists that something horrible might have happened in Naples, and that Mann was either involved in a murder, or witnessed a murder, hmm... [*Audience laughing*] and that this guilt was then registered in the notebooks, which have been destroyed... [*Laughing continues*] and therefore the guilt is visible in all of his work in one way or another... [*More laughter in the audience*.] It is a little bit like the shocking scene in the Dostoevsky's The Possessed... [*Quietly*: in the famous censored chapter, where Stavrogin confesses to the monk about the rape of the young girl and which was not published... (*Mumbles indistinctly*).][4] But in Mann, the victim would be, I take it, the pimp who is the first figure of the devil — this disreputable red-haired creature who appears already in Death in Venice, and then in other works. Regarding Maar, I believe that he did not have the, hmm... [*Quietly:* how should I put it...?] There is no scholarly or investigative rigor here. He could have gone to search for the crime records in Naples, in order to find out if anybody was murdered during the period when Thomas Mann was there. Because this sounds a little bit like Freud's seduction theory, which, as you know, he proposed in the 1890s to explain the root of neurosis in light of childhood trauma, and which was first thought to be the real cause, but then it turns out it took place in most of the bourgeois households... [*Quietly*: and then Freud decided to shift to the famous Oedipal theory, something which, of course, was... (*Mumbles indistinctly*).] Anyway, but this is an interesting article to learn about their relationship, and how Adorno served as musical advisor to Mann, and what Mann thought about Adorno.

[*Long pause.*]

Okay, I think that with that maybe we will go on to the presentation on Adorno and film. [*Looks at student.*] You gonna show us something?

STUDENT ONE: Yea...

JAMESON: Oh, good, good, okay, so we should put this down... [*Pulls down retractable screen.*] What are the arts that we associate Adorno with...? [*Pounds his fist on the desk.*] Well, it is the temporal arts in a sense; music, first of all, but he also wrote on plays, on Beckett, he wrote on novels, he wrote on Proust. I don't know if there is enough interest in what he had to say about novels; he was a reader of novels, he was very intelligent, very cultured, and so on, but I don't remember anything he said about novels that is very striking. There is the second essay in Notes to Literature, on the first person of the epic narrative, and that's very interesting, but it's not about any specific novel.[5] [*Pause.*] And painting... [*Quietly*: I mean, obviously he knows a lot of painting, and he knows the avant-garde, but I don't remember anything he said about painting that was intellectually memorable.] But his comments on film are the least known and, given his nervousness about... [*Chair scrapes the floor*] Benjamin's work, in that respect, and his overall hostility to mass culture and the mechanical reproduction and aura, he would not have been a person to say anything important about film. But "Transparencies on..." [*Looks at student.*] This is part of a collection on film translated by Thomas Levin...

STUDENT ONE: Yes, it's a short piece called "Transparencies on Film."[6]

JAMESON: But this is now in English, right, in a collection?

STUDENT ONE: I don't know anything about the collection...

JAMESON: You don't know about the English collection of essays?[7]

STUDENT ONE: No, I only know about the special issue of the New German Critique, where "Transparencies on Film" first appeared in English.

JAMESON: Oh, yeah, New German Critique is another place for specifically German stuff, because they have done a lot of pioneering translations. Okay, but anyway, please proceed.

Student Presentation: Adorno and Film

STUDENT ONE: I'm going to speak today about Adorno and film, but I will also talk briefly about Benjamin, given his influence on film studies. I will start with a clip from Dziga... [*Cough in the audience*] Vertov's Three Songs about Lenin, which I believe was released in 1934. As you know, Benjamin wrote and was very much influenced by early Soviet cinema,[8] he praised the use of montage and the ability of radical filmmakers to convey a sense of collective experience and revolutionary potential. [*Pause.*] I will first show a short clip, then I will share with you some of my notes....

[*Presses "Play" button on the VHS player. Shows a clip from Dziga Vertov's* Three Songs about Lenin.]

[*Presses "Stop" button on VHS player.*]

STUDENT ONE: Benjamin's ideas about film are contained in his famous essay, "The Work of Art in the Age of Mechanical Reproduction," which we already discussed. [*Chuckles.*] Therefore, I will only give a very short summary before we move on to discuss Adorno and film.

[*Page flipping.*]

Benjamin's understanding of film is informed by Marx's critique of the capitalist mode of production, which holds that capitalism's increasing exploitation of the masses will ultimately bring political struggle and new conditions for art and culture. He examines some of the key transformations in art, brought

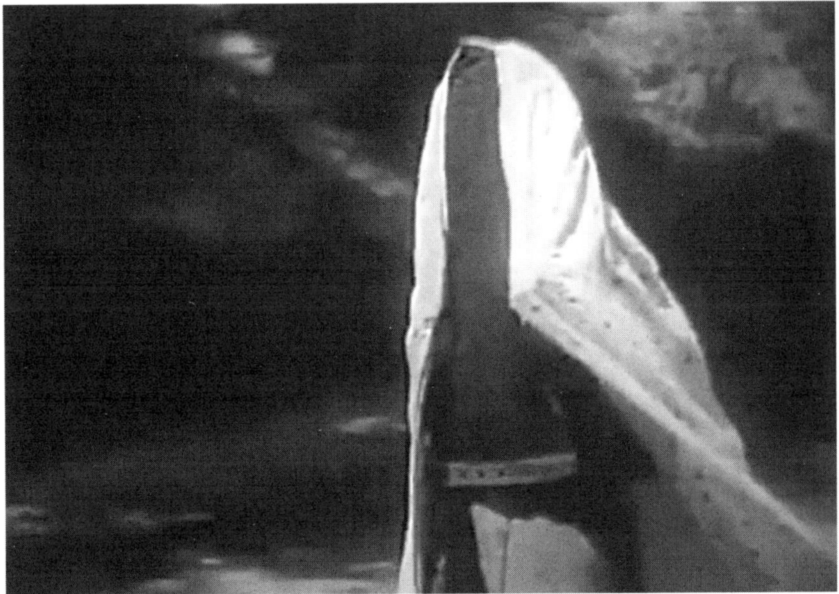

Screenshot from Dziga Vertov's Three Songs of Lenin (1934). Public Domain.

about by the technological innovations which open new revolutionary potential in art and politics, both for democratic politics and reactionary... [*Quietly*: radio, film, mass communication serves as a tool for nationalists and fascists.] The new political function of art is the result of the loss of aura... [*Quietly*: which we have already talked about.] Mechanical reproduction frees art from the bondage of myth and ritual, but it also cancels the aura, which has to do with... [*Thunder rumbling outside*] the uniqueness or presence authenticity of the work of art. The loss of the aura impacts art in major ways, leading to a shift in the way art is perceived and valued. First, it bridges the gap between the subject and object, enabling the modern viewer to meet new products of culture halfway... [*Door slams shut*] and secondly, because of the category of production, functions independently of the original... [*Chair-back creaks*] has great potential for democratization. Emancipated from its parasitical dependence on ritual, a new era begins for art, which is based on another practice: politics. The loss of the aura has its base in contemporary politics... [*Quietly*: I quote:] "...the increasing significance of the masses in contemporary life. Namely, the desire of contemporary masses to bring things 'closer' spatially and humanly, which is just as ardent as their bent toward overcoming the uniqueness of every reality..."[9] in short, to see it as the "mark... [*Quietly*: and this is also Benjamin] of a perception whose 'sense of the universal equality of things' has increased..."[10] Benjamin names film as the most powerful agent of art's political function; just ten years after the screen talkies, Benjamin predicted a great political future for the cinematic media. [*Pause*.] For Benjamin, the accessibility of film makes it a more democratized art, more representative of the masses. Film allows an event or performance to be recorded and be available for countless number of people to see. Mechanical reproduction makes possible the involvement of the masses in culture and politics, making possible both mass culture and mass politics. Not only a simultaneous collective experience has been made possible by the advent of film, but the accessibility of information means greater potential for collective action... [*Pause*.]

[*Page flipping*.][11]

I will turn now to Adorno. One encounters Adorno's thoughts on film in several of his works: from "The Culture Industry" chapter in the Dialectic of Enlightenment, to his later essay "Transparencies on Film," and a book called Composing for the Films... [*Quietly*: which was initially published in English with Hanns Eisler as the only author. Apparently, Adorno withdrew his authorship in order to avoid falling under the investigation of the House of Un-American Activities Committee that was looking into Eisler and Eisler's brother's political activism.] Composing for the Films was reprinted in West Germany in the late 1960s, and then Adorno decided to add his name as co-author.[12]

[*Page flipping*.]

In Dialectic of Enlightenment, Adorno and Horkheimer have a very elitist view regarding film, which later on, Adorno at least, tried to backtrack. They state that "films, radio and magazines make up a system which is uniform as a whole and in every part."[13] Writing in the time of the golden age of Hollywood, Adorno and Horkheimer claimed that "movies and radio need no longer [*Stressing*] pretend to be art"[14]; they openly admit being businesses and have no problem with calling themselves "industries." Technology itself is not blamed for its cooptation by the ideological system, whose main function is to transform each viewer, or listener, into a consumer. [*Pause.*] Rather, Adorno and Horkheimer believe that the functioning of technological entertainment is strictly under the monopoly of capitalism. Taking an inverse path to that of Benjamin, Adorno fails to distinguish between properties of the medium exploited by capitalism and these properties as they could have or could be utilized under other conditions of production or different politics... [*Door creaks open.*] At this stage in his career, Adorno expresses fundamental mistrust of the visual... [*Achoo. Sneeze in the audience*] immediacy of film, which, as we know from the Dialectic of Enlightenment, is one of the culture industry's most effective mechanisms of ideological cooptation. The authors of "The Culture Industry" chapter do not see film as autonomous artistic practice, and they cannot identify an aesthetics for this medium — anything that could be aesthetically redeemable or that could be called an independent work of art. [*Pause.*] The perfect synchronization of word, image and music adds to the claim that the film's main goal is to ensure an affirmative stance towards the full system, since there is no antithesis and no connection. There is only affirmation. Negation is only possible in an autonomous work of art, which is mediated knowledge of the present irreconcilable social contradictions, which are inscribed in the form of the work of art. Affirmative works affirm rather than negate, falsely reconciling the general and the particular, and come to partly reconcile the mass audience with the status quo.

[*Page flipping.*]

Another concern of Adorno and Horkheimer regards the impact of the culture industry, and film in particular, on the viewer, as when he states that even... [*Quietly*: I quote:] "Kant's formalism still expected a contribution from the individual, who was thought to relate the varied experiences of the senses to fundamental concepts," but then the culture industry empties out the individual, or "robs the individual of his function." [*Quietly*: End of quote.][15] Only automatic, programmed reactions are possible by the viewing subject of cinema or sound film, as there is no more room for imagination or reflection on the part of the audience. Spectators have no choice but to witness the predictable unraveling of the narrative, which nonetheless requires dedicated observation, as the spectator is made sure not to miss on the chain of displayed facts. Ooh... [*Clears throat*.] Mass culture resorts to regressive mechanisms, according to Adorno and Horkheimer's account, not simply because it reflects the general state of reification and "mummification of the world..." [*Quietly*: and here I quote Miriam Hansen:] "but, on the contrary, because they mask the stage, disguising script as pure image, as natural humanized presence."[16] This doesn't just happen because people become passive absorbers of ideology, but precisely because the spectator is interpellated as an expert, and is encouraged to be an active reader, to second-guess the mysteries of the plot; "it is in the shift of the viewer's attention to the 'how' by which the trivial resolution is achieved."[17]

[*Long pause*.]

Generally, Adorno's film writings... [*Cough in the audience*] are less of a question for aesthetics than part of the field of cultural sociology. Film is not a traditional form of art for him, and one of the reasons lies in the technological origins of cinema. In "Transparencies on Film," which is a text written in the 1960s, and where he tries to modify some of his early elitist views on film, Adorno states that... [*Quietly*: I quote:] "The late emergence of film makes it difficult to distinguish between technique and technology as clearly as is possible in music."[18] [*Quietly*: End quote.] He relies on Benjamin to state that, since the cinema has no original but is reproduced on mass scale, this mass product is the thing itself. Adorno continues to doubt an aesthetic theory or norm of criticism for cinema, suggesting that: "the aesthetics of film will do better to base itself on a subjective mode of experience which film resembles and which constitutes its artistic character."[19] [*Quietly*: End of quote.] The technological process of film, the representability of the medium, highlights the significance of the object and objectivity, which is something as... [*Quietly*: and I quote:] "foreign to subjectivity, than aesthetically autonomous techniques; this is the retarding aspect of film in the historical process of art."[20] In opposition to Kracauer, he writes that "there can be no aesthetics of the cinema, not even a purely technological one, which would not include the sociology of the cinema."[21] The negativity of the medium is not in the eternal logic of its technological origin... [*Quietly*: as is the case for Benjamin] but rather in something of which Adorno accused Benjamin: the confusion of technique and technology. Miriam Hansen explains the two terms, which have often been confused by translators, by distinguishing between artistic technique, or "technique"... [*Quietly*: in German is Technologie] and "technology" in the broader sense... [*Quietly*: which, in German, is Technik.] Adorno criticized Benjamin's "The Work of Art" essay in a famous letter by stating: "You under-estimate the technicality (Technizität) of autonomous art and over-estimate that of dependent art."[22] As Hansen states: "an aesthetics of film would have to emphasize its inherent affinity with subjective modes of experience as well as to acknowledge the role of intentionality in both representation and construction."[23] [*Quietly*: End of quote.] The "Transparencies on Film" essay can be regarded as another dialogue with "The Work of Art" essay, and here Adorno states that Benjamin does not elaborate on some categories related to film... [*Quietly*: such as "exhibition," "test"] ignoring their relation to the commodity form, which he opposes.[24] And so, Adorno concludes that the only hope that cinema may have to become art is in the practice of montage, which... [*Quietly*: I quote:] "does not interfere with things but rather arranges them in a constellation akin to that of writing."[25] So, if... [*Quietly*: end quote.] So, if you imagine a memory, which appears like a slide show of discontinues of images in your mind, this is the subjective mode of experience that, for Adorno, serves as an example of how film's mimetic impulse might be rescued from its... [*Achoo. Sneeze in the audience*] of the culture industry. Adorno writes... "It is in the discontinuity of their movement that the images of the interior monologue resemble the phenomenon of writing: the latter similarly moving before our eyes while fixed in its discrete signs."[26] The movement of these internal images in film is then comparable to what the acoustic world is to music and the visible world is to the art of painting. "As the objectifying recreation of this type of experience, film may become art. The technological medium par excellence is thus intimately related to the beauty of nature (tief verwandt dem Naturschönen)."[27] [*Quietly*: End quote.] And later, in Minima Moralia, Adorno would pick up on this thought and write that film should replace superficial realism with radical naturalism.[28]

[*Long pause.*]

In his thoughts on montage, Adorno was clearly influenced by the German author, philosopher, academic and film director Alexander Kluge, for whom literary discourse is at the center of his literary practice... [*Quietly*: we don't have any of his books here in the library.] In his montage theory, Kluge emphasized the "empty spaces between shots (Leerstellen)"[29] as the sites of resistance to the power of the image... [*Quietly*: in this, Kluge is different from Eisenstein's theory of montage that prioritizes the image.] He argues that only within these empty spaces that the imagination of the spectator is activated, as meaning does not reside in the film but in the spectator. Adorno, as well, maintains that the cinematic image should require to reveal its construction rather than offer a predictable script. [*Page flipping.*] Perception thus should be closer to the activity of reading rather than to automatic consumption. "The liberated film would have to wrest its a priori collectivity from the mechanisms of unconscious and irrational influence and enlist this collectivity in the service of emancipatory intentions."[30] Something like soft-focus shots, superimpositions, flashbacks; these, for Adorno, are ludicrous technological effects that simply fill in the narrative gaps of basic cinematic realism. None of these fetishistic uses of technology... [*Cough in the audience*] are necessitated by individual works are simply conventions. For Adorno, the only hope for cinema to become an artform lies in is its interaction with other media, such as music or other arts, using montage, as he sees in some instances of television. Not that the absence of intentional meaning is possible in montage, but the directors refuse to interpret the sequence of images as in itself a subjective act, and as such... [*Loud chair screech across the floor*] a priori. He writes: "The individual subject who remains silent speaks not less but more through silence than when speaking aloud."[31]

[*Long pause.*]

So, finally, I'm going to show you a clip from Charlie Chaplin's The Great Dictator. The reason I've chosen Chaplin is because both Adorno and Benjamin wrote about Chaplin... [*Quietly*: Adorno met Chaplin at a party in California... (*Zipper unzipping*).] They both admired his work, not so much the excited or funny portrayal of action, but Chaplin's themes and variations... [*Softly*] composition. Benjamin once remarked that Chaplin "directed himself toward both the most international and most revolutionary affect of the masses — laughter."[32] And although Adorno has treated laughter with suspicion, particularly in the Dialectic of Enlightenment, where he calls the laughing audience "a parody of humanity,"[33] he was also sensitive to the political nature of Chaplin's film and seemed to be ready for a reconsideration of laughter. I will start with... [*Pulls down retractable screen.*] This clip is from Charlie Chaplin's The Gold Rush... [*Quietly*: I presume everyone knows it.] [*Audience murmuring.*] It is a silent film made in 1925 and is considered Chaplin's personal favorite of all time... [*Cough in the audience. Student One presses "Play" button on the VHS player.*]

STUDENT ONE: [*Talks while the silent film rolls.*] Here the main character is going to Alaska and is being stalked by a bear... [*Giggles.*] The movie is set during the Klondike Gold Rush of the

Scene from Charlie Chaplin's The Gold Rush (1925). Public domain.

1890s, and it follows the story of Tramp... [*Quietly*: played by Chaplin] as he travels to the Yukon in search of gold. It depicts the adventures of the little Tramp as he meets Big Jim, played by Mack Swain, and a girl, Georgia, with whom he falls in love... [*Laughter in the audience.*]

[*Silent movie rolls.*]

AUDIENCE: [*Laughing.*]

JAMESON: [*Laughing.*]

AUDIENCE: [*Laughter gets louder and louder.*]

STUDENT ONE: [*Presses "Stop" button on the VHS player.*] Okay, that's it.

AUDIENCE: [*Loud laughter continues.*]

JAMESON: [*Laughing.*] Okay, thank you. A few things about Chaplin. He was pretty much on the left, as you know, although he denied being a communist. You have Miriam Hansen's book on silent cinema in America, what is it called, hmm... [*Tries to remember*] Babel something,[34] and we must have it in our department library, along with some of her essays on Adorno and film...

STUDENT ONE: Yes, I found them online in various issues on the *New German Critique*...

JAMESON: Hansen is one of the major writers on all of these people, Benjamin in particular, and Adorno, hmm... [*Hesitates*] and Kluge... [*Choo-choo. Amtrak train whistle in the distance.*]

STUDENT ONE: She has an interesting article called "Mass Culture as Hieroglyphic Writing"...

JAMESON: Is that the one about Kracauer?

STUDENT ONE: It's on Adorno, Derrida, [*Stressing*] and Kracauer.

JAMESON: Ah, okay. Is it about the movie *Intolerance* and... [*Mumbles indistinctly*]?

STUDENT ONE: She talks about Griffith's 1916 movie *Intolerance* in her book *Babel and Babylon*. In here writings she has these interesting theories on Adorno's position on mass culture and film by way of writing, as an attempt to put forward an aesthetics of film. [*Pause.*]

STUDENT TWO: I have a question about reproduction. I was under the impression that, for Benjamin, the means of mass reproduction, which is to say bookmaking and engravings, came earlier. Do you have any sense of how Benjamin sees the qualitative differences between the earlier forms of mass reproduction, like manual engravings, Guttenberg, and the mechanical ones, like photography and film?

STUDENT ONE: In "The Work of Art" essay, Benjamin mentions the pre-modern or pre-mechanical modes of reproduction, like woodcut, etching and engraving, and also later in the nineteenth century, how lithography played a role in the artistic production of the time. But I guess the main difference here... [*Whispers*: the way I see it, of course] is reproducibility for [*Stressing*] mass reproduction, because the earlier forms of reproduction were still not possible for mass distribution, but only for privileged groups. It was not reproduction for the [*Stressing*] masses.

JAMESON: I think technologies, like movies or radio, are a little bit different from newspapers or the circulation of engravings all the way back. Benjamin has written on engraving not only as part of reproducibility, but also in relation to his theory of allegory...[35]

STUDENT TWO: But did he feel that engraving was not anymore relevant as form of artistic reproduction?

STUDENT ONE: When it comes to reproducibility, we should also think about the intention of the work. The way I see it, engraving is still part of the so-called "cult value," rather than "exhibition value," of art. The latter is the case for modern forms of art, and photography or film in particular. [*Pause.*] The older forms of reproduction are part of the "ritual purpose" of art, and that only changes with the introduction of photography and cinema, when art shifts to so-called "exhibition purpose," as it now becomes available to the wider masses...

JAMESON: There is a set of multiple things going on here. One is reproducibility, the other is cult versus secular, and that's why it gets very complicated in Benjamin's "The Work of Art" essay... [*Quietly*: and then there are also three versions of this essay anyway.] So, it's not a single shot theory at all...

STUDENT TWO: And then secularization also plays a role as well...

JAMESON: That's another side of it... [*Pause.*] That is the audience, and that's not necessarily why it should be the same as reproducibility... [*Quietly*: clearly, it's not.] On the other hand, I suppose with engravings, hmm... [*Hesitates.*] For example, in Holland, there were people living in particular cities and who were very skilled at engravings, so painters like Rembrandt and Rubens had to go to Leiden or some other place to enlist the services of these highly skilled engravers in order to distribute their works. During that period, that was art's main means of reproduction and distribution. But like the dialectic of enlightenment, when you get on to a new stage, then the past stage seems to have acquired a certain aura of its own, an aura that it didn't have at the time, and I am not always sure if this dialectic is very visible in Benjamin...

STUDENT TWO: Right... [*Pause.*] And this is also the case for so many other painters from the past, like when art historians talk about Veronese copies, that there was very difficult to talk about a painted original...

JAMESON: Yeah, yeah. Exactly. So, these concepts are not always crystal clear. [*Agitated.*] You see, many of these things are oppositions, and any opposition becomes fatally good or bad. Then you think, alright, which one is good, and which one is bad...? [*Cough in the audience.*] You may think, okay, aura means bad because of the loss of the original and authenticity, and all that kind of stuff, and the new modes of reproduction are good as they are part of the progress. But then, the descriptions of aura may sound different, and what's interesting about the dialectic, and confusing at the same time, is that you will never unequivocally identify the opposites in clear-cut terms of "good versus bad." Dialectical opposites mean they shift all the time according to situation, and they are not anymore considered in terms of "good" and "bad," but of something else: "above" or "beyond" and "new" versus "old" or... [*Mumbles indistinctly.*] Mm-hmm. Are there other comments, questions? [*Addresses Student One.*] When was this "Transparencies" essay written, do you know?

STUDENT ONE: It was written in 1960, hmm... [*Hesitates*] 1964, maybe?[36]

JAMESON: Oh, that is very late. The New Wave... [*Tries to remember.*] When does the New Wave film movement with Renoir, Bresson, Kluge in Germany begin? [*Pause.*] In the late 1950s, right? Kluge was also a lawyer, and so he drafted the famous German New Wave statement, which is associated with a place in Germany, what is that town called... [*Tries to remember. Raps his knuckles on the desk.*]

STUDENT THREE: Ober... [*Pause.*] Oberhausen?

JAMESON: Oberhausen, yes, exactly! The "Oberhausen Manifesto," do you know what the date of that document is?

STUDENT THREE: Fifty-eight?

JAMESON: I think it's a little bit later than that,[37] but that's... [*Pause.*] So, Adorno was well aware of these new practices in film, as he was well aware of the new kinds of music. He wasn't stuck in classical bourgeois music, but on the other hand, I don't know if he ever wrote about these latest developments... [*Pounds his fist against the desk.*]

STUDENT ONE: Miriam Hansen says that one of the reasons that motivated Adorno to write the "Transparencies" essay was to show support for a new and independent New German cinema.[38] She claims that Adorno was trying to change his earlier critical fixations on film, which, in the Dialectic of Enlightenment, they dismissed as a branch of "culture industry" that aimed at reproducing consumers. [*Pause.*]

JAMESON: Yeah, that may be so... [*Pause.*] But Kluge was indeed his beloved disciple, as Adorno was very close to Kluge. And I do think we have some of his books in our library... [*Tries to remember.*] It is a collection of translations...

STUDENT ONE: [*Addresses audience.*] Anyone else knows anything about this...?

JAMESON: [*Softly.*] Okay, then maybe we should stop here.

[*Audience applauding.*]

JAMESON: One word that I think does not get mention enough here by Benjamin... [*Quietly*: and it is not necessarily that it should] but this is the word... [*Chalk strokes on the blackboard*] M-O-D-E-R-N and M-O-D-E-R-N-I-T-Y. It is clear that this business about the "aura" is about modernity, because technology is very much associated with that. And remember that Adorno always takes a modernizing position... [*Quietly*: for him, the most advanced form of cultural production is the best] but on the other hand, you don't want to reify and fetishize the technological component. [*Pause.*] But the technological element is always there. In music, for example, the nineteenth century brings all sort of technical novelties with regard to the audience, and to the orchestra. With Berlioz, there is a breakthrough... [*Door creaks open. Footsteps*] in the orchestra as he is expanding the range of instruments, adding new instrumental colors and effects. Then Wagner adds his own innovations, which we all know, and these are: stage design, costumes, lighting, leitmotifs, the musical drama and so forth. It is a bit harder to see what the innovations in literary production are, unless you want to include things like the serialization of the newspapers… [*Quietly*: Dickens' and all sort of other people's writings that are now part of serialized fiction that is being distributed in portions.] You can also see this important distinction that you mentioned between "technique" and "technology," as when Adorno is implying that Benjamin [*Stressing*] reifies technology in some sense. And I think that if you read the final version of "The Work of Art" essay, you come away with some of that feeling. [*Pause*.] Now, hmm… [*Raps his knuckles on the desk*.] Part of this feeling comes from the fact that Brecht has been removed from that essay… [*Quietly*: as I mentioned to you the other day, they made him get rid of Brecht.] For example, you mentioned Adorno's reference to "test." [*Softly*.] What is test? [*Pause*.] Well, these are words from the vocabulary of modernization, of Taylorism, and of the new mode of production that is transformed into a science. In film, "test" means you have a film that, hmm… [*Hesitates*.] There was, for example, a famous problem that no one could figure out in human history, namely, the movement of a galloping horse. This is sometimes called the "flying gallop" debate. And it was only when Eadweard Muybridge made his famous albums for the study of animal locomotion using stop-motion photography, or long exposure photography, that it became clear how horses run. [*Footsteps*.] Test films then work a little bit like that — you make something in order to study your theme before you proceed to large-scale production. Nowadays, you would use video to do some tests… [*Quietly*: make a video of some athletes running in order to see what the best angle is to shoot that performance, and so on.] That's what Adorno meant here by [*Stressing*] test, and you can see that this comes up very closely to Brecht's idea on how the audience is supposed to evaluate the actors.[39] So you put on stage a businessman, then some Salvation Army missionaries, then some factory workers... [*Quietly*: folks from the poor houses] and you have to decide who's got the power? Who is winning the struggle?[40] Are they doing it right? Shouldn't they be doing something else? That was Brecht's idea of testing what one should do... [*Softly*.] And this is not exactly didactic — it's not Agitprop, for Brecht doesn't see it like the Chinese... [*Cough in the audience*] where you have Uncle Sam dressed in a red-white-and-blue suit, and the worker, as this often appears in the most orthodox forms of socialist realism. [*Pause*.] It is nothing like that. Rather, you have a [*Stressing*] situation, and you have to sit back, smoke your cigar, and make some judgments about what you see. And if you add that perspective back into Benjamin, then his technological fascinations start to look a little bit different. It no longer seems like a reification of technology.

[*Long pause*.]

Now, regarding moder... [*Clears throat*] regarding modernization or modernity. Well, in Dziga Vertov's Three Songs about Lenin, you can see what this is all about. [*Pause*.] You have the old and the new, the remains of the past and the achievements of the Soviet state that meet at the May Day parade, where you see the impact of socialism on the ethnic minorities. [*Pause*.] These populations... [*Quietly*: allegedly lost in pre-history] are now listening to radios or are working on the latest agricultural machines, tractors, and everything else in the kolkhoz fields. In a funny kind of way, the aesthetic [*Stressing*] technique of Dziga Vertov, which you probably know from the much more famous Man with a Movie Camera,[41] is also part of the content, and the content too, it's about modernization. And then, this aspect of modernization in the USSR takes a more complex form. As you know, there is this great opposition between Sergei Eisenstein and Dziga Vertov. Has anybody seen Eisenstein's great political film called The General Line... [*Quietly*: also known as Old and New?] [*Silence*.] It's a film about collectivization, which was a very dangerous subject when he was filming it at the time, so he had to redo it... [*Quietly*: because, as you know, this was the period of the great turning point in the Soviet history, the beginning of Stalinism.] In The General Line, there is the famous scene, which Eisenstein called the "Holy Grail and the Milk Separator"...[42] [*Quietly*: where the sexual and the sacred appears in the work of this new machine that the collective farm bought in order to modernize the production of milk.] But then, at the end... [*Agitated*.] I was very surprised to learn very recently that, in the Soviet Union, they've never seen the end of this film, which we've known very well over here. So here you have the collective farm being modernized through the actions of the main hero, this young peasant woman who is pushing them to get all of these new technologies. Then an aviator comes in from outside, and in the very last scene... [*Quietly*: here is the gender revolution] the aviator is in peasant clothes driving a tractor, while the peasant woman is shown trying to become an aviator. In this, you have all kind of statements about the Soviet revolution and its relation to modernity, and evidently, that final scene was pulled from the film because they were not ready yet to swap gender roles... [*Sound of student struggling with a stuck zipper near the microphone*.]

[*Long pause*.]

Now, you can see in the last chapters of Negative Dialectics Adorno's views of Brecht, and his, hmm... [*Quietly*: nervousness about Benjamin, too.] Some of this has to do with the entrenchment in East Germany of the vulgar form of Marxist criticism called Diamat. You all know what that is, right... [*Chalk on the blackboard*] D-I-A-M-A-T. It stands for "Dialectical Materialism." This was Stalin's philosophy, implemented as the official state ideology in the USSR, and it was used to justify his policies and actions, but also to interpret works of art. [*Pause*.] But Brecht, who moved in 1949 to East Berlin and established his theatre company there, the Berliner Ensemble, could get away with many things, and this was because he didn't arrive in the baggage of those German communists who spent the war in Moscow exile, of people like Ulbricht,[43] who was brought to East Berlin by the

Soviets. In fact, someone told me once that some of these Soviet army officers admired Brecht's work; apparently, they knew about him and really wanted him there... [*Quietly*: but of course, there was always great tension between them.] Later on, however, the orthodoxy takes over, although one could also say that East Germany preserved the experimental tradition in culture, which partially comes out of Brecht. [*Exhales deeply*.] So, it is against such a background that Adorno likes to argue very much against the East, and Brecht. He is fighting on several fronts here, constantly going back and forth between two poles: one is against the old Nazis... [*Cough in the audience*] still working in the West German academia, and all sorts of other reactionaries, and the other is against all those in East Germany associated with this Diamat tradition that Stalin imposed on everyone else in the postwar period. And then there is also a third front, and this is the American "mass culture," or the "culture industry," as he liked to call it. And because he was fighting on these multiple fronts, this makes his position look like aestheticizing, or in a defensive posture of supporting a [*Stressing*] purely art-for-art's-sake aesthetics, which is often considered bourgeois and incompatible with Marxism. [*Pause*.] When viewed in this way, the position appears to be an aestheticist one, but if one shifted the polemic a little bit, hmm... [*Hesitates*.] As I'm trying to say it over and over again, the insistence on production in Adorno is... [*Achoo. Sneeze in the audience*] crucial to the interpretation of art, as you could imagine. In other words, when taking into account the politics of his time, his Aesthetic Theory is not at all revisionist or purely aestheticizing.

[*Long pause*.]

But there are other things here in Adorno and film that are very interesting, things that will be restated in a different way when we get to the modern polemics, like those appearing in the French Tel Quel and English Screen magazine in the late 1960s. These were the two cultural avant-garde periodicals in the 1960s to also cover film, especially Screen magazine.

This notion that you've mentioned earlier of the unification of sound and image, this is very much the [*Stressing*] disguising of the traces of production... [*Quietly:* and this is his definition of reification. I mean, it is not strictly Adornian, for you find it already in Marx in some sense.] But that particular formula for reification — the effacement of the traces of production on the object — is sort of the philosophical substrata of this whole new form of modernist leftism, the sort of Maoist leftism that you find in the French and other places, in the 1960s... [*Quietly*: as I said it already, this is Tel Quel and Screen that will soon become the orthodoxy of the new left in that period.] And there the attack is phrased in terms of [*Softly*] representation, and this is a word that they got from Heidegger somehow, although it will not look the same. But Adorno's emphasis is very similar, in that the unification of sound and image, or the use of certain film techniques like shot and counter-shot... [*Quietly*: in dialogues, for example, when somebody is speaking, then you show somebody listening, then you show somebody speaking again and so on] and the fact that this is considered natural, and not just a way of suturing over or editing all these disconnections, this becomes a critique of ideology. It is an ideology — the ideology of realism, and realism itself, in that sense, is an ideology. Representation is an ideology, and therefore it follows that all you want to do is to show that, and accordingly, there is a lot of modern film production in that period that pulls these representations and realisms apart in order to reveal its tricks.

[*Long pause.*]

Now, Adorno wrote this other book on music and film with Eisler. [*Softly.*] Eisler wrote a lot of it, but later on, Adorno thought that it was too political, and he withdrew his authorship from the first edition. Eisler was a great composer anyway, and only now are we getting all of Eisler's works on CDs... [*Quietly*: you can buy all of them now.] One of the things that he, or they, insist on in this book is something that only began to come out in the period of the New Wave, namely the [*Stressing*] non-synchronicity between various levels in film, like image and sound. Famously, I think, what people consider the very first major breakthrough examples is in the Diary of a Country Priest, directed by Robert... [*Chalk on the blackboard*] B-R-E-S-S-O-N, which is based on a novel by Bernanos,[44] where the diary is [*Stressing*] dyssynchronous with the action... [*Chair-back creaks.*] The voiceover is separate from what it illustrates, and this holds image and sound apart. This was the way Adorno thought... [*Quietly*: and Eisler, or whoever wrote those pages] thought that music and movies should function. [*Pause.*] If they are synchronous, then you are getting pure rhetoric; that's when the movie tells you, "oh, now feel some emotion..." [*Chuckles*] and "now be afraid because something terrible is gonna happen" [*More chuckles*] and this is the rhetorical way that music must mirror the function or help the image. But in their theory, there must be this gap between music and, hmm... [*Hesitates*] this lag or anticipation between music and image — each of them must remain semi-autonomous and entertain this [*Stressing*] dyssynchronous relation to each other. I'm not sure that Eisler and Adorno's... [*Cough in the audience*] language conveys the whole theory the way those late 1960s avant-garde journals did, but I think it comes very close to that.

[*Long pause.*]

What's also interesting in this is the matter of construction. Remember that, if you look for positive things in Adorno, they would be productivity, as I already said, and then construction. [*Pause.*] Whenever we have the choice in here — in this constant back and forth between mimesis and construction, between emotion, expression, and construction — Adorno always seems to come down on the side of construction. When we have a choice between subjectivity and objectivity, we come down on the side of objectivity... [*Quietly*: Hegel versus Kant.] But for a real dialectical method, there must also be something of the matter with construction and objectivity, right, as we're ought to, hmm... [*Hesitates*] there should be another shoe drop in here, and we ought to then turn around and find some flaws with construction. [*Pause.*] Well, I think in the last chapter, and I don't know if we will have time to get to that, but I would recommend that you take a look at the pages... [*Page flipping. Talks to himself*: Where are those pages...? (*Mumbles indistinctly*) Yes, starting with page 222.] Here, he suddenly seems to be saying, yeah, but construction is [*Stressing*] static and we have to preserve what he calls the "temporal..." [*Tries to remember*] the "temporal something," but in German, this is the "time-kernel" — der Zeitkern in the artwork. [*Pause*.] Construction tends to make us believe that it's really an object... [*Zipper unzipping*] at least completed construction makes us forget the process, and I think something like that seems to be going on a little bit here, in this discussion on page 222, because all of the sudden it is very interesting the way he puts it. It seems as though Adorno is trying to say ... , [*Impersonates Adorno*] "Look, I know I told you art is objective, but you're likely to forget that objectivity, and you may even favor something else." [*Pause*.] So, now we have to insist on the opposite, and instead of objectivity, let's make it subjective, let's bring up the subject on the side of this process, and instead of representation and realism, let's bring out montage... [*Quietly*: and so forth.] It's aaa... [*Pause*.] And the montage, it's like a constellation which brings us back to the familiar Benjaminian world. But that's also a kind of suspicious thing, you know, or rather old-fashioned thing. A lot of theories see film as virtual dream, as association of ideas, as internal monologue... [*Quietly*: you got that already in Eisenstein, his work was quite... (*Mumbles indistinctly*).] But when you look at famous examples of [*Stressing*] subjective cinema... [*Quietly*: those look very weird today.] Stream of consciousness, in the older silent films, those were the ten-day wonders of the period, and I think that today they look incredibly tedious to insist on... [*Feet shuffling*] subject position. The more recent film theories always insist that the camera takes the place of the subject, but it isn't the subject, and it isn't subjective. When they first started to imitate, hmm... [*Hesitate*.] You could have a nightmare sequence or... [*Quietly*: and there also some great films, I shouldn't... (*Mumbles indistinctly*) generalize] but those are not terribly subjective. And remember that the dream could be an object. If you think of the famous subject-centered films, when you turn it back, hmm... [*Excited.*] I think that everybody agrees that it was Welles who wanted to make a film from the point of view of the character, and he was going to make Heart of Darkness... [*Quietly*: which didn't happen.][45] So the first one turned out to be Lady in the Lake,[46] where Robert Montgomery starred as Marlowe and directed the film, and this is exactly an all-point-of-view film. [*Pause.*] You see the entire film through the main character's eyes, and you only see Marlowe in the mirror, or in other kind of reflective surfaces, in shadows. [*Sighs.*] But I also think that everybody agrees that it is tedious... (*Mumbling quietly*)] it does not seem to me that such movies solve the problem of subjectivity. I see them as traces of some other old-fashioned kind of taste, but nonetheless they do allow us to see a little bit this problem, and how this approach to an aesthetics of pure subjectivity works in art and cinema.

[*Long pause.*]

Now, distraction, yeah, this is very funny idea. It's the idea that, hmm... [*Pause. Agitated.*] I... [*Pause.*] I think it's better to think about it in cinema, because of the fact that you can't see everything in the frame. Adorno's reference to distraction in this last chapter is a reference to Benjamin,[47] who talks about distraction and attention in "The Work of Art" essay. You know that, at some point in the history of cinema, there was a big polarity between montage editing and the so-called "deep focus" — the deep-focused one-shot sequences. In the late 1940s, André Bazin talked about a revolutionary mode of filmmaking which he saw in Welles, and that was the deep focus. That is to say, Welles, rather than Eisenstein, because in Welles, famously, you have this really deep shots which are relatively static and where the action takes place simultaneously on several planes. Bazin called that "continuum..." [*Quietly*: I could think of some scenes in Citizen Kane that are very dramatic, like when Mrs. Kane is in the living room when she signs the paper, and you can see through the window the boy playing outside... (*Words indistinct*).] In this valorization of the deep focus, it is clear that you can't see everything, and that's what Benjamin means by distraction: it is the opposite to attention, or being able to focus on a single thing, and therefore presumably he is making a comment about the mass audiences, but in a kind of mediated way. [*Pause.*] The masses seek distraction, but how could the mass audience be expected to develop the kind of habits of perception that only film critics and experts in specialized studies possess? That is all tied into the way in which something like the deep-focus technique functions in cinema. That's at least the way I read Benjamin, for he is using distraction in terms of architecture. Architecture is perceived habitually in a state of passive distraction... [*Quietly*: that is when you're walking in a building and, unless you're doing something else, you gotta pay your parking ticket, or something else, you are experiencing the building around you in a passive distractive mode.] This is the opposite to the way we concentrate on a work of art; it is now a specific way of experiencing modern art, film — it's an experience of non-experience... [*Pause.*] But I suppose, for Adorno, given his interest in either the hatred of art by the philistines, and the emptiness of the culture industry, this idea of distraction did not... [*Mumbles indistinctly.*]

[*Long pause.*]

As with Kluge, very briefly, I think he is a wonderful filmmaker. Now he makes late-night productions, like he gets ten minutes at three in the morning where he interviews someone, and he puts it on German television... [*Quietly*: it's quite a crazy operation.] He is also a wonderful writer, the little collection of stories that you might wanna look at is called, hmm... [*Agitated.*] Well, we published one of them, which is called Learning Processes with a Deadly Outcome,[48] that was translated by our university press, and here the key novella is the story of the Nazis' space astronauts on the moon... [*Mumbles indistinctly.*] It was first published in Germany in 1973, and it is a mixture of fact and fiction and also images, made in this quasi-documentary style that combines science fiction with reportage — very remarkable. He's also a philosopher, his big book hasn't been translated and it's called "History and..." [*Raps his knuckles on the desk*] something, which is a large book also with pictures and a whole theory of history.[49]

[*Long pause.*]

The one other thing I wanted to point out in this... [*Page flipping*] last chapter of Aesthetic Theory... [*Pause.*] You could see in this last chapter that the argument is constantly moving into political issues. First of all, Brecht ... , [*Impersonates Adorno*] "Yeah, yeah, he was a great poet, but that's because he was doing something [*Stressing*] other than what he thought he was doing..." [*Quietly*: this is Adorno's classic way of dealing with such issues.] But I think the much stronger argument, and one worth pondering on, is Adorno's move, which is always there — it's the move that he always makes when he says, "art is not political, art is social." [*Pause.*] Political is an intention, and intentions are sort of worthless, they are like... [*Excited.*] It is not ideology. In ideology, he says... [*Cough near the microphone*] — and that's a great statement too — you could have ideology and truth content; those things could go together, for no work of art can be non-ideological. But even with the bad ideologies, they could have truth content. But when it comes to art with political intention, which is what he considered the very bad art of East Germany, and the Soviet Union during the Stalinist period, those are radically to be distinguished by the way in which the form of the works express social reality. [*Softly.*] The social is an ontology. The political is just a set of wishes, ideals, intents, goals, and so on.[50] It is a very powerful argument, and eventually you could go on and say that the kind of politics that you practice at a given moment, it's also social.

[*Long pause.*]

One other section that I would have liked you to look at is on pages 244 and 245... [*Page flipping.*] This is the other way he makes the argument about objectivity, which is simply by form and content still. You want to do your politics in content — let's rather do it in form. The content expresses some political intentions, but the form expresses social categories and social experiences. As I say, this is more or less the way this is done in Adorno. [*Pause.*] The other important thing that you will see here, which I think we could have anticipated... [*Page flipping*] is on page 244, where he talks about the eclipse of the subject. First of all, the subject in art is social... [*Quietly*: not private.] Whenever you say, and a lot of modern criticism is... [*Cough in the audience*] personal pronouns — the pronouns are not personal. After all, you get it in the linguistic period, the pronouns have to be social, they are part of language... [*Quietly*: I don't invent my own word for "I," for example, which only I could... (*Mumbles indistinctly*).] These pronouns are "shifters" in Jakobson's vocabulary,[51] which is to say everyone has to say "I," but what could be personal about it, and that's only the beginning of the whole argument about the way in which voice is always social in art.. [*Zipper zipping up.*] The narrative of the private and the ineffable in art, this is all simple rhetoric; the private does not come through in the work of art in that way. If you have an art of the inexpressible, about anxiety and neurosis, think about Schoenberg's Erwartung or any other expressionist work from the period, they rely on these beliefs in the possibility of art to express the private, but that is social too... [*Pause.*] "Me" is social. And my anxiety and neurosis, they are social too. Therefore, you can see how this is dialectically converted into the thing about the subject. What is the relationship with the subject in art? And this is what these pages talk about regarding the [*Stressing*] eclipse of the subject. He says, [*Impersonates Adorno*] "Art does not express something or someone, you do not project stuff into this like a personal home..." [*Quietly*: isn't that wonderful, that I will express something so that someone could feel my pain, my frustrations, and feelings or senses.] The subject of experience of so-called "great art..." [*Quietly*: because, as you know, that's what Adorno was dealing with; but then you could also say that anything that does what he says is "great art"] has to do with the eclipse of subjectivity, with the depersonalization of the ego. What we feel to be personal, and our own, and what we call the "subject" is generally the ego, as with Lacan. Whereas when you try to think what would [*Stressing*] not be the ego anymore here is the destruction of art... [*Achoo. Sneeze in the audience*] and the emergence of the shudder. [*Page flipping.*] "The shudder is a response, colored by fear of the overwhelming; by its affirmation the music at the same time speaks the truth about untruth. Nonjudging, artworks point-as with their finger-to their content without its thereby becoming discursive."[52] And further down... [*Door creaks open. Footsteps*] "Shudder, radically opposed to the conventional idea of experience [Erlebnis], provides no particular satisfaction for the I; it bears no similarity to desire. Rather, it is a memento of the liquidation of the I, which, shaken, perceives its own limitedness and finitude."[53] [*Pause.*] Well, and right away, a few lines down, we have Kant's sublime. The point about the experience with the sublime is that it does not preserve the person — it destroys the person, and this is the experience of the radical liquidation of the subject. And this is why we have Adorno's emphasis on the objective, because everything we call subjective is probably attached to the "I" as ego, and all of those personal things. All of this is extremely modern, and it seems to me contemporary... [*Mumbles indistinctly*] and is deliberately inserted into this political chapter by way of a trying to wrest away, and get from the political intentions.

[*Long pause.*]

Oh... [*Pause.*] Okay, that is that then, and I look forward to reading your papers... If you have questions or issues to discuss, or if you need anything, letters of recommendation and... [*Heavy chairs scratching against the floor*] come see me in my office.

Audience stands up. Objects drop on the floor. Door squeaking. Students returning chairs to other classrooms. Some in the audience form a line to discuss their assignments with Jameson. General noise. Screeching microphone noise.

[*Microphone turns off.*]

CURTAIN

NOTES

INTRODUCTION

1 For the treatment of beauty in one of the Platonic dialogs, see, for example, the conversion between Socrates and Hippias in Paul Woodruff *Plato's Hippias Major*, trans. with commentary and essay (Indianapolis: Hackett Publishing Company, 1982). For the Hotho Transcript see G.W.F. Hegel, *Philosophie der Kunst: Vorlesung von 1826*, ed. Annemarie Gethmann-Siefert, Jeong-Im Kwon and Karsten Berr (Frankfurt: Suhrkamp, 2005). In English, G. W. H. Hegel, *Lectures on the Philosophy of Art. The Hotho Transcript of the 1823 Lectures*, trans. Robert F. Brown (Oxford: Clarendon Press, 2014). Adorno's seminars on aesthetics, which he delivered in Frankfurt in 1958/1959, have been published as Theodor W. Adorno, *Ästhetik (1958/59)* ed. Ederhard Ortand (Frankfurt am Main: Suhrkamp Verlag, 2009). This volume was translated as: Theodor W. Adorno, *Aesthetics (1958/59)* ed. Ederhard Ortand, trans. Wieland Hoban (Cambridge: Polity Press, 2018).

2 Since Jameson's seminar used the Minnesota University Press 1997 edition of *Aesthetic Theory,* all the references, quotes and pagination that appear throughout this book will be made from this particular version of the book cited as: Theodor W. Adorno, *Aesthetic Theory*, trans. Robert Hullot-Kentor, eds. Gretel Adorno and Rolf Tiedemann (Minneapolis, MN: University of Minnesota Press, 1997). For the dictation of the early drafts of *Aesthetic Theory,* see Gretel Adorno and Rolf Tiedemann, "Editors' Afterword" in: Adorno, *Aesthetic Theory*, 363.

3 "The definition of beauty as the 'sensual appearance of the idea', which was central for the reception of Hegel's aesthetics, does not feature in any of the surviving transcripts of Hegel's lectures on aesthetics in Berlin (1820/21, 1823, 1826, 1828/29). It is now assumed that this phrase was not coined by Hegel himself but by his student

and editor H.G. Hotho." See editor's Note 8 to "Lecture 1, 11 November 1958" in: Adorno, *Aesthetics (1958/59)* [unpaginated].

4 For voice as "intimate kernel of subjectivity," see: Mladen Dolar, *A Voice and Nothing More* (Cambridge, MA: The MIT Press, 2006), 15.

5 Fredric Jameson, *Late Marxism: Adorno, or, The Persistence of the Dialectic* (London: Verso, 1990), 51.

6 Susan Buck-Morss, *The Origins of Negative Dialectics: Theodor W. Adorno, Walter Benjamin and the Frankfurt Institute* (New York: The Free Press, 1977), xiii.

7 See, for example: Stefan Müller-Doohm, *Adorno: A Biography*, trans. Rodney Livingstone (Cambridge: Polity Press, 2005), 487.

8 For a more detailed discussion on the split between science and art, see Adorno's "The Essay as Form" in: Theodor W. Adorno, *Notes to Literature*, ed. Rolf Tiedemann, trans. Shierry Weber Nicholson (New York: Columbia University Press, 2019). On Adorno's hostility to assimilate philosophy and art, or aesthetic writing and the "absolute differentiation of philosophical thought from artistic production," see also: Jameson, *Late Marxism*, 66.

9 "The book must, so to speak, be written in equally weighted, paratactical parts that are arranged around a midpoint that they express through their constellation." Adorno quoted in: "Editors' Afterward," Adorno, *Aesthetic Theory*, 364.

10 Adorno, *Aesthetic Theory*, 366.

11 See the beginning of "Editor's Foreword," Adorno, *Aesthetics (1958/59)* [unpaginated].

12 Fredric Jameson, *Marxism and Form: Twentieth-Century Dialectical Theories of Literature* (Princeton, NJ: Princeton University Press, 1971); Jameson, *Late Marxism*.

13 See the interview "Live Jameson" in: Ian Buchanan, *Fredric Jameson: Live Theory* (Bloomsbury Publishing Plc, 2007).

14 At the time of the seminar in 2003, there were four figures (Jean-Paul Sartre, Wyndham Lewis, Theodor W. Adorno and Bertolt Brecht) to whom Jameson dedicated full-length books. Today this number has increased to six, adding in the past decade Walter Benjamin and Raymond Chandler.

15 See: Robert Kaufman, "Red Kant, or the Persistence of the Third

Critique in Adorno and Jameson," *Critical Inquiry*, vol. 26, no. 4 (Summer, 2000), 708.

16 Ibid., 684.

17 Many interpretations of *Aesthetic Theory* do not stress enough the relation between these aesthetic dimensions. Some interpreters tend to prioritize "mimesis" as the central protagonist of Adorno's speculative anthropology, thus overlooking the complex relation to other modern aesthetic drives of "expression" and "construction." They tend to reduce Adorno's aesthetics to pure mimesis. See, for example: Karla L. Schultz, *Mimesis on the Move: Theodor W. Adorno's Concept of Imitation* (Frankfurt am Main: Peter Lang, 1990). For more recent examples of accentuating mimesis at the expense of other drives, see: Brian O'Connor's "Aesthetics" in: *Adorno* (New York, Routledge, 2013). Jameson has been among the critical voices (along with Martin Jay) who recognized early on the close interrelationship between the three drives. For the discussion of the interrelation between mimesis, expression and construction, see: Jameson, *Late Marxism* and Martin Jay, "Mimesis and Mimetology: Adorno and Lacoue-Labarthe" in: *The Semblance of Subjectivity: Essays in Adorno's* Aesthetic Theory," edited by Tom Huhn and Lambert Zuidervaart (The MIT Press, 1997), 29-55.

18 Adorno, *Aesthetic Theory*, 1.

19 Adorno and Horkheimer are not the only critics working with the idea of mimesis at the "origins" of art, knowledge, and progress. There have been numerous anthropologists, from James George Frazer, *The Golden Bough* (1890) to Count Bégouen, "The Magical Origin of Prehistoric Art" (1929), and more recent anthropological studies like Leroi-Gourhan Andre, *Gesture and Speech* (1964-65). Many art critics and historians, such Arnold Hauser's *Social History of Art* (1951) and Aby Warburg's *Bilderatlas Mnemosyne* (1932), have also dedicated extensive studies to the role of mimesis at the dawn of human civilization.

20 R.G. Collingwood, *The Principles of Art* (Oxford: Oxford University Press, 1938).

21 On the "enigma" of art in Adorno, and its comparison with Benjamin's notion of "aura," see: Shierry Weber Nicholsen, "*Aesthetic*

Theory's Mimesis of Walter Benjamin" in *The Semblance of Subjectivity*, 56-91.

22 See: Jacques Derrida, "Scribble (Writing-Power)" in *Yale French Studies*, no. 58, (1979), 117-147.

23 See the more extensive note on the treatment of expression by Martin Jay and Fredric Jameson in Lecture 2 of this book. Jameson has pointed out that one other place where the notions of "expression" and "construction" have been discussed in aesthetic terms is Collingwood. Indeed, in Collingwood, one could find a discussion of the principles of "expression" and, to a lesser degree, "construction," and "mimesis" (via magic). However, Adorno's anthropological or historical take on these drives significantly differ from their more "technical" treatment in Collingwood. See R.G. Collingwood, *The Principles of Art* (Oxford: Oxford University Press, 1938).

24 For a more detailed discussion of the "weathering of experience" and of death in Adorno, see: J. M. Bernstein, "Why Rescue Semblance? Metaphysical Experience and the Idea of Ethics" in *The Semblance of Subjectivity*, 177-212.

25 Peter Weiss, *The Aesthetics of Resistance*, vol. I (Durham, NC: Duke University Press, 2005). The second volume of this novel was published by the same press in 2020.

LECTURE ONE

1 On the number of drafts and the stages of writing *Aesthetic Theory*, see: Chapter 16, Gretel Adorno and Rolf Tiedemann, "Editors' Afterword" in Adorno, *Aesthetic Theory*.

2 Theodor W. Adorno died of a heart attack on August 6, 1969. *Aesthetic Theory* appeared posthumously in 1970. On Adorno's preoccupations with aesthetics, and the beginning of dictating the first draft of *Aesthetic Theory* in October 1966, see: "The Divided Nature of Art," in Part IV, and note 105 in: Müller-Doohm, *Adorno*, 470-474.

3 Reference is to the last three so-called "chapters" of *Aesthetic Theory*: Chapter 14, "Paralipomena;" Chapter 15, "Theories on the Origin of Art Excursus"; and Chapter 16, "Draft Introduction."

4 For a discussion of the structure and what was included or omitted from *Aesthetic Theory*, see: Gretel Adorno and Rolf Tiedemann, "Editors' Afterword" in: Adorno, *Aesthetic Theory*, 361-67.

5 For the German edition of *Aesthetic Theory*, see: Theodor W. Adorno, *Ästhetische Theorie* (Frankfurt am Main: Suhrkamp Verlag, 1970).

6 As stated in the Introduction, the seminar worked with the 1997 University of Minnesota Press edition of *Aesthetic Theory*, whose Table of Contents includes an index of topics. In the German edition of the book, the index of topics appears at the end.

7 Reference to the first English translation of Theodor W. Adorno, *Aesthetic Theory*, trans. Christian Lenhardt (London: Routledge and Kegan Paul, 1984). Lenhardt's translation has been criticized on many occasions. Lambert Zuidervaart, who reviewed this translation in 1985, writes that Lenhardt broke up sentences into shorter ones in order to make "Adorno's highly wrought, idiosyncratic prose" more accessible for the English reader. See: Lambert Zuidervaart' review of *Aesthetic Theory* by T.W. Adorno; C. Lenhardt; Gretel Adorno; Rolf Tiedemann, in *The Journal of Aesthetics and Art Criticism* vol. 44, No 2, Winter 1985, 95. Similarly, Robert Hullot-Kentor pointed to numerous errors, emissions, and simplifications, suggesting that Lenhardt was indifferent to the formal concerns of Adorno's *Aesthetic Theory*, turning it into a "guide to aesthetics" in order to give the reader the illusion of secure trip by inserting such transitional phrases as "let us remember," "art, we said," "we can see," "as we saw," or getting rid of many foreign words (some sources have suggested that these were demands made by the publisher). See Bob Hullot-Kentor, "Adorno's *Aesthetic Theory*: The Translation" in *Telos* 65 (Fall 1986), 143-47. For a reply from the translator, see: Christian Lenhardt, "Reply to Hullot-Kentor" in: Ibid., 147-52.

8 The seminar worked with the 2001 Cambridge University Press edition of Kant's third *Critique*. Immanuel Kant, *Critique of the Power of Judgment*, trans. Paul Guyer, ed. Eric Matthews (Cambridge: Cambridge University Press, 2001).

9 First Part: Critique of the Aesthetic Power of Judgment.

10 See: Adorno, *Aesthetic Theory*, 10.

11 Reference to Sigmund Freud, "Creative Writing and Daydream-

ing" in: *The Standard Edition of the Complete Psychological Works of Sigmund Freud*, ed. James Strachey, vol. 9 (London: Hogarth, 1959), 143-53.

12 On the circumstances of writing and publishing *Doctor Faustus*, see: Thomas Mann, *The Story of a Novel: The Genesis of Doctor Faustus*, trans. Richard and Clara Winston (New York: Alfred Knopf, 1961). The first English translation made by Helen T. Lowe-Porter appeared in 1948 (one year after the German version) with A. Knopf in New York.

13 "On 13 November 1948 Schoenberg dispatched an angry open letter, specifically aimed at Mann, to the *Saturday Review of Literature*. He complained that Mann's reference in the postscript to 'a contemporary composer and theoretician' only served to 'belittle' his own work and character: 'Yet in two or three decades we shall see who is the contemporary of whom.'" On the details of the angry exchange between Schoenberg and Mann, see: *Theodor W. Adorno and Thomas Mann: Correspondence 1943-1955*, eds. Christoph Gödde and Thomas Sprecher, trans. Nicholas Walker (London: Polity Press, 2006), 30.

14 Martin Jay, *The Dialectical Imagination: A History of the Frankfurt School and the Institute of Social Research, 1923-1950* (Los Angeles: University of California Press, 1973).

15 Rolf Wiggershaus, *The Frankfurt School: Its History, Theories, and Political Significance* (Cambridge, Mass: MIT Press, 1994).

16 Adorno's studies included the 1924 dissertation thesis on the phenomenology of Edmund Husserl, and the 1927 *Habilitation* dissertation, "The Concept of the Unconscious in the Transcendental Doctrine of the Soul." For a more detailed discussion of his studies, see: Part II of Müller-Doohm, *Adorno*, 77.

17 Reference to Adorno's books on Schoenberg, Mahler and Berg are available today in English. See Theodor W. Adorno, *Philosophy of Modern Music*, trans. Anne G. Mitchell and Wesley V. Blomster (New York: The Seabury Press, 1973); A newer translation of the same book is Theodor W. Adorno, Philosophy of New Music, trans. Robert Hullot-Kentor (University of Minnesota Press, 2006); Theodor W. Adorno, *Alban Berg: Master of the Smallest Link*, trans. Juliane Brand

and Christopher Hailey (Cambridge: Cambridge University Press, 1991); Theodor W. Adorno, *Mahler: A Musical Physiognomy*, trans. Edmund Jephcott (Chicago: The University of Chicago Press, 1992).

18 Theodor W. Adorno, *Beethoven: The Philosophy of Music*, ed. Rolf Tiedemann, trans. Edmund Jephcott (London: Polity Press, 1998).

19 Reference to what was published in English as Theodor W. Adorno, *Notes to Literature*, 2 vols., ed. Rolf Tiedemann, trans. Sherry Weber Nicholsen (New York: Columbia University Press, 1991-92).

20 Theodor W. Adorno and Walter Benjamin, *The Complete Correspondence, 1928-1940*, ed. Henri Lonitz, trans. Nicholas Walker (Cambridge: Harvard University Press, 1999).

21 Theodor W. Adorno, *In Search of Wagner*, trans. Rodney Livingstone (London: Verso, 1983).

22 It is not clear what other book on Wagner Jameson is referring to; it may be the larger study published in 1939 in *Zeitschrift für Sozialforschung*, under the title "Fragments on Wagner." Müller-Doohm, *Adorno*, 238.

23 Thomas Mann, *Freud, Goethe, Wagner* (three essays), trans. H.T. Lowe-Porter and Rita Matthias-Reil (New York: Alfred A. Knopf, 1937).

24 Gödde and Sprecher, eds., *Theodor W. Adorno and Thomas Mann.*

25 Herbert Marcuse, "On the Affirmative Character of Culture," in *Negations: Essays in Critical Theory*, trans. Jeremy J. Shapiro (Boston: Beacon, 1968), 88-133.

26 See: Theodor W. Adorno et al., *The Positivist Dispute in German Sociology*, trans. Glyn Adey and David Frisby (London: Heinemann, 1976).

27 On nominalism and repudiation of universals, see also: Fredric Jameson, *Postmodernism or, The Cultural Logic of Late Capitalism* (Durham, NC: Duke University Press, 1991), 152.

28 Reference to the so-called "Hegel's Doppelsatz," which appeared in the preface to his *Philosophy of Right*: "What is rational is actual; and what is actual is rational." See G.W.F. Hegel, *Elements of the Philosophy of Right*, ed. Allen W. Wood, trans. H.B. Nisbet (Cambridge: Cambridge University Press, 1991), 20.

29 Theodor W. Adorno, "Trying to Understand *Endgame*," *New German Critique*, no. 26, (Spring-Summer, 1982), 119-150.

30 Reference to Wittgenstein's well-known motto, translated into English as "Whereof one cannot speak, thereof one must be silent." Ludwig Wittgenstein, *Tractatus Logico-philosophicus*, trans. Frank Ramsey and Cecil K. Ogden (London: Routledge & Kegan Paul, 1922), proposition 7.

31 Theodor W. Adorno, *Minima Moralia: Reflections from Damaged Life*, trans. E.F.N. Jephcott (London: Verso, 2005). Max Horkheimer and Theodor W. Adorno, *Dialectic of Enlightenment*, trans. John Cumming (New York: Continuum Press, 1972).

32 Reference to European writers who published books after visiting the United States in the nineteenth century: Alexis de Tocqueville's *Democracy in America* (1835); Harriet Martineau's *Society in America*, (1837); Charles Dickens' *American Notes* (1842).

33 Adorno used the name "Wiesengrund," or "Wiesengrund-Adorno" until 1938, when he was thirty-five. He followed the suggestion of Friedrich Pollock, who "asked him to drop 'Wiesengrund' because there were too many Jewish names amongst the members of the Institute for Social Research." Simon Jarvis, *Adorno: A Critical Introduction* (New York: Routledge, 1998), 3.

34 Reference to the passage in *Doctor Faustus* dedicated to the Arietta theme in Beethoven's final Piano Sonata 32, Opus 111, where the main motif of the Arietta is constructed to the syllables "Wies-en-grund," which is the middle name of Adorno. See the German original: Thomas Mann, *Doktor Faustus. Das Leben des deutschen Tonsetzers Adrian Leverkühn erzählt von einem Freunde* (S. Fischer Verlag, 1967), 75-76. For the English, see: Chapter VIII, Thomas Mann, *Doctor Faustus: The Life of the German Composer Adrian Leverkuhn as Told by a Friend*, trans. John E. Woods (New York: Vintage, 1999), 58-59. See also: Lecture Fifteen in this book.

35 Georg Wilhelm Friedrich Hegel, *Introductory Lectures on Aesthetics*, ed. Michael Inwood, trans. Bernard Bosanquet (London: Penguin, 1993).

36 It is not clear whether the seminar was on Camus's novella, *L'étrang-*

er, which is only 159 pages (and per the latest editions, 123 pages). Perhaps it was Camus's *La Peste*, which is 320 pages.

37 Another most commonly encountered translation of this sentence is: "Philosophy, which once seemed obsolete, lives on because the moment to realize it was missed." See: Theodor Adorno, *Negative Dialectics*, trans. E.B. Ashton (New York: Continuum, 1983), 3.

38 Adorno, *Aesthetic Theory*, 1.

39 Reference to Erich Maria Remarque's anti-war novel, *All Quiet on the Western Front* (1928). The original German title is *Im Westen nichts Neues*.

40 The Sartrean idea of art as process of derealization of reality into the imaginary, or the construction of mental imagery, was first discussed in Sartre's *L'imaginaire* (1940). See the English translation: Jean-Paul Sartre, *The Imaginary: A phenomenological psychology of the imagination* (New York: Routledge, 2004). Later, Sartre returned to the topic of derealization in: Jean-Paul Sartre, *The Family Idiot: Gustave Flaubert, 1821-1857*, Volume 5, trans. Carol Cosman (Chicago: University of Chicago Press, 1989).

41 Possibly a reference to the following passage: "Art's substance could be its transitoriness. It is thinkable, and not merely an abstract possibility, that great music — a late development — was possible only during a limited phase of humanity." See: Adorno, *Aesthetic Theory*, 3.

42 Timothy Clark, *Farewell to an Idea: Episodes from a History of Modernism* (New Heaven: Yale University Press, 1999).

43 Reference to Peter Bürger, *Theory of the Avant-garde,* trans. Michael Shaw (Minneapolis, MN: University of Minnesota Press, 1984).

LECTURE TWO

1 Peter Sloterdijk, *Critique of Cynical Reason*, trans. Michael Eldred (Minneapolis: University of Minnesota Press, 1987).

2 Reference to Bertolt Brecht's career in the German Democratic Republic (GDR). Brecht moved to East Germany after the war, where he contributed to the construction of new socialist culture, and where he enjoyed many privileges not available to other intellectuals. For a more recent discussion of some controversies, and of Brecht's years

in the GDR, see: Mark W. Clark, "Hero or Villain? Bertolt Brecht and the Crisis Surrounding June 1953," *Journal of Contemporary History*, vol. 41, no. 3 (July, 2006), 451-475.

3 For Adorno and the police incident, see: Esther Leslie, "Introduction to Adorno/Marcuse: Correspondence on the German Student Movement," in *New Left Review* 1/233 (1999): 118-33. On Habermas' role and position in the student movement in the 1960s, see: "Habermas and the Student Movement" in Matthew G. Specter, *Habermas: An Intellectual Biography* (Cambridge: Cambridge University Press, 2010).

4 Gretel Adorno took notes, and then retyped the entire manuscript from dictations made by Adorno and Horkheimer. On the circumstances of writing the *Dialectics of Enlightenment*, see: "Messages in a bottle, or, How to create enlightenment about the Enlightenment" in Müller-Doohm, *Adorno*, 278-287.

5 "Thematization" is an important term in Jameson's vocabulary, to which he will return in subsequent lectures. The term is borrowed from the late writings of Paul de Man and is used to refer to a form of thematic reification. See: Jameson, *Postmodernism or, The Cultural Logic of Late Capitalism*, 91.

6 Adorno, *Aesthetic Theory*, 138.

7 Ibid.

8 Ibid., 3.

9 Ibid., 5.

10 Ibid.

11 In *Exiles and Émigrés*, Terry Eagleton discusses the role played in early-twentieth-century English literature by such "outsiders" as the Pole Joseph Conrad, the Americans Ezra Pound and T.S. Eliot, or the Irish writers James Joyce and W. B. Yeats. The English writer and poet D.H. Lawrence was driven into exile. See: Terry Eagleton, *Exiles and Émigrés: Studies in Modern Literature* (London: Chatto and Windus, 1970).

12 Adorno, *Aesthetic Theory*, 6.

13 Ibid.

14 Adorno, *Minima Moralia*, 92.

15 Ibid.

16 Ibid., 93.

17 Reference to Adorno's first sentence in *Negative Dialectics*. See previous chapter.
18 Adorno, *Aesthetic Theory*, 7.
19 Ibid.
20 Ibid.
21 Ibid.
22 G.F.W. Hegel, *Aesthetics: Lectures on Fine Art*, vol. 1., trans. T.M. Knox, (Oxford: Oxford University Press, 1998), 76.
23 In English, the sentence has most often been translated as: "Hence, imperfection of the artistic form betrays itself also as imperfection of idea." See: G.F.W. Hegel, *The Philosophy of Art: Being the Second Part of Hegel's Aesthetik* trans. W.M.M. Bryant (New York: D. Appleton and Company, 1879), 1-2.
24 Hegel, *Aesthetics: Lectures on Fine Art*, 78.
25 Possibly a reference to one of the early Roman-era Greek treatises, titled *On the Sublime* (in Latin: *De sublimitate*), attributed to Longinus.
26 Edmund Burke, *A Philosophical Enquiry into the Origin of our Ideas of the Sublime and the Beautiful* (London: Dodsley, 1759).
27 Reference to Edmund Burke, *Reflections on the Revolution in France* (1790).
28 The reference is likely to Luc Ferry, who served as France's minister of education (2002-2004). In his book *Homo Aestheticus* (1990), Ferry delivers a critique of modernism and of the aesthetics and politics of the 1960s, calling for a return to non-metaphysical humanism, anti-historicism, beauty and the judgment of taste, all in the name of freedom and liberal democracy. See: Luc Ferry, *Homo Aestheticus: The Invention of Taste in the Democratic Age*, trans. Robert de Loaiza (Chicago: Chicago University Press, 1993). Jameson would refer several times in the seminar to Luc Ferry, associating his name with an aesthetic conservatism that calls for a return of the beautiful.
29 See: Hans Robert Jauss's study, *Ästhetische Normen und geschichtliche Reflexion in der "Querelle des anciens et des modernes"* (Munich: Eidos, 1964).

LECTURE THREE

1 Adorno, "Trying to Understand *Endgame*" in: Adorno, *Notes to Literature*, 237-71.

2 It is not clear to what article in the *Times* Jameson is referring to here. It could be Anne Midgette, "Twelve-Tone Works Pitched to the Emotion of Protest" in: *New York Times* (Sep 30), 2003, E3.

3 The reference may be to Barnett Newman, whose "little strip of color on bare canvas" was shown in a large retrospective at the Philadelphia Museum of Art in 2002.

4 Here Jameson makes a quick reference to the relation between Kantian categories of theoretical reason in the *Critique of Pure Reason* (quantity, quality, relation, modality) and the "prerequisites" for the judgment of taste (disinterestedness, universality, subjective purposiveness, and necessity), as they are introduced in the *Critique of Judgment*. For a more detailed discussion of this correspondence, which is part of a broader intention in Kant to put forward beauty or art (and the *Critique of Judgment*) as a so-called transition (*Übergang*) or articulation (*Mittelglied*) between the theoretical and practical reason, between understanding and reason, knowledge and freedom, see: Derrida's *Truth in Painting*, in particular chapter two, "The Parergon." Jacques Derrida, *The Truth in Painting*, trans. Geoff Bennington and Ian McLeod (Chicago IL: University of Chicago Press, 1987).

5 This is a description of the distinction between understanding and reason in Kant's own words, as it appears in a nineteenth-century translation: "The understanding may be a faculty for the production of unity of phenomena by virtue of rules; the reason is a faculty for the production of unity of rules (of the understanding) under principles. Reason, therefore, never applies directly to experience, or to any sensuous object; its object is, on the contrary, the understanding, to the manifold cognition of which it gives a unity a priori by means of conceptions — a unity which may be called rational unity, and which is of a nature very different from that of the unity produced by the understanding." See: Immanuel Kant, *Critique of Pure Reason*, trans. John Miller Dow Meiklejohn (London: Henry G. Bohn, 1855), 213.

6 In the seminar, we used Werner Pluhar's translation of Kant's third *Critique*. See: Immanuel Kant, *Critique of Judgment*, trans. Werner S. Pluhar. (Indianapolis: Hackett Publishing Co, 1987), 52/210.

7 Ibid., 53/211. [Emphasis in the original.]

8 For their last issue, the *Little Review* (1929) had a questionnaire in which they asked everyone whose work they had printed to answer a number of questions. "One of the questions was, what do you feel about modern art. I answered, I like to look at it. That was my real answer because I do, I do like to look at it, that is at the picture part of modern art. The other parts of it interest me much less." See: Gertrude Stein, *Lectures in America*, in Digital General Collection at <http://quod.lib.umich.edu>. Accessed June 10, 2014. It also seems that, for the original questioner of *Little Review*, Gertrude Stein answered simply: "I do like to look at it." The rest of the sentence may have originated later in her memoirs.

9 Kant, *Critique of Judgment*, 220/64. [Emphasis in the original.]

10 "There is no disputing about taste." Kant, *Critique of Judgment*, 210/338

11 Reference to David Hume, *Of the Standard of Taste* (1757).

12 Kant, *Critique of Judgment*, 84/236 [Emphasis in the original.]

13 Ibid., 90/240. [Emphasis in the original.]

14 Ibid., 92/242.

15 Reference to Vico's principle *verum factum* which first appeared in Vico's *De antiquissima Italorum sapienta* (1710) and was later reformulated in *La scienza nuova seconda* (1730). Vico's "*verum* is *factum*," which means "truth is made," is often seen as the origins of historicism.

16 Ibid., 100/247. [Emphasis in the original.]

17 Ibid., 101/248. [Emphasis in the original.]

18 "By the same token, a liking for the sublime in nature is only *negative* (whereas a liking for the beautiful is *positive*)." Ibid., 129. [Emphasis in the original.]

19 The most common examples of Kantian "sublime objects" are St. Peter's Basilica in Rome, the Alps, the Pyramids, the sky, the stormy sea. For a short discussion of these objects and other references,

see: Robert R. Clewis, *The Kantian Sublime and the Revelation of Freedom* (Cambridge: Cambridge University Press, 2009), 67, n. 22.

20 Ibid., 108-109/252-253

21 Kant, *Critique of Judgment*, 111/255. [Emphasis in the original.]

22 Ibid.

23 Ibid., 124.

24 Ibid., 121-122/262-263.

25 Ibid., 129. [Emphasis in the original.]

26 Jean-François Lyotard, *Lessons on the Analytic of the Sublime*, trans. Elisabeth Rottenberg (Stanford, CA: Stanford University Press, 1991).

27 Kant, *Critique of Judgment*, 213/341.

LECTURE FOUR

1 Reference to the collection of Adorno's essays, *Notes to Literature*.

2 Reference to two plays in the Lulu-cycle by Frank Wedekind (1864-1918): *Die Büchse der Pandora* (Pandora's Box), 1904, and *Frühlings Erwachen* (Spring Awakening), 1891.

3 Reference to film by the Austrian film director and screenwriter Georg Wilhelm Pabst (1885-1967) and his silent film, *Pandora's Box* (1929).

4 Reference to Austrian composer Alban Berg's last opera, *Wozzeck* (1924). The original source material for the opera is the play "Woyzeck" written by Georg Büchner in the 19th century. When Alban Berg adapted the play into an opera, he chose to use the spelling "Wozzeck" instead. Therefore, there are two different spellings used in this book: "Woyzeck" when referring to Georg Büchner's drama or Werner Herzog's film, and "Wozzeck" when mentioning Alban Berg's opera.

5 The so-called "beauty chapters" are the three chapters following the chapter "Situation." These are chapter three, "On the Categories of the Ugly, the Beautiful, and Technique"; chapter four, "Natural Beauty"; and chapter five, "Art Beauty: Apparition, Spiritualization, Intuitability." See table of contents (index) in: Adorno, *Aesthetic Theory*.

6 Jean-François Lyotard, *Le Différend* (Paris: Les Éditions de Minuit, 1983). In English: Jean-François Lyotard, *The Differend: Phrases in*

Dispute, trans. Georges Van Den Abbeele (Minneapolis, MN: University of Minnesota Press, 1988).

7 Lyotard taught and lectured at many universities in the United States: Johns Hopkins University; University of California, Berkeley; Yale University; Stony Brook University; University of California, San Diego; University of California, Irvine.

8 Reference to Friedrich Schiller's *Über die ästhetische Erziehung des Menschen in einer Reihe von Briefen (On the Aesthetic Education of Man)*, first published in 1794.

9 In Lyotard, the concept of "enthusiasm" marks the transition from his Freudo-Marxist preoccupations with libidinal politics and culture to his later interests in ethics. In this transition, Lyotard departs from the Kantian notions of beauty and, most importantly, of the sublime in Kant's *Third Critique*. Lyotard's writings on enthusiasm, which he started in a small paper in 1981, then continued in *The Differend*, were later published in a short book called *Enthusiasm: The Kantian Critique of History* (Sandford, CA: Stanford University Press, 2009). For a concise discussion of the concept of "enthusiasm" in Lyotard's work, see: Georges Van Den Abbeele, "Enthusiasm" in *The Lyotard Dictionary*, ed. Stuart Sim (Edinburgh: Edinburgh University Press, 2011), 67-68.

10 Edmund Burke, *Reflections on the Revolution in France* (1790).

11 Reference to Franco-American literary critic Francis George Steiner (1929-2020).

12 See: *The Iliad of Homer. In the English verse translation by Alexander Pope. Illustrated with the Classical designs by John Flaxman* (New York: Heritage, 1942).

13 Reference to movie by Martin Scorsese, *Gangs of New York* (Miramax Film Corp. 2002).

14 Jameson reads from Book Three of the *Iliad*; the part describing the battle between the Greeks and Trojans, as offered by three translators: George Chapman in late seventeenth and early eighteenth century, Alexander Pope in the eighteenth and Richard Lattimore in the late twentieth century.

15 It is not clear from what edition of Pope's translation of Homer Jameson is reading. I cite the passage from an American edition by

Samuel Johnson, *The Poetical works of Alexander Pope, Esq. [Including his translation of Homer], to which is prefixed the life of the author* (Philadelphia: J.J. Woodward, 1836), 231.

16 *The Iliad of Homer, Prince of Poets*, trans. George Chapman (London: John Russel Smith Soho Square, 1857), 62.

17 Homer, *The Iliad*, trans. Richard Lattimore (Chicago, IL: University of Chicago Press, 2011), 117. For a more recent discussion of this part, see also: Fredric Jameson, *Allegory and Ideology* (London: Verso, 2019), 5.

18 In this seminar, Jameson discusses several oppositions: between beauty and the sublime in Kant (via Lyotard and Burke); between unity and multiplicity, Greeks and Trojans (via Homer's *Iliad*); and between Freud and Kant in the second part of the lecture.

19 Johnson, *The Poetical Works of Alexander Pope*, 231.

20 Ibid.

21 Reference to Alexander Pope's "An Essay on Criticism" (1711).

22 A reference to the Line/Color debate and the historical exchange between the proponents of Neoclassicism and Romanticism. The Color/Line Debate, within the French Royal Academy, unfolded at the same time with the Quarrel between the Ancients and the Moderns. In art, the debate took the form of an exchange between the proponents of line and drawing, who were known as the Poussinists (after the painter Nicolas Poussin) and the Rubenists (after the painter Peter Paul Rubens), who prioritized color.

23 This text has also been translated as "The Relation of the Poet to Day-dreaming." See: Sigmund Freud, "The Relation of the Poet to Day-dreaming" in *Collected Papers*, vol. 4, trans. I.F. Grant Duff (New York: Basic Books, 1959).

24 Ibid., 174.

25 Ibid., 175.

26 Ibid., 178.

27 Ibid., 182.

28 Ibid.

29 Sigmund Freud, *Jokes and their Relation to the Unconscious*, Free eBook by www.SigmundFreud.net, 99-100.

30 Ibid., 100.

31 Sigmund Freud, *Three Essays on the Theory of Sexuality* (1905).
32 Sigmund Freud, *Introductory Lectures on Psychoanalysis* (1917).
33 See: Jean Laplanche and Jean-Bertrand Pontalis, *The Language of Psychoanalysis*, trans. Donald Nicholson-Smith (New York: Norton, 1973), 431-34.
34 See: chapter six in Cornelius Castoriadis, *The Imaginary Institution of Society*, trans. Kathleen Blamey (Cambridge, MA: The MIT Press, 199).
35 Sigmund Freud, *Introductory Lectures on Psychoanalysis*, SE vol. 16, 345
36 Sigmund Freud, "'Civilized' Sexual Ethics and the Modern Nervous Illness," SE vol. 9, 189. [Emphasis in the original.]
37 Adorno, *Minima Moralia*, 214.
38 Sigmund Freud, *Introductory Lectures on Psychoanalysis*, SE vol. 16, 376.
39 Napoleon's phrase translated as "careers open to the talents," which has often being considered the slogan of modern meritocracy.
40 Reference to the German-American developmental psychologist who coined the phrase "identity crisis," Erik Homburger Erikson (1902-1994), born Erik Salomonsen.
41 Reference to Erik H. Erikson, *Young Man Luther: A Study in Psychoanalysis and History* (New York: Norton & Company, 1958) and Erik H. Erikson, *Childhood and Society* (New York: Norton & Company, 1950). The last chapters of *Childhood and Society* are titled "The Legend of Hitler's Childhood" (chapter nine) and "The Legend of Maxim Gorky's Youth" (chapter ten).
42 Reference to early twentieth-century critical traditions, such as Russian Formalism, or in a different cultural context and method, that of New Criticism in the United States. During his Opoiaz phase, Roman Jakobson compared the biographical model of mainstream criticism dominant at that time to the work of the policeman, who goes around to gather biographical evidence in order to build a case.
43 Reference to the only book that Stendhal published under his real name: Marie-Henri Beyle, *The History of Painting in Italy and Rome, Naples and Florence* (1817).

44 Reference to Freud's "pot story" in *The Interpretation of Dreams*.

45 Adorno, *Aesthetic Theory*, 15. [Emphasis in the original.]

LECTURE FIVE

1 For a more detailed discussion of Jameson's role in China, see: Xudong Zhang, "Modernity as Cultural Politics: Jameson in China," in *Fredric Jameson: A Critical Reader*, eds. Sean Homer and Douglas Kellner (New York: Palgrave Macmillan, 2004), 169-195.

2 Discusses the plan for the next class to show the German silent film directed by Georg Wilhelm Pabst, *Pandora Box* (1929). Pabst's film was based on two plays in the Lulu-cycle by Frank Wedekind (1864-1918): *Die Büchse der Pandora* (Pandora's Box), 1904, and *Frühlings Erwachen* (Spring Awakening), 1891.

3 Reference to the nineteenth century writers and dramatists Georg Büchner (1813-1837) and Frank Wedekind (1864-1918), regarded as major precursors of German Expressionism, as well as most influential on twentieth-century German dramatists, such as Bertolt Brecht or Friedrich Dürrenmatt.

4 Reference to book by Gotthold Ephraim Lessing, *Laocoön: An Essay on the Limits of Painting and Poetry* (1767).

5 Reference to the *Aeneid*, the Latin epic poem written by Virgil between 29 and 19 BC.

6 The date of the marble sculptural group representing an episode from Book II of Virgil's *Aeneid* is disputed. The sculpture is believed to be a work of the 1st century AD, made in the stylistic tradition of the sculptures of Hellenistic Pergamon. It is not known whether the sculpture discovered in 1507 and placed in Vatican is an original or a copy based on an earlier Greek work. See: Luca Leoncini, "Laokoon" in *Groove Art Online*, <https://doi.org/10.1093/gao/9781884446054.article.T049232>

7 Reference to Benjamin's 1933 essays, "On The Mimetic Faculty" and "The Doctrine of the Similar."

8 Adorno, *Aesthetic Theory*, 359.

9 Reference to the Scottish anthropologist James George Frazer (1854-1941) and his influential work, *The Golden Bough: A Study in Compar-*

ative Religion (1890), retitled from the second edition as *The Golden Bough: A Study in Magic and Religion*.

10 Jameson will return to the concept of "mimesis" in Lecture Nine, and then later it will be discussed in relation to two other key concepts: "expression" and "construction." In his early book, *Late Marxism*, Jameson declared mimesis "a kind of pseudo-totality" (*LM*, 50), calling it the "enigmatic concept of 'mimesis'" (74), and insisting that "'mimesis' in Adorno [is] a foundational concept [which is] never defined nor argued but always alluded to, by name, as though it had preexisted all the texts like Benjamin's notion of *aura*, which otherwise has nothing to do with it" (64). Such statements, regarding the "Adorno's omnipresent theme of mimesis" (52), have been later cited by numerous interpreters. Mimesis is indeed a ubiquitous yet also surreptitious concept in Adorno's writings on art, where one has the impression that mimesis is always around, ready to pop up at any moment in order to remind us of the anthropological "origins" of knowledge and art. According to his view, science and art begin — and to an extent — end with or *in* mimesis. Mimesis is the oldest epistemic drive; it is the original sin — the archetypal relationship that humans had with the object, nature, external reality, from the earliest time. Even in its modern configuration, mimesis is present — albeit in a sublimated form, discussed in more detail later — in the subject's nonconceptual or intuitive relation to the other, or self, and which, as it will be argued later, goes by the name of "expression." As a central concept of Adornian aesthetics, mimesis lies at the foundation of his speculative anthropology and/or natural history. Adorno and Horkheimer deal with the anthropological aspect of mimesis in one of the chapters of the *Dialectic of Enlightenment*. Mimesis points to art's origins in primeval magic, ritual or prehistoric myth. The primitive mind depends for its survival on the intuitive enactment or imitation of the forces of nature, which it seeks to bring under control. It is the law of self-preservation that motivates early mimetic behavior. But as humanity entrusts its fate to reason and modern science, following on the pathway to progress and enlightenment, the role of mimesis — as non- or pre-conceptual impulsive ritual of identification with the other, as practiced by early

humans — began to diminish. With the advance of modern rationality, mimesis did not disappear but was turned into a sublimated drive, a deeply buried instinct in the modern human psyche. The history of mankind, one may say, is the history of reason progressing through different forms and modes of mimesis: from the primitive one, when early humans mimicked their natural surroundings out of fear for the unknown forces of nature, to mimesis as simulation of the deeds of the mythical hero in the classical ancient age, to a form of counter-mimesis present in the historical process of disenchantment, or demythologization, and the substitution of magic and myth with modern science. One of modern mimesis' great paradoxes in the age of progress is that, even though modern rationality, instrumental reason, the thinking of *Verstand*, positivism, and the likes, work hard to dethrone magic, myth, religion and superstition, it ends up constituting itself into a new myth — the myth of modern natural science as the *only* form of knowledge or truth permissible. This reversal, which displaces old forms of knowledge with new ones, could be also interpreted in terms of a negative mimesis. In the urge to overcome ancient myth, modern rationality builds a new myth of positive or natural sciences as the only valid form of cognition. In this dialectic of reason and nature, art is at the other pole. Art stands with, or *for*, what enlightened modern rationality seeks to bring into subjection. With the rise of historical romanticism, in the early phase of industrial capitalism, art proclaims itself the sole ally and defender not only of nature but also of suppressed forms of knowledge and truth (such as magic, myth, religion). The romantics, the modern magicians of poetic imaginary worlds, drew on play, mimicry, assimilation, and the occult as a counterreaction to rationalistic disenchantment. While modern science seeks new epistemic virtues, capable of providing "pure" objectivity, and it does so by detaching itself from the object — seeking to erase the trace of all that interfered with "scientific objectivity" in the factual regime of science — art, on the other hand, looks for ways to preserve its relation to nature. Art keeps deploying old techniques of imitation and simulation for some time, as one can witness in the naturalist and realist art and literature of the early industrial capitalism in the eighteenth and nineteenth centuries, or even in various forms of "magical," "social," or "socialist" realisms that have survived in some place until late in the twentieth century. It is also through mimetic impulse that art negates the abstract logic of capital, utility, commodity, and the new alliance between capital and applied science or technology that forge the main instruments in the ongoing conquest and destruction of nature. But art is also part of the Spirit, and it cannot completely separate itself from other forms of knowledge. Art looks into more efficient ways of defending nature, into practices and techniques that depart from the simple mimetic identification. Therefore, in the art of high modernism, artistic mimesis also manifests negatively — that is to say, as a repressed drive coded into more modern aesthetic impulses of expression and construction. And even though every valid work of modern art secretly seeks to free itself of the initial sin, of the spell of ancient imitation (secretly believing perhaps that it will neither relate nor save the world or nature) mimesis remains the most basic drive or immanent force of art. [*Fragment from the transcriber/editor's research for the seminar, updated and rewritten in 2021-2022.*]

11 On the importance of the notion of mimesis, see: "The Concept of Enlightenment" in Adorno and Horkheimer, *Dialectic of Enlightenment*.

12 Harry Braverman, *Labor and Monopoly Capital: The Degradation of Work in the Twentieth Century* (New York: New York University Press, 1998).

13 Reference to Charlie Chaplin 1936 movie, *Modern Times*.

14 Jameson meant to say in chapter two. *Entkunstung* translated as "deaestheticization" first appears in chapter "Situation." See Adorno, *Aesthetic Theory*, 16.

15 Reference to Paul Samuel Whiteman (1890-1967), successful American bandleader, orchestral director often referred to in Hollywood as the "King of Jazz."

16 Perhaps a reference to Ferdinand Joseph LaMothe (1890-1941), known as Jelly Roll Morton, American jazz pianist and composer who played jazz in the brothels of New Orleans.

17 See the section "Deaestheticization of Art: Critique of the Culture

Industry" in chapter two, "Situation." Adorno, *Aesthetic Theory*, 16-18.

18 See note 7 to chapter one about content discussed in terms of "Inhalt" and "Gehalt." Ibid., 368, n. 7.

19 See: "Art, Society, Aesthetics," and then again in the "Draft Introduction." Adorno, *Aesthetic Theory*, 6, 350.

20 In his presentation, the student relied heavily on chapter four, "Lord Chandos and His Discontents," from a book by Richard Sheppard, *Modernism-Dada-Postmodernism* (Evansston, Ill.: Northwestern University Press, 2000), 89-97. The student acknowledged his indebtedness to Sheppard, whom he calls "my tutor at Oxford," even though, in some parts of the presentation, the text was identical with Shepperd's chapter. For this reason, the editor significantly modified the student's presentation due to copyright and liability issues.

21 Hugo von Hofmannsthal, *The Lord Chandos Letter and Other Writings*, trans. Joel Rotenberg (New York: New York Review of Books, 2005), 117-18.

22 Sheppard, *Modernism-Dada-Postmodernism*, 91.

23 Hofmannsthal, *The Lord Chandos Letter and Other Writings*, 119-120.

24 Ibid., 120.

25 Sheppard, *Modernism-Dada-Postmodernism*, 92.

26 Ibid.

27 Hofmannsthal, *The Lord Chandos Letter and Other Writings*, 122.

28 Sheppard, *Modernism-Dada-Postmodernism*, 94-95.

29 Ibid., 95.

30 Ibid., 96.

31 Ibid., 99.

32 Ibid.

33 Ibid.

34 Hofmannsthal, *The Lord Chandos Letter and Other Writings*, 127-28.

35 Sheppard, *Modernism-Dada-Postmodernism*, 100.

36 A line from the poem "This Is Just To Say" (1934) by the American poet William Carlos Williams (1883-1963).

37 The distinction universal-particular-singular (the latter sometimes

is translated as the "individual") is the Hegelian reinterpretation of Aristotelian logic. For a more detailed discussion of this relation, see: Book Two in Georg Wilhelm Friedrich Hegel, *Science of Logic* (London: Routledge, 1969), 599-618.

38 See: Adorno, *Aesthetic Theory*, 16.

39 Reference to David Fernbach's review of Robert Norton, *Secret Germany: Stefan George and His Circle* (Ithaca and London: Cornell University Press, 2002). See also: David Fernbach, "Prophet-Pariah" in *New Left Review* 18 (Nov/Dec. 2002).

40 Arnold Schoenberg, *Verklärte Nacht* (Transfigured Night), Op. 4. (1899).

41 Reference to the French painter Pierre Puvis de Chavannes (1824-1898).

42 Arthur Rimbaud, *Une Saison en Enfer* (A Season in Hell), an extended poem in prose published in 1873.

43 Walter Benjamin's essay "Goethe's Elective Affinities" was first printed in Hofmannsthal's journal, *Neue Deutsche Beiträge* (1924/25).

LECTURE SIX

1 See the 1997 Japanese film, "Welcome Back, Mr. McDonald," directed by Kōki Mitani.

2 Alenka Zupančič, *Ethics of the Real: Kant, Lacan* (London: Verso, 2000).

3 Mladen Dolar, *Wenn die Musik der Liebe Nahrung ist...: Mozart und die Philosophie in der Oper* (Wien: Turia und Kant, 2001).

4 Mladen Dolar, "The Object Voice" in *Sic 1: Gaze and Voice as Love Objects* (Durham: Duke University Press, 1996).

5 Mladen Dolar, "Cogito as the Subject of the Unconscious" in *Cogito and the Unconscious*, ed. Slavoj Žižek (Durham: Duke University Press, 1998), 11-40.

6 V. I. Lenin, *Revolution at the Gates: Selected Writings of Lenin from 1917*, ed. Slavoj Žižek (London: Verso, 2002).

7 Slavoj Žižek and Mladen Dolar, *Opera's Second Death* (London; Routledge, 2001); the "book on ethics" is most likely Slavoj Žižek's *On Belief: Thinking in Action* (London; Routledge, 2003).

8 See: pages 16-17 in the chapter, "Situation." Adorno, *Aesthetic Theory*.

9 It is not clear to what production of Georg Büchner's 1837 drama *Woyzeck* was the student referring. Perhaps the student is talking about Werner Herzog's 2000 movie, *Woyzeck*.

10 Reference back to the beginning of the chapter "Situation," in which Adorno starts with the discussion of the materials that have also lost their self-evidence (like the categories of art discussed in chapter one). Adorno, *Aesthetic Theory*, 16.

11 Reference to Thomas More's book, *Utopia* (1516).

12 Marx's denunciations of Proudhon appear in many books. The most concentrated attack is in Marx's *The Poverty of Philosophy* (1847). Here, Jameson may be referring to Marx's *Grundrisse: Foundations of the Critique of Political Economy*, chapter two. See also Jameson's discussion of the same issues in: Fredric Jameson, *Archaeologies of the Future: The Desire Called Utopia and Other Science Fictions* (London: Verso, 2007).

13 Adorno, *Aesthetic Theory*, 17.

14 Adorno, *Ästhetische Theorie*, 33.

15 Reference to Deleuze and Guattari's critique of "ideology" in *Anti-Oedipus* and *A Thousand Plateaus*. "There is no ideology and never has been." See: Gilles Deleuze and Félix Guattari, *A Thousand Plateaus: Capitalism and Schizophrenia*, trans. Brian Massumi (Minneapolis: University of Minnesota Press, 1987), 4.

16 On practice and ideology, see: Fredric Jameson, "Architecture and the Critique of Ideology" in Joan Ockman, ed., *Architecture, Criticism, Ideology* (Princeton: Princeton Architectural Press, 1985), 53.

17 Reference here to an essay by Marcuse, "On the Affirmative Character of Culture." See also: Lecture One.

18 For Adorno's late 1930s visits to Berlin or Frankfurt, see: Stefan Müller-Doohm, *Adorno: A Biography* trans. Rodney Livingstone (Cambridge: Polity, 2005).

19 Adorno, *Aesthetic Theory*, 19.

20 Ibid.

21 The short exchange between Jameson and the student touches upon a crucial point of disagreement in the interpretations of modernism.

The poles of the debate are represented by Clement Greenberg (and, to a degree, Michel Fried) on one side, who regard modernism in terms of reductionism, and the supporters of modernism as "practices of negation," represented by such Marxist critics as T.J. Clark or Peter Bürger, and as we see above in Jameson's own interpretation of the negating "telos" of modernism, related to the Marxist notion of "mode of production." For T.J. Clark, modernism proceeds by ever more extreme acts of negation of meaning. According to this position, modernism proceeds by casting off or negating art's norm and codes, in order to arrive at some bare minimum that suffice to be called "art." These acts of radical negation, which Marxist critics have emphasized in their interpretation of modernism, are often motivated by politics. The reductionism of art to its bare essentials is sometimes linked to the meaning and place of art in modern society (for example, in Peter Bürger's thesis regarding the "political program" of the historical avant-garde that sought to bridge the gap separating art and life, as a reaction against bourgeois aestheticism). Greenberg and Fried do not agree with the interpretation of modernism in terms of practices of negation of meaning. Greenberg's interpretation of modernism — which Fried has partially supported adding his own interpretations of "literalness," "absorption," "theatri cality" — rests on reductionism and the discovery of the essence and "flatness." As Greenberg famously put it, modernist painting seeks to come to terms with the manipulation of canvas and paint. In completing the reduction, the modernist painter sought to discover the irreducible essence of painting that would constitute panting's *source of value*. For Fried, the value is not of painting as such — and in all times — but for *that* particular historical moment (from mid-nineteenth to mid-twentieth century). To quote Fried: "the task of modernist painter is to discover those conventions which, at a given moment, alone are capable of establishing his work's identity as painting." For a more detailed discussion of the debate between two conflicting interpretations of modernism, as outlined in Greenberg's "reductionism" and in T.J. Clark's "negation," see: Michael Fried, "How Modernism Works: A Response to T.J. Clark," *Critical Inquiry*, 9, no. 1, 223. For an interpretation of Fried's account of modernism, see also: Stephen Melville, "Notes on the Reemergence of Allegory, the Forgetting of Modernism, the Necessity of Rhetoric, and the Conditions of Publicity in Art and Criticism," *October* 19 (Winter 1981), 55-92.

22 Reference to Michael Fried's trilogy of books on French pictorial modernism, consisting of: *Absorption and Theatricality* (1980); *Courbet's Realism* (1990); and *Manet's Modernism* (1996).

23 Antoine Compagnon, *The Five Paradoxes of Modernity*, trans. Franklin Philip (New York: Columbia University Press, 1994).

24 Jameson referred several times to Luc Ferry, who served as France's Minister of Education (2002-2004), and who wrote a critique of modernism in his acclaimed book, *Homo Aestheticus* (1993). See also: note on Ferry in Lecture Two.

25 Reference to *The Letters of Madame de Sévigné (Lettres de Madame de Sévigné: de sa famille et de ses amis)*, published in several editions in the early eighteenth century.

26 Adorno, *Aesthetic Theory*, 21.

27 Reference to Yvor Winters, *In Defense of Reason* (Routledge and Kegan Paul, 1960). The book consists of three parts: "Part 1: Primitivism and Decadence: A Study of American Experimental Poetry"; "Part 2: Maule's Curse: Seven Studies in the History of American Obscurantism"; "Part 3: The Anatomy of Nonsense. The Significance of The Bridge, by Hart Crane, Or What are We to Think of Professor X?"

28 Reference to Albert C. Barnes (1872-1951), a wealthy physician and collector of modern art and the founder of The Barnes Foundation in Philadelphia. His collection of modern art was considered too radical for Philadelphia of the 1920s.

29 Possibly reference to Adorno's discussion of genius in a later chapter, "Subject-Object." See: Adorno, *Aesthetic Theory*, 170.

30 "This prohibition falls on what provincials ultimately hoped to salvage under the name 'message': appearance as meaningful." See: Adorno, *Aesthetic Theory*, 22.

LECTURE SEVEN

1 Adorno, *Aesthetic Theory*, 22.

2 Reference to Schoenberg's statement: "a discussion of harmony is not on the agenda at present" in Adorno's essay, "The Function of

Counterpoint in New Music." See: Theodor W. Adorno, *Sound Figures*, trans. Rodney Livingstone (Stanford, CA: Stanford University Press, 1999), 135.

3 Arnold Schoenberg died in 1951 in Los Angeles, California.

4 Reference to Japanese film director renown for the simplicity of composition and minimal camera movement, Yasujirō Ozu (1903-1963). See also: Stanley Aronowitz, "Film — The Art Form of Late Capitalism" in *Social Text*, no. 1 (Winter, 1979), 110-129.

5 Reference to Jean Baudrillard, *The Mirror of Production*, trans. Mark Poster. (St. Louis: Telos Press, 1975).

6 Adorno, *Aesthetic Theory*, 22.

7 Ibid., 23.

8 Jameson often uses this quote in his books. It appears in *Late Marxism* and *Postmodernism Or, The Cultural Logic of Late Capitalism*. "Every masterpiece came into the world with a measure of ugliness in it... It's our business as critics to stand in front of it and recover its ugliness." Quoted from Thornton Wilder's introduction to Gertrude Stein, *Four in America* (New Haven, CT: Yale University Press, 1947), xi.

9 Adorno, *Aesthetic Theory*, 23.

10 Jürgen Habermas, *The Philosophical Discourse of Modernity: Twelve Lectures*, trans. Frederick G. Lawrence (Cambridge, MA: The MIT Press, 1990).

11 Reference to Jürgen Habermas's theory of communication, developed in a series of books that began with the *Theory of Communicative Action* (1981).

12 Jameson does not name the slogan, but it can be inferred that he is still referring to the Habermasian denunciation of "irrationalisms." Jameson discusses Habermas' critique of Adorno and Horkheimer in terms of "irrationalism," due to their condemnation of reason and progress. For Habermas, progress is an incomplete project, and the path of Enlightenment rationality must proceed to further democratization by means of what he calls "communicative reason." The latter is Habermas's alternative to what his mentor Adorno, with Horkheimer, denounced as the byproduct of Enlightenment, calling it "instrumental reason."

13 Adorno, *Aesthetic Theory*, 23-24.

14 Reference to his writings on the postmodernist subject. This subject is determined by increased reification and commodification under late capitalism, which leads to an end of the bourgeois sentimental ego. In his book on postmodernism, Jameson talks about signs of shrinking subjectivity in terms of the "waning of affect," by which he means the disappearance of bourgeois sentimental and emotional life as part of a process of de-subjectivation. On the "waning of affect," see: Jameson, *Postmodernism or, The Cultural Logic of Late Capitalism*, 11-16.

15 The phrase "the war of all against all," or "the war of every man against his neighbor," or "the war of every man against every man" is associated with Thomas Hobbes' *Leviathan* (1651).

16 Possibly a reference to Mallarmé's *Livre*. which was a great influence on many futurists.

17 It is not easy to hear the name from the recording, but the reference may be to *A New History of French Literature*, a volume edited by Denis Hollier. It was written by 164 "literature specialists," with essays introduced by dates and arranged in chronological order: from 778 to 1989. The table of contents include such topics as: "842 — The Birth of Medieval Studies [R. Howard Bloch]"; "1127 — The Old Provençal Lyric [Stephen G. Nichols]"; "1528 — Manners and Mannerisms at Court [Nancy J. Vickers]" "1968, May — "Actions, No! Words, Yes!" [Denis Hollier.]" See Denis Hollier, ed., *A New History of French Literature* (Cambridge: Harvard University Press, 1998).

18 See; "Defense of Isms" and "Isms as Secularized Schools" in Adorno, *Aesthetic Theory*, 24-25.

19 Reference to Harold Bloom's concern for the Western literary canon, and his insistence on studying the masterpieces. For example, in *Shakespeare: The Invention of the Human*, Bloom insists that Shakespeare wrote thirty-eight plays and that only "twenty-four of which are masterpieces."

20 Reference to Walter Benjamin, *The Origin of German Tragic Drama*, trans. John Osborne (London: Verso, 1998).

21 Adorno, *Aesthetic Theory*, 25.

22 Ibid., 26.

23 The full sentence in Adorno: "The truth of the new, as the truth of what is not already used up, is situated in the intentionless." Ibid.
24 Ibid.
25 Ibid., 28.
26 Ibid.
27 Ibid., 29.
28 Ibid.
29 Reference to the postmodern encyclopedic novel by David Foster Wallace, *Infinite Jest* (1996).
30 Reference to Hans Robert Jauss (1921-1997).
31 Adorno, *Aesthetic Theory*, 32.
32 Ibid.
33 Ibid.
34 Ibid.
35 Ibid., 33.
36 Adorno, Ästhetische Theorie, GS.7, 94.
37 Adorno, *Aesthetic Theory*, 59.

LECTURE EIGHT

1 See the film *Predictions of Fire*, directed/written by Michael Benson (Kinetikon Pictures and RTV Slovenia, 1996), DVD.
2 Although Jameson warned against treating the categories of mimesis, expression and construction individually, or in "substantive" terms — reminding everyone in the seminar that they should be grasped "relationally," or how they play against each other in the production of a work of art in a particular historical epoch — these fragments (from the paper researched for the seminar) also look at these categories individually. This long note is dedicated to expression. Expression is a key category of modernism, with a long prehistory in German idealism. In the aesthetics of high modernism, and Adorno in particular, expression designates the subjective aspect of aesthetic experience. "There is no expression without a subject," states Adorno in *Aesthetic Theory* (42). Expression is dialectically intertwined with mimesis, and the complex relationship between the two drives manifests on several levels. Adorno's interpreters do not always agree whether expression is an opposite or a corelative of

mimesis. In *Late Marxism*, Jameson treats "mimesis" and "expression" as irreconcilable opposites (159), whereas Martin Jay interpreted "expression" as part of "mimesis" and together in opposition to "construction" (*MM*, 37). My interpretation is closer to that of Jay, but not completely irreconcilable with Jameson's, as I believe that mimesis and expression could be both opposites and identical, given their dialectical reflection or determination into each other. In Adorno's constellations, one could easily imagine the relation between these two aesthetic poles as constantly changing, or producing new relations based on the perspective from which they are considered. Expression and mimesis could be viewed as opposites, and at the same time, as historically predetermined. One way to imagine expression is in terms of a gradual waning of the archaic impulse of mimesis. The unfolding of mimesis through different periods, epochs, and modes of production (or "scenarios," as outlined by Karla L. Schultz in the influential *Mimesis on the Move*) contributed to the emergence of self-consciousness and modern subjectivity. For Adorno, there was an anthropological time, when consciousness could relate to the other, or nature, only by way of mimickry. With the advance of modernity, however, the mimetic form of knowledge is banned, and what has remained of it has spilled or sedimented into other categories of aesthetic experience. Expression is precisely one such consequence of mimetic sedimentation. When viewed from this perspective, the relation between mimesis and expression appears (in a Hegelian light) as complementary opposites. In his *Aesthetics (1958/59)* lectures, Adorno stresses that "expression itself is a memetic residuum" (Lecture 5, 2 December 1958, unpaginated). In *Aesthetic Theory*, Adorno resorts to a Freudian psychological language in order to discuss various aesthetic impulses in terms of repressed drives, desire, or biological instincts. Expression then could be also understood in terms of a repressed form of mimesis, a mimetic residuum — a radically transformed remnant of the early archaic practices of knowledge achieved through imitation, simulation, assimilation. There is imitation in expression as well, but unlike ancient mimesis, which is imitation of the other, of nature, or simulation of a collective myth — performed in the name of the law of self-preservation — the modern impulse of the expression drive is imitation performed by the alienated subject. Expression is enunciation without reference to nature, or mimesis by the subject caught in the proverbial "desert of the real", to use the Hollywood metaphor from the *Matrix* derived from Jean Baudrillard's 1981 book *Simulacra and Simulation,* that was adopted by many contemporary practitioners of ideology critique). Expression is a form of negative mimesis, or mimesis as *lack* — that is, imitation of what, or when, nothing is left to imitate. In this respect, expression resonates with the postmodernist simulacra — as copy without original, or expression without a subject (that is, a *wholly* constituted subject) — and it is certainly related to what Jameson, in *Late Marxism*, defines as the problem of modern aesthetics in terms of a crisis of semblance, of aesthetic appearance, or *Schein* (discussed in more detail in another note). In other words, modern subjective expression is a kind of ban on mimesis — or rather, it is repressed mimesis transformed into an unconscious drive that compels the subject to imitate its own lack and emptiness. This comes as an outcome of the suppression of nature, performed in the name of the law of self-preservation, by the forces of progress; it is suppression of both internal-subjective and external-objective nature. Given its place in the genealogy of knowledge, and the fact that mimesis has been complicit with the forces of reason, expression is the voice or cry of nature, as it endures violence at the hands of *ratio*. Expression gives voice to that which has been muted, suppressed or has fallen under domination by reason — that is, when "humans have subjected both external nature and internal nature" (Adorno, *Aesthetics 1958/59*, Lecture 6, 4 December 1958, unpaginated). Expression then is a kind of mimesis of emptiness, brought about by modernization and technologization of every aspect of life under the commodity logic of capital. As such, expression is itself the product of "second nature" of capitalism (unlike mimesis, which, in its archaic form, seems more suitable as the drive of representation for the "first nature.") Most prominent in modern art — consolidated into such important historical movements as Expressionism — expression is also a mode of experiencing the *crisis* of life under the conditions of modernity. It is not only the voice of the disappearing nature, but also the pain of life when "life does not live" (to use Ferdinand Kiimberger's statement that Adorno frequently uses, and which he also chose as the epigraph for *Minima Moralia*). One of the major aporias of expression is that, in seeking a particular language — or an artistic form most suitable for giving voice to broken nature — the drive of expression further sunders itself into even more minuscule fragments, or into artistic singularities (most clearly perceived in the aesthetics of contemporary art that Jameson later would call "The Aesthetics of Singularity.") Like many other positions in Adorno, expression is fundamentally aporiatic. Unlike mimesis — harassed by the positive sciences, and even earlier on by Platonism, or by the ban on graven images imposed by some Abrahamic religions — expression is a self-annihilating drive. Artistic expression is fueled by a demand for particularization, individuation, or individualization. The demand is powered by the logic of the "new," as it constantly seeks to elevate works of art out of, and above, any existing conventions, and when it does so, Adorno says that valid or successful works of art begin to imitate themselves. We made a full circle, to realize that expression is a form of self-mimesis. Put in other words, expression is a modern form of (repressed) mimesis, or mimesis in its last, or latest, phase. In this last phase of mimesis, expression only imitates itself, as when most authentic works of modern art resemble nothing but themselves. Thus, expression is both a remnant and a surplus of mimesis, as the latter recedes, along with nature, which it once helped subdue — a relation that follows Hegel's logic, where something has its truth in something other than itself. And yet, despite their dialectical relation, expression is to be separated from mimesis. As a quintessential *modern* drive, expression is the artistic impulse through which art takes the side of the other. Expression preserves its fundamental opposition to mimesis — the archaic form that has evolved into the instrumentality of science with regard to the other (i.e., animals, environment, nature). Therefore, Adorno calls expression a form of articulation of suffering. [*Fragment from the transcriber/editor's research for the seminar, updated and rewritten in 2021-2022.*]

3 Adorno, *Aesthetic Theory*, 42.

4 Reference to *New Criterion*, a New York monthly magazine of neoconservative aesthetics. It was founded in 1982 by a former *New York Times* critic Hilton Kramer and the musical critic Samuel Lipman.

5 It is not clear to what "just published" book about the return of beauty, by a distinguished Irish critic, Jameson is referring to. There were several books on the revival of beauty published around the time of the seminar, but their authors were not Irish critics. See, for example: Vernon Hyde Minor, *The Triumph of Beauty* (2004); Konrad Oberhuber, *The Return of Beauty: A New Look at German Renaissance* (2002).

6 Reference to the so-called "beauty chapters" of Adorno's *Aesthetic Theory*: chapter three, "On the Categories of the Ugly, the Beautiful, and Technique"; chapter four, "Natural Beauty"; and chapter five, "Art Beauty: Apparition, Spiritualization, Intuitability."

7 Reference to Fichte's *Concerning the Concept of the Wissenschaftslehre* (1794), where Fichte lays out his system *Wissenschaftlehre*, or the Doctrine of Science. In the *Foundations of the Entire Science of Knowledge* (1794-1795), Fichte introduces the "Not-I" (*Nicht-Ich*).

8 Johann Wolfgang von Goethe and Friedrich Schiller, *Correspondence Between Goethe and Schiller, 1794-1805*, trans. Liselotte Dieckmann (New York: Peter Lang, 1994).

9 Friedrich Schiller, *Naive and Sentimental Poetry*, and *On the Sublime: Two Essays*, trans. Julius A. Elias (New York: F. Ungar Publishing Company, 1967).

10 Friedrich Schiller, *On the Aesthetic Education of Man in a Series of Letters* (English and German facing), ed. and trans. Elizabeth Wilkinson and L.A. Willoughby (Oxford and New York: Oxford University Press, 1983).

11 Jameson is referring here to what, in Kantian studies, is sometimes called the "Kantian *Übergang*," namely the aesthetic judgment as discussed in the *Critique of Judgment* (the third critique) as a transition (*Übergang*) between nature (in the first *Critique of Pure Reason*) and freedom (the second *Critique of Practical Reason*).

12 Reference to the famous dictum by Le Corbusier: "Architecture or revolution. Revolution can be avoided." See: Le Corbusier, *Towards a New Architecture* (New York: Praeger, 1965), 269. In the same vein, Ludwig Mies van der Rohe states: "If we succeed in carrying out this

industrialization, the social, economic, technical, and also artistic problems will be readily solved." See: Ludwig Mies van der Rohe, "Industrialized Building" in *G* (June 10, 1924).

13 For a published translation of this passage, see, for example: "On Naïve and Sentimental Poetry" in Friedrich Schiller, *Essays*, eds. Walter Hinderer and Daniel O. Dahlstrom (New York: Continuum, 1993), 180-181.

14 Jean-Paul Sartre, *Saint Genet: Actor and Martyr*, trans. Bernard Frechtman (Minnesota: Minnesota University Press, 2012), 265.

15 Ibid.

16 Ibid., 265-266.

17 Ibid., 266.

18 See: John Barrell, *The Dark Side of the Landscape: The Rural Poor in English Painting 1730-1840* (Cambridge: Cambridge University Press, 1980).

19 Sartre, *Saint Genet*, 266.

20 Reference may be to György Lukács, "Zur Ästhetik Schillers" (1935) in *Beiträge zur Geschichte der Ästhetik* (Berlin: Aufbau, 1954).

21 "An inane Wilhelminian army joke tells of an orderly who one fine Sunday morning is sent by his superior to the zoo. He returns very worked up and declares: 'Lieutenant! Animals like that do not exist!'" See: Adorno, *Aesthetic Theory*, 82.

22 Possibly a reference to the French dramatist and poet Paul Claudel's play, *Le Soulier de satin* (The Satin Slipper) on the subject of the conquistadors during the Renaissance.

23 Adorno, *Aesthetic Theory*, 46.

24 Reference to passages about nature in Herbert Marcuse, *One-Dimensional Man: Studies in the Ideology of Advanced Industrial Society* (1964).

25 Adorno, *Aesthetic Theory*, 47.

26 Reference to William Leiss, *The Domination of Nature* (New York: George Braziller, 1972).

27 Adorno, *Aesthetic Theory*, 47.

28 Reference to the so-called "archaic smile," which appears in the sixth century BC to indicate that the person was alive.

29 "If one originated in the other, it is beauty that originated in the ugly, and not the reverse." See: Adorno, *Aesthetic Theory*, 50.
30 Ibid., 50-51.
31 Ibid., 52.
32 Ibid., 53.
33 From the description, it may be the dystopian thriller *Soylent Green* (1973).

LECTURE NINE

1 Reference to Peter Weiss's The *Aesthetics of Resistance*. The first volume was published as Peter Weiss, *The Aesthetics of Resistance*. vol. I (Durham, NC: Duke University Press, 2005). The second volume of this novel was published by the same press in 2020.
2 Adorno, *Aesthetic Theory*, 50-51.
3 Ibid., 51.
4 The full sentence reads: "Following an internal logic whose stages will need to be described by an aesthetic historiography that does not yet exist, the principle of montage therefore became that of construction." Ibid., 56.
5 A search for the word "Nietzsche" in Thomas Mann's novel *Doctor Faustus* did not find any reference.
6 Jameson considers the concept of "mimesis" foundational in Adorno, adding that Adorno neither defines nor explains this term but is always alluding to it. (See *Late Marxism*, 64 and note 10, on page 700 in this book.) Not all critics have agreed with the view that mimesis is undefined in Adorno. Not all critics have agreed with this view. Peter Osborne, for example, once suggested that mimesis was in fact very well defined in Adorno, pointing to the first English edition of *Aesthetic Theory*, translated by Christian Lenhardt (see above page 687 note 7 of this book). See: Peter Osborne, "A Marxism for the Postmodern? Jameson's Adorno" *New German Critique*, Spring-Summer, 1992, no. 56, Special Issue on Theodor W. Adorno, 177.
7 The reference is to two texts by Benjamin, written in the early 1930s and unpublished during his lifetime. See: Walter Benjamin, "On the Mimetic Faculty" (1933) and "The Doctrine of the Similar" (1933) in

Selected Writings, vol. 2, 1927-1934, eds. Michael W. Jennings, Howard Eiland, and Gary Smith (Cambridge, MA: Belknap Press, 1999).

8 "Adorno met Benjamin in Frankfurt in 1923. The meeting was arranged by their mutual friend Siegfried Kracauer at the Café Westend am Opernplatz." See: Susan Buck-Morss, *The Origin of Negative Dialectics*, 5-6.

9 In Vienna, Adorno edited the *Musikblätter des Anbruch*, known after 1929 as *Anbruch*. On the details of his unofficial editorial work with *Anbruch*, as well as other sources, see: "Theodor W. Adorno to Thomas Mann, Los Angeles, 5.7.1948" in *Theodor W. Adorno and Thomas Mann: Correspondence 1943–1955*, eds. Christoph Gödde and Thomas Sprecher; trans. Nicholas Walker (London: Polity Press, 2006), 26, n. 11. Adorno broke up with the *Anbruch* when the editors decided to turn the magazine into a tool of pure political propaganda. See: Susan Buck-Morss, *The Origins of Negative Dialectics*, 34.

10 On "Tuis" and "tui-intellectuals," see also: Jay, *The Dialectical Imagination*, 201-202. For a more recent discussion of "Tui" and "Tuism," which is the Brechtian acronym formed from "Tellekt-Uell-Ins," and used by Brecht to critique intellectual posturing or "passive politicking," as he saw it in Thomas Mann, Andre Gide, Georg Lukács, and the "Frankfurtists," see: Philip Glahn, "Brecht, the Popular, and Intellectuals in Dark Times: Of Donkeys and 'Tuis,'" in *Philosophizing Brecht: Critical Readings on Art, Consciousness, Social Theory and Performance*, eds. Norman Roessler and Anthony Squiers (Leiden/Boston: Brill Rodopi, 2019), 121-123.

11 For Marcuse's letters to Horkheimer, see: Herbert Marcuse, *Collected Papers of Herbert Marcuse*, ed. Douglas Kellner, vol. I, *Technology, War and Fascism* (New York and London: Routledge, 1998).

12 Reference to the discussion of Adrian's father of exotic moth and butterfly (i.e., *Hetaera esmeralda*) in the opening chapters of *Doctor Faustus*, see: Mann, *Doctor Faustus*, trans. Woods, 17.

13 See, in particular: Roger Caillois, "Mimétisme et Psychasthénie légendaire" (Mimicry and Legendary Psychasthenia), published in the Surrealist journal *Minotaure* in 1934 and 1935.

14 James George Frazer, *The Golden Bough: A Study in Comparative*

Religion, Volume 1 and 2 (New York and London: MacMillan and Co., 1894).

15 Frazer distinguishes between "sympathetic magic" (also called "imitative magic") and "contagious magic." See: Frazer, *The Golden Bough*.

16 Adorno's anthropomorphizing and anthropologizing of the notion of "mimesis" is made in the context of art. In Adorno, mimesis is immanent to art. It is art's memory and the inerasable trace of art's origins in magic, rituals, and other ancient incantation practices. The mimetic drive begins with magic and continues through myth and metaphysics to be contained and transformed into fantasy or imagination. From imitation or impersonation of demons in ancient magic to simulation of the gods' wishes in myth, mimesis finally transforms into artistic fantasy or imagination. And in this latter stage, art represses the early forms of the mimetic impulse: namely, imitation and simulation. In modern autonomous art, mimesis is art's suppressed memory, and as much as "advanced" art would like to hide its relationship to the imitative impulse — or magic and myth, which the greatest works of high modernism have so emphatically done — mimesis as such cannot be eradicated, but only repressed and conserved in a new guise. The modernist repression of mimesis, or the taboo imposed on the nonconceptual, or image-based relation to the other (i.e., object, nature, animal, social reality), has a long history: from the ban on graven images in certain religious practices, to the persecution of vagabond entertainers, gypsies, actors, and fools. The mimetic ban becomes the keystone in the ontology of the modern bourgeois subject. For the latter, art is forbidden to emulate or encourage daily utilitarian needs of the bourgeois subject, and instead must persist in the great Kantian aesthetic tradition of disinterested contemplation. The repression of mimetic comportment in art triggers a resistance mechanism that calls into play the dialectics of other and more modern aesthetic impulses, namely that of expression and construction. When radical modern art expresses or constructs the raw material, rather than resort to imitation, identification, or simulation, it wishes first of all to hide art's origins in ancestral magic, shamanism, and other enchantment practices that the "enlight-

ened" bourgeois reason decided to eliminate. Therefore, Adorno sees mimesis as directed at itself, stating on page 145 of *Minima Morlia* that: "Even the rejection of mimesis... in art is mimetic." He places imitation and mimesis not only at the origins of art, but also of *ratio*, or scientific rationality. Early or proto-scientific practices, such as alchemy, astrology and witchcraft, also drew heavily on the mimetic impulse, which continued until these practices have been banned by the ideology of progress and scienticism. The rise of positivism, technology and applied science advocate the elimination of archaic mimetic comportment of identification in order to increase the distance between the subject and object, in the name of non-interference and greater objectivity. According to the modern virtue of scientific objectivity, the knower must eliminate any trace of the object. Reason, and modern science, breaks with magical mimesis, continuing to pursue its nefarious goal of suppressing nature by turning into negative mimesis, or what Adorno and Horkheimer called "mimesis into death" (*Dialectic of Enlightenment*, 57). With the separation of science from magic and myth, mimesis finds refuge in art. The latter still practice imitation by trying to recover and bring back to life what the "enlightened" reason leaves behind: its path of destruction. The split of knowledge into science and art, with the latter being relegated to entertainment and disinterested pleasure, scientific rationality in the name of objectivity seeks to eliminate direct identification with the object. Therefore, it is art that, for some time, continues the tradition of magic and myth by continuing to imitate or identify and simulate the other (object, nature, society). Art takes the side of the oppressed and opposes the oppressor: reason. And even though, for Adorno, art is the other of reason, or science — it constitutes resistance of what is left in nature after reason has done violence to it — art cannot but also move along with Spirit and reason in the general process of disenchanting the world. "Art's disavowal of magical practices — its antecedents — implies participation in rationality" (*Aesthetic Theory*, 53). Art is a form of rationality that is critical of the rational, and this constitutes art's principal aporia. On the one hand, modern art represses its original relation to mimesis by turning to the impulses of subjective expression and objective construction, in order to find more efficient means for defending what is left of nature. But modern art also conceals mimesis because, as part of the Spirit, it is complicit in the domination of nature — a conspiracy that art cannot deny being so closely interconnected with reason. Regardless of the complicity, the irreducible trace of mimesis in art is the persistent reminder of art's origin in ritual and superstition; a reminder that modern art both conceals and intimates by mimicking itself.

The anthropological core in Adorno's aesthetic theory, namely mimesis's ancestry in magic and myth, has often been treated with disdain by Marxists, including by Jameson above in this seminar, when he maintains that the Adornian theory of art is anthropological and not historical. Indeed, for a self-proclaimed Marxist, this is suspicious. In the *Origins of Negative Dialectics*, Susan Buck-Morss stresses Adorno's rejection of the Hegelian concept of history, as the identity of subject and object, explaining Adorno and Horkheimer's distrust of history as an effect of their Kantian training with Hans Cornelius (Buck-Morss, 47). Their account of mimesis at the origins of art and reason is that of a natural history, rather than history defined by Marxism in terms of continues class struggle. According to Adorno's cultural anthropology, the archaic humans' relation to magic and assimilation with the other (nature, object) is fear and the urge for survival — the instinct of self-preservation. "Nothing at all must remain outside, because the mere idea of outsideness is the source of fear" (*Dialectic of Enlightenment*, 16). Jameson points above to some influences in Adorno's approach to mimesis. James George Frazer's *The Golden Bough* (1890) was one anthropological investigation into the nature of superstition, magic and religion that drew on early human belief practices, as well as on ethnographic material from different parts of Frazer's contemporary world. At the root of all human superstition, argued Frazer, is what he called "sympathetic magic." The latter assumes that any desired effect (i.e., influencing the forces of nature, such as rain, sun, wind, crops, hunting or gathering, wishing someone ill) can be obtained by imitating it. This is the function of the sorcerer, shaman, magician, or priest in early human societies and, one may add, of the artist in the modern world. Roger Caillois's "Mimicry and Legendary Psychasthenia" (1934-35) discusses the ability of certain animals to change their appearance in response to the threats from the physical environment. But for Caillois, the imitation and mimesis that certain insects or animals adopt with regard to their environment has a negative function, as life depends on preserving the autonomy and difference rather than dissolving it. Insect-mimicry also appears in the opening pages of Thomas Mann's *Doctor Faustus*, where Adorno served as aesthetic "consultant," and the reference to the butterfly *Hetaera Esmeralda*, which imitates a windblown petal. Jameson deals with this aspect of mimesis in the section of the seminars dedicated to *Doctor Faustus*. Finally, one other source of inspiration for Adorno is Walter Benjamin's discussion of mimesis in "The Doctrine of the Similar" (1933) and "On the Mimetic Faculty" (1933), which drew on the mimetic games found in children's interactions with the world. In *Late Marxism*, Jameson called the influence of Benjamin on Adorno "liberation by mimesis" (52), and Shierry Weber Nicholsen has emphasized, in a text evocatively titled "*Aesthetic Theory*'s Mimesis of Walter Benjamin," that even though Adornian mimesis borrows from Benjamin's discussion of mimesis in the context of language, it is however distinctly focused on art. Even though he draws references to other disciplines, the mimetic impulse in Adorno is emphatically an *aesthetic* function. In the spirit of Hegel's aesthetics, art is imitation or simulation of the idea of beauty: the sensual appearance of the idea. It is not necessarily simple imitation of the object, but the impulse to assimilate or turn oneself into the object in order to negate the reality principle. All art, insists Adorno, carries within itself the archaic memory of mimesis as imitation and simulation, which is not necessarily the imitation of the object, but the imitative behavior, "the identification of the entity with that which it is not" and "similarity in itself" (Adorno, *Aesthetics 1958/59*). Art operating through the dialectics of mimesis and its modern variant of fantasy and/or opposites (expression and construction) is to give voice to "first nature" — a concept that Adorno borrows from Lukács, and the latter from Hegel — that is to refer to humanly unmediated materiality against the incursions of the "second nature" — that is, *reified* or mediated social experience under capitalism. Art's relation to "first nature," or "mutilated" and "suppressed" nature, is also an imitation, simulation, or intimation of truth — that is, to what is yet non-reified and non-alienated by the second nature of capitalist relations. [*Fragment from the transcriber/editor's research for the seminar, updated and rewritten in 2021-2022.*]

17 Jameson does not specify which theories he is referring to.

18 For Adorno, construction is the dominant aesthetic principle in the modern age, following the logic of Enlightenment. It is the main mode of interaction with the world, and a way of imposing order over nature. It is the mode that has been at the center of organizing social and economic development (modernization), history (modernity), and culture (modernism). Similarly, aesthetic construction is the modern principle of organizing artistic material, and as such, it must be considered within the broader dimensions of historical progress and Western modernity. When compared to expression — which can be seen as the idealist aesthetic drive conveying the modern subject's suffering in the world, following the "ordering" of nature — construction is the objective or material form of aesthetic interaction. As Adorno suggests, one can encounter construction in its early form already at the dawn of modern age, at the time of the Renaissance, when art sought emancipation from cultic heteronomy, in what was "then called 'composition'" (*Aesthetic Theory*, 57). Pictorial composition is the early form of modernist construction. "What distinguishes construction from composition," however, "is the ruthless subordination not only of everything that originated from outside the artwork, but also of all partial elements immanent to the work" (Ibid.). That is to say that, with modernist construction, the subject urges for "ruthless subordination" — not only of the pictorial elements (line, color, volume, sound, surface and so on), but also the compulsion to subject or organize the outside world, as in the radical practices of early twentieth-century art, wishing to bring art into the praxis of life. Construction and

modern art go hand-in-hand, reaching its peak in the aesthetics of the early twentieth-century European avant-gardes. This constructive impulse manifests in the new identity embraced by the most radical artists of that epoch, an identity that incorporated a range of constructive-organizational practices: from montage (borrowed from the French *monter*, to assemble), to the German *bau* (as in Bauhaus), to Russian *konstruktsia* (in Constructivism and Productivism), and to many other less known variants encountered in different countries of Central and Eastern Europe (i.e., Romanian integralists, Hungarian aktivista, Croatian zenitists and others). Aesthetic construction is also the dominant aesthetic drive of postmodernity or — depending on the favored periodization term — contemporaneity. Most works of contemporary art are produced today by means of constructive principles: from editing, montage, coding, and programming (as in video art, film, expanded cinema, multimedia and web or software art), to various organizational practices (in forming artist associations, or political activism), to installations, assemblages, ready-mades and other inter- and multimedia or cultural modes assembled from splinters of the cultural or the industrial worlds. Terms, which one encounters today in the field of cultural production, such as "organizer," "(cultural) producer," "designer," "programmer," "engineer" (including those of "the human soul"), "curator" — they all convey the meaning of assembling parts, or cultural forms of work rooted in construction. Construction is essentially related to the notion of "totality" — the category used in the modern age, in positive or negative terms, to express the urge for a more coherent, "whole" world, or what Adorno called "socialization." Aesthetic construction has to do with "the interest in the aesthetic totality wanted to be, objectively, an interest in a correct organization of the whole" (*Aesthetic Theory*, 11-12). But, if the "whole" was ever to be achieved (in a utopian future), the radical modernist must take a stance against those attitudes that sabotaged the aesthetic or social totality. Therefore, Adorno sets construction in opposition to both mimesis and expression (Ibid., 44). The radical opposition of construction to expression comes to counteract the subjective pole of high modernism. Since construction is concerned with the objective, with the assemblage and organization of "real" world materials and techniques, with totalities and building a better "whole," it finds itself in a dialectical opposition to subjective expression. Adorno understands the need for construction in modern art in terms of setting up a principle that has been called upon in order "to do away with those dangers or problems that arose from expressionism" (*Aesthetics 1958/59*, Lecture 6, unpaginated). It is the dangers of excessive subjective individualism, as manifested in expressionism and other historical Isms, celebrating the "randomness," "involuntariness," and "accidentalness" of the human action (from surrealists' "automatic writing" and *cadavre exquis*, to tachism, chance, aleatory art, and music within various neo-dada and Fluxus circles after World War Two). Construction is also a way of preventing "destruction," which Adorno attributes to expression, and in his seminars, he quotes his intellectual archenemy Heidegger, who once referred to expressionism in terms of a removal of other forms that resulted in leaving behind only naked substances (Ibid). If the principle of aesthetic construction has been the way of opposing the destructiveness of subjective expression, whose individualistic principle disrupts the wholeness of social or aesthetic totality, construction is also opposed to mimesis. In fact, and in its relation to the outside world, the drives of construction and mimesis seem closer to each other, as they both aim at the Other of nature. And yet, the two remain opposites, as mimesis is "prespiritual" or "contrary to spirit" (*Aesthetic Theory*, 118), and are therefore outdated or archaic forms of aesthetic organization. When it comes to the principle of aesthetic construction, Adorno makes frequent references to θέσει (*thesis*). In the history of Western philosophy, θέσει is often interpreted via Plato's dialogue *Cratylus*, which concerned itself with the relation between names and things. θέσει is the opposite of φύσει (*physei*), which, since Aristotle, has been a reference to nature. In his Frankfurt seminars, as well as in *Aesthetic Theory*, Adorno often alludes to this ongoing dialectic between θέσει and φύσει, as, for example, in this passage: "...and that which is θέσει, the aspect of construction, if I might introduce the term here, [is] the aspect of control over nature" (*Aesthetics 1958/59*, Lecture 6, unpaginated). Thus, Adorno designates construction in terms of thesis and human dominance over nature, a principle that encompasses not only art and other terms sharing the same prefix (artifice, artifact, artisanal), but the modern take on nature. Construction then combines within itself, on the one hand, the objective demand to assume power over natural world and its materials, and on the other hand, a form of resistance to the excesses of modern individualism and loss of touch with φύσει (nature) and reality by completely surrendering oneself to the power of imagination. In the context of modern capitalism, the principle of aesthetic construction is also part of the impossibility of the subject to express or to speak directly (without running into ideological clichés or reified cultural signifiers). Therefore, the modernist artist speaks by means of external things (ready-mades, mathematized symbols, *sachlichkeit*). [*Fragment from the transcriber/editor's research for the seminar, updated and rewritten in 2021*.]

19 Adorno, *Aesthetic Theory*, 57. [Emphasis in intonation added.]

20 Ibid., 59.

21 Ibid. [Emphasize in intonation added.]

22 Reference to the American writer and poet Joyce Kilmer (1886-1918), who is known for a short lyrical poem called "Trees" (1913).

23 Jameson discusses Stravinsky's "squirm" in his discussions of Adorno in: Fredric Jameson, *The Ancients and the Postmoderns: On the Historicity of Forms* (London: Verso, 2015). The Stravinsky reference is in: Robert Craft, *Conversations with Stravinsky* (London: Faber & Faber, 1958), 71.

24 Adorno, *Aesthetic Theory*, 63-64.

25 Ibid., 73. [Emphasis in intonation added.]

26 Reference to "Art perceived strictly aesthetically is art aesthetically misperceived." See: Ibid., 6.

27 Ibid., 47. Reference to Adorno's discussion of *Kulturlandschaft* [cultural landscape.]

28 Possibly a reference to the following sentence in *Aesthetic Theory*: "The 'How beautiful!' at the sight of a landscape insults its mute language and reduces its beauty; appearing nature wants silence at the same time that anyone capable of its experience feels compelled

to speak in order to find a momentary liberation from monadological confinement." Ibid., 69.

LECTURE TEN

1 Reference to a quote by Goethe: "People are always talking about originality; but what do they mean? As soon as we are born, the world begins to work upon us; and this goes on to the end. And after all, what can we call our own, except energy, strength, and will? If I could give an account of all that I owe to great predecessors and contemporaries, there would be but a small balance in my favor." See: Johann Wolfgang von Goethe and Johann Peter Eckermann, *Conversations of Goethe with Johann Peter Eckermann*, trans. John Oxenford (New York: Ravenio Books, 2014), 160.

2 Reference to chapter five, "Art Beauty: Apparition, Spiritualization, Intuitability" in *Aesthetic Theory*.

3 Adorno also deals with the "deaestheticization of art" in other chapters of *Aesthetic Theory*. See, for example: "Situation" (chapter two).

4 For the discussion of silence in Beckett, see also: Adorno's "Trying to Understand *Endgame*," which discusses Beckett's expression of the absence of meaning in *Endgame*. See: Adorno, *Notes on Literature*, 237-267.

5 See: Lecture Five.

6 Adorno, *Aesthetic Theory*, 79.

7 For a more detailed discussion of *Schein* in Adorno, see: "The Crisis of *Schein*" in Part III of Jameson, *Late Marxism*, 165-177.

8 The reference is to Paul Valéry's essay, "Dance and the Soul." See: Paul Valéry, *Dialogues*, vol. 4, trans. William McCausland Stewart (Princeton, NJ: Princeton University Press, 1956).

9 For a discussion of the Marx Brothers, Chaplin and clowness, see: "The Culture Industry: Enlightenment and Mass Deception" in: Adorno and Horkheimer, *Dialectic of Enlightenment*, 137-38.

10 Reference to the French vocabulary of the circus, where the "act" is called *le numéro*, for example: *un numéro de dressage* — an animal act — or *un numéro de haute voltige* — an acrobatic act.

11 Sergei Eisenstein, "The Montage of Attractions" (1923) and "The Montage of Film Attractions" (1924) in *S. M. Eisenstein. Selected*

Works. Writings 1922-1935 vol. I, ed. And trans. Richard Taylor (Bloomington IN: Indiana University Press, 1988).

12 Reference to Erich Auerbach, *Mimesis: The Representation of Reality in the Western Thought*, trans. Willard R. Trask (Princeton, NJ: Princeton University Press, 2003). Here Erich Auerbach is suggesting that Homer privileged the part over the whole.

13 Reference to "Odysseus's Scar" in Auerbach, *Mimesis*.

14 Reference to Duchesse de Guermantes' party scene in Marcel Proust, *In Search of Time Lost* (1913).

15 Reference to Richard Wagner's opera cycle, *Der Ring des Nibelungen* (1876).

16 Reference to British literary critic George Wilson Knight, whose most famous book was *The Wheel of Fire: Interpretations of Shakespearian Tragedy* (1930).

17 For the association of Coriolanus with images of metal and blood, see: G. Wilson Knight, "The Royal Occupation: An Essay on Coriolanus" in *The Imperial Theme* (Oxford, 1931; 3rd ed., London, 1951).

18 Earlier reference to Ibsen perhaps hints at Ibsen's tendency to co-operate with the actors. For Schoenberg's "unheard music," see: Lecture Twelve, dedicated to twelve-tone music.

19 Adorno, *Aesthetic Theory*, 82.

20 Reference to John Locke's response to René Descartes' argument that the idea of a "centaur" must have some objective reality. Locke argued that our ideas of fantastical creatures are constructed by combining ideas received in sense-perception. He gives the example of the centaur, which we have by combining the "horse's head, joined to a body of human shape." See: chapter XXX, "Of Real and Fantastical Ideas" in John Locke, *An Essay Concerning Human Understanding*.

21 Jean-Paul Sartre, *L'imaginaire* (Paris: Gallimard, 1940). Translated first in English as Jean-Paul Sartre, *The Psychology of Imagination* (London: Methuen & Co., 1972). Revised and reprinted as Jean-Paul Sartre, *The Imaginary: a phenomenological psychology of the imagination*, ed. Arlette-Elkaïm Sartre, trans. Jonathan Webber (London: Routledge, 2014).

22 "In homage to *L'imaginaire* by Jean-Paul Sartre." See dedication in

Roland Barthes, *Camera Lucida: Reflections on Photography* trans. Richard Howard (London: Flamingo, 1984).

23 Adorno, *Aesthetic Theory*, 83.

24 Ibid., 83.

25 Ibid.

26 Ibid.

27 Ibid.

28 A reference to David Lindsay's novel, *A Voyage to Arcturus* (1920).

29 Lindsay, *A Voyage to Arcturus*, 53. This passage is also discussed and and quoted in full in Jameson, *Archaeologies of the Future*, 119.

30 Adorno, *Aesthetic Theory*, 85.

31 Ibid., 86. [Emphasis in the original.]

32 Ibid.

33 Reference to what is sometimes considered the Third Surrealist Manifesto: André Breton, *Les vases communicants* (Paris: Cahiers libres, 1932). In this text, Breton deploys a "surrealist dialectics" to mediate between opposite concepts, such as: interior and exterior, waking and sleep, love and revolution, material and oneiric, Marx and Freud. Translated into English as André Breton, *Communicating Vessels*, trans. Mary Ann Caws and Geoffrey T. Harris (Lincoln: University of Nebraska, 1990).

34 In *Lectures on the Philosophy of History*, Hegel coins the expression "ruse of history," which refers to a process by which people realize a historical purpose for mankind without being fully aware of it.

35 A reference to Peter Weiss's three volumes of *The Aesthetics of Resistance*. See: Lecture Ten.

36 Reference to Hegel's *Phenomenology of Spirit*.

LECTURE ELEVEN

1 For example, Benjamin wrote his 1935 essay "Johann Jakob Bachofen" in French for the *Nouvelle Revue Française*, which ultimately rejected it.

2 Reference to Helen Lowe-Porter (1876 –1963), the first translator of most of Thomas Mann's novels into English. She was sometimes accused of inaccuracies in translation, even though Mann appears to have been content with Lowe-Porter's work.

3 Reference to the use of Early New High German in Thomas Mann's *Doctor Faustus*, which Lowe-Porter translated using medieval English vocabulary.

4 Reference to John E. Woods' translation of *Doctor Faustus*, which was first published by Alfred A. Knopf in 1997.

5 Reference to "The Task of the Translator" in Walter Benjamin, *Illuminations* ed. Hannah Arendt, trans. Harry Zohn (New York: Schocken Books, 1969).

6 See: chapter six, "Semblance and Expression" in Adorno, *Aesthetic Theory*.

7 In this edition of *Aesthetic Theory*, *Schein* was translated as "semblance."

8 Adorno's central concept of *Schein*, which is in crisis, has been variously translated as "appearance," "semblance" or "illusion." Jameson has translated *Schein* primarily as "appearance," and in the *Late Marxism* chapter entitled "The Crisis of Schein," he has also used such terms as "aesthetic illusion," "aesthetic appearance," and "fiction." See: Jameson, *Late Marxism*, 165-167.

9 Jameson reads from Helen Lowe-Porter's translation of *Doctor Faustus*. See: Thomas Mann, *Doctor Faustus* trans. Helen Lowe-Porter (New York: Knopf, 1948), 240-241.

10 The full quote by Thomas Mann in the "Foreword" to *The Magic Mountain*: "We do not fear being called meticulous, inclining as we do to the view that only the exhaustive can be truly interesting."

11 Reference to Walter Benjamin, "On Some Motifs in Baudelaire," where he deals with the notion of "shock," drawing on Freud.

12 Martin Heidegger, "On the Origin of the Work of Art" in *Poetry, Language, Thought*, trans. Albert Hofstadter (New York: Harper & Row, 1975), 77.

13 Ibid., 79.

14 Ibid., 17.

15 Ibid., 23.

16 Ibid., 25.

17 Ibid., 27-28.

18 Ibid., 28.

19 Ibid., 33.

20 Ibid., 34-35.
21 Ibid., 35.
22 Ibid., 40.
23 Ibid., 41.
24 Ibid.
25 Ibid., 45.
26 Ibid., 54.
27 Ibid.
28 Possibly a reference to Frederic Spotts, *Hitler and the Power of Aesthetics* (New York: Overlook Books, 2004).
29 Jameson uses the term "defamiliarization" in the context of several traditions of modernist aesthetics. The Russian formalists' concept of *ostranenie*, introduced by Viktor Shklovsky, has been translated as "making strange," "estrangement," "enstrangement" and "defamiliarization." Another version of modernist defamiliarization is Bertolt Brecht's concept of *Verfremdung*, also translated as "estrangement" and "enstrangement," but also as "disillusion" and even "alienation." For a more detailed discussion of the aesthetics of defamiliarization, see: "The Formalist Projection" in Fredric Jameson, *The Prison House of Language: A Critical Account of Structuralism and Russian Formalism* (Princeton, NJ: Princeton University Press, 1972).
30 Pierre Bourdieu, *The Political Ontology of Martin Heidegger* trans. Peter Collier (Stanford, CA: Stanford University Press, 1991). For Habermas's critique of Heidegger, see: Jürgen Habermas, "Work and Weltanschauung: The Heidegger Controversy from a German Perspective," *Critical Inquiry* 15, no. 2 (Winter, 1989), 431-456.
31 Jameson here quotes from another translation of Heidegger, "Origin of the Work of Art," in *Philosophies of Art and Beauty*, eds. Albert Hofstadter and Richard Kuhns (Chicago: University of Chicago Press, 1964), 685.
32 Later in this lecture, Jameson will self-correct himself, suggesting that "the setting-itself-into-work of truth" — where "work" [*Werk*] designates the work of art in Heidegger — is the *aesthetic* way of truth (not the philosophical). See below in the same paragraph.
33 Heidegger, "Origin of the Work of Art," 685.

34 Ibid.

35 Ibid.

36 Ibid.

37 Ibid. For a more detailed discussion of this passage in Heidegger, see also: Fredric Jameson, *Valences of the Dialectic* (London: Verso, 2009), 606.

38 Martin Heidegger, "Building Dwelling Thinking" in *Poetry, Language, Thought*, trans. Albert Hofstadter (New York: Harper Colophon Books, 1971).

39 In his "Letter on Humanism" (1946), Heidegger states that "Language is the house of Being. In its home man dwells." See: Martin Heidegger, "Letter on Humanism" in *Basic Writings* ed. David Farrell Krell (New York: Harper and Row, 1977).

40 Reference to Heidegger's four-volume *Nietzsche* (New York: Harper and Row, 1979-87).

41 Reference to parts in *Doctor Faustus* and *Reflections of a Nonpolitical Man*, where Mann discusses Germany's unique destiny by comparing it to France and Russia.

LECTURE TWELVE

1 Reference to Ernst Bloch's essays, "A Philosophical View of the Detective Novel" (1965) and "A Philosophical View of the Novel of the Artist" (1965), published in: Ernst Bloch, *The Utopian Function of Art and Literature* trans. Jack Zipes and Frank Mecklenburg (Cambridge, MA: MIT Press, 1988). Jameson discusses Bloch's essays in: "Versions of Marxist Hermeneutic" in Jameson, *Marxism and Form*.

2 Reference to the Prague-born Austrian music critic Eduard Hanslick (1825–1904), often regarded as founder of musical formalism. Hanslick's best-known treatise is *Vom Musikalisch-Schönen* (On the Musically Beautiful) from 1854, which is often abbreviated as OMB and is considered one of the great contributions to musical aesthetics.

3 "Forest melody" is Richard Wagner's metaphor, invoked in his essay *Zukunftmusik* (Music of the Future, 1861). He used the phrase to illustrate his new notion of "endless melody," which appears in his opera, *Tristan and Isolde*. See Wagner's essay: *Zukunftmusik*. See also: Oscar

Comettant and Paul Scudo, "Debacle at the Paris Opéra Tannhäuser and the French Critics, 1861," trans. Thomas S. Grey, introduced by Annegret Fauser in *Richard Wagner and His World*, ed. Thomas S. Grey (Princeton, NJ: Princeton University Press, 2009), 347-372.

4 Reference to essay by Arnold Schoenberg, "Brahms the Progressive" (1947), based on a radio lecture delivered in 1933.

5 This declaration was made by Schoenberg in his correspondence to Joseph Rufer (1921 or 1922). For this, and other similar pronouncements made by Schoenberg regarding his "historical figure," see: Richard Taruskin, *The Danger of Music: and Other anti-Utopian Essays* (Los Angeles, CA: University of California Press, 2009), 316, 372.

6 Reference to the journalist, essayist, and cultural critic Henry Louis Mencken (1880-1956).

7 See: Arnold Schoenberg, *Style and Idea: Selected Writings of Arnold Schoenberg*, ed. Leonard Stein, trans. Leo Black (New York: St. Martin's 1975), 284.

8 See: Arnold Schoenberg, "Brahms the Progressive" (1947), in *Style and Idea*, 398-344.

9 "In its most common meaning, the term idea is used as a synonym for theme, melody, phrase or motive. I myself consider the totality of a piece as the idea: the idea which its creator wanted to present." See: Arnold Schoenberg, "New Music, Outmoded Music, Style, and Idea," (1930) in *Style and Idea*. On "musical idea," see also: Arnold Schoenberg, *The Musical Idea and the Logic, Technique, and Art of Its Presentation*, edited, translated, and with a commentary by Patricia Carpenter and Severine Neff (New York: Columbia University Press, 1995).

10 Schoenberg, "My Evolution," in *Style and Idea*, 87.

11 Schoenberg, "The Problems of Harmony," Ibid., 269.

12 "Schenker considered compositions according to the model of life, with its tendency toward reproduction and expansion, while for Schoenberg a piece of music is a linguistic creation that as such can be understood only by mastering the syntactic-grammatical rules on which it is based." See: Gianmario Borio, "Schenker versus Schoenberg versus Schenker: The Difficulties of a Reconciliation," *Journal of the Royal Musical Association*, vol. 126, no. 2 (2001), 273. On the Schenker-Schoenberg tonal polemic, see also: Carl Dahl-

haus, *Proceedings of the Royal Musical Association*, 1973-1974, vol. 100 (1973-1974), 209-215.

13 See Schoenberg's letter cited in: Bryan R. Simms, "New Documents in the Schoenberg-Schenker Polemic," *Perspectives of New Music*, vol. 16, no. 1 (Autumn Winter, 1977), 123.

14 Reference to film theorist and film historian David Jay Bordwell.

15 Reference to Schoenberg's teaching career at UCLA. See: Dorothy Lamb Crawford, "Arnold Schoenberg in Los Angeles" in *The Musical Quarterly*, Spring, 2002, vol. 86, no. 1 (Spring, 2002), 6-48. On Schoenberg's uninspiring attempts to write film music for Hollywood, see: Sabine M. Feisst, "Schoenberg and the Cinematic Art" in *The Music Quarterly* vol. 83, no. 1 (Spring, 1999), 93-113.

16 *Klangfarbenmelodie* (sound-color- melody) is a term derived from Schoenberg's book, *Harmonielehre* (1911). In English: Arnold Schoenberg, *Theory of Harmony*, trans. Roy E. Carter (Los Angeles, CA: University of California Press, 1978).

17 Reference to an article by Pierre Boulez, "Schoenberg is Dead," first published in *Score* (London) in May 1952.

18 Reference to John Cage, *Radio Music, for eight radios* [1956.]

19 Here Jameson gives a composite image of Cage's techniques and works, like the 1940s technique of prepared piano and elements from pieces, in which Cage used radios rattled a radiator.

20 Theodor W. Adorno, "Vers une musique informelle," in *Quasi Una Fantasia: Essays on Modern Music*, trans. Rodney Livingstone (London: Verso, 1998).

21 For a comparison of Berg to Schoenberg and Webern, see: Theodor W. Adorno, "Alban Berg" in *Sound Figures*, trans. Rodney Livingstone (Stanford, CA: Sandford University Press, 1999), 76. See also: Theodor W. Adorno, *Alban Berg: Master of the Smallest Link*, trans. Juliane Brand and Christopher Hailey (Cambridge, UK: Cambridge University Press, 1991).

22 See Adorno, "Anton von Webern" in *Sound Figures*, 91-105.

23 On Adorno's critique of Stravinsky, see: "Stravinsky and Restoration" in Adorno, *The Philosophy of New Music*; and "Stravinsky: A Dialectical Portrait — In Memory of Walter Benjamin" in Adorno, *Quasi Una Fantasia*.

24 See Jean Cocteau, *Le rappel à l'ordre* (Paris: Stock, 1926).

25 Reference to Luigi Russolo's *L'arte dei Rumori* (Art of Noise) 1913 manifesto.

26 "Dissonance is the technical term for the reception through art of what aesthetics as well as naïveté calls ugly." Adorno, *Aesthetic Theory*, 45.

27 Reference to Adorno's two portrayals of Stravinsky in *Philosophy of New Music* (1947) and "Stravinsky: A Dialectical Portrait" (1962).

LECTURE THIRTEEN

1 STUDENT ONE, in this chapter, is Fabio Akcelrud Durão, who defended his dissertation in the Literature Program with the thesis entitled *Modernism and Coherence: Four Chapters of a Negative Aesthetics* (Ph.D. Dissertation, Duke University, 2003). The title is also available as a book: Fabio Ak celrud Durão, *Modernism and Coherence: Four Chapters of a Negative Aesthetics* (Frankfurt am Main: Peter Lang, 2008).

2 Theodor W. Adorno, *Philosophische Terminologie: Zur Einleitung* ed. Rudolf zur Lippe (Frankfurt: Suhrkamp, 1973).

3 Not all of Adorno's seminars were translated at the time of Jameson's seminar. In 2000, Adorno's 1965 seminar on metaphysics was published as Theodor Adorno, *Metaphysics, Concept and Problems*, trans. R. Livingstone, ed. R. Tiedemann (Cambridge: Polity, 2000). Other seminars of Adorno were translated later: Theodor Adorno, "Marx and the Basic Concepts of Sociological Theory: From a Seminar Transcript of the Summer Semester 1962," trans. Verena Erlenbusch-Anderson and Chris O'Kane, *Historical Materialism*, 26, no. 1 (2008); the seminars on aesthetics were translated in 2018 as: Adorno, *Aesthetics (1958/59)*, ed. Ederhard Ortand, trans. Wieland Hoban (Cambridge: Polity Press, 2018).

4 Adorno's Kant and Hegel seminars were translated as: Theodor W. Adorno, *Kant's Critique of Pure Reason*, trans. R. Livingstone, ed. R. Tiedemann (Sanford: Stanford University Press, [1995] 2001); Theodor W. Adorno, *Hegel: Three Studies*, trans. Shierry Weber Nicholsen (Cambridge MA: The MIT Press, 1993).

5 Reference to Gilles Deleuze and Félix Guattari, *What Is Philosophy?*, trans. Graham Burchill and Hugh Tomlinson (New York: Columbia University Press, 1994).

6 Lambert Zuidervaart, *Adorno's Aesthetic Theory: The Redemption of Illusion* (Cambridge, MA: MIT Press, 1991).

7 Marc Jimenez, *Adorno: Art, idéologie et théorie de l'art* (Paris: Union générale d'éditions, 1973).

8 Reference to Jürgen Habermas and Albrecht Wellmer, as leading defenders of the "project of modernity." For the latter, see: Albrecht Wellmer, *Zur Dialektik von Moderne und Postmoderne; Vernunftkritik nach Adorno* (Frankfurt: Suhrkamp, 1985). See also, in English: Albrecht Wellmer, *The Persistence of Modernity Essays on Aesthetics, Ethics, and Postmodernism*, trans. David Midgley (Cambridge: MIT Press, 1991).

9 Shierry Weber Nicholsen, *Exact Imagination, Late Work: On Adorno's Aesthetics* (Cambridge, MA: MIT Press, 1997).

10 Theodor W. Adorno, *Prisms*, trans. Shierry Weber Nicholsen and Samuel Weber (Cambridge, MA: MIT Press, 1983).

11 Wolfgang Welsch, "Adornos Ästhetik: eine implizite Ästhetik des Erhabenen" in Christine Pries, ed., *Das Erhabene: Zwischen Grenzerfahrung Und Größenwahn* (Berlin: Walter de Gruyter, 1989); 185-214.

12 For Jameson's engagement with the idea of beauty, see: "'End of Art' or 'End of History'?" in Fredric Jameson, *The Cultural Turn: Selected Writings on the Postmodern, 1983-1998* (London: Verso, 1998). In his other writings, Jameson often criticizes anti-postmodern cultural critics who have been calling for the revival of "conservative" or "counter-revolutionary" modernist values, like, for example, the journal *New Criterion*, edited by Hilton Kramer in the US; and in Europe, the author and France's former minister of education, Luc Ferry (see Lecture Two).

13 See more on Jameson's comments on Schoenberg's remark in his introduction to Peter Weiss's *The Aesthetic of Resistance*, xii.

14 Harry Lavin, *James Joyce. A Critical Introduction* (Norfolk, CT: New Directions, 1941).

15 Reference to 1948 Knopf edition of Helen Lowe-Porter's translation of Mann's *Doctor Faustus*.

16 At this point in the seminar, Jameson is not yet aware that students could only buy the new 1999 Vintage edition of *Doctor Faustus*, translated by John Edwin Woods.

17 Reference to André Gide's 1925 novel, *The Counterfeiters* (*Les Faux-monnayeurs*) with *Journal of "The Counterfeiters."* Jameson draws very closely here to what Harry Levin's once described *The Counterfeiters* and the *Journal* as: "the diary of a novelist who is writing a novel about a novelist who is keeping a diary about the novel he is writing." Harry Levin, quoted in Gary Saul Morson, *The Boundaries of Genre Dostoevsky"s Diary of a Writer and the Traditions of Literary Utopia* (Evanston IL: Northwestern University Press, 1988), 60.

18 Thomas Mann, *Die Entstehung des Doktor Faustus, Roman eines Romanes* (S. Fischer Verlag, Frankfurt am Main, 1949).

19 Thomas Mann, *The Story of a Novel: The Genesis of Doctor Faustus* (1961).

20 See: Mann, *Doctor Faustus*, trans. Woods, 505.

21 Reference to *Der Untertan* (commonly translated in English as *Man of Straw* and *The Loyal Subject*), which was produced by the German Democratic Republic DEFA Studio in 1951. The film is based on Heinrich Mann's satirical novel, *The Kaiser's Lackey* (1918).

22 Edgar Reitz, *Heimat: A Chronicle of Germany* (11 episodes, 1984).

23 Edgar Reitz, *Heimat 2: Chronicle of a Youth* (13 episodes, 1992).

24 *Heimat 3: Chronicle of a Changing Time* (premiered in 2004, one year after the seminar) covers the post-Berlin Wall decade, 1989-1999.

25 "I did not will this" is a reference to Adrian Leverkühn's final composition, the symphonic cantata *The Lamentation of Doctor Faustus*. See: Mann, *Doctor Faustus*, trans. Woods, 515.

26 The origins of the phrase "a nation of shopkeepers" have been debated, with some pointing to Napoleon and others to Adam Smith as its originator in *The Wealth of Nations* (1776): "To found a great empire for the sole purpose of raising up a people of customers may at first sight appear a project fit only for a nation of shopkeepers."

27 Reference to Thomas Mann's 1918 book, *Reflections of a Nonpolitical*

Man (*Betrachtungen eines Unpolitischen*), which Mann wrote during World War One.

28 Heinrich Mann did not make it to East Germany, despite his attempts to do so. In 1949, he was offered the position of president of the Academy of the Arts in East Germany, a position that he accepted, but he died in Santa Monica (CA) before traveling to Europe. He was seventy-eight years old.

29 Reference to parts in *Doctor Faustus*, where Adrian participates in student fraternities who are discussing Germany's unique destiny. Similar discussions and comparisons of Germany organic *Kultur* versus France and England's "civilization" take place in *Reflections of a Nonpolitical Man*.

30 Reference to the four-part novel by Thomas Mann, *Joseph and His Brothers* (*Joseph und seine Brüder*), which Mann completed in 1943.

31 Reference to Thomas Mann's first novel, *Buddenbrooks: Verfall einer Familie*, published in 1901.

32 Reference to Thomas Mann's last novel, *The Holy Sinner* (*Der Erwählte*), published in 1951.

33 Reference to Theodor W. Adorno, "Late Style in Beethoven," trans. Susan H. Gillespie, in *Essays on Music*, ed. by Richard Leppert (Berkley, CA: University of California Press, 2002), 564–567. See also: Edward Said, *On Late Style: Music and Literature Against the Grain* (London: Bloomsbury, 2006).

34 For a more detailed discussion of the national question and literature in the context of globalization, see: Fredric Jameson, "Third World Literature in the Era of Multinational Capitalism," in *Social Text* 15, (Autumn 1986). See also: Aijaz Ahmad's reaction to this position in Aijaz Ahmad, "Jameson's Rhetoric of Otherness and the 'National Allegory,'" *Social Text* 17, (Fall 1987).

35 Mann, *Doctor Faustus*, trans. Lowe-Porter, 499.

36 Deborah Hayden, *Pox: Genius, Madness, And the Mysteries of Syphilis* (New York: Basic Books, 2003).

37 Mann, *Doctor Faustus*, trans. Lowe-Porter, 31.

LECTURE FOURTEEN

1 Refence to an essay by Paul de Man, "Aesthetic Formalization in Kleist's *Über das Marionettentheater*," in *The Rhetoric of Romanticism* (New York: Columbia University Press, 1984). Here, de Man engages with Heinrich von Kleist's short story, *Über das Marionettentheater* [*On the Marionette Theater*] (1810).

2 Reference to a review by Michael Wood of Hermann Kurzke, *Thomas Mann: A Biography*, trans. Leslie Willson (London: Allen Lane, 2002) and Ritchie Robertson, ed., *The Cambridge Companion to Thomas Mann* (Cambridge University Press, 2002). See: Michael Wood, "Impossible Wishes" in *London Review of Books*, 25:3, 6 February (2003): 3-6.

3 Kurzke's biography was originally published as Hermann Kurzke, *Thomas Mann: Das Leben als Kunstwerk* (München: C.H. Beck, 1999).

4 See page 10 in Mann, *Doctor Faustus*, trans. Lowe-Porter, and pages 12-13 in Mann, *Doctor Faustus*, trans. Woods.

5 Mann, *Doctor Faustus*, trans. Lowe-Porter, 8; Mann, *Doctor Faustus*, trans. Woods, 10.

6 Possibly a reference to Manfred Voigts, *Oskar Goldberg, der mythische Experimentalwissenschaftler: Ein verdrängtes Kapiteljüdischer Geschichte* (München: Carl Hanser, 1988). A more recent book published after the seminar is Bruce Rosenstock, *Oskar Goldberg and the Vitalist Imagination* (Bloomington IN: Indiana University Press, 2017).

7 For a discussion of Erik Erikson's psychoanalytic biography and his book *Childhood and Society*, see also: Lecture Four.

8 See end of Chapter XII in Mann, *Doctor Faustus*, trans. Woods, 106-107.

9 Elizabeth L. Eisenstein, *The Printing Revolution in Early Modern Europe* (Cambridge: Cambridge University Press, 1988).

10 Reference to collection of conversations, anecdotes, and remarks attributed to Luther. See: Martin Luther, *The Table Talk of Martin Luther*, trans. and ed. William Hazlitt (London: H.G. Bohn, 1857).

11 Mann, *Doctor Faustus*, trans. Woods, 40.

12 Ibid., 7. [Emphasis in intonation added.]

13 Mann, *Doctor Faustus*, trans. Lowe-Porter, 5.

14 Reference to the daemon of Socrates. See: Plutarch's *On the Daemon of Socrates*. See also: Plato's *Apology*, where he discusses Socrates' daemon.
15 Reference to Goethe's autobiography, *Dichtung und Wahrheit* (*Poetry and Truth*), which was written in four parts.
16 Mann, *Doctor* Faustus, trans. Woods, 8.
17 Reference to Richard Wagner's epic music drama, *Der Ring des Nibelungen* (1876).
18 Reference to Jean Seznec, *The Survival of the Pagan Gods: The Mythological Tradition and Its Place in Renaissance Humanism and Art*, trans. Barbara Sessions (Princeton, NJ: Princeton University Press, 1953).
19 Mann, *Doctor Faustus*, trans. Woods, 76-77.
20 Ibid.
21 Jacques Attali, *Noise: The Political Economy of Music*, trans. Brian Massumi (Minneapolis: University of Minnesota Press, 1985).
22 Reference to Adorno's remark that human beings should live like good animals. See: Adorno, *Negative Dialectics*, 294/299. For a more detailed discussion by Jameson of this aspect in Adornian ethics, see: *Late Marxism* and *Archaeologies of the Future*.

LECTURE FIFTEEN

1 Johann Sebastian Bach, *Das Wohltemperierte Klavier* (1722).
2 On the equal tempering of the pitch of the intervals in modern music and the "well-tempered society," see: Max Weber, *Zur Musiksoziologie. Nachlaß*, 1921, Max Weber-Gesamtausgabe I/14, ed. C. Braun and L. Finscher (Tübingen, Germany: Mohr [Siebeck], 2004).
3 Reference to Chapter Six in *Doctor Faustus*, which is dedicated to Adrian Leverkuhn's mother; also referencing the milkmaid, Hanne, who gave Adrian his first music lessons. See: Mann, *Doctor Faustus*, trans. Woods.
4 Ibid., 32.
5 Reference to Ferdinand Tönnies's categories *Gemeinschaft* and *Gesellschaft* (translated into English as "community" and "society.") See: Ferdinand Tönnies, *Gemeinschaft und Gesellschaft* (Leipzig: Fues's Verlag, 1887). In English: Ferdinand Tönnies, *Community and Society*, trans.

Charles P. Loomis (East Lansing: The Michigan State University Press, 1957).

6 In English: Johan Huizinga, *Homo Ludens: A Study of the Play Element in Culture* (Boston, MA: Beacon Press, 1944).

7 Reference to Johan Huizinga's classic, *Herfsttij der Middeleeuwen* (1919), translated as *The Waning of the Middle Ages* (1924); *The Autumn of the Middle Ages* (1996); *Autumntide of the Middle Ages* (2020).

8 Fyodor Dostoevsky's *Besy* (1873), translated into English as *The Possessed*, *The Devils* and *Demons*.

9 For a discussion of this opposition, see also: Fredric Jameson, *The Modernist Papers* (London: Verso, 2016), 123.

10 Reference to Chapter XIX in Mann, *Doctor Faustus*, trans. Woods, 513. See also: Thomas Mann's letter to Agnes E. Meyer, explaining the role of the h-e-a-e-es [B-E-E-A-E*b*] motif in the invention of the twelve-tone system, which comes across as the work of the devil. See: E. Randol Schoenberg, ed., *The Doctor Faustus Dossier: Arnold Schoenberg, Thomas Mann, and Their Contemporaries, 1930-1951*, trans. Adrian Feuchtwanger and Barbara Zeisl Schoenberg (Berkley and Los Angeles, CA: University of California Press, 2018), 77.

11 Reference to Pieter Bruegel the Elder, *The Triumph of Death,* (1562) and Hieronymus Bosch, *The Last Judgment*, (circa 1515).

12 Possibly a reference to Kant's late writing, especially his short essay, *Das Ende aller Dinge* (1794), where he engages with the book of the Apocalypse. See: Immanuel Kant, *The End of All Things*, trans. A. Wood, in A. Wood and G. di Giovanni, *Immanuel Kant: Religion and Rational Theology* (Cambridge: Cambridge University Press, 1996), 217-231.

13 Reference to Chapter III of *Doctor Faustus*, which tells the story of father Leverkühn's obsession with mimicry and forms of imitation through the butterfly *Hetaera Esmeralda*. See: Mann, *Doctor Faustus*, trans. Woods, 21-22.

14 Jameson later develops this theme in *The Modernist Papers*. See: Jameson, *The Modernist Papers*, 122.

15 For a more detailed discussion of the role of gestures in Brecht, see: Fredric Jameson, *Brecht and Method* (London: Verso, 1998).

16 Ibid., 23.

17 Nathalie Sarraute, *Tropismes* (Paris: Éditions Denoël, 1939).

18 Mann, *Doctor Faustus*, trans. Woods, 23.

19 Ibid.

20 Wyndham Lewis, *A Reading of Ovid (Tyros)* 1920-21, oil on canvas. See also: the discussion of laughter in Wyndham Lewis in Fredric Jameson, *Signatures of the Visible* (New York: Routledge, 1990).

21 Charles Baudelaire, *De l'essence du rire* (1855). In English: Charles Baudelaire, "On the Essence of Laughter."

22 Reference to the German-American composer and conductor Hermann Hans Wetzler (1870-1943). Mann used Wetzler to create the character of Adrian's music teacher, the stutterer Wendell Kretzschmar. For a more detailed discussion, as well as other earlier sources, see (in German): Heinrich Aerni, "Thomas Mann und Hermann Hans Wetzler: Neue Quellen zum deutsch-amerikanischen Dirigenten und Komponisten Hermann Hans Wetzler (1870–1943) als Modell für Wendell Kretzschmar in 'Doktor Faustus'" in *Thomas Mann Jahrbuch*, 2014, vol. 27 (2014), 171-197.

23 The most recent recording of Hermann Hans Wetzler's music, such as *Visionen/Assisi, Op. 13* (2009), is available online on all major music-streaming platforms.

24 Mann, *Doctor Faustus*, trans. Woods, 77.

25 The reference may be to the musicologist and Beethoven expert Charles Rosen, who wrote a virulent critique of Adorno around the time of the seminar. See: Charles Rosen, "Should We Adore Adorno?", *New York Review of Books*, October 24, 2002, 59-66.

26 Mann, *Doctor Faustus*, trans. Woods, 55.

27 Adorno wrote "Beethoven's Late Style" in 1934 and it was first published in a Czechoslovakian journal before his departure for America. See: "Beethoven's Late Style," in Adorno, *Beethoven: The Philosophy of Music*.

28 Jameson discusses the sonata form in more detail and in terms of the crisis of *Schein* in *Late Marxism*. See: Chapter Two in Jameson, *Late Marxism*. See also: Rose Rosengard Subotnik, "Adorno's Di-

agnosis of Beethoven's Late Style: Early Symptom of a Fatal Condition," *Journal of the American Musicological Society*, vol. 29, no. 2 (Summer, 1976), 242-275.

29 Ludwig van Beethoven, Piano Sonata No. 23 in F minor, Op. 57 (1804-1805) colloquially known as the "Appassionata".

30 Possibly a reference to Chapter VIII in Mann, *Doctor Faustus*, trans. Woods, 69-70.

31 Reference to the 1968 book by Gilles Deleuze, *Différence et repetition*.

32 Quoted in: Leon Plantinga, *Simply Beethoven* (New York: Simply Charly, 2020).

33 Mann, *Doctor Faustus*, trans. Woods, 58.

34 Ibid., 478.

LECTURE SIXTEEN

1 Albrecht Dürer, *Apocalypsis cum figuris* [*Apocalypse with Pictures*] (Nuremberg: Anton Koberger for Albrecht Dürer, 1498).

2 "Die Welt ist alles, was der Fall ist." See: Ludwig Wittgenstein, *Tractatus Logico-philosophicus*, Proposition 1 (1922).

3 Adorno, *Aesthetic Theory*, 335.

4 Adorno quotes such sources as Melville J. Herskovits's *Man and His Work* (1948) and Arnold Hauser's *The Social History of Art*, vol. 1 (1962).

5 Fyodor Dostoevsky, *The Idiot*, trans. Richard Pevear and Larissa Volokhonsky (London: Vintage, 2003), 225-226.

6 Reference to the Epilogue scene in *Doctor Faustus*, where Adrian escapes from the farm house and runs to the pond. See: Mann, *Doctor Faustus*, trans. Woods, 531-532.

7 Reference to the so-called "Gilbert's schema," which provides a summary of Joyce's *Ulysses*, divided into parts. See: Stuart Gilbert, *James Joyce's Ulysses: A Study* (London: Faber & Faber, 1930).

8 From this point in the seminar, Jameson discusses *Doctor Faustus* in relation to the method of allegorical interpretation, on which he has worked in many of his books. Contemporary allegorical reading, based on medieval exegesis, has preoccupied Jameson since early on in his career. Already in *Marxism and Form* (1971), Jameson was

concerned with formulating a model of interpretation inspired by the four-fold patristic hermeneutic of the Church Fathers, as well as by the work of Northrop Frye, whose *Anatomy of Criticism* (1957) Jameson once called a "contemporary reinvention" of the patristic hermeneutic. Jameson worked on his own version of the Marxist hermeneutic, focused on the notions of history as hidden cause, or literary interpretation formulated in relation to modes of production, in *Marxism and Form* (1971), *The Political Unconscious* (1981), *Postmodernism, or, the Cultural Logic of Late Capitalism* (1991), and in a series of articles. More recently, Jameson has returned to the problem of allegory in "Allegory and History: On Rereading *Doktor Faustus*," published in *The Modernist Papers* (2016) and in *Allegory and Ideology* (2019). There is also a vast number of secondary sources discussing his contribution to the methodology of literary interpretation.

9 See also: Jameson, "Allegory and History," 123.

10 Published in English as Jean Daniélou, *From Shadows to Reality: Studies in the Typology of the Fathers*, trans. Wulstan Hibberd (London: Burns & Oates, 1960).

11 Reference to Henri de Lubac's three-volume *Medieval Exegesis*. See: Henri de Lubac, *Medieval Exegesis: The Four Senses of Scripture*, trans. Mark Sebanc and E.M. Macierowski, 3 vols. (Grand Rapids, MI: Eerdmans, 1998-2009).

12 See also: Fredric Jameson, *The Political Unconscious: Narrative as a Socially Symbolic Act* (London: Routledge, 2006), 14.

13 Reference to Isaiah 53 in the Old Testament and the reference to a "suffering servant," which Christians interpret as Jesus. This part is often used as the link between the Old Testament and conviction in the New Testament that the death of Jesus atones for our sins.

14 The levels reproduced here are from Jameson, *The Modernist Papers*, 123.

15 Reference to Dante's epistle to Cangrande della Scala, in which he provides some of his interpretations of the *Divine Comedy*. Many scholars however doubt whether Dante wrote this letter.

16 Jameson, "Allegory and History," 114.

17 Reference to Sergei Eisenstein's silent film, *The Battleship Potemkin* (1925).

18 After the war, Mann did not live in West Germany, but he made a few short visits. The most important one was in 1949, when he visited Frankfurt am Main and Weimar to attend Goethe's 200th anniversary. See: Kenneth H. Marcus, "The International Relations of Thomas Mann in Early Cold War Germany" in *New Global Studies*, 8 (1) 2014: 1–15. <doi:10.1515/ngs-2014-0007>

19 Possibly reference to Mann's last novel, *The Holy Sinner* (*Der Erwählte*), published in 1951.

20 Mann, *Doctor Faustus*, trans. Woods, 520.

21 References to parts in *Doctor Faustus* where Serenus Zeitblom reflects on the process of organizing his writing of the story of Adrian Leverkühn. See, for example: Chapters IX and XIV. Ibid.

22 Reference to a painting by Caravaggio, *Saint Jerome Writing*, or simply *Saint Jerome* (1605-06).

23 Reference to a passage in Mann, *Doctor Faustus*, trans. Woods, 514, and 516.

24 Ibid., 514.

25 Ibid., 28.

26 Ibid., 357-59.

27 Reference to a novel by Gustave Flaubert, *L'Éducation sentimentale* (1869).

28 Mann, *Doctor Faustus*, trans. Woods, 359.

29 It is not clear from the recording what was the abandoned satirical project from which Mann brought the portraits of some of the characters. Jameson also mentions the "satirical project" in "Allegory and History". See: Jameson, "Allegory and History," 118.

30 Mann, *Doctor Faustus*, trans. Woods, 251.

31 Reference to Martin Heidegger's interview for *Der Spiegel*, made in 1966 and published in 1976 after Heidegger's death. See: Rudolf Augstein and Georg Wolff, Martin Heidegger, *Der Spiegel*, (23 September 1966), published May 31, 1976. https://www.lacan.com/heidespie.html (Accessed October 12, 2022).

32 Ibid.

33 Reference to Robin George Collingwood, *The Idea of History* (1946).

LECTURE SEVENTEEN

1 Reference to Georg Büchner's short story, *Lenz*, about the Romantic poet Jakob Michael Reinhold Lenz (1751-1792). For Deleuze's reference to Büchner or Lenz and the "anti-Goethe" romantics, see: Gilles Deleuze and Claire Parnet, *Dialogues* (Paris: Flammarion, 1996). Lenz is also discussed early on in Deleuze and Guattari's *Anti-Oedipus* in relation to the contrast between the schizophrenic taking a stroll outdoors and the neurotic lying on the analyst's couch.

2 Reference to Berg's opera, *Lulu* (1935).

3 Theodor W. Adorno, "Beethoven's Late Style," in *Beethoven: The Philosophy of Music*.

4 Adorno, *Aesthetic Theory*, 26-27.

5 Student One's presentation was difficult to transcribe, as she spoke far away from the microphone. Attempts to contact her were unsuccessful, and the editor chose to omit the rest of the presentation from the lecture, only presenting the subsequent discussion.

6 The reference is most likely to the translation of "Aussage" as "message" in the following German sentence: "Aus den großen Dramen Shakespeares ist so wenig herauszupressen, was sie heute die Aussage nennen, wie aus Beckett." See: Adorno, *Ästhetische Theorie*, 48. This sentence was translated into English as: "What is today called a 'message' is no more to be squeezed out of Shakespeare's great dramas than out of Beckett's works." See: Adorno, *Aesthetic Theory*, 27.

7 Benjamin, *The Origin of German Tragic Drama*, 34. For Jameson's discussion of "constellations," see: "Benjamin and Constellations" in *Late Marxism*.

8 Benjamin's "Epistemo-Critical Prologue" in *The Origin of German Tragic*, 28.

9 Jameson, *Late Marxism*, 59-62.

10 Adorno, *Aesthetic Theory*, 27.

11 Ibid., 26

12 See also: Jameson's discussion of "second reflection" in *Late Marxism*, 210-211.

13 Possibly a reference to: "The conceptual apparatus determines the

senses, even before perception occurs; *a priori*, the citizen sees the world as the matter from which he himself manufactures it. Intuitively, Kant foretold what Hollywood consciously put into practice: in the very process of production, images are pre-censored according to the norm of the understanding which will later govern their apprehension." See: Adorno and Horkheimer, *The Dialectic of Enlightenment*, 84.

14 Adorno, *Aesthetic Theory*, 27.

15 See: Chapter Five in Jameson, *Late Marxism*.

16 Benjamin uses the phrase "reason of state," which he borrows from Paul Valéry's writing on Charles Baudelaire, in "On Some Motifs in Baudelaire," (1939) in Benjamin, *Illuminations*, 162.

17 For a discussion of this reference to Nietzsche in Adorno and corresponding sources, see: Gillian Rose, *The Melancholy Science: An Introduction to the Thought of Theodor W. Adorno* (New York: Columbia University Press, 1978), 24.

LECTURE EIGHTEEN

1 Reference to Latin grammarian M. Terentius Varro, who is said to have forgotten the future tense. See: Ernst Bloch, *The Principle of Hope*, trans. Neville Plaice, Stephen Plaice and Paul Knight (Oxford: Blackwell, 1986), 6.

2 For a longer discussion of "Bloch's hermeneutics," see: Jameson, *Marxism and Form*, 116-159.

3 Ibid., 117.

4 For a more recent discussion of Bloch, see also: Jameson, *Signatures of the Visible*, 96.

5 Reference to Northrop Frye, *Anatomy of Criticism: Four Essays* (Princeton University Press, 1957).

6 Ernst Bloch died in 1977 at the age of ninety-two.

7 Ernst Bloch, *Spuren* (Berlin: Paul Cassirer Verlag, 1930).

8 Jameson, *Marxism and Form*, 121.

9 Reference to the official history of the detective story genre, where Edgar Allan Poe's "The Murders in the Rue Morgue" (1841) is considered the first example, although many critics acknowledge Poe's

indebtedness to E.T.A. Hoffmann's "Das Fräulein von Scuderi," which was written twenty years earlier.

10 See also: Jameson, *Marxism and Form*, 131.

11 Ernst Bloch, "A Philosophical View of the Novel of the Artist," in Bloch, *The Utopian Function of Art and Literature*, 267.

12 See also: Jameson, *Marxism and Form*, 132.

13 "Hegel and Kant were the last who, to put it bluntly, were able to write major aesthetics without understanding anything about art." See: Adorno, *Aesthetic Theory*, 334.

14 Reference to Viktor Hugo's preface to his play *Cromwell* (1827), which is considered a manifesto of Romanticism.

15 Reference to the English writer and one of the most widely read humorists of the twentieth century, Pelham Grenville Wodehouse (1881–1975).

16 Jameson deals with the notion of "philistine" in several of his books. For a discussion of "Adorno's philistine" and anti-Semitism, see: "Parable of the Oarsmen" in Jameson, *Late Marxism*. It is important to mention that, during the time of the seminar, the terms "philistine" and "philistinism" were commonly used to describe cultural elitism by highly educated individuals from the upper-middle-class in Europe and North America. At that time, the term was accepted without awareness of its other connotations, related to the exclusion of marginalized ethnic groups, as is the case of recent discussions on the relation of this word to Palestine, from which the term has been derived.

17 Reference to the break space that appears in the German original. See: Adorno, *Ästhetische Theorie*, GS 7, 4574/514.

18 See: "Little History of Photography" in *Walter Benjamin: Selected Writings*, vol. 2, pt. 2: *1931-1934*, ed. M. Jennings, H. Eiland and G. Smith (Cambridge, MA: Harvard University Press, 1999), 515-17.

19 Ibid., 518.

20 Ibid., 510.

21 Walter Benjamin, "L'œuvre d'art à l'époque de sa reproduction méchanisée," trans. Pierre Klossowski, in *Zeitschrift für Sozialforschung, Jahrgang V* [*Journal of Social Research*, vol. 5] (Paris: Félix Alcan, 1936), 40-68.

22 Reference to Walter Benjamin, *Schriften*, 2 vols., ed. Theodor W. Adorno and Gretel Adorno (Frankfurt a.M: Suhrkamp Verlag, 1955) and Waler Benjamin, *Illuminations*, ed. Hannah Arendt, trans. Harry Zohn (New York: Schocken Books, 1969).
23 Waler Benjamin, "The Work of Art in the Age of Mechanical Reproduction" in *Illuminations*, 221.
24 Ibid.
25 Ibid., 222.
26 Ibid., 223.
27 Ibid., 228.
28 Ibid., 239.
29 Ibid., 242.
30 Walter Benjamin, *The Arcades Project*, trans. Howard Eiland and Kevin McLaughlin (Cambridge, MA: Harvard University Press, 1999), N2a, 3/462.
31 Secondary literature sources this quote from Benjamin's "Letters from Paris" (1936), which was unpublished in his lifetime.
32 Punctum "is this element which rises from the scene, shots out of it like an arrow, and pierces me." See: Barthes, *Camera Lucida*, 26.
33 Reference to Boris Groys, *Gesamtkunstwerk Stalin* (Carl Hanser Verlag, München-Wien, 1988). In English: Boris Groys, *The Total Art of Stalinism: Avant-garde, Aesthetic Dictatorship, and Beyond* (Princeton, NJ: Princeton Unversity Press, 1992).

LECTURE NINETEEN

1 Theodor W. Adorno, "The Essay as Form" in *Notes to Literature*, 29.
2 Ibid., 30.
3 Ibid., 41.
4 Ibid., 43.
5 Ibid., 44.
6 Ibid., 45.
7 Reference to Michel de Montaigne (1533-1592), often credited with the invention of the essay as a literary genre.
8 The expanded version of this line is: "The essayist is a Schopenhauer who writes his *Parerga* while waiting for the arrival of his own (or another's) *The World as Will and Idea*, he is a John the Baptist who goes

out to preach in the wilderness about another who is still to come." See: Georg Lukács, "On the Nature and Form of the Essay: A Letter to Leo Popper" in *Soul and Form*, trans. Anna Bostock (Cambridge, MA: The MIT Press), 16.

9 Reference to "The Oldest System Programme of German Idealism" (1796), which has been attributed to Hegel or Schelling.

10 Reference to the American writer, reporter, and political commentator Walter Lippmann (1889-1974).

11 Georg Simmel, *Philosophie des Geldes* (Leipzig. Duncker & Humblot, 1900). Translated by Tom Bottomore and David Frisby as *The Philosophy of Money* (London: Routledge & Kegan Paul, 1978).

12 Georg Simmel, "The Metropolis and Mental Life" (1903).

13 Reference to Georg Lukács's 1911 collection of essays, *Die Seele und die Formen* (*Soul and Form*).

14 Reference to Walter Benjamin, "The Destructive Character" in *Selected Writings*, vol. 2, 1931-1934, ed. Michael W. Jennings, Howard Eiland, and Gary Smith (Cambridge, MA: Harvard University Press, 1999), 54-543.

15 Theodor W. Adorno, Else Frenkel-Brunswik, Daniel J. Levinson, and R. Nevitt Sanford, et al., *The Authoritarian Personality* (New York: Norton, 1950).

16 Erich Fromm, *Escape from Freedom* (New York: Rinehart, 1941). The book was reprinted later under a new title: Erich Fromm, *The Fear of Freedom* (London: Routledge, 2001).

17 Reference to chapter "The Fragment" in Philippe Lacoue-Labarthe and Jean-Luc Nancy, *The Literary Absolute: The Theory of Literature in German Romanticism*, trans. Philip Barnard and Cheryl Lester (Albany, NY: State University of New York Press, 1988).

18 Possibly a reference to Paul Valéry's distinction between *le vers donné* (which is produced by inspiration or *Einfall*) and *le vers calculé*.

19 For "the canon of what is permissible or forbidden," see: Adorno, "Stravinsky: A Dialectal Portrait" in *Quasi Una Fantasia*, 155.

20 Jacques Derrida, *Spectres de Marx: l'état de la dette, le travail du deuil et la nouvelle Internationale* (1993), translated into English as Jacques Derrida, *Specters of Marx: The State of the Debt, the Work of*

Mourning and the New International, trans. Peggy Kamuf (London: Routledge 1994).

21 Reference to an unfinished book of essays by Marcel Proust entitled *Contre Sainte-Beuve (Against Sainte-Beuve)*, in which he criticizes the method of literary criticism practiced by the French literary critic Charles Augustin Sainte-Beuve (1804-1869).

22 Reference to Proust's translation of John Ruskin's book, *The Bible of Amiens*, published in French as *La Bible d'Amiens* (1893).

23 Reference to Proust's essay "Sainte-Beuve et Balzac," published posthumously.

24 Possible reference to Alexandre Astruc's essay "La caméra-stylo" (The Camera-Pen) (1948), where Astruc argues that contemporary film has the potential to become a powerful artistic medium, much like the pen in literature. Astruc proposes the concept of the filmmaker as auteur by drawing a parallel between the camera and a writer's pen. He argues that the camera should be a flexible tool that allows filmmakers to express their personal artistic vision and convey their thoughts and emotions just as a writer does with a pen. This essay is considered a key text in the development of the French New Wave movement in cinema.

25 Reference to Jean-Luc Godard's *Un ou deux choses que je sais d'elle* (*Two or Three Things I Know about Her*) from 1967. Godard's film about migrant workers housing is possibly a reference to *Le Gai Savoir* (*Joy of Learning*) from 1969 which centers around a dialogue between two characters who discuss various socio-political issues, including the living conditions of migrant workers.

26 "Whereof one cannot speak, thereof one must remain silent." See: Wittgenstein, *Tractatus Logico-Philosophicus* (1921).

27 Reference to Barnet Newman's remark, "Aesthetics is for me like what ornithology must be like for the birds." Also quoted in Robert Hullot-Kentor's "Translator's Introduction" in Adorno, *Aesthetic Theory*, xii.

28 Reference to the English writer and novelist Edward Morgan Forster (1879 -1970), whose aphorism appeared in *Aspects of the Novel* (1927).

29 Adorno, *Aesthetic Theory*, 179-80.

30 For Benjamin's reference to Ranke, see: Walter Benjamin, "Theses on the Philosophy of History" in *Illuminations*, 255.

31 Reference to *Le Séminaire de Jacques Lacan, Livre VIII, Le transfert* (Éditions du Seuil, 1991). In English: Jacques Lacan, *The Seminar of Jacques Lacan, Book VIII: Transference*, edited by Jacques-Alain Miller, trans. Bruce Fink (Cambridge: Polity Press, 2015).

32 Benjamin, "Theses on the Philosophy of History," 262.

LECTURE TWENTY

1 Kira Rosoff, "Schools Gain Little Ground in most Recent Rankings," *The Chronicle,* (Friday April 4, 2003), 1.

2 Friedrich Nietzsche, *The Birth of Tragedy*, trans. Douglas Smith (Oxford and New York: Oxford University Press, 2000), 4.

3 Ibid., 8.

4 Heidegger discusses these "failures" in a series of lectures he gave in the late 1930s, and essays on Nietzsche written in the 1940s.

5 See: Friedrich Nietzsche, "The Case of Wagner", trans. Walter Kaufmann, in *Basic Writings of Nietzsche* (New York: The Modern Library, 2000), 614.

6 Nietzsche, *The Birth of Tragedy*, 48.

7 Ibid., 6.

8 Ibid., 4.

9 Ibid., 48.

10 Another translation of this formulation is: "Everything must be conscious in order to be beautiful."

11 Nietzsche, *The Birth of Tragedy*, 81-82.

12 Reference to Friedrich Nietzsche's *Nietzsche contra Wagner: Aktenstücke eines Psychologen* (1889) and *Der Fall Wagner und Götzen-Dämmerung* (1888). In English: Friedrich Nietzsche, *Nietzsche contra Wagner: Out of the Files of a Psychologist* in *The Portable Nietzsche*, trans. Walter Kaufmann (New York: Viking, 1968), and Friedrich Nietzsche, *The Birth of Tragedy and The Case of Wagner*, trans. Walter Kaufmann (New York: Vintage, 1967).

13 Reference to Nietzsche's older sister, Elisabeth Förster-Nietzsche (1846-1935).

14 See: Gilles Deleuze, *Nietzsche et la philosophie* (1962); in English:

Gilles Deleuze, *Nietzsche and Philosophy*, trans. H. Tomlinson, (New York: Columbia University Press, 1983).

15 This famous pronouncement by Goethe was made to Eckermann (April 2, 1829). "The classical I call the healthy, and the romantic, the sick," is said to have had a great influence on Nietzsche's conception of the Dionysian. See: Walter A. Kaufmann, *Nietzsche: Philosopher, Psychologist, Antichrist* (Princeton, NJ: Princeton University Press, 1950), 155.

16 Reference to Wagner's *Der Ring des Nibelungen* (*The Ring of the Nibelung*).

17 Reference to Hans-Jürgen Syberberg (b. 1935) and his best-known film, *Hitler: A Film from Germany* (1977). (In German, the film's title is: *Hitler, ein Film aus Deutschland*). In the US, this film was translated as *Our Hitler*. His *Parsifal* film was released in 1988.

18 Reference to one of the founders of Frankfurt School, the German social scientist and philosopher Friedrich Pollock (1894-1970).

19 Reference to Herbert Marcuse's 1958 book, *Soviet Marxism: A Critical Analysis.*

20 Marx discusses the concept of "subsumption" in the so-called "unfinished chapter six" of *Capital* vol. 1, and the *Economic Manuscript of 1861-63*.

21 For Mann's late essay on Nietzsche, see: Thomas Mann, "Nietzsche's Philosophy in the Light of Recent History," in *Last Essays*, trans. Richard and Clara Winston and Tania and James Stern (New York; Knopf, 1959).

22 It is not clear to what "report" Jameson is referring here. For a discussion of Nietzsche's abuse of chloral hydrate and "a 'Javanese' sedative from an old Dutchman," see: note 236 in letter "197. To Franz Overbeck" in *Selected Letters of Friedrich Nietzsche*, ed. and trans. Christopher Middleton, (Chicago: University of Chicago Press, 1969). See also: his older sister's account on the impact of drugs on Nietzsche's collapse in Elisabeth Förster-Nietzsche, *Das Leben Friedrich Nietzsche's*. (Leipzig: Naumann, 1897).

23 Reference to the following passage in a lecture by Breton delivered in 1934: "During the last ten years, surrealism has almost unceasingly been obliged to defend itself against deviations to the right and to the left. On the one hand we have had to struggle against the

will of those who would maintain surrealism on a purely speculative level and treasonably transfer it on to an artistic and literary plane (Artaud, Desnos, Ribemont-Dessaignes, Vitrac) at the cost of all the hope for subversion we have placed in it; on the other, against the will of those who would place it on a purely practical basis, available at any moment to be sacrificed to an ill-conceived political militancy (Naville, Aragon) — at the cost, this time, of what constitutes the originality and reality of its researches, at the cost of the autonomous risk that it has to run." See: André Breton, *What is Surrealism?: Selected Writings*, ed. Franklin Rosemont (New York: Pathfinder Press, 1978),

24 William James used the phrase "blooming buzzing confusion" to describe the infant's world in *The Principles of Psychology* (1890).

25 Reference to Georges Seurat (1859-1891).

26 Reference to Heidegger's 1950 essay, "The Thing." On *das Ding* in Lacan, see: Jacques Lacan, *The Seminar of Jacques Lacan. Book 7: The Ethics of Psychoanalysis: 1959-1960*, ed. Jacques-Alain Miller, trans. Dennis Porter (New York: Norton, 1992).

27 Adorno, *Aesthetic Theory*, 186.

28 Ibid., 187.

LECTURE TWENTY-ONE

1 Michael Maar, "Teddy and Tommy: The Masks of 'Doctor Faustus'" in *New Left Review* 20, (March/April 2003), 113-30.

2 Theodor Adorno and Thomas Mann, *Correspondence 1943-1955*.

3 Michael Maar, *Bluebeard's Chamber: Guilt and Confession in Thomas Mann* (London: Verso, 2003).

4 Reference to the chapter "At Tikhon's" in Dostoevsky's novel, *The Possessed* [also translated as *Demons*] (1873), which the editor of *The Russian Messenger* refused to publish.

5 Reference to "On Epic Naiveté" in Adorno, *Notes to Literature*.

6 Theodor W. Adorno and Thomas Y. Levin, "Transparencies on Film," *New German Critique*, no. 24/25, Special Double Issue on New German Cinema (Autumn, 1981-Winter, 1982), 199-205.

7 It is possible that both are referring to the same special issue collection dedicated to New German Cinema in *New German Critique* from 1981-1982.

8 Benjamin wrote about film after his visit to the USSR. See: Walter Benjamin, "On the Present Situation of Russian Film" (1927) and "Reply to Oscar A. H. Schmitz" (1927) in *Selected Writings*, vol. 2.

9 Benjamin, "The Work of Art in the Age of Mechanical Reproduction" in *Illuminations*, 5.

10 Ibid.

11 This student's presentation, which included a long summary of Benjamin's "The Work of Art" essay (already presented in Lecture Eighteen), was significantly reduced in order to focus on Adorno's thoughts on film.

12 Theodor W. Adorno and Hanns Eisler, *Composing for the Films* (New York: Oxford University Press, 1947).

13 Horkheimer and Adorno, *Dialectic of Enlightenment*, 120.

14 Ibid., 121.

15 Ibid., 124.

16 Miriam Hansen, "Mass Culture as Hieroglyphic Writing: Adorno, Derrida, Kracauer" in *New German Critique*, no. 56, Special Issue on Theodor W. Adorno (Spring-Summer, 1992), 50.

17 Ibid., 51.

18 Adorno, "Transparencies on Film," 200.

19 Ibid., 201.

20 Ibid., 202.

21 Ibid.

22 "Adorno, Letter to Benjamin, March 18, 1936" in *Aesthetics and Politics*, ed. Fredric Jameson (London: NLB, 1977), 121. Quoted in: Miriam Hansen, "Introduction to Adorno, 'Transparencies on Film' (1966)" in *New German Critique*, Autumn, no. 24/25, Special Double Issue on New German Cinema (Autumn, 1981-Winter, 1982), 186-198. On the issue of translation of the terms "technique" and "technology," see: note 6 in Hansen.

23 Ibid., 190.

24 Adorno, "Transparencies on Film," 202.

25 Ibid., 203.

26 Ibid., 201.

27 Ibid.

28 "Radical naturalism, to which the technique of film lends itself, would dissolve all surface coherence of meaning and finish up as the antithesis of familiar realism." See: Adorno, *Minima Moralia*, 142.

29 On the "empty spaces," see: Miriam Hansen, "Cooperative Auteur Cinema and Oppositional Public Sphere: Alexander Kluge's Contribution to *Germany in Autumn*" in *Alexandre Kluge: Raw Material for Imagination*. ed. Tara Forrest (Amsterdam: Amsterdam University Press, 2012).

30 Adorno, "Transparencies on Film," 204.

31 Ibid., 203.

32 Benjamin, "Chaplin in Retrospect" (1929), *Selected Writings*, vol. 2, 224.

33 Horkheimer and Adorno, *Dialectic of Enlightenment*, 141.

34 Miriam Hansen, *Babel and Babylon: Spectatorship in American Silent Film* (Cambridge MA: Harvard University Press, 1991).

35 Walter Benjamin discusses engraving in "The Work of Art" essay, and in relation to his concept of allegory in *The Origin of German Tragic Drama*.

36 Adorno's "Transparencies on Film" text was based on an article in *Die Zeit* (18 November 1966). It was also published in Theodor W. Adorno, *Ohne Leitbild* (Frankfurt/M.: Suhrkamp, 1967).

37 Reference to the so-called "Oberhausen Manifesto," signed in West Germany by a group of twenty-six young German filmmakers on February 28, 1962.

38 Reference to Hansen's "Introduction to Adorno, 'Transparencies on Film' (1966)."

39 On "test" and Brecht, see, for example: Brigid Doherty, "Test and Gestus in Brecht and Benjamin" in *MLN* 115, no. 3 (2000): 442–81.

40 See also: Jameson, *Brecht and Method*.

41 Reference to an earlier constructivist silent film by Dziga Vertov, *The Man with a Movie Camera* (1929).

42 See: Sergei Eisenstein, "The Milk Separator and the Holy Grail," in *Nonindifferent Nature*, trans. Herbert Marshall, et al. (Cambridge: Cambridge University Press, 1987).

43 Reference to German communist politician and first secretary of the Socialist Unity Party of Germany (SED), Walter Ernst Paul Ulbricht (1893-1973).
44 Reference to the French author Louis Émile Clément Georges Bernanos (1888-1948), whose novel *The Diary of a Country Priest* (1936) was turned into a 1951 film by the French film director Robert Bresson (1901-1999).
45 Reference to Orson Welles' first feature film, *Heart of Darkness* (1940), a movie that is sometimes described as "never-made"; according to other sources, some footage was produced but is considered lost. The movie was to be an adaptation of Joseph Conrad's 1899 novella, *Heart of Darkness*.
46 Reference to the American film noir *Lady in the Lake* (1947), directed by and starring Robert Montgomery, which was an adaptation of Raymond Chandler's murder mystery with the same title.
47 See Adorno, *Aesthetic Theory*, 245.
48 Alexander Kluge, *Learning Processes with a Deadly Outcome*, trans. Christopher Pavsek (Durham, NC: Duke University Press, 1996).
49 Possibly a reference to Alexander Kluge and Oskar Negt, *Geschichte und Eigensinn* (1981), translated as *History and Obstinacy*, ed. Devin Fore, trans. Richard Langston (New York: Zone Books, 2014). See also: Fredric Jameson, "On Negt and Kluge," *October* 46, (Autumn, 1988): 151-177.
50 See: Adorno, *Aesthetic Theory*, 242.
51 See: Roman Jakobson, "Shifters and Verbal Categories" in Linda R. Waugh and Monique Monville-Burston, eds., *On Language: Roman Jakobson* (Cambridge, MA: Harvard University Press, 1990): 386-392.
52 Adorno, *Aesthetic Theory*, 245.
53 Ibid.

INDEX

G

H

ACKNOWLEDGMENTS

I would like to thank a few individuals for their generous assistance at various stages of this project. First of all, I am grateful to Fredric Jameson for the permission to publish the seminar transcripts, and for our discussions at various points. I am also thankful to Joan Morgan and Wendy Weiher, from the Literature Department at Duke, for help with locating some of Jameson's syllabi and notes. I thank Fabio Akcelrud Durão, who kindly agreed to revisit the presentation on "concepts in Adorno" that he delivered in the seminar (see Lecture Thirteen), and the Beiruti musicologist and serial music composer Joelle Khoury for her generous help and stimulating discussions of Schoenberg's twelve-tone system (Lecture Twelve) and of the sonata form and Beethoven's Piano Sonata No. 32 in C minor, Op. 111 (Chapter Fifteen). Ann Lee was incredibly generous in offering me her notes from this seminar, some pages of which I have reproduced. Additionally, D. Graham Burnett provided me with valuable advice regarding publishers who might be interested in this mode of presenting the material. I am also grateful to Ray Brassier, and to the members of the Repeater team, Tariq Goddard and Josh Turner, who provided valuable suggestions and feedback during the production phase. Finally, and as always, I thank Catherine Hansen and Audra Esanu for their encouragement and support.

Octavian Esanu
Beirut and Tokyo, 2023

REPEATER BOOKS

is dedicated to the creation of a new reality. The landscape of twenty-first-century arts and letters is faded and inert, riven by fashionable cynicism, egotistical self-reference and a nostalgia for the recent past. Repeater intends to add its voice to those movements that wish to enter history and assert control over its currents, gathering together scattered and isolated voices with those who have already called for an escape from Capitalist Realism. Our desire is to publish in every sphere and genre, combining vigorous dissent and a pragmatic willingness to succeed where messianic abstraction and quiescent co-option have stalled: abstention is not an option: we are alive and we don't agree.